CONFRONTING
MORAL WORLDS

Understanding Business Ethics

CONFRONTING MORAL WORLDS

Understanding Business Ethics

Mark N. Wexler

Prentice Hall Canada Inc.
Scarborough, Ontario

Canadian Cataloguing in Publication Data

Wexler, Mark N., 1949–
        Confronting moral worlds

1st ed.
Includes Index
ISBN 0-13-080142-9

1. Business ethics. I. Title.

HF5387.W49   2000   174′.4   C99-930530-1

© 2000 Prentice-Hall Canada Inc., Scarborough, Ontario
Pearson Education Canada, a division of Pearson Canada Inc.,

ISBN 0-13-080142-9

Acquisitions Editor: Mike Ryan
Senior Marketing Manager: Ann Byford
Production Editor: Kelly Dickson
Associate Editor: Sherry Torchinsky
Copy Editor: Jennifer Lambert
Production Coordinator: Jane Schell
Cover Design: Julia M. Hall
Cover Image: Photodisc
Page Layout: Heidi Palfrey

4 5 6 DPC 10 09 08

Printed and bound in Canada.

Bowen H. McCoy, "The Parable of the Sadhu." *Harvard Business Review* (May-June 1997), pp. 54-64.
Reprinted with permission.

This book is dedicated to

Judy A.E. Oberlander

There are no whole truths; all truths are half-truths. It is trying to treat them as whole truths that we play the devil.

Alfred North Whitehead
Dialogues

Contents

Chapter 8: Environmental Ethics and Business   253

Chapter 9: Reputational Capital and Diversity in the Workplace   293

Chapter 10: Encounters With Technology: Ethics and Change   338

Cases

Chapter 7:

Chapter 8:

Chapter 9:

Chapter 10:

Appendix

Figures

Chapter 4:

Chapter 5:

Chapter 6:

Chapter 7:

Chapter 8:

Chapter 9:

Chapter 10:

Preface

In *The Brothers Karamozov*, one of Fyodor Dostoevsky's characters ponders the question of whether or not humans would be willing to acquire ongoing genuine happiness at the cost of a newborn baby being tortured to death. Questions of how to distribute the harms and benefits that occur in and as a result of human actions have been with us since earliest time. Is it fair that people were enslaved to construct the pyramids as burial sites for Egyptian royalty? Do women in hunting tribes have a duty to prepare the spoils of the hunt for their menfolk? Can we say that the decimation of the great plains buffalo to feed those who built our first railways was wrong? Is it fair that a Disney subcontract worker in Haiti made $11.00 (US) a week in 1995 compared to Michael Eisner's $28,000 (US) weekly compensation?

Questions of ethics—what is right and good, and what is not—have been with us always. Our enduring quest for spiritual meaning reflects a yearning for the good life, and what rests beneath our study of ethics is the pursuit of learning—as individuals, corporations, and societies—of how we can both achieve and sustain it. There is, and perhaps ought to be, an ongoing debate over what is and what is not the good life, and how, in our brief time on the planet, we can help bring it into existence.

Business ethics, as we shall discover, focuses on that part of the public debate that asks a simple but powerful question. What is a morally reasonable standard of behaviour for individuals in businesses, for occupational groups in the economy, and for societies as a whole in their distribution of harms and benefits? Within this debate, there are two interrelated orientations or perspectives. The first is descriptive. What, for example, does the Bank of Montreal's code of ethics say about gender equity? How did the union at the Windsor, Ontario Wal-Mart push its cause for certification using moral arguments? How much does employee theft from Air Canada cost the corporation? Are the changes to the Canadian Pension Plan fair to those between the ages of eighteen to thirty when compared to those between fifty-three and sixty-five years of age? The second orientation is prescriptive. What *should* the code of ethics at the Bank of Montreal say about gender equity? How *should* the union at the Windsor Wal-Mart sustain and further its push for certification in other branches using moral argumentation? The descriptive perspective explores the norms, practices, contracts, and technologies within businesses that impact ethical behaviour. To prescribe, on the other hand, is to seek to improve the ongoing manner in which standards governing moral behaviour operate.

The thesis of this book is simple: moral worlds must be confronted. The contemporary and persistent effort to separate technical from moral reflection and decision making is, I will argue, a sorely inadequate means of training business persons for the world they will face. To treat the organization as a technical island in a sea of social and moral problems is to extend a mode of thinking that increasingly has outlived its utility. This mode of thinking achieves its coherence by defining businesses and their operations very narrowly. It goes something like this. The business of running a company such as, say, Maple Leaf Gardens Limited, entails making a profit by winning the support of sufficient numbers of fans (consumers) who will purchase seats, regalia, food, and parking. In other words, the business of business is simply that—doing business in the midst of change. This mode of thinking suggests that morality or ethics rests in the hands, heads, and hearts of others—social workers, therapists, ethicists, public policy analysts—who are trained in dealing with conflicting human values, dashed expectations, or contentious consequences of well-intended public policies. In short, the business of business is business, not ethics or morality.

This view suggests, as the logic of specialization itself implies, that Maple Leaf Gardens Limited has no competitive advantage in working through moral quandaries. Those who work for the company specialize in providing management services to a venue that hosts sports teams, special events, and leisure-related activities. However, whether or not they are competent in the ethical arena, businesses frequently are dragged kicking and screaming into the spotlight. When I started to write this book, Cliff Fletcher, the president of Maple Leaf Gardens Limited, found himself and his firm deeply embroiled in an ethical quandary. It was alleged that at least one ex-employee lured young boys into sexual activities with the promise of hockey sticks and tickets to games and rock concerts. One lad and his parents hired lawyers and brought a lawsuit against the company. It was settled for $60,000, and it is reported that the settlement included a confidentiality agreement. Maple Leaf Gardens Limited, despite its protestations, was dragged into an ethical quandary. As I correct the proofs of this book, the Toronto Maple Leafs are playing their final game at Maple Leaf Gardens.

The fact that businesses may indeed be better at generating profits than at mastering ethical quandaries is no particular reason to expect these issues to remain at bay. We can, in fact, expect ethical issues to visit organizations of all sorts with greater frequency. This book explores why this is, and how we can prepare ourselves by honing our skills in ethical issue diagnosis, both descriptive and prescriptive. To do so, we turn to our investigation of the fascinating and often curious nature of the very moral worlds we are constructing, often unintentionally, in our pursuit of the business of making a living.

The purpose of this book is to provide its readers with the confidence to confront moral worlds within their business lives openly and with conviction. One of the quickest ways to find oneself in what executive headhunters call a "CEM," or a career-ending move, is to be perceived by a boss, one's peers, or the public at large as having crossed the line in one's moral behaviour. This admonition applies to corporations, public or elected officials, professionals, and everyday working men and women. Whether you aspire to be a head of state, CEO of a blue chip company, director of a not-for-profit organization, accountant, computer programmer, nurse, or carpenter, you must know how and why moral lines get drawn and redrawn. This is no simple matter. It calls for a recognition that whether we are ready or not, a great deal of our behaviour in business contexts will be judged not only on our ability to make profits, but also on our capacity to make decisions that are seen as fair, to enhance trust, and to amplify the reputation of our organization as a good corporate citizen.

The mixing of business and virtue is discussed in Chapters 1 through 4. In Chapter 1 we look at the good corporate citizen as a moral line drawing exercise, whereby a firm's claims and actions seem to go beyond the call to maximize stockholder value and are generating genuine public goods and services. Chapter 2 explores the forces at play in the postmodern world that are moving businesses to increase their roles and responsibilities in society. In Chapter 3 we build a vocabulary of five evolving and contending views of social responsibility that mark the debate over how to best structure and create governance over the business community. In Chapter 4, still within our examination of the combustible nature of bringing the search for good citizenship into the operations of business, we look at how to put corporate social responsibility into practice.

Chapters 5, 6, and 7 turn from the prescriptive focus on the good corporate citizen and its role in postmodern society to a more descriptive examination. In Chapter 5 we examine how three different views of the organizational culture concept help us understand moral line drawing in organizations. Chapter 6 explores the idea of "dirty hands" in business, looking at why and how good people like you and I, with well-intentioned motives, can and do cross moral lines. In Chapter 7 we examine the whistle-blowing process in organizations, and discover how seeing others cross the moral line may compel us to call attention to their transgression.

In Chapters 8, 9, and 10 we confront and seek to build a vocabulary of the trends that are stretching our ethical views and causing friction within the business community. Chapter 8 analyzes the reactions of both the public and the business community to varied perceptions of the environmental crisis. The ongoing interaction between business and society is the focus of Chapter 9, which takes up two interrelated themes: how and why organizations seek to manage themselves so as to win the approval of their stakeholders, and why opinion is divided on the merits of equity programs as a means of effectively reflecting changing social concerns. In Chapter 10 we take a close look at how our views of technology temper our understanding of the good corporation and, within it, the good life.

It is impossible for me to write a book on business ethics without acknowledging the many individuals who have contributed directly and indirectly to my understanding of the field. I have included a bibliography of the works of ethicists, practising managers, social scientists, and others who I believe have shown wisdom in their words and actions. On a more personal note, I have twenty-three years worth of students to thank, who have entered into dialogue with me and helped me appreciate the joys of learning as I teach. Each generation seems to come to the study of business ethics with new perspectives and issues to tackle. I delight in this "immediacy" of their concerns and try to show them how and why they, like all of us, are working in a larger tradition and discipline.

Tradition and discipline do not humble our unique experience of the world—they lend it credence and make it accessible. It is in the uniqueness of my relationship with my wife, Judy Oberlander, and step-daughter, Jody Rayher, and the quiet tide that alters the shoreline of False Creek each night, that I seek and have found understanding, acceptance, and change. It is to my parents, Saul and Pearl, I turn when I seek an explanation for my curious tenacity to pose the simple question—why not Eden? why this? They never thought these were the questions of a lazy boy, now man; they never insisted that other questions might lead more easily towards security and prosperity. My colleagues at Simon Fraser University's Faculty of Business Administration, and most particularly Jean Donald, proved invaluable in making my words stick to the page. Finally, I would like to extend my gratitude to Sherry Torchinsky, Patrick Ferrier, and Amber Wallace of Prentice Hall Canada, and Jennifer Lambert for helping me bring this book to the market. It is here—in practical terms—that value is made explicit and the wheat is separated from the chaff.

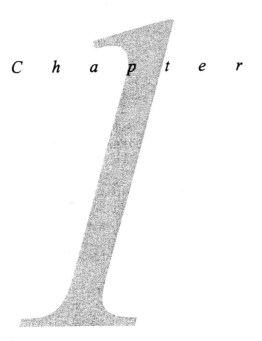

THE GOOD CORPORATE CITIZEN

Since evidence can be adduced and interpreted to corroborate a virtually limitless array of worldviews, the human challenge is to engage that worldview or set of perspectives which brings forward the most valuable life enhancing consequences.

Richard Tarnas
The Passions of the Western Mind (1991)

APPROACHING ETHICS

From earliest tribal life to the present, human beings have had to decide what is good and right for ourselves and for others. Having made these decisions, we seek not only to put them into practice, revising them when necessary, but to transmit these values to the next generation. We cannot envision human relationships as ongoing, stable, and grounded without some agreement, often tacit, as to what (or who) is good and should be rewarded and what is not. Ethics is largely a matter of perspective; to reflect upon or use ethics to evaluate an issue or a relationship is to use moral standards of evaluation. Moral standards, both those adopted unquestioningly and those arrived at by critical reflection, permit us to evaluate things, people, and ideas with reference to our belief in their "goodness" or "badness."

At first blush, readers may feel that a field of inquiry which grounds its core purpose in such general terms as "goodness" and "badness" is too simplistic to reap either intellectual or practical returns. This view fails, however, to take into account how central moral evaluations

1

are to our framing of social, political, economic, medical, and—as is the focus of this book—business issues. Moral standards guide us through uncertain terrain. It is in the shared acknowledgement of moral standards that we agree upon the construction of the "hero" and the "villain" in life.

In this book, we are interested in how and why we consider certain actions of individuals, corporations, and business institutions heroic and laudable, while others are viewed as morally suspect. The importance of ethics as a field of study rests in its ability to make us conscious of how we use, apply, and articulate moral standards. In Canada, as in other societies, we continue to work through certain areas where our moral standards remain grey or controversial. Our ability to discern right from wrong remains complicated in issues related to native land claims, genetic engineering, abortion, the manufacture and pricing of generic drugs, the use of equity programs to help right past wrongs, and the fast-tracking of immigrants with money to invest. Ethics becomes controversial when a people are unsure, within a given realm of activity, which direction leads to the good world.

In this chapter we shall approach ethics as a way to make sense of that moral line which helps us distinguish what we believe is good and ought to be sought, from what we feel is ignoble, base, and should be avoided. Our conception of the "good corporate citizen" points towards a common belief that the good corporate citizen provides stability and, interestingly, innovation in the midst of our experience of dislocating change. The good corporate citizen enhances the socio-moral development of those who come under its influence. It empowers. It creates a web of inclusion which permits individuals to join teams, yet in so doing diminishes neither their autonomy nor their individuality. Good corporate citizens ensure these features in a willingness to sponsor and utilize the tools available—ombudspersons, ethics committees, hotlines, ethics training, harassment coordinators, social/environmental audits, and the like—to establish conditions for open dialogue over values and value conflicts. Lastly, the good corporate citizen is not afraid of controversy and often is willing to engage in principled positions—even those which may be seen as unpopular. The good corporate citizen helps us locate and develop our personal ethics and integrate these with the values at play in society.

"Ethics," write R.C. Soloman and K.R. Hansen, "is first of all the quest for and the understanding of the good life, living well, a life worth living." The good life, as these authors note, involves not only being able to know the good, but also "knowing what is worth wanting and having and knowing what is not worth wanting and having" (1983:9). Our society offers up a cornucopia of options. To some, the good life, simply put, is the pleasurable life. To others, it is a life of hard work, the maintenance of principles, and a sense of obligation. Still to others, if one is not famous, one has not tasted the nectar of the good life. Others envision power as the centre of the good life and they measure their worth and value by how directly they influence others. Yet others quest for balance and harmony, seeking the middle road as their path. Discussion of the "good life" assumes that all of us—robber, artist, banker, priest, accountant, merchant—are on a journey. We are all passing through life aware of time's finiteness, seeking to understand the values which give rise to our actions, in pursuit of the good life.

Business ethics is the application of moral standards and ideas of the good life to the intentions, actions, and technologies used in the business world. Business ethics is that particular branch of applied ethics which seeks to describe the moral standards in use in business practices and to prescribe effective ways to change, raise, or alter these moral standards.

Business ethics is not solely the domain of business ethicists. Each of us, in partaking in the organizational world as a worker, consumer, investor, media analyst, professional, or manager, is fully involved in making business ethics a reality. For example, in Figure 1.1, Anthony Newley just stepped out for lunch and, upon returning quite rested and relaxed, finds himself in the midst of an ethical quandary.

FIGURE 1-1 Anthony Newley Is Out to Lunch

My name is Anthony Newley and I am Director of Nursing Personnel in a large Canadian hospital. During my lunch break on 13 February 1997 I received the following voice-mail message:

"Mr. Newley, you don't know me. You can call me Reisa Kaplan, which is not my real name.

I'm a business student at the University of Manitoba. I'm majoring in public policy and know how important it is to nip ethical problems in the bud. I clean houses as a job to supplement my income and help pay my rising tuition fees.

One of my clients, Margaret O'Shea, is a registered nurse in your Department of Internal Medicine. While cleaning this client's house, I have come across numerous vials of medicine—mostly amphetamines and barbiturates—with the name of the hospital and what I believe to be patients' names written across the vials. This has raised my concerns. Is my client stealing these drugs? Are the patients whose names are on the vials getting placebos instead of the drugs and medicines prescribed to them by their physicians? If indeed Ms. O'Shea is taking these drugs, are they imperilling her patients ... the quality of her judgments ... her relationships with other nurses?

I want you, Mr. Newley, to investigate this matter and do something about it. If I am not satisfied with your investigation or its speed, I will, in time, leak this story, including a tape of this phone call to the newspapers.

Bye now ...."

ETHICS IN BUSINESS

Perhaps the most basic question one can ask when setting out to make sense of ethics in general, and business ethics more particularly, is: why think about ethics at all? Why concern ourselves with these questions? Why become conscious of the conflicting values and demands we place on one another, since we usually manage to stumble through life and have done so in the past? The answer is that ethics, when push comes to shove, is humanity's way of making sense of life, of the world, of the purpose of our being here now. We are a species driven, albeit sporadically, to make sense of things. One of the lenses we must look through in this venture is a kind of "moral squint."

Eric Mount, Jr., writing in *Professional Ethics in Context*, sees the moral squint not as the science of vision, but rather as the exploration of meaning and value in our world. Mount writes:

> With some kind of 'moral squint,' we focus, we scan, we search, we scrutinize, we stare, we give dirty looks. When we look into things, we may take close looks, quick looks, good looks, hard looks, long looks, or honest looks. We look around; we look askance; and we overlook things. We look down on people, up to people, and out for people .... Sometimes when our defenses are down, we get hit between the eyes with something we had no desire to see .... (1990:18, 22)

We cannot get away from ethics. Even the basic act of seeing requires that we visually attend to some stimuli and ignore others. We value certain people, things, and ideas we see; others we do not. We evaluate. We form attachments. We develop models of a world inhabited by those scenes which draw us, and those which—at times for reasons we are unsure of—repel us.

In business ethics, the world we study is purposeful and managed. It is an organizational world in which individuals, as they join, become agents for and work within corporate and institutional policies or standards. It is important at this early stage to realize that—at least in modern, technologically-advanced societies like Canada, the United States, Italy, and Japan—one becomes a member at birth and rarely truly escapes the pull of organizational or managed worlds until one dies. Upon one's death, one's estate and its dispensation, taxation, and eventual destination is largely determined by and within organizational worlds.

Within this book, the organizational world is the business context. It is the world of rules, managers, policies, marketing, finance, competition, and work. It is important not to simply think of your experience of business as that world you enter when you are at work. This emphasis, one not uncommon within the value systems of modern society, focuses solely on your experience of business and its context from the "producer role." You also experience it as a consumer, as an investor, and even as a citizen. Firms of all sorts pervade our life and help us make sense of the world beyond our immediate grasp. We are born, educated, work, die, and are buried in and by organizations. When we enter a school, gymnasium, restaurant, museum, or department store, we are entering a business. In each, we find an ongoing, albeit changeable, nest of rules, expectations, and rewards or punishments for various behaviours. Organizations are sites where, in the study of ethics, the rubber hits the road. Hospitals, courthouses, and sports arenas present us with applied ethical issues. Given economic constraints in the running of hospitals, who is to receive costly treatment; who is not? Given the increasingly high use of our legal system, is it fair to have those seeking justice wait long periods of time until their case can be slotted in the calendar? Given the fascination of youth with sports celebrities, ought our drug laws to be severely enforced when elite and often exceedingly wealthy athletes are apprehended using recreational drugs?

Businesses in the private sector, both large enterprises like Union Carbide and General Motors of Canada, franchises like Pizza Hut Incorporated or McDonald's Restaurants, and small independent retail outlets present many facets to those who seek to understand, monitor, work, consume, invest, and report on or in them. One might use the light passing through a prism or crystal as a useful visual analogy to see the way business ethics is a means of asking important questions about business, business persons, and the effects of businesses upon society. For example, a marketer looks at businesses with an eye to enhancing the ability of the firm to attract, satisfy, and maintain a growing client or customer base. The management information specialist within or consulting for a firm sees the organization as a river of information that requires careful and skilful monitoring so that its policy-making representatives can put their fingers on relevant information at the right time and in a comprehensible form. The public relations expert sees the firm as possessing a reputation which must be enhanced, guarded, and brought where and whenever possible to the public in the best light. The financial analyst sees the business as a ship out on a long journey and requiring sufficient capital, in changing seas and with altering conditions of the crew, to successfully complete its journey and bring adequate returns to all those who have taken the risk of investing in it. The human relations champion sees the organization as a team that is only as good as its personnel.

None of these orientations is wrong. Businesses are complex worlds. We use different lenses to understand them and make them work smoothly. One of the lenses we can use, and are being asked to use more and more, is the business ethics lens. The business ethics facet or lens cuts across functional areas in the firm and can be experienced by members at any level of hierarchy within the organization. Marketing specialists may find themselves challenged by a group of clients, for example housewives, for portraying them in a sexist or stereotypical manner. The management information specialists may find themselves increasing the domain of technology by creating a system which codes clients' confidential files, only to realize later that they have not closely supervised access to these files and are presently under fire for failing to guard their clients' rights. The human relations experts may find that the firm's economic commitment to bolstering the education of key personnel may bring mixed results as more and more employees take paid educational leave, only to move on to new firms, taking with them greatly enhanced skills and technical knowledge.

In this chapter, we shall introduce the notion of business ethics by posing questions surrounding what it means to be a good corporate citizen. How do different analysts, using different notions of the good world, justify their notion of the good corporate citizen? What differing ethical guidelines stem from these conceptions of the good corporate citizen? Business ethics is intended to help us clarify our views and make decisions in the midst of moral ambiguity and conflicting perceptions. In Figure 1.2, we see from three brief cases that there is little unanimity on the sorts of decisions that are required in the midst of ethics quandaries. In fact, when comparing executives to a sample of university students, we may be surprised that in reaction to a survey, the executives were often tougher and more demanding on ethics in organizations than the students.

In making decisions, both the public and business executives are guided by what they see as the good corporate citizen and, within this, the good corporate department and, within this, the good corporate actor. We will discuss four models of the good corporate citizen. Each view of the good corporate citizen guides our understanding of what is an ethical way to act in business. Each, as we shall see in both Chapters 5 and 6, shows how these four views of the good corporate citizen are modified in practice. While we are motivated by ideals of the good corporate citizen, many a problem arises as we are tempted by personal ambition, debt, heated competitive circumstances, dysfunctional organizational politics, and the emergence of organizational cultures which reward careerism, self-promotion, and the willingness to win at all costs.

The first view of the good corporation highlights the good corporate citizen as an agent of change. Organizations are a rational means by which we achieve our goals. Innovations which enhance this ability and bring us closer, more easily, to our goals are seen positively. These help us learn and adapt to change. This view, we shall note, looks at the organization as a tool to attain that societal goal we call and idealize as progress. Aiding and abetting progress through the enhancement of techniques, the introduction of user-friendly technologies, and the improvement of the quality of life of citizens in both the developed and developing economies is viewed as meritorious. To become an agent of change, the good corporate citizen must enhance the skills of employees and act innovatively, while at once attending to the emergence of stakeholder issues and experimenting with projects which enhance the response time of organizations.

The second view of the good corporate citizen portrays it as an "agent of socio-moral development." In this view, using the works of Kenneth Kohlberg and collaborators (Kohlberg,

---

FIGURE 1-2 Decisions, Decisions, Decisions ...

Using a sample of 282 executives and 921 undergraduate students, and exposing them to three brief cases, we can note that the students by and large tend to be more willing to compromise their views than are the executives.

Case: Environmental Lapse

Ralph learns that the chemical plant he manages is generating slightly more water pollution in a nearby lake than is legally permitted. Revealing the problem will bring unfavourable publicity to the plant, hurt the lakeside town's resort industry, and cost well over $1 million to fix. There is a very low probability of the issue being discovered. The violation poses no danger whatsoever to people. It may endanger a small number of fish, none of which is on or near to being on the endangered species list. Should Ralph make the problem public?

Results: 75% of the executives stated that Ralph should expose the problem and pay the costs; 64% of the undergraduates agreed. Only 10% of the executives and 18% of the undergraduates believed Ralph should disregard his duty to report.

Case: Faking the Diploma

Bill has done a sound job for over a year. Bill's boss learns that he got the job by claiming to have a college degree that he never earned. Should his boss dismiss him for submitting a fraudulent resume, or overlook the false claim, since Bill has otherwise shown himself to be conscientious and honourable? Making an issue of the degree might ruin Bill's career.

Results: 53% of the executives recommended dismissal; 39% recommended overlooking Bill's false claim. In the undergraduate sample, 69% recommended overlooking the false claim; 20% recommended dismissal.

Case: Who's Cheating?

Mary, a 41-year-old widow with a dependent mother and a child who is severely disabled, has just discovered that the proprietors of the firm for which she has worked for the past four years are cheating the government out of a substantial amount of money in their taxes. Mary has risen from the ranks and has recently been promoted to a managerial position. Mary is the only employee who would be in a position to know of the tax avoidance. Should Mary report the owners to the taxation authorities at the risk of endangering her job, or should she ignore the discovery in order to protect her family's livelihood?

Results: 52% of the executives and 36% of the undergraduates said Mary should report the owners to the officials; 21% of the executives and 44% of the undergraduates stated that Mary should ignore her discovery so that she can protect her family.

1981; Kohlberg *et al.*, 1983) and Carol Gilligan (1977, 1982, 1988), we view the good corporate citizen as fostering socio-moral development rather than repressing and stifling the moral imagination. The corporation does not become a psychic prison, trapping the moral aspirations of those who come into contact with it. People do not feel used, exploited, or compromised. Rather than reinforcing moral muteness—an unwillingness to raise moral matters and create difficulties—the good corporate citizen, as an agent of moral development, facilitates ethical inquiry. It rewards those who act with moral integrity and establishes an organizational climate in which ethical programs can be inititated and take root.

The third view of the good corporate citizen emphasizes the good corporate citizen as an effective implementer of ethics programs. In this view, the good corporate citizen develops, implements, and revises policies, programs, and corporate positions intended to help manage corporate ethical issues and to achieve a positive reputation for the organization. "Ethics programs" is a generic name for the use of a combination of ethics training programs, ombudspersons, ethics officers, ethics committees, hotlines, social and/or environmental audits, and ethics codes. These ethics programs are most effective when the input for them is inclusive of many positions, when the guidelines are revised with some frequency, and where adherence to the programs is built into the organization's reward system.

The final view of the good corporate citizen presents it as providing moral leadership both to those within the organization and to society at large. The good corporate citizen as a moral leader maintains high ethical principles in its ongoing relations with others in the business community. It goes beyond the letter of the law in attempting to live up to its responsibilities, for example, by using some percentage of its profits in philanthropic endeavours. As a moral leader, the good corporate citizen tries to get involved in issues of empowering the voiceless and homeless. It often seeks to aid the illiterate and provide opportunities for productive individuals with handicaps.

Let us turn to our first view of the good corporate citizen, the positive agent of change fostering innovation and enhancing organizational learning.

THE AGENT OF CHANGE

Business books today propound the popular view that organizations which are healthy and vital innovate. These good corporate citizens motivate employees, not only to excel in routine tasks where programmed behaviour predominates, but also to foster a mindfulness which has been called organizational learning. Innovativeness and organizational learning, when engaged in by corporations, suggest a form of problem solving which not only achieves viable solutions but does so in a creative, often inclusive, manner. Corporations which achieve both are seen not only as economically responsive to their markets, but also morally sensitive and capable of rising to challenges. It is the good corporate citizen who masters markets and yet remains sufficiently aware of societal trends and emerging anxieties to explore issues such as cultural diversity in the firm, or telecommuting for employees. The good corporate citizen, in this context, fosters change—mindful change.

Our present ambivalence to change is modified, and change is made trustworthy when it is mediated by our belief in the good corporate citizen. To comprehend this, let us first look at the roots of our ambivalent attitude towards change, then at the manner in which our belief in the good corporate citizen reduces our perception of the risk entailed in our commitment to change. The good corporate citizen engages in planned, integrated, and responsive change. The good corporate citizen is portrayed as neither an exploitative nor as an opportunistic player.

Our ambivalence towards change is visible in the business literature itself. On the one hand, change, while believed to be ubiquitous, is escalating to the point where it dashes our very sense of order. In the next chapter, in our discussion of postmodern business ethics, we look at the problem of achieving order and moral integrity in a system which lacks a centre, is experienced as being fragmented (Bauman, 1995), and celebrates the virtues of change as a force of renewal, loosely kept under wraps by the marketplace. In our experience of change as disorienting, we experience a series of confusions and dislocations. This is closely aligned to what communication theorists call "noise." Change, in this sense, is experienced as unintegrated, unplanned, and driven by forces beyond our control. This experience of change is disquieting. Change is a form of turbulence which disrupts our lives and to which we react, as one would expect, with resistance. On experiencing bouts of this unintegrated, unplanned, and largely out-of-our-control change, we become nostalgic for the good old days of stability, tradition, and clear routines.

On the other hand, when thought of within the ambit of a controlled, planned, and integrated experience, change is viewed quite differently. Innovation and organizational learning, particularly when tied to organizations, are a means of placing an order, a purpose, and a positive spin on our experience and understanding of escalating change in the contemporary context. Both "learning" and "innovation" emphasize that change is more than a mere dislocation or disquieting experience. While they possess these characteristics, they are short-lived. In learning, we believe we change behaviours, but rather than the new behaviours leading to disruption, we are convinced that they lead to improved behaviours. We do not learn to become drug addicts, liars, or impostors; we learn functional skills, useful abilities, and adaptive means to satisfy our desires. Innovation, too, carries similar connotations. While it is understood that innovation is risky—indeed, that most efforts at innovation fail—we still view innovation as worth the cost of the risk.

In the idea of the good corporate citizen as an innovator and learner, we seek to find instances of organizations such as 3M, Bombardier, and the Bank of Montreal, which not only excel at their tasks—bringing stability and predictability to those involved—but who also innovate and learn, bringing change which is integrated, planned, and largely under the control of those who invest their energies in them. The good corporate citizen in this context provides stability and from it creates a form of change which is highly regarded, valued, and experienced positively. This change is deemed rewarding. We are convinced that we profit from it.

The good corporate citizen, in this view, helps to create a version of the good world in which change is harnessed and directed. The good corporate citizen functions as a mechanism to direct the best minds of our generation to engage in controlled risk. The good corporate citizen acts as a stabilizer while introducing changes which can be diffused throughout society. It is important in this context to realize that all organizations are not good corporate citizens. Some organizations refuse to learn; others take no responsibility for the innovations they unleash upon the public. Still others feign innovation continually using "hype" to pass off old ideas and products as if they were new and vital. Rather than acting as agents of change, these organizations perpetuate a climate of distrust. They project an image in which their statements are out of line with their actions. In Figure 1.3, we see the challenges posed to two different businesses by the innovative potential of the Internet.

Acting as an agent of change does not come without its problems. Old routines must be rewired. Change often heats up opportunities for those seeking to free-ride or lessen their contribution under the guise of a new job description. It often frees up the ambitious and provides them with a chance to bring up old issues under a new name. To take positive advantage of the opportunities that come with change, firms which seek the route of innovation must be prepared to spend capital on educating and training their workforces to live in rapidly changing organizations.

FIGURE 1–3 Internet Chicanery

Kathy Blair, writing in the *Canadian HR Reporter* (1997:2), provides us with an insight into how some Canadian companies are coping with employee abuse of the Internet. For example, Montreal-based CAE Electronics Ltd., a high-technology firm that produces flight simulators and employs a large number of young engineering graduates, has discovered that a few of its highly computer-literate employees are using the Internet to visit Web sites that have more to do with simulated sex than simulated flight.

CAE is one of many Canadian organizations attempting to bring its corporate policies into line with the rapid pace of technological change. CAE has warned employees that visiting particular Web sites is out of bounds. Gilbert Guerin, the human resources development manager at CAE, has noted that, depending on the nature of the indiscretion, particularly frequency, and time taken away from work responsibilities, CAE has fired workers for their Internet chicanery.

The Internet has proved to be a mixed blessing. It is vital to access new information rapidly, but for those seeking to abuse it, opportunity awaits. For example, the federal government has recently been caught off-guard. One of its Department of National Defense scientists was recently charged with possessing, making, and distributing child pornography over the Internet. The lure of the Internet can, of course, tempt employees, not only into acts of outright deviance, but into activities which have nothing whatsoever to do with work.

CAE, reports Blair, plans to develop a formal corporate policy dealing with employees' use of the Internet. The company intends to restrict Internet access to employees who demonstrate a need for it. Another approach to this problem has been taken by the petrochemical firm, Nova Corporation, in Calgary. It permits almost all its employees unlimited access to the Internet and e-mail. Nova employees are made aware that their use of company hardware, time, and software means that their use must be limited to business activities. Bruce Nysetvold, corporate counsel for Nova Corporation, notes that the company monitors all http requests and employees are fully apprised of this. Employees know that there is no right to privacy with respect to the materials they are sending and receiving over the Internet.

At Nova Corporation they have noted a dramatic increase in the number of people using the Internet at lunch time. The company, so far, has turned a blind eye to this "own time" net surfing hoping that it will help motivate employees and keep them in touch with learning possibilities. Daniel Shap, a Toronto lawyer with Goodman and Carr, notes that this is still a legal grey area. Employers are responsible for their employees when they are using the company's hardware and software. Shap tells the story of an incident in which a worker for one company posted disparaging remarks about another company on the Internet without his employer's knowledge. The worker received a letter from the outraged company, as did his employer.

This does not come cheaply. Firms which invest in their personnel are seeking potential dividends from subsidizing the training of their teams. This investment should not be engaged in—at least not at the same rate—by firms whose policy it is to adopt innovations well after they have been tried elsewhere. The strategy of the innovator requires experimentation, something that can occur only within corporations in which error-making is evaluated less seriously than is the willingness to try new options and alternatives. Organizations which stress error reduction (and these are legion) negate the very ethos of experimentation upon which the good corporate citizen as an agent of change is founded.

To make this experimental climate manifest and yet retain stability, the good corporate citizen must remain open to the voices of its stakeholders. This theme will be picked up more fully in Chapter 3. It is sufficient to say here, that to achieve the explosive mixture of "experimentation" required to embrace the ethos of change, while remaining "stable" as required by the structural requisites of maintaining a corporate structure, the good corporate citizen as an agent of change must open its organizational boundaries. What this means in practice is that the organization must be able to hear and respond to the varying views of its stakeholders with regards to any experiment in which it engages. The organization which innovates without a clear idea of how to diffuse the innovation and have it accepted by the groups with which it is interdependent—contractors, suppliers, unions, local community, etc.—is at a loss.

Opening the organizational boundaries, a logic which accelerates learning, is opposed by many organizations. It increases risk. It amplifies uncertainty. It exposes the organization to the criticisms of those not tightly bound by the ethos of experimentation. However, as we shall see in the next section, it brings into contact people who possess very different values than one another. It can, as we shall see, increase or stifle socio-moral development.

SOCIO-MORAL DEVELOPMENT

There is a view in the business ethics literature that the good corporate citizen enhances the socio-moral development of those who come into contact with it. Usually this is not the primary task of organizations. Rather, it is an unintended consequence of making, operating, and sustaining organizations in society over time. In this context, organizations are not merely places of business or work, they are mechanisms which shape and give form to values. They socialize. Organizations in this expanded view are more than tools for task accomplishment; they help to shape our view of life, and provide us with insight into what is feasible and what is beyond our reach.

From the cradle to the grave, most of us will experience organizations. We, especially those of use who consider management important, believe that we influence organizations. We must, as well, realize that organizations influence us. This "built environment" that is ours and that we are managing—an environment that embraces urban settings, stock markets, technologies, and our daily commute—helps, in part, to make us what we are and what we can become.

There are those among us who feel that we, in what we will call the postmodern business environment, are living in an age of moral crisis. This not uncommon view is fraught with the apprehensiveness which comes of losing trust in institutions, systems, and, of course, those within them. The beliefs which have helped establish this view are as follows: that in the (idealized) past, an age marked by family values and characterized by face-to-face interactions and loyalty, ethics were seen as far less problematic; the deterioration of ethics in postmodern environments is due in large measure to the increased complexity of social, political, and economic affairs which have dislodged human virtues from centre stage and replaced them with large, impersonal systems; and lastly, rather than fostering socio-moral development and enhancing the use of ethics as an important tool in coping with life's exigencies, these formal systems foster the belief that winning is everything, that strategic thinking is good thinking, and that remaining quiet in times of questionable conduct is the key to success.

The view that there are universal stages in the moral development of our species has been popularized and imported into the field of business ethics by three very different psychologists: Jean Piaget in the 1930s, Lawrence Kohlberg, while still active, in the 1960s and 1970s, and Carol Gilligan in the 1980s. Each was a practitioner of cognitive developmental theory, which attempts to classify moral outlook on the basis of stages of cognitive development from early childhood to maturity. Piaget, half philosopher, half cognitive psychologist, set the stage for the two more contemporary analysts in his fifth book, *The Moral Judgment of the Child* (1965), originally published in 1932.

As a structuralist (Piaget, 1970; Gardner, 1981) and a radical constructivist (Waite-Stupiansky, 1997), Piaget posited that humans continuously develop new cognitive structures which become organized into even more complex and adaptive structures. Just as intellectual development is no simple matter of a quantitative increase in intelligence, neither, insisted Piaget, is moral development. Rather, through working actively with children orienting to rules and telling stories about themselves and those around them, Piaget concluded that there are definite universal stages to the development of morality. Piaget probed judgments and selected games such as marbles, and got down into the world of children. In seeking the children's spontaneous thoughts about the world, he inquired how they felt about the fairness, origin, and nature of rules.

In the child's world of marbles, a game at which Piaget became very good, he observed four stages of altering moral judgment. At the "motoric" stage of the game, the child experiences no collective rules, but rather a purely individualistic enjoyment of the ritual and its assurance of repetitive motor movement. There follows an "egocentric" stage where, while becoming aware of the existence of external rules governing the game, the child plays separately although in the company of others. In the egocentric stage, it is not the winning that brings contentment, but rather the loose connection to others playing in the game. Next, according to Piaget, a third stage emerges. This stage of "incipient cooperation" reflects the emergence of social activity. While all players attempt to win, there is a vagueness about the rules. These are not generalized from one game to the next. In stage four, called "codification of rules" by Piaget, the fine details of each rule are debated publicly and acknowledged consensually. This shift to formal operations, insisted Piaget, de-emphasizes cooperation and highlights the rules or formal concept of justice.

It was Piaget's conclusion that as long as the child remains embedded in his or her own perspective, the child will be unable to progress in his or her capacity for moral development. When humans of all ages act in their interpersonal relations as if others automatically share their outlook, this egocentrism stifles moral development. There is no basis for even attempting to anticipate the needs, feelings, motives, and views of others. This fusing of the subject and object, the knower and the known, the self and the other, requires disengagement if and when one is to begin moral development. Kohlberg fastened on these Piagetian insights in his articulation of the socio-moral level and stages which accompany our efforts to deal with what are believed to be the vital distinctions between what is right and what, in our view, is not.

Kohlberg began a longitudinal study on moral development with his doctoral dissertation, "The Development of Modes of Moral Thinking." While his thesis was completed in 1958, the questions that Kohlberg and his many collaborators are still probing can be discovered in this initial framework. Kohlberg's first report of this data looked at a sample of 72 boys, all with comparable IQs, drawn from three age groups—10, 13, and 16 years. Ten moral dilemmas, each stressing a choice between an act which would comply with socio-legal rules and one which would violate the rules but serve human needs, were discussed on a theoretical plane. Analysis of the raw data from the two-hour taped interviews produced a pattern of six stages of moral development in three different levels such that each level contains two stages of moral development (Kohlberg, 1981).

Kohlberg followed Piaget in focusing upon moral reasoning as the central issue in moral development; he also took his cue from Piaget in fixing moral judgments in the centre of morality. Where Kohlberg departs from Piaget is that his account of the six moral stages (see Figure 1.4) is strictly structured, hierarchically integrated, and forming an invariant sequence. We can summarize Kohlberg's stipulation of how to use the six stages with the following six general claims:

1. the moral stages constitute distinct, qualitatively different ways of thinking about or solving justice related problems

2. the stages are structured wholes

3. the stages constitute hierarchical integrations

4. the stages form an invariant sequence moving progressively from a less to a more integrated structure such that stages hold universality, are not skipped, and are not substantially affected by historical period, social class, or gender differences

5. the six stages form a complete set

6. one moves through the stages by increasing one's capacity for judgment

In Kohlberg's six stages of moral development people do not enter a higher stage until they have passed through each of the earlier ones. Reaching the highest is, however, not inevitable. Kohlberg maintains that the majority of the population remains at either stage three or four.

Carol Gilligan (1982) views Kohlberg and his mentor Piaget as providing a false impression of socio-moral development because they over-emphasize the very male notion of justice, linear reasoning, and problem solving as central to moral development. In Figure 1.5, we compare Gilligan's morality of care and responsibility to Kohlberg's morality of justice. Gilligan accepts and builds upon the assumption of differences between the nature of men and the nature of women and applies this thinking to the development of socio-moral stages rooted in the "ethics of care," not, as do Kohlberg and Piaget, in "the ethics of justice." Gilligan notes that what marks a woman as unique, also marks her—in Kohlberg's stages—as morally inferior. She writes that "the very traits that have traditionally defined the 'goodness' of women, their care for and sensitivity to the needs of others, are those that mark them as deficient in their moral development (1977:487). Women's moral judgments, Gilligan notes (1982:18), are typically allocated to the third stage—the stage of "mutual expectations, relationships, and conformity," which Kohlberg spoke of in an earlier study as "a functional morality for housewives and mothers," but not for professionals and businessmen (Kohlberg and Kramer, 1969).

Gilligan articulates a three-level, two-transition model of socio-moral development drawn with women in mind (see Figure 1.6). For women, the moral problem arises from conflicting responsibilities rather than from competing rights; it necessitates contextual and inductive rather than formal and abstract reasoning for its resolution. To describe development of this moral orientation, Gilligan provides a model of a morality of care in which one is responsible for both self and others, and thus, at its centre, fairness is superseded by the need for compassion and mercy. Gilligan's basic model is outlined in Figure 1.6.

FIGURE 1-4 Kohlberg's Six Stages of Moral Development

LEVEL I: Pre-Conventional Level
At this level, individuals are self-centred. What is good and right is determined by avoiding pain or punishment and securing pleasure or reward.

Stage 1: *Heteronomous Morality*
What is right and good is obeying others in order to avoid punishment.

Stage 2: *Individual Instrumental Purpose:*
What is right and good is to win at all costs.

LEVEL II: Conventional Level
At this level, group membership and loyalty replace the individualism and egoism of Stage 1. Deference to the group and conformity to rules predominate.

Stage 3: *Mutual Interpersonal Expectation*
What is right and good is meeting the expectations of the group with whom one lives and/or identifies.

Stage 4: *Social System and Conscience*
What is right and good is set by one's duties in society to maintain the welfare of one's society, group, or institution, and to do so out of a sense of conscience.

LEVEL III: Post-Conventional Level
At this level, individuals question the rules seeking to understand the general principles from which they are derived.

Stage 5: *Contract*
What is right and good is the commitment to impartially uphold the nature of sound contracts and obligations.

Stage 6: *Universal Principles*
What is right and good are ethical principles expressed by individuals acting upon the principles of universality, consistency, and logical comprehensiveness.

In each of the three orientations—Piaget's, Kohlberg's, and Gilligan's— there is a belief that it is possible for us to discern the level of socio-moral development achieved by individuals. In the hands of business ethicists, these perspectives have been used to assess how various occupations and/or organizations either inhibit or facilitate the socio-moral development of those involved. Those organizations which inhibit socio-moral development are thought to deprive individuals of the ability to use discretion, to admit error, and to give voice to issues which violate the individual's principles. On the other hand, organizations which facilitate socio-moral development empower the individual, providing him or her with a recognition that their voicing of issues is pertinent, that their use of discretion in decision making is rewarded, and that exploration, particularly insofar as it increases the likelihood of error, is encouraged.

The good corporate citizen selects, trains, and encourages socio-moral development. The motives for this include the following: good corporate citizens see the long-term value

FIGURE 1-5   Comparing Gilligan's Morality of Care and Responsibility with Kohlberg's Morality of Justice

	Morality of Care & Responsibility (Gilligan)	Morality of Justice (Kohlberg)
Components of Morality	• web of relationships • care • harmony • responsibility for self & others • non-violence	• sanctity of individual • fairness • reciprocity • rights of self & others • justice
Core Moral Dilemma	• threats to harmony & relationships	• conflicting rights
View of Self	• committed • member • feeling	• impartial • autonomous • objective
Sense-Making Procedures in Dilemmas	• experiential • inductive thinking • contextual	• formal/logical • deductive thinking • universalistic

of personnel who make good moral decisions; the leaders of these good corporate citizens are themselves individuals at the higher stages or levels of socio-moral development and, as such, place a strong emphasis upon hiring, rewarding, and developing this within the corporation; and lastly, that good corporate citizens gain a competitive edge over others in industries which are vulnerable to issues related to corporate reputation, image, and perceived legitimacy. There are others who argue, in keeping with the spirit of cognitive psychology, that it is a mistake to think that theories of socio-moral development are applicable to units of analysis such as organizations. Not only are organizations complex groupings of individuals, but within them, as we shall see, behaviour may be unrelated to the values of individuals. Individuals in groups or departments often act at variance with the evaluation of their personal values as expressed in reading and answering cases (Kohlberg), playing marbles (Piaget), or responding to questions on abortion (Gilligan).

A third and related body of business ethics literature assesses whether or not an organization is a good corporate citizen based upon whether or not it possesses programs and processes which promote or monitor business ethics. Unlike the view of the good corporate citizen as the agent of socio-moral development with its cognitive take on morality, the view of the good corporate citizen as an implementer of ethics programs takes a behavioural point of view.

ETHICS PROGRAMS

Practically-minded business ethicists suggest that good corporate citizenship involves the explicit development and implementation of strategic policies, programs, and positions for managing ethical issues and achieving a positive reputation for the firm or public sector

---

FIGURE 1-6 Gilligan's Socio-Moral Development Schemata: Three Levels, Two Transitions

1st LEVEL

Orientation to Individual Survival: At the basic and earliest level, the self is the object of concern. Morality at this level is a matter of imposed sanctions on the self. Moral considerations emerge only when one's own needs are in conflict.

1st Transition

From *Selfishness* to *Responsibility*: This level acknowledges a definition of self within the attachments and connections established with others. One's own desires and the responsibilities one has for others are now viewed as defining the conflict between what one would and what one should do.

2nd LEVEL

Goodness to Self-Sacrifice: Moral judgments are derived from social norms and consensus. Concern for others, particularly for the feelings of others and the possibility of inflicting harm, are major concerns for people at this level. Goodness is equated at this level with self-sacrifice and is joined with the desire to care for and aid others.

2nd Transition

From *Goodness* to *Truth*: The situation, intentions, and consequences of an action are of primary importance in this transition—not the evaluation of others. Persons experience a heightened sense of responsibility for moral decisions accompanying the increased attention to one's own self as well as to others.

3rd LEVEL

The Morality of Non-Violence: The conflict between selfishness and responsibility to the self in the principle of non-violence. The injunction against hurting provides a means of applying in equal measures the same principle to the self and the other.

---

organization. If art is what we find in art galleries, then perhaps good corporate citizenship is what we find in those modern organizations which invest in programs to address ethical issues. Just as the controversy over what is and is not "genuine" art drives those of us unfamiliar with the art world to an overly concrete and somewhat circular definition of art, so too the quest to differentiate good corporate citizenship from merely law-abiding corporate behaviour leads us into both an examination of the ethics-related policies and programs of the firm and, counterintuitively, to ethics-related issues which may be skirted by organizations using ethics programs as mere tokens. First, let us look at the policies and programs, then at the possible use or misuse of ethics programs by firms seeking to use the mantle of "good corporate citizen" to carry on a business-as-usual approach.

Ethics programs in modern organizations are essentially an integration of various tools—codes of ethics, ombudspersons, ethics officers, harassment coordinators, hotlines, ethics committees, social/environmental audits, stakeholder-balanced boards of directors, ethics training courses, and the like—used to deal with governance, reputation, and strategic issues involving challenges to the organization's shared value system, its personnel, or the routines it has developed to maintain and sustain itself. Outlined below are of some of the key tools that go into a typical ethics program. The size and scope of ethics programs vary. Some organizations possess only a code of ethics or behaviour; others utilize, in varying proportions, all or most of the aforementioned tools. Heavily regulated industries can point to their regulatory environment as the reason for their extensive investment. Other organizations increase or even initiate their investment in an ethics program following their involvement in a controversy, often made public and framed in the public mind, wherein the organization is portrayed as a "bad" corporate citizen. Still other firms intensify their commitment to an ethics program as a means of locating a market niche rich with consumers in search of a good corporate citizen.

Most firms which self-consciously employ an ethics program do so by first consciously aping the professions. All professions possess a code of ethics which serves to socialize new members, guide veteran members' behaviour, and assure the public that members of a profession can be trusted. Professionals, including physicians, architects, and teachers, claim to self-police. Their logic as occupational groups is simple. Unlike other occupational groups—e.g., labour who join unions—professionals receive their training in a body of knowledge. This knowledge includes not only how to enact the skill required to be a professional, but also the values that accompany the provision of professional services. To assure that members know these values, the professionals make their code of ethics explicit, and operate ethics committees which can, when presented with evidence, disqualify a member from practising the profession. The ethics committees used within the professions loosely adhere to a peer-review model where it is believed that only professionals can assess the rationality, trustworthiness, and decision-making aptitude of other professionals.

Generally, the modern organization, in attempting to embrace ethics programs, has not departed too sharply from this model of the professions. Codes of ethics present the behavioural expectations to members. Ethics committees exist to maintain the ethical tools, champion ethics issues and, as we shall see in our discussion of moral leadership, create an organizational culture which takes the ethics portfolio as a serious platform upon which to make arguments, build ideas, and fight for resources. Ombudspersons, ethics officers, and harassment coordinators are specialists used by the modern organization to deal with conflicts over social values in the operation of the organization.

The ombudsperson, whether a full-time employee or an individual hired on a retainer or per case basis, functions as a value-neutral voice in the organization's effort to mete out ethical judgments in a fair and dispassionate manner. The ombudsperson, like the ethics officer, receives specialized training in problem diagnosis, mediation, and the resolution of conflicts. In the United States, ethics officers receive credentials from a knowledge-conferring body. In Canada, both ombudspersons and ethics officers are hired for their specialized training in law, moral philosophy, or applied ethics. The harassment coordinator, an even more specialized role within the ethics program tool-kit, assesses and collects information, and helps to set the agenda for the mediation or resolution of cases where the misuse of power (often including sexual or racial harassment) occurs. The office of the harassment coordinator can become a lightning rod and barometer of the way in which the organization is maintaining a culture capable of integrating the "new" and the "old" gender issues (including homosexuality and homophobia), racial issues, and increasing complaints about subordinates' loss of privacy, confidentiality, and dignity.

The techniques which can be used to make ethics programs effective include raising the level of ethics awareness, employing social and/or environmental audits, using hotlines, and creating stakeholder-balanced boards of directors and other inclusive governance innovation. These techniques help to fine-tune and pull together a full-blown ethics program. Each accomplishes very different things.

Ethics training, often called by varying names—values clarification, management sensitivity training, or team-building—focuses upon an effort to train selected individuals within the corporation on how to conduct business in a socially responsible manner. The emphasis in this training is upon combining a sensitivity towards diverse perspectives, an attitude of task accomplishment, and the pursuit of fairness in terms recognizable both to the organization's members and to society at large. Ethics training, as readers of this book will learn, involves the practical ability to make sense of and use diverse—often conflicting and contradictory—points of view, and pull them together to accomplish specific tasks and set the agenda for new and challenging ones.

To set the agenda, those at the organization's helm must know what works and what irks. Hotlines are a tool that permit an organization's members or customers and clients to give voice to issues which they perceive to be unfair, unsafe or unsavory, or to contravene either its code of ethics or its corporate culture. As we shall discuss later, the failure to provide members with a variable form of voice often drives them to whistle-blowing. Whistle-blowing occurs when an organization's member, perceiving an ethical lapse, feels powerless and voiceless in attempting to rectify the lapse, while is unable to "let it be." Employees who speak to the media or leak information anonymously may be doing so because with no hotline or other grievance procedure, they feel that the wrong they see may persist. The effectiveness of a hotline relies upon the organization taking this information source seriously.

Information abounds in the modern organization. Audits are serious efforts to assess the health of an organization using the best data available. Financial audits, of course, refer to the accounting procedures used to measure the sustained viability and growth potential of an organization. The data and techniques used in the field are well developed and follow well-established accounting standards and procedures. Social audits refer to the use of accounting procedures to gauge a firm's social values by measuring such variables as days missed due to accidents, customer complaints about service, days lost due to strikes, and court-issued warnings and complaints against the organization for sexual harassment, unjust dismissal, and the like. The skilled social auditor attempts to portray the social values of the organization as compared to other companies of a similar nature, and to the firm itself based upon past social audits.

The environmental audit or assessment collects and measures data on the variability and sustainability of the organization in its physical environment. Good corporate citizens don't endanger the lives of humans who work within or live nearby an organization; nor do they unnecessarily jeopardize the habitats of endangered species. Both the social and environmental audit are most effective when they are done by a qualified outsider—someone with neither an axe to grind nor an issue or group within the firm to favour.

The favouring of a particular view due to the homogenous make-up of the board of directors—or, indeed, the top management team—can, even with the best ethics program in place, skew matters. It has become important in establishing ethics programs within organizations to draw upon diverse points of view and value systems when creating key advisory and strategy-setting teams. "Groupthink," as we shall see in Chapter 6, occurs when an organization sets up a club-like or overly cohesive group as its master planners. The individuals in such an in-group, while often well intended, may find it difficult to understand the origins and merits of points of view which are at variance with their own. The stakeholder-balanced board reduces this propensity and places individuals as agents who represent the organization as a whole.

As suggested at the outset of this section, we must be wary of believing that the existence of an ethics program is itself evidence of good corporate citizenship. Three issues remain embedded in this insight. First, many ethics programs are ineffective. Second, ethics programs are often initiated in order to compensate for a company's bad reputation in this very area. Third, and most subtle, ethics programs can be used to present an organization as a good corporate citizen in order to market it as a distinctive player and thereby attract consumers eager to support capitalism when it shows a friendly face. This issue refers to companies whose self-promoted ethical programs, often touted on advertisements and promotions, do not stand up to close scrutiny.

The management of ethics programs is problematic. Firms often face difficulties in co-ordinating the diverse policies which go into their operation. The resources for ethics programs frequently come from ancillary or supplemental budgets. Half-hearted endorsements by top managers can inadvertently send a chill over a program. Corporate incentive systems, including fast-tracked careers intended for future stars, often bypass ethics programs, which are seen by corporate incumbents as graveyards for promotion. Many hard-nosed executives, in private moments, have likened ethics monitors and ombudspersons to "spoilers." They view ethics programs as a form of political correctness which takes the spontaneity out of corporate culture, and forces individuals' authentic views and attitudes into the recesses of private conversations. This, I believe, is far from a Neanderthal view.

The corporate opposition towards ethics programs arises when they stifle rather than give voice to concerns regarding fairness, justice, and freedom. Ineffective programs either bureaucratize too prematurely, or become the fiefdom of a particular corporate point of view. In the former instance, rules and gestures of compliance, particularly as evidenced in the ubiquity of forms, meetings, and time spent attending to the demands of the program, short-circuit its utility. The organization's members no longer see the process as a quest for justice, fairness, and freedom, but rather as a series of transaction costs to be borne by incumbents. Instead of motivating concerns, members use their intelligence systems to avoid the process, or sidestep its actual intent. In the latter instance, wherein the ethics program is viewed as the domain of a particular corporate point of view, its utility as an impartial arbiter is forfeited. When an ethics program becomes "problem-centred," it is soon viewed as nothing but an instrumental strategy for those who set the problem agenda of the program. If the ethics program is seen—rightly or wrongly—as, let us say, a means of getting the environmentalists or animal rights activists "off our case," then it will be used and treated by incumbents as a form of corporate strategy, not as a means of arriving at fairness, justice, or freedom.

In this manner, ethics programs can be seen as compensatory devices or strategic tools used by organizations to achieve greater legitimacy than would be their due based solely upon performance. Organizations often commit scarce resources to ethics when they either are morally vulnerable or anticipate this possibility. Within this view, organizations seek to invest in their reputations. It is quite clear that the cost of doing business goes down when an organization possesses a sterling reputation: it can borrow money more cheaply, hire top-flight people with greater ease, and, of course, can raise money on the stock market with less strain. When, however, an organization's reputation—essentially its public persona—is cast in doubt, it will dedicate resources to quell, calm, and remediate this deficiency. In

Chapter 9 we shall probe in more detail the relationship between "reputational capital" and business ethics.

Ethics programs can default to or otherwise become part of an organization's public relations strategy. In some sense, and in small proportions, I believe this is acceptable. Organizations which invest their resources in developing and revising codes of ethics, employ ethics specialists, and coordinate programs to educate personnel, can utilize these investments to bolster their image. However, when the image bolstering is the central focus of the ethics program, it ceases to effectively promote the notions of fair governance, societal justice, and individual freedom and personal development. Those within the firm do not see the ethics program as giving voice to emerging concerns of its members; rather, it is seen as a tool to convince *others* that life within the organization is more harmonious than it is. In effect, the devolution of an ethics program into a public relations vehicle creates an insider's realization that the "squabbles" within the family, so to speak, must be hidden from the public.

Finally, there is the possibility that ethics programs, despite the best intentions of those who champion them, may actually help the organization to resist change. Organizational codes are complex. In Figure 1.7 we see the benefits expected from an effective code, which takes time, care, and resources to implement. When these benefits are not forthcoming, the ethics code may do more harm than good. This is counterintuitive. Ethics programs are intended to stimulate the use of the moral imagination in organizational problem solving and governance. Many who champion ethics programs see in them a means of stimulating dialogue and introducing the affective, value-laden, and qualitative skills into a skill set which rewards technical, quantitative, and instrumental reasoning and argumentation. The new skill set, essentially intended to complement the skills of the manager as a director and producer, focuses upon facilitating, mentoring, and innovating. The ethics program is intended to help move the organization's community towards a mindful attitude towards its dealings with others—an attitude of learning.

However, ethics programs can stifle learning, hand out strict compliance messages, and use ethics specialists to bolster the status quo. One of the early—and, to my mind, still effective critiques of the human relations perspective in management—is that, despite its humanistic emphasis upon communitarian values, teamwork, and organizational development, it can be misused. It can be used to siphon off tension and conflict before they require action and change. It can reinforce too much solidarity or group cohesiveness, leading to conformity. The creation of an internal corporate ideology which is too strong, too pervasive, and too preoccupied with its own version of virtue can become an organizational culture which, in its righteousness, becomes parochial and xenophobic.

Ethics programs share with the human relations perspective the assumption that humanistic reasoning, when adapted to the organization, will broaden the organizational community and help it develop skills which will open it to change, learning, and the pursuit of sound values. This can fall apart in practice. Ethics programs can shore up the status quo and put those who seek to introduce change and broaden horizons on the endangered species list. This occurs when ethics programs are rooted too closely in issues deemed to be indisputable, when consensus is achieved by fiat and training, and when rules and compliance replace inquiry and discussion. As we shall see in the next section, organizations develop cultures rooted in the sort of moral leadership which is provided by pivotal players within the firm. Ethics programs don't become moral leadership, but rather become useful mech-

FIGURE 1-7   Benefits of a Corporate Code

Recent research on codes of ethics in business (Foreese, 1997; Frankel, 1989, and Manley, 1992) suggests the following benefits for the firm or professional association that devises a well-drafted code of ethics and remains open to revising it as the need arises.

Provides guidance to and inculcates the company's values, cultural substance, and style into managers and employees:
* The code is a key instrument in socializing new employees both at starter positions and those recently hired higher up within the firm.

Sharpens and defines the company's policies and helps to unify the workforce:
* By establishing a common language, attitude, conduct, and consensus regarding ethics, it is possible to both clarify and unite the often diversified workforce.
* This helps orientate workers to organizational culture and provide them with some assurance, which is useful when uncertainty arises.

Codes help provide overall strategic direction:
* Firms are forced, when either putting a code together or revising a code, to focus upon strategic direction.
* The code, once in place, can help resolve strategic dilemmas by referring back to core values or consistent values.

Contributes instruction on interactions with pressure groups and others outside the firm:
* The boundary-spanning role of individuals in the firm who interact with outsiders is one fraught with ambiguity since the employee often depends upon the outside world to fulfill his corporate assignment.
* The outsider is, by definition, not constrained by corporate directives.
* The code can provide clarity and limitations to the boundary spanner, helping them to point to the code when saying no or yes to outsider demands.

Signals expectations of proper conduct to suppliers and customers:
* The existence of the code signals to outsiders what is and is not licensed by the corporation.
* The code should be clearly understandable to outsiders.

Delineates rights and duties of the company, managers, and employees:
* Codes go beyond job descriptions in dealing with issues that are in the workplace as a whole.
* Codes cut down the diffusion of responsibility that can diminish accountability in departments within the firm.

Responds to anticipated and actual government pressures and rules:
* Self-regulation is often an effective counter-measure to demands for greater external regulation.
* Codes can be used to anticipate impending alterations or revisions of regulations.

anisms for avoiding moral quandaries. Ironically, it is possible that when ethics programs are ineffective, they are doubly problematic; not only do they fail to provide moral leadership, but they exacerbate this with false assurances that—at least in the moral arena— all is well or will be soon.

MORAL LEADERSHIP

Ethics and leadership meet at an unexpected junction; each acts as a guide to conduct. We look towards leaders when we become uncertain and there among us stands an individual, group, or organization confident of a direction and a plan of action. Similarly, in times of uncertainty, we look to ethics to guide us, to give us direction and meaning. It is possible, and surely this possibility will be experienced in a time of great confusion, that organizational leaders guide our conduct in a direction which we experience as going against the grain of our ethical assessment and intuition. Organizations which provide moral leadership and, as such, are good corporate citizens, bring leadership and ethics into alignment. These are firms that "walk their talk" and speak of fairness, justice, personal freedom, and autonomy in their actions.

The notion that it would be desirable to align executive action and character with ethical reasoning is controversial. It is possible to skirt this controversy by assuming that organizations that act as moral leaders are more likely to survive and even prosper than less ethical firms. If this were so and experienced as such, there would be, one ought to conjecture, a flurry of competition by firms seeking to outdo themselves in providing moral leadership. This is not the case. The persistent quip in reaction to my profession—"a professor of business ethics; isn't that an oxymoron?"—touches an element at the root of this controversy.

The perception of "business ethics" as a contradiction in terms derives its momentum from the view that the job of business in society is business. This seemingly self-evident statement requires unpacking. In this view, the job of business involves a commitment to a rough-and-tumble, competitive game whose focus is upon winning. Within the game to win, as we shall see in Chapter 6, leaders must be willing, as agents of the organization, to engage in opportunistic behaviour—to buy low and sell high, to selectively and skillfully extract and divulge information, to build allies, and to broker deals with a constant, if not penetrating, eye upon the bottom line. The leader in the context of business games is the individual skilled at directing the organization to victory over its competitors, and positioning it advantageously for the next round. In this context, the business leader and his or her character are seen as products of the needs of the game. They do and say what is required. Within the "job of business is business" perspective, moral qualms are seen as weaknesses, taking a step or two out of a leader's quick ability to react.

To be fair to this view of business, it does not advocate immorality and law breaking for the business leader; rather, it lauds a technicist's worldview. In this view we rediscover a version of radical specialization. Business does business. The issues of doing good ought to be left for others and other sorts of leaders—church, educational, and government leaders. The best world emerges when those with special competence in moral leadership provide this, and those competent in business leadership provide it. A good business leader is amoral, not immoral. To place morality in the hands of business leaders is to generate an inefficiency. This is not their game. It is not their role. They are agents for the firm, for its stockholders and members—not for society at large.

This view is a decidedly powerful one in contemporary thinking. Its strengths are evident. Business ought to do what it does best, and it is not particularly good at creating, sustaining, and maintaining the rules of conduct we use to distinguish what is right from what is wrong. The business leader is a pragmatist and will use his or her intelligence and other gifts to bend or utilize morality as a means to achieve ends sought by the firm—corporate profits, reputation, labour peace, and the like. Businesses should follow the law, but should not strive to lead in the area of morality. Following the law is one thing; demonstrating moral leadership is another thing altogether.

The "job of business is business" point of view is flawed in five very basic ways. The credibility of this perspective derives from a strong and persistent desire to keep our ethics, which we often think of as existing in a personalized and private domain, separate from our commercial or business activities and their very public domain. This private versus public, sacred versus secular, or expressive versus instrumental values are separate in the "job of business is business" view. In this view, business is a private sector, but psychologically public domain, permeated with secular values and carried out using instrumental reasoning and justification. Ethics, on the other hand, at least as portrayed in the "job of business is business" point of view, is a public sector activity, psychologically rooted in one's private self, replete with sacred values and assumptions and put into practice with expressive reasoning and justifications.

The first flaw with this point of view is that rather than describing how businesses actually run, it prescribes a view on how to run businesses most efficiently. In practice, businesses and, most particularly, business leaders must make decisions and deal with moral issues and claims. Business leaders reward employees for good behaviour and penalize others. In fact, businesses possess governance structures and, within businesses, leaders must decide on whether or not to recall a defective part when the law remains mute on the issue. Business leaders must engage in decisions on whether or not to outsource their work and, if so, whether or not to monitor or audit the working conditions and age of workers hired by external agents. Business leaders must decide whether they will use sex and violence to advertise their products and services, whether they will employ surveillance techniques or drug testing measures to check up on employees, and whether they will subsidize continuing education, daycare, or health insurance. The business of business is business, but this in no way, shape, or form can or ever has excluded ethics.

The second flaw results from taking this point of view too seriously. If one does take it seriously, then one should expect others outside of business, most particularly those claiming to specialize in ethics, to increasingly seek to regulate the moral domain of businesses. We have seen that professional associations of all sorts claim a great deal of autonomy over their operations by claiming to live within a code of ethics. Currently within many societies, governments have moved down the regulatory continuum. Other groups within society—environmentalists, animal rights activists, community groups, AIDS activists, and segments of the mass media—have been placing pressure upon businesses to meet the agenda of moral obligations as set by these groups. It is a weak defense to say you will not do it because you cannot do it as well as social workers, priests, jurists, and the like; it is poor management to allow others to set your business agenda.

The third flaw, like the second, also stems from taking this point of view too seriously. If the job of business is to adapt to change and if this is what businesses do so well, why are they not our first line, indeed a vital one, in handling the moral problems and controversies that come with new technologies and change? When we look at how businesses are pushing exploration on the information highway, in genetic technology, and in the arena of intellectual property, we see businesses working in areas too new for the law to be the guide. These businesses, whether they want the job or not, are pioneering areas of moral concern. It will be harder and harder to duck the responsibilities that come with it.

The fourth flaw in the "job of business is business" perspective refuses to take this point of view seriously. Rather, if the job of business is business, then it is possible to take on the role of moral leadership within one's industry and to extract rents from this, indeed, to make it part of one's business. In other words, the job of some businesses *is* ethics. Businesses that set industry standards, like ISO 9000, consulting firms that provide data to help other firms cope with ethics issues, and businesses such as The Perimeter Group (for whom I act as executive director), that tailor-make ethics programs for companies interested in developing a hold on their moral portfolios, all make ethics the centre of their business. The point here is that morality is not contrary, nor, indeed, is it by logical necessity peripheral to business. It can become central to and even the main output of particular businesses. The importance of this point is more than pointing out a logical flaw in the "job of business is business" perspective; it is intended to show that while we cannot buy and sell morality, we can buy and sell information, techniques, and skills that help us manage the ethical portfolios of businesses.

The fifth and final flaw in this point of view probes the insistence that morality in businesses slows down their ability to adapt to change. The assumption that brings this to the forefront is the idea that to act as moral leaders, firms must engage in consensus-seeking and other forms of participative decision-making that are both costly and time consuming. This belief can, of course, become a self-fulfilling prophecy. If businesses only do what is neither costly nor time consuming, they are severely limiting themselves. To be masters of change, to be ready adapters, it seems apparent that businesses can adapt to the changes of doing ethics well and aspiring to moral leadership. In fact, the very processes that businesses shy away from as costly and/or time consuming may be precisely the processes that will help firms anticipate emerging issues and thereby cut both costs and time-consuming efforts to work on issues once they have become well-entrenched. It is not at all clear, in the "job of business is business" perspective, either why businesses cannot rise to the challenge of ethics and do so with competence, or that if and when they do so, they might not lower both their costs and their time to respond.

The good corporate citizen is an elusive concept. Dale Clutterback, in *How To Be a Good Corporate Citizen: A Manager's Guide to Making Social Responsibility Work—and Pay* (1981), provides a practical overview of what the corporate manager can do to put good corporate citizenship into practical action. On the other hand, the Canadian social commentator, Murray Dobbin, in *The Myth of the Good Corporate Citizen: Democracy Under the Rule of Big Business* (1998), insists that there is no such thing as a good corporate citizen. In Dobbin's view, business—particularly big business—wields more power now than ever before. Its endeavours to put a friendly face over its practised efforts to further its power, Dobbin insists, requires careful scrutiny. However, both Clutterback and Dobbin, representing diametrically opposed views on the nature and existence of the good corporate citizen, would agree that there are questions we can ask of businesses to determine, in relative terms, which among them is compatible with our notion of the good world. In Figure 1.8, I have put together a series of probes that can be used to assess the relative merits (or lack of them) of the various organizations you confront in your everyday life.

FIGURE 1-8 Rating the Good Corporate Citizen: 15 Questions

It is apparent that there is no precise way to determine whether or not a company's effect on its community is ultimately beneficial or exploitative. Here, however, are fifteen questions one can ask which probe the issue:

1. Does the company follow the laws of the community, or has it accumulated fines and penalties for legal transgressions? Does it have a record of questionable activity?

2. Is the company a provider of steady employment?

3. Does the company possess an effective means of dealing with community complaints and issues?

4. Does the company contribute philanthropically to the community?

5. If an accident were to occur due to this company's actions, does it have plans, equipment, and specialists to help the community deal with the emergency? Does the company have practice drills and emergency update exercises?

6. Does the company provide goods and services which the community needs?

7. Does the company pay its fair share of the tax burden, or is it constantly seeking to find loopholes to lower its taxes?

8. What is the company's record on environmental issues?

9. If the management of the company feels compelled to lay off employees or to close down a site, what does it do to mitigate the damage done to the community?

10. Does the company site and design its facilities to maximize their social benefits?

11. Is the company improving the standard of living and quality of life of the community?

12. Does the company encourage employees to get involved in ethical issues within the company and the community as volunteers and active community members?

13. Does the company obfuscate and drag its feet when the community requests information and insight about the company and its plans?

14. Has the company made it clear that it possesses a commitment to a safe workplace? Does the employee safety record of the company hold up to this commitment?

15. Does the company possess a stated policy banning discrimination?

As we shall see in the next chapter, moral leadership by the business community is needed now more than ever before. The era of "postmodern business ethics" will be portrayed as one in which individuals feel fragmented. Expertise, including the centrality of science, is increasingly challenged. Nation states and the governments entrusted with their management are increasingly outsourcing their duties to commercial enterprises and attempting, in their governance structures, to resemble what they perceive to be the more efficient organization of business. Schools and the educational institutions of most countries such as Canada are increasingly measuring their success on how they shape students for jobs. The legal system is beleaguered, overworked, and increasingly questioned by citizens who view it as elitist, ponderous, and costly. Finally, religion, particularly in secular societies marked by an attempt to separate the state from church, has not served as the centre of most lives for some time.

Within this decentred or centreless society, we are alluding to new ideas or recasting old ones to capture this effect—the Internet is one, the market, particularly in its global sense, is another, and the science of chaos is another. Each, at very different levels of abstraction, suits the new *Zeitgeist* of postmodernity. There is randomness here. Boundaries are uncertain and (certainly) fluctuating. There is an order here, but it resists definitive and objective delineation. It depends on what point of view one takes, for the order resides in short-term connections, flexibility, and the absence whatsoever of a centre. From an intellectual perspective, this can be either liberating or crushing, depending upon your point of view. It liberates those who can make sense of things on the run, who can improvise, and whose sense-making abilities do not crumble as ambiguity increases. It crushes those who seek to make sense of things through stable or sacred texts and measures, whose decisions are premised upon established and reliable structures and data, and who prefer to be right rather than merely heading in what has not yet been proven a wrong direction.

In the next chapter, we do look to history as a guide. In it we turn to analysis of postmodern business ethics, paying particular attention to how postmodern optimists portray and/or predict a very different series of scenarios than do their postmodern pessimist colleagues.

CASES AND QUESTIONS

CASE 1-1 The Disabled Worker in Canada

In her recent report, *Living With Disability in Canada: An Economic Portrait* (1996), Gail Fawcett notes that while disabled Canadians are more likely to participate in the workforce now than ten years ago, there are still immense difficulties for both the disabled and for firms seeking to employ them. People with jobs or looking for work among the disabled rose to 56.3% in 1991 from 48.5% in 1986. In 1991, 3.8 million adult Canadians (17.8% of Canada's adult population) had a disability.

Yet despite this, severely disabled Canadians were much less successful in getting employment. Fawcett, a sociologist, found that from 1986 to 1991 the rate of labour participation ranged from 25% for those with severe disabilities to almost 71% for those with milder handicaps. "Discrimination is a barrier that is yet to be overcome in all

workplaces," said Fawcett. "Employers—their hearts are, for the most part, in the right place—are more likely to hire someone with a mild disability than a severe one. The severely disabled just need to get a foot in the door, but in many cases the door will not open for them."

One organization that has helped to bring the disabled into the workforce is the National Educational Association for Disabled Students (NEADS), which represents post-secondary students and graduates with disabilities. The Bank of Montreal is one of about thirty businesses that sit on the NEADS employment advisory council. They are involved in communicating to disabled students what skills are required to find work in their organizations. Tom Proszowski, the Bank of Montreal's national manager of initiatives for people with disabilities, suggests that more work needs to be done to match the educational skills of the disabled with the organization's needs.

Motorola Canada Limited is another example of a business working with community groups to make sure that disabled job-seekers find out about corporate openings. Brenda Jean Lycett, Motorola's manager of workplace diversity, notes that the company attempts to ensure disabled candidates get a fair shot at posted positions by notifying community organizations dealing with the handicapped. Motorola also collects and tries to keep active the resumes of the disabled.

While improvements in the placement of the disabled, particularly those with mild disabilities, are being made, we must heed the warning of Wendy Abel, the executive director of the Training Coordinating Group for People with Disabilities, who notes that the attachment of the disabled to the workforce in Canada remains precarious and marginal. In a time of government retrenchment of social services and corporate downsizing, the future of disabled persons employment in the Canadian workforce remains uncertain. There is currently a debate in Canada whether or not business organizations should move into this area as government cuts back its commitment. Those opposing this position argue that it would not be good for business. Those supporting it argue that in the long run, this is precisely what will be good for business and its profitability. (For further study on this topic, see Chapter 9.)

QUESTIONS

1. Why does the plight of the disabled worker in Canada, as represented by Gail Fawcett in *Living With Disability in Canada*, present us with a dilemma in applied ethics?

2. How is the socio-moral development of the disabled worker impacted when he or she believes that despite the fact that they can do the job well, they are often discriminated against?

3. What are your views about government retrenchment in its expenditures on services to the handicapped seeking work? Would your views alter if: (a) the government had a budget surplus? (b) you had a handicapped person in your family? and (c) handicapped workers were paid 60% of the rate paid for the able-bodied for doing the same job?

4. Make the argument that hiring the handicapped, particularly the severely handicapped, is not good for business. Relate this argument to the position taken by those who argue that the "job of business is business."

5. Make the case for disabled workers faring better in a unionized job site than in a nonunionized one. Then make the argument for disabled workers faring worse in a unionized than in a non-unionized site. Can unions, in your view, support corporations in their efforts to become good corporate citizens, or are they naturally resistant?

6. Make the argument that hiring the handicapped, particularly the severely handicapped, is good for business. What, in your view, do you think Motorola Canada Limited and the Bank of Montreal get from their involvement in NEADS that makes for good business practices?

CASE 1-2   The Tremendous Supermarket Chain

The Tremendous Supermarket Chain has sixteen large stores in Toronto, Ontario. These stores return a satisfactory return to stockholders, are unionized, and attempt to act as good corporate citizens. The chain encourages recycling and reuse. It provides free delivery of purchases greater than seventy dollars to those with a physical disability or over the age of sixty-five. The stores pay equal wages to workers whose tasks are considered equivalent. It presents a corporate image of itself as a moral leader in the business community, stating in its advertisements that "it makes the tough business choices with you, the consumer, in mind."

The company's overt policy is to maintain the same prices in all stores throughout the chain. This is in effect. However, Karl Oppenheimer, the distribution manager, is fully appraised of the fact that the poorest cuts of meat and the lowest quality produce is sent to two stores, both located in the lowest income neighbourhoods within the city. Mr. Oppenheimer, a trained and seasoned professional at his job, justifies his decision by pointing to the empirically verifiable fact that the two stores in question have higher overheads due to such ongoing factors as vandalism, theft, employee turnover, and higher insurance rates. Karl Oppenheimer is sure that his justification supports his decision. In fact, Mr. Oppenheimer feels that to be responsive to the community means just that. In discussions with a representative of a concerned community group from the lowest income neighbourhood, Mr. Oppenheimer was forthright in presenting his decision and concealed nothing. The representative, Mr. Russell, enraged by the fact that Mr. Oppenheimer was justifying poorer quality meats and produce at the same price for those

least able to deal with nutritional problems and least able to shop outside the neighbourhood, threatened to begin a movement to boycott the Tremendous Supermarket chain. Mr. Russell made it clear that he and his community organization would publicize the issue, not only in the neighbourhood, but throughout the city. Mr. Oppenheimer thought that Mr. Russell simply did not understand business.

QUESTIONS

1   How does Mr. Oppenheimer's idea of community responsiveness differ from Mr. Russell's?

2   Is it ethically correct to state that all stores charge the same price when they do so for meat and produce of different quality? Is it right to knowingly find a loophole in an overt public policy used explicitly in one's advertisements?

3   In your view, is the Tremendous Supermarket chain actually a good corporate citizen, or is it using this label to capture the consumer's attention?

4   What is Mr. Russell attempting to accomplish in threatening to initiate a city-wide boycott of the Tremendous Supermarket chain?

5   Would Mr. Oppenheimer be acting as a good businessman if he closed the two stores in the poorest neighbourhoods and opened two new ones in neighbourhoods that had less vandalism, employee turnover, theft, and higher insurance rates? Would he be acting as a good corporate citizen?

6   How, in your view, can Mr. Oppenheimer act so as to be both a good businessman and a good corporate citizen in his operation of the Tremendous Supermarket chain?

CASE 1-3   Competing Voices and the Good Corporate Citizen

Under the direction of Charles Johnson, Canadian Telephone and Telecommunication Limited recently changed its name to Ozone Telecommunication Limited to signal its willingness to enter into the competitive fray of the now deregulated telecommunications industry. Despite its shift from near-monopoly status to the thrust and parry of everyday competition, Charles Johnson continues to promote Ozone as a good corporate citizen. Johnson insists that under the new name and in the new game Ozone will maintain its integrity and continue to be one of the best places to work in North America.

In Thomas Gilmore's "Business Beat" column in *The National Globe's* feature on the telecommunications industry, Johnson claimed he would sustain the fully developed ethics program that sets the tone for Ozone's organizational culture. The program boasts a state-of-the art ethics code that is revised and updated with full employee participation, an ombudsperson and harassment coordinator, training in ethics and value sensitivity for all employees, and an ethics hotline. Johnson added that Ozone would continue to undergo an annual external audit, and its equity program would continue to integrate and advance women, members of minority groups, and the physically and mentally challenged into its organizational culture. Lastly, Johnson was insistent that Ozone would persist in its use of participative teams, and not only provide employees with an empowered voice in major decisions, but make sure that top producers were rewarded.

Eight weeks later, "Business Beat" told a very different story about Ozone's good corporate citizenship. Karl Block, a longtime employee and "ethics sensitivity" trainer at Ozone, revealed to Gilmore that under its new entrepreneurial mandate the company

had hired a personnel consulting firm—Waters, Jones and Girard (WJG)—to provide a template for Ozone to rationalize its operations by downsizing, outsourcing, and re-engineering. Block made it clear that Charles Johnson wanted the study to be kept secret lest it stir up employees, negatively affect clients, and stimulate fear in Ozone's long-term suppliers and subcontractors. However, employees began questioning the presence of WJG poking about and requesting operating data that normally is not made available to outsiders. After being prodded by his senior staff, Johnson sent a memorandum to all employees to announce the study and urge them to keep calm.

Gilmore's column went on to describe how a group of thirty senior employees asked Johnson if they could present their input and views to the consultants. Karl Block, one of the thirty, was caught off guard by Johnson's refusal. Block and his colleagues complained to the ombudsperson. They registered their discontent on the ethics hotline. They called a public lunch-hour meeting in the cafeteria, but discovered that Ozone issued a request that same day for all employees to work through their lunch hours. Only 22 out a possible 1,862 employees turned up at the information session.

In conjunction with the editor of the "Ozone Times," the organization's in-house newsletter, Block wrote an open letter drawing attention to the fact that employees were being shut out from a study that was to guide the company into the future, while Charles Johnson boasted publicly about Ozone's ethics program. The letter called for an open inquiry into the true state of employee empowerment at Ozone, and was signed by each member of the "group of thirty," as they had since been tagged.

Thomas Gilmore ended his second column on Ozone by noting that within a month of the open letter, eight of the "group of thirty" had been let go, twelve were transferred into "dead-end" jobs, and three found themselves demoted. Gilmore posed the question to his readers whether or not "good corporate citizenship" could take on such very different faces.

QUESTIONS

1. What changes are occurring in the once monopolistic telephone and telecommunications industry? What is Charles Johnson doing to keep Ozone Telephone and Telecommunications Limited viable amidst these changes?

2. In your opinion, why is Charles Johnson so vocal about his desire to retain Ozone's ethics program, and to reassure the public that the company will remain a good corporate citizen?

3. Before printing Charles Johnson's views in "Business Beat," should Thomas Gilmore have been more thorough in his research? Should he have spoken to others at Ozone? What is the role of the press and other investigative media in assuring that firms do not falsely promote themselves as good corporate citizens?

4. From Karl Block's perspective, is Ozone acting as a good corporate citizen? Compare and contrast Karl Block's views of Ozone's status as a good corporate citizen with those of Charles Johnson. Which position do you side with, and why?

5. If you had read both of Thomas Gilmore's "Business Beat" columns about Ozone, what conclusion would you have arrived at with regard to Ozone Telephone and Telecommunication Limited? What would you think about the plight of Karl Block and the "group of thirty"?

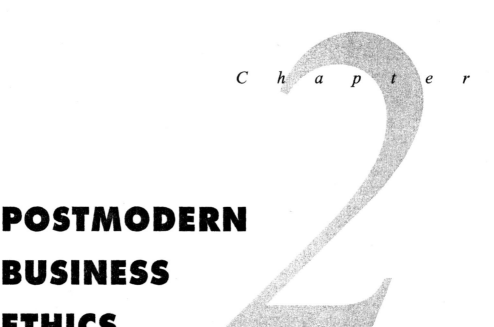

POSTMODERN BUSINESS ETHICS

What is it like to be within modernity's paradigm? Modernity's frame frames us in this way: it tells a story in which reason comes before story-making; reason creates paradigms and observes them from the outside. Postmodernity tells a story in which stories come before reason. Our logic and methods, our objectivity and observations (in postmodernity) are narrated, that is, they are spun within a story.

Joseph Natoli
Primer to Postmodernity (1997)

Our conception of the good corporate citizen is not static. The notion of the good corporate citizen as an agent of change, an agent of socio-moral development, an implementer of ethics programs, and a provider of moral leadership, as outlined in Chapter 1, is being challenged. New requirements for increased social responsibility, as we shall explore in Chapter 3, are being made by society. In this chapter, we will provide the background to understanding the socio-cultural context in which business ethics is coming to the fore. There is a growing recognition that we are in the midst of a revolution in our paradigm, or, in the context of business ethics, in the way we attempt to tell the story of what an organization is, how it functions, how it *should* function, and the relationship between business and our attempts to live in the good world. Joseph Natoli, in *A Primer to Postmodernity* (1997), sets the prologue to this story by noting that postmodernity, the cultural, political, and social forces gripping countries such as Canada, calls for a new and different understanding. This chapter seeks to outline the new story of this place and this time—a story that precedes reason and reveals a deep and growing concern for the social responsibilities of business.

Ours is a time in which bodies of knowledge and their agents are represented to communities by their texts. The names given to this paradigmatic revolution depend upon the texts one selects. Those of you with this particular text in your hand—or more likely, on your computer screen—have grown accustomed to the suggestion that we in the business community are in the midst of one revolution or another. It is variously called the information revolution, the participative revolution, the post-industrial or service society revolution, and the age of globalization where the internationalization of businesses and markets hold sway. Figure 2.1 outlines the business implications, within the postmodern perspective, of each of these four revolutions.

FIGURE 2-1 Paradigm Change Stories in the Business Community, 1970–2000

Revolution	Main Features	Business Implications
Post-Industrial Revolution (service revolution)	• The shift from an economy with an industrial base, marked by the predominance of the factory and mass batch bureaucracies to the service industries, particularly the knowledge-based service industries.	• This revolution entails a shift from a managerial emphasis upon efficiency to one on effectiveness; businesses must remain open to their clients' changing needs and demands.
Globalization Revolution (trade liberalization)	• The shift from business in local and national markets to the international context is seen as a revolution in the nature and type of competition that occurs between firms.	• Globalization gives rise to strategic joint ventures, new partnerships, coalitions, and alliances as a means of businesses entering new markets.
Participative Revolution (flat is better)	• The shift from hierarchically rigid and tall organizational structures to relatively flat, flexible organizations that cut out layers of unnecessary supervision and rely upon cross-trained teams.	• In the new participative, flexible systems, increasing discretion is given to employees, but also a larger percentage of tasks are contracted out or outsourced.
Information Revolution (smart machines)	• Power shifts from land, capital, and labour to information and those who manage and control it; this revolution is rooted in the ubiquity of computers.	• The opening of cyberspace creates commercial frontiers on the Internet and the use of data-mining to sharpen the ability of companies to deal with their clients.

The purpose of this chapter is to explore two versions of postmodernism, the optimistic and the pessimistic, using them as points of departure from which to understand the value changes we collectively are experiencing, and to discuss the implications of postmodern perspectives for students of business ethics. Mixing virtue and business is now part and parcel of our telling of the story of the good corporate citizen. We will see that postmodernism relativizes moral perspectives; places interpretation at the centre of leadership; emphasizes the fragmented pulls of varying stakeholders; reduces the power of the organizational boundary as a means of determining membership; and explains the growing pressure to associate business ethics with both environmentally-friendly capitalism and the apparent democratization of the corporate workforce associated with increasing employee diversity.

The abstract or abstract-like references to premodern, modern, and postmodern contexts for business may seem, at first, to avoid the real problems of ethics. I ask for your indulgence now so that in later chapters we can understand the distinguishing marks of the manager who operates in the premodern entrepreneurial community, the modern community of rational rules and practices, or the postmodern community of fleeting exchanges. We can also understand why, as aspiring business ethicists living in a postmodern context, we cannot simply insist upon a return to a simpler, more decent time where—in our telling of the story of the past—virtue flourished. We'll begin by examining what postmodernism is, how it adds to the already accepted insights of paradigm-change stories used by the business community (see Figure 2.1), and how pessimistic postmodernism differs from optimistic postmodernism. To capture the idea of the emergence of the postmodern world view, it is necessary to compare it with premodern and modern world views.

THREE WORLD VIEWS: PREMODERNISM, MODERNISM, AND POSTMODERNISM

Intimations of postmodernism surround the business student. Commerce rooted in barter and early forms of cash (locally acknowledged) is the model for the premodern world; money recognized as international currency, or cheques and money orders, defines the modern world; and economic exchange with credit or debit cards or Internet commerce characterizes the postmodern world. These are different worlds; in practice, however, we can think of them as co-existing along a continuum. They can be understood in two interrelated ways: first—and in itself a rational, modern world view—we can think of each as a stage within an evolutionary (or devolutionary) pattern; second, all three world views co-exist on the planet simultaneously, but each predominates in an idealized historical time frame. For our purposes, by disassociating it from the mediaeval period and tying it to commercial concerns, premodernism can be thought of as predominating during 1770–1870, modernism during 1870–1970, and postmodernism from 1970 through into the new millennium. These dates should be treated as rough timelines, not as positive historical demarcations.

While the primary concerns of this chapter are with the tensions between modernism and postmodernism, it is important to not lose sight of premodernism, which provides two functions within current discussions. Premodernism is a repository of nostalgic images, which often can be used to soothe and stabilize issues in the transition from the modern world view to the postmodern. Then, too, in the ongoing debate between optimistic and pessimistic postmoderns, the pessimists accuse the optimists of using premodern imagery—albeit set in high-tech frames—as a means of sidestepping the problematic or shadow-side of postmodernism. When we are interested in the premodern world of commerce, we are nostalgic for a world of close, face-to-face exchanges, tightly bound communities, tradition, and a strong, relatively homogeneous belief in the universe as a great chain of being under a firm conception of authority.

In the premodern world view, work is a craft and a calling. It is a means of saving the soul, preserving one's material existence, and deferring to the past as the arbiter of rationality. From a business perspective, the premodern world view is conservative. Authority is steeped in tradition. One remains, as is the will of God, in the social role into which one is born. Men and women achieve their power and influence by adhering to the community's central doctrine, which is often theologically rooted. Power is from God to the Church, to civil authorities, to local authorities. The dominant organizations of the premodern world resonate with an authority believed granted by God; commercial organizations serve the dominant organization and its espoused world view.

The premodern world view resonates with a form of business ethics closely tied to religious belief, doctrine, faith, and tightly held principles. There is a stable centre in this world view. Natural justice prevails, and nature is seen as an unfolding of God's will within the great chain of being. Sacred texts, believed to be God's voice, are heeded as prescribing the good and outlawing transgressions. While great discrepancies exist between the values of communities who have different conceptions of the great chain of being, the overriding propensity is to exclude the other. This, after all, is an age of the local, not the cosmopolitan; valued transactions are those between relatives and neighbours. Commerce that stays in the community gains respect; commerce that goes into ongoing exchange-relations with those with different beliefs, is suspect. Business, in the premodern context, is perceived as successful when it is integrated into and contributes to the belief system of the community, and when it adheres to local understandings of the great chain of being.

While the modern business school (founded around 1910), where managers are taught to manage, is a product of the modern world view with its emphasis upon rationality as a counterweight to faith, many of the ethical ideals expressed therein owe their origins to the premodern world view. Two illustrations make this point more concretely. First, the business ethics interest in communitarianism is rooted in the idea that the instrumental values of business in the modern world view, if tempered by sensitivity to the community and its real needs, would provide a meaning and a limit to human materialism. Another body of literature proliferating on the business ethics scene celebrates management as soul-work, and extols the project of organization empowerment as a spiritual quest. These views are important statements. To place them within the ambit of premodernism is not intended as a criticism, but rather as a recognition that each addresses a world in which there are shared values, a stable centre, and an agreed-upon conception of what is valuable and why.

Modernism turns away from faith in the great chain of being and sees rationality, discoverable pattern, and quantifiable relationships at the core of things. In modernism, talk about God and soul-saving seems archaic. Physics, in the eye of the modern, replaces metaphysics. Everything in nature has a natural cause that humans can discover and use to suit human purposes. Science, the appreciation of rationality and planning, are all human efforts to find ways to develop techniques and patterns to improve upon nature. In the modern world view, nature becomes "the environment," and is usually conceived of as a resource or as a set of phenomena such as weather, which, when out of control, can wreak havoc on human settlements. Nature is not understood, as it is in premodernism, as part of the great chain of being in which mankind is inextricably bound.

Being outside the chain, our species sees society as a human construction, a built environment, in which the adjective "human" modifies the noun "nature" in an orderly fashion. Order is neither ordained nor given—it is made. Society is a maze of social constructs that must be negotiated. In these negotiations, essentially a quest for power and authority, there are winners and losers. Unlike premodernism, in the modern world view rulers do not rule by divine right or decree. Power and influence await those who achieve under competitive conditions. It is assumed that the more competitive the conditions, the greater the contribution to society.

In the modern world view, persons make themselves. Selves, essentially a modern notion, are authenticated or believed to be genuine when the individual feels that he or she has become master of his/her own fate. Mastery and control, unlike the notion of acceptance in the premodern world view, are equated with success. Those who succeed in the material world but whose mastery of the self is problematic, are considered—and may consider themselves—to be in need of psychological repair. Therapy, the psychologization of the self, and the quest for personal development and happiness replace the ideals of faith in God and subservience to the great chain of being as the ethical ideal. Contributions to society are understood within an abstract utilitarian matrix in which, through the operation of efficient markets, individuals continually striving for their personal and familial happiness create the greatest good for the greatest number.

Work and the workplace reflect the shift from the face-to-face small-town and rural roots of the premodern world view to the impersonal, specialized, and bureaucratic modern perspective. The mass-batch standardized factory, using tightly-coupled relationships between workers and machines, and the hierarchically-organized large bureaucracy, typify the notion of order in the modern world view. Critics of the modern world view—and sympathetic to the premodern notion of craft and calling—point out how application of rationality in the workplace has created a sense of alienation, disenchantment, and loss of spiritual grace. Modernism, to be sure, takes the magic out of premodernism and places it in the hopeful, siren lure of technology. The organization of the modern workplace is rooted in techniques of applied rationality modelled after science. It is not at all accidental that the first "bona fide" school of management, founded by Frederick Winslow Taylor in the first decade of the twentieth century, took the name "scientific management." In modernity, the organization is like a machine or system that is initially designed, and then, when problems emerge, re-engineered to achieve specified goals.

Within the modern world view, business ethics is treated as the search for a series of techniques to help in the diagnosis, repair, and stabilization of ethical problems in the behaviour of individuals, departments, organizations, and industries. Business ethics is a problem-solving exercise leaning upon the field of moral philosophy for its theory, psychology for its data, and law or legal studies for its precedents. In practice, business ethics is viewed as a special topic crossing functional areas in the education of aspiring managers, professionals, and administrators. It is believed, within the enlightened point of departure that girds all rationality, that an education in applied ethics can aid those in business to see the forest for the trees—that is, to avoid confusion over ethical issues and make good, ethically rational decisions.

The postmodern world view is self-consciously aware of the fragmentary and ephemeral nature of order as espoused in the modern world view, and simultaneously distrusting of the faith-bound promises tied to the premodern world view. Postmodernism is a broad-gauged reconceptualization of how we experience and explain the world around us. As we shall see later in this chapter, there are two variants: an optimistic or affirmative form of postmodernism that views this world view as an accomplishment, and plays up the romantic and even democratizing elements within it; and a disaffirming or pessimistic reading that stresses postmodernism's radical abandonment of science as a form of nihilism.

In the postmodern world view, nature is reconfigured from its modern world view status as a resource. Rationality has not only been applied badly, with short-term, exploitative zeal, but in itself rationality is no assurance of rectitude. In the postmodern world view there are many instances where there is more than one rational position. Rationality that totalizes or gives a single answer founded by ignoring other perspectives is reason for alarm. In our ongoing treatment of nature, cutting off contending voices, not giving status to species other than our own, and using use value to assess all value of nature has created a separation between humans and nature. Postmodern thinking seeks to reinvent our relationship to nature.

In the postmodern world view, relationships are reinvented. Perspectives prevail. The assumed homogeneity of the small town prevalent in the premodern view is forfeited; the assumption of the privileged contentions of rationality dominant in the modern world view is challenged. The result is that society is seen as a loose coalition of points of view held by those with different agendas, each arguing that theirs is the rational point of view. Data and quantitative methods are often launched as evidence in this or that perspective. Language itself, the basis for social communication and consensus building, is seen as a tool for furthering one's perspective. As a result, society in postmodernism becomes truly polyglot. Many languages are spoken by many different groups, each claiming to speak the "truth." In this context, heightened by access to the media, Internet, and continuous advertising, there is no centre; all is in fragments.

The fragmented experience of postmodernity can be perceived as a severe wounding of the human psyche and community, or as the emergence of genuine choice and local grassroots communities capable of finding outlets for heretofore repressed voices. Fragmentation in the business community is tied to the decentralization of totalizing bureaucracies, and to an ideology that applauds the more organic and flexible organization as an adaptation to sporadic, unpredictable, and unplanned change.

In postmodernism, we are not sure who we really are. There is no authentic or genuine self. We are a series of reflections over our control and management of our public image. The self moves, so to speak, from the soul of the premodern, to the authentic self of the modern, to the surface and malleable self of the postmodern. The surface self is associated with style, image, and impression management. The self, in short, is made. The remaking of the self moves from therapy in the lexicon of the modern, to change of attitude, voice, and style in the postmodern. The self becomes a form of branding and is strategically positioned to help one attain one's ends. Changing one's hair colour, body jewellery, clothes style, topics of speech, and associates is, in postmodernism, the emergence of a new self. To the individual anchored in the modern world view, this seems disingenuous and reveals deep-seated psychological problems within the individual undergoing such changes. To the postmodern, style is essence.

Work, in postmodernism, is a means to learn how to establish, anchor, and create yourself in a public image. It determines your voice, consumption opportunities, and ability to make, follow, or even break the rules at work. While we search for meaning in and at work, we are all replaceable and must increasingly mix our home with our work. The role of the manager alters. In the modern world view, the manager is the voice of authority, the decision maker; in the postmodern world view, teams and coalitions of individuals attempt to work through issues. The workplace becomes a loose coalition of specialists, many on temporary contracts and special assignments or projects. Temporary and contingent bonds replace the assumption of stable and enduring or long-term relationships built into the modern view of organizations. At the level of the organization as a whole, centralized bureaucratic structures give rise to loose coalitions, franchising relationships, joint ventures, networks, industrial associations, and strategic alliances.

Within this context of the ascendancy of the temporary, fragmentary, and uncertain nature of organizational life in postmodernity, the focus of business ethics changes. The assumed stability, certainty, and rationality of the modern world view enhances a view of business ethics as the applied attempt to solve ethical quandaries. In the postmodern world view, points of view as to what is and what is not an ethical quandary for the organization become problematic. Business ethics in postmodernity seeks to assemble and clarify points of view, adding insight and value where possible. In this context, it is important to realize that the organization is no longer a simple, bounded entity with a clear roster of members, a set of pre-specified goals, and a rational and authoritative centre. It is a loose coalition, often unstable, of differing perspectives and points of view, often working on different products or services on different timelines in diverse locations for differing clientele. In this postmodern context, business ethics seeks to provide those interested with perspectives on the origins, thinking, and claims of rationality that meet in and are indispensably part of the organizational environment of the postmodern firm.

These three quick sketches—premodern, modern, and postmodern—should, I believe, locate most of us as modernists with both a nostalgia for the trust and community-held fundamentals of the premodern era, and a growing awareness of the fragmented, interdependent, destabilizing, and increasingly uncertain nature of postmodern forces emerging. As modernists, particularly with our interest in businesses and their operations, we long for a rational formula that would allow us to cobble together the best and most useful from each world view, and bring it to bear on the problems or quandaries in business ethics. This is sound. I encourage readers to think this way and I have, throughout this text, rather self-consciously moved between and among these world views. Now let us examine more closely the postmodern world view, seeing how optimistic or affirming postmodernists turn the world view very differently from their pessimistic colleagues. To accomplish this, we will look closely at five key features (see Figure 2.2) in which postmodernism departs radically from modernism, and in so doing has relevance for business ethics.

POSTMODERNISM FOR BUSINESS PEOPLE

It is only in the past few years that ideas associated with postmodernism have made their way from the humanities, particularly cultural studies (Cantor, 1989; Connor, 1989; Hutcheon and Natoli, 1997), through the social sciences as a whole (Bauman, 1992; Beck *et al.*, 1994; Giddens, 1991; Roseneau, 1992), to texts within the contemporary business school (Berquist, 1993; Boje and Dennehy, 1994; Boje *et al.*, 1996; Clegg, 1990, 1996; Hatch, 1997; Kilduff and Mehra, 1997). The mainstays of postmodernism—the work of Michel Foucault (1970, 1982), Jurgen Habermas (1973, 1990), Jacque Derrida (1981, 1997) and, to a lesser degree, Jean Baudrillard (1975, 1998) and Frederic Jameson (1991, 1997)—have been interpreted

FIGURE 2-2 Key Features of Distinction in the Postmodern World View

Modernity →	Postmodernity →	Business Ethics Implications
Centred	Dispersed	In the process of decentring, organizations tend to overcompensate by moving to radical forms of ethical relativism. Business ethics must search for narratives, locate their meanings, and help sustain dialogue over the ethical standards to be used in an archipelago of loosely coupled organizational systems.
Totalizing	Fragmentary	In the shift from an ideal of management as a formal, planned, rational routine to management as improvisation, brokering of deals, and project master, there is a tendency to manage by short-term directives and opportunities. Business ethics must search for the long-term and for points of view which, in the face of fragmentation, cannot get their voices heard.
Distancing	Involvement	The value-neutral ideology of the manager as an objective administrator and bureaucrat is replaced by the ideal of the manager as a subjectively committed team player. In the shift to the inclusion of personal vision, teamwork, empowerment, and participative forums, the business ethicist must attend to the possible dysfunctions or shadow-side of overzealous forms of participation.
Hierarchy	Networks	This transition has implications for structure and, concomitantly, organizational strategy in that hierarchy is not only flattened but, in the emergence of loose coalitions or networks within the organization, the emphasis shifts from achieving pre-specified goals to adopting opportunistic behaviour. Business ethicists must evaluate the shifting portfolio of opportunities.
Reality	Virtual Reality	Modern management manages reality. Postmodern management believes that reality is humanly constructed, and treats it as image, simulation, or story. Business ethics will be called upon to clarify the ownership claims and rights therein of those who "own" imagined, simulated, and virtual realities.

for those interested in postmodern applications to organizational studies and management (Burrell, 1988, 1994; Cooper, 1988; Cooper and Burrell, 1988). Robert Chia (1996) has, with mixed results, attempted to delineate possible applications of postmodern methodologies, particularly "deconstructive practices," to those pursuing a management education.

Do not let the newness of this literature suggest that it is merely a fad that, like others, will pass. Peter Drucker, the grand master of ideas that stand the test of time, uses the introduction of his book, *Landmarks of Tomorrow* (1957), to signal the importance to managers of coming to terms with the transition to a postmodern world; and in his later piece, "The New Society of Organizations" (1992), Drucker warns that the modern world view requires alteration if managers are to cope with emerging postmodern realities or, as postmodernists prefer to call them, hyper-realities. Conceived of in this fashion, postmodernism is a summative statement of the reconceptualizations analysts are using to make sense of our changing world. Tied to the study of business, it is an attempt to make sense of organizational theories of emerging heterogeneity, strategic alliances, hyper-competitive markets, disorganization, accelerating change, increasing information dependence, decreasing product life cycles, persistent pressures for innovation, and increasing organizational or managerial uncertainties.

To make this connection, let us look at each of the five key features of distinction in the postmodern world view (see Figure 2.2), turning first to the general societal issues connected to each, then more specifically to the relevance for the study of organizations, and then most specifically to the implications for business ethics. In this treatment, we are less interested in predicting the future than we are in examining the present, which often goes undetected in our tendency to enter into debate with our past and speculation about our future. In business, we in fact attempt to locate two sorts of present: the first is the "now" that focuses upon the immediacy of our local experience and the problems at hand; the second, and this is the crux of this exercise, is on the "now" occurring in the larger cultural, political, and economic context in which businesses and business people operate.

THE CENTRE CANNOT HOLD

The first distinctive feature is that while modernity is centred, postmodernity is dispersed. The notions of centredness and dispersion can be understood both spatially and temporally. To possess a centre is to have access to methods, ideas, or persons who, we believe, are able in the midst of uncertainty and equivocality to act as beacons. To have a centre is to trust in its guidance. When the centre is removed or, more precisely, when we no longer feel confident with our selection of a beacon, paradoxically—and this is essential to the tension between the optimistic and pessimistic forms of postmodernism—we are both capable of being lost or found. We become lost when, relative to others, we go off on our own, often in tight circles of others sharing the same perspective. This shrinking of the world is done at the expense of our ability to gather data that reflects the complexity at hand. We are found when, in selecting our direction independently and having it reinforced by the existence of others, albeit in small numbers, sharing our perspective, we manage to live in a big, complex world with increased freedom in a supporting context.

Modernism acknowledges and embraces the expert. In a world with a centre, truth cannot be far away. In a world with a centre, those who access the centre become beacons. They possess methods or techniques for accessing the truth. The centre, in the modern world view, sees further and far more sharply than do those on the periphery. The centre comes by different names—nuclear physicist, supreme court judge, chief operating executive, and the like. The techniques used by those accessing the centre can be learned, codified, and distributed to those on the periphery. This act of public education, in modernity, is one important way in which the modern world view invests in its improvement. Another is to refine and improve upon the techniques and methods used to access the centre.

Postmodernism is decentred or dispersed. Postmodernism is, metaphorically speaking, an ongoing argument, cacophonous in its diversity with contradictory voices often heatedly at odds. Rather than there being *a* beacon, there are many, and each with a small but brilliant flash seems to beckon in a code that some recognize. The argument is more than a functional, pluralist conception of many points of view rendered sensible by the ability of some expert to discern an overall trend. Postmodernists are self-conscious, and perhaps ought to be, in acknowledging themselves as experts. Rather, in postmodernism, truth is believed to be a tightly and strongly-held opinion backed up with evidence from one's experience. It is in postmodernism that science is challenged. Alternative medicines proliferate. Mediators, facilitators, and conflict negotiators challenge the "official" courts as the most cost-efficient and "fair" way to get justice.

The question remains—what decentres modernity? In deciphering this question, we can comment on how those who affirm or embrace postmodernism tell the story of its decentring quite differently than those who see postmodernism as inevitable, but cringe in the apprehension of widespread nihilism and the deterioration of fundamental and shared values. The postmodern optimists portray the decentring of modernity as a result of its very successes. An increasingly educated, democratized, and confident public is coming into its own. The centre is not crumbling or becoming peripheral; rather, the existence of a multiplicity of centres speaks to a new and healthy ordering principle. The new ordering principle, with its dispersion of authority and with a multiplicity of beacons, accelerates choice by providing real options, individual discretion, and learning. Postmodern optimists are not at all concerned with the dysfunctions of accelerating change or future shock. They embrace it.

The postmodern pessimists respond to the question of what decentres modernity quite differently. It is, in their eyes, the failure of modernity that both decentres and makes the emergence of postmodernism inevitable. The emergence of multiple and competing perspectives confuses rather than liberates. The techniques of applied rationality—science, mass education, true democratic electoral politics—have failed or, worse, have not been truly implemented. Nonsense now passes for science. Trivia is the currency of mass education; the hermeneutic treatment of soap operas now replaces Shakespeare in the English class. Electoral politics become increasingly discredited and politicians are viewed as duplicitous. Fewer vote. In this story, the turn to postmodernism is not a celebration of the demise of modernism, but a lament. In postmodernism, the postmodern pessimists insist, nonsense is given the same status as a profundity.

While the postmodern optimists laud the removal of the modern fixation upon a centre, the postmodern pessimists mourn it. Interestingly, when one applies the first distinctive feature—the shift from a centred modernity to the dispersal of postmodernity—to organizational studies, the ensuing story is dominated by the postmodern optimists. Organizations presuppose orderliness. The decentring processes are easily absorbed as instances of decentralization. Postmodernism, seen in this light, is viewed as an empowering or granting of greater autonomy to the peripheral organizational units. As uncertainty increases, businesses are accustomed to relaxing the tightly-bound rules of bureaucratic structuring, and permitting greater decision-making power to peripheral units. The breakdown of the mechanistic and the emergence of organic organizational structures can easily be read into the postmodern optimists' take on organizations.

The postmodern pessimists in organizational studies view the shift from a centred modernity to a dispersed notion of postmodernity as creating greater difficulties for the manager and less security for all organizational members. Decentring raises organizational costs; it increases organizational vulnerabilities. For example, postmodern pessimists argue that the newly-emerging postmodern organization (see Figure 2.3) handles crises—defined as organization-threatening issues requiring swift and centralized coordination of action—poorly. The loose network or coalition of semi-autonomous units are, the postmodern pessimists argue, rather fine at increasing the potential to innovate and explore new possibilities, but they defend themselves poorly against a concerted and massive threat. Inherent in the postmodern pessimists' position is a distrust of the time-consuming participative process required to create high-quality, quick-response reactions to growing threats.

The logic in this portrayal of the postmodern optimists' versus the pessimists' view of the organization is a function of how each attenuates certain features of the postmodern organization (see Figure 2.3). The optimists see the dispersal of authority under the auspices of the turn to postmodernism as a rational reaction of management to increasing uncertainty and risk. To them, the questioning of the expert is good and healthy when it is highly likely that "the" expert is less likely to be knowledgeable or possess useful knowledge as uncertainty elevates. Many experts, each close to the source of uncertainty, loosely federated, is, the postmodern optimists suggest, a reasonable response. The move away from formal planning, pre-specified goals, mass markets, specialization in training, long-term employment contracts, and standardized quantitative data (see Figure 2.3), rather than slowing down managers, makes them more responsive.

The postmodern pessimists look at Figure 2.3 and worry the loss of clarity and hierarchy in the postmodern organization. The manager as a facilitator loses the ability to truly lead (direct) in hard times when consensus is unlikely and participative procedures are time- and capital-consuming. Managing without a formal plan, the postmodern pessimists insist, is not managing at all—it is surfing. In postmodern organizations, managers will try to use smoke-and-mirrors or rhetoric to convince others, in the absence of standardized data, that either everything is far better than in fact it is, or, on the other hand, level blame for troublesome issues at the feet of others. Postmodern pessimists see the dispersal of authority as a loss of order and clarity. In the loose coalition emerging in postmodernism, the manager is given responsibility but insufficient authority.

From the perspective of business ethics, the centredness of modernity turning to the dispersal of postmodernity not only increases indeterminacy, it increases the controversies over what is an acceptable standard of behaviour for figures in public affairs and business. The absence of a centre, while conducive to exploration and the posing of questions, rarely leads to clear, authoritative answers. With the absence of the centre and its replacement by many competing centres, perspectivism replaces a single, definitive, and clearly correct answer. Business students, no doubt, are getting accustomed to the quip, "it all depends," when probing issues in business. This response, a wise one in the postmodern context, hedges. It implies that it is hard to give a definitive answer until we know all the facts, know from what point of view the question is being asked, and understand the agenda that rests beneath the question posed.

Postmodernism both complicates ethical debates by removing an authoritative and legitimate centre as an expert arbitrator, and increases the number of ethical controversies emerging. The magnified interest and concern regarding business ethics as we turn to postmodernism is no accident. It is, in the eyes of the postmodern optimists, a search for a new centre—a value coalition rooted in an open and participative dialogue between and among stakehold-

---

FIGURE 2-3 The Modern and the Postmodern Organization: A Managerial Perspective

Modern Organization

- Manager as director or authoritative centre of an organization with fixed goals.
- Manager is most effective when working from a formal plan—one that maps out a series of future actions.
- Management succeeds best when it closely monitors the performance of the units using standardized evaluation criteria and close supervision of workplace processes.
- Managers are primarily specialists hired because of their expertise in the tasks at hand.
- Management of personnel is rooted in employment contracts that tend to be vertical, relatively enduring, and based upon authoritative controls.
- Managers can separate their private lives from their work lives. Although commitment is expected, one's private life is still one's own.

Postmodern Organization

- Manager as facilitator or coordinator of specialists in projects in many fields working on many goals simultaneously.
- Improvisation predominates managerial planning as issues of an unexpected nature occur with great frequency.
- Greater autonomy is given to the units and monitoring is moved to reams, quality control analysis, and the monitoring of the technology used by employees.
- Managers are increasingly generalists who rotate and are expected to learn new skills on the job.
- Management of personnel is rooted in subcontracts, networking, and joint ventures that tend to be short-lived, more horizontal, and less authoritative.
- Managers are expected to meld their corporate life and private life. To become a life-long learner is to treat all data and experience as useful.

---

ers in an ethical quandary; for postmodern pessimists, the rise in concern for ethics in business is a distraction from the task at hand. As one would expect, postmodern optimists welcome business ethics as a natural concomitant of the processes of dispersing power and authority. One cannot be genuine in one's empowering of others when one refuses to hear their issues, particularly those that are rooted in differing values. The postmodern pessimists, on the other hand, view business ethics as a distraction, since, in their eyes, empowerment should be limited to the task at hand, not to underlying issues of meaning, value, and identity.

As we become more proficient in business ethics, there are times when we will be sensitive to the voices of the postmodern optimists, others when we shall be so to the views of the postmodern pessimists. When we embrace the view of the pessimists, we may feel comfortable locating an ethical quandary in the jurisdiction of the individual in their "private" life, not in their work life. Imagine a well-paid couple, each partner earning about $100,000, having their first child and approaching each of their companies for a subsidy to help with the cost of their daycare expenses. The companies in question do provide subsidies towards the daycare expenses of families of employees whose total household earnings is less than $28,000. The couple files two grievances, one against each of their firms, for discrimination.

On the other hand, we may feel more comfortable with the optimistic postmodern position in dealing with the decentred moral world when we feel that the discrimination seems to be unfairly contributing to the victimization of the individual. Imagine in the same circumstances a couple who together earn $27,000 a year and apply for the daycare subsidy, but are told that although both have been employed for more than 4 years, since each works only part-time (25–28 hours a week), unlike full-time workers (36–40 hours/minimum 1-year employment) they are not eligible to receive any portion of the daycare subsidy. Moreover, since the couple is gainfully employed and neither collects government assistance, they are not eligible for public funding. As business ethicists, we may not feel as comfortable throwing the quandary of the part-time couple back onto the individuals in their private life. We may want to create a dialogue between the couple, the two corporations, and the government agents entrusted with distributing childcare subsidies.

It is in the complex differentiation of small and distinct centres—the couple, the two corporations, the government agents, and their policies—that postmodern optimists differ from postmodern pessimists. The postmodern optimists view dialogue between and among those involved as a prerequisite to working through the quandary. Perspectives vary. The couple, the two corporations, and the government agency each frames the issue differently. Each uses language to defend its point of view. Each brings an argument (often several) which, from its point of view, seems to be clear, consistent, and to carry the ethical high road. The task of the postmodern optimists is to remain sensitive to the narratives supporting the dispersed points of view. Listening deeply is a prerequisite to the skills required of the optimistic postmodern business ethicist. In the act of interpretation, the task is one of aiding the participants to re-frame their perspectives to allow for mutually beneficial compromise and even, at times, genuine recognition that one's initial arguments in support of one's position may be flawed. As an interpreter, the optimist greets postmodernism with the belief that rationality is not dead; rather, with care, skill, and the involvement of those within a dialogue over what is and is not right, it can be reinvented.

The postmodern pessimist, in longing for a return to the rational centre of the modern era, chooses the role of the legislator, not the interpeter. As legislator, the ethicist provides the perspectives with an answer. In arguments with differing centres, the ethicist with an expert's body of knowledge acts as a centre. Ethicists solve problems. The modern context, in its celebration of the expert, resolves by judgment. Neither, keeping with the postmodern view, is superior. Each should be used when most appropriate. Essentially, one is a postmodern optimist when one seeks to interpret and facilitate points of view within ongoing, unending differences in values expressed by participants; one is a postmodern pessimist when one seeks to reinstate the centre by ethics itself, and ethicists themselves bring answers to disputes over what is and what is not valuable.

Let us now turn to the second key feature in the postmodern world view—the belief that in modernity one requires a map or model of one's territory before one can effectively manage it. This totalizing impulse, essentially a belief in the ability to simplify a complex reality by formal planning, analysis, and scientific-like thinking, is tested and found wanting in the fragmented, quickly-changing, postmodern context.

THE FOREST FOR THE TREES

In modernity, one often loses sight of any particular tree, but one always knows the forest; in postmodernity, the experience of the trees predominates. The logic of totalizing (see Figure 2.2) is to seek generalities and avoid looking too closely at differences. The big picture predominates. This, after all, is expected in a world with a centre and confidence in expertise. The big picture is possible because it is believed that what is known effectively represents what is experienced. In the turn to postmodernism, the big picture fragments. The experience of participants is of a world in which the map created and authorized by the centre does not correspond to the territory. Change is ubiquitous and believed to be accelerating. Instability permeates. Trends, outlooks, and opinions replace stable, factual projections. Just as we are cautioned when purchasing stocks or mutual funds that the past performance of a mutual fund is no indication of its future performance, so too, postmodernism cautions us to modify our formal plans. Uncertainty prevails.

Totalizing entails making assumptions that some elements of one's plan or model will remain constant or stable. Totalizing often takes a very long perspective. For example, models of population ecology applied to organizations often take a time frame of several centuries. Totalizing also makes assumptions that rational men and women are all pretty much the same, want the same things, and make decisions in a similar fashion. On the other hand, fragmenting—the processes pervading the turn to postmodernity—tears away at these assumptions. Stability is a rare and fleeting state. Due to this, the shorter the time frame, the more descriptive the representation. In postmodernity, organizing (with its emphasis upon processes) replaces the "organization" as a set and stable structure. This replacement treats the organization as a loose network of systems that are continually reacting, adapting, learning, and changing.

The postmodern pessimists mourn the diminished ability to totalize, and seek to find new ways to totalize in the postmodern context. While admitting the increasingly chaotic nature of postmodernity, many postmodern pessimists insist that it is still not only possible but entirely necessary to build a science of chaos. Chaos theory is essentially a field of mathematical application, aided by the new developments in computers, which permits one to see organization and order in what would otherwise seem like unique and random events. Just as Freud, the epitome of the rational totalizing modernist, would argue that there are not real accidents in the psychological lives of individuals, the postmodern pessimists insist that even in the most apparently chaotic and complex occurrences there is an underlying order. For the postmodern pessimists, to relinquish this belief is to lose their way.

The postmodern optimists, on the other hand, celebrate the manner in which the diminishing credibility of totalizing enhances a close examination of assumptions. The optimists assert that postmodernism is a healthy period of questioning. While the postmodern pessimists lament the postmodern questioning of the apparent rationality of, let us say, science, the postmodern optimists applaud. They see the questioning of basic assumptions as helping to remove the comforting blinders that seem to lull people into believing that others, in this example scientists, will look after us. The absence of a totalizing plan empowers. Moreover, the postmodern optimists warn us against false, disingenuous empowerment. They remind us that one cannot become empowered when those in power grant power. Rather, empowerment arises when the periphery begins to question the totalizing techniques of the centre and finds them wanting. In lieu of viewing postmodernity as an archipelago of warring points of view, each having lost confidence in the big picture, the postmodern optimists portray the breakdown of totalizing as providing for the blossoming of many differing perspectives, each offering viable alternatives.

Within the context of the business school, the shift from totalizing strategies to fragmentation has created a deep doubt concerning the most appropriate methodologies to use in both studying and operating businesses. In the modern period (see Figure 2.4), using planning as our example, we can note how the shift has left a questioning of the very notion of how to best imaginatively rehearse the events likely to become decisive in the future of the firm. In the modern context, planning is seen as a form of rational, science-like behaviour engaged in by top managers or those who advise them. This behaviour, like science itself, is formal, quantitative, objective, and replicable. The last notion means that if all the planners in a firm were, to state an extreme hypothetical instance, killed in an airplane crash, the new planners hired to replace them would, given the same data, come up with pretty much the same plan. In fact, the rationality of a plan is believed to be sufficiently pervasive that new plans must be tied to the ones that preceded them. Planning, like science, totalizes; it grows incrementally. It adds new positions to correct old ones. If followed, progress results. One is, it is clear, never lost with a good plan.

Postmodern planning, to the ear of a modernist, is a pure oxymoron. It is hard for modernists to view the breakdown of totalizing as providing a clear direction. Postmodernists see

---

FIGURE 2-4 Modern vs. Postmodern Views of Business Planning: The Turn from Totalizing to Fragmentation

Modern Planning

- Is formal, quantitative, and rooted in science. It is portrayed as an objective account of the direction in which to move the firm in the future.

- Incrementally-based. The new plans are tied to preceding plans such that the image is of the firm on a journey, changing its direction now and then to deal with an unforeseen problem.

- Is always done before action and is intended to guide action and keep it on course. The rationality in planning is primarily predictive.

- Reality-based. Planning is done on the real (one) world out there and plans, to be good plans, must fit the facts or data.

- Works best when the plans percolate down from the top of the organization, which has the responsibility for planning, to the bottom, which has the responsibility of implementing the plans.

Postmodern Planning

- Is viewed as a story, rooted in the organizational culture that forms a discussion of what different members think is likely to be the direction for the firm in the future.

- Revolutionary-based. The new plans savage their predecessors. The image is one of planning as improvisation. New problems and issues cannot easily be fitted into the grand plan. New ones, often contradictory ones, proliferate.

- Often follows upon action and is a justification for actions taken. The rationality, if existent at all, has a retrospective tinge.

- Cognitively-based. Planning is done on the interpretations of what those doing the planning believe to be occurring. Good plans ease the anxieties of those who use them.

- The separation between the design and implementation of the plan is a false dichotomy. Planning works best when it is inclusive. Participants should include agents of the key stakeholders of the organization.

planning quite differently. To them, planning is rooted in the stories and other sense-making devices used by those in the organization to evaluate and locate it vis à vis a stream of ongoing events—the actions of competitors, alterations in government regulations, or new product developments, to name a few. Rather than being science-like, planning in the postmodern world view is a political forum in which varying and often contending perspectives vie for a place on the agenda. Vested interests abound. Much of what is called planning may be a form of justificatory logic, far more retrospective than predictive. For example, in the modern take on planning, it is assumed that budgets and budgetary allocations follow the plan. Units that are made more central in the new plan and require more resources will have their budgets increased; those that are deemed less central will have theirs curtailed. The postmodern view suggests that at times the logic is reversed. Those who receive large budgets due to their purported increased centrality will oppose future plans that drastically reduce their budget. The plan, rather than creating a reality, may in fact be a means of perpetuating the status quo, and—what is most interesting—justifying it.

In business ethics, the fragmentary nature of the turn to postmodernism is viewed as a challenge. As we shall examine more fully in Chapter 9, the diminishing credibility of totalizing leads to the problem of finding a common vocabulary for dealing with the different perspectives in the organization. Totalizing helps to create standards. In everyday operational terms, the greater the totalizing (in our example the reliance upon a formal, objective, science-like plan), the greater the reliance of the organization upon routines. Standard operating procedures, the bulwark of the modern organization, are possible since it is believed that the organization can use its past operating procedures and its plans for the future to slowly modify them. This line of reasoning has got to the point that most modern organizational analysts recommend that the "healthy" company have an operational crisis management plan on hand—a plan to be regularly revised and updated. The crisis-management plan—in essence, a plan for the rapid disintegration of the firm's standard operating procedures—will provide the firm with direction, coherence, and confidence in the face of imminent threat. The totalizing is complete. The plan extends from the everyday operations of the firm in fair weather to the operations of the firm in the midst of unexpected storm-tossed seas.

Postmodernism, in its turn to fragmentation, plays havoc with standards, including the ethical standards used to assess what is and is not acceptable moral behaviour in public life and the business community. The postmodern optimists see this as an inevitable adaptation to the altered role of the organization in postmodern life; the postmodern pessimists see the dissolution of clear standards as the equivalent to a moral meltdown, and they argue for a return to a clearer, more totalizing approach to moral education in the business school. One can speculate that one reason for the increasingly large sums of money being left by business people and public-minded citizens to universities to pursue business ethics in the core of the educational curriculum, is their fear that the moral meltdown being talked about in the last decade of the twentieth century, unless checked by effective and vigorous education in moral standards, will spread like untreatable cancer cells into the millennium. Let us first turn to the postmodern optimists' view of the present state of fragmented moral standards, and then to the pessimists' call for a return to a revised form of totalizing.

In business ethics, the postmodern optimists herald the fragmenting of voices, the breakdown of totalizing, as a breath of fresh air. Theirs is an enlightenment argument. Put simply, we learn best and most deeply about ourselves and our ethics when we choose to live in and among those whose values are different than ours. It is in the experience of the other as other, not as an extension of the impulse to totalize, that we challenge the self to grow, love, and make commitments. To make this thinking less esoteric, let us filter the post-modern optimists' view through the now-orthodox thinking of Thomas Kuhn in his book, *The Structure of Scientific Revolutions* (1970). Kuhn argues that paradigm changes or revolutions in scientific thinking do not occur when scientists critically study the data of their colleagues. This "normal science," argues Kuhn, reinforces or helps to totalize the views of the initial work since each agrees to use the same standards to engage in the test. Paradigm breakthroughs occur when new voices with distinct approaches re-frame the issues and provide a new vocabulary to make sense of them.

The postmodern optimists see business ethics as the emergence of new voices, perspectives, and framing procedures. The fragmentation of moral standards is not equivalent to the disappearance of morality. In fact, it signals a renaissance in curiosity about what is and is not ethical. Points of view that challenge one another call the issue into attention. We become, as it were, mindful when challenged about our standard, if not sometimes packaged and facile conception of the good world. In the postmodern cultural context, the proliferation of many contradictory voices—feminists, old-school males, new age sensitive males, religious fundamentalists, gay and lesbian activists, environmentalists—keeps us from mindlessness when it comes to our conception of what are or seem to be acceptable ethical standards.

The postmodern pessimists give little truck to what they believe to be the wishful thinking of postmodern optimists with regard to the enlightenment potential of ethical fragmentation. To the postmodern pessimist, Kuhn is correct—new views re-framing the old perspectives give rise to revolution in paradigms. But, they insist, once a paradigm is revolutionized, another, totalized to the hilt, replaces it. Totalization is not, in the lexicon of postmodern pessimists, associated with mindlessness. Rather, totalization is conceptualized as an ideal state in which a working equilibrium among different perspectives is not only established, but built into ongoing systems of exchange and trust. The stability of totalizing is not accomplished by blinding the participants to difference, or repressing the idea of the other, but rather represents a working-through of how dialogue between and among contrary points of view can be held in a public and workable forum with each perspective adhering to certain basic conventions and standards. The postmodern pessimists see the lack of standards in postmodernity resulting in a wild free-for-all with an anything-goes attitude in which only the most rhetorically flamboyant make it through the maze of voices.

FOLLOW YOUR BLISS

The third key feature of distinction in the postmodern world view (see Figure 2.2) is the shift from actors distancing themselves or claiming dispassionate objectivity, to actors' subjective involvement and active participation in the story they tell about what is good and important in their world. Modernity privileges processes of distancing. To partake in a world that values totalizing, one must be able to get outside one's self and one's perspective and thereby see, if not embrace, the big picture. Postmodernism, on the other hand, emphasizes an involvement or commitment to a perspective, and the willingness to participate with others—often irksome others—in finding one's bliss. The subjectivism and participative ethos of postmodernism are not seen as contradictory. It is in activities with others that one either discovers the fitfulness of one's present path or journey, or one modifies it.

While modernism is about mastery and control, postmodernism is formulated around a notion of the self that is exploratory, tentative, and grounded in the image of life as a changeable journey. If one is a student accustomed to taking exams, then one might conjecture that modernism is like an exam in a course in which one's responses are either right or they are wrong; postmodernism is like an exam in a course in which one is supposed to show one's opinions and values. Not surprisingly, showing one's opinions and values moves ethics from the back burner to the centre of analysis. In the former, it is evident that the opposite of a correct answer is a false one. In postmodernism, the opposite of a profound response may be an equally profound one. To master an exam given in the modern context, one must, within the rules and conventions of the game, eliminate false responses. This is hard. It takes incredible work and attention to the rules of the game. In this sort of work, one distances one's self from one's opinions and personal inclinations. The answer is right or it is wrong— no matter what you like to think or believe. To master an exam in the postmodern context, one aspires to profundity. Since, in the last analysis, oneself or one's peers (those with whom one shares a perspective) are the best arbiters of one's profundity, it is difficult to put aside opinions and personal inclinations.

The postmodern adage, "follow your bliss," is seen by the modern temperament as a form of weak-kneed narcissism. The conceptions of the self, distanced in modernity and involved in postmodernity, are very different (see Figure 2.5). In a centralized, totalized world, the task of a human is both to contribute to the needs of the whole and to attempt to influence the centre. The game, like the problem set in the modern exam, is given. Reality precedes the individual. The self in the modern context is believed to mediate the relationship between the individual and this reality. The individual must, using the self, adapt to reality by playing the game at its centre. In postmodernity, a dispersed fragmentary world,

---

FIGURE 2-5 Conceptions of the Self: The Turn from Distancing to Involvement

The Modern Self	The Postmodern Self
• Rationally involved with discovering order and authenticity in a stable and consistent line of action.	• Playfully rehearsing other aspects to the self that can be brought forward; inconsistent and searching.
• Self-disciplining and self-managing in order to eliminate costly mistakes.	• Exploratory and searching for emancipative options, particularly in freeing the self from self-imposed discipline.
• Hard to access, inconsistent, and a poor basis upon which to make important decisions.	• Easy to access, inconsistent, and the primary source upon which to make important decisions.
• Internally split. One frequently argues with oneself or finds that one's sense of conscience is in conflict with one's desire to have fun and let loose. Conflict is driven inward.	• One externalizes the argument with others who may represent parts of oneself with whom one may be in conflict. Conflict is driven outward.
• Conformist and seeks the approval of others when in doubt.	• Nonconformist and seeks the approval of a small group with whom one shares a perspective.
• Self-development is tied to the ability to function and do well in the social, political, and work worlds.	• Social development is tied to the ability to find one's bliss and locate a personal sense of fulfillment.

the game is not given—the centre being absent. It must be selected from the many that are available and that can be both imagined and invented. Reality does not precede the individual. In fact, in postmodernity, it is through the self that individuals make and remake realities. They do so with their ability to change perspectives, languages, attitudes, beliefs, lifestyles, and the like. Just as environments are built in postmodernity, so too, selves are made. Rather than seeing themselves as self-absorbed narcissists, postmodernists see the self, particularly themselves, as exploring the worlds they are making.

The turn from distancing to postmodern involvement has become central to what a growing number of analysts have called the revolution in workplace participation. Involvement, of course, increases when the self is brought into close contact and evaluated on more than just the ability to accomplish the task. In Figure 2.1, the participative revolution in the workplace is shown as heralding the emergence of cooperative-based strategies and the ideology of participative and inclusion-focused decision processes. These replace the modern organizational analysts' fixed focus on the rugged individual, often with loose commitments to the workplace and requiring a heavy dosage of encouragement to raise his or her motivational level. The participative revolution requires participants to become full members— thinking, dreaming, and worrying about the team. It also brings, as we shall see in the next chapter, a call for social responsibility. The workplace requires the whole individual and is thus responsible to the whole community that shapes both the individual and the workplace.

The two images—modernity and its strategies of distancing, postmodernity and its strategies of involvement—can best be understood by looking at work and the worker in the two world views. We can look at the modern context with two sorts of workers in mind. First, the elite or well-paid professional or manager in the modern context seeks to succeed by "winning" at the work game quickly, proving his or her competence, achieving material success, and retiring early. Second, the everyday worker in modernity views the job as something one must put up with. One engages in it for as much money as one can extract per hour, but when the whistle blows, one turns quickly to one's genuine interests and passions. The tale in the postmodern world is quite different. The elite worker uses his or her cunning and power to delay retirement—work having become a prime site for identity-building, belonging, and membership. In postmodernity, the everyday worker finds it more difficult to separate the public world from the private, genuine interests from work interests and, of course, personal principles from organizational practices.

The postmodern pessimists see the turn from the modern stress upon distancing to the postmodern heightening of involvement, as a costly emphasis upon personnel in an age in which, due to technology, personnel are increasingly replaceable (see Chapter 10). The postmodern pessimists worry that what they see is a contradiction. In essence, the organization's heightening of involvement through its use of teams, consensus-based decision making, and participative management builds loyalty and the expectations of it precisely when the firm is likely to engage in selective downsizing or other cost-cutting strategies. Rather than heighten worker trust, it leads to a complex chain reaction: first, those let go in cost-cutting efforts break up the interdependent and ongoing cohesion achieved in smoothly-functioning teams; second, those who survive the downsizing feel guilty for carrying on as usual (no time for mourning) despite the devastating plight of their best friends, colleagues, and coworkers; and thirdly, those who are hired after a round of cost-cutting are fully aware of the contradiction between the ideology of involvement and participation and the reality of the norms in use within the organizational culture.

Postmodern pessimists see the turn to involvement and participation as a strategy used by firms to get more from workers for less cost. They point out that—in practice, not in theory—the ideology of involvement and participation is very cost-effective. Teams reduce the need for costly middle managers as supervisors. When people work in and are rewarded on the basis of their team's performance, there is less need to closely monitor process. Teams, particularly high-involvement teams, use guilt and social control mechanisms to reign in the slack worker or to compel the knowledgeable worker to lend assistance to his or her struggling team member. In fact, rather than being a deep and meaningful shift in intentions, the new emphasis upon involvement and participation is still the old iron fist of "profits first"—but now covered in the velvet glove of involvement.

The optimists do not see the modern turn from distancing to the postmodern emphasis on involvement as either a complicating issue or a deceptive practice. The postmodern optimists view involvement as an adaptation of organizations to the changes occurring in postmodern culture. As workers become more educated, they seek tasks with greater discretion. Moving towards participation and involvement is not an attempt by managers to win the loyalty of their workers; it is, rather, an attempt to use educated people in the new workplace in an efficient manner. The new workplace involves rapidly changing tasks and projects, a multiplicity of changing skills needed on each different project, and the ability to learn as one works. Teams and participative worker involvement satisfy these. Teams permit "multi-skilling," by bringing together workers of all sorts—permanent, part-time, contract work—with varying skills to deal with rapidly changing tasks. It enhances learning by providing a peer context in which team members teach each other in a non-intimidating context.

The postmodern optimists do not see participation or involvement as contradictory to cost-cutting or downsizing exercises. These occur whenever competition heats up and, in the post-industrial context, competition, insist the postmodern optimists, is superheated. But in this context, involvement and participation are ways to assure that even cost-cutting can be done with a human face. Rather than defend cost-cutting, the postmodern optimists point out that this is always a test—and a hard one—for organizations that are stressing involvement and participation. Involvement and participation are more than a velvet glove—they represent the future possibility that more and more people of all sorts, not solely those employed by the firm, will become involved in organizational life.

Where the postmodern pessimists build their case most convincingly is on the notion that worker participation and involvement is far less altruistically motivated than most managers would have those that they employ believe. This is a fair point. Where the postmodern optimists build their case best is by widening the idea of involvement to include the organization's stakeholders by shifting from the well-entrenched modernist focus on the struggle between management and labour, to the struggle between the organization and its stakeholders. The postmodern optimists hold out hope that through the development of trust and dialogue, education in the sensitive area of issues and management, and the ability to transcend their roles as legislators and move towards interpretive roles (see Chapter 4), organizations will, by extending involvement and participation to stakeholders, drastically increase their public responsiveness.

It is clear, even to those who have no interest whatsoever in developing skills in the area of business ethics, that increasing one's involvement and commitment plays havoc with justice. Being fair to one's children or husband involves a different sense of being fair than being fair to strangers in a supermarket queue. In the former, we are subjectively involved.

With, for example, our husband, we possess a great deal of robust information. We know his idiosyncrasies, and these often modify or put into context any moral evaluation we may have of any particular behaviour. With those in line with us at the supermarket, we have low involvement, possess little information, and are likely, should one of them push ahead of us in the line, to have no qualms about evaluating his or her behaviour as morally impoverished and dreadfully insensitive.

In the context of modernity, business ethics adheres to a notion of justice that is rooted in distancing. It is dispassionate. It is objective. Codes of conduct or ethics codes in corporate life have this air. They suit the tone and tenor of bureaucracy. No exceptions are permitted unless clearly specified. The concept of justice in most codes, even very good corporate codes of ethics, is worked out with an emphasis upon the position, not the person. These codes are intended to show lines of expected conduct, denote where one ought to aspire, and even, at times, explicitly prohibit behaviours by labelling them as unethical. These codes, to be effective, must be updated continually and written in language that can be understood easily by the employee new to the firm or new to the position within the firm.

As involvement increases in postmodernity, codes of ethics must be altered. Rather than retain a prescriptive or "this is not to be done" approach, these codes of ethics become increasingly aspirational. Aspirational codes are easy to tie to the corporate mission statement or the corporate philosophy. Rather than delineate areas of ethical transgressions, aspirational codes, like the postmodern optimists, point out what the individual or team should try to become as a member of the organization. They shift the locus of concern from behaviour to attitudes. Aspirational codes are open-ended and accommodate, at least in the eyes of postmodern pessimists, too much room for justifying even the most crass moral behaviour. The postmodern pessimists lament the shift from prescriptive to aspirational codes. They see in this a relativizing of important ethical imperatives, a tendency to allow interpretation to take too big a part in establishing moral parameters.

The debate between postmodern optimists and pessimists over the turn from distancing to involvement is not easy to score, since each seems to agree that involvement is increasing in postmodernity and that this alters the notion of justice used in corporate life from an objective to a more subjective reading. The postmodern optimists see this as permitting an exploration of organizational moral worlds and even, in time, the likelihood for involved organizational members to develop moral imagination—the skill of anticipating and managing ethical quandaries. The postmodern optimists worry that codes, particularly prescriptive ones, reinforce moral muteness, that is, the belief that it is best not to confront moral issues but leave them to others. On their side, the postmodern pessimists remain contrite. The subjective and interpretist nature of aspirational codes fails to set a behavioural agenda. It is possible to argue, even in the most blatantly unethical circumstances, that one's intentions were noble and that one had the best interests of one's team in mind.

The postmodern pessimists are quick to point out that as involvement increases and justice becomes more subjective, the problem of "fairness" to those perceived as out-groups increases. The reasoning here is rooted in the belief that the greater one's involvement with a specific team, the more likely other, more distant, teams or players—including those outside the corporation—may be seen as out-groups. Since one has increased one's commitment to one's focal group or team, one's commitment to out-groups may radically diminish. In modern contexts, the employment of prescriptive codes acts as an excellent countervailing force to potential ethical abuse or misuse of out-groups. The postmodern pessimists argue that aspirational codes lack this countervailing force. In fact, in their eyes, the fragmented, dispersed, and involved nature of business in the postmodern context fails to provide clear guidelines on what is and is not ethically permissible.

The postmodern optimists agree, but they argue that it is not only impossible to provide clear guidelines in organizations on what is and what is not ethically permissible, but that it would be dysfunctional. It is not possible because, in postmodernity, change is ubiquitous. And, while it is clear that not everything is ethically permissible, it does a disservice to try to prescribe areas in which change and controversy prevail. Moreover, the postmodern optimists see prescriptive codes as dysfunctional since they claim to make clear and solid what is still being worked through. They curtail innovation in moral issues and create moral outlaws of those whose temperament for ambiguity may be higher. Lastly, and perhaps most importantly, argue the postmodern optimists, no one is aided when, in a world of subtle shades of grey, a document purports to show all concerned what is black and what is white. It may be, the postmodern optimists argue, hard to "follow your bliss" when it is not prescribed.

WITHER HIERARCHY, WITHER ...

The fourth key feature of distinction in the postmodern world view is the turn away from hierarchy, so dominant in the modern world view, towards the loose coalition of networks, joint ventures, strategic alliances, and contracted arrangements emerging in the postmodern world (Figure 2.2). We have already noted in our discussion of the turn from modern totalizing to postmodern fragmentation, that structure, understood as a form of solidity, is in retreat. In fact, two of the ordering principles in postmodernism—the hyper-competitive market and the Internet—both point, not only towards the absence of a centre, but also towards a diminishing reliance upon hierarchy. In the hyper-competitive market, competition shifts from a state of equilibrium to one in which new players or players from distant markets can and do enter new markets suddenly. This, as we shall see in greater depth in Chapter 5, has placed great pressure upon the normative stability or ethical climate in many organizations. Hyper-competition accelerates change. Hierarchy responds to change poorly. The Internet and Internet communication not only suit hyper-competitive markets, but exist without either a hierarchy or a centre.

Hierarchy is neither old-fashioned nor remarkably inefficient. As Max Weber (1947), the German sociologist and legal scholar, made clear, hierarchy, particularly in its bureaucratic form, adds rationality, stability, and just standards. Bureaucracy—in its specialization, rules, applied standards, and proceduralism—evolves to deal best with issues and parameters whose outcomes are well known. It is a poor platform upon which to build an effort to deal with innovation, accelerating change, ill-defined problems or issues, or to deal with unique and idiosyncratic cases of justice. Weber himself was attracted to the orderly efficiency of bureaucratic form, but lamented its lack of artistry and soul. Using Weber's thinking, the business ethics student might be tempted to conclude that what postmodernism requires is artistry and soul—both of which are difficult to achieve in hierarchicalized environments. This would be only half right. In Weber's writing, it is the tension or turn from the premodern to modern that preoccupies his intellect. Postmodernism wants both the artistry and soul of premodernism and the orderly efficiency of modernity.

In society at large, the struggle between the desire for artistry and soul, and the postmodern fascination with magic, mysticism, and new age notions of the sacred, are being made to fit with computer simulated realities, corporate retreats, and the literature on soul-making in the workplace. The marriage, to be sure, is not an easy one. Perspectives proliferate. The so-called "culture wars" prevalent in places such as Canada are attempts to work through how much of one's soul or artistic temperament is being sold out in order to find material security; or reverse the perspective: how much of the material well-being of a culture is being frittered away on an individual's archaic efforts to find his or her soul, child within, or artistic temperament?

To business students, the "culture wars" have very little to do with the turn from the modern emphasis upon bureaucracy and hierarchy to the postmodern proliferation of networks, joint ventures, strategic alliances, and the like. Yet, the postmodern optimists point out, the new organizational forms, in their turn from hierarchy, not only increase the climate of participation, but create the bases for organizational cultures that permit a greater expression of what is truly valued by the individual. Like the artist, it is more possible in the new organizational forms to mix one's private aspirations and dreams with the goals of the team in the project. The liberating capacity of the new organizational forms, argue the optimists, is a way to express oneself, yet, at the same time, achieve security within the context of a stable and effective system.

The postmodern pessimists view the new organizational form—an accommodation between the human quest for artistry, soul, and self-expression and the equally strong desire for certainty, goal attainment, and security—as unattainable. It is, insist the pessimists, only attainable if hierarchy is kept intact. It is, in this sense, that the postmodern pessimists look upon the so-called new organizational forms as actual extensions of bureaucracy rather than a move away from it. For instance, they see the emergence of loose coalitions, networks, joint ventures, and strategic alliances as all forms of contractual agreements in which hierarchy still plays a central role. The pessimists point out that when two bureaucracies form, let us say, a joint venture to enter a politically unstable territory where each seeks to hedge its bets, this is hardly a disappearance of hierarchy. The pessimists point out that one must not confuse the fact that in many cases businesses are getting smaller with the diminishment of hierarchy.

Hierarchy in organizational studies, the postmodern pessimists point out, becomes more subtle but even more entrenched in postmodernism than it was in modernism. The extensive boom of the small entrepreneurial organizations, they argue, exists mostly as outsourcing outlets for large hierarchical organizations. The rules of these hierarchical organizations are not sidestepped by the small, outsourcing outlets, but are built into the contracts and monitoring used by the larger, more powerful party within the contract. The postmodern pessimists also argue that with regard to the extensive boom in franchising operations in countries such as Canada, despite the apparent small-business feel of the typical 7-11 or Wendy's, it would be erroneous to assume that they are not tied through rules, standards, procedures, and the like to the requirements of their head office. The postmodern pessimists argue that it is a strange position to suggest that hierarchy evolves to handle uncertainty, and then to argue, as they insist the optimists do, that in the midst of accelerating change and uncertainty, rational business people are moving away from hierarchy.

The postmodern optimists, in their rebuttal, insist that the pessimists are not distinguishing hierarchy as structure from the experience of hierarchy. The optimists insist that their opponents are using circular reasoning and reification to make their position plausible. The accusation of circular reasoning rests, the optimists insist, in the postmodern pessimists' insistence that hierarchy persists because rules, standards, procedures, and other features associated with bureaucracy persist. The postmodernist optimists insist the bureaucracy can persist, but it is how we react to hierarchy that is central. We now flatten levels of hierarchy. We learn to express ourselves within rules and procedures as all artists must. Moreover, we are no longer blindly following procedures. We insist in the new organizational forms that—within the procedures—people think and use discretion. Blind rule-following, the logic of a totalized system, is no longer the stuff of which organizational heroes are made. The movement away from hierarchy, the postmodern optimists insist, celebrates the individual who is mindful, morally prepared, and creative. This movement can be understood in the postmodern optimists' willingness to embrace a phenomenological epistemology—one in which an individual's personal experience and feelings are seen as valid and reliable data.

The phenomenological position taken by the postmodern optimists is rooted in the position that it is how people feel about their experience of hierarchy in the new organizational forms that is germane, not whether or not contracts made by bureaucrats contain the obvious (to the postmodern pessimists) seeds of hierarchy. In taking this position, the optimists try to show how those who work in the new organizational forms feel more free to express themselves, find it easier to tie their creativity to their work, and feel that those working with them see them as peers. In the midst of this new experience of the workplace, both postmodern optimists and pessimists agree that the discussion of what is acceptable behaviour in business is renewed, and with vigour. Freedom of expression often brings with it the need to align one's so-called freedom with that of others.

The turn from hierarchy, so dominant in the modern world view, to the loose coalition of networks, joint ventures, strategic alliances, and contracted arrangements emerging in the postmodern world (see Figure 2.2) has implications for students of business ethics. The postmodern optimists' view of the emancipating potential of the new organizational forms waves red flags for the business ethicist. As we shall see more fully in Chapter 7, personal idealism and public-mindedness often go against the perceived needs of one's team members in even the loosest coalition or network. In their vilification of modern bureaucracy, the postmodern optimists may be failing to note how, in the new organizational forms, other forces of conformity and repression arise.

Typically, and somewhat simplifying the matter, the postmodern optimists see hierarchy as repressing individual freedom, artistry, and soul because of its attenuation of vertical power. Vertical power is top-down power. It is best understood in the dynamics between a subordinate and a superordinate. The former owes obeisance, in an almost feudal manner, to the latter. This, to some, is kept under control. Superordinates can not abuse subordinates. Rules, codes and, of course, the fact that most superordinates are subordinates to others within the hierarchy, help to prevent the abuse of vertical power. In this power context, individuals, even superordinates, feel stifled and, in time, develop highly conformist approaches to their work lives—indeed, the optimistic postmodernists argue, even to their lives as a whole. It is not accidental that when we call someone a bureaucrat, in pointing to his or her obedience to the hierarchy, we are not being particularly complimentary.

From a business ethics perspective, it is important to remind postmodern optimists that horizontal power, that associated with the newly emerging organizational forms, can also stifle creativity and suppress individual freedom. In Chapter 6 we shall explore how, in "groupthink," the very cohesiveness of teams can increase the propensity towards low-quality decisions, over-conformity, and dubious ethical behaviour. While it is clear and intuitively sensible to expect one to conform or suppress one's genuine feelings and expression when confronting one's boss (vertical power), it is less clear and intuitively sensible that one may suppress one's genuine feelings and expression when confronting one's best friend (horizontal power). Peer conformity is rampant in many instances where individuals, in their quest for peer approval, suppress personal expression and conform to the group expectations. Business ethics students should be aware that a classic dilemma in the "professions" (occupations governed by horizontal power) is how to get physicians, lawyers, engineers, and the like to speak up when they detect that a colleague is incompetent even to the point of endangering his or her clients.

On the other hand, the postmodern pessimists, in pointing to the persistence of hierarchy and its insidious inherence in the contracting arrangements girding the emergence of the new organizational forms, neglect certain issues pertinent to business ethics. The postmodern pessimists are intent upon rediscovering hierarchy in the midst of joint ventures, strategic alliances, franchising agreements, and all the new contracting arrangements heralded by the postmodern optimists—not because they are spoilsports; they truly believe that hierarchy is the most efficient way to achieve order and the most effective way to achieve accountability and stability in the structuring of organizations. Hierarchy, to harken back to our previous point, helps to identify the centre, facilitates the creation and maintenance of a plan that totalizes, and enhances objectivity and distancing. It is the ideal structure for an analyst seeking stability in modernity. Let us, for the sake of seeing where it leads, accept this belief. If we do, we still find that, within their reasoning, there are problems for the student of business ethics.

The problems emerge when we realize that postmodern pessimists are arguing that in postmodernity there is a proliferation of small and recurring organizational forms that all have hierarchy at either their cores or built, albeit subtly, into the contracts that bind them. The logic that hierarchy creates order, accountability, and stability, if accepted, leads one to question how differing hierarchies, each with its sense of order, accountability, and stability, can act as the basis for guidance or aid in determining what is and is not ethically acceptable behaviour across different hierarchies. Is a subcontractor to several firms in an international consortium to hire child labour (as is done by one firm in the consortium), to refrain from these practices (as do two other members of the consortium), or to determine its own position? The proliferation of interdependent hierarchies can create a nightmare of cross-cutting ethical practices, each licensed, as it were, by a hierarchy, and generating ongoing debate and controversy. Figure 2.6 illustrates how different hierarchies can arrive at different views over the same ethical issue. Business ethics thrives when controversy produces debate.

Both the postmodern optimists and the postmodern pessimists agree that our relationship to hierarchy is altering. Each, however, sutures their story by interpreting what is occurring in postmodernity quite differently. It is this insight that leads us to believe that making sense in postmodernity is more like reading a text in which multiple realities and interpretations coexist than it is like mastering a machine. As we shall see in the next section, we cross an important boundary when we use postmodernism to help us make sense of business ethics. Reality is no longer what it seems; it must be interpreted and deconstructed.

CROSSING THE BOUNDARY: FROM REALITY TO VIRTUAL REALITY

The fifth, last, and most science-fiction-like of the key features of distinction in the postmodern world view, is the turn from the set but malleable reality of modernity to the hyper-reality of the world and organization as text (see Figure 2.2). It is a topic we will revisit in less theoretical terms in Chapter 10. This, for students coming to the idea of postmodernism for

FIGURE 2-6 Examples of Controversies Licensed by Differing Hierarchies: Making Sense of Postmodern Pessimism

Controversy

Polar Positions

Equity issues

- Some organizations support the principle of equity, extending it to the ideas of equal pay for equal work, even to efforts to hire more visible minority group members and handicapped workers, and to advance women in the hierarchy. Other organizations feel that markets are best at determining both pay and hiring issues. To tinker with getting the best person at the best price is to create unintended consequences and problems.

Gift giving/ gift receiving

- Some organizations have explicit guidelines of the circumstances and/or monetary value of the gifts an individual working in a hierarchy can give and receive in order to make friends and accomplish the work of the firm. Other organizations remain mute on the issues, preferring either to follow the law of the land on "bribery," or to deal with gift giving and gift receiving by examining situations as they arise.

Use of sexual imagery in advertising

- Some organizations not only adhere to the advertising guidelines surrounding the use of sexual imagery in stimulating the consumer, but do not try to push the boundary or circumvent the issue. Other firms seek not only to employ sexual imagery, but to go as far as the guidelines can be stretched.

Buying client/ consumer data profiles from third parties

- Some organizations buy client consumer data acquired from third parties (magazine subscription lists, contest entry sheets, survey companies, warranties) to get a better handle on how to appeal to new clients. Other firms prohibit this purchase and provide their employees with no direction in this matter.

E-mail and Internet use surveillance

- Some organizations monitor their employees' use of e-mail and/or the Internet in order to assure that these are not being misused or that the employee is not wasting time pursuing personal interests at corporate expense. Other firms not only do not use this form of surveillance, but actually encourage the personal but productive use of e-mail and the Internet. It is seen as a learning tool that helps develop human resources and enables dialogue across departments and divisions.

Doing business with countries with dismal human rights records

- Some companies attempt to keep business with countries with dismal human rights records at a minimum. Other firms leap at the opportunity to enter into business deals with countries others will not deal with. In these contexts, competition diminishes and excellent rents can be extracted due to the pariah-like treatment of these states. These companies argue that it is government's business to deal with the human rights records of other governments.

the first time, is the most outlandish and incredible of the five turns we have addressed. There is, for most students, a strong boundary between what is real and what is virtual, between fact and fiction, or between what is actual or material and what is imagined or illusory. This boundary is, within the auspices of modernity, no simple convenience. It is, after all, the basis for the "modern" claim to sanity, rationality, and membership in a society that believes it has a relatively strong consensus on what is real and what is not. Line drawing in moral worlds requires, the modern world view insists, an agreement on what is and what is not. Without facts, we are lost.

There are many ways to tell the story of how and why the firmness of the boundary between what is real and what is not is wavering as we turn from a modern to a postmodern culture. In Figure 2.7 three stories are summarized, each of which, I believe, can best be heard by individuals aspiring to learn more about the business world, particularly business ethics. In Figure 2.8 we look at each of these three variations on a theme from the perspectives of the postmodern optimists and from those who see the turn to postmodernism as inevitable, but note its shadow-side (the postmodern pessimists).

The first variation on the turn from the modern emphasis on reality to the postmodern fascination with virtual reality is the emergence of meaning-management as a valued skill. As we rely more and more upon the media and institutional sources for our data, we turn from empirical experience to a more abstract interpretation. When the world becomes, as postmodernists argue, less centred, more involved, loosely connected, and unplanned, ambiguity rises and the search for meaning intensifies. Things are not what they seem. Both postmodern optimists and pessimists see postmodernity as an intensification of anxiety. The optimists happen to think that we are adapting meaning-management strategies to keep this anxiety in check; the pessimists do not. The postmodern pessimists believe that we are developing meaning-managing techniques that exacerbate our anxiety, accelerate our levels of stress, and drive us to want to escape from a realistic appraisal of our condition.

Whether or not meaning-management is a form of escapism or an attempt to deal maturely with the changing nature of our experience of the postmodern world largely depends on what we think meaning-management is all about and why it is so central. The answer to this can be understood best if we can, using images from the business school, understand why society is becoming more abstract or meaning-dependent. Without simplifying too much, let us look at the idea of the shift from goods-producing firms to service generation as the basic backbone of postmodern economies.

Most students who study the nation state and its economies quickly recognize that many nations (Canada included) are now economies in which the vast majority of the employed population work in jobs for organizations that at the end of the day produce nothing that is tangible or can be stored. The service revolution (Figure 2.1), a well-recognized paradigm-change story in the business community, denotes an economy in which the majority of the employed population no longer work in either the primary sector (farming, fishing, hunting, mining), nor in the manufacturing sector, but now work in the generation of services. A service society is one in which producers, or those who work in organizations, increasingly do so in firms that produce intangibles; it is a society also in which more and more clients/consumers are interested in such intangibles as security, health, transportation, and hospitality. The shift to services opens a Pandora's box of issues. All intangibles must be interpreted. The boundary separating the service organization from its customers collapses. Managers, to cope with the abstract nature of commerce in the service society, must develop meaning-management skills.

FIGURE 2-7 Three Variations on the Turn from Reality to Virtual Reality: Business Implications, Business Ethics Implications

Variation 1: The Emergence of Meaning-Management

Major Premises	Business Implications	Business Ethics Implications
Increasingly, power is vested in the abstract nature of information. We increasingly buy and sell intangibles—security, health, transportation, hospitality, etc. All intangibles must be interpreted. Managers shift from managing things in real space and real time to managing meaning.	Organizations are seen as devices that help people make sense in a disorderly world. Organizations must still get things done, but in the postmodern world this is accomplished by managing meaning. Image, style, logos, and reputation become important. Managers are seen as symbolic. They help create organizational cultures.	Business ethicists worry about the degree to which organizations increase their tacit manipulation of symbols, signs, images, rituals, and cultural accoutrements as they seek to manage meaning. In postmodernism there is concern that the organizational control over employee emotions, cultural symbols, and sacred ideas may be out of control.

Variation 2: The World and Organization as Text

Major Premises	Business Implications	Business Ethics Implications
If managing is increasing the management of meaning, then the world and the organization are more like a text than they are a machine or a system. Texts are representations of stories told from a perspective. To know what is going on in a text, the manager must be able to read and decode varying perspectives.	As texts, organizations are equivocal; they resonate with uncertainty and multiple interpretations. The modern view of the organization as a "container" of instrumental actions is challenged. The organization must provide direction and meaning. It must stand for something. The task of the manager is to take an influential reading of the text (organization) and overcome alternate readings.	The multiple-reality, multiple-meaning view of organizations can lead to an "anything goes" organizational culture. This shadow potential of the organization as text is preventable if the organization builds an organizational culture capable of countervailing interpretations of the organization as text where arguments are treated with respect and minority positions given clear voice.

Variation 3: Reality Stretching and Deconstruction with Technology

Major Premises	Business Implications	Business Ethics Implications
Deconstruction is a form of decoding others' readings, pointing to new possibilities. It sets the course for action in interpretation. It creates influence. It becomes most influential when tied, not only to an argument, but to a technology that is believed to be a portal to a newly-interpreted or virtual world.	In the turn to virtual reality, the organization seeks to not only interpret reality but, in its interpretation, to stretch or make it. Deconstruction is the means to the end. Organizations create not only a sense of order, but a sense in which a new order is possible. The task of business is to point towards markets and help usher in these new possibilities.	The possibility of new and virtual worlds increases the call for corporate social responsibility. Ushering in new and virtual realities requires that those who are its prime movers and provide direction, capital, and decision-making power must, as well, take responsibility for its possible failings. Worries surround new ways of reality-creating since this holds revolutionary possibilities.

This logic requires some extension. "All intangibles must be interpreted" means that when we as clients to a service organization purchase an intangible such as an education, we cannot, despite our desire for instant gratification, go to the shelf and pick one up. This, of course, is and should be the case with our purchase of a pair of shoes. In entering a commercial transaction for an education, we cannot, as it were, try on the education as we would a pair of shoes. When we purchase an education, we must interpret what—at the end of the experience of being educated—we will possess. The educational organization, no doubt, will attempt to draw our attention to issues that may ease our fears. It may point towards its stability by emphasizing that it was founded a century ago. It may point out, often by testimonial, the degree to which the education from that particular institution has furthered the career and personal satisfaction of this or that well-placed individual. It may point out, using pictures and images, that a comfortable learning environment with healthy students as colleagues provides a life-long social network of contacts who, upon graduating from that institution, will be there for us should we need them.

Well, the astute reader of this text may ask, "Are the 'marketing efforts' of the educational institute not the same or similar to those of the shoe manufacturer?" They are and they are not. They are in the sense that marketing is a service and all abstracted services have this in common. They are not since the marketing effort here is done on behalf of a goods-producing firm. While all efforts by organizations to get scarce resources (called customers) are promissory, the service organization must consummate the economic transaction without the client "trying on" the education, the kidney transplant, or the law case. The purchaser of services must take the service on faith. We must try to deconstruct or decode the actual competency of the service provider through the service provider's rhetoric. We must assure ourselves that we are not being conned. We must wade through the lists of testimonials, professional associations, and credentials and decide whether or not to buy the service—which always remains obscured.

Meaning-management thrives in contexts where information is abundant, but due to our inability to use our senses (empiricism) to directly assess outcomes, we must rely upon background data. In this context, things are not what they are, as in the example of the shoes. Rather, they are what some people whom we trust, or believe are authorities, or who have more experience than us, say they are. In the turn to services, a small feature of postmodern culture, the business student can be expected to anticipate the mediating nature of interpretation and meaning. Turning to culture, we must note that the modern newspaper, a compendium of fact, is, in the turn to postmodernity, an array of commentaries and opinion. Postmodern culture, like commerce, creates the condition where meaning-making provides guidance and fact gathering becomes more and more difficult. Reputation, including corporate reputation, as we shall discover in Chapter 9, is an exercise in meaning-making in which facts may count less than optics or perceptions. Recall that style and image indicate depth in postmodernity. In modernity, style and image exist only on the surface.

When reality is perceived to be stable, knowable, and our problem, clear fact gathering is the way to proceed. Postmodern analysts insist that fact gathering is near impossible in the postmodern context. The world is no longer perceived as stable. The world is presently mediated by too many commentators, points of view, and interdependent positions to be easily knowable. The ideals of the renaissance citizen, knowledgeable in many fields simultaneously, is no longer possible in what is euphemistically called the "200-channel world." The allusion to channel surfing with the remote control is a helpful image. In this image, one does not master or become proficient in "a" channel; rather, in channel surfing, one learns how meaning is made within a context. To make sense of abundant, multi-streamed realities, one must be able to understand the purpose of the image, who this image seeks to address, and how it is funded. We do not want to confuse the news with an informercial, or a soap opera with a documentary. Meaning-making involves far more than merely repeating what it is we do in a technical sense when we "surf" television, but how in making meaning we become selective interpreters of very complex images. This selectivity applies, of course, not just to channel surfing as a metaphor for reality in postmodernism, but also to our selectivity in attending to reality with the Internet or other postmodern technologies (see Chapter 10).

Meaning-making "means" that due to increased choices, interdependence and selectivity, what we believe to be real is real. This does not mean that humans, if they believe they can fly by jumping from mountain tops, will fly, or that men, if they believe they can give birth to babies, will give birth to babies. Rather, meaning-making "means" that what it means to fly or what it means to give birth is not fixed but, rather, is made by men and women and will alter. Humans do indeed fly. Men and women, trained in hang-gliding, can, when jumping from mountain tops, be said to fly. While it is not quite clear what verb we will use when a baby is cloned from the cells of a human male, it is not apparent that it will not be derived from or related to our present verb "to give birth." Since meanings are not given but are made, the emergence of meaning impacts business quite centrally.

The business implications of Variation 1 (see Figure 2.7), will be drawn out more fully also in Chapter 5. Meaning-making occurs when men and women seek to alter the way they and others make sense of the world. Culture evolves to accomplish this. In the modern world view, culture provides its inhabitants with their understanding of what is and is not real, what is and is not valuable, and what is and is not good. In the postmodern world view, culture is made, at times, self-consciously—at other times, unconsciously—by men and women. Organizations have cultures. It is with greater and greater frequency, as we shall see in Chapter 5, that managers try to manage culture. Managers are increasingly aware that their skills have a symbolic side. They help to create and alter the organizational culture.

The business ethics implication of Variation 1 are related to the fact that the values of organizational participants are expressed in and through the organization's culture. Some organizations, as we shall see more fully in Chapter 5, emphasize and privilege different ethical views. For example, some organizational cultures or subcultures within a larger organization, emphasize and privilege a utilitarian cultural perspective where arguments as to what is and is not an ethical line of action for the organization are assumed to be those in which it can be "shown" that the largest number of members benefit. Another example, group hedonism, flourishes in the decentralized postmodern context. In group hedonistic organizational cultures, arguments supporting the greatest and most immediate benefit to the group are selected. A last example from Chapter 5, a compulsively neurotic organizational culture where stress is placed on doing things exactly as planned and where arguments that show how to act in accordance with the specified plan, rise to ascendancy. In fact, it is in the emphasis and privileging of differing arguments over what is good, supportable, and to be rewarded that managers consciously and unconsciously manage meaning and, by altering the organization's culture, influence corporate ethics.

The second variation on the turn from reality to virtual reality (see Figure 2.7) em-phasizes that the meaning-making that prevails in postmodernism necessitates an alter-ation of the metaphors we use to make sense of reality. In the modern world view, the apparent stability of "things," their clear boundaries, their measurement and meaning, are all, to a large degree, assumed; the postmodern world resonates with the uncertainty of "intangibles" that do not possess stable boundaries, are difficult to measure, and whose meaning largely depends on the perspective that one elects to take. As students of business ethics, we can think of the organization in the modern world view as a thing. In so doing, we can think of it, for example, as a machine, rationally engineered to accomplish a spe-cific task or tasks. As an intangible, within the auspices of postmodernity, the organization can be thought of as a text into which different groups read different interpretations and un-derstand different stories.

The text metaphor licenses perspectivism. In the next chapter, in looking at stakeholder theories of the organization, we shall hear that shareholders tell the story of what the orga-nization is and ought to be very differently than do unionized employees, who, in turn, weave a tale quite distinct from the local community in which the organization operates. The text-like understanding of the world and organizations can also be seen filtered through the increasing reliance we place in postmodernity on realities we do not experience directly, but access through the interpretations of others. Do we recognize fully that despite the de-throning of the expert as the centre there is no end to many competing expert views magnified by the technology of satellite television, cable, and the Internet? We see and understand the world and texts like the organization, not directly, but through the composite lens of commentators, analysts, opinion polls, plays, television entertainment, and the news. This, to be sure, is a mediated world in which symbols, images, and motives coming under our scrutiny must be assessed. Who is it that is conveying this reality? What is their take? Do they represent a special interest group? Do they have an axe to grind? Have I heard a different take on this same reality?

This process of questioning, looking at points of view, attempting to distinguish among the messages the agenda and the hidden agenda are all necessary to make sense of things when the world and organization are text. The surface of the text must be broken. One attends to the mean-ing beneath the meaning. This decoding or deconstruction is not at all sensible in the modern world view. In fact, one would consider it, if taken to the extreme, a form of paranoia. What is, after all, presented by the centre is objective, validated by the best minds, and achieved using state-of-the-art techniques. In postmodernism, with no centre and many claimants to contra-dictory directions, all of them claiming rationality, all of them advocating ideas of what is and is not ethical, it is difficult to be certain that one has selected the right direction.

Turning to the business implications of the "world and organization as text," it should be clear that postmodernism will be resisted by managers who require high degrees of cer-tainty before they act. The text, as we have seen, does not eliminate equivocality; rather, it is a way of ordering it and making the uncertainty useful. The organization as a text lends meaning and direction in the midst of uncertainty. The text is a compilation of voices and traces of perspectives, all adding to authorship. The postmodernist claim that the one-author view of the world and organization as text is dead. Managers may feel uncomfortable with this since it presumes to limit their power, but organizational analysts accustomed to the importance of other issues in determining the fate of organizations—government regulations, shifts in currency value, war—may find the metaphor of the organization as text attractive.

As text-like, the organization is seen as requiring a particular attention to language. The organization is not only a web of stable routines leading to expected outcomes, as is predominant in the modern world view, but is now, as well, a web of perspectives located in language that guides notions of meaning and sets the stage for decisions that precede action that breaks routine. Postmodernism sees the breakdown of routine as a sign of organizational viability. Postmodernism presupposes that routine no longer contains human anxiety. It is in our growing anxiety that we become willing to explore perspectives that heretofore were seen as "merely" peripheral. The attractiveness of the text-like nature of organizations rests less in its definite guidance in times of accelerating change, but in its Zen-like reminder to remain mindful, to remain aloof from the promises of a quick fix, and to listen deeply to the voices and their meaning as they occur in the organization and its environment.

In business ethics, Variation 2 (See Figure 2.7) in the turn from reality to virtual reality is looked upon as both a problem and as an interesting solution to a problem—"pluralistic ignorance"—prevalent in the ethics portfolio of the organization in the modern world view. The problem is easy to apprehend and has no doubt been anticipated by the keen student of business ethics. The multiple reality, multiple meaning view of organization is great in theory, but in practice might it not lead to an "anything goes" organizational culture? The smart and persuasive can, within the loose ordering and accountability procedures of the organization as text, justify his or her actions—even the most ethically callous. Related and equally troubling is the old but nonetheless wise adage that one of the best ways to colonize a people is to divide and then to conquer them. The organization as text provides fertile ground for those who would be autocrats. The divisions are many. There is no centre. Uncertainty prevails. While postmodernist optimists would like to read democracy into the formulation, postmodern pessimists see the preconditions for totalitarianism (see Figure 2.8).

The business ethics problem that Variation 2 helps to resolve is that of pluralistic ignorance. Pluralistic ignorance is a problem that plagues organizations in the modern world view. Pluralistic ignorance occurs when smart people doing excellent jobs in highly-structured organizations discover that no one is handling problems—i.e. ethics problems—that fall between the cracks of the existing functional structure. This becomes problematic as many see the organization and its members as complicitous in the concealment, delay, or stonewalling of issues. In the organization, everyone assumes that someone else is tackling the issue. The scenario of pluralistic ignorance is less likely in the text-like treatment of organizations. Interpretation requires that issues outside functional areas be a focus of attention. The generalist striving to make sense of new and emerging issues has a different attitude towards the boundaries of functional specialists. Being project-based, loosely-coupled, and based on networks, implies that the postmodern organization is accustomed to dealing with issues that would otherwise fall between the cracks.

The third and last variation (see Figure 2.7) on the turn from the reality of modernity to the virtual reality of postmodernism points to the fact that not only are postmodern organizations interpreted and managed as if they were multiple realities, but also that organizations stretch reality, particularly in their use of technology. The result is that in postmodernity, organizations self-consciously create new realities. In modernity we have become accustomed to the fact that organizations help build new environments. Pictures of pastoral fields or stream-laced forests remind us that where our cities now sit, other realities once were. When we visit Disneyland or immerse ourselves in the darkness of a movie house, we understand that the reality we are partaking in is made, financed, and packaged in the modern organizational context. From a business ethics point of view, the very making of a reality, even a make-believe one, requires in important and real terms that the makers become responsible for the consequences of that reality should it go wrong. Building a shopping mall whose roof collapses on opening day requires that those central to the fault-line in the newly-built environment claim responsibility.

Postmodernity, and we are only on its edge, involves the use of technologies to alter the way we sense the world. Virtual realities are realities in which it is difficult, if not impossible, to distinguish between the original and the facsimile. In virtual realities, one can participate and interact in models as three-dimensional space, somewhat like *being in* rather than watching a movie. The movie, however, in virtual reality, may be a computer program attached to a visor or a bodysuit that gives one the experience of being involved in a created or simulated reality. Just as the wisdom of the East requires us to be sufficiently mindful to remember to ask the question "what is reality and what is the dream?" so too, the stretched technology of postmodernism asks us "which is the original and which the technologically-stretched reality?"

This question leads us to why postmodernists suggest that deconstruction, the strategy of critically examining texts by focusing upon contradictions, oppositions, and actual agendas, be brought to the fore. In the postmodern context, deconstruction is a prerequisite for managing in a multiple-meaning, multiple-interpretation world where technologies stretch and bend realities. The turn from positivism to deconstructionism in business studies, a turn resisted by analysts accustomed to relying upon the appropriation of the term "science" to get their voices heard, calls for competent business actors to be aware. The awareness is a critical call to solicit the voices of experts, but then to trace their logic—to read them, so to speak, as if they were a text, to compare their views with others purporting to address the same issue, and to piece together lines of action. While the postmodernists in the business community may be seen as indecisive, theirs is a point of view that calls for competent business actors to be wary of pat solutions and to begin to educate themselves to lead in a very intangible, quickly-altering, multi-reality, multi-interpreted world.

We, of course, are already in the postmodern world view and have been so throughout the past decade. In the business world, we have grown accustomed to the emerging virtual reality of the increasingly cashless society. Credit cards, debit cards, cash cards, and Internet all have helped to create an environment in which money shifts hands by movement of pixels that make up digits on a computer screen. Transactions are abstracted. One's identity is attached to numbers, such as credit card numbers, and exchanges in real time and real space—shop floors, dentists' offices, racetracks—are converted into exchanges in virtual space and time. The emerging virtual reality in this instance simulates the original reality, abstracting from it the economic exchange, and thereby determining which of many different piles of figures (the credit card companies, the consumers' accounts, a line of credit) ought to be recalibrated in line with the actual economic transaction. Now, of course, the reality of the actual transactions themselves can be altered. Economic exchanges can be engaged in over thousands of miles, different time zones, by parties who have never met in reality but know each other, so to speak, in virtual reality.

I am not a futurist, but a business ethicist. My purpose here is not to portray a version of the future, but to try to address a sense of the "now" that has come into our lives and is modifying our understanding of what is good and what is not in our organizations. In Figure 2.8, the postmodern optimists' and the postmodern pessimists' turn from reality to virtual

FIGURE 2-8 Three Variations on the Turn from Reality to Virtual Reality: Postmodern Optimists, Postmodern Pessimists

Variation 1: The Emergence of Meaning-Management

Postmodern Optimists

Meaning-management liberates. The turn to virtual reality is subsumed beneath a glossy reading of the service revolution or post-industrial society. Service workers are depicted as knowledge workers. Society escalates its emphasis upon education. Workers are given more freedom in order to put their knowledge into practice.

Postmodern Pessimists

Meaning-management helps to tighten the iron cage. The new service worker is typically a retail clerk, cashier, or "gopher." The turn to virtual reality is a new and more efficient way to extend supervision and control. Supervision is now built into the use of technology, which provides accurate data on one's output.

Variation 2: The World and Organization as Text

Postmodern Optimists

The metaphor of the text for the world and organization is celebrated as a triumph of pluralism and the democratization of power. The postmodern optimists see the malleable text as both adaptive and genuine. The flexibility comes from the fact that the organization as text has multiple authorship, diverse perspectives, and an openness to new interpretations.

Postmodern Pessimists

The metaphor of the text for both the world and organization is lamented because, without a centre or dominant read, there is no direction—no up, no down, no right, no wrong. Multiple authorship licenses an "anything goes" attitude. This exacerbates the smooth and efficient functioning of systems.

Variation 3: Reality Stretching and Deconstruction with Technology

Postmodern Optimists

Reality is stretched with deconstruction and technology so that new possibilities emerge. Deconstruction creates the search for alternatives to old, imposed answers to problems. We test reality more quickly and honestly when we seek to become inclusive and open to new voices. Technology creates new possibilities and opens the portal to heretofore undreamed options.

Postmodern Pessimists

Reality is not stretched at all with deconstruction and technology. It is shrunken. Deconstruction creates the illusion of public debate and the open search for new options. In fact, it is dominated by forms of political correctness wherein people do not dare say what they truly believe. Technology goes, always, to the powerful. Its promises are rarely realized.

reality are presented. It is important to see that in each variation of the story—"The Emergence of Meaning-Management"; "The World and Organization as Text"; and "Reality Stretching and Deconstruction with Technology"—there is both a dark side and one promising new light and liberty.

The postmodern optimists view the turn from reality to virtual reality as an emancipating and liberating moment. In their hands, technology bends reality in line with the most noble intentions. Variation 1, "The Emergence of Meaning-Management" (see Figure 2.8), empowers a whole new wave of knowledge—workers riding the crest of the service-based economy. The postmodern pessimists, however, see neither the service economy, nor its computer technology, in the same light. The pessimists view the service economy as providing part-time programming and retail jobs in fast food outlets. In these, the technology of postmodernism tightens the ability to monitor employees. Clients and consumer databases can be built from the smallest transactions (see Figure 2.9). Rather than liberating and democratizing the organization, the postmodern pessimists see the turn to meaning-management as coercive and limiting the freedom of individuals.

The dystopian theme of the postmodern pessimists is kept alive in both the second variation, "The World and Organization as Text," and in the third variation, "Reality Stretching and Deconstruction with Technology" (see Figure 2.8). The postmodern pessimists see the text metaphor as illusive. In licensing multiple interpretations and multiple readings, it confuses nonsense with substance. Moreover, in cleverly concealing the role of the author in setting the agenda of the text, the postmodern optimists package power and politics as if it were dialogue. And in the "Reality Stretching and Deconstruction with Technology," postmodern pessimists see escapism and a retreat from dealing with what they acknowledge is an increasingly stressful and anxiety-ridden world.

The postmodern optimists push utopian buttons. In both Variations 1 and 2, the turn from modern reality to postmodern virtual reality is celebrated. The text-like character of organizations encourages pluralism and gives rise to previously suppressed voices in the working-through of issues. This diversity accelerates the learning potentials within organizations and permits the education of managers in directions that encourage inclusiveness and deep listening. As to "Reality Stretching and Deconstruction with Technology," the postmodern optimists herald the technologies leading to virtual reality as new highways for commerce. The reality stretching technologies, girded by the deconstructionist skills of managers, suggest new possibilities for solving not only problems of the material comfort of our species, but building environments that simulate excitement, sexual involvement, meditative calm, and the like.

The shift from modernity to postmodernity is ongoing. A first-rate student of mine in a business ethics seminar once asked, "While we live in the postmodern world view and experience this daily, we still think in models from the modern world view, and often dream in images and symbols from the premodern view. What are we to do when things are out of whack?" This, I believed then and still do now, is an excellent question. When things are out of whack we look for responsible people to aid us in bringing things back into line. We turn to those who, we believe, can make things happen. Increasingly, with our confidence in government as an arbiter of effective action diminishing, we are turning to business and the organizational world. We are calling for businesses to act responsibly—to increase their social responsibility; to provide an institutional means for us to employ some of our collective energy, wealth, and power; to redress our sense of dislocation; and to provide a sense that the good world is once again within our grasp.

In Chapter 3, we turn to the theoretical premises that underlie our increasing interest in corporate social responsibility and what we think it can do. In Chapter 4, we will look at how to put social responsibility into practice to deal with issues in the premodern world view (i.e. trust), modern world view (i.e. issues management), and postmodern world view (i.e. interpretation of information). The discussion of corporate social responsibility in these two chapters will pave the way for our descriptive treatment of business ethics in Chapter 5, of organizational cultures in Chapter 6, and of whistle-blowing in Chapter 7.

FIGURE 2-9 Everyday Surveillance: Postmodern Data or Spying?

Item	Uses
Warranty Cards	Warranty cards, when filled in by the consumer, are data mines for marketers; the data is often sold to others.
Prescription Drugs	If you employ your company health insurance to purchase your pharmaceuticals, your employer may have access to the details.
Bank Machines (ATMs)	Each and every time you use an automated teller, the bank records the date and location of your transactions.
Sending E-mail	In many offices, e-mail is considered to be part and parcel of your job; your employer is allowed to read it—many bosses do just that.
Supermarket Scanners	Many grocery stores let you register for and use discount coupons that are used to track what you purchase.
Cellular Phones	Your calls can be intercepted and your access numbers cribbed by eavesdroppers using easily acquired police scanners.
Credit Cards	Everything you ever charged is in a database that police and others in authority could, without too much difficulty, access.
Making a Phone Call	The phone company does not need a court order to note the number you are calling or who is calling you.
Using the Internet	You are being "watched" even as you browse; search engines index your postings to public forums, such as Usernet, by your name.
Mail Order Transactions	Many firms, including mail order houses and publishers, sell their lists of customers.
Employee ID Scanners	If you rely on a magnetic stripe pass to enter the office, your whereabouts are automatically recorded.
Surveillance Cameras	They are in banks, government buildings, apartment lobbies, public garages—even houses of worship; it is now estimated that in a large urban centre like Toronto, the typical citizen is on a camera up to twenty times a day.
Satellites	Commercial satellites are on the market that are eagle-eyed enough to catch you—and maybe a companion—lounging by the swimming pool.

CASES AND QUESTIONS

CASE 2-1	New Wave of Unionization in Canada: Postmodern Optimism vs. Postmodern Pessimism

Jane Jenson and Rianne Mahon (*The Challenge of Restructuring: North American Labour Movements Respond*) present the thesis that unions are in the grips of a massive restructuring. Clive Thompson (1998) echoes this idea, arguing that there is a new postmodern wave of unionization spelling a fundamental shift in the retail service sector in Canada. That new wave is driven by a fundamental change in how workers view the low-paying, often part-time, retail service sector. Twenty years ago, many of these jobs were seen as ways to assist individuals to pay their way through college, over a rough spot in their quest for a career, or in order to make some money for travel while living with their parents. Times have changed. These stepping-stone jobs are now in many instances the career itself; they are at the centre of actual job creation and employment in Canada.

In the postmodern era, both young contingent workforce employees and unions are adapting to the abandonment of the old industrial rules of the game. Youth are buttressed against two factors: higher educational attainment than preceding generations, a factor that bolsters expectations; and, in Canada, a high youth unemployment with oodles of low-paying, low-level service jobs, but few career-path opportunities. On their side, union membership in Canada hit the wall in the 1990s. In 1997, unions had lost almost 300,000 members. True, unions still represented a relatively healthy 30% of all workers, but the future is not hard to read. The losses in the nineties came almost

entirely from Canada's industrial sector. Between 1976 and 1997, the proportion of Canadians working in goods-producing companies diminished to 27% from 36%, according to Statistics Canada, and is due to decline even more in the next decade. In the same period, the proportion of the working population employed in service industries rose to 73% from 65%. Union leaders realized that if they wanted to serve in the postmodern context they had to look at service work for new members.

This required a revolution in the thinking of many union leaders. The big unions had developed a leadership that had learned their union skills in the customary fashion— as hard-core labour in the mines and forests, or as shop-floor workers in heavy industries. Young, part-time workers, telemarketers, and retail service workers were not even on their radar screens. This neglect was aided by the economics of unionizing small service outlets. It can be a sinkhole for union money at a time when falling union membership means fewer dues in the unions' coffers and a strategy of lessening rather than increasing their propensities to take on costly and risky ventures.

The cost for a union to develop an organizing drive in a single outlet of a store like Starbucks or McDonald's can be as much as $30,000, demand years of expensive servicing, have a high probability of failure, and, if it succeeds, bring in only a fraction of the costs of the investment in union dues. Adding to the tactical nightmare of unionizing the small service organization is the fact that these firms, often organized in a franchise manner, fight back with very deep pockets furnished by headquarters. This often increases the cost of keeping the union going as the branches, even when unions enter, are characterized by high staff turnover, irregular schedules, and a low barrier between branch management and branch labour. In fact, many workers are "acting" branch managers during those hours when the actual branch manager is off.

Yet more unions, like the United Steelworkers' of America (USWA), are beginning to take an active interest in this sector. The USWA has moved into concerted efforts to unionize Ontario's loose constellation of security guard firms. It was a field ripe for the picking. The industry is booming and profits are large. Yet, despite this, the workers are fed up with near minimum wage, shift work, part-time wages, low benefits, poor training, unsafe working conditions and, for many, an exposure to the risk of violence and bodily harm. The industry subcontracts to other industries, and primarily competes on price and claims of technological sophistication in security and surveillance when, in fact, the industry is labour-intensive and relies almost exclusively on the labour of the guards for its services.

Other unions thought the USWA was out to lunch. They felt they would fall flat on their faces. These workers were just too hard to reach. The standard logic in the field of union organization is that if you cannot meet face-to-face with the workers in organized meetings, the union will not take. In the case of security guards, it would take 24-hour, often one-on-one organization. Despite this, the security guards were not only responsive, but were relatively eager to become part and parcel of the USWA. Within four years, the USWA had signed up more than 7,000 security guards in Ontario.

With such a large base for power, bargaining became easier. The USWA has been able in a short time to usher in some substantial improvements, including limitations on the frequency of security guard transfers to new locations, and small but regular wage increases tied to seniority. This foray into the small retail service sector has enabled the USWA to alter its Canadian membership profile. Nearly 60,000 of its 180,000 Canadian members are now in the service sector, and the number is expected to rise steadily. Postmodern optimists point to this trend as one of the ways the fragmented, decentralized economy is providing power and voice to its less powerful members.

The postmodern pessimists scoff at this reading of the story and point to others. The successes at Starbucks, although high profile, are extremely rare and isolated. They, like the unionization of a small proportion of security guards in Ontario, are the exception, not the rule, as is emphasized by the fact that they make the news. The major trend in Canadian society may be reflected more realistically by looking at the recent case of efforts to unionize McDonald's, and looking even more closely at the so-called successful unionization of a few branches of Starbucks. McDonald's Canada is more the rule than the exception. Essentially, in postmodern contexts when franchise branches threaten unionization, the head office can and does revoke the franchise, perhaps settling issues economically with the owner-operator. In February 1991, the Teamsters were closing their efforts to successfully launch a union at the St. Hubert, Quebec branch of McDonald's. The franchise owners, Tom and Mike Cappelli, shut the operation down. The Cappellis said that they had been throwing good money after bad in keeping the franchise going and it was time to pull the plug. McDonald's head office responded curtly, noting that the location of the franchise had not proven itself as economically suitable and that they would not be re-opening a franchise on that site. The union not only lost its investment in trying to organize the franchise, but saw the possibility of organizing other branches of McDonald's in Canada as meeting a similar plight.

The postmodern pessimists require that we look more closely at high-profile successes like the unionization of several outlets of Starbucks in Vancouver. The complaints by workers at Starbucks typify the small retail service sector—wages are extremely low, few people work a full forty-hour week, and shifts are erratic. In fact, Starbucks uses a computer software program, Starbucks' Star Labour Software, to match employees' working hours to the projected level of business at any particular time of the day in 15-minute increments. This format, as Clive Thompson points out, can result in a shift that begins at 5 a.m. and ends at 9:30 a.m. Coming across town for a four-hour shift at $7.00 per hour (starting) wage can be very difficult for young college students attempting to finance their studies.

The move to unionize Starbucks was set back and complicated by the atmosphere of meaning-management that pervades Starbucks. Starbucks' managers have tried, despite the size and big-business aspects of the international firm, to invoke the quaint, nostalgic, and participative ideals of a bygone era. The company is described to employees and consumers as a "family," and the low-wage employees are spoken of, in reverential terms, as the "team." Despite the ongoing jostling by staff for better hours, higher wages, and their union, Starbucks calls its employees "partners." Coffee servers are told they are professionals in a noble craft and referred to by the exotic-sounding title, "baristas". The baristas are put through three days worth of training sessions on coffee knowledge—caffeine levels, types of beans, grinding for different filters, etc. Lastly, employees are told that they are entrusted with a mission that far surpasses the brewing, serving, and selling of coffee. They are an important force in postmodern society providing a cherished "third space" for their clients—a place of refuge or safety outside of home and work—a necessary, public space for the busy citizen. John Bowman, the Canadian Autoworker (CAW) representative who worked with several employees to unionize a branch of Starbucks, likens them to a cult. Starbucks, Bowman insists, tries to instil in its employees a belief that what they are doing is far more than just making coffee. They are serving a social function in which there is an important social good.

John Bowman and the CAW have had, by their own admission, mixed success with Starbucks. They have invested a great deal of time and effort. Wages have risen by about $.75 per hour, but on other issues the employees seem still caught in the intricacies of part-time scheduling, short shifts, and a lack of upward mobility in their careers. In the meantime, the CAW is pleased with its foray and plans much more in the future. Other unions are seeing possibilities here of moving unionization forward. The Steelworkers are already working on organizing other Wal-Mart stores now they have had a victory in Windsor.

It is clear that the postmodern optimists see the new wave of unionization as a radical effort to empower and give voice to the previously neglected and somewhat marginalized Canadian workers in the small retail service sector. The postmodern pessimists see this as business as usual. The unions, desperate for new areas of growth, are moving into a new sector, and rather than liberate and provide voice to the contingent or part-time force in this sector, they will usher in a new level of rules that exclude the marginal worker, penalize part-timers, and reward those who now must master two sets of rules—those of the union and those of management.

QUESTIONS

1. How is the new wave of unionization in Canada different from the old wave? What is postmodern about the new wave? Why do the postmodern pessimists see business as usual even after unions enter into small retail service outlets?

2. Why, in your view, are unions getting increasingly interested in the small service retail outlets? Make this case from the point of view of the postmodern optimists. What ethical argument attaches itself to this view?

3. Are the part-time workers in small retail outlets exploited? Is their disgruntled status justified? Why? Why not? What would you do if you were the franchise owner of a service retail outlet that was in the process of vying for unionization? Why?

4. Using the third key feature of distinction in the postmodern world view—the shift from distancing to involvement—discuss what the workers in the small service retail outlets expect from their new unions. What do you think are their chances of attaining this? Are you, in this matter, a postmodern optimist or a postmodern pessimist?

5. Analyze Starbucks' use of cult-like jargon and a sense of higher purpose as an incidence of the emergence of meaning-management in the shift from a modern insistence on reality to a postmodern fascination with virtual reality. Discuss how part of the union drive to organize is an attempt to provide workers with a new key to decode management's effort at meaning-management.

6. Evaluate the arguments of the postmodern pessimists vs. postmodern optimists with regard to the new wave of unionization. What are the ethical implications of the postmodern pessimists' position? What are the ethical implications of the postmodern optimists' position? What, in your view, are the best ways to provide part-time, marginal, low-earning workers in the retail service sector with a voice?

CASE 2-2 Looking Back Ten Years in the Business Ethics Field

Business Ethics (July/August 1991) recently celebrated its tenth anniversary. To mark the event, Editor Marjorie Kelly compiled comments by noted authors, advocates, and activists assessing the progress—or lack of it—made in their particular areas of expertise. A sampling of these comments indicates the challenges that face a new generation of business ethicists.

Milton Moskowitz, Author of *100 Best Companies to Work for in America*:

> Having spent 30 years in this field, I'm tempted to trumpet how much has been accomplished: more than 30 mutual funds using social screens; diversity on boards of directors; new organizations (Business for Social Responsibility, Social Venture Network, Social Investment Forum, CERES); and new socially conscious companies (Ben and Jerry's, Aveda, Odwalla, Whole Foods, Stoneyfield Yogurt, Hanna Anderson, Tom's of Maine). Looks impressive, doesn't it?
>
> But when all is said and done, those activities remain blips in an economy that has exploded. To most people in business, they're invisible. When you talk about social responsibility to business people in Hong Kong, Tokyo, or London, they don't know what you are talking about.
>
> In short, we haven't changed the basic way businesses operate or the ways in which they are measured and evaluated. That's not to say we've had no effect. But it's been mostly at the margin. I recently saw an essay in *Financial*

Times that sums it up. A professor of Oxford's business school wrote: 'Shell should care about the environment and human rights because it is the best way for it to go on making money.'

Martha Peak, Group Editor, American Management Association magazines:

There's been a lot of talk about progressive, responsible business, but the results have been less than overwhelming. Too many of us have been jerked around by empowerment policies that didn't, by human capital planning that wasn't, and by equality programs that couldn't.

Too many of us are survivors of euphemisms such as 'restructuring' (translation: your job's at risk) and 'rightsizing' (translation: you're fired!). Is there anyone who doesn't choke when the mantra 'people are our greatest asset' is intoned? It didn't start out that way, but somehow it's ended up that way. I'm concerned that the fabric is unravelling. I'm even more concerned that we have become so complacent about it.

Jeffrey Hollender, CEO, Seven Generation:

When the green products industry first started, prices were substantially higher than traditional products, and performance was far inferior. Today, most of our products—such as paper towels and cleaning agents—are comparably priced. On a per-unit basis, some are less than major brands. That's a big change.

Secondly, I've seen consumer awareness shift from things like saving trees to issues like the health effects of dioxin. Health issues are now a stronger driver than environmental issues. With good reason. Indoor pollution is five to ten times greater than outdoor pollution. Male sperm counts are down 50 percent from 50 years ago. Girls are reaching puberty earlier. These issues are integral to the products we sell. Environmentally

friendly household products are seeing sales growth twice that of the natural products industry—which is itself growing 22 percent a year. Our sales increased 63 percent last year, and we could continue strong growth just in natural products stores. But we're also getting into some upscale, mainstream stores like Tops and Food Emporium. We've grown from $1 to $5 million in two years, and we aim to continue growing at 50 percent a year. Consumer interest has barely been tapped.

In the larger environmental perspective, I don't think we've turned the corner yet. We've made progress on water and air pollution. But there are areas that don't get attention where we're not progressing. Alligators in Florida can't reproduce. Bird shells are so thin offspring can't survive. Animals are being born with organs of both sexes. Wiping out the rainforest is simple and visible—but this stuff is subtle. And the systems we've designed to protect us aren't working. Companies are creating so many new chemicals, the EPA can't even read all the tests they submit. The whole way we define 'safe' is about what causes cancer—but that misses 90 percent of what's going on. It's the responsibility of chemical manufacturers to determine if their products are safe. But the scientist who created DDT got a prize for it. It took 20 years to understand it wasn't good.

I'm an optimist by nature, and I don't believe all these problems mean we can't find solutions. But I'm struck by the complexity of it all.

Carl Frankel, Editor for *Tomorrow* magazine:

Have we progressed in environmental responsibility? Yes and no. Transnational corporations have progressed on the technical side, reducing emissions. The data on Toxic Release Inventory chemical reductions is impressive. But it's also misleading. The TRI reports on less than 1 per cent of all the chemicals that are used. And it leaves out all the millions of small companies that aren't required to report at all.

At large companies, there also seems to be a trend for people to be internal environmental champions, and then get the legs cut out from under them. Bryan Thomlison of Church & Dwight was an effective environmental champion, but was laid off last year. Mark Eisen of Home Depot was recently let go as well. We like to say corporate environmentalism is institutionalized, but that's not necessarily the case for activities that aren't strictly compliance-oriented. With less conventional environmental strategies, champions need active support from above. When it goes, they're exposed. All too often it's *sayonara* to proactive environmental visions.

On the positive side, the insurance industry is now expressing concern about climate change—that's significant. The CEO of British Petroleum just came out with an impressive expression of concern about climate change. And the CEO of Monsanto is deeply committed to sustainability. But corporate performance tends to have many faces. For instance, Monsanto has been rather heavy-handed in its regulatory and marketing efforts to bring genetically engineered products to market. So it's four steps forward, three steps back.

But over time, the base-line shifts. It keeps getting pushed forward. You have to ask, where is the leading edge relative to where it was, say, six years ago? At the Fortune 500, it's further along. I'm less persuaded that smaller socially responsible businesses are further along than they were. Of course, they were pretty far along to start with. And the movement in some ways is maturing, for instance in how it opens itself to criticism. But I have trouble with socially responsible companies when they define themselves in polarity to mainstream companies. It's time to move beyond reactive positioning to an integrative stage.

It's important to do things like develop best practices and environmental performance metrics. But technical steps like that are not enough. Sustainable development keeps taking you deeper and deeper. Ultimately, I believe it requires businesses to give greater value to the quality dimension of life.

The philosopher Ken Wilber writes of a triad, 'it', 'we', and 'I'. Historically, business has focused almost exclusively on the 'it' dimension, the empirical face of the world. Quality, as I think of it, lies mostly in the 'we' and 'I' dimensions—social and intrapsychic. Both culturally and industrially, we need to get beyond our fixation with technical measurement. We need to give greater value to quality, and develop more sophisticated strategies for measuring quality. That's the next great challenge, figuring out how to measure, or at least account for, the unmeasurable. The roots are forming, in early community and corporate attempts to develop sustainability indicators. But we're only at the beginning.

QUESTIONS

1. From his statements, would you classify Milton Moskowitz, author of *100 Best Companies to Work for in America*, as a postmodern optimist or a postmodern pessimist? Why? Why does Mr. Moskowitz feel uncomfortable with the summative statement, "Shell should care about the environment and human rights because it is the best way for it to go on making money"?

2. If we see the shift from the modern notion of reality to the postmodern notion of virtual reality as licensing the treatment of "the world and organization as text," what sort of text does Martha Peak see in the postmodern context? What is it about "empowerment policies" that Peak sees as "jerking us around"? Why is the postmodern text strewn with euphemisms that require translation? If one becomes truly committed to the organization, what happens to one's ability to make these "translations"?

3. Is Jeffrey Hollender, CEO of Seven Generation, a postmodern optimist or a postmodern pessimist? Are you happy with the incrementalist position taken by Hollender? Is Hollender's view steeped more in the postmodern or modern world view? Why?

4. Carl Frankel, editor for *Tomorrow* magazine, makes sense of the progress—or lack of it—in the field of applied business ethics, noting that "it's four steps forward and three steps back." Select a recent story in the news with some business ethics content that seems to reflect Carl Frankel's position. What, in your view, is the best way to measure progress in the field of applied business ethics? Relate the difficulty in measuring progress in the field of applied business ethics to the shift from modern notions of totalizing to postmodern emphases on fragmentation.

5. Given what these commentators say regarding their views of the past ten years in the field of business ethics, what do you think? Are you a postmodern optimist, a postmodern pessimist, or some combination of the two? Give examples from your own experience to support your position.

6. Deconstruct Carl Frankel's use of Ken Wilber's triad of "it, we, and I." What is your interpretation of Frankel's use of this triad? What is the implication of this interpretation for technology? Why is Frankel so emphatic on figuring out how to measure, or at least account for, the unmeasurable?

CASE 2-3   Benetton: Getting Attention in the Era of Information Overload

The $2-billion fashion empire with 7,000 franchise stores in over 100 countries that we now know as Benetton, had humble beginnings. In 1965, Luciano Benetton and three siblings established a small business, Fratelli Benetton, near Treviso, Italy. The business that originally was designed to sell a few thousand colourful sweaters now manufactures over 80 million pieces of clothing each year. A key to Benetton's growth and prosperity, particularly in the past decade, has been its controversial advertising campaign.

This advertising campaign has been instrumental in Benetton's success in the fashion world by both extending the firm's name recognition and, equally important, associating the company with a broader set of political and cultural values. In 1984, Luciano Benetton hired Oliviero Toscani, an award-winning photographer, to take the reins of its advertising campaign. Toscani's early efforts focused upon linking the colours of Benetton to the diverse colours of its customers from all over the world. Young people from different racial groups all sporting Benetton clothes were photographed engaging in a variety of aimless and playful acts. The themes of racial harmony, world peace, and the good life of youth were linked in the thematic structure of these photographs. The slogan "United Colours of Benetton" was adopted by Toscani as a recurring trademark.

In 1991, Toscani began to use Benetton's $80 million (US) global advertisement budget to publish controversial and disturbing photographs on billboards and in magazines and newspapers. These included a number of confusing and compelling images that were intended to have a provocative effect. These images included a nun kissing a priest on the lips, a row of test tubes filled with blood, variously coloured, blown up condoms floating tranquilly in the air, and a newborn baby girl still attached to her umbilical cord and covered in blood. In 1992, Toscani intensified the advertising-publicity campaign. He chose a series of highly-charged, photojournalistic images referencing, among other things, violence in the streets, the AIDS crisis, war, exile, homelessness, natural catastrophe, and environmental disaster. The photographs appeared in various magazines, billboards, and newspapers throughout the world. On each the written text was limited to the conspicuous insertion of the green and white "United Colours of Benetton" logo located in the margins of the photograph.

Reaction to the campaign commenced in 1991 was swift. Benetton was both condemned and praised. The company was lauded for incorporating urgent social concerns into its advertising. It was condemned for its appropriation of serious issues to sell goods and call attention to itself. In many instances, Benetton advertisements were refused by specific magazines or, more significant, banned from particular countries. An example of one of the more controversial advertisements depicted David Kirby, an AIDS patient, surrounded by his family shortly before he died. This advertisement became the subject of heated debate over the bounds of advertising. The presence of the logo, "The United Colours of Benetton," suggested to many that Benetton was not interested in the issue for its own sake, but rather as a vehicle to convey its name and portray itself as socially active, concerned, and "out there."

The company defends its position by either condemning the criticism as a form of censorship, or criticizing other advertisement companies for merely pandering to false consumer images. A statement that appeared in Benetton's Fall/Winter 1992 advertising campaign states: "Among the various means available to achieve the brand recognition that every company must have, we at Benetton believe our strategy for communication to be more effective for the company and more useful to society than would

be yet another series of ads showing pretty girls wearing pretty clothes."

When accused of the commercial use or abuse of sensational journalistic photographs like body parts tattooed with "HIV-Positive," or the image of a black soldier with a rifle strapped over his shoulder holding the skeletal remains of another human being, Benetton spokespersons respond that this is all part and parcel of a deliberate educational program. Images like this, insist Benetton, serve as a vehicle for social change by arresting public attention and riveting it upon important issues. The call to a "truth" that is shocking is an attempt to get people to awake from their slumber and attend to the social problems that pervade modern life.

Opponents argue the opposite, that Benetton's photo-realism decontextualizes real political and violent events and makes them appear staged and even safe. The ubiquitous logo, "The United Colours of Benetton," is a visible reminder that these photographs are within our safety zone. They are advertisements. The images they depict are completely under the control of the photographer and, more importantly, are subservient to a social system that values the commodification of "shock" as a means of moving product. Rather than educating people to act on their ethical or political understanding, these ads foster passivity. The framing of shock as nothing but an ad confuses realism with amusement. Public truths made manifest in Benetton's ads, regardless of how shocking or horrifying the images, are not a corporate force for social responsibility, but rather a concerted search for a means of cashing in upon controversy. Benetton uses the controversy to further its marketing campaign, get is name in the papers, talks, interviews, articles, and, I am sure the critics would say, case studies such as this.

QUESTIONS

1. What is postmodern about Benetton's controversial advertising campaign? What is the image of the person and of the self in the advertisements described? Why is controversy often the centre of attention? Why does controversy tend to persist when the centre and its expertise are, as prevails in postmodernity, dispersed?

2. Make the case for Benetton's controversial advertising campaign from the point of view of a postmodern pessimist. What are, in your view, the ethics of using factual photojournalism to sell sweaters? Do these advertisements educate?

3. Make the case for Benetton's controversial advertising campaign from the point of view of a postmodern optimist. How do these advertisements put social concerns into advertising? What are the ethics of Benetton's controversial advertising campaign from the point of view of a postmodern optimist?

4. Do Benetton's advertisements foster passivity or do they stir activism? Take an example of one of the advertisements depicted in the case and make your argument. What are the ethical implications of the passivity or the involvement that you point towards?

5. From a management perspective, outline the risks and benefits likely to ensue from using controversy as the basis for an advertisement campaign. Are these risks and benefits the same or similar to those you would come up with if you did your outline of the risks and benefits from the perspective of society as a whole?

6. In the shift from the fixed reality of modernity to the virtual reality of postmodernity, how does the advertisement campaign at Benetton stretch reality? Analyze who is responsible for the new meanings produced in a campaign based on controversy. Does this sort of controversy actually stimulate dialogue, or does it simulate it?

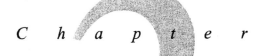

CORPORATE
SOCIAL
RESPONSIBILITY

In 1995, Multinational Monitor in the USA published a list of ten 'Worst Corporations' as a means of re-establishing shame as a driver of good corporate behaviour. The list included such august names as Shell, Dow Chemicals, 3M. Is this state of affairs peculiar to business? Absolutely not. Religious institutions, political parties, governments, judicial bodies and even educational and medical establishments around the world are held in increasingly fragile esteem by ordinary citizens. It may be that this new culture of discontent and disrespect arises directly from the replacement of past certainties with new insecurities, particularly about livelihoods and social cohesion.

David Wheeler and Maria Sillanpää
The Stakeholder Corporation:
A Blueprint for Maximizing Stakeholder Value (1997)

What social responsibility entails and, more to the point, to whom the postmodern organization is and ought to be responsible, are questions worthy of debate. David Wheeler and Maria Sillanpää see this debate as occurring in a postmodern context wherein "new insecurities, particularly about livelihood and social cohesion" are replacing past certainties. In this context, the debate over corporate social responsibility takes on a new urgency. However, the idea of corporate social responsibility (hereafter CSR) is neither new nor radical. While primarily an invention of the second half of the twentieth century, echoes of CSR can be found in biblical sources. Deuteronomy 24:10–13 and 25:13–16 both enjoin that in business or commercial transactions we seek to be fair and to utilize our abilities to further the needs of the community, including those less fortunate than ourselves—the handicapped, the infirm, those caught in the midst of poverty, and those who are excluded or marginalized.

More recently, Adolf A. Berle, Jr. and Gardiner C. Means, in their seminal work, *The Modern Corporation and Private Property* (1933), warned readers about the increasing power of the then new organizational form drawing its resources and power from stock market offerings and left in the hands of a new decision-making elite—managers. Berle and Means, writing over sixty years ago and in a decidedly modern temperament, worried about the upcoming clash between the broader interests of society and the claims of the corporate owners (stockholders) and their hired managers (1933:356). The former seek to use the profits and energy of the corporation for social purposes and the common good; the latter seek to extract rents, as befits owners of private property, for their own benefits.

The clash alluded to by Berle and Means is at the centre of more contemporary attempts to work out the positions within the CSR debate and to provide direction in their anticipation of the fragmentation we now call postmodernity. The core issue in this debate is *not* whether or not the modern corporation should be socially responsible, but rather upon whom this social responsibility should be conferred. Berle's and Means' prescient take on the problem recognized the two most polarized of the five positions within the debate. In their view, a tension would arise between those who advocate that the corporation is socially responsible when it serves the needs of its stockholders (the minimalist CSR view), and those further towards the political left who would insist that a corporation is socially responsible only if it uses a portion of its profits and energies to solve social problems (the stakeholder [stewardship] model).

The five positions within the CSR debate are: (1) the minimalist CSR view; (2) the self-interested CSR model; (3) the social contract perspective in CSR; (4) the stakeholder (management) model; and (5) the stakeholder (stewardship) model. If one is politically inclined it is possible, without too much distortion of ideology, to shift from the political right to the political left while moving through positions one to five (see Figure 3.1). It is the political right which, in its embrace of the conservative notion of the status quo, worries about the apparent moral meltdown that it believes is ushered in by the tolerance of the left-leaning postmodern optimists.

Different ideological dimensions may be traced within this movement. Travelling from the minimalist CSR view to the stakeholder (stewardship) model, we move from an emphasis upon the individual and his/her rights, to the idea of community and citizens' duties; from an enshrining of private property, to a call for a respect for the public good; and from a notion of the "job of business is business," steeped in a technical or amoral perspective, to an insistence upon business as a value-rooted activity requiring moral leadership in order to make a better world. In viewing this right versus left ideology imbedded in the continuum of CSR positions, we ought to do what we can to avoid becoming prisoners of too simple a world view—one in which, because we feel ourselves sympathetic to ideas on the political right or left, we cannot see the reasoning of positions that contradict and oppose our views. To be unable to do so limits one's ability to see the origins and system of reasoning from whence other views—challenging views—emerge.

FIGURE 3-1 **The Five CSR Positions: Differing Forms of Collective Responsibility**

CSR Position	Responsible to Whom	The Responsible Corporation
Minimalist CSR view	Stockholders or owners	A responsible corporation maximizes its profits, therein assuring that it succeeds in its specialist role of providing goods and services that are of high quality and can be afforded.
The self-interested CSR model	Stockholders or owners and those who can impose high costs upon the corporation	A responsible corporation does good for others when this furthers its quest for growth and profits.
The social contract perspective in CSR	All with whom it makes legal and social contracts	A responsible corporation does more than follow the law. Rather, it attempts to live up to the spirit of the commitment and obligation it incurs in doing business.
The stakeholder (management) model	Those who attempt to influence the direction and fortunes of the organization	Responsible corporations develop strategies for satisfactorily dealing with the often-changing and, at times, contradictory demands of stakeholders.
The stakeholder (stewardship) model	Those who are not directly in the firm's market—future generations, non-human species, society as a whole	The responsible corporation uses a significant portion of its profits and energies to contribute to the solution of social problems that it did not directly cause.

In Figure 3.1, the five CSR positions are summarized—who within the organization ought to be responsible and the key implications of each for understanding the good corporate citizen is reviewed. Let us look at each position more fully, drawing out the key differences. To do so, it will help us to identify how each of the CSR conceptions is rooted in a different conception of the good world. In the second part of this chapter, we shall look at the changing notion of community in which we formulate the idea of responsibility.

THE MINIMALIST CSR VIEW

The minimalist CSR view is also referred to as the "traditional stockholders' model" (Bruono and Nichols, 1990), or CSR "fundamentalism" (Klonoski, 1991). The terms "minimalist," "traditional," and "fundamentalist" signify that this view adheres very closely to the neo-classical view of the firm and the nature of competitive markets espoused by Adam Smith. Milton Friedman (1962, 1970, 1983) is probably the most vocal and clear-headed representative of the minimalist CSR view. Within this view, business managers have a responsibility to shareholders, as owners of the corporation, to maximize the firm's value. In effect, managers in their role as agents of the shareholders have no mandate to embark on socially responsible projects that fail to enhance the income-generating capabilities of the firm. Managers should not refrain from profitable investments that satisfy all legal constraints but fail to conform to the manager's personal social agenda. The minimalist orientation is stated clearly by Friedman's pronouncement that "there is one and only one social responsibility of business—to use its resources and engage in activities designed to increase profits so long as it stays within the rules of the game, which is to say, engages in open and free competition without deception or fraud" (1970).

The minimalist CSR view, as represented by Friedman, is rooted in a version of the good world in which competition, rugged individualism, and the primacy of the law are central. Competition does away with waste and inefficiency as well as keeping individuals motivated. Friedman notes: "Few trends would so thoroughly undermine the foundations of our free society as the acceptance by corporate officials of a social responsibility other than to make as much money for stockholders as they possibly can" (1962:133). The individual property or shareholder is paramount in Friedman's insistence that under the law the corporation is an autonomous entity owned and run by a freely constituted group of shareholders who, given the nature of competitive markets, have instructed their agent, the manager, to make money without breaking the law.

Harvard professor, Theodore Levitt, echoes the minimalist CSR perspective: "... in the end, business has only two responsibilities—to obey the elementary canons of face-to-face civility (honesty, good faith, and so on) and to seek material gain" (1958). The minimalist CSR view warns that to detach the corporation from the market by directing profits away from material gain is to toy with the foundations—private property, pursuit of individual happiness, and competition—that gird the very notion of freedom in a capitalist system. It is implied within the positions of both Friedman (1970) and Levitt (1958) that to tinker with the minimalist CSR position is to open an explosive series of possibilities that will test the very core of capitalism and free markets. These possibilities include the diminished efficiency of capitalist enterprise and, equally frightening, the rise—albeit a slow one—of regulatory regimes that smack of socialism and other forms of centralized planning in the name of the "public good."

The minimalist CSR position is tested severely by postmodernism. It is at its strongest when propped up by two historically-grounded assumptions. The first is that capitalism is threatened by egalitarian forms of communism, and second that government, if left to its own devices, will naturally over-regulate and strangle free market capitalism. Both premises hold less credibility in the 1990s than they did in the years when Levitt (1958) and Friedman (1970) were writing. Capitalism, with its emphasis upon private property, individual happiness, and competition, is no longer seen as challenged by communism with its state-owned notion of property, collectivism, and emphasis upon government regulation and planning. Then, too, business no longer seems threatened by overzealous efforts by governments to reign it in. Rather, increasingly in postmodernity, governments are acting as if they were businesses. The tight separation between the public and private sector, so prevalent in Friedman's and Levitt's heydays, seems less pressing now. Businesses now operate prisons; manage the removal of garbage; operate police forces; run hospitals; test for environmental toxins; manage blood banks; and administer schools, social work agencies, and special events for heart disease. Daniel Yergin and Joseph Stanislaw, in their highly readable *The Commanding*

Heights: The Battle Between Government and the Marketplace That is Remaking the Modern World (1996), argue that postmodernity increasingly places government and the nation state on the same side of the ledger as the business organization.

In the midst of these waning dichotomies, the insistence that the corporation be responsible to its stockholders hardly seems debatable. The insistence that it should be responsible "only" to the stockholders has, however, fallen upon less and less fertile ground. Even small stockholders, those with holdings in mutual funds and through their pension funds, feel left out of this very restricted notion of responsibility. When push comes to shove, the minimalist CSR position advocates that corporations remain responsible to those large stockholders who can, with their block of votes, make a difference. Others must find a way to be heard. Those who can do so by appealing to a firm's economic goals can be heard in the self-interested CSR model.

THE SELF-INTERESTED CSR MODEL

The self-interested CSR model is compatible with the minimalist CSR view, but it takes it one step further, expanding the minimalist view into three different conceptions of social responsibility, and then arguing that two of these—if in moderation and tied closely to economic reality—may in fact be helpful to the long-run profitability of the firm. The self-interested CSR model proposes that both Friedman's and Levitt's views that the very term "social responsibility" means that this behaviour will not be in the best interest of the shareholders, is needlessly provocative and careless in the degree to which it vilifies a possible area of corporate growth, profit, and long-term financial well-being. Peter Drucker (1989, 1992, 1993) captures this view in the words of an accessible management analyst.

Drucker underscores the three types of instrumental or corporate-centred socially responsible actions. The first type, essentially a mismanaged form of social responsibility, not unlike that made central in Friedman's minimalist CSR position, requires that "we had better be watchful because good intentions are not always socially responsible. It is irresponsible for an organization to accept—let alone pursue—responsibilities that would impede its capacity to perform its main task and mission or to act where it has no competence" (1992:99). Drucker, like Friedman, would concede that this is nothing but folly.

In the second type of social responsibility, unlike Friedman, Drucker sees other forms of direct or indirect acts of social responsibility as capable, if managed well, of both satisfying community needs and helping the corporate bottom line. Money spent by a high-technology corporation, to take an example, in implementing flex time may not only alleviate the 5:00 p.m. to 5:45 p.m. traffic that clogs the community's highways, but may help to retain highly-trained employees wishing to adapt their work time to their changing family needs. This second type of social responsibility succeeds in possibly increasing the profits of the firm by benefiting the community. This win-win formulation within the self-interested CSR model argues that to act with CSR a firm must be responsible to its investors *and* can be responsible to others as long as care for the shareholders is taken duly into account. This not only amends the minimalist CSR position (the firm is acting with CSR when it is responsible only to its shareholders), but makes it seem that the minimalist CSR position is one in search of a controversy.

The third form of social responsibility Drucker advocates is philanthropic giving that indirectly furthers corporate goals. A corporation giving a sum of money to construct a wing of the public library in the community in which it operates may reap admirable tax benefits, associate the corporate name with learning, youth and knowledge, and raise the literacy rate and knowledge base of potential employees within the corporation's recruiting terrain. Philanthropy is a voluntary activity of the firm. Just as individuals seek to share their well-being with others less fortunate, corporations, insist Drucker and advocates of the self-interested CSR model, should also have this option. To suggest that philanthropy is equivalent to irresponsible management, as is implied in the minimalist CSR position, is to deny the instrumental benefits that arise to the "giver" in a philanthropic gesture. The topic of reputational capital, as an example of the legitimacy thesis in a business and society perspective on business ethics, will be taken up more fully in Chapter 9.

In the self-interested CSR model, as evidenced in Drucker's work, "the job of business is business" but, unlike the minimalist view, social responsibility is one of the tools available to corporations seeking long-term financial health. It should not, Drucker insists, be used blindly. But to argue that it should not be used, as the minimalist CSR advocates do, is to compete with other managers without the full advantage of all the tools in one's tool kit. The distinction between Drucker and Friedman is evidenced by the example of how Julius Rosenwald, through self-interested CSR, breathed financial health into Sears Roebuck. Drucker writes:

> In the early years of this century, a Chicago clothing merchant, Julius Rosenwald, took over an ailing mail-order house called Sears Roebuck. Within ten years, it had become the world's largest and most profitable retailer. One reason was Rosenwald's recognition that, to prosper, Sears needed a healthy farm community. But the American farmer at the beginning of the century was in desperate straits.... Rosenwald invented the Farm Agent to act as the change agent on the American farm. (1989:91–92)

Rosenwald took a rather enlightened self-interested approach to Sears. For over a decade he funded aid from his own pocket to the troubled farmers. When it proved to be a grand success, the United States government took it over. By then the farmers—through heeding the advice of the farm agent—had acquired sufficient economic power to purchase what Rosenwald offered in his Sears catalogue. Drucker notes that had Milton Friedman—or other minimalist CSR types—been consulted, Rosenwald would have been advised to stick to business and leave concern for the farmer to the government. It is clear, to a minimalist CSR advocate, that diverting profits from Sears to fund the Farm Agent System in the United States for ten years would be sheer folly. To the self-interested CSR advocate, community responsibility such as concern for a healthy and prosperous community is not philanthropy gone wild but, as the Sears case makes clear, is self-interest.

The self-interested CSR model still adheres to the traditional or minimalist CSR understanding of the corporation, but modifies it by pointing out that profitable opportunities await the firm that wisely and judiciously uses CSR to its advantage. The conception of the organization in both the minimalist and the self-interested CSR models is that of an economic institution with solely economic responsibilities: these latter are rooted in the notion of the corporation as private property tied to society through the legal requirements placed upon a group of people (stockholders) and their agents (managers, employees). On the other hand, the conception of the corporation in all the varying sorts of social contract theories is that of a social institution. Unlike the minimalist and self-interested CSR positions, the social contract perspective assumes that business and society are not separable. Social contract perspectives in CSR, such as that advocated by Amitai Etzioni, attempt to forge the roots of neo-classical economics—replete with its competitive individualism—with a community form of contractualism. In his book, *The Moral Dimension: Toward a New Economics*, Etzioni's version of socio-economics generates a form of "communitarianism," which suggests that business, like other social institutions, can only succeed if they play the game, either competitively or cooperatively, within a recognition of their responsibilities to the larger community.

THE SOCIAL CONTRACT PERSPECTIVE IN CSR

There are three origins of the treatment of corporations as social institutions, and each can be taken to lead to a "weak" or a "strong" call for social responsibility. Weak calls, when push comes to shove, turn the social contract perspective into a form of self-interested CSR; strong calls, on the other hand, push the social contract toward the stakeholder models (see Figure 3.1). Those companies that claim to be social institutions and do the community "talk," may not be particularly good at creating processes for employees (unions), suppliers, and customers to give "voice." Rather, these weak social contract positions are found in companies that react predominantly to their shareholders but pay lip service to others. The stronger the social contract position, the greater the degree to which the firm is socially responsive to the needs of stakeholders other than the shareholders—indeed, even taking a stewardship role in attempting to help solve pressing social problems such as illiteracy or racism.

The first origin of the treatment of the corporation as a social institution is the view that the modern corporation is a moral, not solely an economic, person. The ascription to corporations not only of legal personhood, but of rights as well, has caused some to question why the strict legal and economic interpretation of the firm cannot be extended. If the firm has rights, and this has been the strict interpretation in the law, it is argued that the firm, as well, must have responsibilities. This means that, like a socially-embedded "moral person," a corporation can not only be held responsible for the contracts its agents sign, but for the implicit understandings it leads others to expect in the course of its actions and statements. Becoming a partner in a relationship, assuming the same household, sharing property, but failing to sign a marriage contract does not mean that either party to the relationship, within this context of common-law marriage, can dissolve the relationship without taking responsibility for the other. This, of course, becomes particularly so in cases where children are the result of the well-intended but ill-fated relationship. Just as we require the moral person to be responsible for his or her implicit social contracts, so too, within this argument, we expect the moral corporation to be responsible for its implicit social contracts.

Richard DeGeorge (1990) maintains that corporations as collectivities can be said to act like individuals. Peter French (1990) concludes that "corporations should be treated as full-fledged moral persons and hence … have whatever privileges, rights, and duties as are, in the normal course of affairs, accorded to moral persons." As a moral person, the corporation not only has a conscience (Goodpaster and Matthews, 1983), but must utilize this conscience in its operations. The use of conscience invokes a notion of rationality (Ladd, 1970) that requires the agent or manager to ask more than whether management ought to adhere to a written contract, but also whether implicit contracts based on social expectations are to be honoured, and at what cost. Those who perceive modern corporations as "moral persons" requiring an honouring of social contracts, are calling for a widening of corporate accountability and social responsibility.

A second and frequently taken route in arriving at the view of the modern corporation as a social institution starts with tying the modern corporation into the historical tradition that has grown up around social contracts. From Hobbes, Locke, Rousseau, and Kant, philosophers have made it clear that there is a need to achieve social agreement in order to create the evolving abstraction we call society and, within it, those activities we recognize and call business. Without this social contract and the trust it conveys, social and economic exchange fall apart and commerce grinds to a halt. The social contract is rooted in shared information, values, and a belief in the ability of those in social institutions such as business to retain its core contracts—social obligations—in the midst of social change and dislocation. Melvin Anshen (1983) argues that there is a need for a "highly implicit social agreement" that lays out the duties and rights of individuals at the micro-analytical level and between business and society at the macro level. This implied and often tacit understanding between business and the communities in which it operates is not static. It evolves. "The good corporation, new social contract, and corporate responsibility," writes James Post, "are conceptual extensions of our need to articulate principles of conduct among people and organizations." (1996:62).

Perhaps the most postmodern derivation of this perspective is called "Integrative Social Contracts Theory (ISCT)," and its key advocates, Thomas Donaldson and Thomas W. Dunfee (1994, 1995) speculate on how to make sense of the relationship between economic and communitarian points of view. Essentially this theory fixes upon how tacit consent arises. Donaldson and Dunfee posit a macro-social contract that is tied to the rational expectations of persons within a society, and then a level of micro-social contracts in which latitude must be built into the heart of the social contract. The micro-social contract, with its built-in latitude, acts as a buffer between the two levels—macro and micro. With this buffer, the contracting partners begin to experience tacit consent, a zone wherein little is written but much is expected. Social contract perspectives seek to explore the unwritten or tacit social contract by seeing business as a social institution with vested interests in adjusting quickly to changing realities by relying upon tacit consent and discretion. The concession to the shifting realities of postmodernism is not easily built into formal contracts. The greater the degree of freedom in a contract, the more adaptable the business; yet the greater the degree of freedom, the greater the need for responsibility.

The third means of deriving the "social institution" perspective bolstering the social contract perspective in CSR, fixes upon the increasing power and scope of modern businesses. Large corporations now possess the power to control the lives of employees, customers, shareholders, and the residents of the local communities in which they operate. In *When Corporations Rule the World* (1995), David Korten points out that of the world's 100 largest economies, 51 are corporations and 49 are countries. It has been estimated by the Worldwatch Institute that the top 500 corporations in the world control 70 per cent of world trade and 30 per cent of world gross domestic product. David Wheeler and Maria Sillanpää note that "on a strictly financial basis, Mitsubishi has sales turnover bigger than Indonesia (the country with the 22nd biggest economy in the world). General Motors outweighs Denmark (number 23 in the list of national economies). Ford is bigger than Hong Kong and Turkey (the 25th and 26th largest economies)" (1997:31). It is clear that a single corporate decision can irrevocably alter the lives of thousands upon thousands of people.

In *Normal Accidents: Living With High-Risk Technologies* (1984), Charles Perrow shows, within the postmodern corporate context, how the concentration of technology, often of an experimental fashion in the hands of corporations, places a heavy burden of responsibility upon them. In industries in high-risk areas (nuclear energy, explosive materials, toxic substances, etc.), with increasing technological interdependence between and among operating systems, the risk of very real accidents increases. Bhopal, the explosion of the

Challenger, and the frequent loss of crude oil by tankers at sea are the sorts of accidents likely to increase in frequency. With the concentration of technologies in corporations with tasks that can—and most likely will—at some time go awry, brings the power, mostly inadvertent, to dramatically affect the lives and property of many people and other species. With power comes responsibility to do more than merely follow the law.

Underlying the social contract perspective in CSR is the belief that legal solutions, while necessary, are not sufficient. If corporations are like social persons, requiring tacit agreements for their operations, and have grown as powerful as entire nations, then not only must they be responsible for following the minimum morality of the law, but they are in the process, whether they like it or not, of establishing the rules we live by. Christopher D. Stone, in *Where the Law Ends: The Social Control of Corporate Behavior* (1975), points to two gaps—the time and information gaps—in calling for greater corporate social responsibility from the modern corporation.

The law, argues Stone, is and ought to be primarily a reactive institution, whereas business is primarily an engine for and of change in society. The law, in a functional sense, lends stability to society. It is a conservative force changing slowly over time. The law, if and when it errs, seeks to do so on the side of tradition. On the other hand, business is all about bringing change—innovating, restructuring, relocating—to society. Most analysts of the contemporary business scene argue that these changes are accelerating (Nevis, Lancourt, and Vassall, 1996) and seem likely to continue to do so. Given this difference between law as a social institution and business as a social institution, there "may" exist a significant period of time between when a problem is recognized and when the legislature can manage to pass a law to solve or otherwise deal with the problem. The social contract perspective in CSR argues that responsible managers, as agents for socially responsible firms, should not exploit this situation by acting swiftly before the law can, as it were, catch up.

The information gap, argues Stone, occurs between lawmakers and corporate managers due to the different information mandates under which they operate. The lawmaker is primarily a generalist, seeking information in broad areas in order to enact effective legislation and coordinate this into the larger legal system; the corporate manager is a specialist in a particular industry with a mandate to increase knowledge and information in specific areas of potential growth. The result is that businesses working in specific areas of specialization get more and more particular or focused information; the law seeks to gather universalistic information or data that applies to all firms. When it comes to passing laws in a specific industry, the industry often knows more about the issue than the law—in essence, an information gap. When investigating particular problems within a specific industry—pollution rates, lead levels, product safety—the companies who have ready access to the best available information often become secretive. The recent admission by cigarette manufacturers that cigarettes are addictive seems to have been information kept out of the hands of legislators. Stone notes that firms go beyond the law and engage in the social contract when they make such information available to the lawmakers (1975:96).

In Figure 3.2, the ideal-type relations between economic, legal, social and, as we shall take up in the stakeholder models in the next section, the ethical responsibilities are mapped. It is an ideal-type because it suits the theories, but not the complex nature, of our experience or reality. In our experience or reality, we cannot separate ethical responsibilities from, let us say, social responsibilities. All responsibilities are experienced at the same level, although at times we are forced to pay more attention to one than another. Those, like Friedman, who see economic responsibility as the basis for a business morality are not wrong; while those, like

Stone, who call for the existence of a social contract, are right. The issue here is one of understanding the way differing conceptions of CSR are rooted in different assumptions. The reasoning in Figure 3.2 is a modification and adaptation of Archie B. Carroll's (1991) "pyramid of corporate social responsibilities."

In this figure, we locate a pyramid of responsibilities that the corporate manager faces in dealing with survival and growth in competitive non-monopolistic contexts. If we think of firms as a whole, this pyramid may be used to place different notions of CSR and to locate different firms. If we think of particular managerial decisions or decision contexts, we may note that some firms in some decisions act with their economic responsibilities as a priority, while at other times their social responsibilities take precedence. If we think of the pyramid as a hierarchy, we may, as Carroll does, argue that firms must fulfill their economic and legal responsibilities before they turn to try to meet their social and ethical responsibilities (1991). Each reading selectively highlights a way of thinking about CSR.

THE STAKEHOLDER (MANAGEMENT) MODEL

The social contract perspective in CSR argues for the existence of the corporation as a functioning social institution capable not only of acting as a moral person and remaining responsible for what have become increasingly powerful actions, but also of establishing implicit social contracts based upon social expectations. The firm in the social contract model in CSR must be efficient or economically responsible, follow the law, and act fairly with regard to those whose involvement with the firm results in implicit contracts (see Figure 3.2). The stakeholder (management) model fills in to whom the firm should act fairly. The stakeholder (management) model comes in two interrelated versions—the influencer model, where stakeholders are depicted as capable of influencing the firm and its operations, and the model in which the stakeholder is a risk taker. In this latter model, the stakeholder is not only capable of having an influence on the firm, but they have a stake or take a risk in their involvement with the firm. With our eye upon CSR, let us take a broad look at the stakeholder (management) model, followed by its two most popular forms—the stakeholder as one who has a stake in the firm, and the broader, influencer version of the stakeholder.

Managerial stakeholder models seek to concretize and put a strong form of the social contract model of CSR into practice. The managerially-oriented stakeholder model has had, within the perspective of the young discipline of business ethics, a relatively long tradition. John Donaldson (1992) suggests that the term "stakeholder" was created by the sociologist Robert K. Merton in the 1950s to account for the changing pressures society was beginning to place upon publicly-traded corporations in the United States and Canada. The term, according to Donaldson, enjoyed a revival in the 1980s and 1990s as business commentators sought to capture the way social groups of all sorts moved in to compensate for the regulatory vacuum created as governments moved towards the political right, and consumers, trade unionists, environmentalists, and agents of local communities, to name a few, sought to more directly impress their needs upon the firm. Unlike Donaldson, Kenneth Goodpaster (1983) feels that the term stakeholder appears to have been invented in the early 1960s as a deliberate play on the word stockholder.

Within management circles, the Stanford Research Institute, in 1963, defined the stakeholder concept to include those groups without whose support an organization would cease to exist. Its list, intended for the practising manager, included stockholders, employees, customers, suppliers, lenders, and society. The members of the Stanford Research Institute

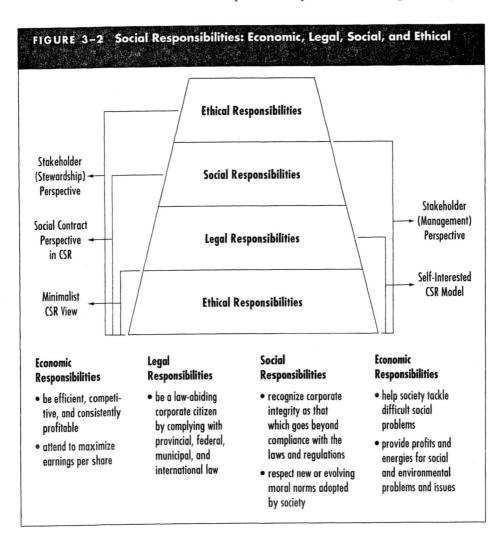

FIGURE 3-2 Social Responsibilities: Economic, Legal, Social, and Ethical

Ethical Responsibilities

Stakeholder (Stewardship) Perspective

Social Responsibilities

Social Contract Perspective in CSR

Legal Responsibilities

Stakeholder (Management) Perspective

Minimalist CSR View

Ethical Responsibilities

Self-Interested CSR Model

Economic Responsibilities

- be efficient, competitive, and consistently profitable
- attend to maximize earnings per share

Legal Responsibilities

- be a law-abiding corporate citizen by complying with provincial, federal, municipal, and international law

Social Responsibilities

- recognize corporate integrity as that which goes beyond compliance with the laws and regulations
- respect new or evolving moral norms adopted by society

Economic Responsibilities

- help society tackle difficult social problems
- provide profits and energies for social and environmental problems and issues

had a prescriptive purpose in mind. They argued that if managers did not understand the needs and concerns of the organization's multiple constituents or stakeholders, they would be far less likely to manage effectively. In this early work, very much in the "influencer" tradition, the emphasis was upon managing multiple constituencies in order to achieve organizational and managerial effectiveness; CSR, later to be made central, was treated as an unintended consequence. Managers sought to manage and this, in itself, required dealing with consumers, unions, suppliers, contractors, and the like. This recognition of the organization as an "open system" was treated initially as an enlargement of the manager's portfolio. It was only later that stakeholder analysis was seen as "the sine quo non of business virtue," and treated as desirable in itself (O'Toole, 1991:19).

In 1967, James Thompson, in a book entitled *Organizations in Action* (which I used as a student), made much of the shift in management as a series of skills moving from profit maximization (the old perspective) to uncertainty minimization (a then new perspective). To make his point, Thompson viewed the manager's task as more complex. The manager, in the modern perspective, had to deal with more than one dominant interest—the stockholder. The modern manager had to develop strategies to cope with the growing power of stakeholders or, to Thompson, "those groups that make a difference." To Thompson's thinking, unlike Donaldson's, the increased power of these "groups that make a difference" was due not to the regulatory vacuum, but to the increasing complexity of the modern corporation and its growing interdependence with others outside its organizational boundaries. Thompson— as we shall see in Chapters 4 and 8— began to direct managers to look at the "organizational environment" as a new portfolio to be managed. This new direction to management thinking would stimulate a concern for strategic management.

In 1984, in *Strategic Management: A Stakeholder Approach*, R. Edward Freeman attempted to lend a synthesis and a theory to the "black box" view of the firm as an entity responsible for dealing with a wide array of stakeholders. This work, unlike Freeman and his collaborators' later efforts (Freeman and Phillips, 1996; Freeman and Evan, 1990; Freeman and Gilbert, 1988), falls clearly within the instrumentally motivated influencer model of the stakeholder. Central to Freeman's (1984) approach are suggestions to managers on: how to map the dynamic and changing coalitions possible among and between the firm's stakeholders; how to monitor and measure the firm's responses to and anticipation of stakeholders' altering tactics; and how to govern stakeholders by engaging in strategic and rational trade-offs among and between them. Freeman's work is seminal; it gathers together the strategic options and monitoring tools available to managers who seek to manage responsibly the postmodern corporation.

Freeman (1984), despite his sage advice to managers and clear synthesis of the literature on stakeholders, confuses or makes little distinction between stakeholders as influencers and stakeholders as having a stake in the enterprise. "It is important," write Donaldson and Preston, with an eye on Freeman's work, "to draw a clear distinction between influencers and stakeholders: some actors in the enterprise (e.g. large investors) may be both, but some recognizable stakeholders (e.g. the job applicants) have no influence, and some influencers (e.g. the media) have no stakes" (1995:16). This is a vital distinction when attempting to delineate the strategic options available to managers who must steer between and among the pressures placed by stakeholders upon the modern organization.

To make this distinction, as in Figure 3.3, we will use Freeman's definition of a stakeholder as "any group or individual who can affect or is affected by the achievement of the organization's objectives" (1984:46). In Figure 3.3, I have drawn a holistic generic stakeholder map of a typical publicly-traded corporation and have distinguished those with stakes from those with influence. Primary stakeholders are those who are affected and can affect the firm through the marketplace. All primary stakeholders have both influence and a stake. The competitor's stake in the focal organization rests in avoiding the troubling visibility and likely regulatory consequences resulting from a firm eliminating all its competitors.

No tertiary stakeholder, as indicated in Figure 3.3, has a clear stake in the focal organization, but each possesses a moral claim and, through it, a means of influencing the focal organization. The moral claims of all tertiary stakeholders, an issue central to the stakeholder (stewardship) model, cannot be made directly by tertiary stakeholders. They must be represented by groups who claim to speak for them. Thus natural environment is represented by a multiplicity of views, all held by environmentalists whose perspectives may differ quite drastically from one another. The same holds for those, of course, who purport to represent what is best for society as a whole—and there are many groups in many different post-

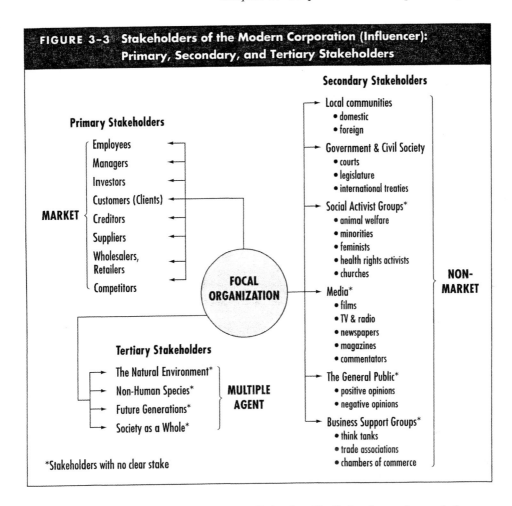

FIGURE 3-3 Stakeholders of the Modern Corporation (Influencer): Primary, Secondary, and Tertiary Stakeholders

modern debates who can claim this dubious distinction. Similarly, those who speak for non-human species and future generations present a multiple-agent agenda to the focal organization. With the absence of a clear take and the articulation of a moral claim, with many versions of the claim argued by well-intended tertiary stakeholders, it should be clear why, within the stakeholder (management) model, tertiary stakeholders, in my view, get the most rhetoric but the least action.

A great deal of attention in the pragmatically-oriented stakeholder (management) model is given to the primary stakeholder. As is made clear in Figure 3.4, primary stakeholders, like employees, seek to achieve their desires—stable, high-paying employment in a safe environment that provides recognition and intrinsic satisfaction—by bargaining for power by threatening to withdraw labour, work to rule, or otherwise generate negative publicity for their employer. Managers, investors, customers/clients, creditors, suppliers, wholesalers/retailers, and competitors all can be considered primary stakeholders since all seek to use the marketplace as the primary means of achieving their objectives and mobilizing their influence. While the moral claim of tertiary stakeholders is high, the practical means to achieving the results of this claim are weak. With primary stakeholders, the moral claim often is embedded within an explicit contract; at other times, as with employees, the contract is tacit or social. The contract and real dependence of the focal organization upon primary stakeholders gives the primary stakeholder a very real power base from which to work their moral claims. As outlined in Figure 3.4, primary stakeholders, like employees, have aspirations that are usually clear to the organization, are frequently presented by agents tied closely to the primary stakeholders (unlike tertiary stakeholders), and have a power base from which to attempt to realize these aspirations.

In the list of primary stakeholders, investors or stockholders are not privileged as they are in both the minimalist CSR perspective and the self-interested CSR perspective. They possess a moral claim—ownership—and a power base. However, neither their moral claim nor their power base puts them at the front of the list. Rather, the stakeholder (management) view is one that deals with stakeholders, including managers themselves, on a very pragmatic level. If one were to be skeptical, one might note that within this view "the squeaky wheel gets the grease." If one were more complimentary, one would note that in this perspective the organization is open to many market forces and seeks to manage them skillfully. This involves not only greasing the wheel, but also acting in a way which, in the case of employees, may make the workplace safer; in the case of customers or clients, may lessen the use of sexually explicit advertisements; or, in the case of the managers themselves, may provide increasing challenges and stock options.

Lest we forget, however, the stakeholder (management) view of corporate social responsibility is one of "real organizational politics." There are trade-offs. Increasing the stock options to retain very skilled managers may reduce the amount of capital available to invest in making the workplace safer for employees. Reducing the sexual explicitness of the advertisements in response to complaints from a small but highly-organized segment of consumers may ease the torrent of bad publicity, but will scuttle an "effective" advertisement campaign, thereby reducing world-wide sales and adversely affecting the focal firm's price per share. It is the trade-offs, not only among primary stakeholders, but across primary, secondary, and tertiary stakeholders, that make the stakeholder (management) perspective a favourite among business people who see business as a game and enjoy strategic management. The idea of strategic management is not only to maintain a keen gaze on economic reality—and utilize this to deal with the trade-offs among and between stakeholders—but also to try to make sure that one's policies are tied to one's abilities to create coalitions, at times temporary, among and between stakeholders. This entire affair is complicated even further by secondary stakeholders.

Secondary stakeholders—local communities, government, social activist groups, the media, the general public, and business support groups (see Figure 3.5)—utilize primarily non-market or social or, in government's case, political means to achieve their influence over a particular corporation. As we shall explore more fully in Chapter 9, firms can gain operating advantages—making the lives of management that much easier—when they enhance their reputation.

A firm with an enhanced reputation, other things being equal, will find it easier to enter into partnerships and strategic alliances, to borrow money at excellent rates, and to attract the very best personnel. Secondary stakeholders make life easy or, at times, hard for the firm by acting in a manner that either enhances or detracts from the firm's reputational capital. For example, the local community that raises a stink about the opening of a new plant will, through this NIMBY (not-in-my-back-yard) reaction, often work in tandem with another secondary stakeholder—the media—in order to influence a third—government. Businesses

FIGURE 3-4 **Primary Stakeholders: Requirements and Powers**

Primary Stakeholders	Nature of Requirements "Stakeholders aspire to ..."	Power Base "Stakeholders influence firm by ..."
Employees	• retain stable, high-paying employment with benefits • work in a safe setting • receive recognition	• union or professional association bargaining • using publicity • working to rule or withdrawing labour
Managers	• upward mobility with increases in pay and challenge • stock options • growing perquisites	• threatening to exit • developing new strategic plans • restructuring • acquiring new firms and properties
Investors	• attain a satisfactory return on investment (dividend) • achieve appreciation in stock value over time	• exercising voting rights based upon share ownership • employing rights to inspect company books and records
Customers/ Clients	• attain fair exchange value and quality for economic outlay • purchase safe, reliable products or services	• purchasing goods and services from competitors • setting up boycotts when firm's policies or actions are deemed unsatisfactory
Creditors	• receive repayment of loans on time and at the stated rates • collect debts, interest, and penalties if any accrue	• calling in loans if payments are not made • employing legal authorities to repossess or take over property if loan payments are severely delinquent
Suppliers	• be paid promptly for supplies delivered • receive steady orders for goods and/or services	• supplying to competitors • refusing to meet orders when conditions of contract are breached
Wholesalers/ Retailers	• receive quality goods and/or services in a timely fashion at reasonable costs • offer reliable service and/or products that consumers trust and value	• buying from other suppliers if the terms of the contract are unsatisfactory • boycotting companies whose policies and/or actions are not satisfactory
Competitors	• become and remain profitable • see the industry (as a whole) grow • achieve a larger share of the market	• charging lower prices • innovating, thereby forcing competitors to keep up

FIGURE 3-5   Secondary Stakeholders: Requirements and Powers

Secondary Stakeholders	Nature of Requirements "Stakeholders aspire to ..."	Power Base "Stakeholders influence firm by ..."
Local Communities	• ensure that the local environment and community are protected from negative externalities (pollution, noise, toxic substances) • employ local residents in the company • ensure the company is a good corporate citizen	• making by-laws and zoning issues problematic for the firm and its operation • generating negative publicity • lobbying governments • NIMBY actions (not-in-my-back-yard)
Government and Civil Society	• promote economic development and material advancement • encourage social improvements • enforce the commercial and criminal laws • raise taxes and public goods	• granting permits to do business • issuing regulations, licenses, permits, and fines • providing subsidies or incentives or removing these • building infrastructure that supports businesses
Social Activists	• monitor the company's actions and policies to ensure that it adheres to legal and ethical standards • raise the legal and ethical standards in areas where it believes the public (or a segment of the public) good is not being met	• achieving broad public support through publicizing the issue(s) • raising awareness, particularly to youth, regarding the issue(s) • politicizing the issue(s) • organizing opposition to the company industry or business issue(s)
Media	• attain business as advertisers in their medium • keep public informed on issues related to their economic, social, and political well-being • monitor company actions, paying particular attention to deviant or 'pariah' corporations and industries • develop ongoing, reliable sources and contacts for news and information within the business community	• publicizing events, people, and issues that have an impact upon the public • highlighting errors, bad judgment, and losses engaged in by the company • negatively evaluating the company's future (plans, products, services) • excluding the company from mention in areas where it has excelled

FIGURE 3-5 (Continued)

Secondary Stakeholders	Nature of Requirements "Stakeholders aspire to ..."	Power Base "Stakeholders influence firm by ..."
Business Support Groups (e.g. trade associations)	• provide legitimacy and good public relations to the wider industry in which the firm operates • provide research and information that will assist the company or industry as a whole performing in a changing world	• creating legal or political support beyond that which the company can provide • providing advertising or a social relations function for the industry • providing staff and resources for development endeavours in the industry

often seek to control their secondary stakeholders by mobilizing public relations campaigns, engaging in social marketing, or seeking to set up "think tanks" or business support groups favourably disposed toward the business or the industry in which the organization operates.

In Figure 3.5, we see the aspirations and influence strategies of typical secondary stakeholders mapped out. Activists, for example, are influencers who often, from a managerial perspective, can be seen as having no stake. To their peril, many managers fail to build plans for dealing with activists until the publicity that surrounds their campaigns begins to become costly. Within management circles—and speaking quite generally—all things being equal, managers attend to primary stakeholders before secondary, and tertiary stakeholders last; within each category, stakeholders with stakes can make themselves heard, all other things being equal, before those who possess influence but have no stake.

The stakeholder (management) view of corporate social responsibility sees the responsible firm as one which manages its primary, secondary, and tertiary stakeholders so as to minimize uncertainty and attain organizational longevity. It is not intended to maximize returns to investors, nor to provide in some important way for the betterment of society as a whole. In Chapter 5, we will discuss how efforts to imbue organizations with a specific form of culture must compromise within the realities of instrumental and, at times, pressing needs of the problems at hand. So it is, in the stakeholder (management) view of corporate social responsibility, that the need to satisfy the moral claims and cope with the countervailing power bases of the various stakeholders means that most organizations take a "good enough" view of corporate social responsibility. This means that within the stakeholder (management) perspective, the problem of social responsibility is treated as a management problem. As a management problem, corporations are, in the views of their managers, responsible when the majority of stakeholders are satisfied, or at least quiet. This emphasis upon satisfying stakeholders, or at least keeping them sufficiently busy to remain quiet, leads to "short-termism."

When people accuse the private corporation of short-termism, they are at some level aware that it is difficult for managers, even well-intended managers, to give tertiary stakeholders—future generations, non-human species, the natural environment, and society as a whole—top priority. These stakeholders are all influencers, but none, at least as seen from a management perspective, has a stake in the firm. These stakeholders are usually represented by secondary stakeholders. For example, the general public or even, at times, government may claim to speak for society as a whole. Activists may claim to speak for or act as agents for the natural environment and non-human species. What, however, is important with tertiary stakeholders (and we shall grasp their importance more fully in Chapter 9) is that they influence the ideological debates over how to operate businesses in the long run so as to overcome the fragmented and opportunistic calls of primary and secondary stakeholders over how we distribute our wealth and concerns in society. The stakeholder (stewardship) perspective attempts to compensate for this by insisting, as a principle, that corporate social responsibility is met by precisely the firm that goes beyond its social responsibilities, and acts in a principled fashion by seeking to address the issues represented by the most neglected tertiary stakeholders—future generations, non-human species, society as a whole, and the natural environment—none of which speaks for itself.

THE STAKEHOLDER (STEWARDSHIP) MODEL

Corporate social responsibility within the stakeholder (management) model is a result of the effective manager/leader who balances the needs of stakeholders, paying particular attention to those more likely to impact the organization, while piloting the firm towards stability, growth, and prosperity; CSR in the stakeholder (stewardship) model is a result of the efforts of an involved team of stewards who partner with stakeholders in order to serve those who might otherwise not be served. Authentic service, the means by which one integrates private life with work and public persona, is essentially a search for greater meaning and purpose. The role of the steward in the stakeholder (stewardship) model is motivated by a quest for service and meaning. In this context, Robert K. Greenleaf, in his work at AT&T and in his book, *Servant Leadership: A Journey in the Nature of Legitimate Power and Greatness* (1977), depicts the servant leader as a model of stewardship in practice. The servant leader exists, not to self-actualize, as in Abraham Maslow's conception of the fully-realized leader, but to serve his or her followers by establishing a community diverse in perspectives, yet capable of developing partnerships rooted in trust. For a further exploration of the ethics of workplace diversity, see Chapter 8.

The stewardship model is unabashedly idealistic in its depiction of the ethical potential of businesses in society. Rather than describing the actions of firms rooted in either the economic model of man (meaning human beings in general), the tenets of legal rationality, or even the social rationality of implicit contracts, stewardship theory seeks to establish an ideal of how the firm might act if it were able to go beyond the confines of self-interest and compliance with the laws of the land. "In stewardship theory," write James H. Davis and his colleagues, "the model of man is based on a steward whose behavior is ordered such that pro-organizational, collectivistic behaviors have a higher utility than individualistic, self-serving behaviors" (Davis, Schoorman, and Donaldson, 1997:24). Davis and his colleagues add to a literature that contrasts agency theory with stewardship theory (Fox and Hamilton, 1994).The former seeks to understand how to keep agents (managers) from using their power in the firm to out-fox principals (owners/stockholders). The answer, within stewardship theory, is to build conditions in which trust flourishes and partnering is emphasized.

The term stewardship means to hold something in trust for another. The origins of the term are steeped in history. Initially, stewardship was an obligation to protect a kingdom while those rightfully in charge were absent, or, more often, to govern with dignity and fairness in the name of an underage king. Peter Block, in his first-rate book, *Stewardship: Choosing Service Over Self-Interest* (1993), addresses the stewardship stakeholder model when he writes, "The underage king for us is the next generation. We choose service over self-interest most powerfully when we build the capacity of the next generation to govern themselves" (Block, 1993:20). The voices of other tertiary stakeholders can be heard in the call for stewardship of the natural environment by Dorothy J. Howell (1997) and Barbara and James Peters (1991); of non-human species by Michael Fox (1990) and Tom Regan (1982); and of society as a whole in the works of Amitai Etzioni (1988) and Paul Hawken (1993).

Peter Block (1993:41–42) notes that the ideals of service through stewardship have been with us in a religious context where it reveals itself in different but related guises. The sacred texts of many religions direct us to care for the earth. The second use occurs wherein many of our religious institutions have practised stewardship for centuries, primarily as a means of achieving financial responsibility. These stewardship committees function as fund-raising groups and, at times, take a position in deciding how to distribute funds to causes within the community. The tone and inflection on the word "giving" varies between the manager and stewardship stakeholder models. It is this difference that makes stewardship theory, and more particularly the stakeholder (stewardship) model, a difficult sell to managers. In fact, Peter Block (1993) calls stewardship theory a form of teaching "revolution to the ruling class."

Within the stakeholder (management) model, "giving" can be understood as instrumental. The leader/manager of the corporation seeks to use a proportion of its profits to deal with those who are affected by and can affect the corporation. While the stakeholder (management) model does not directly address maximizing profits, it does address and, what is more important, it makes suggestions on how to minimize uncertainty and achieve some stability over time. This logic is heard (perhaps not as easily as is the directive to maximize profits) by managers of "blue chip" corporations. These corporations, in their use of conservative growth strategies over long periods of time, rely heavily on achieving stability and building a solid corporate reputation (see Chapter 9). The stakeholder (management) model addresses the needs of those who must compete for social legitimacy, credibility, and customer loyalty over time.

The inflection given to the term "giving" employed in the stakeholder (stewardship) model is more difficult to sell to managers. Selling revolution to the ruling class is difficult because the ruling class always enjoys the conditions that led to their acquisition and employment of power. The managerial elite, the actual ruling class in most managed systems seeking its ideal in the image of the efficient corporation, views competition as central. Within a world view that enshrines competition as an indispensable element in corporate governance, it is difficult to sell the idea of using one's scarce time, energy, and resources, even in relatively small amounts, to help others who are unlikely to be of direct benefit to the corporation. Giving, in a trade-off sense, to stakeholders who can go on strike (employees), impact your public image (the media), cause you difficulties in getting permits and licenses (local communities), is one thing; giving to future generations, non-human species, and the like, is another thing entirely.

Yet to respond to the challenge, advocates of the stakeholder (stewardship) model posit three reasons why a firm that already has achieved economic, legal, and social responsibility, ought to dedicate some time, energy, and resources to the stewardship model. The first reason, the most intuitively comprehensible to the business person, is that firms that adhere to the stakeholder (stewardship) model will be able to attract and maintain the very best and brightest of talent. The stewardship model provides the employees of the firm with a belief in and an understanding that work is done to serve a larger, more meaningful, purpose. If social analysts are correct and people are looking for a sense of meaning and purpose in their work, then firms that successfully implement and develop a stewardship model may possess a competitive advantage. This competitive advantage, of course, is most useful for those organizations that utilize highly-talented, not easily replaced, human resources as their primary strength.

A second justification of the stakeholder (stewardship) model suggests that by moving towards the implementation of this model, the firm will become more flexible, resilient, and have the capacity to anticipate problems and thereby learn more effectively. The key to this position rests on the assumption that to implement a genuine stakeholder (stewardship) model, the managers of the firm must engage in changes to the organization's structure that will make the firm more responsive. As an example of the sorts of changes they have in mind, advocates of the stakeholder (stewardship) model point to the need to reconfigure and highlight the role of the board of governors. In the typical firm, the board of governors is composed of industry insiders who meet infrequently, but frequently act as a rubber stamp, provided dividends are being paid. In the firm genuinely involved in the stakeholder (stewardship) model, the board of directors includes knowledgeable industry insiders mixed with a fair representation of knowledgeable or articulate stakeholders. Boards that are more inclusive keep the firm, advocates of the stewardship model insist, on its toes. They pose questions outside the standard operating procedures of the firm and, in rising to the challenge, the firm stretches and learns.

The third and last justification of the stakeholder (stewardship) model applauds the model as providing an ideal to which everyday managers can aspire. The advocates of the stakeholder (stewardship) model are looked upon as radicals by advocates of the minimalist CSR position, and as idealists by advocates of the management stakeholder model. They are both. As radicals, they seek to suggest that the goal of business is not only to make profit, but to use this profit wisely and well; as idealists, they dream the dream of a time in which, in our secular, everyday roles as business people, we find a greater meaning and purpose—a sense of the sacred—that is rooted in our willingness to deal with issues and problems beyond the immediate gratification of our needs, the quest for material comfort and security.

The five models of corporate responsibility that we have discussed indicate that CSR means different things to different analysts. The minimalist CSR position bound to a view of CSR as a neo-classical form of economic rationality privileges the owner of the corporation or its shareholders. The self-interested CSR model does as well, but notes that it is possible and responsible to serve the owners or shareholders, at the right time and in the right proportion, by giving a concession or a portion of the profits to others. This should, in the self-interested CSR model, be done opportunistically such that the profits of the firm are increased by the concession. The contract perspectives in CSR, both the formal and social, insist that to be responsible, firms must honour their promises to others. The formal contracts involve explicit legal promissory documents; the social contract perspective includes implicit understandings and notions of "rational" expectations. The stakeholder perspectives in CSR, both managerial and stewardship, insist that to be socially responsible, the firm must be able to deal with primary, secondary, and tertiary stakeholders in minimizing uncertainty, attaining legitimacy and, of course, operating a viable business. The management stakeholder perspective, in an instrumental fashion, attends to the stakeholders with the greatest ability to influence the focal organization. The stewardship stakeholder perspective, in an idealist and prescriptive fashion, urges members of the focal organization to rise to the challenge of coping with not only those who can threaten the organization, but also with the moral claims of tertiary stakeholders.

Now, in the next section, let us look at the three notions of community girding the views of CSR—the traditional community, the rational rule-based community, and the community as a loose coalition. Each reflects, within the business community, the period in which it rose to ascendancy: the traditional community in the premodern context, the rule-based community in the modern context, and the community as a loose coalition in the postmodern context. Each, when we look to our next chapter, prepares us for an understanding of the key dilemmas in putting CSR into practice.

BUSINESS AS COMMUNITY

Responsibility is born in community and in collective action. Community requires that we attend to the other, align our actions, and take responsibility for the consequences of our actions within and upon the community. When we ask the question, "What is corporate social responsibility (CSR)?", we are asking what conception of community binds our thinking about the organization. In Figure 3.6, we note that within our scrutiny of the five CSR perspectives, three notions of community prevail. When we speak of community, we address our sense of obligation and who it is we think we should worry about when we take risks or engage in activities with uncertain outcomes. It is our perception of the community with whom we are involved when we do business that sets our understanding of for whom we should feel responsible. Our notion of community has, of course, altered from premodern, to modern, to postmodern world views. This shift towards the postmodern notion of community has had an impact upon business. Not surprisingly, in postmodernity the business community is a loose coalition of fleeting exchanges in which much of the exchange is between anonymous interacters who offer different elements to the transaction.

It is important in this discussion not to confuse business as a community with the concept of organizational culture that we will probe in Chapter 5. When we speak about organizational culture, we are talking about the values and beliefs shared by participants within the organization. Organizational culture, if we were to put words into an organizational member's mouth, "is the way things are done around here." When we speak of business as a community, we are looking at the role of business in society. How does business see itself in society? As a community of people doing business, what does it see as its role in society? If it, as a community, were doing well, who would benefit and why?

Let us now turn to each of the three views of business as community—noting the following premises as underlying axioms in our interpretation. The shift from business as a traditional entrepreneurial community (premodern), to business as a community of rational practices and rules (modern), to business as a loose coalition of fleeting exchanges (postmodern), does not mean that the concerns of business as either a traditional community or as a community of rational practices and rules no longer exist. They do; and many, as we shall see, do try to use "trust"—essentially an idea embedded in business as a traditional community—to solve the notions of CSR in the postmodern context. Or, still germane, many try

FIGURE 3-6   Three Views of Business as Community: Responsibility in What Context?

Type of Community	Context/CSR Perspective	Responsibility is ...
• Business is a traditional entrepreneurial community	• "Premodern" • Minimalist CSR view • Self-interested CSR model	• Duty to one central obligation in the business/community • Trust, predictability, and continuity • Meeting obligations
• Business is a community of rational practices and rules	• "Modern" • The contract (social and formal) perspectives in CSR	• Following rational practices and rules, altering outmoded practices and rules, and reducing uncertainty • Carefully assessing which new and emerging issues deserve organizational attention
• Business is a loose coalition of fleeting exchanges	• "Postmodern" • The stakeholder (management and stewardship) perspectives	• To have sufficient confidence in your sense-making ability to deal with others who see the world very differently, and still enter into exchanges that can create new options, new coalitions, and alternative possibilities

to use the notion of the contract, particularly the social contract, an idea emerging in the modern context as a means of coping with business as a loose coalition of fleeting exchanges. What this is intended to convey to the reader is that a historical reading of the three views of business as a community is possible. It should not, particularly if you are given to postmodern forms of analysis, predominate.

A second axiom useful to move from Figure 3.6 to a closer reading of the three views is to realize that in each view, a predominant problem seems to emerge. In business as a traditional entrepreneurial community, the tight boundaries of the business community play havoc with "trust." Within the firm, investors do not trust managers, employees do not trust employers and, of course, nobody within the firm trusts government, competitors, contractors, suppliers, and certainly not those who advocate what the firm sees as activist issues. In the modern context, business as a community of rational practices and rules, the predominant problem is how to recognize and manage emerging issues—those that do not seem to easily fit into the existing rule and rational practices. In the postmodern context, wherein business is a loose coalition of fleeting exchanges, the predominant problem is to provide participants with the tools to engage in interpretive forms of sense-making. This last, of course, is required when one is compelled by the nature of postmodern business to deal with a multiplicity of positions, each having the right to be heard.

BUSINESS AS A TRADITIONAL ENTREPRENEURIAL COMMUNITY

In Adam Smith's *Wealth of Nations* we are introduced to the traditional entrepreneurial community. Competition prevails. Some firms thrive, others go out of business. There is, in this community, a frontier spirit. Anything goes—as long as it is not detected as illegal—if it aids one in competing successfully. The firm in the traditional entrepreneurial community is considered to be the property of its owner or owners. Rights within the traditional entrepreneurial community are extended to owners. Even within the array of owners, those whose claims are heard easiest are those owners in control of dominant firms. As indicated in Figure 3.7, power and authority go to those who succeed in the jungle-like atmosphere of the traditional entrepreneurial community. In game-theoretical terms, the traditional entrepreneurial community is a win-lose forum. The powerful are winners; those who fail to survive and flourish are losers.

This is far from a planned community. Both the minimalist CSR perspective and the self-interested CSR model best approximate the notion of responsibility in the traditional entrepreneurial community. Government is seen as an interloper. The task of government is to make and enforce the laws fairly, and then stay out of the way of the business community. Government regulation and "intervention," as it is called in the traditional entrepreneurial community, are seen as troublesome forms of meddling that take business away from its central goals. Efforts by government to ensure workers' rights, for example, to a safe workplace or

FIGURE 3-7 Power and Authority: Three Views of the Business Community

Power		
Traditional Entrepreneurial Community	**Community of Rational Rules and Practices**	**Community of Fleeting Exchanges**
Power goes to those who succeed in a community that is like a jungle. This social Darwinian perspective applied to business speaks to the survival of the fittest. In it, the powerful colonize and control the less powerful.	Power goes to those who make the rules. To make the rules, one must make a claim as an expert. Others will attempt to override your claim. If you succeed in establishing it, you will accede to power.	Power goes to those who are central in networks and can cut deals. To be central in networks, one must have the ability to deal with and thrive under high degrees of uncertainty.
Authority		
Traditional Entrepreneurial Community	**Community of Rational Rules and Practices**	**Community of Fleeting Exchanges**
Authority goes to those who can legitimize their power. Power in the traditional community is legitimized when it can be shown that the business has influence over others. Size, wealth, and longevity of the business confer authority upon it.	Authority goes to those who, once having made the rules, now get to enforce them. Enforcing the rules is associated with vertical power. Those at the top of vertical power games held together by rules possess authority.	Authority goes to those who see and can tell the story of how to put into practice even more new coalitions and deals. These new options often break the rules of authority in the community of rational rules.

one that does not discriminate along lines of age, gender, or race, are looked upon as infringements upon the freedom of the business community. Actions by activists to try to draw attention to what some may see as failures of the business community are also treated as infringements upon the freedom of the community.

The traditional entrepreneurial community justifies its need for freedom from what is sees as "interventions" since, its advocates insist, it is under the control of free markets. To be socially responsible, business must respond to the very real and ever-present play of the forces of demand and supply. Firms that provide leadership in the traditional entrepreneurial community successfully compete and, over time, dominate markets. As market leaders, they influence others in the business community. This influence grows as long as the firm can retain the power and authority of its market dominance. The skill of those in the traditional entrepreneurial business community is not tested solely in rising to positions of market leadership, but also in developing techniques to sustain this leadership over time. These techniques include attempting to retain one's control over resources and thereby reducing one's vulnerability to the strategies of others in the traditional entrepreneurial community.

It is, to the astute business ethics student, a contradiction to label the traditional entrepreneurial as "premodern" (see Figure 3.6), and then to note that one of its central problems rests in the absence of trust in the community. The premodern context, as discussed in Chapter 2, was portrayed as a traditional society in which close, face-to-face interaction led to a great deal of trust in members. This is true. But one must recall that while members tended to trust each other, there was complete and utter distrust of outsiders. Outsiders were strangers, carried odd perspectives, and were from "away." These perspectives challenged the world view of the premodern society, and caused those who held them to be denied membership, to be treated with distrust, and to be marginalized. In short, the premodern context as discussed in Chapter 2 exacerbated a view of privileging the voices of the "in" group and derogating those of outgroups.

In the traditional entrepreneurial community, membership with full rights, as we have seen in the minimalist CSR view and the self-interested CSR model (see Figure 3.3), is severely restricted to owners or dominant shareholders and their agents, the firm's team of managers. All others, even within the firm, are seen as instruments to be employed in the service of the business community. It is in the context of the traditional entrepreneurial community that the field of industrial relations rises to prominence. Employees in the traditional entrepreneurial community try to develop countervailing powers in their unions and professional associations as a way to get their voices heard. Those living in neighbourhoods proximate to these businesses will have a hard time getting their concerns about issues that may be lowering their property values and decreasing their quality of life on to the agenda of businesses in the traditional entrepreneurial community. Even the consumer, an individual one might think should be sovereign in this community, often finds it difficult to be heard. The consumer can, of course, take his or her business elsewhere, but to be heard, he or she must influence sufficient numbers of consumers so as to threaten the bottom line. In this context, consumer groups may be formed to monitor the behaviour of particular firms.

Trust within the traditional entrepreneurial community is high between and among owners. In this (in effect quite small) setting a handshake often will be sufficient, just as in the premodern context, to get a deal going between businesses. Unlike the postmodern business community with its fleeting exchanges transacted via mediating technologies and in a global context, exchanges in the traditional entrepreneurial community occur in a fish bowl.

Violations of trust will be broadcast and amplified within the grapevine or the rumour mill of the traditional entrepreneurial community.

This bifurcated treatment of trust between full members with rights, namely dominant owners and their agents (managers), when compared to the struggle of others to be heard by this community, plays havoc with socio-moral development in the traditional entrepreneurial community. In Figure 3.8 we note how ethics in the traditional entrepreneurial community is tied to the honouring of the strongest and the fittest. Sensitivity to others is understood as either the ability to intuit weaknesses and to capitalize upon them, or to recognize and utilize others' strengths to help attain one's own victories. The tone of these insights is Machiavellian. The competitive milieu in the traditional entrepreneurial community fosters a belief that others are to be used or out-foxed. Winners serve as models. Those who move from the minimalist CSR perspective to the self-interested CSR model may seek to use others humanely and out-fox them fairly, but the relationship between self and other is still one of an effort by self to colonize the other.

To be fair, those embedded in the social Darwinian aspects of the traditional entrepreneurial business community do not view themselves as Machiavellian strategists. Rather, in their view, they are sensitive to others. They provide employment for large numbers. They pay taxes on their wealth. They are constantly seeking to improve their services and products to either get ahead in their competitive markets, or to sustain their market position. In their view, personal morality is unrelated to business acumen. The separation between their personal morality and business strategy is understood to be a prerequisite of full membership in the traditional entrepreneurial community. With this separation, the owner or investor can and will sensibly go into any business venture—armaments, tobacco, clear-cutting of timber, distribution of sexually explicit videos—as long as it is legal and is perceived to be an area in which the probability of success is high.

It should come as no surprise, given the separation between personal and business morality, to learn that in the traditional entrepreneurial business community, business ethics are kept to a minimum (see Figure 3.8) Those who seek to right a wrong, insist members of the traditional entrepreneurial community, should use the existing legal system. It would be irresponsible for the firm to create a format for justice-seeking. Even grievances between and among participants should be worked out by the participants. In the ideology of the traditional entrepreneurial community, the entire ethos of ethics programs runs counter to the social Darwinism that serves as the lifeblood of this community. Ethics programs are seen as protecting the weak. This is hardly the way to ensure that the best, toughest, and fittest rise to the top.

The ethics of the traditional entrepreneurial community reward those who are able to succeed by dint of hard work and effort (see Figure 3.8). Pleasure in a job well done, in winning in open competition, is its own reward. But there is far more than hedonism girding this position. It can be argued that the traditional entrepreneurial community is the bedrock of a version of frontier capitalism. In it we seek people with great skills, stamina, and drive to pilot the social system into and through areas of high risk, novelty, and uncertainty. Since these are high risk areas, we insist that the risk takers use their own money and, as such, get to call the shots. We become uneasy with this version of frontier capitalism when we rely on it in contexts in which the firms themselves get very large and powerful, in some instances possessing economies larger than the nation state. We worry about this "anything goes" attitude when it is brought to bear in the operation of hospitals, nuclear facilities, banks, and air-

---

FIGURE 3–8   Ethics and Ethics Program Implementation: Three Views of the Business Community

Ethics

Traditional Entrepreneurial Community	Community of Rational Rules and Practices	Community of Fleeting Exchanges
Ethics in the traditional community is rooted in the glorification of rugged individualism and the celebration of the pleasures that go to the strongest, fittest, and the winners.	Ethics in the rational rules community focuses on the procedures of fairness. The entire community system seeks to develop new rules to deal with controversies in which grievances emerge.	Ethics in the community of fleeting exchanges takes a situational perspective. Unlike the search for rules of fairness, as in the community of rational rules, the emphasis here is on interpreting situations.

Ethics Program Implementation

Traditional Entrepreneurial Community	Community of Rational Rules and Practices	Community of Fleeting Exchanges
Ethics programs are kept to a minimum. Those who seek to right a wrong can use the courts or straighten things out by contests of power and resources. Ethics programs just protect the weak. The traditional business community addresses the survival of the fittest.	Ethics programs are rule-based efforts with a bureaucratic system to deal with value conflicts and moral controversies that otherwise might impede the smooth flow of rational and fair work practices. The attempt to make things fairer often itself leads to controversy, and many ethics programs become ineffective.	Ethics programs emerge to handle the divergent views of those within loose coalitions. To make things work within interdependent but loosely-bound exchanges, there must be agreement on basic principles and values.

---

ports. In these instances, we look for a more stable, less volatile ethos—one grounded in a very different conception of community.

The following section examines the business community operating in a matrix of rational rules and practices.

THE COMMUNITY OF RATIONAL RULES

In Max Weber's work (1947) and in other work on bureaucracy (Albrow, 1970; Blau, 1956; Crozier, 1964; Nohria and Berkley, 1994), we are introduced to the idea of business as a collective pattern of action, in essence, of community rooted in a rather formal matrix of rules and practices. As in our discussion of the "modern" world view, rationality, planning, the centrality of the expert, and hierarchy are woven tightly into the fabric of the community of rational rules. This is not the basis for frontier capitalism, nor the context in which the entrepreneur is lionized. The traditional entrepreneurial community accelerates risk-taking, individualism, profit maximization, and personal liberty. The traditional entrepreneurial community explodes with superstar entrepreneurs and the meteoric rise to prominence of particular organizations. However, it provides little stability. It, we might conjecture, is like a sleek automobile designed for speed but awkward in the stop-and-go, wait-and-be-patient traffic typical at rush hour in a Canadian city.

Business, operating as it if it were a community of rational rules and practices, offers and provides stability. At the centre of this community is not the charisma of the entrepreneur, but the rational notion of "position." Positions are designed by experts as an assemblage of tasks and skills believed necessary in order for a member to provide a function. The function, or the person who provides it—the functionary—is the basic building block in the community. All functionaries are, however, not equal in terms of power and authority (see Figure 3.7). A hierarchy, stretched most notably along its vertical axis, prevails. At the top within any organization and at the top of the most central bureaucracies within society, we can locate functionaries with power. Power here accrues to those who make, enforce, and select the rules to be applied in particular circumstances. When this power is enacted within the rules by someone sufficiently high up in the hierarchy, it is seen as authoritative.

Since, as we shall see, even top-level functionaries cannot easily remove lower-level ones except within the rules, there is an ongoing need in the community of rules to turn one's power into authority. This is not a pressing issue in the traditional entrepreneurial community, where the master in his or her castle can remove others with much greater ease. Authority in the bureaucratic context means that power is being, and is seen to be, enacted within the rules. This, clearly, is not the context of rugged individualism, accelerated risk, profit maximization, and personal liberty.

It is, however, the domain of stability. Managers succeed by anticipating issues, and problem solve by bringing them into the rules and standard operating procedures of the organization. Stability is built into the community by placing rules at its centre and requiring, as it were, that one follow the rules to change the rules. In fact, decisions as to whether or not to commit to one line of action rather than another, within the community of rational rules and practices, must be justified by making a clear case using the rules. As in the "modern" world view, the use of quantitative evidence rooted in precedence and a close examination of data prevails. Language becomes, within each level of the hierarchy and in areas of particular expertise, highly specialized. To weigh the evidence for and against committing resources to one line of action rather than another, expert opinion is relied upon. These experts are often members of professional associations, the source of their credentials, and owe a dual allegiance to the firm that pays their salaries and to the professional associations that license their competencies.

In this context, contracts prevail. The "formal" and "social" contract perspectives in CSR replace the dominant "minimalist" and self-interested CSR models that prevail in the traditional entrepreneurial business community. It is clear, in the community of rules, that functionaries have rights. These are conferred in the contract between the organization in the community of rational rules and practices, and groups of functionaries hired to fill particular functions. There are two differing sorts of rights and, concomitantly, accompanying duties in this context. The first are the explicit contractual relations between the firm and its participants. The second, and we shall explore these in greater length in our discussion of organizational cultures in Chapter 5, are rooted in the implicit social expectations, word-of-mouth agreements, and evolution, over time, of the relationship between and among members in the business community formulated around rational rules and practices.

When one works in a business fully enveloped in the community of rational rules and practices, one usually gets a rather large binder full of procedures, practices, expectations, and rules. When, on the other hand, one works in the traditional entrepreneurial business place, one receives a page to sign, a handshake, and a time at which one is expected to show up for work. Many of us feel crushed by the weight of the rules in bureaucratic settings. There are rules on how to register an official complaint. There are directives stating what one must do in order to be considered for promotion. Based upon your seniority and status within the hierarchy, there is a formula to calculate how many (paid) sick days will be countenanced. Outlined in the binder, you may find what one is to do in case of a fire or a computer emergency within the firm. The rules are, of course, a double-edged sword—they protect you when you can get them to work on your behalf and they increase your vulnerability when you violate them—or are perceived to have violated them—and must pay the consequences.

Even though you may have to pay the consequences for violating rules, it is evident that the very existence of these rules, both formal and implicit, alter the "trust" problem so explicit in the traditional entrepreneurial community. In Figure 3.6 we see how business in a community of rational practices and rules creates a new problem. The problem here, ironically, emerges because of the very stability achieved by this community. The duty of all functionaries is to adhere to rational practices and rules. This creates conditions for increasing reliability, consistency, and fairness. The "anything goes" element in the traditional entrepreneurial system accelerates change, risk-taking, and rugged individualism, but, as we have seen, it plays havoc with trust. In the community of rational rules and practices, the very use of precedent and rational rules makes it extremely difficult for this notion of community to be responsive to newly-emerging issues, trends, and exceptions. Exceptions, by definition, violate or call into question the standard operating procedures of rule-based communities.

The precedent-based nature of the business community of rational rules and practices prohibits an easy response to new and emerging issues. The responsibility of this community is to reduce uncertainty and to produce stability. The good world, in this community, is the stable one that permits one to predict accurately, make rational rules, and generate plans that will, given the circumstances, cover all eventualities. Functionaries use the rules and practices even after they have become outmoded. They are not to blame. The entire reward structure is tied to the rational rules and practices. Selection to and promotion up the levels of hierarchy in the community are premised on the incumbent's knowledge of and willingness to place faith in the rational rules and practices of the firm. Success or failure in these communities is much more difficult to discern than it is in the traditional business community where a failure to sustain or surpass one's last quarterly performance signals trouble. Signals of trouble are much more difficult to read in businesses operating in the community of rational rules and practices. In fact, most functionaries feel that it is the very abandonment of the rational rules and practices that indicates trouble.

To be responsible, the business community immersed in rational rules and practices must be able to diagnose, anticipate, and manage emerging issues. This community shows leadership when it works the rules effectively (see Figure 3.9). This requires developing a feedback system to detect when and where rules central to the organization's operations require revisions and alterations. Attentiveness to the connection between the assumption that the rules are rational and—as a consequence—that they are effective, must not be allowed to lapse. To sustain this, the organization must be willing to become self-critical and reflexive. The adoption of a defensive posture towards critics, a feature aided by the authority of many of the experts in the organization, may curtail efforts to make sense of and incrementally alter the rational rules and practices at the heart of the community.

When a defensive posture is adopted, the socio-moral development of participants in the business as community of rational rules takes a conformist and self-satisfied turn. The conformity arises out of the explicitness of rewards for rule-following. The self-satisfaction

FIGURE 3-9 Leadership and Socio-Moral Development: Three Views of the Business Community		

Leadership

Traditional Entrepreneurial Community	Community of Rational Rules and Practices	Community of Fleeting Exchanges
Leadership in the traditional community is tied to the abilities of the firm to dominate others. This dominance is a sign of its ability to compete in markets.	Leadership in the community of rational rules is held by the firm that work the rules best. This rule working involves adapting the organization to changes. The approach to staying ahead is incremental.	Leadership in the community of fleeting exchanges is held by the firm that has the confidence to interpret and put into practice new ideas. Leadership involves the use of radical change to stay ahead.

Socio-Moral Development

Traditional Entrepreneurial Community	Community of Rational Rules and Practices	Community of Fleeting Exchanges
Socio-moral development is tied to winning and dominating. Sensitivity to others is understood as the ability to intuit weaknesses and to capitalize upon them. Hearing others' views is useful only if these can be appropriated.	Socio-moral development is measured by one's ability to keep one's commitment, both formal and implicit. The notion of justice here is tied to keeping one's word and remaining true to one's promises. To fail in this regard requires a very good justification.	Socio-moral development is related to one's ability to be sensitive to others' views so that one can help bring together new teams and outlooks that can help participants. Caring for others is its own reward, since to be truly secure, one must be involved with genuine others.

develops as a result of the functionary's belief that within his or her system of rational rules and procedures, the ego is well protected. What is worrying is that when conformity is high and egos are well protected, learning is made difficult. Mimicry and obeisance to policy take over. On the positive side, there is a concerted effort within this context to arrive at a working definition of fairness that must go across levels of hierarchy, include clients, and be publicly justified. The proliferation of contracts, both formal and implicit, necessitates the emergence of efforts to resolve value conflicts and disagreements over what is acceptable in the community and what is not.

The search for what is and is not fair in the operations of business as a community of rational rules and practices is conducive to an elaborate and often extensive series of committees entrusted with the task of coming to terms with ethical problems. Ethics program implementation in this context is problem based (see Figure 3.8). Ethics creates the sort of controversies difficult to handle by rational, universalistic rules. In businesses operating in the community of rational rules and practices, there is a search to hire ethics experts to set the template for the ethics programs. Task forces and special project teams of functionaries culled from their own areas of specialization seek to put the ethics programs into practice. This often proves to be difficult, given the propensity towards red tape and proceduralism. To make ethics programs viable in businesses operating in the community of rational rules, the organization must avoid confusing the following of their rules with the accomplishment and realization of fairness and justice.

The ethics of the business community immersed in rational rules and practices is rooted in a problem-solving perspective. Ethical issues create uncertainty. People take different views. They argue. Controversy emerges. Sides get drawn. Moral views are presented. These moral views are difficult to rein in and control by creating rational rules and practices. In fact, it is hope that by creating rational rules and practices and revising these, ethical issues can be turned from problems with crisis potential to standard operating procedures. This is precisely why businesses operating in the community of rational rules look to ethics experts and the committee system to resolve these issues. Resolution entails building these into the template that is used to socialize new members, justify policy, and allocate resources.

BUSINESS AS A COMMUNITY OF FLEETING EXCHANGES

Relying upon a template, even one rooted in rationality, can be problematic when the firm operates in contexts where exchange is fleeting, views radically diverge, and the community turns to loose coalitions of stakeholders. In the works of Zygmunt Bauman (1992, 1993, 1995), David Boje (1991, 1996), and his colleagues (Boje *et al.*, 1996), we are given an introduction to the community of fleeting exchanges from a perspective useful to the business student. This community marries the frontier spirit of the traditional entrepreneurial community to the stability and quest for fairness pursued by firms operating in the community of rational rules and practices. It seeks to put together the gas pedal of the traditional entrepreneurial community with the brakes of the inertial community of rational rules and procedures. In so doing, those who seek proficiency within it must try to: 1) reduce the mistrust originating in the "anything goes" elements inherited from operations within the traditional entrepreneurial community; 2) perpetuate a means of anticipating, diagnosing, and managing emerging issues, something sorely lacking within the community of rational rules; and 3) consolidate these in the ability of participants to interpret rather than legislate. Postmodern management presents no small challenge.

To interpret requires that participants in business as a loose coalition of fleeting exchanges recognize the multiple-constituency, multiple-reality nature of organizations in the postmodern world view. In Chapter 2 we formulated the logic whereby the "opening" of organizational boundaries came less from the ability of organizational participants to handle larger amounts of uncertainty, than it did from their inability to fortify the community of rational rules and practices to withstand the bombardment of opposing and cross-hatched demands placed upon it. Stakeholding takes root when membership is extended or, in a more political sense, is won. In the traditional entrepreneurial community, membership and its privileges are accorded to owners or large shareholders; in businesses operating in the community of rational rules and practices, membership is extended to functionaries or employees and, through guarantees and other contracting procedures, to clients. In the community of business as a loose coalition of fleeting exchanges, membership is extended to stakeholders—primary, secondary and, even in the case of firms arguing a stakeholder (stewardship) position, to tertiary stakeholders.

To thrive in this context, organizations must be able to form coalitions with others. This includes other businesses or stakeholders such as government, unions, contractors, or suppliers, as the situation requires. To succeed, participants in the community of fleeting exchanges cannot merely dominate, as was the rule of thumb in the traditional entrepreneurial community, nor assert rational rules and practices, as do businesses in the community of rational rules, but must have the ability to interpret and negotiate deals. Deals here are not those of the traditional entrepreneur, but those of the broker who must bring together participants to an exchange. This emphasis upon process, not structure and rules, places power in the community of fleeting exchanges within one's abilities to remain central to and within altering networks.

Figure 3.7 illustrates how in the community of fleeting exchanges, power requires the ability to not only maintain one's centrality in altering networks, but to do so by managing uncertainty. Members come and go. Allies turn and threaten. Partners try to acquire one's power base. It is, of course, in this context that the term "strategic" increases in its frequency of use in businesses. The long-term reliable plan of business in the community of rational rules is retained, but treated as a rough approximation of a generalized direction sought by the firm. Strategies become ways to implement moves, to remain central in a network, or to reposition oneself in a new network. Authority goes to those who can see and tell the story of how to put new strategies into practice. Authority comes when one can grant or deny others access to a network. To speak for the network, one's centrality or power must exist, but not threaten, the other coalitions.

Speaking for others, not threatening others, is the essence of leadership in business done in the community of fleeting exchanges (see Figure 3.9). The agent for the coalition has to have the confidence of its members. As it disappears, so too do the members. This confidence is won, not only by being reliable, as one would expect in businesses immersed in the community of rational rules, but also by inspiring members with one's interpretation of what is possible in the newly-emergent coalition. In this sense, leadership not only brokers innovative deals and puts them into practice, but also captures the imagination of participants. The use of rhetoric and language that influences members who come from different perspectives is central to this form of leadership. The leader as a radical agent of change, unlike the leader in businesses in the community of rational rules, formulates options from differing perspectives and helps those involved to see their common interest within these alternatives.

In terms of socio-moral development, business in the community of fleeting exchanges is very demanding (see Figure 3.9). It requires the ability to listen deeply to others, to win their confidence, and to refrain from exploiting them. The ability to sustain centrality in networks comes not solely from satisfying coalition members, but from educating them and receiving an education from them. This education focuses upon what is possible and how to achieve it. This is much more difficult to accomplish than it is to say. Most people I have worked with, particularly the more powerful, prefer to surround themselves with people "like themselves," that is, with people who have somewhat similar values, goals, and lifestyles. This, to their way of thinking, makes management easier. They are right, of course, if we think of management in the community of rational rules. Who, after all, is more rational than people who we believe mirror our views and privilege the same outlook? In socio-moral terms, the community of fleeting exchanges brings together an ongoing clashing of perspectives requiring that we are sufficiently secure in our views and self-knowledge that we do not turn defensive when others seem to challenge us. Moreover, we can, when challenged, respond with challenges of our own that if done with integrity, can stimulate joint search and dialogue rather than regress to one-upmanship.

It is the desire to avoid privileging a point of view that could tear apart a loosely-formulated coalition that gives rise to the implementation of ethics programs in organizations within the community of fleeting exchanges (see Figure 3.8). As in organizations operating in the community of rational rules, committees prevail. But, unlike the community of rational rules, organizations operating in the community of fleeting exchanges downplay expertise in ethics and emphasize the team or special project nature of the issues in the program. Expertise is downplayed since, in organizations in the community of fleeting exchanges, what one seeks is representativity from the varying perspectives that make up the coalition. Teams, rather than communities, are highlighted, since the ethics programs in organizations operating in the community of fleeting exchanges are intended to facilitate dialogue and increase the frequency of contact and communication from those taking different perspectives.

The problem-solving purpose of ethics programs in organizations immersed in the community of rational rules and practices is downplayed in organizations operating in the community of fleeting exchanges. The predominate position of ethics programs in organizations within the community of rational rules, is for experts in the area of ethics to come together with experts in that functional area of the organization believed to be experiencing the ethics quandary, and hammer out a rational set of pertinant procedures as a solution. In the organization operating within the community of fleeting exchanges, the emphasis is upon bringing together diverse perspectives to the ethical issue in order to build an interpretation of it. The interpretation, in practice, is an amalgam of compromises between the perspectives taken by members of the coalition—a working model. The model persists until some of those in the coalition put it back on to the table again for reformulation.

In organizations operating in the community of fleeting exchanges, ethics is not a problem that goes away, once solved, with the organization returning to standard operating procedures. Rather, ethics is ongoing, recurrent, and situational (see Figure 3.8). As the coalition alters frequently, the ethics issues, once interpreted and put into a working model, are opened again. The recurrent call for reinterpretation is time-consuming and costly. The very decentralization and relative autonomy of members of the coalition is beneficial because it brings together different views, orientations, and contacts. The effectiveness of relying upon people from different perspectives rests in developing shared interpretations that are sufficiently robust to hold the tension built into the very nature of the "differences" in question. It is within the context where creative tension becomes a core competence that ethics moves from legislating solutions to clearly-defined problems, to the interpretation of working agreements.

Each of the five CSR positions formulates a distinct understanding of to whom the corporation is—and sometimes should be—responsible. As we have seen, each CSR position is rooted in a version of community, for it is in the idea that organizations are part of an integrated collectivity or open system that we begin to see and appreciate the need for responsibility to others. Rooted in the premodern, modern, and postmodern world views discussed in Chapter 2, we fixed upon three ideal-type communities, each drawing our attention to a specific and predominating ethical problem. The premodern origins of the traditional entrepreneurial community, with its emphasis upon profit maximization, bold risk taking, and the "anything goes" approach, generate the ongoing problem of building and sustaining trust among the participants in the business community. The rule-based community in the modern context, emphasizing uncertainty-minimization and relying heavily upon the use of precedent, requires an ongoing means of adapting to and anticipating changing issues. The business community as a loose coalition in the postmodern context necessitates that managers, in order to make sense of fleeting exchanges, must develop and diffuse the skills of the facilitator and interpreter.

In Chapter 4, we close our look at CSR by attending to the problems and opportunities of putting trust, issues management, and interpreters' skills into the operations of the contemporary organization. In this discussion we see that CSR entails far more than simply claiming to act responsibly.

CASES AND QUESTIONS

CASE 3-1 **The Stoltmann Wilderness and Beyond: Whose Social Responsibility?**

John Schriener (1997) notes that environmentalists are taking lessons from business marketers. The Western Canada Wilderness Committee (WCWC) is learning the well-worn business technique of personalizing and humanizing complex issues. The WCWC is personalizing huge tracts of ancient British Columbia forests by lending them specific names and highlighting sunlit images of the forest in well-priced, upscale posters. A hot seller eight years ago was the Carmanah Valley poster. This poster helped to drive Macmillan Bloedel Ltd. from Clayoquot Sound. Paul George, Executive Director of the WCWC, says of the poster and marketing campaign, "It's a formula, but it works."

There are currently efforts by WCWC to use the name of Randy Stoltmann, an environmentalist killed in a 1994 skiing accident, to personalize a tract of 200,000 hectares of ancient BC forest. The poster shows a photograph of a hiker at Sims Creek, dwarfed by the sun-dappled canopy of trees that seem to glisten with life. The caption below the heading, "Stoltmann Wilderness," reads "Living Trees, Not Dead Stumps." The awe-inspiring image sets the stage for a far less gentle war brewing in BC forests.

Eco-activists and environmentalists have raised their aspirations, in a very public manner, on how much of British Columbia they would like to set aside for wilderness and preservation. As the BC government approaches its 1992 target of setting aside 12% for preservation, Greenpeace now seeks 36% and the 25,000-member WCWC views Alaska's 38% for preservation as the desired ratio. To achieve these ambitious goals, environmentalists are targeting more forest companies, bolstering their boycotts, and remaining poised with camera-friendly acts of civil disobedience. For example, a letter from the San Francisco-based Clayoquot Rain Forest Coalition has gone to over 5,000 American companies, discouraging them from buying products derived from the old-growth forests of British Columbia. In May1997, Greenpeace's blockades effectively stopped Western Forest Products Ltd. from working the forest in an area the eco-activists have named the Great Bear Rainforest.

The forest firms, the provincial government, the unions, the residents of small timber-reliant BC towns and, increasingly, the native community, have not taken kindly to the escalation of strategic efforts to curb timber-related activity. William Dumont, the chief forester for Western Forest Products, a subsidiary of Doman Industries Ltd., notes: "This is a vicious circle, to be playing the boycott game … but we have a plan in place." Premier Clark, whose New Democrat Party has a substantial majority in the BC legislature, has called attention to the boycott-oriented environmentalists as "enemies of BC." The industry-backed Forest Alliance of British Columbia says its polls indicate that 80% of British Columbians no longer support the more aggressive environmentalists. The labour unions are organizing small BC towns and their merchants by suggesting that locals refuse to do business—denying them gas, provisions, boat moorage, accommodations, and the like. As well, a significant representation of First Nations members are turning a cold shoulder to the environmentalists. One Indian band labelled Greenpeace activists nothing but "environmental colonists."

The tactics of the increasingly polarized players indicate that the BC forests are a hotbed of conflicting values and points of view. The government has sought to reassure the market that excesses in BC logging would be curbed by the 1994 Forest Practices Code, described by both the government and industry as the world's toughest forestry standards. Groups like the Clayoquot Rainforest Coalition, WCWC, the Sierra Legal Defense Fund, and Greenpeace note that the onerous red tape seems to have a far greater bark than bite. They point to a paucity of fines for non-compliance with the Forest Practices Code. Greenpeace, for instance, alleges that, "Since the introduction of the Forest Practices Code in 1994, Doman Industries and its subsidiaries have been found in non-compliance of its regulations 96 times." Moreover, insists Greenpeace, the issuing of these non-compliance fines and the warnings that are attached hardly seem to be altering the behaviour of Doman Industries or other forest companies.

This war in the woods is creating a very confusing image of the state of the temperate Canadian rainforests. From the point of view of the forest companies, BC is on the leading edge of the new forestry and its practice of sustainable harvest. The provincial government portrays the forest as a haven for tourists with its parks and campgrounds, for the environmentalists with its miles and miles of preserved wilderness, and for the small lumber towns who flourish in the timber-based economy. Labour and natives portray the forests as an embodiment of a lifestyle (a somewhat different one in each case) that is being threatened by the arrogant intrusiveness of eco-activists. The aggressive environmentalists portray the BC forests as an opportunity to save the last of the temperate rainforests still intact, an opportunity that cannot be squandered.

QUESTIONS:

1. What, in your view, is the difference in outlook on CSR taken by the forestry firms like Macmillan Bloedel Ltd. and the environmental group known as Western Canada Wilderness Committee? Which is taking a stakeholder (stewardship) model of CSR? Which is trying to move from a minimalist CSR view to a stakeholder (management) perspective? Why is it hard to move from one to the other?

2. Those in Macmillan Bloedel Ltd. see the members of Western Canada Wilderness Committee as acting from a self-interested CSR view. Support this labelling of the WCWC, and then defend the WCWC from this classification.

3. How does the Indian band's labelling of Greenpeace activists as nothing but "environmental colonists" fit into views of the traditional entrepreneurial business? Can a not-for-profit organization using volunteers dominate an ethical issue? How?

4. Who, in your opinion, is managing the loose coalition of the forestry firms? The provincial government? The unions? The residents of small timber-reliant BC towns? The native community? In this community of fleeting exchanges, what do the members hold in common? Are there rational rules available to simply put an end to this hotbed of conflicting values and points of view?

5. Who, in your view, is responsible for bringing peace and harmony to the forests of British Columbia? Why do each of the participants have a different image of the state of the temperate Canadian rainforests? How do you think those in other countries are reacting to this war in the woods?

6. How would an analyst immersed in the ethics of organizations in the traditional entrepreneurial community handle this war in the woods differently from an analyst favouring the ethics of organizations practising in the community of rational rules? Which is most likely to conclude with a comprehensive plan of future action?

CASE 3-2 — Magna International Incorporated: Corporate Social Responsibility and Sexual Harassment

Janet McFarland and Greg Keenan (1997) report that a sexual harassment lawsuit against Canadian car parts giant, Magna International Inc., has opened a Pandora's box of alleged improprieties, particularly in dealings with the big three automakers— General Motors, Ford, and Chrysler. The claims of impropriety arise out of the concerted efforts taken by employees of Magna to secure lucrative contracts with the big three. The allegations include wooing top purchasing officers of the car companies with lavish gifts and entertainment—golf games, tickets to sporting events, trips to topless bars, and an excursion to Las Vegas.

These claims became part of the public domain as they emerged in court documents arising from a sexual harassment lawsuit filed in Detroit, Michigan by a female employee, Lorrie Beno, who worked in an important Magna sales division in a suburb of Detroit. Lorrie Beno alleges that within weeks of joining the company she was grabbed and kissed by a manager at a company Christmas party. After the incident, the manager tried to embarrass her at meetings, look up her skirt while she was at the fax machine, and pass her messages. The sexual harassment case documents allege that women in Magna's sales division were routinely patted and touched and referred to as "cupcakes," "ice princesses," and other suggestive names. In one example cited in the case materials, an employee avowedly tossed M&M candies down a woman's blouse.

Magna International headquarters in Markham, Ontario vehemently denies the allegations and contends that it will defend itself vigorously in court. The huge firm, which has an annual revenue of about $8 billion, does not like the insight into the organizational culture at Magna that the case is creating. In gathering the deposition for the sexual harassment case, it has been alleged that Magna officials say they routinely took purchasing agents from the big three automobile manufacturers to strip clubs in and about Detroit, and paid for lap dancers, private booths, and private dances in upstairs chambers.

McFarland and Keenan note that a Magna employee—Mr. Raymond Iavasile, an account manager in the Livonia, Michigan office—said, for example, that he not only entertained customers at topless bars on a routine basis, but also spent more than $1,000 (US) per week on gifts to clients. Iavasile said that he accompanied and paid for golf trips for customers to Las Vegas and lavished Mont Blanc pens ($85 US) upon prospective clients. David Wojie, an executive director in Magna's interior systems division states that he spent $84,852 (US) in an 18-month period (1994–1995) to attract clients.

The plot thickens when one realizes that such gifts clearly would violate the ethics policies of the three Detroit-centred car manufacturers that remain Magna's biggest customers. In fact, Scott Priest, an account manager for Magna, said in a deposition that many officials from the car companies did not want their names to appear on expenses because the entertainment violated the car manufacturers' ethics policies.

The case has not yet gone to trial. Nevertheless, the deposition testimony suggests that the organizational culture at Magna International Incorporated may be in for a necessary examination. (See Chapter 5 for more on organizational culture.)

QUESTIONS:

1. Using the five CSR positions outlined in Figure 3.1, which one or combination best characterizes Magna International Incorporated in its response to Lorrie Beno's allegations? Support your selection of a perspective or combination of perspectives.

2. Utilizing the self-interested CSR perspective, justify the alleged behaviour—sexual harassment, strip clubs, lap dancers, and favours to purchasing agents from the big three automobile manufacturers. Can these behaviours help a firm grow and employ more personnel? Discuss.

3. Within the minimalist CSR position, how, in your view, will the shareholders react to these allegations? Still within the minimalist CSR position, how will the big three automakers—General Motors, Ford, and Chrysler—react to their purported involvement in these matters?

4. Mr. Raymond Iavasile and David Wojie, two employees of Magna International Incorporated, have revealed that Magna seems to have spent large amounts of money on gifts and favours to attract and maintain customers. Within businesses operating in the traditional entrepreneurial community, how would this be looked upon? Within businesses operating in the rational community of rules, how would this be looked upon?

5. In this case, what sort of loosely-formulated coalition is likely to arise among the big three automakers—General Motors, Ford, and Chrysler? What do they now have in common?

6. If you were to characterize the organizational culture of Magna International Incorporated, given the emerging allegations, what would you say of its corporate social responsibility? What would you say if you were Lorrie Beno? How would you characterize the organizational culture if you were Raymond Iavasile?

CASE 3-3	**Herbalists Protest Bureaucratic Regulations, Rules, and Corporate Social Responsibility**

Taped to the glass outside Gaia Garden Apothecary on West Broadway in Vancouver, BC—a store that sells herbal remedies of all sorts—is a list of newly restricted herbs. The enlarged print reads: "The Food Directorate considers these (herbs) unfit for human consumption," and the list includes a large array of herbs, including barberry, khat, and kava. Another list headed by the words, "The Drugs Directorate considers these herbs drugs, under certain conditions," and names hawthorn, arnica, valerian, yellow dock, and other herbal remedies.

Customers of Gaia Garden Apothecary and other health food stores, herbal treatment centres, and alternative medicine outlets in Canada are upset. These individuals believe that the federal government is attempting to restrict their access to folk remedies which, like echinacea (a cold remedy) and gingko biloba (said to improve brain functioning), have been available to people from many folk cultures since time immemorial.

A grassroots consumer movement has sprung up to fight the tighter controls that Canada's Health Protection Branch plans to erect over herbal and folk remedies effective 1 July 1997. The members of this grassroots movement feel: (a) that a society that seeks to regulate herbs as if they were drugs, but allows alcohol and tobacco to be freely sold outside the drug category, has its priorities confused; (b) that the paternalistic and costly scrutiny of herbs is unnecessary since people around the world have used these substances for centuries with relatively little harm; and (c) the Canadian government, in the midst of its cutbacks to education, health care, and other necessary services, is expending taxpayers' money to protect taxpayers in an area that few, if any, want or need.

The Canadian Coalition for Health Freedom has staged rallies in Vancouver, Calgary, and Toronto urging the Canadian government to desist in its regulatory fervour. The coalition insists in its literature that the adverse effects from consuming natural health products are "almost nonexistent"; moreover, that if the herbs in folk remedies are classified as drugs, then garlic, chocolate, expectorants, rehydrators, and stimulants—all presently treated as nondrugs—must be reconsidered.

On the other side of the issue, the Health Protection Branch officials defend the changes, insisting that the herbal and health food industries are not being singled out for special treatment. To their thinking, the herbal products industry has grown up and is no longer a fringe component in Canada's health care delivery system. The industry is now at a healthy $175 million dollars in annual sales, and services a growing alternative medicine clientele. The Health Protection Branch argues that it is time for this industry to bear its fair share of the cost of assuring the public that its products are labelled correctly, proper dosages given to clients, and potential dangers nipped in the bud. Dennis Shelley, who heads the Drug and Environmental Health Protection Branch's western region, points out that all drug manufacturers—herbal and pharmaceutical companies alike—are required to help pay the costs of regulating the industry by Ottawa's Drugs and Medical Devices Directorate.

The health and herbal remedy business in Canada feels that it is being selected for abuse; Ottawa insists that, quite the opposite, it is now being taken seriously and is included in the way government treats health care delivery. Ironically, it is the very success of herbal remedies that has influenced government's decision to regulate the industry.

QUESTIONS:

1. What is the view of corporate social responsibility taken by the Canadian Coalition for Health Freedom? Why are they opposed to the expertise of officials at the Health Protection Branch?

2. How would you recommend that the Health Protection Branch utilize the stakeholder (management) and stakeholder (stewardship) perspectives to help them deal with the emerging grassroots consumer movement? Which of the two perspectives is most likely to be used? Why?

3. How is the coalition of grassroots consumers attempting to get others to interpret the Health Protection Branch's recent treatment of the health and herbal remedy business in Canada? What are the strengths of their interpretation? The weaknesses?

4. How is the Canadian government's Health Protection Branch attempting to get others to interpret the treatment of the herbal remedy business in Canada? What are the strengths of their interpretation? The weaknesses?

5. If we think of Gaia Garden Apothecary as a business in the traditional entrepreneurial community, what actions should it engage in to deal with Canada's Health Protection Branch, which operates as an organization in the community of rational rules? How does the notion of socio-moral development differ in these two communities?

6. If the Health and Protection Branch were to implement an ethics program to deal with the emerging controversy with the coalition of health and herbal remedy businesses and their consumers, how would it proceed? What could be done to improve this ethics program?

CORPORATE SOCIAL RESPONSIBILITY (CSR): IN PRACTICE

Business has become, in this last half century, the most powerful institution on the planet. The dominant institution in any society needs to take responsibility for the whole—as the church did in the day of the Holy Roman Empire. But business has not had such a tradition. This is a new role, not yet well understood and accepted. Built into the concept of capitalism and free enterprise from the beginning was the assumption that the actions of many units of individual enterprise, responding to market forces and guided by the 'invisible hand' of Adam Smith, would somehow add up to a desirable outcome. But in the last decade of the twentieth century, it has become clear that this 'invisible hand' is faltering. It depended upon a consensus of overarching meanings and values which is no longer present. So business has to adopt a new tradition which it has never had throughout the entire history of capitalism. That is, as the most powerful institution on the planet, to take responsibility for the whole. Every decision that is made, every action that is taken, has to be viewed in the light of—in the context of—that kind of responsibility.

Willis Harmon
World Business Academy Perspectives (1992)

The implication in Willis Harmon's call for social responsibility is simple but controversial. In *Transforming Communication, Transforming Business: Building Responsive and Responsible Workplaces* (1995), Stanley Deetz agrees with Harmon's call for a new ethos of corporate social responsibility, noting that, "We have entered a new political and economic situation in which old concepts and ways of doing business no longer apply" (29). The "new" situation calls not only for a realization that business must become more responsible for its actions, but, and more germane to our concerns in this chapter, also that there be demands for organizations to develop and apply techniques relevant to business community relations. Corporate social responsibility (CSR) comes with the new business climate. Governments have moved regulatory concerns to the back burner. Unemployment rates in countries such as Canada are at seven to ten per cent. Organizations and their participants are redirecting the energies and resources of the planet. The world we are building is increasingly one resulting from this mobilization. Responsibility, it is argued, comes with this territory.

In Harmon's and Deetz's view, the new call for a "practice" of social responsibility is neither simply nor quickly fixed by returning to the so-called "welfare state," nor by turning otherwise to government regulation as the sole solution. Business in the postmodern context is a brand new game. Neither Harmon nor Deetz is nostalgic for "the good old days," nor do they believe that tighter government controls on business will, in time, return to favour. Rather, like those calling for the "stewardship model" of CSR, or the "radical environmentalists" who will be discussed in Chapter 8, both men think that a fundamental change is required in the way we think about and operate business. This fundamental change calls for business, just like individuals, to be responsible for its actions. This responsibility, argue Harmon and Deetz, requires business to rethink its values and reconsider what is essential to "the good life."

Those calling for CSR insist that the need for a radical reformulation of business in both theory and practice is due to a lag resulting from efforts to bring modern, industrial thinking about business into the postmodern era. In the modern world view, all that was needed for business to thrive and contribute to the greater good of society was a "level playing field." It was assumed that, under the rules of fair play and open competition, the invisible hand of the market would effectively keep all players honest and efficient. When this failed—and it was believed that failure would be rare—social policy or legislation under the auspices of a duly-elected government could be mobilized to make things right. We are now aware that business growth is a mixed blessing; while it does bring benefits, increasingly we have become cognizant of the social costs.

Figure 4.1 reviews some of the external diseconomies or social costs now believed to accompany business. The sensitivity to these rising social costs can be detected in the proliferation of communities seeking to keep businesses with these external diseconomies out of their neighbourhoods. City planning in North America and Europe is heavily influenced by the growth of what many analysts call the NIMBY (not-in-my-back-yard) syndrome. The view that business must fit into the community rather than reverse, is at the centre of the growing public call for corporate social responsibility.

Deetz's and Harmon's desire to put CSR into practice can best be understood within the framework of the three business communities outlined in Chapter 3. Businesses operating in the traditional entrepreneurial community, wherein "anything goes" as long as it is legal, and where owners or dominant shareholders are privileged members, must solve the problem of trust. Businesses immersed in the community of rational rules—which grows out of the traditional entrepreneurial community—must not only solve the problem of trust, but must develop ways to anticipate, diagnose, and manage newly-emergent issues. Lastly, within

---

FIGURE 4–1   Social Costs of Business: The Public Costs of Private Corporations

Corporate finances, particularly those rooted in standard business accounting procedures, measure a firm's profits and losses. The accounting standards, in practice in most of the world's firms, do not make allowance for external diseconomies or social costs—that is, costs inflicted on society that are not incurred by the corporation itself and for which the corporation makes no sacrifice.

Ralph Estes, in his books, *Corporate Social Accounting* (1976), and *Tyranny of the Bottom Line: Why Corporations Make Good People Do Bad Things* (1996), provides us with an interesting, albeit broad and partial, listing of the social costs involved with a typical corporation.

Cost	Examples
• in the workplace	• workplace injuries; illness; death; sexual harassment; physical and emotional stress; paid care required when parent(s) work
• in the consumption of natural resources	• depletion of energy resources; elimination of important habitats for endangered species; depletion of wildlife
• corporate crime and fraud	• cost of imprisonment for white collar criminals; direct costs of fraud, embezzlement, shoddy products, and deceptive practices
• in the manipulation of public opinion	• lobbying; advertising and the promotion of products that induce unhealthy behaviour such as cigarettes or fatty foods
• in congestion	• rush hour; pressure on school systems where the population converges to take advantage of industrial concentration
• in waste	• pollution; sewage; trash; landfills; hazardous and toxic waste
• in taxation to taxpayers	• inspectors; industrial accidents and disasters; commercial litigation and the use of courts to deal with business problems

---

the postmodern context, in loosely-coupled coalitions of businesses in a community of fleeting exchanges, to be socially responsible, businesses must generate trust; anticipate, diagnose, and manage emergent issues; and develop an interpretive rather than a legislative framework for dealing with divergent perspectives within the community.

Applying CSR in the postmodern business community is no simple task. It tests the mettle of the well-intended businessperson. However, it is a challenge that cannot be left on the back burner for long.

TRUST AND CSR

Trust always is seen as a solution in the premodern world view and, of course, like that world view, it retains its resilience and vitality in the postmodern context. Trust, like faith in God or in community elders, simplifies decision making. Trust provides those imbued with it with the belief that others have sufficient incentives, information, and fellow-feeling to provide a way out of quandaries, including moral quandaries. In the context of modernity, trust turns from a reliance upon God, elders, or sacred texts, towards experts with credentials. These credentials are important in proving or establishing the trusted other's access to rational practices and rules. In modernity, we turn to family counsellors, psychiatrists, and business ethicists to help us work through ethical quandaries. In postmodernity, where fragmentation, the absence of a centre, and the appearance of multiple plausible realities are operative, we trust those who represent our point of view and values, those who we select to represent our views and with whom we identify.

In all three world views, trust is essential. From a functional perspective, trust permits individuals to live with confidence in the midst of change and uncertainty. Trust is indispensable in the CSR portfolio of businesses in their relations to society; trust lubricates the controversies that pervade CSR debates. Figure 4.2 illustrates how within each CSR position the "change issues" alter, placing the trust/distrust dynamics on a different footing. Thus, for example, in the minimalist CSR view it is the heightening of competition that increases the desire of investors or owners to monitor their managers. Where there is the desire to increase monitoring, trust diminishes. Monitoring others in order to assure they act as they say they will is costly. Also, the greater the monitoring, the more difficult it is to get those accustomed to heavy surveillance to increase their use of discretion. CSR portfolios immersed in the minimalist CSR view work by increasing the costs for those whose behaviour departs from what is programmed in the heavily-monitored system.

In the self-interested CSR model, CSR is utilized as a strategy to increase the firm's visibility and bring it opportunities that it otherwise might not possess. CSR program advocates seek to sell managers on aspects of CSR based on the simple but powerful slogan, "ethics brings increased profits." CSR, like all management processes, is a risky affair. The firm may associate itself with a good cause which, due to the rise and fall of issues, may bring more controversy than goodwill. The CSR portfolio may, by bad fortune, attach itself to a spokesperson whose "real life" is, in time, found to represent the virtues of the goodwill effort rather poorly. In short, advocates of CSR campaigns must win the trust of managers, who in turn must loosen the corporate purse-strings in a CSR-favourable direction and, as well, win the trust of consumers. If CSR is to be successful within the opportunistic framework, consumers must not come to the conclusion that a firm's CSR portfolio is merely the work of spin doctors.

In the social contract perspective on CSR, in both its formal or legal treatment and its informal or implicit contract, distrust emanates from the perception by those in the contract that the other is in violation. Workers may feel and argue that surveillance cameras in the workplace are a violation of their understanding of the employment contract. When they first came to work in the company, these cameras were not in place. Norms and expectations were implicit in the initial contract. In their view—with the eyes of growing distrust—the firm is violating the contract. It is not seeking to negotiate the initial understanding, but is acting in what they perceive as an authoritarian manner. Meanwhile, the firm actually sees this as part of its desire to act with greater CSR. In the minimalist CSR, the intensification of monitoring can be seen as a way to cut down on shirking. Moreover, it can be argued that this is beneficial, not only for the investors, but also for those employees who are working exceedingly hard but being slowed down by those who free-ride. Trust in the social contract

FIGURE 4-2   The Five CSR Positions: Participants, Trust, and Change

CSR Position	Key Participants	Change Issues	Trust/Distrust
Minimalist CSR View	• Investors/ stockholders • Owners/managers	• Hyper-competition • Globalization	Trust grows when performance meets expectation; distrust is engendered when the firm fails to meet expectations.
Self-Interested CSR Model	• Owners/managers • Program advocates	• Competition • Reputation enhancement	Trust grows when problem advocates deliver an enhanced corporate reputation; distrust is engendered when problem advocates fail to do so.
Social Contract Perspective in CSR	• Managers/owners • Those with contracts with the firm	• Need for flexibility • International-ization	Trust grows when the firm keeps its legal and social contracts over time; distrust is engendered when the firm is willing to violate contracts.
Stakeholder (Management Model)	• Managers/owners • Primary and secondary stakeholders	• Information access to firm increases • Systems open for scrutiny	Trust grows when stakeholders feel included in the firm's decision making; distrust is engendered when stakeholders are excluded.
Stakeholder (Stewardship) Model	• Owners/managers • Spokespersons for tertiary stakeholders	• Pressure to include tertiary stakeholders • Worry about environment	Trust grows when the firm is willing to negotiate with spokespersons for tertiary stakeholders; distrust is engendered when the spokespersons for tertiary stakeholders are excluded.

perspective develops as the firm identifies its contracts, maintains them, and learns to slowly, carefully, and consistently modify them with the participation of others.

In both stakeholder models—management and stewardship—the openness of the firm to the greater participation of stakeholders, when intensified by change, creates distrust. In the stakeholder (management) model, distrust prevails when stakeholders feel that they are being short-changed in their treatment by the focal organization. Trust grows when they feel that the trade-offs made by the focal organization are reasonable vis-à-vis their own expectations and relative to their perception of what other stakeholders are receiving. In the stakeholder (stewardship) model, distrust surrounds the perceived ability of the firm to live up to its explicit commitments to tertiary stakeholder values and not "sell out." In this manner, trust in the stakeholder (stewardship) model increases when the focal organization includes agents representative of the values of tertiary stakeholders on relevant decisions. If, however, the focal organization is perceived to be co-opting tertiary values and using them in an opportunistic CSR fashion, the distrust will again raise its head.

The adage, "develop trust to establish CSR," in one's business dealings sounds simple enough. We all nod sagely when we hear the word "trust," since each one of us can point to someone or something that we, albeit in varying degrees, trust. But this short-circuits careful analysis. Trust is a complex process. It exists at several levels, with different units of analysis, and can be won, lost, and feigned. Let us turn to an analysis of the dynamics of trust and/or mistrust (suspicion), paying particular attention to how, at several different levels in our relations with others, we rely on trust to act in a manner we consider socially responsible. When trust is fleeting or totally absent, we remain apprehensive. We search for techniques to gain assurance that the other will respect our needs.

THE DYNAMICS OF TRUST/MISTRUST

The dynamics of trust/mistrust are complex. While trust is indispensable for CSR because it lubricates complex social exchange, it is a double-edged sword. When we trust others, we become increasingly dependent and reliant upon them. It is precisely this dependence that helps to simplify complex social exchanges and permit us to engage in uncertain collective action with a reliance that others will do as they say, act with competence, and signal to us when things are not as they seem. The double-edged sword of trust manifests itself when we feel betrayed. We only feel betrayed when, having trusted and grown interdependent, we discover that the trusted other has been cheating—indeed, that they did not do as they said, that they acted with far less competence than we initially assumed, or that they failed to signal to us when things were not as they seemed. CSR in practice is complicated by the fact that the greater the trust between and among participants, the greater the potential for betrayal. Given this insight, it is not surprising that participants in CSR relationships often feel a strong ambivalence towards the process.

To make this ambivalence—the attraction/resistance—to trust and betrayal more lucid to the business ethics student, it is important to understand that to build CSR one must realize that trust exists at four levels simultaneously. To become proficient at utilizing trust/distrust and betrayal dynamics in building CSR, one must realize that doing so at only one level, while necessary, is insufficient. In my consulting practice, I work with organizations of all sorts to provide them with a means to realize their CSR objectives. Some executives intuitively make the connection between CSR and trust, but they see trust primarily at the individual level. For them, one builds trust by choosing one's personnel wisely and delegating the CSR function to a person who can deal with the "intuitive" side of people.

At the individual level of trust, the emphasis is upon trust as an aspect of the unique character of individuals. There seems to be a highly personal aspect to trust that arises out of personality differences in individuals' readiness to trust or distrust. Some analysts have focused their explanation of this readiness to trust on particular life events. Erikson (1963, 1968) and Bowlby (1973) highlight basic models of early psycho-social development which, they argue, stress trust development—parents who provide children with unconditional love and those who, when they do bargain with their children over unmet needs, fulfill the conditions of the bargain. In this fashion, individual-level trust is incubated in the early relationship with caregivers. The adequacy of this relationship is central in determining whether or not the individual develops a core orientation of trust and trustworthiness or of distrust, suspicion, and cynicism.

In the same vein, but rooted more in psychology and epistemology than in psychiatry and psycho-biography, some researchers see individual-level trust as the faith that individuals possess in humanity. This understanding of faith in humanity—or the lack of it—stems from the work of personality theorists like Rotter (1967, 1971), whose work has also been germinal in conceptualizing trust at the interpersonal level. Rotter viewed trust as a generalized expectancy that others will do as they say (verbal promises, written statements, gestures) and to Rotter, trust is a generalized response of confidence derived from the reinforcement-history of previous interactions. To others (Wrightsman, 1966, 1972; Yamagishi and Sato, 1986), this history results in a personal philosophy of life that includes one's view on trust, and the willingness to rely upon others in the face of uncertain information and on issues that are perceived to be important. Within the study of business, we try to make sense of why some managers are excellent at delegating important tasks, while others try to do as much as they can without relying upon others.

Individual-level trust functions to provide confidence in the face of uncertainty. It permits the individual to reduce complexity and develop expectations of others that foster interdependence and mutuality. People with a disposition to trust must not automatically be thought of as innocents—trust at this level develops slowly and is rooted in a history of previous exchanges which, in the language of the researchers working in this area, have been positively reinforced. At the interpersonal level, people with this predisposition are readily able to supplement explicit and formal contracting with pliable forms of implicit contracting. This, as Kenneth Arrow (1974) points out, pushes the limits of the organization, making it capable of greater flexibility in its dealings with stakeholders.

In practical terms, four suggestions predominate for building trust at the individual level in the organization. First, it is essential that managers, particularly those to be entrusted with the CSR portfolio, are selected from a pool of employees who are seen to possess this disposition. In a nutshell, people with the predisposition to trust and to win others' trust are capable of suspending cynicism until exchange violation warrants its existence. These individuals are calm, confident, and willing to engage in negotiations with others who take a different position without assuming that wheeling and dealing is the only road to success. Second, it is important to select and groom individuals for the CSR portfolio who have some knowledge and shared interest with those with whom they will be working. Selecting a virulent, anti-environmentalist to deal with the environmental side of the CSR portfolio is clearly problematic. Third, the individuals or individual selected to head the CSR portfolio should be provided with sufficient discretion to engage in implicit contracting. Fourth and finally, CSR should not be treated as a battleground with the expectation that the individuals selected will win; the CSR portfolio should be configured as a harmony-building exercise with a long-term horizon.

At the interpersonal level, trust may be thought of as the willingness of one person to increase his or her vulnerability to the actions of others. The unit of analysis here is the exchange relation (Blau, 1989) that occurs between individuals. Dyadic exchange, two-person interactions, are the procrustean bed upon which we build cooperation. Blau, and social exchange theorists in general (Eisenstadt, 1995; Kramer and Messick, 1995; Landa, 1994), conceive of trust as rooted in the belief that the other in a dyad will reciprocate. These theorists declare this expectation the essence of the goal of achieving mutual cooperation. Those in an exchange who are accommodative create the conditions for trust; those who are exploitative, on the other hand, generate a sense of mistrust. Betrayal in interpersonal trust results from realizing that one has misplaced one's trust, increased one's vulnerability, and rather than being rewarded, can expect punishment (Akerstrom, 1991).

Interpersonal trust, when established, permits one to expect continued exchanges in the absence of monitoring or enforcement mechanisms, since trust within this context is faith that the others "will not cheat with impunity" (Kahneman, Knetsch, and Thaler, 1986). It is these repeated interactions that breed familiarity, interdependence, and continuity. They do so because they establish mutually clear and beneficial expectations and do not violate these. It is this continuity that creates the cooperation sought. It is important—and in Chapter 9 we shall treat this theme more analytically—in order to realize that in embedded structures (Granovetter, 1985), where third parties become involved in the dyadic exchange, trust grows. Third parties function, just as witnesses do, to keep things honest. When third parties are privy to the terms and consequences of an exchange, both parties to the exchange must calculate the costs to their reputations of cheating or cutting corners. As exchange becomes embedded in corporate structures and as the history of the exchange builds momentum, trust not only grows between participants, but they can, with some confidence, lower their costs of monitoring the exchange.

When interpersonal trust does not develop, transaction costs rise. Parties to an exchange must increase their monitoring of others. This attempt to reduce other parties' discretion, the essence of control, is relaxed when interpersonal trust flourishes. This flourishing of interpersonal trust aids the firm in developing a CSR portfolio, not only by lowering the transaction costs, but also by permitting parties in an exchange to use discretion. This attracts to the exchange those interested in giving voice to issues that can be connected to their experiences, and keeps away those interested only in the "official" line. As a consequence, increasingly attracting those willing and empowered to use discretion in the exchange accelerates the ability to make deals, amalgamate viewpoints, and create dialogue. As this happens, participants to an exchange begin to build into the exchange points of view that call into play the social, moral, and contextual issues surrounding the pure economic exchange.

To foster interpersonal trust in the CSR portfolio of the organization, participants in CSR discussions must be empowered to use their personal discretion. Participants to the CSR exchange from the focal organization and the stakeholder groups must interact with some frequency over time. Interpersonal trust develops through repeated interaction with others. To build familiarity, continuity, and interdependence into the CSR, exchanges should be held even when no heated problem exists, rather than saving them for crisis situations. The small and incremental process of negotiating positions will generate interpersonal trust, while quick, sharp wins and losses will polarize positions and drive interpersonal trust into the background. To structure meetings between members of the focal organization and the stakeholders for the purpose of CSR exchanges, it is necessary to avoid privileging a point of view. Others will experience this as a power play—or worse, as patronizing. Lastly, it is recommended that organizations see CSR exchanges as analogous to long-term investments. Involvement with the participants to a CSR exchange involves not only a confidence in the process and outcomes of the exchange, but also confidence in the other's goodwill, which can be assumed only if one's own is brought clearly, honestly, and directly to the exchange.

The third level of trust, organizational-level trust, seeks to portray trust as a cost-efficient means of achieving, sustaining, and, over time, diffusing cooperation within and between organizations. In this context, trust is depicted as the salient factor in determining the effectiveness of many relationships, particularly those in which a leader sets the agenda (Zand, 1972). In keeping with this idea, it is apparent that the dominant portion of the work on leadership in organizations conceives of the leader as a developer, not a controller, of followers (Fairholm, 1993, 1994). The leader's task is to be aware of the existence and potential significance of trust, and of the cultural beliefs and norms in the organization's culture—and to broaden these through use. Peter Koestenbaum, in *Leadership: The Inner Side of Greatness* (1991), epitomizes this view. In his book, he presents a "diamond theory" of leadership composed of four facets: vision, ethical behaviour, reliability, and courage. The combination of these four characteristics in the hands of an effective leader greatly enhances the emergence of an organizational culture in which trust enhances problem solving, lowers monitoring costs, and generates the opportunity for functional dialogue between the organization and its stakeholders.

At the organizational level, trust is a form of social and moral capital that operates in a fundamentally different manner than physical capital (Husted, 1989). Within organizational cultures, as mobilized by effective leaders, the supply of trust increases rather than decreases with use; indeed, trust becomes depleted if not used. Friedland (1990) and Michalos (1990) argue that organizational trust is neither a form of altruism nor of *naïveté*; rather, unlike unconditional cooperation, it functions to enhance cooperation, innovation, and reputation all within a pragmatic framework. Cooperation, as we have seen at the interpersonal level, is enhanced by the slow and growing expectation of reciprocity between exchange partners. In directing his attention to executives, Clawson reminds us that "you can't manage them (followers) if they don't trust you" (1989:10). Trust, as we have seen, permits both a questioning of the status quo and, when it answers effectively, a support for it. It is this willingness, in the concept of organizational trust, to test relationships—not only between managers and workers, but between organizations—that helps to keep relationships healthy. Lastly, reputation is enhanced as organizational-level trust, when enduring, signals to others that the corporation can be expected to deliver upon its promises.

At the practical level, building organizational-level, identification-based trust in the CSR portfolio of firms falls beneath the auspices of two general categories—leadership and organizational culture. Under the rubric of leadership, five points are salient; beneath that of organizational culture, two issues are germane. Techniques that engender organizational-level trust in the CSR portfolio under the leadership and leader's behaviour designation are:

1. Predictable leader actions and consistent behaviour help to build organizational trust (Bennis and Nanus, 1985). This organizational-level trust can be extended to the CSR portfolio when leaders are provided with incentives to bring this consistency to exchanges with stakeholders. The career of a manager in the CSR portfolio of the firm should be assessed by how well the incumbent extends organizational-level trust to stakeholders.

2. Leaders must show confidence in other organizational leaders, particularly so when expecting this from their followers (Fairholm, 1994). Applied to CSR, corporate leaders must extend confidence in stakeholder leaders if they expect their own members to do so with the members of the stakeholding group.

3. Leaders who seek to perpetuate organizational-level trust must align their actual behaviour with their stated objectives—letting others know when and why these become

disconnected (Sinator, 1988). In the firm's CSR portfolio, leaders must "walk the talk" and avoid obfuscation, stonewalling, and denial as ongoing strategies for dealing with corporate critics.

4. A consistent record of service to followers is critical in helping to initiate and heighten the goodwill implicit in organizational-level trust (Greenleaf, 1977). In CSR activities, this means that corporate leaders must be able to (and be seen to) provide benefits to stakeholding groups.

5. Leaders must be (and be seen to be) competent, caring, and willing to defer taking advantage of followers' known vulnerabilities (Zand, 1972). In CSR dealings, this involves an ability of the corporation to demonstrate competence, care, and, most vitally, the ability to resist using its power to temporarily remove its critics.

Insofar as organizational culture is concerned, organizational-level trust can not be demanded; it must emerge in a corporate culture in which corporate leaders are sufficiently secure to seriously include stakeholders in the corporate identity, and, secondly, where corporate leaders recognize the value of constructive controversy, seeing it as essential to open dialogue (Fisher and Ury, 1981). The topic of organizational cultures and the way these influence views of the "good enough world" will be discussed more fully in the next chapter.

At the last level of trust, the systems level, trust is portrayed by sociologists, economists, anthropologists, and educational researchers as a necessary lubricant in the aligning of institutions and complex institutional arrangements (Lewis and Weigert, 1985; Luhman, 1979, 1988; Neu, 1991; Williamson, 1975, 1981; Zucker, 1986). At this level, trust can be conceptualized, both as a phenomenon within and between institutions, and as the trust individuals put into institutions. In this regard, Georg Simmel (1978), an early twentieth-century sociologist, points out that money is possible as a reliable economic and social medium of exchange because people trust that behind it rest real institutions with real power and wealth willing to stand by the currency. In essence, Simmel anticipates the problem of trust in postmodern institutions when he highlights the concern we have that substance (actual value) underlies the symbol (money) in which we increasingly place our trust. Institutionalists of all sorts worry about the gap between the image—a marketable event in contemporary society—and the reality. The moral panic that surrounds priests, physicians, and teachers who abuse their trust and exploit those in their care (Arent, 1991; Canadian Conference of Catholic Bishops, 1992; Gallagher, 1990; Pellegrino *et al.*, 1991), focuses attention upon the possible disjuncture between professions as social symbols and the actual behaviours of particular renegade professionals.

Within the systems level, we might paraphrase the concerns of many institutionalists by pointing out that their concern with the question, "How paranoid should a rational citizen become in order to cope with his or her times?" is a good one for postmodernist discussions. In the fragmented, centreless society, those who claim authority are viewed with suspicion. We suspect the existence of a hidden agenda. The tendency to view language as both a mechanism for persuasion and a leadership skill, suggests that we in postmodern contexts expect the text or image, as in advertising, to be quite distinct from the actual experience or behaviours, and indicates our recognition that we must remain critical of rhetoric. The citizen must be taught to deconstruct text, symbols, and images, and determine what is, in effect, being conveyed. In this context, one might be tempted to say that the rational citizen today, in a postmodern society, is expected to be far more suspicious than his or her relatives living in a traditional society.

In this context of growing skepticism and sophistication, institutional trust develops when individuals must generalize their personal trust to large organizations and systems made up of individuals with whom they have low familiarity, low interdependence, and relatively low continuity of interaction. Debra Myerson, Karl Weick, and Roderick Kramer, in their work, "Swift Trust and Temporary Groups," point out that in the epitome of the postmodern social and economic system—the film industry—knowing how to make a permanent contribution based on temporary systems requires the interweaving of competence-based trust into temporary contracts such that all become interdependent within the project (the film). These authors point out that violators can win small victories, but must bear the taint that comes from working in an industry that maintains a lively and ongoing interest in one's ability to become a team player. In counselling individuals in this temporary and somewhat chaotic system, Myerson *et al*. note that "ultimately, of course, knowing when to confer trust quickly and when to withhold or withdraw it may be crucial to the success of the temporary system" (1996:192).

The techniques for building systems-level trust in the CSR portfolio of organizations require that managers and systems leaders establish a corporate image and reputation for standing behind their products, services, and operations. The idea is that business as a system of activities must be seen as legitimate. This idea will be discussed far more thoroughly in Chapter 9, when I utilize the idea of "reputational capital" to explore the "legitimacy thesis" in business and society. This legitimacy is tested when businesses, for example, profit by marketing cigarettes to children or do business with political regimes notorious for their scorn of human and civil liberties. At the systems level, trust is rooted in putting together and stabilizing the trust achieved at each of the three other levels. At the individual level of trust, the system must be able to select, promote, and train individuals capable of building trust into positions of power and influence; at the interpersonal level, the system must be able, through repeated interactions, to build familiarity, interdependence, and continuity into ongoing exchanges; and at the organizational level, systems leaders or managers must be able to build a vital, adaptive organizational culture. With these three in place, systems-level trust is possible when the systems stand behind their corporate image. This requires that systems leaders and managers maintain a working awareness of the values and core competencies of the system, and work to align these with systems actions.

At the systems level of trust, CSR is sorely disrupted when the system purports to maintain values out of whack with its behaviours. This problem seems to have many origins—all of which lead to a schism between image and reality. Systems that seek to paste together systems-level trust through public relations or advertisement campaigns often fail to align their campaigns with the other levels of trust. Systems that hastily and all too frequently import new leaders to change the image of the system often flounder. Systems-level trust evolves slowly, but, as all students of business ethics know, can be dealt a blow quite swiftly. The image of a system which, for example, handles the issue of product safety in the Ford Pinto, or the issue of environmental safety in the *Exxon Valdez*, can be, despite years of trust, reduced quite swiftly. How systems and their managers diagnose issues, manage them, and learn from them is another key ingredient in developing a practical perspective on CSR.

ISSUES MANAGEMENT

Firms that practise CSR recognize that their continuance as profitable and adaptable enterprises are, to some extent, reliant on their abilities to anticipate, understand, and manage issues as they arise (Chase, 1984; Heath and Nelson, 1986; Wartick and Rude, 1986). "The over-riding objective of an issues management system," writes William Renfro, in *Issues Management in Strategic Planning*, "is to enhance the current and long-term performance and standing of the corporation by anticipating change, promoting opportunities, and avoiding or mitigating threats" (1993:93). Issues management systems are self-conscious efforts of those within the firm to create committees, project teams, or functional areas (public affairs, community relations, corporate social responsibility units) intended to set an issues agenda for the corporation. "An issue," writes James K. Brown, in *This Business of Issues: Coping With the Company's Environment*, "is a condition or pressure, either internal or external to an organization, that, if it continues, will have a significant effect on the functioning of the organization or its future interests" (1979:1).

The model of the organization in the issue management literature is that of an open system bombarded from both internal and external sources by a continuous stream of ill-defined events that must be made sense of by management. The term "issues" is used to describe developments or events that have not yet achieved the status of a "decision event," yet are believed to have the potential to influence the organization's current or future strategy (Ansoff, 1980; King, 1982, 1987). In this fashion, issues do not activate decision-makers' attention in packaged form; the issues often fly below the radar of bureaucratic organizations. Issues management comes to the forefront the more postmodern the organizational context—redolent with environmental turbulence, controversy over priorities, and a rapidly changing agenda. In this context, issues, as we shall see in the next section of this chapter, require interpretation.

It is a belief in the issues management field that issues, if untended, will have a far greater possibility of turning into a costly crisis for both the firm and, at times, society at large (Lerbinger, 1997; Pauchant and Mitroff, 1992). The perception that crises may originate in firms from non-market issues such as ethics is of particularly recent vintage (Baron, 1996:37). The term "issues management" was coined in the mid-1970s (Chase, 1976), and represents what Robert L. Heath and Richard A. Nelson, in their book, *Issues Management: Corporate Public Policy Making in an Information Society* (1986), call "a new ball game." The competent, contemporary manager must not only lead the firm to economic well-being, but also place it such that social, political, and moral issues do not overcome it and threaten its very existence. This manager manages not only the firm's bottom line, but must, as well, learn to monitor non-market events, communicate on issues important to the firm's various publics, and, as we shall see in greater depth in the last section of this chapter, develop confidence in his or her ability to interpret multiple realities presented by groups with very different points of view.

Many current ethics textbooks (e.g., Boatright, 1997; Shaw and Barry, 1992; Velasquez, 1988) use an issues-based orientation tied to the functional areas of the firm—finance (insider trading), human resource management (privacy rights of employees due to increased surveillance technologies), marketing (depiction of healthy lifestyle images to sell tobacco), accounting (client confidentiality), and the like. This approach, while useful within the university context wherein specialized knowledge is often imparted by the functional areas of the firm, fails to provide a holistic approach to issues management. Each issue is seen as a distinct problem to be tackled by, in our examples, the finance, human resource, marketing, or accounting specialist. There are three problems with this perspective: first, the ill-defined, often emergent nature of heretofore unseen issues is forfeited when we assume (often for pedagogical reasons) that each falls easily within the agreed-upon domain of the functional specialist; second, it is often assumed that competent handling of issues begins and ends with the functional specialists' increased understanding and sensitivity to issues; and third, that issues are best handled by functional specialists (e.g., marketers, accountants), and not by issues specialists.

The issues management perspective takes a broader, more holistic, and strategic view of issues. Issues—moral, social, political, economic, legislative (regulatory), technological, environmental, community-based, and those emerging in the postmodern context (e.g., AIDS, cyberspace commerce)—come in varying sizes, intensities, technical sophistication, public interest, and from varying sources. They do not come in neat functional packages. Often issues impact and call upon the skills of many of the firm's functional areas simultaneously. Issues can impact one functional area (e.g., a sexual harassment case in the accounting department), yet call upon the skills of other areas (e.g., legal and human resources) to move it towards resolution. The issues management perspective seeks to identify, diagnose, communicate, and move issues towards resolution so that the firm learns and develops systems to cope with and use them as opportunities to reorientate corporate strategy, smooth public and corporate relations, and establish a consistent and clear approach to CSR.

WHAT ARE ISSUES?

Issues, in the context of issues management (Wartick and Rude, 1986), are those controversial matters that people argue over in good faith and which, if left unresolved, would have a detrimental impact upon the firm. Issues management is the process by which the corporation can identify, evaluate, and respond to those social, political, and ethical pressures that may impact significantly upon it. In the context of this section we focus on ethical issues, but the framework presented here can be applied to strategic issues (Cammillus and Datta, 1991; Dutton and Jackson, 1987; Zenter, 1984) and public policy issues (Arrington and Sawaya, 1984; Bigelow *et al.*, 1991; McMillan and Murray, 1983). Issues management, when engaged in by a firm as a systematic, effective, and responsive reaction to emergent issues, not only serves to minimize that firm's surprise and uncertainty, but also serves as a coordinating and integrating force within the firm and between the firm and its external environment. While not a panacea for CSR, issues management, if done in good faith, is a solid and practical step towards CSR.

To understand what an issue is requires that we think of the organization in a different manner than traditionally done in the business school. Traditionally, organizations are conceptualized as complex systems or tools designed or having evolved to accomplish particular goals—make profits, educate students, collect taxes, and defend the nation. In this depiction, managers succeed by attending to the "problems" that directly impede the bottom-line attainment of these goals. Management, in this view, is a form of problem solving where it is quite apparent what is and is not a problem. Problem diagnosis takes a small amount of time relative to problem solving. The reverse is true of organizations in this issue management perspective. Issues are pre-problematic. Issues require identification, interpretation, and classification before it is known (subjectively) whether or not they are problems, opportunities, or merely noise. Organizations facing high degrees of turbulence or discontinuous change in their environments, features not uncommon in the postmodern context, must not assume, as in the rule-bound traditional model, that they know what requires their attention.

The organization, as suggested earlier, does not experience one issue, but is constantly stimulated by a cacophony of simultaneously occurring issues, very few of which make it to the front burner of strategic action. Issues come in highly variable shapes, sizes, and sources.

Issues that originate in the external environment of the organization—from government, clients, suppliers, competitors, and the like—increase the probability of getting on the management agenda for different reasons. The more threatening the issue is to the dominant coalition in the organization, the more likely it may be directed in two very distinct directions. The more threatening the issue and the more public, the greater the likelihood of the dominant coalition seeking to fast-track the issue by placing resources at the disposal of those who claim to be able to dismantle the threat. On the other hand, when the issue is believed to be threatening to the organization's dominant coalition but can be kept localized, the more likely it is that the issue will be stifled.

Issues become public when either they 1) originate from sources external to the organization and are amplified through the media, or 2) come from internal sources where either whistle-blowers (see Chapter 7) make issues known to the media, or internal organizational politics enhance the probability of issue amplification. As issues become public, they become harder to bury. Diverse publics, either external or internal to the organization, shape the issue and interpret it in manners consistent with their outlook. Issues are interpreted to fit the cognitive maps (Dutton *et al.*, 1983) or frames of reference (El Sawy and Pauchant, 1988) of individuals and groups who seek or find themselves compelled to make sense of an issue. The cognitive maps or frames of reference shift as information, often of a contradictory nature, is assembled by diverse publics. It is, to be sure, easier to contain issues and reduce the negative impact they carry where there is a consensus as to the meaning and means of dealing with an issue.

Ethical issues arising external to the organization emerge when the organization is perceived to be responsible or involved in a controversy involving moral issues (Logsdon and Palmer, 1988). The accusation by a human rights group that a prosperous Canadian organization is employing child labour—albeit through subcontractors—is bound to capture headlines that give the issue an ethical framework. In Figure 4.3, adapted and modified from Peter Bartha (1982), four different types of issues are presented. Each is managed differently. Part of the strategy of those seeking to make issues known or those attempting to handle them as swiftly and effectively as possible, is to shift the framing of an issue from, for example, a "universal issue" to a "technical issue." Technical issues, with their accompanying legions of experts, scientific evidence, and courtroom procedures, are one of the strategies used so successfully for decades by the tobacco and tobacco-related industries to keep health and addiction related connections to tobacco use from becoming common and accepted knowledge (universal issue). It is only recently that the floodgates on this framing have been altered; tobacco is no longer as easily defensible on technical grounds.

Each issue requires careful examination lest the neophytes in the study of issues management believe that, as in the tobacco example, firms prefer technical-issue framing. A manufacturing firm accused by the municipality of polluting a stream may elect to attempt to shift the framing from a technical to a universal issue by avoiding expert testimony and claiming that employment and benefits that accrue to the community far outweigh the sort and level of pollution that exists throughout the municipality. The problem of pollution, implied in the firm's attempt to shift the issue from a technical to a universal one, is everyone's problem, and therefore requires a thorough examination of whether or not the municipal government is off-loading its responsibility to what, due to its employment record, may be an organization practising CSR.

Advocacy issues are those issues external to the firm that are taken up by and pursued by groups claiming to represent broad public interests. Typically, when students hear this, they

FIGURE 4–3   A Typology of Issues: External Sources

	Issue Type			
	Universal	**Advocacy**	**Selective**	**Technical**
Locus of Concern	• Issues that impact large numbers of people in a matter linked to business or particular business.	• Issues led by groups claiming to represent broad public interests (environmental and consumer groups) that push for change.	• Issues of concern to special interests in which the special interest gains by promoting the issue.	• Issues the public does not believe it possesses the knowledge to assess; it is willing to leave them to experts.
Examples	• Pollution; unsafe products; sexual and/or violent images made available to children.	• Consumer boycotts; calls for corporate daycare; media campaigns; educational material.	• NIMBY syndrome or "not in my back yard" out- breaks; college students opposing their depiction in a corporate advertisement.	• Greenhouse effect; soil leeching; pharmaceuticals safety.
Pressures	• General public, often in a political vein.	• Activists and highly organized professional groups.	• Population segments by region, occupation, gender, age, lifestyle, or other criteria.	• Interest groups; government bodies such as commissions.
Amplification (Role of Media)	• Reflect and enlarge on public mood often through com- mentary and public opinion.	• Identifies the issue as an important one; sets an agenda; takes sides on the issue.	• Draws public attention to the outbreak of the event; seeks to move it into an advocacy frame- work.	• Specialized reporters educate the public by popularizing and simplifying issues.
Management Perspective	• Business must deal with the inevitable government pressures to regulate and legislate solutions.	• Persistence of the activist lobby requires the establishment of ongoing commu- nications with the issue source.	• One nature of these issues requires a form of corporate preparedness to deal with the unexpected.	• The management requires hiring specialists and building well- reasoned and documented arguments.

immediately think about groups like Mothers Against Drunk Driving (MADD), Greenpeace, The Sierra Club, or animal rights activist groups. They are right, but they typically fail to see how businesses, often in their industry-wide associations through Chambers of Commerce or even through advocacy advertising (Sethi, 1977, 1979), frame issues as advocacy issues. In British Columbia, The Forest Alliance, a coalition of large- and medium-sized forestry firms in the province, captures public attention by seeking to point out the factual errors, omissions of fact, and hyperbole engaged in by groups seeking to terminate clear-cut logging. The Forest Alliance, as well, seeks to portray the industry as the backbone of an economy that has clear vested interests in protecting the forest for future use and re-use.

Advocacy groups, whether of the small activist sort or the large coalition of firms such as The Forest Alliance, seek not only to advocate a position, but also to oppose one. Advocacy issues entail a "rival camps" form of political game in which victories to the advocate are clearly losses to the opponent. When the beef industry of Alberta promotes meat eating, it is attempting to deal with the view that the cholesterol in red meat lessens one's probability of living a long and healthy life. The clear oppositional logic in framing issues as advocacy issues requires a close monitoring of one's rival and a professional use of the media. The aim is to both upgrade one's influence and diminish that of one's rival. The advocacy-issues game is one for deep pockets. Many of the smaller or fringe activist groups attempt to overcome this problem by using volunteer and often true-believer labour and their small size to capture the moral rectitude of the underdog. They try to frame themselves as a David in what they would like to portray as a David-and-Goliath struggle.

While the rival-camp struggle in advocacy-issue framing often moves to the level of social archetypes—good versus evil, just countering the unjust, caring versus greedy, and domestic versus foreign—selective-issue framing carves out a much more restricted turf (see Figure 4.3). Selective issues impact populations external to firms segmented by region, occupation, gender, age, lifestyle, or other rather specific criteria. A firm seeking to operate a giant incinerator to get rid of garbage far more efficiently than existing land-fills, may find those communities in which it seeks to operate resisting it. The NIMBY (not-in-my-backyard) syndrome refers to a community's reaction to the externalities of business (pollution, noise, traffic, toxic waste, etc.). This regional or community reaction, for example, is often amplified by the local media who seek to portray it as an advocacy issue.

The typology of external source issues differs from internal source issues in that the latter become public or are amplified by whistle-blowers or the internal politics of coalitions within the firm. Whistle-blowing, a topic we will take up in greater depth in Chapter 7, is the act whereby employees or other insiders go public with issues fomenting within the firm. Ideally, whistle-blowers first seek to trigger the issue or call attention to it internally, and when and if this goes unheeded and the issue festers, they then go to the media, political agents, or other "public representatives" (commissions of inquiry, ombudspersons, regulatory bodies, etc.). Internal politics, on the other hand, bring corporate issues to the public due to the advantages accruing to the corporate group that publicizes the issue. Union members may find it in their best interest to publicize their firm's poor record on occupational safety and health; management may find it advantageous to counter the union's data with its own, which shows (favourably) the firm's accident rate compared to its competitors.

Internal issues emerge and require management when the standard operating procedures of internal governance break down. Distribution issues (see Figure 4.4) are rampant in organizations where the internal organizational culture is fractious, competitive, and resources are believed to be scarce. Distribution issues often surround the politics of budgetary allocation within firms and are rooted in group comparisons. Complainants feel that, relative to other groups or departments within the firm, they have been hard done by; or, relative to their past allocation, a recent injustice has been created. Distribution issues become heated when, comparing themselves to others believed to be in some way similar (seniority,

FIGURE 4-4   A Typology of Issues: Internal Sources

	Issue Type			
	People Issues	**Information Issues**	**Technology Issues**	**Distribution Issues**
Locus of Concern	• Issues that arise out of different views and lifestyles held by people working in the firm.	• Issues created when information is seen as violating individuals' rights or being appropriated without consent of owners.	• Issues arise with the change, modification, and replacement of employees with technology.	• Issues arise when groups within the firm compare themselves and claim injustice as others are better off.
Examples	• Accusations of homophobia, sexual harassment, mistreatment of minority employees.	• Accusations of violation of confidentiality; plagiarism of ideas; failure to check on information.	• Safety of new technology for special groups like pregnant women; noise issues; obsolescence of workers.	• Gender issues of equal pay for equal work; variations in benefit packages for employees in different regions.
Pressures	• Issues become impossible to ignore when taken to the courts or official complaint centres.	• Issues become acute when costly, recurrent, and requiring a major readjustment of corporate routines.	• Issues grow in intensity as the firm moves to be an early adopter of innovative technology.	• Issues reach heightened proportions as groups go public and politicize their grievances.
Amplification (Media or Coalition Politics)	• The issue gets on the agenda by either getting to the media (whistle-blowers, investigative journalism), or when useful in the internal politics of organizational power.	• The same as in people issues except, when these go public, the media fixes on individual rights and freedom of expression.	• The same as in information issues except the media fixes on victimization aspects and loses sight of experimental nature of new technology.	• Media highlights issues of injustice, particularly in contexts where it can give a David & Goliath spin to the story.
Management	• Businesses must move quickly to put systems in place that can surface these issues early and deal with the conflict.	• Businesses must be aware of their use, storage, and sharing of information since there is a tendency to lose sight of this resource if used the way it always has been.	• Businesses must monitor technology and use adequate procedures before committing to new technology.	• Businesses must provide complainants with internal procedures for grievance and provide a full disclosure of the reasoning for distribution inequities.

job type, work qualifications), individuals or groups feel cheated and threaten to take action. Distribution issues often arise when power is being re-aligned within the firm. Those from whom it is being taken often find it in their best interests to go public. Whistle-blowers often arise with the sincere belief that, by pointing out the inefficiencies of other departments or groups, they are serving not only their own, but also the public good.

People issues (see Figure 4.4) often predominate in the human resource management approach to business ethics. In this perspective, people issues arise out of different views and lifestyles held by people working in and for the firm. Gender, sexual preference, racial and, increasingly, age related issues emerge by constituent publics to the firm who feel that they are being exploited (to varying degrees). In a quest to rectify these perceived and often heart-felt inequities, individuals, either through whistle-blowing or internal corporate politics, put pressure on the firm to alter its ways. These issues gain momentum the more they threaten the firm's dominant coalition. At other times, the dominant coalition does not even see or register the pressure.

Information issues internal to the firm (see Figure 4.4) are created when information used by the firm is seen as violating individual and/or group rights of the firm's constituent publics. Most frequently information issues combine with technology issues (see Figure 4.4) to give rise to some variant of people issues. The increasing accessibility of technologies enhancing surveillance, drug testing, character testing, and the like, raise the information issues of confidentiality, privacy, and personal rights. Those who see information as power raise the fear that, within the ambit of postmodern business, the organization, in its ability to amass information, creates a reputation for itself as a form of hyper-reality (Rosenau, 1992). In hyper-reality, the reality of the individual pales before the sense-making abilities of markets that quickly and unerringly adjust to new information. The sense prevailing in postmodernity that the organization is "more real" than the individual, is tied closely, it can be argued, to the privileged status of the organization as the nexus of emerging technology.

Technology issues (see Figure 4.4) arise in the context of the firm's attempt to adapt to change. Technology, as we shall see in further detail in Chapter 10, is more than the machinery used by the firm in the production of goods and services, but is also the techniques, processes, and systems employed to achieve an ongoing orderliness in the face of an altering reality. As firms alter technologies as a response to competitive forces and other alterations in their surface calm, they alter, often unintentionally, the conventions of life as lived and as expected in the organization. As these conventions alter, for example, job descriptions as automation increases, or salaries as more responsibilities are added to some jobs and not to others, so too are altered those questions posed by internal constituents as to what is and is not fair. The changing conventions facilitated by altering, even fine-tuning, technologies are amplified when the media fixes upon and makes the issue public. At times, like that of the alleged health problems of pregnant employees trapped too long before computer screens, the issue is made public early on in its life cycle. When this occurs, the media often polarize the technological issue and avoid the complex middle ground in which the debate takes on nuance and subtlety.

Both external issues (see Figure 4.3) and internal issues (see Figure 4.4) must be managed if they are not to rise in troublesome intensity, cost and, of course, problem status. As issues get out of control, CSR becomes problematic for the focal organization. This occurs not only for issues that threaten, but also for opportunities. Hazel Henderson, co-director of the Princeton Centre for Alternative Futures Incorporated, has devised a seven-stage vertical hierarchy to show the life cycle of issues (1978:321). In Figure 4.5, this model has been adapted to show the life cycle of issues in terms of how it builds up concern and requires management by either a governmental organization with its ability to create or interpret legislation, or a private firm with its capacity to redesign or engineer workplaces. One must realize that, in practice rather than theory, a firm rarely faces one and only one issue. For heuristic purposes, the management perspective highlighted in Figure 4.5 simplifies the fact that while a firm may be in the midst of its issue action phase on working through a serious bout of sexual harassment cases, a new issue, such as the threat of a community campaign to force the firm to enlarge its parking facilities, may be occurring simultaneously.

The firm that identifies issues early is typically one that possesses "leaders" rather than "managers." In the context of the life cycle of issues management, leaders are sensitive to events both internal or external that break the surface calm of organizational life; managers, on the other hand, tend to run the organization by relying upon standard operating procedures which, if disturbed, are forced or jimmied back into working order. In other words, leaders see the organization as an ongoing experiment in coping with new and often unprecedented events before they impact the important transactions at the core of the organization's technical system. Leaders anticipate events; managers identify events usually when they are already driving costs up or threatening to drive the company's stock evaluations down by impairing its reputation.

The major management problem at Stage 1 of the issue life cycle is the leader's ability to overcome denial and define the issue. Denial is a defense mechanism used by individuals and groups to avoid having to deal with realities that call into question central assumptions. In the area of ethics issues, most leaders feel that their organizations, as reflections of themselves, are essentially well-intended and good corporate citizens—that is to say, at least as good as most of the players in their industry. To catch ethics issues early on in the life cycle, one cannot rely upon this common assumption as anything more than tentative hypothesis. As William Renfro speculates in *Issues Management in Strategic Planning* (1993), to overcome denial, the leader must not become captured by the past, even the most successful past, because this leads away from being able to see events that threaten or opportunities that may cause the break-up of the surface calm.

To lead successfully in Stage 2 of the life cycle, the leader must balance concerns for the past—precedent, tradition, and the status quo—with apprehensions that surround new and challenging issues. It is not the "newness" of issues that is germane to the successful issues champion, but the degree to which they are relevant. Issues that are relevant at this early stage are difficult to spot. This is because there are many of them, and each is often championed by someone in the firm or some stakeholder group. In Stage 2 the leader selects, out of this jungle of contending issues, several that are believed germane to the dominant elite in the corporation. It is important to realize that, since corporate attentiveness is selective, those in control often select and identify issues that suit their agendas.

However, we must not get cynical since issue selection even in the emergent phase is not solely in the hands of the dominant corporate elite. Pressure groups within the company, often those with views discordant with the dominant elite, can use strategies to get their issues on the agenda. These include: forming coalitions with others, both inside and outside the firm; providing evidence, rhetoric, and testimonials as to the corporate significance of the issue; re-framing issues accepted by the dominant elite in such a manner that the issue, when re-framed, contains components of other issues. External issues are often forced upon an unwilling corporate elite by publics that threaten to boycott the firm, raise negative publicity, or otherwise continually deride the corporate elite's failure to deal with "reality."

FIGURE 4-5 Life Cycle of Issues: Management Perspective

Stage	Name	Description	Issue Phase	Management Problem
1	Surface calm breaks	Signs of standard operating procedure breakdown.	Emergent	Overcoming denial.
2	Leader concern	The dominant elite begins to see the issue as a threat or opportunity.	Emergent	Identifying the issue and giving it a name.
3	Public/ organizational member identification	Leaders disseminate the issue in terms that mobilize others.	Involvement	Communicating the issue in the right terms to relevant others.
4	Public/ organizational member concern	The public (external issues) and organizational members (internal issues) become concerned.	Involvement	Indicating what is in it for those who get involved.
5	Organizing the involvement	Mobilizing others to join into new teams or project groups to deal with the issue.	Involvement	Having a plan or design for mobilizing those who are aroused by the issue.
6	Acting on the issue	Motivating those who seek to get involved to follow through on initial interest.	Issue action	Focusing attention on the issue and its solution while still running the organization.
7	Assessing one's actions	In a dispassionate way, measuring one's success or failure in issue management.	Issue action	Fine-tuning the issue management effort and putting in place a way to stabilize the issue.

The recognition in issues management that there are, in postmodern business ethics, multiple realities is easier for most leaders when dealing with external issues. It is assumed in Stage 3 that "outsiders" or stakeholders are more difficult to communicate with and to justify corporate issue attentiveness. The task of the leader in Stage 3 is to get others involved in the issue. This is the beginning of the involvement phase and in it the leader must disseminate the issue in terms with which others identify. It is typical at this stage for the leader to begin to encourage involvement by selecting individuals and groups readily disposed towards the issue and empowering them to bring the issue to the attention of others. There is a formal and informal side to this communication. The formal communication centres on explicit texts—

memoranda, e-mail transmissions, public newsletters, and annual reports; the informal communication at Stage 3 entails the judicious use and selection of appropriate opinion leaders, both inside and external to the organization, to increase the issue's visibility and salience.

The politicization of issues becomes most apparent in two distinct but interrelated circumstances. In the first, and this becomes relevant in the transition from Stage 3 to Stage 4, the leader, as representative of the dominant organizational elite, believes strongly in the importance of an issue but is unable to successfully motivate others either within the firm or external to it. This signals that the dominant elite is unable to use its dominance to alter the attention and routines of subordinates. The second instance, usually related to the first, occurs when the leader, in drawing attention to an issue, is not the formal or hierarchical manager of the organization and is able to get others to attend to the emerging issue.

Stage 4 is where the issue "takes" or does not. To get issues on the agenda and, as we shall see, to keep them on it, leaders must go beyond involving those most likely to respond to the issue (as in Stage 3) and motivate others. Motivating others to become involved in an issue entails three separate realms. The first, and this is dealt with most explicitly by the typical business school, involves convincing others that the benefits of seriously attending to the issues far outweigh the costs; second, that the issue is meaningful and carries significance for the future of the organization and its strategy; and third, that there is something very concrete and real, albeit not too unsettling, that can be done to deal with the issue. For the issue to take, others must see a rational argument, backed by a meaningful explanation tied to a plausible line of action. Exciting rhetoric can call attention to the issue, but only when no other options for placement on the agenda contend can rhetoric alone succeed in getting the issue to "take."

The involvement phase is complete in Stage 5, when those supporting an issue produce a plan or design for mobilizing the organization and its interested stakeholders in dealing with it. The plan, in effect, alters the existing policies, procedures, and/or systems of the organization by calling for new or different activities from individuals and groups. The plan must be clearly communicable yet sufficiently robust to permit improvisation as may be required by even further unexpected events. The plan should identify the key personnel to be involved in dealing with the issue, their accountability, and lines of communication. It is wise, in the early stages of the plan, to build in a mechanism for assessing the effectiveness of the unit, whether it be a project team, permanent unit, or contracted-out issue. Issues that stay on the agenda, in time, are built into the standard operating procedures of the organization. This is, of course, not to say that they are done automatically or without discretion being given to the incumbents but, rather, that they become part and parcel of the division of labour within the firm.

The issue action phase, made up of Stages 6 and 7, puts the plan into action and develops effective ways to measure the issue handlers' success—or lack of it. In organizations that evolve ongoing issue-handling entities—public relations departments, community affairs units, or corporate social responsibility specialists—the emphasis is upon hiring and training specialists to handle issues. Other organizations that utilize special committees, project teams, and other temporary or cross-functional teams to handle issues, emphasize training the firm's employees to be aware of emergent issues and to devote some proportion of their time to committee assignments that focus upon issues. Each has its benefits. Organizations that utilize full-time issue handlers or departments and units have specialists on hand (or near at hand in the case of retainers), to deal with the issues as they emerge. This approach, however, may ghettoize or prevent the significance of the issue from being integrated into the organizational culture. The use of temporary project teams and voluntary service of employees to deal with issues integrates the substance of the issue into the organizational culture, but these teams often lack the knowledge to move an issue towards a technical resolution.

The life cycle of the issue ends when the organization normalizes the issue and, in a dispassionate way, establishes methods to measure how well or poorly it is handling it. CSR becomes a possibility when organizations are able to reach Stage 7, in which the focus is upon evaluating the action taken to manage the issue. What we measure, in organizational life, we respect, because when we measure we seek to evaluate whether or not we are succeeding or failing. We have decided, when employing the tightly-focused attention required to measure, that the issue in question requires careful assessment and the use of techniques to ensure that our measures live up to our expectations. Management issue systems that bring an issue to Stage 7 not only have learned to live with an issue, they have made it part and parcel of ongoing organizational processes.

While Figure 4.5 calls our attention to the rise and, in time, fall of concern regarding an issue, it only hints at the relationship between issues management and organizational change. This is an important area of inquiry. The business ethics student intuits that there is a relationship between ethics and the pressures being placed upon organizations to change. The process is an uneven one in which organizational environments trigger issue-impact evaluation, giving rise to efforts by organizations to develop strategies to handle issues believed to have the greatest impact. These strategies, even those that manage to contain the issue, lead to change—much of it, of course, incremental, but at times even radical organizational or transformational change. The next section examines how management issue processes create a front line in our efforts to understand organizational changes which, at times, push organizations towards CSR and, at other times, in directions that stonewall, cover up, or exacerbate ethical lapses.

MANAGEMENT ISSUES AND ORGANIZATIONAL CHANGE

Issues emerge, not from the dark, but rather from managers' interpretations of the changing environments in which organizations operate. If there has been a revolution in the education of aspiring managers during my career as a management professor in various business schools, it has been upon the improvisational skills required by managers in postmodern contexts. The initial educational thrust of teaching managers that organizations are tightly bound (closed) systems that can be designed or engineered to maximize output has been replaced. Today, the pedagogical emphasis is upon teaching that the organization is an open system that must adapt to its environment. The new pedagogy fixes upon the manager as an adaptive innovator or strategic broker working on a multiplicity of interdependent and poorly-defined (ambiguous) issues within a changing context in which little can be taken for granted. With the uncertainty of the postmodern era, managers (at least in training) are shifting from technical, legal, science-based forms of thinking to innovative, creative, and strategic thinking.

Issue management necessitates that managers broaden their outlooks and learn to anticipate which issues will impact the organization, whether as a threat or an opportunity. Attending to the origins of issues involves teaching managers how to manage issues by "scanning environments" (Aguilar, 1967; Ewing, 1987; Fahey and King, 1977, Stoeffels, 1994). Environment scanning, as seen in Figure 4.6, is a form of information gathering used by organizations to make sense of and identify issues that are beyond the organization's current and planned environment. As an organization's environment becomes more turbulent and complex, the motivation and pay-off for successful environmental scanning increases.

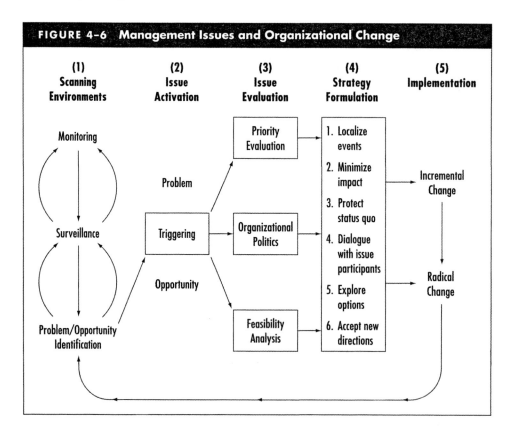

FIGURE 4-6   Management Issues and Organizational Change

The functions of environmental scanning are threefold—to monitor the organization's environments, to increase surveillance over issues that might heat up, and, of course, to problem solve. Monitoring entails persistent and regular efforts by managers to broaden their information-search horizons to include trends, altering social, economic and political issues that are not directly tied to the planning horizon or strategy of the firm. Monitoring, within the context of environmental scanning, requires time, patience, curiosity, and personnel with broad interests and a willingness to read widely and meet people (network) beyond the confines of the usual industry functions. The monitoring function in environmental screening is intended to prevent the organization from becoming too parochial in its approach to its problems, too caught up and entrenched in thinking with the same circuits and connections.

The surveillance function in scanning the environment fixes upon prioritizing certain occurrences being monitored as requiring more specific attention and more in-depth or robust information. Just as good maps blow up or enlarge the information detail for sites that are complex or deemed important, so too, in surveillance, one seeks to broaden one's insights. How one selects sites to enlarge is usually a cognitive process called "tracking" (El Sawy and Pauchant, 1988). Tracking involves bounding the issues being monitored due to the expectation that there exists the probability of an opportunity or threat associated with the tracked item(s) (Heath and Nelson, 1986). Items tracked are followed up more formally than those monitored. Technical specialists, in what Henry Mintzberg (1983, 1989) calls the "technostructure" of the typical organization, are often delegated the task of conducting a more in-depth investigation into issues being tracked. The information becomes a form of intelligence used by firms to make sense of their turbulent environments. In the next chapter, we shall probe how the values held in the organizational culture, to some degree, determine how organizations employ their intelligence.

The last and key function of environmental scanning is to identify problematic or opportunistic issues. Tracked issues are those believed to be of potential relevance to the firm. The more issues are studied, the more those gathering information upon them begin to understand and feel that action may be appropriate. Once identified and studied, problems are seen to have actionable solutions; opportunities, likewise, are viewed as requiring a timely and often innovative response. The identification function in scanning disaggregates and focuses upon an issue as either promising (an opportunity) or threatening (a problem). Once identified as issues, the organization and those within it must decide or, at times, react to it. The issue is given a name and a priority. It begins to get mentioned in memoranda and conversations as an explanation of what seems to be changing in and about the organization.

Those issues that are taken seriously by the firm so as to potentially alter the status quo, enter the "issue activation" phase (see Figure 4.6). Issue activation not only breaks the surface calm by going beyond the monitoring, surveillance, and identification functions of environmental scanning, but in doing so requires that the organization evaluate the problem potential (priority evaluation), or do a feasibility analysis of inherent opportunities. At the point of triggering, the issue must either be moved towards strategy formulation or looked at more closely before being returned to regular scanning functions. Issues revert back to the scanning function when they are given a low priority or are perceived to be "interesting" but not easily acted upon at a particular time. Timing is key in triggering. The same issue may move from scanning functions to issue activation several times before it is triggered into strategy formulation.

The salience of a problem in the issue evaluation phase (see Figure 4.6), like that of an opportunity, is dependent upon two different types of thinking. The first, and this is highlighted in most business schools' curricula, focuses on a rational or calculating assessment of the issue's impact. When the issue is triggered as a "problem"—and, as we shall see, this is prevalent in issues framed as "ethics" issues—then the issue moves to strategy formulation when it is viewed that the costs of failing to deal with the issue will far outweigh the benefits of returning it to the scanning function. This so-called cost-benefit may be done rigorously using data or, as is more prevalent in many issues management programs, it may be accomplished by eye-balling the "forces" at play and roughly estimating the impact. When the issue is triggered as an "opportunity," the rational calculation turns from a cost-benefit form to a feasibility approach. In the feasibility approach, the organization seeks to make sense of how "actionable" the opportunity inherent in the issue may be for the firm and it stakeholders. In essence, the more feasible the issue opportunity, the more likely it enters into strategy formulation; conversely, the less feasible it is deemed, the more likely the issue opportunity returns to the scanning function.

Issue evaluation can also be connected to another source—organizational politics. Organizational politics is the fight for resources, including recognition and career mobility, fought over by its members. As we shall see in the following chapter, different organizations possess varying degrees of internal competitiveness over resources, but all possess some. In this competition, some issues can help one further one's personal or departmental goals, or one's view of the organizational goals. In this perspective, issues are not in themselves of value; the value is in that which issues may bring about. Helping to trigger the issues, for example, of sexual harassment, may bring more resources to the human resource department, heighten its profile, and provide it with an opportunity to make new hires.

It would be incorrect to see the priority evaluation of problematic issues and the feasibility analysis of opportunities as rational, while classifying the organizational politics assessment as irrational. The two, in practice, collapse. Organizational politics may be built into the apparently objective cost-benefit analysis or, indeed, into the arguments for and against feasibility. This occurs because incumbents doing the apparently objective forms of analysis are entrenched in the organizational culture that they use to make sense of the issue's salience and impact. The data utilized to measure impact and salience is tied to members' perceptions and projections. These latter are formulated within the competitive milieu of organizational politics.

Once an issue gets to the strategy formulation phase, there are six possible strategic options for dealing with issues (see Figure 4.6). Strategy formulation is the process of tying the now salient issues into the plan for the operation of the organization now and in the future. Issues that make it to the strategy formulation stage are candidates for changing the organization either incrementally or radically. It is precisely this possibility that makes issue management so central in practical discussions of CSR. Issues that require the organization to modify its ways are powerful, for not only do they directly impact the organization in question, but they often serve as an exemplar for other organizations seeking to avoid issue-related problems or to capitalize upon issue-related opportunities.

When triggered as a problem and passing through priority evaluation and/or organizational politics as an issue with salience and impact, the first strategy formulation is to localize events. This is the strategy of containment. Of the six strategy options, it is the least likely to lead to radical organizational change. Organizations seek to localize events for three reasons: First, in keeping with the cost-benefit analysis inherent in evaluating priorities, it can help keep costs down; second, in keeping with organizational politics, it can limit the embarrassment and reputational fallout that is likely to occur when issues heighten; third, it sets no precedents or rewriting of policy for the organization as a whole. The probability of localizing events is greater when the event arises internally and those involved have neither the means nor the interest in getting the issue diffused. However, it is important to realize that even when issues are contained and localized, they must be dealt with. The change required to deal with the issue is restricted but, if frequent enough, change—albeit incremental—does take place.

The second strategic formulation is also most commonly applied when the issue is triggered as a problem. Containment involves buffering the issue from the organizational core. Since the issue increases vulnerability, this strategy entails admitting the issue while protecting the important parts of the organization from the fallout. Filtered through the lens of organizational politics, the strategy of minimizing impact involves distancing one's group, department, or indeed one's career, from the inherent fallout. Impact can be minimized by four means: acting swiftly to deal with the issue; explaining the issue such that the impact is shared with other institutions; locating specific others (often scapegoats) to take the brunt of the impact; and buying time by setting up a special "blue ribbon committee" to deal with the impact. Incremental change results from the strategy of minimizing impact because there is an acceptance that the issue will have impact—in other words, that the firm will take a hit. However, the hit can be minimized. How the organization prepares itself to cope with the impact of the hit and how it learns from the impact of the issue, both determine the nature of the incremental change.

The third strategic formulation, and one primarily reserved for issues triggered as problems, is to protect the status quo. The status quo, or "the way we do things in organization X," is the organizational member's understanding of the difference between incremental and radical change. Incremental change is perceived as fitting into the status quo—a form of fine-tuning or adjustment. Issues that mobilize strategies 1 (localizing events), 2 (minimizing impact), and 3 (protecting the status quo), all essentially seek to limit change to within the existing dominant organizational paradigm. None of these three strategies asks the incumbents to question key assumptions. When, however, the organization cannot protect the status quo, it must—often pushing and screaming—look to strategies 4 (dialoguing with issue participants), 5 (exploring options), and 6 (accepting new directions).

Those issues triggered as opportunities and filtered through forms of feasibility evaluation and tied to organizational politics lead to radical change. This is so because, in approaching opportunities, organizational members tend to be quick to associate themselves with the issue rather than distance themselves from it. Organizations that seek dialogue with issue participants are eager to broaden their horizons. If this comes via the problem trigger, organizations see dialogue with issue participants as something that has been foisted upon them. This latter framing comes out of a desire to protect the status quo, to not empower "outsiders" with a voice on important issues. Dialogue is thus most successful when the trigger frames the issue as an opportunity, and organizational members buy this framing. While it threatens change, it does so by suggesting that associations with the change will confer benefits—indeed, outsiders are important resources in the possible radical reformulation of the future organization. The issue that presents itself as a joint venture, of course, presents itself very differently than an issue that is framed as a critique of the status quo.

In the postmodern cultural context, as we have seen, voice is very important in making change possible. Dialogue with issue participants alters the "voice field" used in the first three containment-oriented strategies by legitimizing the perspectives of issue participants. This broadens the discussion and moves it away from strategic efforts to contain the issue perspectives. To make dialogue with issue participants possible and more than token gestures, it is vital to permit these voices to give rise to alternate options. This movement away from the status quo is threatening when issue participants are seen as troublemakers, impractical idealists, or self-serving entrepreneurs. Dialogue is possible when both organizational participants and issue participants experience the dialogue as a search for ways to improve both the organization and its long-term viability, and to satisfy the voices of the issue participants.

The options that emerge in dialogue must not only be allowed to be heard by the organization, they must be explored. The fifth strategic formulation accepts the possibility that the status quo can no longer be protected in a blind fashion but, rather, that the options arising from dialogue with issue participants require investigation. The exploration of options involves enlarging the organizational vocabulary to include points of view heretofore neglected. This vocabulary is tested when the organization is willing to accept new directions and procedures.

This last strategy and embodiment of radical organizational change is the organization's acceptance of new directions. There are two possible approaches to strategy 6. The first involves compliance. In this formulation, the organization accepts the new direction begrudgingly. It has heard new voices, looked at the options, and accepted the new directions. However, closer inspection may reveal that the organization seeks to revert to the status quo once the monitoring of stakeholders diminishes, or the issue abates. This compliance requires ongoing vigilance, even legislation, to make the new directions stick. The second approach involves the organization becoming an "issue champion," and absorbing the new directions into its basic operations. This latter state is facilitated when the dominant elite of the corporation buys into and is able to convince others of the benefits of the new directions. It is secure when the new directions become industry norms.

Issue management, while not an assurance of CSR, is a clear attempt by organizations and those who run them to react to some issues as they arise and take on growing importance. Not all firms practise issue management; some feel that this is a distraction from the real "bottom line pursuits." Those who do practise issue management either link this pursuit to the long-term pursuit of the bottom line, or see issue management as a necessary investment in bringing the organization into the postmodern context. Those firms that seek to engage in issue management require managers with particular skills and abilities, neither of which are central to the education of managers in the postmodern business school. Moreover, when issue management is taught, it will be argued, it is confused with forms of political correctness. Let us turn to the education of issue managers and conclude this chapter with suggestions on how to enable issue management to deal with the CSR opportunities of the interpreter.

EDUCATING INTERPRETERS FOR CSR

If the CSR portfolio of the firm requires the skills of those who can engender trust and manage a diversity of ill-defined issues, we must ask ourselves what sort of skills these would be and how we educate individuals, groups, and organizations to put CSR into practice. The literature on organizations and management in the postmodern context (Berquist, 1993; Boje, 1996; Chia, 1996; Clegg, 1996; Kilduff, 1993; Power, 1992) provides a clue. Like Zymunt Bauman in *Legislators and Interpreters* (1987), this literature distinguishes between three skill sets: calculating, legislating, and interpreting, each of which rises to ascendancy respectively within the premodern, modern, and postmodern business contexts.

The traditional entrepreneurial community, that which we associate with the premodern context, selects and rewards those whose skills permit them to legitimately dominate or take the power of ownership—and with it the right to control—within a very competitive context. The skills of the calculator or entrepreneur are legend. These skills, calculators argue, are best learned in the school of hard knocks. The calculator is the stereotypical "boss" in the organizational context. What he or she says is the will of the organization. The calculator seeks to take legitimate power and control in the organizational context. Winning is a sign of prowess. Winning is necessary in this competitive dog-eat-dog business context. To win, the calculator seeks to increase, in as short a time as possible, the profitability of the organization. Problems are impediments to profitability that are to be solved only if the solution is less costly than the price of the problem. Improvisation is sought, but only insofar as it can be understood to move the bottom line.

The calculator is not wedded to a particular organization, but will radically shift its focus if this is a feasible means to capitalize on profitable opportunities. If we attempt to understand the calculator as a trust builder (see Figure 4.7), we would see how the calculator seeks to utilize market-oriented, economic calculation by comparing the outcomes resulting from creating and sustaining relations to the costs of maintaining or severing them. The calculator maintains trusting relations with those who continue to offer greater economic benefits than costs. Betrayal comes easily to the calculator and is considered "nothing personal." Relationships—even longstanding ones—will be severed once they prove costly or can be replaced by more profitable ones. This behaviour grows most tenaciously in power-asymmetric relations in which the calculator seeks to increase his or her power, and thereby learns to trust the other by having the power to thoroughly monitor them.

When it comes to issues management (see Figure 4.8), the calculator tends towards the deployment of the self-interested CSR perspective. The calculator attempts to use issues to make profits and avoid losses. Short-term economic calculations help the calculator determine whether or not an issue is to be triggered. Despite the desire to use opportunistic issues and stay clear of costly, problematic issues, the calculator does not spend much time or effort scanning organizational environments. Rather, the calculator tends to react to issues, even to capitalize upon them,

---

FIGURE 4-7 Calculators, Legislators, and Interpreters: Building Trust

Skill Type	Trust Base	Dynamics
Calculators	• The calculator bases his or her trust in "deterrence." Deterrence in a relationship arises when the potential costs of discontinuing the relationship in whole or in part outweigh the short-term advantage of acting in a distrustful way. Deterrence flourishes in markets, in the courts, and in hierarchies—all of which mete out penalties to cheaters.	• The ability to levy costs on potential cheaters is central. Trust is achieved in a relationship when the benefits of cheating in any one exchange pale in comparison to the advantages created through the possibility of continuing ongoing profitable exchanges.
Legislators	• The legislator bases his or her trust on "knowledge." The capacity to predict, with accuracy, others' behaviour means that it is possible to make plans, investments, or other decisions contingent on knowledge of others' behaviour. Trust flourishes when each has knowledge of the other's moves and is able to act with it.	• The ability to possess knowledge of the other is rooted in information. The more points of contact and the more transparent the parties are in the transactions, the better and more reliable the information.
Interpreters	• The interpreter bases his or her trust on an "identification" with the other. This requires the sharing of basic assumptions and values attained through dialogue and interdependence. Identification with the other stems from the perception of a shared destiny. This destiny is rooted in a belief that each party to the exchange is tied to the others. As exit options diminish, voice and loyalty begin, albeit slowly, to gain ground.	• The ability to identify with the other lowers the need to deterrence and removes the search for relevant information. However, these relationships take a great deal of commitment, time, and energy. As one partner to the exchange changes, the other must be willing to internalize the new dynamics.

---

once the issues are well along in their life cycles. On the whole, the calculator, in his or her quest for ownership and control, tries to keep stakeholders, including government, at a distance, since they often bring social, moral, and political issues to bear in their transactions.

The calculator's skills emerge in competitive contexts in which winning and losing is understood in economic calculations. While the entrepreneurial basis of the calculator's skills is lauded by the public, it is not held in particularly high esteem by the legislator. Legislators in organizational contexts try to minimize uncertainty rather than maximize profits. Unlike the risk-seeking calculator, the legislator tends whenever possible to avoid risk. Like the functionary or bureaucrat, the legislator relies upon precedent embedded in known rules and procedures. In the university or college context, we make an attempt to train entrepreneurs, but it is only an attempt. While the calculator emerges through the school of hard

FIGURE 4–8   Calculators, Legislators, and Interpreters: Issue Management Perspectives

Skill Type	Issue Management Strategy	Dynamics
Calculators	• Attempt to use issues to make profits and avoid losses. Do not spend much time scanning organizational environments, but rather react to issues that are well along in their life cycles. They tend to use the two extreme strategies of localizing events if the issue is perceived as a problem, or accepting new directions if it is seen as an opportunity.	• Calculators' skills rest in focusing upon winning. Issues can become a means to this end or, if mishandled, they can raise the price of doing business. Calculators seek to keep stakeholders, including government, at a distance. They fear infringement on their control. Within a CSR format, calculators tend to use minimalist or self-interested perspectives.
Legislators	• Attempt to create rules, programs, and committees to handle issues. Experts hired by legislators spend large amounts of time scanning the environment and passing trends on. The goal of legislators is to minimize uncertainty and avoid a head-on confrontation with issues. Legislators try to use the strategy of setting up dialogue with issue participants.	• Legislators learn issue-management skills by hiring those proficient in information gathering techniques, public opinion polling, using focus groups, forecasting trends, and the like. The legislator's task is to synthesize this data and build it into rational rules, practices, and structures. The tendency is to use social and formal contracts and— sparingly—the stakeholder (management) perspectives on CSR.
Interpreters	• Attempt to provide a meaningful story translated into the languages of participants that permits them to orient to an issue. Interpreters make sense of positions to those who are unable to do so. This requires scanning environments at a very early stage. The goal of interpreters is to make sense of change. Interpreters use the strategies of exploring options and accepting new directions.	• Interpreters' skills rest in their ability to be excellent ethnographers. They understand alternate perspectives and take a creative attitude towards the thematic structure underlying different views. They are not worried about ambiguity, fuzzy logic, or chaos. They try to figure out what the firm stands for. Interpreters try to introduce a full-bodied stakeholder (management) perspective on CSR and articulate a stake-holder (stewardship) perspective on CSR.

knocks, the legislator is trained in the modern techniques of the business school. Master of business administration (MBA) students are inundated with the legislator's skills.

The legislator is trained as an expert in the rational rules and procedures taught in the business school in various functional areas—finance, marketing, accounting, human resource management, information systems, and strategy. It is the legislator's task to synthesize these areas and bring them to bear in designing a comprehensive plan for the organization. Key decisions are to be tied to the plan. The legislator, in the design of a rational system, is to identify and nurture the core competence of the firm, develop it technologically, and shield this from disruption. The long-term goal of the legislator is to achieve organizational longevity with slow but steady growth.

Legislators are not innovators. Seeking to minimize surprises, they tie procedures, when and wherever possible, to standard operating procedures. This fits the tone and temperament of the rule maker or legislator. In this model, problems are solved. Opposition is co-opted into the legislator's plan. The plan by which the legislator rules conforms to the general model used by many organizations facing the same problems, because legislators in competitive business contracts understand the utility of organizational mimicry. They learn by benchmarking and importing—albeit with modifications for the specifics of organizational culture—the successful rules and procedures used elsewhere. The manager as legislator proceeds with a rational plan based on the best practices of other firms, plants, or organizations.

Figure 4.7 shows the legislator as someone who builds trust using information rather than the deterrence employed by the calculator. In the context of the manager as legislator, trust entails the ability to predict and anticipate events. Information, particularly clear, measurable, valid, and reliable information, is indispensable in this matter. For example, it is clear, at least from a rational rules perspective, that the more we know about the "other" in an interpersonal context, the greater is our ability to anticipate and predict their behaviour. However, unlike the calculator who relies upon monitoring to get information, the legislator relies upon the rational rules that make up the organizational plan. Legislators trust those who are free to do what they want within the rational rules as long as they are committed to and retain a loyalty to the plan. This breeds interdependence rather than the dependence of the calculator.

The legislator trusts those who are competent. Competence entails adhering to the rational rules and procedures while showing an appreciation for the organizational plan. In turn, the legislator is trusted as long as he or she remains subservient to the rational rules and procedures. Competence is established in a context where credentials, titles, memberships, and diplomas address one's socialization to a rigorous body of rational rules. Legislators surround themselves with engineers, technical planners, information analysts, accounts specialists, corporate lawyers, communication experts, accountants, public relations specialists, demographers, marketers, financial analysts, and the like. This is not the world of the self-made entrepreneur, but the context in which the pedigree of a first-rate degree from a good school, connections, and ability will raise one's star.

The legislator is someone who must anticipate issues. The legislator attempts to create rules, programs, and committees to handle issues. This is in line with the need to reduce uncertainty and generate organizational longevity with slow but steady growth and development. The legislator turns issues management over to experts who run the process. The legislator ties the issues management program to the organizational plan, and makes sure that the ideas generated in contact with stakeholders can be co-opted into the organization. The legislator uses stakeholder representatives on pertinent committees. Focus groups are employed to pick up on key constituents' views on particular issues. Public opinion polls and trend-lines are developed. Consultants who claim to understand the logic of key stake-holders—environmentalists, NIMBY participants, consumer activists—are brought into the organization for their insights. The consultants who succeed at this role are those who can make the views of these stakeholders clear within the legislator's ambit of rational rules and practices. Stakeholders' views that can be tied to the organizational plan stick; those that do not tend to fall by the wayside. Legislators may see these as well-intended, but too woolly-headed to be of use in planning the long-term well-being of the organization.

The legislator uses the strategies of minimizing the impact of issues, protecting the status quo, or—when push comes to shove—entering into dialogue with issue participants (see Figure 4.6). The desire to anticipate issues in the skill set of the legislator is motivated by the desire to minimize the impact of issues, which bring uncertainty, challenge the rational rules and practices, and call for change. It is within this situation that the legislator tends to use contracts—both formal and social—CSR perspectives, and when the stakeholders raise a sufficiently clear threat, the legislator turns to the trade-offs required in the stakeholder (management) perspective on CSR. Contracts, particularly the formal or rational-legal sort, is the mechanism preferred by the legislator. The legal contract is rational. Its interpretation, while possibly debatable, can be decided within a very clear procedural context. Contracts are time-specific. They are placed in the hands of experts. They are written down. They can be tied to the organization's plan.

Social or implicit contracts are, to the eye of the legislator, inevitable but messy. Contracts grounded in social expectations, cultural norms, and moral arguments require the sort of interpretation that cannot be as easily determined by rational procedures as can the legal contracts. These social contracts are not written down. They are not time-specific. They trouble legislators. The whole domain of organizational culture, a topic examined in the next chapter, violates the assumptions of the legislator but plays strongly to those of the interpreter. This is because organizational cultures cannot be legislated. They refer to the beliefs and values of the collectivity and the way these get expressed in everyday organizational activities.

When the legislator cannot contain issues, he or she is forced to explore the management (stakeholder) perspective in CSR. This increases the participation of those who want, even at times demand, a say in reformulating the organization's plan. The legislator, when stakeholders demand a greater say, begins to feel that a measure of uncertainty has been thrown into the organization's plan. The strategy taken by many legislators in turning to management (stakeholder) perspectives in CSR is to try to domesticate the stakeholders. There are several ways to do this. The first is to select members from the stakeholder groups who have a thorough understanding of the rational rules and practices of organizations. The second strategy involves co-opting the stakeholders' agents by giving them responsible jobs within the organization. Once they are on the payroll, it is possible to develop a third strategy—to fully socialize these stakeholders (now employees) to the rational rules and practices. The fourth and last strategy used to dampen or minimize the impact of utilizing the management (stakeholder) model is to enter into dialogue with stakeholders, but use stalling tactics. This is greatly aided by the long time frame of the typical bureaucratic organization, and its tendency to use committee procedures, documentation, and formal channels.

In all, legislators are key players in postmodern business contexts. While not at the forefront of CSR, it is impossible to render an adequate description of CSR practices without an awareness of the views of the legislator. If one is an ardent advocate of greater CSR in postmodern society, the legislator is a vast improvement over the calculator. He or she can hear economic issues. The long time frame of the legislator suits the needs of CSR advocates. The major problem is that the legislator, to put it simply, deals with varying perspectives only if they can be understood within the rational rules and practices of the organization. The legislator is skilled at bringing organizational rationality to others' perspectives, but he or she has a hard time bringing others' perspectives into the organization.

Speaking metaphorically, the legislator runs the organization as if it were a solid; whereas the interpreter treats the organization as if it were a fluid. It shifts shape depending on what sort of container it is placed in. Changing the interpretation of the organization and getting this accepted by others is the interpreter's ongoing task. Design found is soon abandoned. The abandonment is not due to an error in adaptation, but rather because of the organization's need to alter its routine to deal with new and emerging issues. The interpreter assimilates voices and, when successful, helps to turn the organization into a chorus. At the centre of this chorus is neither repetition nor even a variation on a theme, but consistently divergent perspectives licensed by management and taken by key players. It is, when push comes to shove, this divergence in response to complexity that not only calls forth the authority conferred to those who possess the skills of interpretation, but also generates the creative tension that is required in the postmodern era.

Rather than maximizing short-term profits as does the calculator, or minimizing uncertainty while pursuing organizational longevity as does the legislator, the interpreter thrives on making networks of loosely-coupled organizations eager to develop new goods and services. To do so, the interpreter seeks to be responsible to even peripheral voices. The business ethics student should not confuse "responsive" with the desire to satisfy all views and perspectives. The loose coalition of fleeting exchanges seeks to integrate the energy and dynamism of the profit-seeking traditional entrepreneur with the stability and rational planning of the strategic-minded functionary by brokering deals and innovating.

The interpreter brokers deals and innovates by being responsive to what is meaningful and valued in a society marked by accelerating change, fragmentation, and a questioning of authority. Building trust is rooted in identification-based trust (see Figure 4.7). This trust is rooted in the ability of the interpreter to make sense of others' needs, choices and values, and tie these together into a workable instrumental culture. The loose coalition of fleeting exchanges at the core of the interpreter's efforts does not rely on compliance (as does the calculator's), nor prediction (as does the legislator's), but on the building of shared meaning. This helps the interpreter to create a sense of shared destiny.

The shared destiny created by the interpreter is made real for the participants since exit from the loose coalition, given its rootedness in fleeting exchanges, is relatively easy. It is the task of the interpreter to sustain a meaningful story that enhances the participants' desire to retain coalition membership. In Figure 4.8, the interpreter succeeds when he or she makes sense of change. This, as we shall see more fully in the next chapter, provides participants with a means of reducing their anxieties over issues and mobilizing their skills in a manner they find both economically rewarding and morally responsible.

This is not to say that managers as interpreters always act ethically, but rather that they must be aware of the values they select and build into their coalitions. Interpreters lead by helping to shape opinion and give credible promise to people's aspirations. These aspirations are tied to the economic rationality of the calculator, the rational rules and practices of the legislator, and now also to the moral views of the incumbents. It is important to realize that the interpreter, true to the multiple realities or divergent viewpoints of postmodernism, does not turn his or her back on the calculator's or the legislator's story of what is required to make the good world, but rather seeks to integrate them and add to them the useful perspectives being explored by less-established but articulate others. This desire to integrate stories, to see things afresh, is realistically stimulated by the globalization of business and, within this, the discovery that in an international context the texts and stories of others can help us make sense of the good world.

In this chapter we have seen that putting CSR into practice involves no simple prescription. Trust, issues management, and interpretive skill development are difficult to build into the agenda of the organization that believes that it is doing well enough just to remain economically viable. This is understandable, and we must have sympathies for the immediate or proximate reality of many a business person. To make sense of this, the next three chapters describe where and how it is that values and value controversies arise in organizations. I have selected three illustrations of this descriptive perspective in ethics. In the next chapter we shall explore three different models for making sense of "organizational culture"—how organizations create and impact human values. In Chapter 6 we shall examine examples of processes that can lead good people morally astray, giving them "dirty hands." Finally, in Chapter 7 we shall look closely at the process of "whistle-blowing," by which employees choose to make their perception of corporate wrongdoing public. Each of these descriptions—culture, dirty hands, and whistle-blowing—gives us some understanding of the ethical processes that are ongoing in corporate life.

CASES AND QUESTIONS

CASE 4-1 Building Systems-Level Trust: Public Education and the Business Community

The 1990s have ushered in an intensifying debate over business involvement in public education. Jennifer Lewington (1997) sees this debate as a proxy for a much larger political struggle between those who see as inevitable and desirable a growing partnership between the private sector and the institutions of public education, and those who see this as neither inevitable nor desirable. Trust is difficult to build when the systems are believed to be guided by very different values.

Many business leaders believe that due to changing economic realities, global competitiveness, and fewer protected or subsidized domestic markets, there must be clear ties between the classroom and the corporate world. Eric Newall, CEO of Syncrude Canada Ltd., notes in this regard that "the only way to handle rapid change is to work together and make the workplace an extension of the classroom" (Lewington, 1997). The new links between business and the Canadian classroom go from commercial sponsorships and donations, to multidisciplinary projects with business and community groups, to promoting student learning and teacher education.

The growing ties between private sector businesses and education excites Ian Barret, the coordinator of Education/ Community Projects for the Etobicoke Board of Education. Mr. Barret estimates that his board has an approximate 555 deals with business and the local community. "It is in an explosion mode." says Barret. "We're at the beginning of the wave and not close to the crest" (Lewington, 1997). Mary Ann McLaughlin, director of the National Business and Education Centre for the Conference Board of Canada, estimates that across Canada there may be as many as 15,000 deals of the sort alluded to by Barret. McLaughlin approves of the trend, noting, "It's good to have broader community collaboration because it allays the fears that a particular partner will wield undue influence."

Proof of the benefits to be accrued in the partnership do exist. Hewlett-Packard (Canada) Ltd. worked with teachers to develop a workload for mathematics and computers pitched at Grades 4, 5, and 6, with a particular emphasis on girls. The material, which comes with a Hewlett-Packard computer, was tested in five provinces to meet the provincial ministry goals, and has been successfully integrated into the education process. Another success story is TV Ontario and Spar Aerospace's production of a video, a teacher's guide, and a Web site to support the ministry curriculum on science and technology for Grades 4 through 6 students. Using these tools, students are taught to navigate on the Internet, to do research, and to take part in experiments on life in space. The students, it seems, have been thrilled with these tools.

The other side of the debate must be heard. From this point of view, the increasing links between private sector businesses and the public institutions of education rests on the concern that the corporate sector will take advantage of schools as lucrative, captive markets for their products or services, or use them as training camps for future employees. Erika Shaker of the Canadian Centre for Policy Alternatives, which is actively monitoring the role of business in the Canadian education system, does not see business involvement in education as a necessary tool to equip schools and their students for the twenty-first century. Shaker argues that many of the so-called education/business partnerships are skewed, with the power in the relationship being decidedly in the hands of business. Words like "partnership," insists Shaker, distort the issue and lead us to believe that this is a relationship between equals and not a business-centred relationship (Lewington, 1997).

As an example of the high cost to education of the business/education partnership, many point to the $1.2 million deal between Pepsi-Cola and the Toronto Board of Education in 1994. John Doherty, one of the trustees of the Toronto Board of Education who voted for the Pepsi deal, notes that "It's become a symbol of corporate intrusion in the schools." In hindsight, the board did not explain the deal nor its motives (which still are open to debate) to the public. To the public, it seemed that the school board was striking a special deal with a manufacturer of a type of beverage that many parents seek to discourage their children from drinking. Moreover, the public worried about Pepsi-Cola's desire, one eventually rejected by the school board, to sponsor motivational school rallies and give away corporate paraphernalia to students.

Lewington is correct: our attitude towards business/education partnerships is ambivalent. When done well and with safeguards upon educational quality, there seems to be room for developing systems trust and exploring the relationship further; when done with an eye to capture a captive market or by the schools to offset the cost and/or responsibility for developing and assuring quality education, then these partnerships establish nothing but distrust and public controversy. It is through understanding how, when, and why to build trust that partnerships at the systems level become possible to create, manage, and sustain.

QUESTIONS

1. Why, in your view, do advocates of a growing partnership between the private sector and the institutions of public education distrust those who do not see this growth as either desirable or inevitable? Why is this not an individual-level problem of trust? How would the calculator, legislator, and interpreter attempt to lower the level of distrust?

2. Why is the possible commercialization of the institutions of public education a social issue and not strictly an economic issue? What trigger in the management of social issues seems to indicate to the participants in the issue activation stage whether the growing partnership between the private sector and the institutions of public education generates an opportunity or a problem?

3. Evaluate Erika Shaker's argument against the partnership. Is she trying to establish dialogue with issue participants? Is she exploring new options? Is she protecting the status quo?

4. What skill set would it take to bring all the participants into a loose coalition? What story, in your view, could best sustain the opposing parties? What values are highlighted in this story? Why these values?

5. Using the "life cycle of issues management perspectives," at what level of concern is this issue? What, in your view, would push it further down or exacerbate the distrust? If John

Doherty is correct, what can be done to rectify errors made in developing an effective partnership between business and the institutions of public education?

6. How would someone using the minimalist CSR view attempt to make sense of this case differently from someone using the stakeholder (management) perspective on CSR? Within the stakeholder (management) perspective, who in your view are the key stakeholders? Give an example of how "safeguards on the quality of education" can be used to generate trade-offs between stakeholders in the case.

CASE 4-2 A Social Issue Emerges at Palindrome Toys Incorporated

Mr. Samuel Sammler, the CEO of Palindrome Toys Incorporated, a world-wide manufacturer of children's toys located in southwestern Ontario, slammed the phone down in disgust. He had just received word from his Director of Marketing, Lawrence Rae, that another area—Brazil—had just banned their hottest new toy, the Sweet Soaker. This meant that 6 countries, 48 municipal governments, and over 700 schools had, to the knowledge of Kay Arnold's team in research, acted quickly to ban the use of the Sweet Soaker.

Palindrome had worked hard and long, devoting over $2 million and the best minds of its research department in a one-year development blitz to out-manoeuvre Kaymer Toys, its chief rival in the upscale squirt gun market. The Sweet Soaker, by Palindrome, is a high-pressure, high-volume squirt gun that comes in several sizes and enables its owners to fire shots of liquid with extreme accuracy for distances as long as 45 yards. Mr. Sammler had farmed out the manufacture of the air compression system and the gun's high-accuracy scope to Birchmount

Road Engineers. They had done an excellent job bringing both parts in to Palindrome on time, within budget, and with the specifications required. Harold Nemiroff, the engineer who had worked on the project for Birchmount Road Engineers, explicitly warned Mr. Sammler that Palindrome should attach a clear warning to users of the Sweet Soaker. The guns and rifles so equipped could be dangerous if used to surprise drivers, people working with dangerous machinery, and the like.

Mr. Sammler, always a thorough executive, ran this by his executives. They felt that they should make sure the advertising, packaging, and promotion of the gun expressed the need for due caution by users. The legal department, headed by Kendrick Clark, fully concurred with this view. The promotion and packaging thus warned that users should take care to use the Sweet Soaker for fun, but to be advised that it was capable of startling those unaware that they were targets of water-sport adventures.

The Sweet Soaker went to market at the onset of the summer vacation. Despite its cost—the most elaborate gun selling for $118.00—the gun was an instant success. The squirtguns were all the rage. For six weeks Palindrome Toys Incorporated was on top of the toy world. On 23 August, in Eugene, Oregon, it was reported that an eleven-year-old had loaded his Sweet Soaker with bleach and blinded his best friend. Within days the newspapers were inundated with reports of injuries, even a death, caused by the Sweet Soaker.

With the news growing, large stores like Woolworth's, Wal-Mart, and The Bay are taking Sweet Soaker off the shelves. Lawsuits are being prepared. In several television news reports, Palindrome Toys Incorporated has been singled out as an example of a socially-irresponsible corporation.

QUESTIONS

1. What could Mr. Samuel Sammler of Palindrome Toys Incorporated have done to anticipate the social issues? What stage in the life cycle of the issue is Palindrome in as of 25 August? Using the typology of internal sources, is this a people issue? information issue? technology issue? or distribution issue? Or is it some combination of these four issues?

2. In your view, is Palindrome Toys Incorporated morally responsible for the injuries and the death described in the case? How would the minimalist CSR perspective frame the notion of trust here? How would the management (stewardship) model of CSR frame the notion of trust here?

3. The legal department of Palindrome, headed by Kendrick Clark, has suggested that Mr. Sammler attempt to cast aspersions on Birchmount Road Engineers for failing to assure that substances other than water should not be used in Sweet Soaker. Using the calculator's approach to CSR, evaluate this option. In your view, is it fair if Palindrome Toys Incorporated goes bankrupt because of Sweet Soaker?

4. Using the legislator's frame of reference, what would you do to minimize the impact of this social issue on Palindrome Toys Incorporated? What rational rules and practices might help mitigate the issue now that the horse, so to speak, is out of the barn?

5. Using the interpreter's frame of reference, what is the best path to follow? What, in your view, is the role of the interpreter in the midst of a crisis? What, in your view, is the role of the calculator in the midst of a crisis?

6. At each of the four levels of trust in this case—individual, interpersonal, organizational, and systemic—how has a violation occurred? At the systemic level, what concrete suggestions can you make that would reduce the probability of violations like this occurring?

CASE 4-3   Canadian Mutual Fund Companies: Fun in the Sun

Andrew Willis (1997) writes that "Ethics, or lack thereof, are a hot topic in the mutual fund industry these days." The mutual fund sales personnel act as agents for the buyer, but this may not, as Willis points out, be clear to include the lavish trip to Hawaii supported by Fortune Financial Management Incorporated (FFMI) in the winter of 1996.

It seems that the Toronto-based financial planning organization, with educational purposes in mind, set up 100 of its sales staff and spouses with beachside rooms ($515 US per night) at the Four Seasons Hotel in Maui.

To complicate matters, FFMI sought to cover some of the $1,250,000 (Cdn.) cost of the excursion by requesting mutual fund companies whose products its sells to cough up to $100,000. While a few refused to have their arms twisted, Willis reports that eleven prominent fund managers did contribute to the Maui excursion. Before the employees left on the trip, FFMI issued a memorandum to those employees bound for Maui. The memo expressed gratitude to all those who supported the Maui trip, and named the companies that had loosened their hold on their wallets. Then, to cap it off, the memo aimed a barb at the money managers called the Berkshire Group, which runs the successful AIC group of Canadian mutual funds. The memo read: "NOTE: AIC, who received the 3rd highest volume of Fortune's business, is not supporting our conference. We know who our friends are!!!"

The "NOTE" was clearly a message, as Willis makes clear, to the sales staff of FFMI to soft-pedal the funds. This is a shame. AIC has been a remarkably sound performer. Willis notes that from August 1996 to August 1997, the $1.7 billion (Cdn.) AIC Advantage fund returned 82.9%, establishing it as the hottest Canadian equity fund in the nation. This was no fluke. The five-year numbers for AIC Advantage fund come in at a very healthy 35.4% annual gain. Once again—the best in Canada.

It is within the rules of the game for FFMI to ask mutual fund companies to pay for a portion of its sales staff to put on an educational forum in Maui. The rules at the Investment Funds Institute of Canada, of which FFMI is a member, prohibit a single fund company paying for more than 10% of the cost of the trip. The rules are mute on the nature of communications—that is the memo between the company offering the trip and its employees, in this case the sale staff going on the Maui excursion.

When asked to comment on this episode, Glorianne Stromberg, a commissioner at the Ontario Securities Commission, and a cru-

sader for raising the integrity of the Canadian mutual funds industry, noted that, "We've reached a point where fund managers now regard distributors as clients and this memo confirms that in spades."

QUESTIONS

1. What Fortune Financial Management Incorporated has done is legal, but is it ethical? What social issues are raised? What stakeholders are involved?

2. Analyze the memo written by Fortune Financial Management Incorporated from the point of view of the calculator, the legislator, and the interpreter. Which do you think would turn to the Ontario Securities Commission and ask for a study or report? Why do you argue this?

3. What, from the point of view of AIC Advantage Fund, is the trigger in this issue management case? Is this a people issue? a distribution issue? an information issue? or a technology issue? Why?

4. Why should the Canadian mutual fund buying public worry about the activities of Fortune Financial Management Incorporated? How, using the legislator's orientation, should this be dealt with? Who is in the best position to utilize the legislator's frame of reference in the case? Why?

5. Discuss the implications of Glorianne Stromberg's comments. How could this best be handled using a self-interested CSR perspective and then a management (stakeholder) CSR view?

6. Although we are only starting to think about organizational culture, how would you characterize the organizational culture of Fortune Financial Management Incorporated? Will it, in your view, take the strategy of minimizing impact and protecting the status quo, or of exploring new options and accepting new directions? What, in your view, will it take to get Fortune Financial Management Incorporated to explore new options?

ORGANIZATIONAL CULTURES AND THE GOOD ENOUGH WORLD

At Disneyland and Disneyworld, every person who comes onto the property (the 'set') is called a guest. Moreover, should you ever write the word at Disney, heaven help you if you don't capitalize the G.

T.J. Peters and N. Austin
A Passion for Excellence (1985)

To be a "Guest" with a capital G at Disneyland or Disneyworld, as T.J. Peters and N. Austin make clear, is to enter into an organizational culture quite distinct from that which one experiences on registering as a guest at a roadside motel (1985:41). The ethos of the first is clearly steeped in a different series of norms, values, and beliefs than the second. This also holds true for organizations engaged in similar businesses. Working for Toyota of Canada, I am told by those who do it, is quite different from carrying on the same or similar tasks at Chrysler of Canada. In my own field of work, teaching business ethics at Simon Fraser University in Vancouver involves quite a difference experience than one would have teaching business ethics at SFU's cross-town rival, the University of British Columbia.

Human cultures, understood generally, arise from peoples' ongoing struggles to manage uncertainties and create some degree of order in their lives. Clifford Geertz, in his seminal work, *The Interpretation of Cultures,* notes that "culture is the fabric of meaning in terms of which human beings interpret their experience and guide their action" (1973:140). In an organizational context, corporate or organizational culture refers to the shared beliefs, attitudes, and norms that individuals, departments, and divisions use to interpret their experiences and guide their actions (Allaire and Firsirote, 1984; Alvesson and Berg, 1992; Schultz, 1994;

Smiricich, 1983). Organizational cultures both give rise to and provide the context for the interpretation of values as they are expressed in the workplace. When organizational cultures support the values of integrity, justice, and open inquiry, we can speak of them as being ethical; on the other hand, when they nurture values that reward duplicity, enhance scheming, and look upon disputatiousness as a coveted characteristic of incumbents, it would not be out of hand to suspect such organizational cultures of being ethically problematic.

Our purpose in this chapter is not to provide an overview of the application of the concept of corporate culture to management, but to refine this topic by looking more specifically at how the concept can and is applied to understand business ethics. Figure 5.1 provides an overview of the three very different schools of thought we shall cover in this chapter. The first view, pioneered by ethnographically-minded social scientists working on business ethics (Jackall, 1988; Toffler, 1986; Martin, 1992; Mathews, 1988), proceeds by observing how the organizational culture impacts the moral behaviour of individuals, departments, and divisions within the corporation. The second perspective, advocated by contemporary moral philosophers (Boatright, 1997; DeGeorge, 1990; Freeman and Gilbert, 1988; Velasquez, 1988), articulates a normative code grounded in rights, justice, utilitarianism, and virtue—ethics that can, these philosophers conjecture, raise the level of moral behaviour in the business community. The last view, pioneered by psycho-dynamically minded analysts (Baum, 1987; Denhardt, 1981; Diamond, 1993; Hirschhorn, 1988; Schwartz, 1990), focuses on the importance of unconscious processes in determining the moral behaviour of participants in the corporate culture.

BEHAVIOURAL ETHICS VIEW OF ORGANIZATIONAL CULTURE

The idea that organizations have specific cultures, which impact their efforts at marketing, strategic planning, personnel management, and budgetary processes, has become commonplace in business literature during the past two decades. A 1980 article in *Business Week*, titled "Corporate Culture: The Hard-to-Change Values That Spell Success or Failure," opened the floodgates for a series of highly popular and eminently readable books (Deal and Kennedy, 1982; Ouchi, 1981; Peters and Waterman, 1982) that not only argued organizations had cultural properties, but that they could, with sufficient effort, be used to increase substantially the effectiveness and survival potential of the firm. This literature drew the analogy between the functions of a healthy culture in society and the functions of a healthy culture in organizations, conceived of as "societies writ small" (Allaire and Firsirote, 1984), replete with their own values, beliefs, legends, myths, stories, rituals, and ceremonies.

Rooted in the anthropological notion of culture, organizational culture has become a highly recognized but rather vague concept used in many different ways and at different levels of analysis by concept advocates (see Figure 5.2). Some use it to designate business done in the international context, where Canadians, for example, show a higher deference to authority than Americans in their business dealings. At this level the behaviour, including decision making, of organizational members is clearly influenced by the national culture in which they operate. This becomes of greater interest when organizations globalize—and operate as such—influenced by more than one national culture. The same logic holds true for regional cultures. Imagine a manufacturer of snack foods operating in six different regions in North America. From a product-design point of view it might be wise to alter the salt

FIGURE 5-1 Three Views of Organizational Culture: A Business Ethics Perspective

View	Main Premise	Ethical Implications
Behavioural Ethics View of Organizational Culture	Organizational culture is a pattern of shared artifacts, values, and basic assumptions that the group has learned to solve its problems of external adaptation and internal integration. It has worked "good enough" to be taught to new members.	In the organizational culture, the artifacts, values, and basic assumptions that are rewarded, built into structures, and taught to new members guide moral behaviour and justify actions. Ethics is an integral part of the organizational culture that can be made more effective if the culture is well-managed.
Normative Code View on Organizational Culture	The challenge is to make the organization a moral community rooted in a responsible form of capitalism. This requires that all the stakeholders of a company be respected and their claims given full recognition.	Draws on an array of philosophers from Aristotle to John Rawls to present a normative code they believe to be applicable to modern business. This code provides guidance to those seeking to make a moral business culture.
Patterns of Unconscious Organizational Culture	Organizational culture is a protection against anxiety. It functions like a defense mechanism for coping with difficult and contradictory situations. Organizational culture contains the emotionally-charged actions of members.	Ethics in organizational culture is a working-out of the group's fantasies. These include ideas of the organizational ideal, the heroic act, the responsible leader, and the "good enough" organizational culture.

content and packaging to suit the tastes of customers in regions as different as the southwestern USA and northwestern Canada and Alaska.

Industry-wide cultures (see Figure 5.2) focus on the shared beliefs, values, and norms that evolve in particular industries such as the pharmaceutical or hospitality industry. Within each industry, competing organizations develop means of problem solving to deal with similar, recurrent problems. The company-managerial culture (see Figure 5.2) is by and large the most predominant level at which behavioural ethics is addressed in works that see organizational culture as primarily a management problem. This literature views organizational culture as one more tool in the arsenal of effective managers. As we shall see, it is a tool that seems capable of solving a myriad of problems.

Beneath the company-managerial culture are organizational subcultures. These evolve within the larger organizational culture with some degree of autonomy. The professional culture within an organization refers to the shared values, belief norms, and attitudes of various

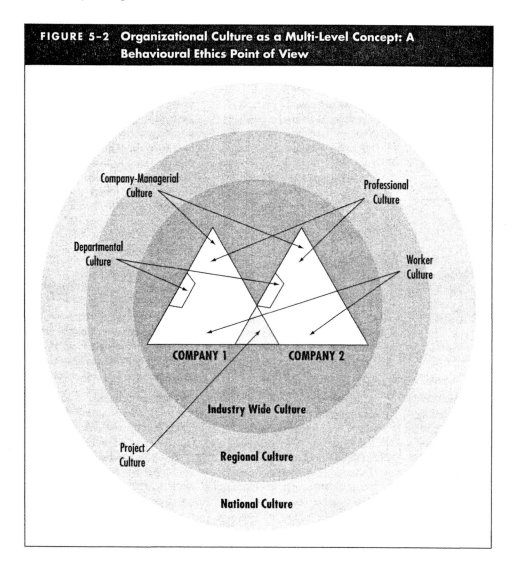

FIGURE 5-2 Organizational Culture as a Multi-Level Concept: A Behavioural Ethics Point of View

professionals (lawyers, accountants, information analysts, ethics ombudspersons, engineers) who may be housed in the firm. Professionals owe their allegiance not only to the firm that hires them, but also to professional associations from which they receive their credentials. Project cultures may be shared between two or more companies, or emerge for temporary assignments within one firm. They often have a special assignment. They bring together people from different parts of the organization with different skills and often different views. Worker cultures receive attention when there is a perceived misalignment between the worker culture and the needs of the organization as a whole. This becomes particularly relevant when the worker culture is unionized, or when it resists changes sought by management.

We need not exhaust the permutations and combinations that can occur when, in using the concept of organizational culture, analysts slide—often without signalling their intentions—from one level to the next. This is because the behavioural ethics view of organizational culture retains a strong functional orientation—even when it is tinged with the postmodernist view of these cultures as complex webs of symbols. Functionalist views of organizational culture—whether rational, structural, or symbolic (see Figure 5.3)—all perceive it as helping the organization and its members to cope with uncertainty and to achieve some confidence that the "way things are done around here" serves a purpose.

In *Organizations: Rational, Natural and Open Systems* (1992), W.R. Scott—leaning upon the work of sociologist Talcott Parsons—notes the following needs of an organization enabling it to act as a small society:

1. Adaptation: the functional necessity to acquire sufficient resources to persist over time

2. Goal attainment: the functional necessity of achieving the objectives that the organization consciously pursues

3. Integration: the functional necessity of maintaining solidarity or coordination among the subculture (worker culture, departmental culture, project culture, etc.)

4. Latency: the functional necessity of transmitting values and know-how that enables the organization to retain its distinctiveness over time

These functions are met, the behavioural ethics advocates insist, not only by the formal structure of the organization, but also by its organizational culture. Functionalism seeks to discern the use-value or utility of a social or, as in our discussion, organizational structure.

Rational functionalism, the most pragmatic of behavioural ethics views of organizational culture, treats it as a management tool. In their groundbreaking work, *In Search of Excellence* (1982), Tom Peters and R.H. Waterman portray organizational cultures in highly effective organizations as those that promote the values of responsiveness, integrity, innovativeness, team building, and learning. Moreover, the authors suggest that by emulating these characteristics, managers in less effective organizations can reap many of these features of excellence. R. Kilmann and his colleagues compiled a book called *Gaining Control of the Corporate Culture* (1985), which champions this form of rational functionalism. In their eyes, organizational cultures can be managed so as to achieve better results. The secret rests in being able to utilize key tracks and levels within the culture to close cultural gaps and bring the expectations of participants closer into alignment with the reality of the organizational culture.

As Figure 5.3 makes clear, the rational functionalist perspective highlights the manager's use of organizational culture to manage, solve problems, and get results. Stories, rites, rituals, symbols, and values do not simply evolve to meet the needs of adaptation, goal attainment, integration, and latency, but, in the hands of the rational functionalists, organizational cultures can be used consciously by managers to solve certain problems. In this orientation, organizational culture is treated as a tool that can be manipulated—with sufficient dexterity—to meet specific ends. Within the rational functionalist perspective it can be argued that if the organization's dominant elite manages the organizational culture effectively, it may be possible, for example, to minimize the costly demands of unions or to accelerate organizational learning and innovation.

This discussion has been extended to argue that it is possible to get beyond merely influencing the task-performance of organizational incumbents, but also to "manage" their display of emotions in order, for example, to get fast food workers to smile during their interactions with customers, or to get check-out clerks in chain stores to make eye contact and show positive feelings towards customers as they leave after paying. This, from an ethical perspective, is worrying. It addresses the possibility that in postmodernity, organizations

Perspective	View of Organization	View of Organizational Culture	Ethical Implications
FIGURE 5-3 Three Orientations in the Behavioural Ethics Approach to Organizational Culture: Ethical Implication			
Rational Functionalism	The organization is a means designed to attain efficient ends.	Organizational culture is one of many tools useful in achieving the organization's goals.	Organizational culture can be manipulated. This view of organizational culture as a form of control can be ethically disquieting.
Symbolic Functionalism	The organization is a human expression of a complex set of symbolic actions.	Organizational culture is an ongoing effort to work out meaning in the context of complexity and change.	Organizational culture can be used to explain and justify any ethical behaviour.
Structural Functionalism	The organization is a collective or community that seeks to survive by performing the necessary functions.	Organizational culture is a shared pattern of artifacts, values, and basic assumptions emerging to help cope with problems of external adaptation and internal integration.	Organizational culture evolves to deal with ethical issues. Business ethicists worry about surfacing tokenistic adaptations to external issues and internal integration.

seek to purchase more than merely one's time, but one's emotional demeanour as well. Nowhere is this more clear than in the socialization and training of new employees. The "emotional quotient" of members to the organizational culture becomes as important as the "intelligence quotient." The emotional quotient measures the member's ability to retain his or her emotional resilience in the midst of troublesome and personally compromising situations. The ethics of emotion management by the corporation has been tacit in most theories of bureaucracy. In these it is assumed that emotions get in the way of a value-neutral reliance upon rules and objective reason. In this context the "good enough world" is one in which the organizational culture can be used by management to increase the firm's effectiveness and probability of survival.

From a business ethics perspective, the rational functionalist view assumes a cavalier attitude that organizational culture is and ought to be in the service of managers. As we shall see when we look at the "normative code" view of organizational culture, this is because a good deal of time is spent attempting to educate managers to a notion of rights, justice, and utilitarian reasoning as a means to assure that those in the organization's governance structure have some idea of the ethical issues that go into an enlightened organizational culture. The rational functionalists duck this responsibility. In their zeal to sell the idea of organizational culture, they seem to insist that—if handled properly—it can reap substantial returns to the patient manager.

In fairness to the advocates of the rational functionalist view of organizational culture, they do position themselves in an interesting manner. They view their investment in the rites, rituals, ceremonies, stories, and language of the organization as a costly but "deep" and persistent way in which to introduce change. They contrast this with the "off the shelf" quick fixes of many consultants. The use of organizational culture, insist the advocates of the rational functionalist position, compels consultants to work closely with the actual organization, tailoring their intervention to the specifics of the culture in question. While not educating managers directly, as do those calling for the normative code, they can and do claim to be involving managers or their agents in the fashioning of the intervention.

Symbolic functionalists (see Figure 5.3) view the organization as a human expression of a complex set of symbolic actions (Alvesson and Berg, 1992; Gagliardi, 1992; Pondy *et al.*, 1983). Linda Smiricich characterizes organizational culture as "webs of meaning, organized in terms of symbols and representations ... to study social significance—how things, events and interactions come to be meaningful" (1983:63). The symbolists, while still rooted in creating and "understanding," which will help the organization meet its functional requisites, take the problem-solving edge out of the rational functionalist conception of organizational culture.

To the symbolists, organizational culture consists of the members' socially defined and meaningful realities that reflect the specific organization's special way of life. The myths, organizational stories, and rituals permit members to discover and invent meaning within the context of the collective. This meaning is neither frivolous nor part of the "informal organization," but an integral part of the way important events are coded, rewards are distributed, and strategic realignments are created. The symbolic nature of organizational culture signifies that meaning is achieved; it can not simply be assumed. Whereas the rational functionalists assume that the task is to make the organization more effective by managing the shared meanings within the organizational culture, the functional symbolists ask first how meaning is created in organizational cultures, and then how it becomes shared.

Symbols thus provide indicators of meaning and meaningfulness in organizational cultures. Symbols differ from signs in that a sign makes reference to what it represents whereas a symbol stands for something else. The red stop sign tells drivers that they must bring their automobiles to a full stop and wait until the intersection is free of traffic, both vehicular and pedestrian, before proceeding. The symbol of the Canadian flag, on the other hand, stands for home and a way of being in the world that we call Canadian. When one uses the flag, the meaningfulness of home remains, yet the specifics of a home in Dartmouth, Nova Scotia or Yellowknife, Northwest Territories vary. The symbol evokes membership in a culture in which shared meanings are tied to unique experiences.

The symbolic functionalists classify symbols based on their degree of visibility, the level of consciousness in their formation, and, of course, their function within the organization. In essence the symbolic functionalist distinguishes among the different types of symbols in the organizational culture—physical symbols (physical layout, logos, attire, graphic design of memos); behavioural symbols (rituals, ceremonies, rites); and verbal symbols (myths, sagas, stories). The task of the symbolist is to put together how organization members, including stakeholders, create shared patterns of meaning that link the organization's symbols to a larger world view and—most important for business ethicists—to an ethos. The world view is the way in which, given organizational culture, participants make sense of how what they are doing contributes to the larger world—the idea of self, society, nature, and the economy. The ethos, on the other hand, refers to the moral concerns that are raised within a world view.

In the symbolic functionalist perspective on organizational culture, the emphasis is upon exploring the ways in which humanly constructed symbolic worlds like that of the post-modern organization influence participants. The approach here, as with rational functionalism, is ethnographic and descriptive. The symbolic functionalist view distinguishes between symbols like rituals, stories, and uniforms—that are functional and enhance meaning—and those that add little, even detract from making events, things, and relationships meaningful. We have all grown accustomed to this in our understanding of metaphor as a useful symbol. In the hands of some of the most competent symbolic functionalists (Barley, 1983; Morgan, 1986; Raspa, 1992), metaphor is given a special pedagogical role, that of helping people to widen their understanding of what is meaningful. The "like" in the metaphor associates two items in such a way that each is put into a new light. However, it is clear that some metaphors, for example, the leg of a table or the analogy between a king and a lion, once chock-full of implications, are now rather passé.

So, too, symbolic functionalists must distinguish between and among those organizational cultures that are functional in terms of stimulating shared meaning and those that are not. Ethical concerns emerge. Symbols can be used to overcome an individual's sense of self-worth, to stereotype, and to demean. Symbols now become open to conscious management by those interested in ends that might depart from the ethnographies of the symbolic func-tionalist. It may be important for marketers to know what symbols provide a deep sense of personal involvement and meaning for various demographic groups. It may be important for those fully immersed in a power culture to utilize the symbolic functionalists' analysis of or-ganizational cultures to learn which stories and legends function best in getting others to come under their influence. It is clear, as the symbolists tell us, that leadership is increasingly a language (symbol) game. It may be problematic for many of us in the study of business ethics to learn that a community of scholars motivated by scholarly concerns is inadver-tently revealing that the game has set moves, opening gambits, and symbolic formulae with proven track records.

The third orientation in the behavioural ethics approach to organizational culture (see Figure 5.3), the structural functionalist approach, depicts it as a shared pattern of artifacts, values, and basic assumptions evolving as a means of solving ongoing organizational prob-lems. The seminal book by Edgar Schein, *Organizational Culture and Leadership* (1992), provides a good conceptual base for this perspective. The popular book by Charles Handy, *Understanding Organizations* (1985), can be used to illustrate how ethical quandaries are dealt with differently in four kinds of structural functionalist organizational cultures.

In Schein's book, the organization is treated as if it were a biological organism; it must successfully perform several vital functions in order to perpetuate itself and survive. Schein makes it clear in his structural functionalist approach to organizational cultures that the or-ganization must resolve two fundamental and ongoing problems: first, the organization must survive in and adapt to the external environment; second, the organization must integrate or coordinate its internal processes to assure continuity.

In Schein's structural functionalist reasoning, organizational culture arises as an unin-tended by-product of the organization's attempt to survive. It is a means whereby organizations link together or create a metaphorical "glue" that permits the components to adhere and yet re-tain sufficient degrees of autonomy and discretion to enhance the probability of survival. As well, organizational culture evolves to facilitate the organization's need to adapt and change in an organizational world in which it is dependent on others outside itself for its survival.

While integration and adaptation are necessary to an organizational culture, they are in themselves not sufficient. The organizational culture must be seen as good enough at accomplishing these ends that it becomes the unquestioned way in which things are done in the organization.

While different organizations face the same fundamental problems, each develops a unique organizational culture. Organizational culture functions as the basis for a survival-learning process that is embedded in the organization's ability to generate shared assumptions. These shared assumptions, insists Schein, do not come about magically, but rather they are found in three discernible levels within the organization. Figure 5.4 outlines the three different levels: (1) artifacts, (2) values, and (3) basic assumptions. Whereas values and artifacts are the organization's more surface or conscious manifestations, the basic assumptions or "taken for granted" aspects of the organizational culture often remain buried and difficult to access.

In Schein's thinking, the artifact level comprises visible and audible behaviour patterns among the organization's members, as well as a number of technological and physical components. Artifacts exist at the surface and function to solve the problems of internal integration and external adaptation.

In Schein's structural functionalist approach, values are imbued with the normative code (see Figure 5.1), which we shall take up more fully in the next section of this chapter. They orient action. They guide in learning and evaluation. Schein writes that "all group learning ultimately reflects someone's original values, someone's sense of ... what is right and what is wrong, what will work or not work ..." (1992:19). Values thus can be assessed. They consist of what the participants within an organizational culture say during and about situations. They are not the doing itself but the reflection upon it—the response to the question of "why." Schein reminds us that organizations do not evolve cultures that reveal linear or logical assemblages of values. When we create value lists of organizational cultures we will find that contradictions abound in even the most functional of them. People give explanations for their behaviour that do not match their actual behaviour. In fact, in the hands of the unconscious organizational culture analysts (see Figure 5.1), much of the value as expressed in organizations is seen as useful collective fantasies permitting members to avoid confronting the contradictions between what they do and how they explain it.

In Schein's third level of organizational culture in the structural functionalist perspective, the basic assumptions are neither visible, audible, or otherwise detectable by human sensory organs, nor self-reflexively available (see Figure 5.4). They are deeply buried within the culture and seem self-evident to fully-fledged members of the organization. These basic assumptions "tell group members how to perceive, think about, and feel about things" (1992: 22). The basic assumptions "have become so taken for granted that one finds little variation within a cultural unit" (1992:21).

It is in the structural functionalist perspective on organizational culture that we begin to see how an individual's ethical behaviour, values, and basic assumptions can be formed and altered through membership and/or participation in the organization. Basic assumptions are not critically tested by new members of the organization. This easy acceptance of premises is bolstered by a system in which one's mentors inadvertently communicate the basic premises, which in turn are reinforced by the reward system. The stories of key events are framed in terms that tacitly imprint them upon new members. What the structural functionalists formulate for the business ethicist is the possibility that some organizations not only engage in questionable ethical behaviour, but that they have these premises buried deep within the unexamined basic assumptions of the organizational culture.

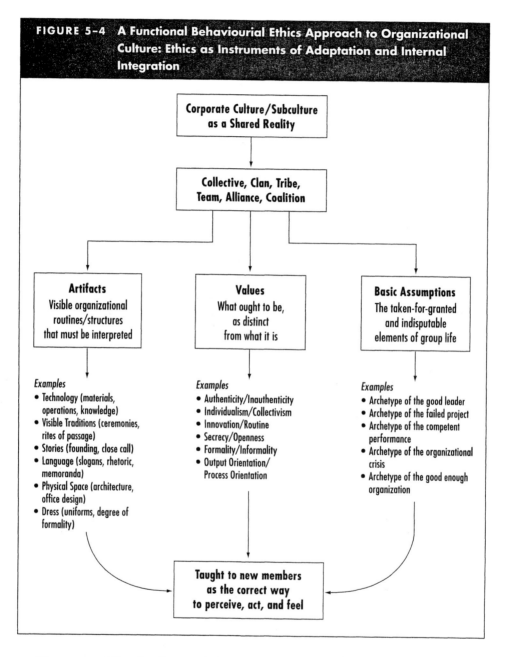

FIGURE 5-4   A Functional Behaviourial Ethics Approach to Organizational Culture: Ethics as Instruments of Adaptation and Internal Integration

Corporate Culture/Subculture as a Shared Reality

Collective, Clan, Tribe, Team, Alliance, Coalition

Artifacts
Visible organizational routines/structures that must be interpreted

Examples
- Technology (materials, operations, knowledge)
- Visible Traditions (ceremonies, rites of passage)
- Stories (founding, close call)
- Language (slogans, rhetoric, memoranda)
- Physical Space (architecture, office design)
- Dress (uniforms, degree of formality)

Values
What ought to be, as distinct from what it is

Examples
- Authenticity/Inauthenticity
- Individualism/Collectivism
- Innovation/Routine
- Secrecy/Openness
- Formality/Informality
- Output Orientation/Process Orientation

Basic Assumptions
The taken-for-granted and indisputable elements of group life

Examples
- Archetype of the good leader
- Archetype of the failed project
- Archetype of the competent performance
- Archetype of the organizational crisis
- Archetype of the good enough organization

Taught to new members as the correct way to perceive, act, and feel

The structural functionalists remind us that individual ethics can be greatly influenced and modified—at times unbeknownst to the individual—by the adoption of the artifacts, values, and basic assumptions of the organizational culture. This absorption into the culture clearly increases with one's commitment to and central identification with the organization. In the name of its survival and growth, individuals can become accomplices in collective actions—such as pollution and sensitivity to the needs of others—which as individuals they rail against.

To illustrate the structural functionalist view of organizational culture, let us turn to Charles Handy's simple but powerful delineation of four ideal types of organizational culture: the role culture, the task (achievement) culture, the power culture, and the person (support) culture. In *Understanding Organizations* (1985), Handy illustrates how each of the four ideal organizational cultures handles the organizational problems of internal integration and external adaptation.

The role culture utilizes tight job descriptions, task specialization, and interdependence to integrate internal components. External adaptation entails uncertainty avoidance, where every effort is made to protect the hierarchy of roles within the organization and to retain the basic assumptions of the organizational culture. The role culture seeks to separate itself where and whenever possible from its environment by emphasizing its external boundaries as a form of closure or separation.

In the task or achievement culture, the entrepreneurial personality is the basic ingredient of the organizational culture. Individualization is everything; the personalities of key players are given full rein. The internal integration is tied to the delegation skills of the entrepreneur. This often limits the size of task or achievement cultures. When they become large they are usually made up of small functional areas loosely held together by a coalition. What predominates is the small functional unit, suited to the skills, ability, and/or charisma of the entrepreneur. External adaptation is achievement-based. The task culture is a problem solver and innovator, quick to utilize new technologies or adapt old ones to new problems and applications. The innovations in the task culture are usually stimulated by a heavy degree of competition. Rather than avoiding uncertainty, as does the role culture, the task culture seeks it out.

The power culture, like the role culture, is rooted in control by regulation. However, in the power culture, control is hierarchical but governed by direct supervision rather than relying upon impersonal rules. The key players in the power culture are not the gifted entrepreneurs of the task culture, but strong personalities capable of imposing their wills upon others. In many instances the governing elite in these cultures retain their positions over time. Power culture prevails in large, family-run enterprises and nepotistic networks, which are embedded in oligopolistic forms of organizational governance. Diana C. Pheysey, in *Organizational Cultures: Types and Transformations* (1993), is only half-joking in her use of the Mafia as an example of a power culture. The power culture adapts to the external environment by confrontation and conquest.

The last of Handy's four ideal types is the person or support culture. Within the ambit of discussions by contemporary business ethicists, the person culture is often treated as exemplary. In fairness to the insights we get from the structural functionalists, the person culture evolves to handle the problems of internal integration and external adaptation in ways that may not prove feasible in all organizational cultures. These organizations emphasize the mobilization of dialogue through the building of an appreciative culture that emphasizes mutuality, relationships, and connectedness. The person culture seeks to deal with the problems of internal integration by reinforcing collaborative control with mutual accountability. This increases the generativity of the culture. The person culture adapts to its external environment by increasing dialogue and involvement with stakeholders. Rather than raise the boundaries in an effort to achieve closure and separation (as does the role culture), the person culture lowers its boundaries and turns to a strategy of inclusion. It is clear that personal cultures take free flow of ideas as their key resource.

Each of these four ideal-type cultures will express itself with different artifacts, values, and basic assumptions. But what is most important is that ethical quandaries pertinent to each of them are rooted deeply in their basic assumptions. Figure 5.5 outlines how, as we move from one culture to another—i.e. the role culture to a task culture—particular ethical issues are expected to arise. In effect, Figure 5.5 maps not only how the four ideal types give rise to ethics issues, but also how the hybrids of organizational cultures that rest between and among the four wrestle with ethical issues.

As we explore organizational cultures from the behavioural ethics view, we begin to develop the skills to interpret basic assumptions. In doing this we become aware that organizational cultures not only encourage a particular way to handle ethics issues, but also point to ways in which arguments will be made as one organizational culture is bombarded with views from those in another. In Figure 5.5 we see how the role culture normally seeks to handle ethics quandaries by establishing efficiently administered ethics programs and committees. When viewed from the task or achievement culture this methodology is seen as too legalistic, bureaucratic, and proceduralist. The task culture, as we have seen, seeks to handle its ethics quandaries by searching for innovative solutions and opportunities. From the point of view of those immersed in the role culture, the task-culture approach to ethics looks like a form of withdrawal, or an escapist attitude towards very real problems. For example, the role-culture advocates see the true believers of the task culture as failing to deal with the issues of global warming and environmental degradation, and relying too optimistically on unproven technologies and quick-fix solutions.

To take another example, this time along the diagonal or interior axis, let us look at how the person culture deals with incumbents from the role culture and vice versa. The person or support culture handles ethics quandaries by relying upon a strategy of inclusiveness and dialogue. In the business literature this participative or team-based ideology is highly prized. However, from the perspective of the role culture with its specialized experts, these teams, dialogue, and the ethos of participation are seen as inefficient, inconsistent, and subjective. On the other hand, members of the person culture are disappointed by the role culture's strategy, which is viewed as too static, impersonal, and hierarchical to deal with the ethics of caring.

While we will not exhaust the permutations and combinations of views illustrated in Figure 5.5, this mapping suggests that business ethicists can learn much from attending to the behavioural ethics view of organizational culture. The rationalist, symbolic, and structural functionalist views suggest that organizations evolve cultures that can give shape to values and basic assumptions, and that these are moral worlds that are more or different than the sum of the moral values of the individuals within them. Where the behavioural ethics view lets us down is in its failure to tell us how to establish an ethical culture. It sees organizational culture and the values and basic assumptions therein as an adaptation to the organizational exigencies it describes. Even when it turns prescriptive it merely describes how organizations can mimic or emulate other organizational cultures, those which, in the eyes of the analyst and no doubt in profit ledgers, are perceived as excellent.

THE NORMATIVE CODE

Tom Donaldson, in "The Third Wave" (1989), explores three waves in the development of the field of business ethics since the 1970s. The first wave, in Donaldson's version of the early years, were texts full of admonitions regarding caring capitalism, corporate responsibility, and due diligence. These texts were atheoretical, well-intentioned, and fully cognizant of

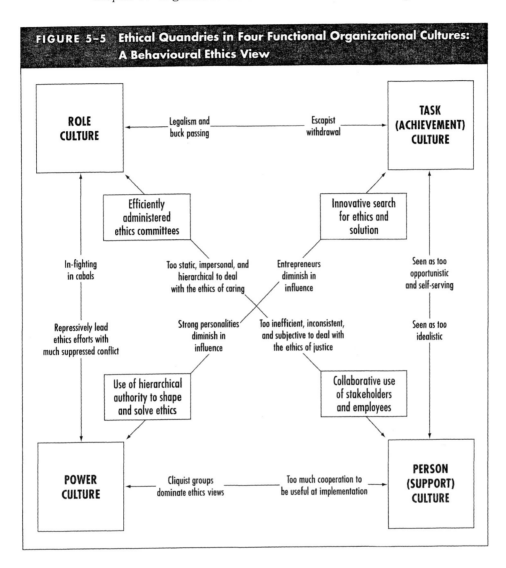

FIGURE 5-5 **Ethical Quandries in Four Functional Organizational Cultures: A Behavioural Ethics View**

business ethics as an issue. The second wave, in which the normative code on corporate culture was born, brought in a bevy of moral philosophers interested in bringing classical moral philosophy to practise in the business school. The third wave, of which this book is an example, is an attempt to turn business ethics into a recognizable body of interdisciplinary views brought to bear on the very real nature of business as a moral world that must be confronted with a moral language.

This second wave is now well established in a series of successful textbooks (Beauchamp and Bowie, 1983; Boatright, 1997; DeGeorge, 1990; Shaw and Barry, 1992; Velasquez, 1988). These, along with others, draw on normative principles long embedded in the history of Western thought. These authors draw on Aristotle, Plato, and lesser classical thinkers, and conjoin these with an interpretation of the works of Thomas Hobbes, Jean-Jacques Rousseau, Immanuel Kant, Adam Smith, John Locke, David Hume, Jeremy Bentham, John Stuart

Mill, and most contemporaneously, the works of Robert Nozick and John Rawls. "From this philosophic stew," writes William C. Frederick in *Values, Nature and Culture in the American Corporation,* they have "extracted the essence of a normative code thought to be applicable to modern business practice" (1995:219). This normative code provides a series of insights on how to best build an organizational culture.

There are four pillars upon which the normative code view of organizational culture rests: rights, justice, utilitarianism, and virtue. The simplified moral philosopher's formula reads: $EBB - R_k + J_r + U_{\beta m} + V_A$, wherein EBB equals, within this prescriptive view, ethical business behaviour; R_k stands for Kantian reasoning on duties and rights; J_r represents John Rawls' views on justice applied to organizational cultures; $U_{\beta m}$ signifies the utilitarian reasoning of Jeremy Bentham and John Stuart Mill, modernized under the guise of act and rule-utilitarianism; and lastly, V_A is the need for organizational culture to facilitate the building of character or virtue, in the Aristotelian sense, at its very heart.

Before we look at each of these pillars in the moral philosopher's version of the normative code of organizational culture, we must note that this view, unlike the behavioural ethics view, does not seek to present examples of best business practices, or the views of accomplished managers as guides to the good enough organizational culture. Advocates of the normative code comb the texts of moral philosophers, selecting ideas which, they argue, when put into the educational curriculum of management education and into practice by corporations, will result in ethical behaviour. Their methodology is interpretive. However, rather than turn to the organizational culture's artifacts, values, and basic assumptions of life as their interpretive data, the normative code looks at the texts of philosophers who, over the last two thousand years, have attempted to elucidate how to build the ethical community.

Figure 5.6 outlines all four of the pillars. The first pillar in the typical normative code espoused by moral philosophers is drawn from an interpretation of Immanuel Kant's "categorical imperative," which requires that everyone should be treated as a free person equal to every other person. That is, as Manuel Velasquez writes, "everyone has a moral right to such treatment and everyone has the correlative duty to treat others in this way" (1988:90). Kant takes what advocates of the normative code on organizational culture term a deontological or non-consequentialist position on determining what is and is not ethical behaviour. Kant argues that we can determine what is and is not ethical behaviour *a priori,* or by principles and reason alone, and not by a calculation of whether its benefits outstrip its costs. This is in contrast to the utilitarian reasoning that makes up part of the normative code perspective (see Figure 5.6). Kant's ethics contend that we do not have to know anything about the likely results of, for example, an employee of a large firm offering a bribe to a government official to get a contract, in order to know if it is moral or immoral.

The advocates of the normative code perspective rely on two formulations of Kant's "categorical imperative" and its application to the postmodern organizational context to solidify this first pillar of the code. The two formulations can be summarized as follows. The first formulation, often called the "maxim of universality," argues that to act morally you should do what you would expect anyone else to do in the situation in which you find yourself. In operationalizing the first formulation you cannot allow yourself to pick or choose which bills you will settle this month, if any, unless you would also be happy that those who are indebted to you can do precisely the same thing. The second formulation, often called the "maxim of respect," argues that what makes an action right is that the organization or its agents treat human beings as ends in themselves. To normative code advocates, the maxim of respect means treating individuals with a full recognition that they must give

FIGURE 5-6 Components of the Normative Code: Premises and Implications for Organizational Culture

Duties and Rights

Components	Premises	Implications for Organizational Culture
Kant's Categorical Imperative	Two premises are combined in Kant's Categorical Imperative. The first states that an action is morally right in a situation when others would be allowed, for the same reason in similar situations, to do the same. The second views a moral action as one that does not use others to advance one's own interest, but respects their capacity to choose freely for themselves.	Kantian rights prescribe that businesses treat others as if they were entitled to respect, and the principle of universalizability insists that the actions in the organizational culture should be consistent with people asking the question "What if everyone did that?"

Justice

Components	Premises	Implications for Organizational Culture
Rawls' Justice as Fairness	To act fairly, Rawls suggests that we combine two principles. The "principle of equal liberty" states that each person has an equal right to the most basic liberties compatible with similar liberties for all. The "difference principle" states that social and economic inequalities be arranged so that they are both to the greatest benefit of the least advantaged persons and attached to offices and positions open to all under conditions of fair equality of opportunity.	Organizational cultures should act so as to value freedom, equality of opportunity, and a concern for the disadvantaged. This view is compatible with the market system, work incentives, and specialization. The community is tended to by the wealthy assisting the disadvantaged; however, individuals are free to pursue their interests.

Utilitarianism

Components	Premises	Implications for Organizational Culture
Bentham's and Mill's Social Costs and Benefits	Utilitarian reasoning insists that, to act ethically, one weigh one's alternatives and select the one that brings the greatest benefits to the largest numbers. In its classical statement, benefit is tied to hedonism; in its more contemporary form in both act- and rule-utilitarianism it's tied to an overall conception of well-being.	Organizational cultures must weigh alternatives with care, not only with regard to personal gain or even to economic gain, but to select options that have the highest probability of returning the greatest benefit to the greatest number. The inclusion of stakeholders is encouraged by advocates of the normative code.

Virtue (Character) Ethics

Components	Premises	Implications for Organizational Culture
Aristotle's Practical Wisdom	Rather than see ethics as a constraint on what we can do, virtue ethics asks the question of how to best build character in communities that are successful. The position of contemporary virtue ethics in business argues that business means achieving the good life. This includes rewarding, fulfilling work, honesty in actions, and a respect for oneself and others.	Organizational cultures must build character that is rewarded for the virtues of honesty, benevolence, compassion, courtesy, dependability, friendliness, loyalty, and accountability. These virtues are facilitated when the culture facilitates the individual in his or her pursuit of community, excellence, membership, integrity, good judgment, and an understanding of the big picture.

free consent to their behaviours, and that the firm has an obligation to develop each person's capacity to make choices pertinent to their role within the organization.

Kant, from the viewpoint of most practising business persons, is idealistic. Modern advocates of the normative code perspective do not employ Kant's work to provide a neat list of rights and duties to which the ethical business person ought to adhere. Rather, within the code, Kantian ethics are mobilized to accomplish three tasks that to some degree are not easily accomplished in the Rawlsian perspective on justice, the interpretation of utilitarianism stimulated by a modern reading of Bentham and Mill, or in the application of Aristotelian virtue ethics. The advocates of the normative code perspective liberally interpret and mobilize Kant's deontological ethics to: (1) show that these are reasonable principles underlying moral problems; (2) that the determination of the good in business is rooted in the principled intentions of the actors; and (3) that the primacy Kant gives the individual reflects the essential function of business.

The importance of showing that there are reasonable principles that can be assessed by reasonable men and women as underlying moral problems is a key virtue of Kantian ethics. We are warned by the normative code advocates not to treat moral worlds as subsets of efficiency problems. We are warned that re-engineering, altering job descriptions, or even developing a better means of testing for the moral development of key personnel will not suffice as responses to moral quandaries. Kant's ethics are not dependent upon the personalities of the players, the depth of one's career involvement, or the consequences likely to ensue from selecting one rather than another option. Like an Old Testament prophet, but one calling for reason over faith, Kant appeals to and makes sense in the postmodern world view. Lying, for example—no matter how much good may come from misrepresenting a product, or from a government under-representing to its citizens the casualties suffered in an international conflict—can never be ethical. Using the maxim of universality, it is clear that one would feel uncomfortable universalizing a view that all firms could misrepresent their products when doing so would increase profits, stimulate corporate growth, and therefore enhance a region's employment rate. Equally so, we would feel remiss if we licensed a view that all countries in battle could under-represent their casualties so that troop motivation, the support of the general population, and therein the ability to mobilize resources to the front would not be affected adversely.

The normative code advocates utilize Kant's notion of duty and rights to stress the centrality of motivation and of acting on principle. The deontological view advanced by Kant and highlighted by advocates of the code focuses on the fact that it is not enough to do the right thing; an action has genuine moral worth only if it stems from a sense of duty. This sense of duty is understood as the desire to do the right thing for its own sake. When Gordon Gekko, in the movie *Wall Street,* argues that "greed" is a good thing, he is, in the eyes of a modern Kantian, rationalizing. This occurs when people, most often in highly competitive contexts, believe that they truly are promoting others' interests when they promote their own. Kantian notions of duty serve as a strong and, in the eyes of the normative code advocate, necessary tonic to this view. The instrumental ethos in the respect maxim bears the same caution. Within a Kantian perspective it is difficult to argue clearly that one is doing good by treating others as means to ends that you seek and they do not.

Lastly, Kantian ethics, as refurbished by the moral philosophers advocating the normative code, elevates the individual and individual dignity and freedom. The view is humanistic. Morality is not merely a search for constraints to rein in the greedy and libidinous side of the business person; it is, as well, an emancipating quest. The morally motivated business person finds his or her moral centre in relationship to the dignity he/she is able to confer upon others. The admonition not to treat others instrumentally is also a suggestion to provide others with the freedom to choose, grow, and develop. This search for the inherent worth and dignity of human beings is much needed in business today, where the encroaching of surveillance techniques, drug testing, and downsizing all help to formulate a vocabulary that places the individual in the service of the system.

The second pillar of the normative code perspective (see Figure 5.6) is the notion of justice, particularly distributive justice, rooted in John Rawls' *A Theory of Justice* (1971). Disputes in business, whether between or among individuals, departments, or branch plants within a divisionalized corporate structure, are often interlaced with references to "justice" or "fairness," or of the lack of these. "Justice," writes Richard T. DeGeorge in *Business Ethics*, "in an age of its formulation, consists in giving each person his or her due, treating equals equally and unequals unequally" (1990:104). DeGeorge, like other normative code advocates, notes that there are basically four different kinds of justice useful for students of business ethics. Compensatory justice, as we are learning in Canada's efforts to come to terms with its moral obligation to Native Canadians, entails compensating others for past injustices or transgressions, and/or attempting to ameliorate a harm the other has suffered. Retributive justice involves punishing one who is believed to have acted illegally, unethically, or both. Procedural justice is a concept that preoccupies those pursuing justice in bureaucratic contexts, and is employed to designate that the practices, agreements, and decision procedures are enacted as specified. Distributive justice, the notion of justice that is central to the normative code advocate, arises when different people or divisions put forth conflicting claims, in a context of scarcity in which all claims can not be satisfied.

Given these different conceptions of justice, what we need is a comprehensive normative theory that can draw these views together into a logical perspective. Rawls' *A Theory of Justice*, thought to be the most influential work of the postwar period, is the closest advocate of the normative code approach to fit the bill. Velasquez writes that "John Rawls provides one approach to distributive justice that at least approximates this ideal of a comprehensive theory " (1988:100). This theory does not reduce justice to social, economic, or political utility, but is grounded in a Kantian view. Rawls' theory purports to arrive at principles of distributive justice that are acceptable to all rational persons.

To this end two main features of Rawls' theory are very important: 1) his hypothetical-contract approach; and 2) the two principles he derives using the hypothetical-contract approach. To present an overview of Rawls' theory one must attend first to his methodology, which is unlike that employed by most analysts one reads in business ethics. Rawls' strategy is to ask us as rational persons what we would select as the basic principles to govern a human system if we were to meet for this purpose in what he calls "the original position." In this original position, Rawls asks us to pretend that we are meeting with other free and equal persons desirous of advancing their own interests. We are going to attempt to arrive at unanimous agreement on the fundamental rules of distribution in our human systems. Furthermore, in the original positions we are beneath what Rawls terms the "veil of ignorance" (1971:136). Under the veil of ignorance, all people are equally ignorant about their personal predicaments. They do not know if they are tall or short, white or black, men or women. The veil of ignorance, in effect, forces people in the original position to be objective and impartial when pursuing their interests.

Rawls then argues that since the circumstances of the original position are authentically equal and fair, then the principles that rational persons agree upon under these conditions have a strong claim to be considered the principles of justice. Rawls reasons that rational, self-interested persons in the original position behind the veil of ignorance would be conservative in their strategy. In setting up the ground rules for the system they are in fact determining their own fate. They will not, given the lack of information beneath the veil of ignorance, try to gamble with their future. Rawls conjectures that people in the original position will adhere to what game strategists call the "maximum rule" for making decisions. This rule "holds that it is rational to maximize the minimum outcome in choosing between different alternatives" (Boatright, 1997:90). This rule suggests that you should choose the option under which the worst thing that could happen to you is better than the worst that could happen to you under any other alternative.

It is Rawls' view that rational people in the original position beneath the veil of ignorance will, in time, endorse two principles as the fundamental justice issues, the first principle taking precedence over the second:

1. Each person is to have an equal right to the most extensive total system of basic liberties compatible with a system of liberty for all

2. Social and economic inequalities are to be arranged so that they are both: (a) to the greatest benefit of the least advantaged; and (b) attached to offices and positions open to all under conditions of equality of opportunity

Rawls' principles of justice play an important role in the normative code perspective of organizational culture. Rawls conceives of systems such as the organization as all-inclusive co-operative ventures. It is a conception of justice grounded in fairness based on rationally derived principles, not upon the assertions of the powerful or the expression of the needs of the elite of a given system. What emanates from Rawls, as interpreted and brought to the fore by the normative code advocates, is a modern recasting of the social contract in the tradition of Hobbes, Locke, and Rousseau, but one tied to the realities of a competitive system in which individuals seek to develop a fair way to advance their interests.

The normative code advocates find Rawls' conception of justice useful because he does not work out the details of applying justice, but insists that others closer to the context in question—economists, sociologists, anthropologists, business ethicists—work out the application of these general principles of justice in particular human systems. As Velasquez writes of Rawls: "the theory fits easily into the basic institutions of western societies; it does not reject the market system, work incentives, nor the inequalities consequent on a division of labour" (1971:113). Yet despite this fit, it speaks the language of power through its recognition of the pursuit of self-interest, and ties this skilfully to individual liberties and a reminder that the system is truly only as good, in the moral issue, as its least advantaged members.

The third pillar in the normative code view of organizational culture (see Figure 5.6) rests upon a revision and application of the classical form of utilitarianism to the field of business ethics. Unlike the previous two pillars—the Kantian emphasis upon duties and rights, and the Rawlsian focus on justice—utilitarianism is rooted in a teleological rather than a deontological theory. Teleological theories hold that the moral worth of actions or practices is determined solely by the consequences of the action or practice. The reasoning behind utilitarianism is neither *a priori* nor rooted in the apparent rationality of certain principles. Utilitarianism is grounded in the basic thesis that an action or practice is right, when compared to alternatives, when it leads to the greatest possible balance of good consequences or to the least possible balance of bad consequences in the world as a whole.

Neither Jeremy Bentham [1748–1832] nor John Stuart Mill [1806–1873] was espousing an ivory-tower philosophy; both were action-oriented analysts with strong interests in legal and social reform. They employed the utilitarian mode of reasoning to assess and critically examine the institutions of their day. Each utilized four foundations or cornerstones in developing utilitarian thinking. John R. Boatright, in *Ethics and the Conduct of Business* (1997), views classical utilitarianism as rooted in:

1. consequentialism: a view which assumes that the rightness of actions or practices is determined solely by their consequences

2. hedonism: in this view utility is identified with pleasure or the absence of pain—hedonism asserts that pleasure, or in a modern form, happiness, is ultimately good

3. maximalism: an action or practice that is morally right is not merely one that has some good but in fact the greatest amount of good consequences relative to bad when compared to other alternatives

4. universalism: the consequences to be analysed in classical utilitarianism pertain to everyone, not merely those directly involved

In its classical form, utilitarianism assumes that we can measure and add the quantities of benefits produced by an action or practice and subtract from these the quantities of harm that the action will have, and in so doing arrive at the greatest total benefits or the lowest total costs. In the hedonistic form of consequentialism called act-utilitarianism, we must be able to measure pleasurable and painful states in order to decide which is greater, and greater not only for those directly involved but for everyone. Bentham, for example, offered a "hedonistic calculus of six actions for evaluating pleasure and pain solely by their quantitative differences." By the use of this "hedonistic calculus," Bentham argued that we allegedly can measure and compare individual happiness, and in time discern which act or practice will, when compared to others, provide the greatest happiness to the greatest number.

In the modern context, efforts to apply the classical utilitarianism of Bentham and Mill have led to the building of a ten-step method for utilitarian reasoning. Figure 5.7 overviews how one would go about following a classical act-utilitarian method of reasoning. In its modern guise, with prices and subjective preferences substituting for the measurement of pleasure and pain, business analysts have attempted to utilize "cost-benefit analysis" (Layard and Glaister, 1994; Nas, 1996; Zerbe and Dively, 1994) or behavioural theories of "social exchange" (Blau, 1989; Cook, 1987; Molm, 1997) in lieu of the well-intended but rather clumsy notion of Bentham's "hedonistic calculus." In recent efforts to borrow from classical act-utilitarianism, the notion of utility replaces happiness and individual preferences expressed in behavioural or monetary terms are used in the calculation. In monetary terms, utility is measured by what a person purchases at a particular price, or in behavioural terms, what an individual opts to expend his or her energies upon. Within a classical act-utilitarian frame applied in the modern context, to maximize an individual's utility is to satisfy him or her by providing alternatives at a price, or with the enthusiasm, which would lead to their selection. To realize the thesis of "universalism," to act in a utilitarian fashion is thus to maximize the utility of the aggregate.

Act-utilitarianism does not hesitate to break the rules if the breaking will lead to the greatest utility of the largest number. As a result, within classical act-utilitarianism, violat-

---

FIGURE 5-7 Overview of the Utilitarian Method of Reasoning

Step 1: Attempt to accurately describe the action that is to be morally evaluated.

Step 2: Specify, to the best of your ability, all those who are directly and indirectly affected by the action under consideration (see Step 1).

Step 3: Delineate all the relevant good and bad consequences of the action for all those affected—as far into the future as seems appropriate—and imaginatively consider various possible outcomes and the probabilities of their occurrence.

Step 4: Attempt to weigh the total good results (the degree of happiness produced) against the total bad results, taking into account such issues as the intensity, quantity, and duration of the harms and benefits involved.

Step 5: Continue the same weighing, if required, for those indirectly affected and for society as a whole.

Step 6: Generate a summative statement of all the good and bad consequences likely to ensue as a consequence of the act.

Step 7: If it is determined that the action produced more good than bad, then that action is morally right. If, on the other hand, it is found that the action is likely to generate more bad than good, it is morally wrong.

Step 8: Now consider whether there are various alternative actions to the one being worked upon in Steps 1–7. Carry out an analysis on these alternatives similar to that done in Steps 1–7.

Step 9: Compare the results of all the alternative actions. Select as the moral action the one that produces the greatest good or the least bad.

Step 10: Act in line with this selection. This is, from a utilitarian position, the moral thing to do.

---

ing a contract, deceiving a colleague, or lying should be engaged in if as a result of these actions, when compared to other options, the greatest good will arise for the largest number. This is because act-utilitarianism, as DeGeorge writes, "holds that each individual action, in all its concreteness and in all its detail, is what should be subjected to the utilitarian test" (1990:65). This approach to "each action" seems natural since act-utilitarianism aims at maximizing value, and it is clear that the most direct means to do so requires maximizing value on each and every single occasion.

To modify this and introduce a deontological or reasoned and principled edge to utilitarianism rule, utilitarians hold that rules have a central position in morality and these cannot be compromised by the demands of particular situations. In effect, rule-utilitarians argue that the utilitarian test should be applied not to individual actions but to moral codes as a whole. For the rule-utilitarian, classes of actions as in the rules "don't deceive," "don't violate promises," or "don't bribe," apply to systems of actions rather than to given individual actions. In line with early thinking on rights and duties (deontological ethics), the rule-utilitarian asks what moral code or set of rules should a society, or in our case an organization, adopt to maximize happiness. The principles that compose that code thus become the basis for determining which actions are morally right and which are not. Using the rule-utilitarian framework leaves open the possibility that a particular right action might not maximize benefits, but would be rooted in an optimal moral code. Rather than suggest, as do the act-utilitarians, that we sometimes obey and sometimes disobey rules depending on the circumstances surrounding the test of utility, rule-utilitarians insist that we try to determine the specific set of principles which, if adhered to, would best promote total happiness in the system.

As Boatright makes clear, "Act- and rule-utilitarianism each has its merits and there is no consensus among philosophers about which is correct" (1997:39). However, taken together, act- and rule-utilitarianism are, as Boatright and other advocates of the normative code make clear, entirely compatible with business ethics. There are four apparent reasons for this. First, utilitarianism is entirely compatible with the business emphasis upon efficiency and the desire to use hard data to quantify and test for ways to achieve it. Second, utilitarianism is, as Velasquez, writes, entirely compatible with the intuitive criteria that practical people use when discussing moral conduct: "When people explain, for example, why they have a moral obligation to perform some action, they will often proceed by pointing to the benefits the action will impose ..." (1988:71). Third, utilitarianism, particularly as advanced by rule-utilitarians, enhances the ability of business persons to assess ethical codes and their precepts when attempting to either introduce an ethical code into an organizational culture, or to modify an existing but flawed code. Fourth and last, utilitarianism in both its act and rule formulations focuses upon a method that narrows the selection of the right action or the optimal moral code down to one, thus suiting the business person's need to make decisions that are reasonable but bounded by very real constraints on time and budget.

Within the method of utilitarian reasoning, the advocates of the normative code view of organizational culture warn us that there are costs and benefits arising from the often made utilitarian assumption that it is possible and desirable to quantify the harms and benefits likely to ensue from an action or adherence to a moral code. There is little problem in intuitively understanding that some actions are more pleasurable for us than are others. The decision to go to a hockey game is often the result of a judgment that attending the game will give us more pleasure, at that time, than any available alternative. When we are provided with a range or menu of alternatives, we can often rank items in order of the pleasure they offer. Difficulties ensue, however, when we try to determine both how much pleasure each action or adherence to a moral code entails, and how to get this reading for others who may enjoy attending hockey games far less than you or I. The shift from subjective assessment of pleasure to market values simplifies but leaves unresolved other issues. It is not clear that the sole photograph of your deceased mother valued at $1.22 on the market is valued by you less than the $72.00 ticket to the hockey game.

What Boatright (1997), Velasquez (1988), and DeGeorge (1990 are doing is not dependent on a blind reliance upon cost-benefit analysis, but rather is an informal and judicious use of act- and rule-utilitarianism combined with the Kantian notion of rights and duties, the Rawlsian concept of justice, and the last pillar, virtue ethics (see Figure 5.6). Virtue ethics was conceived upon Aristotle's *Nicomachean Ethics*, as interpreted and brought to the fore by Alasdair MacIntyre, in *After Virtue* (1981), and brought into the normative code perspective by Robert C. Soloman, in *Ethics and Excellence: Co-operation and Integrity in Business* (1992).

Virtue ethics alters the questions we have been looking at so far. The virtue ethics question asks: what kind of person best expresses our understanding of the good life? This is quite different from the questions: what acts are right? what is the moral code which if fol-

FIGURE 5-8 Ten Core Values: A Virtue Ethics Approach to Organizational Culture	
1. Caring:	The virtue of treating people as ends in themselves, not means to an end.
2. Honesty:	The virtue of being truthful and not deceiving, distorting, or misinforming.
3. Accountability:	The virtue of accepting the consequences of one's actions and accepting the responsibility for one's decisions and their consequences.
4. Promise-keeping:	The virtue of keeping one's commitments over time.
5. Pursuit of excellence:	The virtue of striving to be as good as one can be.
6. Loyalty:	The virtue of being faithful to those with whom one has dealings.
7. Fairness:	The virtue of being open-minded, willing to admit error, avoiding arbitrary and capricious favouritism, and not overreaching.
8. Integrity:	The virtue of employing independent judgment, avoiding conflicts of interest, and restraining from both self-aggrandizement and succumbing to economic pressure.
9. Respect for others:	The virtue of recognizing each person's right to self-determination and dignity.
10. Responsible citizenship:	The virtue of taking societal and cultural values into one's decisions, and of realizing that the action, to be accepted, must take place within a community.

lowed will bring the greatest happiness to the greatest number? what principles of justice would we select in the original position, behind a veil of ignorance? The virtue ethics question focuses on the character of the person in determining what is and is not a virtue (see Figure 5.8). It locates within the character of individuals and groups a series of traits and characteristics that are perceived as virtuous.

In turning to virtue ethics, advocates of the normative code perspective of organizational culture remind us that the nature of the agent making the choice may be as important as the consequences of the choice. Moral virtues are neither rules nor the consequences of acts, but personal characteristics or propensities by people to behave in one kind of way rather than another. In Aristotle's *Nicomachean Ethics*, the role of ethics is to facilitate our ability to lead successful, rewarding lives in the community. The notion of the "good life" in the "good community" is formulated in the spirit of inquiry that seeks to determine how—by selection, training, education, and development—character is fostered. The Aristotelian ethics of virtue espoused by Alasdair MacIntyre defines virtue as "an acquired human quality the possession and exercise of which tends to enable us to achieve those goods that are internal to practices and the lack of which effectively prevent us from achieving any such good" (1981:178).

As examples of virtues, Aristotle lists, among others: courage, temperance, liberality, a sense of self-worth, gentleness, modesty, justice, and wisdom. William Shaw and Vincent Barry, in *Moral Issues in Business* (1992), see Aristotle as saying much more than "good acts are those performed by the good (virtuous) person." Instead, they ask you to imagine that you have lost your way in a deep and impenetrable jungle in which the way out is neither clear nor even possible. In this context, what would you hope for in order to extricate yourself? Shaw and Barry write: "I would want neither a map nor a survival handbook. Since I don't know where I am, to begin with .... Since the handbook cannot hope to cover every situation that might be encountered, it can only be marginally helpful. Rather, I would like a person who is experienced in the ways of the jungle to act as my guide. I think that Aristotle saw moral problems in much the same way" (1992:98). To Shaw and Barry, the good person, in Aristotle's sense of virtue, possesses *phronesis,* or practical wisdom.

This is not to say that rules and reasons have no place in morality, any more than that they have no place in business. But the advocates of the normative code remind us that rules and reason can take us only so far, and we may reach a point when wisdom, experience, imagination, good judgment, and what Shaw and Barry call "practical wisdom or intelligence," may have to be our guides. In *Ethical Decision Making in Everyday Work Situations* (1990), Mary E. Guy highlights two virtues or core values as necessary to build the idea of "aspiration" into the conception of the good life in organizations. David L. Norton, in "Character Ethics and Organizational Life" (1988), agrees, seeing the modern moral minimalism that pervades organizational cultures as dampening aspiration and in fact turning attention away from examining morality to much more instrumental preoccupations. Norton seeks to remind us that we must look to character, including our own, and not solely to the laboratory and market for our answers to the pressing moral questions of our business lives.

Robert C. Soloman pushes Norton's insights along, putting Aristotelian virtue ethics at the centre of business ethics. In Soloman's rendering, the purposes of business are not given but rather created by the participants in the business community. Business, if thought of as a community of individuals all seeking the good life, opens up the important question of what the purpose of business is and ought to be. Soloman's interpretation of Aristotelian virtue ethics emphasizes ethics as a means to achieve happiness and the good life, rather than as a constraint on what it is that we are permitted to do. Business in practice is the search, insists Soloman, for excellence: genuine excellence, which entails making the good life a possibility for as many people and other species as is possible. As with Norton's, the emphasis in Soloman's virtue ethics is upon building the idea of business as a community that aspires to the good life and attempts to achieve this by rewarding the emergence of character traits— honesty, fairness, trust, toughness, friendliness, honour, and loyalty—that not only lead to success in life, but that facilitate our ability to cooperate in the business world. Soloman insists "that the precondition of business is the virtue of its participants," and it is in this sense that "such notions as honest advertising and truth in lending are not simply legal impositions upon business life ... they are rather the preconditions of business and, as such, the essential virtues ..." (1992:208–09).

Virtue ethics challenges but remains compatible with the culture of business. It asks participants to question the status quo, to become critically reflexive in an effort to integrate their personal notions of virtue with the public and ongoing commitments they make to others in their business dealings. The good life cannot be attained when we make a virtue of selfishness in our workplace and then assume that we can build a thriving, healthy life by maintaining family values in our domestic affairs. The normative code advocates ask us to reflect on what sort of moral education we are creating when we create business cultures. These cultures are made of a web of relations that surpass our need for immediate gratification and speak to the need for meaning, purpose, and a sense of self-worth.

Selecting among and between the four pillars in the normative code view of organizational culture is no simple matter (see Figure 5.6). The normative code perspective serves, I believe, as an excellent vocabulary to start thinking about organizational culture from a business perspective. But it assumes by and large that ethics within organizational culture is a function of rational choices and deliberations engaged in by participants. This emphasis, prevalent in moral philosophy at large, does not take into account the possibility that organizational culture, to a large degree, may be the product of unconscious processes where neurotic organizations are unsuccessfully seeking attention, excitement, and adventure, or attempting to cope with depression and even schizophrenic cultural tendencies. In the next section of this chapter, borrowing from the title of a book by Manfred F.R. Kets de Vries, we will look at organizational cultures and their ethics as if they were on the psychiatrist's couch. In *Organizations on the Couch* (1991), and with his co-author, Danny Miller, in *The Neurotic Organization* (1984), de Vries and others with a clinical perspective on organizational culture open our horizons to the third and last view of the ethics of organizational culture—the unconscious organizational culture (see Figure 5.1).

PATTERNS OF UNCONSCIOUS CULTURE

Up until now, in both behavioural ethics and normative code views of organizational culture, we have recognized organizational culture as a function of the conscious and reasonable behaviour of participants. Even the "basic assumption" of the structural functional perspective within the behavioural ethics view of organizational culture was conceived of as deeply embedded but discernible through an examination of the surface artifacts and the deconstruction of the stories, legends, and ceremonies that are always part and parcel of the functioning organizational culture. The normative code perspective of organizational culture acknowledges the existence of forces—the market, legal codes, the charter of rights— outside the control of organizations, but never directly probes the manner in which unconscious processes impact the ethical component of an organizational culture.

In Figure 5.9 we see two interrelated but distinct views of the organizational culture as unconscious patterns. In the first view, organizational cultures as adaptations to anxiety, the organizational culture is seen as a defense mechanism. In this view organizational cultures exist to aid in: (1) task accomplishment; (2) social lubrication; and (3) containing deep-seated anxieties. When looked at as any of eight defense mechanisms—denial, disavowal, fixation, grandiosity, idealization, intellectualization, projection, and splitting— organizational cultures often contain anxiety but may sabotage efforts to introduce ethics. The second view, organizational cultures as neurotic adaptation and collective fantasies, emphasizes the dark side of organizational culture. Neurotic cultures are preoccupied with collective fantasies that, while reducing anxieties, generate dysfunctions. For example, we see how the "persecution" fantasy predominates in the paranoid organizational culture. In the paranoid culture the need to have a menacing face "out there" helps to unite the culture but produces an ongoing atmosphere of suspicion.

Of these views the first is the most elemental and basic approach. Early works (Bion, 1959; Jacques, 1951, 1955; Menzies, 1960) all conceive of the organizational culture as a

FIGURE 5-9 Two Orientations to Organizational Culture as Unconscious Patterns: Ethical Implications

View	Main Premise	Ethical Implications
Organizational Cultures as Adaptations to Anxiety	Organizational cultures serve, not only to accomplish specific goals, but also as a means to contain and deal with human anxieties that arise from a lack of control, a fear of death, and the need to find meaning. Organizational cultures thus act like defense mechanisms.	In this view of the organizational culture as a defense mechanism, ethical behaviour can be rooted in fanciful, delusional, and self-serving information. Defense mechanisms, once established, divert ethical behaviour.
Organizational Cultures as Neurotic Adaptations and Collective Fantasies	Organizational cultures can take on neurotic forms of adaptation when collective fantasies take root. These collective fantasies prevail when the organization, in its attempt to contain anxiety, loses touch with reality.	Whether we look at the persecutory preoccupations of the paranoid culture or the fantasy of control in the bureaucratic culture, we see that ethics becomes part and parcel of the collective fantasies of organizations. Rather than deal with ethical issues, organizations are often working out their flight from reality.

social system functioning so as to contain the experience of human anxiety. Wilfred Bion, working with psychoanalytic techniques at the Tavistock Institute, claimed in his pioneering work, *Experiences in Groups* (1959), that to comprehend the task culture we must understand the unconsciously-driven root assumptions that often sabotage the more consciously-driven task group. Bion, working with groups, demonstrated how in trying to get things accomplished, we unconsciously take one of three routes—dependence, pairing, and what Bion termed "fight-flight." A culture or subculture that unconsciously pulls towards "dependence" expends enormous energy, often at the expense of task accomplishment, searching for a strong leader to protect and shield the group from threat. "Pairing" involves the group in the unconscious belief that the potential merger or a reconciliation of views by two members in the group will usher in a time of hope and rebirth. "Fight-flight" preoccupations pull the group towards the quest for a leader to help them successfully flee or fight what is perceived to be a common enemy.

In a more contemporary view, although working through the same premises as Wilfred Bion, Elliot Jacques and Isabel Menzies argue in a very intellectually stimulating fashion that organizations and the cultures therein are external self-systems intended to help us cope with our anxieties. Robert Denhardt's *In the Shadow of Organizations* (1981), Burkard Sievers' *Work, Death, and Life Itself* (1993), and Michael A. Diamond's *The Unconscious Life of Organizations: Interpreting Organizational Identity* (1993) all point out, albeit in different manners, how human's knowledge of their morality hastens their search for connections to that which can lessen the anxieties that this often produces. Organizations provide such a connection. They transcend the individual. They help provide routine and a set of priorities. They aid us in our quest for meaning and relevance. They provide a justification for spending or passing our time on the planet in a manner recognized by ourselves and others as useful.

We need not, of course, rise to the levels of death-related anxiety to explain how organizational cultures may help us adapt to our anxieties. When we talk about our motives for joining organizations we usually speak about money. In the hands of the unconscious analysts of organizational culture our worries about survival are taken literally, and what is probed is how in organizing we create containers, called organizations, that are efforts to lessen and direct our anxieties. This may seem like a rather fanciful, even confused view, since rather than containing human anxieties, organizations seem to exacerbate them. Rather than lessening, for instance, our fear of death, organizations may be viewed as creators of pollution, global warming, and chemical spills that threaten rather than contain our anxieties. This position is reasonable, but it fails to acknowledge that it is the organization's failure to control our anxiety that surprises.

When organizational cultures are seen as adaptations to anxiety they serve as defense mechanisms. When defense mechanisms break down, we are startled to find that we are not in the reality we had assumed. It is important to stress that these defense mechanisms are not, in themselves, pathological. They are often the source of very creative action allowing organizations to remain focused and survive traumatic events. It is when these defenses are used extensively or blindly that they distort information sufficiently to render organizations dysfunctional. The eight defense mechanisms rooted in the technical literature in this field (Argyris, 1990; S. Freud, 1926; A. Freud, 1966; Hampden-Turner, 1981; 1989; Kohut, 1977) help organizational cultures to deal with complex, potentially threatening situations that, if acknowledged, would overwhelm their ability to cope.

Denial is when organizational cultures refuse to acknowledge a threatening reality or realities. Denial flourishes when the organizational culture deflects, sidesteps, buries, or mystifies information revealing an imminent threat. This, of course, functions to reduce anxiety in the short-run, but like the ostrich sticking its head in the sand while being attacked by a tiger, it does little to prepare the organization to cope with the threatening reality. In the field of ethics, denial operates in organizational cultures to curtail the voices of critics, whistle-blowers, and advisors with complex-change messages. Denial works to maintain the organizational culture in the midst of trauma and can, of course, be functional when the trauma is fleeting and bears no lesson for the organization. However, it is very dysfunctional when for the sake of short-term avoidance the organizational culture inadvertently exposes itself to greater threat.

Disavowal occurs when the organizational culture acknowledges a threatening reality but downplays or minimalizes its importance. Disavowal is functional when it permits the organizational culture to return to the threatening reality when it is more able, and thereby more capable; it is dysfunctional when the unconscious use of the disavowal defense mechanism enhances the organization's ability to dismiss what is in fact a realistic threat. Disavowal remains buried within the organizational culture, for it entails the recognition of threats but the use of poor judgment in not taking them seriously. The poor judgment, after the fact, is seen as the fault of an individual in the act of evaluation rather than the result of a propensity within the culture are a whole. The organizational culture that enhances disavowal penalizes those who come forward with threatening issues and rewards those who take copious note of all issues but draw no attention to those that threaten. The good citizen in the organization that leans towards disavowal tracks ethical issues, but when the crunch-time comes, avoids too close an association with the quarrels and controversies that can and will most likely ensue.

Fixation in organizational cultures is established in those which attempt to alleviate the experience of anxiety by adhering to procedures. This reduces uncertainty and provides members of an organization with a sense of control. The procedure-following tends, however, to be automatic and mindless. This permits the group to go about its work-life without questioning. Fixation can be functional in organizational tasks that are highly repetitive and require an ongoing repetition of closely-sequenced behaviour. Fixation is dysfunctional when it is turned to complex problems that require nuancing issues, innovating, and preparing for contingent options. It is important to realize that in a fixated organizational culture, ethics programs will likely be reduced to a series of simple procedures. These fixed procedures will serve as a substitute for the close examination of ethical quandaries. Within organizational cultures employing the defense mechanism of fixation, a close examination of ethical quandaries causes anxieties. It addresses the possibility that procedures may have to be amended—indeed, at times jettisoned—in order for an organization to engage in ethical action.

Grandiosity emerges in those organizational cultures that reinforce the view of themselves as omnipotent. Ironically, this occurs in organizations that are successful in keeping anxieties at bay. They are led by protective, successful managers who claim to see (in the sense of a visionary manager) what the future will bring. The organization is usually a large market leader accustomed to success and believing that it has the best technology, the best personnel, and the best strategic plan for dealing with impending threats. The organizational cultures of the large North American automakers at the time of the oil embargo, and the concomitant shift by consumers to small (foreign) cars, is indicative of how the self-satisfied nature of grandiosity can sabotage economic performance. From an ethics perspective, grandiosity deadens the organizational culture's ability to take account of others. The belief that the organization is all-knowing and all-powerful subverts well-intentioned efforts at implementing ethics reform.

In grandiosity, the organizational culture ascribes omnipotence to itself, whereas in idealization, the organizational culture projects omnipotence onto others. This is not magical thinking. Many an owner of a small franchise may feel totally protected, not because of his or her abilities, but because of the belief that "headquarters" has a strategic plan and experts in place to deal with all possibilities. The insurance industry flourishes as an outlet for many who believe that despite their vulnerability, they are safe and protected by a large pool of resources. Idealization plagues the ethical portfolio of organizational cultures since it fosters dependence. Under the "guardian-angel illusion," organizations, like individuals, often fail to attend to moral claims, which are perceived as mere irritants that can be shoved aside and in time taken care of by the protector. This regression to child-like behaviour may be seen by some as innocence; from a practised ethical eye it may, as well, be understood as the shirking of responsibility.

Intellectualization is the defense mechanism that requires an elaborate rationalization or plan prior to committing to a line of action. Impulse and intuition are not trusted. They, if left unchecked, result in a heightening of anxiety due to an increased exposure to threatening experiences. To curtail this, the organizational culture must plan before it acts. This insistence upon eliminating uncertainty prior to action is problematic in two senses. In the first sense it reinforces fixation as the organizational culture tends to repeat, almost ritualistically, its past successes and avoids any foray into new (but dangerous) territory. In the second sense, intellectualization in its high demands for detailed planning can produce paralysis by analysis. Paralysis by analysis occurs when in the name of minimizing uncertainty and avoiding errors, the organizational culture does nothing at all but study the issue. In this second sense, many an organizational culture would rather investigate or study the feasibility of an ethics issue than act.

Projection by individuals in organizational cultures reduces threats and anxiety by truly viewing these as arising from and impacting others, not themselves. Projection is the defensive act of getting rid of an unwanted part of the organizational culture by placing it onto someone external to the organization. In other words, one throws out what one refuses to recognize in the organizational culture. The offering of bribes may be seen as the result of the character of those to whom the bribes were offered. The offering is not truly acknowledged—the character of the other, in the defense mechanism of projection, called forward the bribe. This, again, is not magical thinking. It flourishes in organizational cultures that refuse to look inward, or only do so when they find something praiseworthy. Organizational cultures that project, do not acknowledge failings as their own. Organizational cultures marked by incidences of projection are functional in that they show a high degree of loyalty to members; they are dysfunctional when these members are incompetent and/or morally suspect.

Splitting, the last defense mechanism we will discuss, flourishes in organizational cultures that internalize their enemy in the guise of other subcultures or component parts of the organization. These organizational cultures are fragmented and badly politicized. In this context ethical issues are viewed as part of the political process. Moral arguments are viewed with suspicion. Within moral controversies in the split organizational culture, some subcultures are seen by others as advancing themselves as arbiters of the good, at the expense of others. Splitting contains anxiety by locating the enemy and, most importantly, locating one's friends. Splitting is functional when the subcultures utilize the conflict to create a viable dialogue; it is dysfunctional when the splitting brings about neurotic forms of paranoia. In split organizational cultures, small cliques and warring factions often predominate. All perceive the others as suspect, including morally suspect; all believe themselves to be the hero-archetype. Within this setting, moral disputes within the organizational culture can be understood as holy wars.

A second body of literature has taken these defensive mechanisms and shown the dark or neurotic side of organizational culture (Hirschhorn, 1988; Kets de Vries, 1984, 1991, 1995; Kets de Vries and Miller, 1984, 1991; Schwartz, 1995). This literature emphasizes how organizational cultures become dysfunctional or preoccupied with irrational psychological forces (Bowles, 1991; Diamond and Allcorn, 1984), which rather than merely aiding in reducing anxiety, become an end within themselves. Neurotic organizational cultures are of interest to business ethicists, since within them organizational participants often find it difficult to develop a reasoned sense of what is good ethical behaviour and what is not. The values in a neurotic organizational culture resound with collective fantasies. In fact, the unconsious view of organizational cultures as neurotic adaptation and collective fantasies (see Figure 5.9), emphasizes the collapse of rational decision-making due to the intrusion of the fantasies of the group onto the normal functioning of an integrated organizational culture, the growing isolation of the neurotic organizational culture from reality-testing, and the example we shall use in our discussion, the imposition of the dominant personalities of the leader or dominant elite upon the organizational culture.

De Vries and Miller (1984 and 1991), when conjoined with Michael A. Diamond and Seth Allcorn ("Psychological Barriers to Personal Responsibility," 1984), help us to identify five neurotic cultures. These are: 1) the paranoid organizational culture; 2) the avoidant organizational culture; 3) the histrionic organizational culture; 4) the compulsive organizational culture; and 5) the schizophrenic organizational culture. In each of these we see how one can draw parallels between common neurotic styles of behaviour and dysfunction within the organizational culture. Diagnosing these neurosis does not require that the CEO exhibit the neurotic behaviour in question, but that the psychological style of key organizational members is a major determinant of the shared fantasies that unconscious analysts believe to permeate all levels within the organizational culture.

The paranoid culture is dominated by suspicion and distrust. Things are not what they seem. People are not to be believed. Secret agendas guide important events. What is known and certain is not to be counted upon. Information is not believed to be distributed to everyone. It is opaque and must be decoded. It is apparent that a major preoccupation of participants in the paranoid organizational culture is to be prepared, on guard, and ready for any attack either imagined or real. The leaders who rise to the top in paranoid cultures perpetuate the paranoia by engaging in overtly persecutory acts with subordinates, who in turn act out their hostility towards their subordinates. Originally the paranoid culture arose to cope with life in highly competitive settings. When this is linked to good knowledge of threats and opportunities it can be functional. However, when it distorts threats and opportunities, disenchants members, produces unnecessary insecurity and distrust, it paralyses ethical activity in the firm. Values are not discussed for they reveal too much of one's genuine inner workings. Concealment and bluff rule the day.

The avoidant organizational culture is mired in the fantasy of dependence or hopelessness. The underlying neurosis is that of depression, deep and demanding. Depressive cultures arise when organizations feel powerless to affect outcomes yet remain sufficiently viable to avoid going out of business. The avoidant organizational culture is often found when organizations are totally dependant on other organizations for their well being, are confined to depleting or dying markets, or possess a weak competitive posture due to poor product lines. Rather than search for greater independence, altering their market positioning, or improving their product lines, the avoidant organizational culture elects to stay the course. In the depressive style, organizational members possess feelings of inadequacy and worthlessness. They feel inferior to others, but cannot admit it. These organizational cultures do not retain risk takers or dreamers, but prefer leaders who will stay with the status quo. Given that the reality they want to retain is not good enough, these organizational cultures turn their hostility inwards. A problem that prevails here has been termed moral masochism. As de Vries and Miller note of members of the avoidant organizational culture: "They may seek psychic pain as a redemptive act, as a means of assuaging their guilt about wishes that are perceived as unacceptable. Defeat is seen as a just reward" (1991:251).

The histrionic or charismatic organizational culture is functional when the strong and dramatic leadership-style that predominates provides the momentum for the organization to either pass through the crucial start-up phase of the firm or to revitalize itself. However, this organizational culture becomes neurotic or histrionic when the fantasy of grandiosity so crucial for dealing with the liabilities of newness and oldness is seen as the style for every-day organizational life. There is as well a recurring element of narcissism in the charismatic culture. The leaders want drama. They covet romance. They want to be admired and cherished. In this context subordinates tend to idealize their charismatic leaders, ignoring their faults and proclaiming their virtues. In the desire of the subordinates to please their charismatic leaders—and in the desire of the charismatic leaders to be nourished by the acclaim of their subordinates—the charismatic culture becomes hyperactive, impulsive, and dangerously uninhibited. Rather than deal prudently with issues, it throws caution to the wind and can become cult-like. In the charismatic organizational culture ethics follows the course of the bond between charismatic leader and his or her followers. In the name of this bond commitments to others can be pushed aside, promises broken, and in the name of renewal, old loyalties severed.

The bureaucratic organizational culture is the most intuitively available to business ethicists. We all know bureaucratic cultures are functional when they generate fine material controls, efficient operations, and high degrees of accountability. However, these cross over and become neurotic when the fantasy of control turns to compulsion. Compulsive-style executives strongly attempt to counteract their fear of being at the mercy of events. Compulsives disdain spontaneity and prefer the calming effect of repetition. The bureaucratic organization is neurotic when the controlling executives are not willing to relinquish sufficient control over operations to allow others to grasp the meaning and relevance of the policies. In lieu, company policies become clear manifestations of the compulsion of the key executives rather than adaptive requirements. Ethics programs in bureaucratic organizational cultures become rituals. They are not subject to discussion or reflection; they become yet another layer of compulsiveness.

The political organizational culture is functional when the fragmented components competing for resources stimulate dialogue, innovation, and corporate profitability; it is dysfunctional when it is dominated by schizoid personalities nestled in subcultures. The subculture, the schizoid believes, can be built into an empire. This is a detached style in which the components of the culture fragment into subcultures, each seeking its own freedom and power. Involvement is engaged in order to become free of the organization and to set a new agenda. This fantasy of involvement and detachment in the service of power is divisive. Individuals feel ambivalent towards the larger organization but totally committed to their work units, which promise them greater freedom and detachment from the organization as a whole. In the political culture emotions are guarded, reciprocal exchanges with those outside one's subculture are difficult. Within the political organizational culture ethics becomes two-faced. The notion of responsibility, rights, duty, justice, and virtue in the in-group of the subculture are not reflected in the culture of the organization as a whole, nor in the relationship between the organization and the broader society.

As this chapter has illustrated, organizational culture is viewed quite differently from the behavioural ethics, normative code, and unconscious perspectives. Each organizes and frames how we think about ethics in a very different light. In Chapter 6 we turn to investigate the ways in which good persons can, within the context of organizations, engage in unethical behaviour. This discussion of "dirty hands" sets the stage for our descriptive account of what and why whistle-blowers do when they make public moral claims regarding their employers.

CASES AND QUESTIONS

CASE 5-1   Feeling Trapped

Monique Letourneau, a bookkeeper in a small, not-for-profit agency focusing on employment opportunities for 18- to 24-year-old residents of Sherbrooke, Quebec, did not know what to do next. Ms. Letourneau's work was supervised by Dennis Lussier, the agency's business manager. Ms. Letourneau was responsible for maintaining the books, billing clients, and following up on unpaid bills. Ms. Letourneau was good at her job and during the past four years claims were filed promptly, follow-ups were carried out diplomatically, and the books were deemed sufficiently meritorious for Ms. Letourneau to be designated as employee of the year.

However, Mr. Lussier was starting to have personal problems of which Ms. Letourneau was fully apprised. Mr. Lussier and his wife of eleven years were on the verge of separating. Issues regarding custody of the children and speculations upon the existence of "another man" plagued Mr. Lussier. He started missing meetings, deadlines were left unheeded, and, in all, the quality of his work deteriorated rapidly. He was late processing vouchers for reimbursement. He took numerous "leave" days. Filing of insurance claims fell behind schedule. Ms. Letourneau clearly saw that her supervisor's personal problems were jeopardizing the good of the agency. Being a forthright and fearless woman, Ms. Letourneau talked to him to let him know that, because he was a supervisor, others, like herself, required his signature, vigilance, and normal good judgment in order to keep the agency on track. Mr. Lussier thanked her for the talk, commented on her loyalty to the agency, and promised to do what he could to get back on schedule and clear his mind of distractions.

Despite Mr. Lussier's best intentions, his work worsened. Ms. Letourneau did not know where to turn. The organizational culture in the agency was rooted in the belief that one ought not to go beyond one's supervisor with complaints, and there was a belief that people's private lives ought never to become the basis for agency gossip. Ms. Letourneau knew the culture well. She felt trapped.

QUESTIONS:

1. What would you recommend Monique Letourneau do to lessen her anxiety over feeling trapped? From a functionalist perspective, characterize the role between Ms. Letourneau and Mr. Lussier. What symbols do you expect would prevail in this organizational culture? Why?

2. From a normative code perspective on organizational culture, what is amiss at the not-for-profit agency that employs Ms. Letourneau? What is the problem with the balance of rights and duties here? What element of injustice seems to prevail? What virtues do you feel would be celebrated in this culture? Why?

3. What would you do if you were Mr. Lussier? How does this organizational culture handle and integrate problems that arise in employees' private lives? What, from a rule-utilitarian perspective, are some of the harms and benefits that may ensue if a firm seeks to increase its attention to the private problems of its employees?

4. What role do the defense mechanisms of denial, disavowal, and idealization play in what is expected of Ms. Letourneau? How, in this case, are these defense mechanisms dysfunctional? What, in your view, can be done to make them less dysfunctional?

5. Discuss this organization as an example of an avoidant culture; then make the case for it as a compulsive or bureaucratic culture. Using each diagnosis, discuss what you would do to alter the organizational culture so as to enhance its ability to deal with its ethical portfolio.

6. What, in your view, is the ethics quandary at the heart of this case? Does this alter when we move from (a) Monique Letourneau's point of view, (b) Mr. Lussier's point of view, and (c) that of the 18- to 24-year-old clients dependent upon the small, not-for-profit agency to help them get jobs?

CASE 5-2   Investigating the Organizational Culture at HRA

Mr. Arnold Robb and his younger brother, Karl, are respectively the CEO and president of operations of a Vancouver based high-tech company that we will call HRA (an acronym for high resolution animation). The company was founded in 1989 by Larry Carriere, a charismatic "wonderchild" who, at the tender age of fifteen, created and patented a device that added dimension and clarity to animated figures projected on screen. The three-dimensional effect surpasses present holograms and can be accessed without using cumbersome three-D glasses.

The Robb brothers, teachers at a technical college in suburban Vancouver, discovered Larry's brilliant innovation and convinced the young man to throw in his lot with HRA. Arnie and Karl would handle the business while Larry dealt with the technical side of things. The company grew in the first two years to thirty-five employees with sales nearing $1 million. It was during this period that Arnie, Robb, and Larry set the template for HRA's organizational culture. They were true believers in their product—respectful, thoughtful, and empathetic men driven by high technical and ethical standards. The company evolved naturally and spontaneously out of the trust and genuine respect between the three men.

In the first two years, the company culture was marked by hard work, high trust, and high rewards. Bonuses and incentives made it entirely possible for employees in the technical side of the business to earn well over $100,000 per year. The clerical staff also worked long hours, and earned 25 to 40 per cent more than their corporate peers. Moreover, the personnel at HRA were like a large, comfortable family. They believed in their product, worked 60 to 80 hours a week, and frequently took their leisure in the company of other HRA employees.

By 1998, HRA employed 1,256 employees and was doing over $500 million in sales. The company went public in 1992, when it had reached $30 million in sales. At this time, Burke Hampton and a cadre of executives were hired from large companies such as General Electric and Monsanto to bring routine and sanity to HRA, which was growing like a cancer cell. Burke Hampton, a savvy senior executive with thirty-five years of experience in large corporate bureaucracies, ushered in a new era at HRA. Within one year, Hampton had mobilized the managers he hired, stocked key committees, rewrote the company's basic strategic plan, and ingratiated himself with key shareholder groups. Arnie Robb sold his shares and is now a happy millionaire operating a restaurant chain in Sydney, Australia. Karl Robb was given the symbolic title of Vice President of Public Relations and a salary of $900,000 per year plus stock options. Larry Carriere was made the President of Operations and given a seat on the Board of Directors.

Burke Hampton vowed to perpetuate HRA's organizational culture and maintain the high ethical standards, trust, and integrity that marked the empire's origins. Management still celebrates the company's relatively few layers of hierarchy and its efficient, open communication via the electronic mail system established by Larry Carriere. Almost all communication within HRA is conducted by electronic mail. HRA employees on the road keep in touch via their laptops. Those telecommuting maintain close ties via their computers. To support the cultural value of open communication, a feature kept from the early years is that the system permits messages to be sent anonymously.

Despite the surface calm, things are not all that rosy. Not long after Burke's arrival, long-time employees, led by Karl Robb and Larry Carriere, began to question top management's genuine commitment to all aspects of HRA's organizational culture. It is a common view amongst "old-timers" that

Burke Hampton's highlighting of commitment and hard work is genuine, but that trust has fallen to the wayside. Hampton is seen to "talk the talk," but not to "do the walk." He is perceived to be engaging in questionable conduct and, what's more, to be licensing this sort of conduct for his friends at HRA. To add to this combustible mixture, HRA has been experiencing a marked slowdown in its growth. The company needs new products, new blood, and new ideas to sustain the growth that Hampton has led others to expect is HRA's due.

The informal culture or grapevine at HRA is all in a flap about a recent "ethics" quandary. This quandary and the general unease making its way through HRA has prompted Burke Hampton to set up an ethics committee to look into the issues. Below are two e-mails—available to all at HRA—spelling out the issues at stake. The first was authored by Burke Hampton; the latter was written anonymously. The grapevine believes that Karl Robb and Larry Carriere's position is manifest in the anonymous e-mail.

E-mail Communication from Burke Hampton:

To: All HRA Employees
From: Burke Hampton, President and CEO of HRA
Regarding: Establishment of HRA Ethics Committee
Date: March 23/98

HRA believes that the actions of the corporation can provide a model for companies seeking to create ethical corporate cultures. The culture we have built at HRA is resilient and capable of sustaining challenges, both from external and internal sources. This is because we enshrine the following values:

1) While the goal of any business is to make a sound profit, we at HRA do not compromise our integrity in the name of profit.

2) HRA is altering the manner in which people spend their time. Our products are important. We are having an impact. We must establish and retain an example of leadership and credibility in all our corporate endeavours.

3) We pride ourselves on our honesty and fairness in all transactions with our customers, suppliers, shareholders, and each other.

4) At HRA we deal with issues responsibly. We respond fairly, swiftly, and with care to honest criticism.

To put these values into action and to maintain focus on ethical behaviour throughout HRA, I have created a taskforce—The HRA Ethics Committee—consisting of Red Sherrington (Chair), Rubin Mendosa, Susan Hall, and Carol Abramovitz. The Ethics Committee is entrusted with the task of examining the following issues in detail and providing me with concrete remedial actions, if necessary. The issues are:

- HRA's ability to protect company assets and intellectual property
- HRA employees' activities with outside business
- HRA's handling of complaints by employees, customers, suppliers, and contractors

You are hereby empowered and, as an employee of HRA, have an obligation to report circumstances that you evaluate to be in conflict with HRA's standards. The Ethics Committee will be glad to hear your views and to build these, when useful, into their report.

To keep HRA successful, we must remain true to our ethics. It is only by working hard to tie our beliefs to our actions that we will fulfill our mission. This is not an easy task. It takes work, honesty, loyalty, and the willingness to fully commit to the company. Let's get to work on this now!

If you would like to comment on the Ethics Committee and its work, please e-mail me. You know I am always here for you.

Sincerely,
Burke Hampton

E-mail Communication from an anonymous employee of HRA:

To: All HRA Employees
From: ****
Regarding: Nomination of HRA for "Hypocrite of the Year Award"
Date: April 15/98

HRA's newly-appointed Ethics Committee has unearthed a gold mine of ethical questions that suggest that rather than walk the talk, we have been talking while we skirt around the edges of acceptable behaviour. The Ethics Committee at HRA is, in my view, doing its job and doing it well. Red Sherrington, Rubin Mendosa, Susan Hall, and Carol Abramovitz have been diligent at attempting to make sense of the feedback they are getting from employees and concerned friends of HRA. However, the news, at least what I have been able to piece together, is bleak. Rather than pat ourselves on the back, the following five breaches of conduct require us to rethink the supposed ethical culture we are so proud of. The issues are:

1) Those of you who have taken the time to read the 1997 annual report of HRA (available in the public relations department) will learn that of the 11-person Board of Directors, 10 voted to give themselves, all non-employees of HRA, stock options worth $94,000 dollars each. The one abstaining member benefited anyway since the motion was passed. It was not challenged by management. Estimates of the average annual income of members of HRA's Board suggest that each earns about $180,000. It is not clear why, when HRA had a relatively slow year, the Board should enrich itself.

2) Morris Glantz, the President of Marketing at HRA, has steered HRA into a contract with Samuels Advertising Agency, owned by Nathan Samuels, Mr. Morris Glantz's son-in-law. The contract, worth more than $2,000,000 a year, is the largest signed by the Samuels Advertising Agency in its three-year history. On file recommending Samuels Advertising is a glowing evaluation of the firm's campaign outline for HRA. The letter is written by Morris Glantz who, in no way, shape, or form, reveals that Nathan Samuels is his daughter's husband.

3) Burke Hampton, our charismatic leader, has had more than a 400% raise in salary, stock options, and bonuses since arriving at HRA—despite the recent serious slowdown in our earnings. The next highest raise in total compensation is for Morris Glantz, who received a 161% raise in the past three years. The average employee at HRA has, in the past three years, received a 7% raise in earnings, stock options, and bonuses. It is not clear what sort of fairness we are talking about when we talk the talk but do not do the walk.

4) Carla Sherman, well known at HRA as one of our most productive sales representatives for the past three years, has just successfully sued HRA for unjust dismissal. The actual sum to be allocated to Ms. Sherman, who now works for Rosy Animation Systems, is still to be determined by the courts. The court transcript revealed that she was fired from HRA by Burke Hampton for refusing to release customer information that HRA had assured both her and the clients to be confidential and anonymous. Moreover, it was revealed by Ms. Sherman that HRA offered her $200,000 to go quietly. Ms. Sherman refused on ethical grounds, claiming that she could not stomach the hypocrisy at HRA. She may, I believe, have a point.

5) Last, but certainly not least, Robert Corcoran in shipping, a young man who has worked for HRA for nearly two years, has made it known that due to a blood transfusion received prior to the close scrutiny of blood donors, he has AIDS. HRA summarily dismissed Mr. Corcoran for poor attendance, falling quality of work, and the inability to keep up with his colleagues. Mr. Corcoran is seeing the same lawyer used by Carla Sherman. I, for one, wish him well in trying to bring justice to his case and to open our eyes to the way in which we are no longer what we once were. We must wake up and smell the corruption.

To close, be aware that we cannot remain complacent. The Ethics Committee at HRA has its hands full. We cannot permit a whitewash of the facts. I personally would be glad to hear from others who would like to dispute my version of the facts. We can only receive accolades for our ethics when we acknowledge the possibility that we have been hypocrites. I nominate us, and this includes myself, for the "Hypocrite of the Year Award."

QUESTIONS

1. From a behavioural ethics perspective, compare and contrast the organizational culture at HRA in its first two years with its later reincarnation under the charge of Burke Hampton. What are the ethical implications of alterations in the basic assumptions in HRA organizational culture in this period? As a rational functionalist, what would you recommend Burke do to tame the growing disenchantment at HRA? Why is it difficult, from a structural functionalist position, to retain the ethical climate at HRA as it grew from 35 to 1,256 employees?

2. Within the normative code perspective, what is the prevailing notion of justice in the organizational culture at HRA? What virtues of leadership have been lost in the transition from the Robb brothers and Larry Carriere to Burke Hampton and his management team? Utilize Kantian thinking to suggest what is ethically problematic in the five points raised by the anonymous author of the second e-mail.

3. HRA's Ethics Committee has its hands full. What do you recommend it does with regards to: (a) its initial mandate; (b) information given by employees of HRA; (c) dealing with the accusations raised by the anonymous e-mail; and (d) setting out a means to establish genuine dialogue in the organizational culture at HRA?

4. Compare and contrast Burke Hampton's e-mail with that of the anonymous author. From an unconscious perspective on organizational culture, what defense mechanisms are operative at HRA? Are they functional? What can be done to make the use of some of these defense mechanisms more functional? What is nostalgia? What role does it play in ceasing tensions between the organizational culture of the Robbs and Larry Carriere and that associated with Burke Hampton?

5. Using the four pillars in the normative code perspective on organizational culture, what, in your view, is the best way to help HRA gain a hold on its ethical portfolio? What role does act utilitarianism seem to play in Burke Hampton's working out of the organizational culture? How can Burke Hampton work the virtue ethics of Larry Carriere back into the organizational culture at HRA?

6. From the unconscious perspective on organizational cultures, what sort of neurotic culture seems to be predominating at HRA? What combination of neurotic cultural elements seems to be at work here? What can be done to turn these dysfunctional elements into functional ones? Who can help in this role? How?

CASE 5-3   Kathy Alexander: Incoming Calls

Kathy Alexander received her first job after graduating from Dalhousie University with a Generalist Degree in Arts. Kathy was planning to work her way up in a good firm, and then use her experience to apply for a graduate degree specializing in public relations. When Kathy applied to Atlantic Car Leasing Incorporated and received a job with the "telephone unit," she was pleased. The telephone unit takes incoming calls; these usually involve client requests for information, and complaints. Kathy felt that the work with the public, particularly with client complaints over their car leases, would prove a solid, ground-floor learning experience for one seeking to develop expertise in public relations.

The job was difficult. Employees dealt hour after hour with phone calls of all sorts, types, and sizes. Kathy tried hard to focus her attention, know the facts, and handle all calls with professional dignity. Kathy felt she was good at this job and that her coworkers and supervisors in the telephone unit shared this evaluation.

After four months with the telephone unit, it was Kathy Alexander's time for quarterly evaluation. This review would determine the amount of merit-pay increase Kathy could expect. As her supervisor, Mrs. Linkovsky went over the various sections of the review sheet. Kathy agreed with her evaluation until they reached the area devoted to the topic of productivity. Having received high grades in every area so far, Kathy was surprised when she received only an average mark in the category of productivity. Kathy politely questioned Mrs. Linkovsky as to why this mark was given, but Mrs. Linkovsky's response was not acceptable to Kathy. Mrs. Linkovsky argued that since it was hard to measure productivity in the telephone unit, all supervisors had decided to give all workers in this unit an average rating. Kathy checked with her coworkers, and not only were all given an average, but several who had been there several years told Kathy that they had never received anything but an "average" for productivity.

Despite the acceptance of an average mark in productivity by the other workers in the telephone unit, Kathy was angry. She found Mrs. Linkovsky's and the other supervisors' logic, insofar as the measurement of productivity in the telephone unit was concerned, unacceptable. Kathy began a barrage of communications to the supervisors' supervisors. Kathy argued that if the best rating workers in the telephone unit could receive was an average, where was the incentive to better performance? Moreover, Kathy insisted that the problems in measurement of productivity were not the fault of the telephone unit workers but were, in effect, an issue that required innovation by those doing the quarterly evaluations—the supervisors.

Kathy Alexander was successful in her campaign to get the issue investigated. Kathy's fellow workers were eager to see the results of this investigation and ascertain whether or not their merit pay would, under the new assessment, take a small jump upward. They were not only sourly disappointed, but soon blamed Kathy Alexander for making their work lives all that more difficult.

The supervisors responded to the ensuing investigation by their supervisors by requiring the phone workers to complete additional paperwork while processing incoming phone calls. This data, the supervisors argued, would help them differentiate the average from above average or even excellent producers in the telephone unit. This barrage of paperwork increased the difficulty of the task required of the employees in the telephone unit and lowered the amount of time they had to deal with important calls.

Kathy Alexander quit her job in disgust only seven months after her first happy days at Atlantic Car Leasing.

QUESTIONS:

1. Describe the organizational culture at Atlantic Car Leasing. How would you characterize the ethical climate at Atlantic Car Leasing? What might you have done differently than Kathy Alexander? How might it have improved things for the "telephone unit" at Atlantic Car Leasing?

2. What, in your view, are the prevailing values at Atlantic Car Leasing? How do these connect to the basic assumptions of the firm? Given these two, what sort of rituals, legends, and stories do you expect might prevail in an organizational culture like that experienced by Kathy Alexander at Atlantic Car Leasing?

3. Utilize all four components of what we have called the philosopher's formula to assess the ethical portfolio at Atlantic Car Leasing. Which of the four seems to be most strongly supported at Atlantic Car Leasing? Which the least? Explain your reasoning.

4. What merits are there in Mrs. Linkovsky's evaluation and treatment of the members of the "telephone unit" with regard to their quarterly evaluation? How does Mrs. Linkovsky's position square with the Rawlsian notion of justice? How does Mrs. Linkovsky's position square with the Kantian position of rights and duties?

5. Was it right, in your view, for Kathy Alexander's fellow workers in the telephone unit to blame her for her attempt at reform? What does this reveal about the level of paranoia in the culture? What does it say about Atlantic Car Leasing as a compulsively-driven bureaucratic culture?

6. What lesson do you recommend Kathy Alexander take from her relatively short and troubled work experience at Atlantic Car Leasing? Which of Charles Handy's four ideal organizational cultures predominates at Atlantic Car Leasing? In what direction was Kathy Alexander to push the organizational culture? What could Kathy Alexander have done to modify these reactions?

DIRTY HANDS
AND CORPORATE
LIFE

*A leader who does not hesitate before he sends his nation into battle is
not fit to be a leader.*

Golda Meir
My Life (1975)

WHEN THE GOOD IS EVASIVE

It would be simplistic to assume that having selected a version of the good world, all that is
needed is to choose the leader and develop the organizational culture that can transport us
there. As Golda Meir makes clear, in a situation that provides no good option, the good
leader must still act. The good leader's value reveals itself not in avoiding the dilemma,
but in acknowledging it and hesitating before boldly proceeding. In practice, particularly in
the competitive milieu of business in which action is under constraints of time and money,
business leaders must make "tough" decisions. Tough decisions occur in a context in which
it is difficult to discern what is good. Ethics involves not merely deciding between options
that clearly represent themselves as good and bad, or even among choices that are all to
various degrees good, but also between "tough" choices, between one wrong and another.

In *How Good People Make Tough Choices* (1995), Rushworth Kidder makes the point
that few of us have trouble with the "right vs. wrong" choices. With some exceptions, we all
recognize that lying, cheating, stealing, and harming innocent others are wrong. As good people trying to be good, what we do have trouble with are those choices in which we are
rushed, over-committed, possess inaccurate data, have just inherited the problem, or remain
unaware of who is actually responsible for it, and thus genuinely cannot discern what is

right from wrong. Unlike cases in an ethics book, businesses must deal with ethical issues in the flow of organizational processes where there are many red flags—technical, economic, political, strategic, operating, and, of course, moral. Rushworth reminds us that in these contexts it is relatively easy to locate an ethical lapse "after the fact," but that it is important to understand the process wherein, during the flow of things, people, departments, and systems may get their hands "dirty."

In this chapter we shall explore the concept of "dirty hands" in business. Our aim is descriptive; we are not concerned with analyzing those "deviants" who consciously cross moral and legal lines in order to benefit themselves. Rather, our focus is upon the well-intentioned good corporate citizen who, in seeking to satisfy the needs of his or her organization, traverses moral and legal boundaries. "I was just doing my job" has become the plaintiff's logic in many cases of corporate moral transgression. Most of us, particularly the dutiful, seek to succeed at work. We can, however, become swept away, ending up with dirty hands. Organizations are unintentional incubators of dirty hands problems. In competitive organizational contexts we can rationalize our actions. We work under constraints of time and resources and are rewarded for quick and daring action that quells costly problems. We act within groups where it is easy to conform to the group interest. We are asked to work in teams where we learn to cover for the deficiencies of our colleagues, just as we expect them to do likewise for us. Moreover, we are rarely looked upon with great promise when we admit our errors, go public with our moral qualms, or seriously question either the intentions or consequences of decisions taken by our superiors.

We shall begin our review of the dirty hands problem by looking at the organization as an incubator of moral choice. Then we shall look at the requisite of all dirty hands problems—that we must act in situations where it is difficult to decide what is good and right and what is not. To illustrate processes that aid good people in making bad moral decisions, we will look at how workaholism, "groupthink," escalation processes, and diffusion of responsibility all create opportunities for questionable moral behaviour.

ORGANIZATIONS AS MORAL INCUBATORS

The behaviour we engage in as agents of organizations is perceived quite differently than our behaviour outside of them. Organizations—and this, of course, means the people in them—make demands of us, and our efforts to interpret what the demands are and then to fulfill them are what most of us call our work. We are paid to represent the will and satisfy the demands of organizations. This occurs not only within the workplace, but also in our relationships to other social institutions—schools, banks, and governments. Organizations focus our energy into action. In trying to fulfill the demands of organizations, we must come to terms with whether or not these demands are both rational and in line with the organization's social responsibilities. Organizations require that we compromise our views; when we are in the minority on a decision, we are advised not to insist that energy be spent revisiting it.

It is possible, of course, to think of a moral transgression as nothing but the act of a few bad apples. This view is usually greeted with sighs of relief all round. Dirty hands are the acts of deviants—those who have been improperly socialized, who know better but seek to advance their careers at all costs, by cutting corners, misappropriating intellectual property, or misrepresenting themselves in their wheeling and dealing. However, another possibility is that organizations are moral incubators. They often reward good people for making questionable moral decisions.

In his classic article, "Why 'Good' Managers Make Bad Ethical Choices" (1986), Saul Gellerman sees the issue as more than the acts of a few bad apples. Gellerman asks, for example, how top-level executives at the Manville Corporation could have suppressed evidence for decades that proved asbestos inhalation was killing their own employees. His response is that the modern business organization provides very fertile ground for four interrelated rationalizations. The first is a belief that the questionable activity is within reasonable ethical limits. This rationalization occurs because the organization requires individuals, groups, and systems to make decisions along a continuum. The issue is not to distinguish between sharp and shady practices, but rather to determine when and under what circumstances the sharp becomes shady. The issue is complex, and will remain so as individuals, groups, and systems seek to innovate in the name of corporations. Put enough bright and hard-working people, Gellerman insists, under stressful conditions in ambiguously-defined situations, with some edge given to those who do the job best—defined in corporate terms—and the line between sharp and shady gets pushed slowly but surely towards the shady.

In the context of a collective like the organization, it is easy to rationalize this shift from the sharp to the shady when the incumbent genuinely believes that in so behaving a large number of people will benefit. This second rationalization—the belief that the activity is in the corporation's best interest—is supported by the ambiguous communications systems set up between top executives and their subordinates. Top executives rarely directly ask their subordinates to do things that both know to be imprudent. The process is one in which the boss, in his or her expression of exasperation, implies that a certain activity would be in the organization's best interest. This leads to a complex sort of shadiness. The executives distance themselves and "keep their hands clean" (Gellerman, 1986:89), but, by either their ambiguous silence or their oblique directives, encourage subordinates in the name of the larger good to push the continuum towards the shady.

Gellerman suggests that the organization is fertile ground for the rationalization of shady behaviour, since it is believed that activities done for the good of the organization are safe. They will be kept quiet. The organization is a complex web of responsibilities and interdependencies. It creates a team environment whose members stick together and help out those who stray somewhat. As Amar Bhide and Howard Stevenson write, in "Why Be Honest if Honesty Doesn't Pay?" it is accepted that "punishment for the treacherous in the real world is neither swift nor sure" (1990:121). Due to the complex, often impenetrable nature of who is accountable for what behaviour, "a great deal of prescribed behaviour escapes detection" (Gellerman, 1986:89), and this is the third rationalization for shady dealings.

Shady dealers often escape detection thanks to the fourth rationalization, which goes something like this: "I may as well do it since it will advance my career, make money for the firm, and when others (who think just as I do) see this, they will cover for me." While the third rationalization focuses on the difficulty of detecting shady practices, the fourth looks at what the social psychologist Irving Janis called the process of "groupthink." Gellerman points out that at Manville Corporation a small group of executives and a long succession of medical directors tacitly agreed to keep the facts about the lethal characteristics of asbestos out of the public domain for decades. These were not "evil" men and women. They convinced themselves within their organizational culture that they were acting in both the long-term interests of Manville Corporation and for society in general. They insisted their data was not scientifically conclusive and, given this, they were reluctant to pull the rug out from under a thriving industry, rocking the economy and forcing workers, often in impoverished regions, out of jobs. More troubling still, they claimed, was the billions of dollars that would have to be spent in taking asbestos out of the built environment.

Figure 6.1 locates what Laura Nash, in her highly readable *Good Intentions Aside: A Manager's Guide to Resolving Ethical Problems*, sees as persistent difficulties. "These," she writes, "are not hot-house problems that occur once in a career, they are familiar dilemmas. A company has at least twenty on the table every day .... What I find equally impressive is their elusive nature. These are the kinds of situations that seem obviously wrong from a distance, but are so embedded in other concerns and environmental circumstances that the demarcations between right and wrong are blurred" (1990:8). Laura Nash is not asking us to be sympathetic to wrongdoers; she is asking us to be aware that it is often not clear when one has crossed the line.

Aspects of this moral line-crossing are illustrated by Bowen H. "Buzz" McCoy's account of an incident that occurred when he took a six-month sabbatical from his job to trek in the mountains of Nepal (McCoy, 1997). Buzz was a managing director of Morgan Stanley Company Inc., the president of Morgan Stanley Realty, and an ordained ruling elder of the United Presbyterian Church. Thirty days into the trek, Buzz and his party—an American anthropologist named Stephen and several Sherpa guides and porters—were ascending to a mountain pass at 18,000 feet. At this point the group was halfway through the Himalayan section of the trip. Their goal was the village of Muklinath, an ancient holy place for pilgrims. At 16,500 feet, in the area of the Everest base camp, Buzz had an attack of pulmonary edema. Stephen, as well, was suffering from a less acute, but still debilitating form of altitude sickness.

As Buzz, Stephen, and the Sherpa guides ascended the trail, they were met by a New Zealander from a party ahead of them on the path. The New Zealander, stumbling under a load covered with blankets, approached the group and dumped the almost naked, barefoot body of an older Indian holy man—a sadhu—at Buzz's feet. Gasping for breath and near exhaustion himself, the New Zealander said that he had found the pilgrim on the ice, shivering and near dead from hypothermia. The New Zealander was angry. In taking responsibility for the freezing holy man, he had endangered himself by cutting off from his group. He insisted that Buzz and his group deal with the sadhu. He justified this by pointing out that he had to catch up with his group since they were carrying his gear and food—that he must move quickly to get across the pass before the sun melted the snow, as his group had no guides or porters.

Buzz and Stephen sprang into action, opening their packs and clothing the sadhu from head to toe. Although revived, the sadhu was too weak to walk or to explain what he was doing at that altitude without shoes and clad in skimpy cotton robes. After taking his carotid pulse, Buzz was assured that the man would live if he were taken to safety. Below them, Buzz and Stephen spotted a Japanese party with a larger entourage of guides and a horse. Telling Stephen that he was worried about the altitude and needed to cross the pass himself, Buzz took off after some porters who had gone on ahead.

Several hours later, Stephen, tired and exhausted, rejoined Buzz at the summit. Stephen was angry. He explained that both the Japanese climbers and their porters refused to take the holy man down to the village, claiming they would require all their energy to get over the pass. Stephen persisted, finally convincing the Sherpas to carry the sadhu down a few thousand feet to a rock in the warm sun. The Japanese gave the sadhu food and drink and, when they last saw him, he was listlessly tossing rocks at the Japanese party's dog.

FIGURE 6-1   Typical Lapses in Moral Judgment and Action in the Organization: Typical Rationalizations

Typical Lapse in Moral Judgment and Action	Typical Rationalization
• Using others to climb the corporate ladder (e.g., appropriating the ideas of subordinates without giving due recognition to them).	• People who work for me will be very well rewarded as I climb the corporate ladder. I take care of my people.
• Remaining mute when an unethical practice occurs (e.g., failing to reveal that one's colleagues are engaged in selling some of the firm's so-called "secret ingredients" to competitors).	• My job description does not involve squealing on my co-workers. The company has not increased our salaries in two years, while the bosses get raises every year.
• Obedience to authority, however unethical and unfair it may seem (e.g., carrying out the company's orders to fire an individual ostensibly due to poor performance but actually because of his/her demanding personality).	• We are good soldiers here. We do as we are told with an understanding that the bosses have more data and can see the big picture to which we have no access.
• Neglecting one's family, health, and/or commitments to the local community due to one's commitment to work (e.g., immersing oneself in work in order to avoid dealing with a failing marriage).	• Work is the way I take care of myself and those I love. There is nothing more caring than providing others with material goods. This is genuine love.
• Ducking one's responsibility for injurious practices (e.g., passing the buck and attributing responsibility to the "testing" department despite their thorough warnings that the product has faults).	• We follow the letter of the law, hire the best researchers, and test our products carefully. Errors can happen. We learn from them.
• The use of cover-ups and distortion in reporting and control procedures (e.g., using creative bookkeeping procedures to understate accident hours lost).	• The reporting procedures are just a ritual. We fill them in for government purposes, but no one seems to pay much attention.
• Selectively using data to exaggerate the benefits of a plan as a way to get support (e.g., employing the best possible data in a series of data points and never revealing the selection bias when introducing a new marketing campaign and its reaction by a test group).	• We have to commit to an option and quickly. Equivocation will kill us. If I am wrong and my plan fails to achieve the ends I have suggested, I will be held to account. I accept this. Now, let's get on with my plan.

Both Stephen and Buzz were distraught. When they inquired about the sadhu on their descent, no one had seen or heard of the holy man. Stephen and Buzz were certain he had perished. Stephen, a Quaker with a committed moral vision said, "I feel that what happened with the sadhu was a good example of the breakdown between the individual ethic and corporate ethic. No one person was willing to assume ultimate responsibility for the sadhu. Each was willing to do his bit—just so long as it was not too inconvenient" (McCoy, 1997:60).

When we look closely at this story, we can identify factors that are common to business. The problem of the holy man came unexpectedly, just as the mountaineers were preparing themselves to deal with a very challenging and demanding experience. The New Zealanders, the Japanese, and Buzz and Stephen were all focused on their own goals. They were under great stress—physical and time pressures were evident. As well, each thought that the others were better equipped to deal with the problem. There was no process on the trail for developing a consensus. Each group felt that it had done enough to act morally towards the sadhu.

McCoy writes that "real moral dilemmas are ambiguous and many hike right through them, unaware that they exist" (1997:60). Participants cannot avoid action; failure to act as a participant is a decision itself. It is clear that on the trail to Muklinath McCoy learned that "in contrast to philosophy, business involves action and implementation—getting things done." Getting things done involves understanding how one's hands get dirty. Men like Buzz McCoy help us become conscious that business ethics is part of what good people, with good intentions, must take seriously. There are too many who think that business ethics is for the "other guy": the cheater, the liar, and the thief.

DIRTY HANDS WITHIN BUSINESS

Within business ethics, the dirty hands problem involves dealing with real life decisions, which, at times, place the leader in a position of having to select between such options as the use of deceit, force, or threats of litigation as a means of achieving an appropriate resolution to a pressing problem. In Figure 6.2, the plight of Nick Mennel speaks to the issue of dirty hands. Niccolo Machiavelli's *The Prince*, published after his death in 1532, brings to the forefront the dirty hands problems in politics. Machiavelli reminds us that to govern an institution or a state, "it is often necessary to act contrary to faith, charity, humanity, and religion in order to maintain the state .... If possible, he (the leader) ought not, as I have said before, turn away from what is good, but he should be able to do evil if necessary" (cited in Thompson, 1980:312). In Machiavelli's view, it is "dangerous" to select as a leader an individual whose respect for honesty, fair dealing, and a good reputation will paralyze him or her when none of these can be achieved within the options presented. Machiavelli, a realist and early founder of managerial strategy, viewed as a requirement of leadership the ability to make tough decisions.

While there are many versions of the dirty hands problem, the most serious faces us when the goal absolutely must be attained, but the only way to reach it is morally unacceptable. Carl B. Klockars (1985) uses the 1971 film, *Dirty Harry,* to explore the dirty hands problem in police work. Clint Eastwood plays a detective who tortures a psychopathic killer in order to force him to divulge the whereabouts of a missing child. The aggressive detective, who goes by the well-chosen name of "Dirty Harry," is clearly in contravention of the rules governing police work, but time is short and the psychopath is his

---

FIGURE 6-2   Photojournalist in the Jungle

Nick Mennel, a young Canadian journalist, tells of his "dirty hands" problem in the jungles of South America. While on assignment to cover guerrilla warfare in jungle territory between Guyana and Surinam, Nick, cameras in hand, runs into a group of fourteen "freedom fighters" holding captive the citizens of a village. Unaccustomed to movement in the jungle, Nick and his two assistants, Katherine Napier and Michael Debenham, are easily apprehended by the guerrillas.

Realizing that Nick and his colleagues are journalists and capable of ready transmission of photographs and stories to major world news centres, the head guerrilla came up with a plan. Nick is ordered to go with seven of the freedom fighters to a town eighty kilometres distant, take photographs, and establish that the main thrust of the guerrillas' attack is along a string of towns quite far from their actual line of attack. Nick realizes that the guerrillas' tactic is to throw their pursuers off the scent and have townsfolk remain unprepared.

The leader of the guerrillas states that unless Nick does this, all the people in the village will be killed along with his companions, Katherine and Michael. In fact, to make this threat evident, the head guerrilla calls one of his men forward. The guerrilla brings with him a young man from the village and promptly puts a bullet through his head. Nick is appalled. Katherine and Michael realize the hole they have placed themselves in.

The guerrilla leader tells Nick that one person from the village will be slain every day until he receives word from his companions in the region's major centre that the false information has been published in the world news. At that date, the guerrilla leader gives his word that Nick's two companions will be held safely for three weeks, along with those villagers still alive. The leader explains that three weeks will give the guerrillas ample time to achieve their territorial goals unopposed.

Nick is driven off with seven guerrillas towards the decoy village. This fictitious case leaves Nick—as an agent for the lives of his colleagues and the villagers—in a real dirty hands problem.

---

sole source of information. The effectiveness of torture is not relevant to the moral issue in this particular film; the child is found, but too late. What is most unsettling, and remains the grievance upon which the viewers' sympathies go to Dirty Harry and not to the administrators within the police force, is that the psychopath is set free. Dirty Harry not only broke the rules by extracting information by violent means, but due to his violation the evidence he gained about the killer's guilt was not admissible in a court of law. Our sense of injustice (sympathy for Dirty Harry) is part of our recognition that there are times when immoral means to a necessary goal (the child's life) seem supportable.

Three issues are embedded in the dirty hands problem, and each sheds light upon the tension between theory and practice in the field of ethics as applied to business. The first comes from the playwright, philosopher, and novelist, Jean Paul Sartre, from whose play, *Les Mains Sales* (1960), these problems are coined. From Sartre's existentialist position, men and women of decisive action must at times compromise their ideals. Decisive action is goal-directed, and to achieve one's goal—particularly if it is vital—requires that one must do things that otherwise one would rather not. In organizations and business we are often asked to compromise our ideals, not only in the name of the organization, but also in recognition that our principles must be brought into line with those of others and, of course, be made consistent with other principles we hold.

In this context, Sir Adrian Cadbury provides an interesting story. Sir Adrian Cadbury, of Cadbury Schweppes, notes how his grandfather was caught between two cherished moral principles that forced him make a "tough choice" (Grace and Cohen, 1995:51). Sir Adrian's grandfather was so opposed to what he took to be the senseless brutality of the Boer War that he bought a British newspaper in order to disseminate his views. He was also vehemently opposed to gambling, and so insisted on eliminating all references to horse racing and other forms of betting in his paper. As a result of this purge, the paper's circulation fell dramatically, which rather defeated his original design. Sir Adrian's grandfather put himself in an ethical bind—report on the races and retain a large audience for his anti-war message, or stick to his principles regarding gambling and forfeit his anti-war voice. He decided to compromise his views on gambling for the greater good of having his anti-war, anti-brutality message reach a larger readership.

Unlike the tough decision in *Dirty Harry*, it was expedient for Sir Adrian's grandfather to suppress one moral principle in order for another to flourish. This is more than merely prioritizing values; acts of compromise can be thought of in two ways. They can be seen as lapses of principle, a form of "selling out." Alternatively, acts of compromise can be seen as the cost one must bear to put principles into action. Action requires us to choose among or between what may be conflicting values.

A second issue germane to the dirty hands problem is the suggestion that business is nothing but a game and that acts of deception, exaggeration, and selective fact-giving are merely strategies used within the rules. Probably the most influential article discussing this is Albert Z. Carr's "Is Business Bluffing Ethical?" (1968). For Carr and other advocates of the business-is-a-game metaphor, we cannot employ everyday ethical truisms such as "tell the truth," or "take time to consider others' positions," within the context of business. Business is a special context in which everyday ethical truisms are worked out and interpreted quite differently. Just as in hockey or boxing it is permissible, even advisable, to use bodily force to impede one's opponent (and not expect him/her to cry foul), so too in business one is expected to bluff, exaggerate, and use facts selectively in order to enhance the probability of winning. Carr insists that those who play the game know its rules and rise to the challenge of their opponents' abilities.

Moreover, what is key is that efforts to use non-business rules to assess the game of business are bound to fail, just as using the rules of etiquette are bound to fail to explain the on-ice behaviour of competitive hockey players. Ethicists who seek to interpret business moves as if they were issues to be assessed using everyday ethics fail to take into account the nature of the game.

On the surface, Carr provides an explanation for the dirty hands problem, but it poses as many questions as it answers. The game metaphor, with its emphasis on bluffing and strategic deception to achieve corporate goals (win), must be treated with care. First, we should not confuse this description of what sometimes occurs in business with a recommendation that this is the way business *ought* to be practised—or, for that matter, that those who engage in questionable practices or, in Carr's language, "play the game hard" (1968), are most likely to win.

What remains even more problematic in the business-is-a-game metaphor is the assumption that all involved are "players" and, as players, they know the rules. In hockey, everyone on the ice develops sound expectations within a game of how rough it will be (particularly given the referee's assessment of penalties). The boundaries are clear. The ice is spatially delineated by the boards and temporally delineated by the game clock. A player who believes a cheap shot has been taken by an opponent may elect to call for a fight. This fight will be dealt with by the rules of the game (and the referee's discretion) and a penalty (2 minutes, 5 minutes, etc.) will be meted. However, if the same player thinks that a fan has taken a cheap shot and decides to use hockey-is-a-game logic to settle the score, he or she may find that the fight with the fan (a non-player) will be assessed quite differently. The same, of course, holds for a hockey player after the game (when the game clock stops) who feels that his wife or neighbour has "taken a cheap shot," and uses hockey-is-a-game logic. In these instances, unlike in the game, assault charges may ensue.

The same clear spatial and temporal boundaries that divide spectators from players in games like hockey or tennis are not so easily established in the "game" of business. Distinguishing between players and non-players is no simple task. Are consumers players? Are people who live in proximity of a plant that discharges questionable amounts of lead players? As well, it is not clear in the game of business when the game clock has run its course. This is particularly relevant for the increasing number of people who work at home or take their business home with them. Carr's analogy is useful in exploring the dirty hands problem, but it fails to establish that business is indeed a game just like others.

The third and final issue pertinent to the dirty hands problem in business ethics, and one related to the treatment of business as if it were a game, is the separation it implies between private and public morality. In Figure 6.3 we can see these dynamics at play. In the game of business, it is argued, one must engage in activities quite apart from what one would teach one's children as standard and acceptable practices. John Ladd (1970), like Niccolo Machiavelli, distinguishes between personal actions and values and organizational actions and values. The logic in this distinction is not unlike that used by sociologists and social psychologists when they talk about socialized men and women enacting "roles."

In role theory, it is important to realize that one is playing not a game but a role. The business metaphor shifts from hockey, soccer, tennis, and poker to the theatre. The role of manager, the role of union representative, the role of member of the board of directors all require that one pursue private goals and values in an official or public capacity. Not only is compromise required but, within the formal rationality of organizational life, putting personal values and aspirations ahead of the public role requirements is deemed wrong. The chief operating executive who jeopardizes the viability of a newspaper—which employs hundreds of people and keeps thousands, if not millions, of readers informed—because of his/her personal principles, is seen as a distortion of the role of the competent newspaper owner. In this regard, Bernard Williams has argued that "in public life ... sometimes the 'right' thing to do is something that is not moral," and sometimes this has the result of allowing that there is a "morally disagreeable remainder" even after one has done the right thing (1978:75).

Within public life, for example political life, morality is fraught with a tension between doing what is expected or proper to a situation (playing one's role competently) and remaining true to one's convictions (personal beliefs and values). This is fertile ground for the emergence of dirty hands problems. As Steve Buckler, the author of *Dirty Hands: The Problem of Political Morality*, writes, "the dirty hands problem is important here because it gives us a sense in which politics, when it disappoints our moral expectations and moral sensibilities, does so for reasons other than mere malpractice" (1993:3). The idea of "selling

FIGURE 6-3 Gunter Voss: Dirty Hands and a Very Good Zoo

James MacGowan's (1997) discussion of the life and career of Gunter Voss is an interesting study of how the dirty hands form of leadership can be extremely effective.

Gunter Voss was a pioneer and leader in the creation and management of zoos. Voss came to his vocation early, and at fifteen began his career as zoo manager by combining his precocious studies in zoology with his volunteer job at the local zoo in his native Germany.

He was the right man to set up the "World's Greatest Zoo," built on 287 hectares in Scarborough's Rouge Valley. Voss had worked in zoos in both Germany and Winnipeg, where he served for eleven years as the director of the Assiniboine Park Zoo. He was supremely confident, a gifted man at the peak of his craft, when he met with Toronto's Metro Zoo planners in 1970 and told them, "Gentlemen, you have a very nice place for a zoo here, but we are going to have to make a lot of changes."

Changes were made and implemented with impeccable precision by Voss. The traditional practice of keeping animals in cages was ended. Animals, he insisted, would be housed within five geographical zones representing Africa, the Americas, Eurasia, Indo-Malaysia, and Canada, roaming freely in open-air enclosures. Barriers were to be minimized and, wherever possible, these were made to blend in with the environment. Voss's ideas were radical for the day.

He insisted that the Metro Zoo "... was not Disneyland. We are not a midway. We have educational values and important conservation aims. The onus will be on visitors to behave. Parents must watch their children and not let them frighten or harass the animals. We are offering a very special experience, but the freedom for us to continue will depend on our guests." With his strong views, educational mission, and impeccable credentials, Voss helped to make Metro Zoo one of the best in the world.

However, Voss's leadership of the zoo was controversial, particularly the manner in which he seemed to enrich himself in purchasing animals. MacGowan reports that Voss did an inordinate amount of business with a New Rochelle, New York wild animal dealer named Fred Zeehandelaar. Voss paid extra for top quality and received from three to six per cent of each purchase back. Some would later view it as a form of kickback. Voss defended the purchases vehemently. The return to the zoo director, insisted Voss, was common practice.

Voss, on the day of his conviction for using his post unwisely and unethically, handed Metro Zoo officials a cheque for $21,582—his share of the money received for animals purchased. Twelve years have passed since Gunter Voss stocked the Metro Zoo, and there remains an active debate over whether another more accommodating and gentler individual could have moved so decisively in making the Toronto Metro Zoo the exemplar it has become.

out," particularly in the realm of politics, is understood as having compromised one's ideals in order to survive and sustain a line of action before formidable opposition.

Business, like politics, is fraught with "opposition," both real and at times strategically conjured. Politicians and business persons, by adhering to their public roles, can and do utilize the existence of an opportunity to justify their recurrent need to amend previous commitments, ethical principles, and personal ideals. The public role as agent responsible for the collective, the decision-maker at the heart of the enterprise, requires the good politician and manager to place personal and private values to the side and put actual accomplishment of ends to the forefront. Many of us can arrive at the rationalization that "the ends justify the means," but few can support it as easily as the politician and manager, by pointing towards a public role.

The problem of dirty hands, write Grace and Cohen, "is essentially one of whether evil may ever be done, not just in exceptional circumstances—which most people are apt to find excusable—but as an inevitable part of human life" (1995:57). The possibility that business—like all human activity—may have a "darker side" requires our attention. A closer look at some pathologies that can and do accompany our business practices speaks to the systematic way in which dirty hands problems get a start in the everyday practices of business. To illustrate these processes, let us turn to (1) workaholism, (2) groupthink, (3) escalation processes, and (4) diffusion of responsibility as examples of the darker side of what some consider to be the essence of rationality—business processes and commitments. Figure 6.4 outlines the four processes we use to illustrate the dirty hands problem and their ethical implications.

WORKAHOLISM

The term "workaholism" was coined in 1971 as an analogy to the term "alcoholism" and refers to people who behave with work as others do who are addicted to alcohol (Oates, 1971). While workaholism has become a household word, it has not yet been accepted into either the official psychiatric or psychological nomenclatures. There is a growing recognition that workaholics find themselves caught in a vicious cycle of symptoms which, from early to late stages, include:

1. *Hurrying and remaining busy:* Workaholics possess an inability to say "no" to work-related matters. They are haunted by a continued sense of urgency. They constantly think about work. They need to have many things happening at once, and enjoy it when they are—or believe themselves to be—at the centre of these.

2. *Taking control:* Workaholics possess an exaggerated belief in both their centrality in work-related affairs and their own abilities. They seek to control others before others control them. They have difficulty delegating. They abhor uncertainty, surprises, or unpredictable events.

3. *Perfectionism:* Workaholics' obsessive concern with avoiding uncertainty places a strong emphasis upon getting things just right. In order to achieve this compulsive avoidance of mistakes, the workaholic becomes single-minded and focused upon rigid ideas. The statement, "If you want it done right, do it yourself" is a classic sign of standards that are difficult for others to achieve largely because they do not know or share them with the workaholic.

4. *Compulsive work behaviour:* Workaholics not only work long hours, but seek these long hours as a way of minimizing relationships, which they cannot control. The social life of workaholics diminishes rapidly. Workaholics give up relationships and relationship obligations in order to increase their commitment to work and the workplace.

5. *One-sided workplace relationships:* Given that workaholics diminish their non-work relationships, one might expect them to find friends at work. This is not the case. Workaholics' relationships with others at work is very formal. This enhances the issues of the workaholics' desire for control, predictability, and perfectionism.

```
FIGURE 6-4   Dirty Hands Processes: Business Ethics Implications
```

Process	Major Dynamics	Business Ethics Implications
Workaholism	For personal and often societally-approved reasons, the individual uses work as a means of avoiding his or her other problems. This compulsive fastening of personal identity to success at work can have dysfunctional consequences for the individual, those dependent upon him or her, and the workplace.	The fixed focus on work lends itself to faulty moral decision making. A "success at any cost" attitude prevails. Others are seen as means to a desired end. The obsession is justified by pointing out how success at work makes the individual a major contributor to the greater good.
Groupthink	Overly cohesive in-groups create the process where conformity and obedience to the group overrides critical evaluation of data. This conformity is rewarded by members reinforcing each other's views and escalating promotions and upward mobility.	The over-conforming nature of the groupthink process lowers the quality of moral decision making. The groupthink process internalizes its own expertise and fails to assess its own moral position from an out-sider's perspective.
Escalation Processes	As sunken costs rise in business settings, decision makers feel trapped. This sense of entrapment often puts the decision maker in the position of throwing good money after bad. In escalation, poor decisions are made rather than admitting error.	The entrapped administrator in escalation processes fails to deal with threatening situations because these will prove that a previous decision taken and championed by the decision maker was wrong. In covering up, the decision maker plays loose with the facts.
Diffusion of Responsibility	In organizations, individuals, groups, and systems specialize and are accountable for their specialization, but are not accountable for events that are, it is argued, the responsibility of other specialists. Good people in good groups in good systems often feel that they are not responsible for moral issues.	Moral dilemmas in business settings are particularly susceptible to diffusion of responsibility. Few see their primary task in the organiza-tion as attending to the moral portfolio. It often lapses or is taken seriously only when it becomes a crisis.

6. *Attempts to change fail:* Workaholics get messages from their spouses, children, co-workers, and good friends to change their obsessive preoccupation with work. At first they deny its existence, stating that all of this is done for others (spouse, children, etc.). When they do "hear" these pleas, they often find that they cannot "cut back" on their addiction.

7. *Difficulty relaxing and having fun:* The obsession with doing rather than being haunts the lives of workaholics. They are often fatigued due to overwork. This fatigue absorbs their leisure time. When it does not, workaholics find themselves irritable and easily aggravated. These symptoms seem to be alleviated by going to work.

8. *Physiological signs:* Workaholics experience, although are often slow to acknowledge, such symptoms as ulcers, chronic headaches, backaches, high blood pressure, depression, and "emotional numbness." These symptoms are caused by the self-neglect that accompanies "work binges." Work binges occur when workaholics seek to escape periodically and completely into the work regime and will often work around the clock, even sleeping at work. This behaviour is often justified by pointing to a deadline or the importance of the deal. Work binges are accompanied by an adrenaline high and followed by a work hang-over, complete with withdrawal, anxiety, and depression. In the later stages, workaholics often conceal the work binge in order to sidestep the disapproval of those outside work.

9. *Brownouts:* While alcoholics have blackouts, workaholics have brownouts. These are memory losses of events, conversations, and promises due to physical exhaustion, mental preoccupation, and absorption with a very fixed and often narrow task. Family members have been known to worry and suspect neurological problems, even Alzheimer's disease.

10. *Self-neglect:* Workaholics have long passed neglecting family members and friends in order to feed their work addiction. At this stage workaholics' physical, emotional, and social isolation all take their toll. Problematically, workaholics deal with these by throwing themselves even more assiduously at their work.

In portraying this downward spiral, Dianne Fassel (1990), Bryan E. Robinson (1989), and Barbara Killinger (1991), each posits that unless they can pull themselves out of it, workaholics end up in a world of moral and spiritual bankruptcy, clinging to the illusory belief that if only they could master their work all their problems would neatly disappear. Sad as is this portrayal of workaholics, our society is quite ambivalent about this affliction and often rewards the overly work-committed individual with a position high up in the pecking orders of commerce, public administration, science, and the arts.

The image of the inventor, artist, scientist, or business person working through the night and waking up in the morning still wearing working clothes is used in our popular culture—films, stories, legends—to convey the committed individual whose focus benefits society. The entertainment industry often portrays the genius as obsessed with work to the point where neglect of the family or social obligations is simply an expected part of his or her role in society. Although we see how workaholism can lead to family breakdowns, mental illness, even death, admissions of this obsessive-compulsive behaviour are frequently made either jokingly, or with an air of self-satisfaction and pride on the part of the confessor. My students tell me that they readily claim to be "workaholics" to prospective employers when asked to divulge their most pressing character flaw. Workaholism is the sort of flaw, so their logic reveals, that a prospective employer would likely see as a source of future profits.

Workaholics may make no better employees than they do spouses, parents, or friends. Frank Minirth and his colleagues point out in *The Workaholic and His Family* (1981) that just as the workaholic plunges into work to fill an emotional void, the family, in the absence of the workaholic, experiences a similar void. Workaholics play havoc with family dynamics as well as other personal relationships. And while it is intuitively clear how the workaholic may prove a costly complication to family and friends, let's examine how in over-committing to work and the workplace the workaholic may be equally problematic to the organization. Recall the symptoms that accompany workaholism as it progresses: workaholics work long hours; they are very rigid, controlling, and perfectionist; they do not share information with others; they are not team players; they do not delegate; in their frantic attempt to over-function in order to meet unmet emotional needs, they create a pressure-cooker atmosphere for others. Figure 6.5 outlines the high cost of workaholics in key organizational roles.

The relationship between workaholism and ethics is neither subtle nor inspiring. We can trace the origins and consequences of ethics and workaholism at two different but interrelated levels of analysis: first, the individual workaholic; second, the workaholic organization as a

FIGURE 6-5 Interpersonal Skills in Management: Effective vs. Workaholic Manager		
Management Skill Area	**Effective Manager**	**Workaholic Manager**
Conflict Management	• is able to utilize confrontation and collaboration skills • is flexible • appeals to common interests	• uses avoidance, accommodation, and denial • is rigid • divides and controls
Delegation	• is able to relinquish control • trusts others • provides useful feedback	• retains control • distrusts others • engages in critical feedback
Communication	• exchanges feelings and emotions • seeks feedback • is open to options	• avoids expression of feelings • seeks only positive feedback • focuses totally on goal at hand
Motivation	• attempts to understand needs of others • rewards performance • deals with the context	• expects compliance from others • punishes failure • goes by the rules
Leadership	• provides vision • plays a developer role • has realistic expectations • uses power and authority to challenge others to learn • is open to cooperation when feasible	• micro-manages • plays caretaker role • has unrealistic expectations • uses power and authority to gain control for personal security • views cooperation as increasing uncertainty
Ethical Consideration	• seeks stakeholders' tradeoffs • is open to critics • seeks to understand others' values • seeks balance	• focuses on task accomplishment • is closed to critics • seeks others as means to an end • seeks success

whole. In line with our discussion of workaholism up to this point, at the individual level of analysis, workaholism is depicted as a problem borne by the well-intentioned individual bruised by life and attempting to cope by turning to a socially-acceptable addiction. Yet the addictive process for the workaholic is similar to that of the cocaine or heroin addict. Not only do workaholics suffer problems with health, family and friends, and time allocation, but they also have difficulties with issues of honesty, cheating, and open human relations.

"Ethical deterioration," write Anne Schaef and Dianne Fassel, "is the inevitable outcome of the immersion in the addictive system" (1988:67). Workaholic workers use work as a fix. They become heavily invested in their workplace persona. It is their firm belief that, if and when they get work to go "just right," all other problematic aspects of their lives will fall into place. Workaholics protect their workplace persona, often at the expense of the truth. They will hide, deny, or derogate the sources of negative feedback on their projects or the status of their assignments. Critical others are easily and stubbornly cast in the role of enemy. Workaholics tend to split the world into those who support them—an instant in-group—and those who do not. Out-groups are easily used, lied to, cheated, or treated shabbily, for they do not "count" in the eyes of the workaholic. The origins of the view that ambitious people often have more trouble with their ethical portfolios may be an insight that confuses ambition with workaholism.

Within the second unit of analysis, it becomes possible to characterize an organization as possessing the traits of the workaholic. The origins of this insight may be due to more than merely a lazy analogy. Workaholics often dominate organizations, particularly so in competitive win-lose organizations. We have already seen at the individual level of analysis that workaholics tend to create an in-group/out-group orientation and that those deemed to be part of the out-group are perceived as obstacles. When we look seriously at how the workaholic builds an in-group, we find an individual driven by the need to have the corporation reflect and thereby affirm the value of his or her work addiction. Powerful workaholics often dominate the managerial structure of certain organizations and stamp their imprimatur deeply into the corporate and administrative value system

The workaholic manager or chief executive officer seeks to have men and women about him or her who reflect his/her own values and drives. Yet this in-group, in the case of workaholics, rarely form functional teams. Rather, the in-group, created in the midst of prevailing workaholism, draws together people with basic insecurities and anxious attachments to the workplace. Each is driven to succeed, but finds it difficult to share information, to trust others from other departments or projects, and to collaborate. As a result, workaholic-dominated organizations often exist as a loose assemblage of highly driven cliques or small groups, each committed to a narrow and selfish version of the successful workplace. Each insists that its views are truly indispensable for the task at hand and that others, while giving the appearance of busyness, are off the mark. The centrality of the small group or clique around a forceful workaholic creates a web of political intrigue and suspicion in corporate life. It results in a firm in which ethics becomes a prisoner to the politics of group life and morality is a tactic used to improve one's abilities to get the task done—at any cost.

The workaholic firm, like the workaholic individual, is preoccupied with task achievement as a means of compensating for an inner void. In the individual, this inner void stems from a particular form of early-childhood experience in which the child was taught and experienced love, attention, and genuine caring only if he or she competed successfully or outshone others. On the organizational level, workaholic individuals are placed in or rise to positions of power and centrality. The organization as a whole seeks to win and comes to believe that in winning not only will it grow and prosper, but that happiness, love, and approval will, as a direct result, ensue. Both workaholic individuals and workaholic organizations get their fix in the confusion in which winning is taken as the sole means of solving problems, and the effort to look beyond the battle to the war—or even beyond the game to its enjoyment—is neither inculcated nor developed as an insight worthy of further inspection and development.

Workaholism is increasingly becoming an international problem. In Figure 6.6, we see how "karoshi," the Japanese term for workaholism, is taking its toll.

FIGURE 6-6 "Karoshi": Workaholism, Japanese Style

The Japanese are reported to work more hours per year than do citizens of any other country. William Brown and his colleagues (1994) studied "karoshi," or workaholism, in Japan. They point out that it is not atypical for a Japanese worker to work more than fourteen hours a day, not including a rather lengthy commute. While the Japanese work approximately 2,500 hours per year, American and Canadians work 1,900 hours, and the French, for example, work 1,600 hours. The Japanese figure corresponds to a society that emphasizes achievement and insists on a strong separation between work and home life. Not surprisingly, karoshi is a growing problem.

As defined by Tetsunojo Uehata, the Japanese medical authority who coined the term, "karoshi" is a work-related addiction in which workers persistently push themselves beyond their physical and psychological endurance for long periods of time in order to satisfy their need for achievement and group approval. Karoshi results in poor health, poor decision making, and ethical issues including addiction to other substances (most frequently alcohol), and suicide. J. Fallows speaks of this mixture of alcoholism and work addiction in his experience of the late-night train from Tokyo: "Once or twice a week I take the late train home myself and feel as if I'm in the middle of Japan's most depressing tableau. Half the salary men are red-faced from their beer or whiskey. As many as can rest their heads against the train windows or their neighbours' shoulders are passed out cold—drunk, slack-jawed, slumped boneless in their seats as though flung there by a mighty hand" (Fallows, 1991).

Work is tied so closely to success and achievement that those who fail or believe they have, often commit suicide. In one often-repeated example, a baseball team manager felt such a strong personal responsibility for his team's under-performance that he took his life. G. Garcia, covering the story for the American popular press, wrote: "In his sixth week as managing director of the Hanshin Tigers baseball team, Shigno Furuya, 56, ended a phone call to his wife, Akiko, with 'sayonara' (good-bye) instead of his customary 'oyasumi' (have a good night's sleep). Sensing something wrong, Akiko summoned a taxi and sped 300 miles from the family home in Ashiya in south western Japan to his hotel in Tokyo. By the time she arrived, early on the morning of 19 July, Furuya had leaped from the staircase outside his 8th-floor room to the garden 92 feet below" (Garcia, 1988).

The problem of karoshi has grown so extensively that since 1988 forty-two hotlines have been started to deal with the thousands of Japanese addicted to work. The problem has become so serious that Ako Morita, the highly revered founder of Sony, has told his employees they no longer have the option of not taking their two-week vacation. Some organizations in Japan are even closing down for several weeks or even a month each year to get workers to take time away from work and achieve a more balanced appreciation of their lives. The Japanese government is trying to take a stand on karoshi. It is setting a national target of 1,800 work hours per year and hopes to achieve this before the end of the century.

GROUPTHINK

When Donald C. Hambrick (1995) conducted in-depth interviews with twenty-three chief executives of major international corporations, he found they felt that "groupthink," an excessive like-mindedness in top management groups, was a major problem. The executives questioned felt that groupthink created a harmonious, amicable, and even smooth-running corporate team, but one that failed to deal with the hard, often morally-rooted issues that confront business. The comments—"we're all too much on the same wavelength," "there's a lack of genuine debate," "we're too comfortable, too self-congratulatory"—all indicated the executives' fear that the pleasant conformity produced by groupthink processes may undermine the organization's effort to apprehend and confront issues that may call into question the group's basic assumptions.

It was well over two decades ago that Irving L. Janis coined the term "groupthink" to apply to a "mode of thinking that people engage in when they are deeply involved in a cohesive in-group, when the members' striving for unanimity overrides their motivation to realistically appraise alternative courses of action," in essence, "a deterioration of mental efficiency, reality testing, and moral judgment that results from in-group pressures" (1972:9). Groupthink refers to a restrictive mode of thinking pursued by a group that emphasizes consensus rather than careful and realistic analysis of the decision alternatives. The fundamental problem underlying groupthink is the manner in which the group concedes to pressure to conform. Conformity in and of itself is not harmful. However, when conformity subverts the meaningful pursuit of issues and opinions relevant to the problem at hand, it can produce disastrous results. Groupthink analysts call this conformity "concurrence seeking," and illustrate its destructive potential: Kennedy's decision to invade Cuba at the Bay of Pigs; Lyndon Johnson's decision to escalate the war in Vietnam (Janis, 1982); the decision to launch the *Challenger* space shuttle (Esser and Lindoerfer, 1989); and the decision by cult leader, David Koresh, and his followers to remain behind their barricaded compound in Waco, Texas (Wexler, 1995).

The possibly disastrous consequences of the groupthink syndrome are particularly strong in a management environment that encourages teams and fosters group decision making and participation as central ingredients in a healthy corporation (Neck and Manz, 1994). Janis, and those extending and critically modifying his model of groupthink (Aldag and Fuller, 1993; Mohamed and Wiebe, 1996) point towards eight main symptoms of groupthink:

1. *An illusion of invulnerability:* The group's expertise and past successes, as proven by their selection to this highly-valued decision making group, provide a sense of detachment and over-confidence in their collective abilities.

2. *A faulty grasp of its own moral principles:* The group's cohesiveness and desire to smooth over differences are rooted in the assumption, often unstated, that group members possess the same values. This assumption is reinforced by members' evaluation of others within the group as having been selected because they have similar backgrounds, educational experiences, and histories.

3. *The skills for intellectualization and rationalization:* The group is left-brained, analytical, and usually highly invested in arriving at the one right answer to its problem. It is quick and its members entirely able to explain away criticisms and employ analytical techniques to deal with those who would question too deeply the basic premises upon which the group proceeds towards its conclusions.

4. *Advanced capabilities in stereotyping others:* The group's ability to downgrade critical comments issuing from outside the group is rooted in both the group's high estimation of its abilities and its perception that those outside the group do not actually count for very much. This self-perceived elitism is often fostered by the organizational culture and shared by those selected to the powerful executive function of group decision making.

5. *A willingness to self-censor:* The group is composed of individuals who are willing to censor their doubts in order to assure their continued good standing and high status within the group. Those who, over time, fail to self-censor are given clear signs that a modification of this behaviour would be met with group approval. The processes are subtle, but ongoing.

6. *A desire to act with unanimity:* The group not only seeks the right answer to the problem, but insists that all those in the group concur. The insistence is not made explicit, but rather introduced by pointing out how a minority view will delay implementation and raise doubts and red flags.

7. *The ability to put direct pressure on dissidents:* While the group utilizes rewards to foster self-censorship (see #5), it employs punishment or the threat of it to deal with those in the group whose thinking moves away from consensus. These punishments include movement out of key sub-committees, failure to be recognized when seeking to be heard, social ostracism, the perception that one's reputation has been tarnished. These are particularly effective given the power and perquisites that issue from being a member of good standing within this group.

8. *Reliance upon self-appointed mind guards to maintain a belief system of the group:* The group develops a culture with members whose role is to assure the smooth continuity of the group. This culture is rooted in the known preferences for outcomes sought by the group leader and promoted by his or her lieutenants or key people.

These eight symptoms are precisely the dynamics feared by Hambrick's (1995) chief executive respondents. They thrive in corporations with a tendency to use a recurring group of elite corporate members to make key decisions. Janis and his colleagues (1972) point to the issue of faulty "moral judgment" as a dimension underlying the poor quality decisions that frequently result from the groupthink process. Groupthink decision making is not only rooted in the group's "faulty grasp of its own moral principles" (see symptom #2), but also in its inability to represent the values of the larger group for which it is making decisions. Ideally, within consensus-based decision making, those who come to the decision making group are expected to represent others for whom they act as agents. Thus, the decision elite, at its best, represents the diversity of points of view held within the company. In groupthink, this is forfeited. The insulated group disavows external points of view, assumes value homogeneity and, with its analytical predisposition, insists that the decision be made on technical grounds.

The rush towards the value-neutrality of technical discussion within the groupthink process excludes the need to open the question of morality. Moreover, technical discussion, given the shared education and training of corporate decision makers, is an issue which, when differences arise, can be resolved by appeal to an expert. Since expertise within groupthink is assumed to exist within the group, the search goes inward and the group functions as its own expert. This failure to turn outward in both the act of representation (political rationality) and the search for expertise (technical rationality) make reliance upon the groupthink process (an example of organizational rationality) dangerous. There is no balance here; there is a detachment from reality, a complacency growing in and among the members of an elite decision-making unit, and a tendency of these very same members "to ignore the ethical and moral consequences of their decision" (Moorhead, *et al.*, 1991:543).

The groupthink concept provides a useful warning to managers who believe that if and when they get organizational rationality just right—use of teams, participative management, and high commitment of personnel—they need not worry about the ethics of their organization. Students of groupthink, particularly when expanding upon and modifying Janis's insights in an experimental or laboratory setting (Courtright, 1978; Leona, 1985), remind us that too much group cohesiveness, despite its desirability from a human relations perspective, may actually prove dysfunctional. The team, when its members meet recurrently, becomes insulated, self-referential and complacent, avoiding ethical issues and making poor decisions.

Richard M. Hodgetts, in *Modern Human Relations at Work*, attempts to spell out what the effective manager can do to overcome both the concurrence-seeking and ethics-avoidance issues that characterize groupthink. Hodgetts provides four suggestions. He writes, "First the manager must encourage the open airing of objections and doubts. Second, one or more outsiders should be invited to challenge the values of the members. Third, one member of the original group should act like a lawyer or devil's advocate and challenge the views of others. Finally, after reaching a preliminary decision, the group should hold a 'second chance' meeting in which every member expresses, as vividly as possible, all his or her doubts ... before making a final decision" (1984:114–15). Harvey Brightman, in *Group Problem-Solving* (1988), recommends the following seven principles to help managers reduce the probability of organizing teams with a groupthink propensity: the manager should (1) foster critical thinking in members; (2) not proselytize the members to his or her preferred outcome; (3) assign the devil's advocate role to one or two (and let everyone know that their duty is to challenge assumptions and point out costs); (4) insist upon full and open participation by all members; (5) emphasize reality testing rather than consensus as the test of the solution to be implemented; (6) have a second-look meeting; and (7) foster, at set times, the group's examination of its problem-solving processes (1988:63–69).

Brightman's (1988) and Hodgetts' (1984) suggestions encapsulate some useful suggestions on how the manager can reduce or eliminate the problematic aspects of groupthink, but they fail to capture fully how the manager, within groupthink, is part of the process, not part of the solution. The groupthink manager is an intricate part of the dynamics that are at the heart of the groupthink syndrome. The manager selects members who do not rock the boat and who get along well with him or her and the other group members. The manager elects to use this elite decision group over and over again, keeping the membership roster intact. The manager reveals his or her preferred outcome to the group early and often—influencing others toward this outcome. The manager is interested in neither dissent nor criticism since each is seen to violate the norm of "clubbiness" that the manager takes to be inherent in good participative management. The manager becomes an integral member of a group that seeks to make decisions without too deeply introducing their doubts.

One can conjecture that managers who permit others to express their doubts, who do not have—or let others know of—a preferred outcome, and who have a second-look meeting are not likely to be selected as the head of the elite decision-making team. As we shall see in our discussion of escalation processes, these elite units are not a home for the facilitator or mentor whose task involves developing human resources; the elite decision unit believes itself to be fully developed. Its task is to arrive at a reasonable line of action and implement it.

ESCALATION PROCESSES

The people who televise late-night movies understand and employ escalation processes effectively. Have you ever noticed that at the beginning of a televised movie, the commercial messages are relatively few and far between, but as you invest more of your time in following the film, the frequency and duration of time given over to advertising increases? The more money, time, identity, and status or prestige we have invested in a line of action, the more difficult it becomes to quit or move on to another activity. Other individual-level instances of escalation abound. How much money should one put into a deteriorating car or house? Do we throw good money after bad in attempting to reclaim the losses incurred by a declining stock? Pouring our identity into a marriage or job increases the difficulty, if it goes bad, of leaving it behind. The more prestige or status one derives from an association or membership in an organization, the more committed we feel, even when this relationship may require us to act in ways which collide with our ethical principles. We feel "locked in" because we believe we "have too much invested to quit" (Teger, 1980).

Although the literature on escalation goes by different names—sunk costs (Arkes and Blumer, 1985), and escalation situations (Ross and Staw, 1986; Staw and Ross, 1987)—the emphasis within each is upon how and why over-commitment to a line of action, particularly within the public domain of organizational life, can lead one to persist in a failing option. Thus, in our discussion of workaholism, the issue of dirty hands can be framed as the outcome of a compulsion. In groupthink, it is the pervasive and comfortable group cohesion that results in uncritical concurrence-seeking; in escalation processes, it is the individual or organization's over-commitment to a line of action (Bazerman, 1998; Staw, 1976).

Recent popular management books hail commitment and describe actions executives can take to increase members' commitment (Deal and Kennedy, 1982; Ouchi, 1981). One must take care, however. Too much commitment (Kiesler, 1971; Salancik, 1977), the creation of over-committed members, those who have "too much invested to quit" can cause immense problems for themselves and their organizations. To become over-committed to an organization, a line of action, a relationship, or even an aspect of your identity is to enter into a sort of blindness. In everyday parlance, we call this "stubbornness," and sometimes attribute virtue to those who persist in their commitments through thick and thin. We reward those who stay on course for their loyalty. However, when they stay on course and all good information suggests that doing so is heading for a collision, we call them foolhardy and ponder their deficiencies and the processes that may have held them captive. Entrapment is the process whereby organizations, when they are led by over-committed leaders, have too much invested to quit.

The questions that students of escalation processes probe are everyday realities. Why did Iran and Iraq keep on fighting a stalemated war for more than seven years? Why did the United States continue pouring people and equipment into the Vietnam War? Why did the Concorde project go ahead despite dubious results? Even closer to home, why do we continue to have referendums to determine whether or not Quebec will stay in Canada? An example from the corporate sector also reveals the tendency towards escalation. The Long Island Lighting Company (Ross and Staw, 1993), a public utility servicing the New York area, sought to diversify its capacity to produce energy by building a nuclear power facility. In the 1970s the company began the construction of the Shoreham Nuclear Power Plant, projected to cost $70 million. Due to a long series of cost over-runs, regulatory delays, and changes in public opinion regarding nuclear energy, the cost rose to more than $5 billion. The Long Island Lighting Company stayed with Shoreham for nearly twenty years. In the end, the company's escalating commitment to a line of action was far from rewarded. Shoreham was sold to the State of New York for the grand sum of one American dollar. The plant was never operated at a commercial level. It was eventually dismantled and pieces sold to scrap dealers.

Once we become over-committed to a line of action, we tend to ignore the consequences, particularly the costly ones. We distance reality. We gather information selectively. We use our justifications of eventual payoffs to continue and hearten us in the midst of our immediate losses. We become trapped. We are committed to a line of action. When bad news arises regarding this line of action, we do not take it seriously. We increase or escalate our commitment even further. Our motives are complex. It is too simple to believe that we are simply covering up for our earlier error. When we question people after escalation situations, when the damage is done, we find that they become true believers in their selected line of action. They actually believe, despite the warning signs, that they are doing what is good for the company. With hindsight, they see themselves as having been trapped.

For purposes of clarification, we can identify a number of situational and behavioural traits that characterize entrapment. The situational components of escalation include the following four characteristics: (1) a prior investment in the pursuit of the goal; (2) a choice between getting into (or staying in) or getting out of a situation; (3) conditions of uncertainty surrounding the decision; and (4) the necessity of a repeated series of investment decisions to achieve these objectives. The behavioural or response component seems to be composed of three elements: (1) with each decision to continue, the debate or conflict over future steps increases and highlights both "avoid" and "attract" features; (2) trapped decision makers or administrators eventually shift from a rational and economic to a social and psychological involvement in the situation; and (3) entrapment behaviour tends to be self-perpetuating as each additional investment increases the degree of commitment until the administrator is over-committed.

In business ethics, the trapped administrator is ripe for discussion within the dirty hands perspective. Here is an individual attempting to be a good and loyal agent to the organization. Due to an incremental decision process that has increased sunk costs and tied the career of the administrator, if not the unit, to a line of action, the administrator may overlook negative feedback. Denial, distortion, and self-justification preoccupy the administrator who seeks to go ahead despite increasing criticism, losses, or skepticism regarding success. The trapped administrator will point to past successes to manage doubts. There will be a tendency to over-emphasize early benefits of the current line of action and project them into a very rosy future. This results in a building of momentum, a single-minded or fixed focus, which plays havoc with efforts to act fairly and ethically toward those who see things in a different light.

We can sense this momentum by looking at the social and structural variables that underlie the escalation process. When we examine escalation decisions and those who make them, we discover that they do not occur in a social vacuum. In escalation situations, social factors may promote a desire for face-saving (Brockner, *et al.*, 1981) and external justification (Fox and Staw, 1979) in decision makers. Saving face involves forms of impression management by the trapped administrator, which emphasize the competence of the decision maker and, in so doing, neutralize the interpretations of the critics. Critics in an escalation process are those who argue for de-escalation or switching to a new line of action (Drummond,

1995, 1996) and, in derogating these options, the trapped administrator seeks not only to save face, but to quell the calls for his resignation or the build-up of powerful opposition to the status quo. The trapped administrator seeks to portray himself as "standing firm" and refusing to fold his cards at the early signs of bad news. In social terms, the trapped administrator seeks to portray himself as heroically persistent and acting in concert with "the plan," which has in the past brought great success.

In terms of structural factors enhancing the escalation process, Staw and Ross (1987) point out that within the context of organizations, particularly large, bureaucratic ones, even when the decision maker's desire is to change a line of action, the over-commitment of the organization as a whole may be too great. Administrative inertia, the tendency of organizations to change slowly, often reinforces the trapped administrator's realization that even when he or she is ready to switch lines of action or quit old and well-entrenched patterns, the organizational costs of initiating change are high. Related to administrative inertia is the difficulty administrators may have in selling or getting "buy in" on the new vision or line of action. Certain long-standing programs and technical equipment might require jettisoning. These often have their champions. These champions will do whatever is in their power, and this may be formidable, to retain these vestiges of the status quo. As political rationality reveals absence of strong support for the new line of action at critical points in the shift, it may become difficult to overturn no matter the economic, social, and ethical costs of the prevailing line of action.

Escalation does not happen just to the weak, stupid, or cowardly organizational player. It is built into the very training we get as competent corporate players. We are taught and rewarded when we act decisively and commit fully to a line of action, get others to buy into our vision, and remain steadfast in the face of opposition. It is not surprising when those who rise to the top, those selected with these traits, find themselves in escalation situations. To offset this propensity, we must try to separate early decision makers from those who are asked to finance and implement programs. Escalation can be held in check, or at least the risks it engenders can be minimized, when we create an organizational culture in which questioning is not only reinforced but built into the implementation process. It is in these circumstances that we permit status players to retain their honour and dignity after admitting that they have made a mistake and are eager to change their minds.

DIFFUSION OF RESPONSIBILITY

It was with shock that the urbanites of New York City learned about the violent death of Kitty Genovese (Latane and Darley, 1970). Surrounded by numerous high-rise residents, this woman had screamed and frantically fought as her assailants raped and killed her. Analysts puzzled over why citizens, safe in their apartments and close to telephones, failed to call the police until the event had dragged on. Journalists and others scoured the vicinity, interviewing apathetic bystanders. They found that each was concerned and moved by the plight of the screaming woman, but each also assumed that others within earshot had already phoned the police. It was concluded that when responsibility is diffused and people believe that they are only partially responsible for outcomes, individuals often act differently than when they believe that they are solely or primarily responsible.

Urban life, with its high population density, specialized division of labour, and large degree of interdependency among its citizens, provides just the conditions for what Garret

Hardin has called "the tragedy of the commons" (1968). Hardin asks us to imagine early village dwellers who have two sorts of responsibilities. First, they have the care and maintenance of their livestock on their private land, where they are solely responsible for the care, maintenance, and sustainability of their land and its value. Second, since they graze their livestock on the commons, the shared village pasture, they collectively have responsibilities to care for this as well. Hardin illustrates how and why citizens tend to the first responsibilities very carefully, but treat the diffused responsibilities of the commons quite poorly. There are temptations, as in the Kitty Genovese crime, to assume that others will tend to these problems. Moreover, when and if they fail to do so, one is not personally to blame. The system, it is argued, failed.

Organizations, particularly as they become more complex, with high degrees of differentiation and interdependency, specialized technologies, human resources, and capitalization, place increasing responsibility on the system. This is not to suggest that in organizations people are not responsible. They are. However, in corporate endeavours, Hardin's commons is central. In the corporation, outcomes often are not due to the actions of an individual but to large, interdependent groups of individuals tied together with technologies, policies, and markets. Decisions made by committees diffuse responsibility. When organizations lapse morally and are found wanting, it is not as clear who is accountable or, to put it bluntly, who is to blame.

Within corporate bodies, there is no lack of volunteers when the distribution of kudos is at hand; however, in incidents involving organizational error, lapses in morality, or complaints against the organization, one is usually met with a deafening silence. If one imagines, as does Jackall in his book, *Moral Mazes: The World of Corporate Managers* (1988), that the organization is like a giant game of snakes and ladders, then kudos is a ladder and, as such, enhances one's upward mobility, while blame, like a snake, signifies a far less enviable corporate future. In Jackall's depiction, career-ending moves are less a function of the costliness of one's transgression than the unwillingness of one's work-group to cover for you. The failure, often an instance of scapegoating (Bonazzi, 1983; Tober, 1972; Wexler, 1993) arises as the workgroup loses confidence in your ability to remain loyal to its needs. In *Moral Mazes*, as in Erving Goffman's (1959) portrayal of interaction in everyday life, getting through life's events is less a matter of how well or poorly you do, but rather how well you present yourself and protect this image.

In this sense, corporations are not merely mechanisms to hedge one's bets and reduce economic risk, but also ways to reduce the risk of blame to the self. It is in this sense that the use of committees, teams, and special projects to deal with strategic issues in the private sector, and special task forces, commissions, and research teams to deal with pressing problems in the public sector can be seen in two ways. The first focuses on how specialization in organizations lowers accountability, and how, as accountability diminishes, the opportunity for dirty hands actions by individuals increases. The second focuses on how rationality itself is specialized in organizational worlds and why technical rationality, social rationality, and political rationality all are necessary in organizations. However, since these three forms of rationality see the "good organizational world" quite differently (see Figure 6.7), it is difficult to hold any person or even committee responsible for choices made by organizations as a whole. First let us turn to the dirty hands problem in increasing specialization in organizational worlds. Why doesn't simply reducing specialization rid us of the diffusion of responsibility in organizations?

FIGURE 6-7 Specialized Rationalities: The Diffusion of Responsibility

Rationality	Main Function	Perspectives on the Good
Technical Rationality	The function of technical rationality is to make decision making and organizational action more efficient within circumstances in which competition prevails.	Efficiency of Process
Political Rationality	The function of political rationality is to broker deals and secure resources, with favourable terms, from others.	Enhancement of Strategic Positioning
Social Rationality	The function of social rationality is to minimize conflict and create a sense of organizational integration.	Harmony in the Workplace

Specialization arises in organizational contexts as the organization takes on more complex tasks. To be functional, specialization requires that decisions be made not only within the specialist's domain, but also applied across the domain's problems—those in which specialists must confer and come to some agreement as to a line of action. The contemporary call for teams and shared responsibility is not accidental. This is precisely what one would expect as uncertainty rises. For as it rises it is necessary to bring together people with different skill bases to provide insight and information on the complex problem. However, when we create these teams, committees, special projects, and the like, we not only increase opportunities for cooperation and sharing, but we also lessen the degree to which we can hold any specialized group or individual accountable for problems caused by their input into the process.

This is not to deny the wisdom of teams, committees, or task forces when things go well. As we have seen, praise and the rewards that accompany it are easy to receive. All participants in the team, task force, or committee will stress their central role in the proceedings. The logic, of course, is reversed when things go poorly. All participants will claim that they warned the team, committee, or task force regarding the error of their ways but were overlooked. In these circumstances, we may have "victims" who have suffered the downside of decisions made and actions taken in organizations, but there is no one to blame. The committees, task forces, and teams often disappear as members disavow their responsibility.

This is no small issue. In society at large it is hard to hold organizations and systems accountable for costly moral lapses. Usually these lapses are detected long after the events in question. With the diffusion of responsibility, it is difficult to pinpoint just who did what when, and who is to be held responsible. Blame games prevail. New investigative committees are struck. Remedies are necessary to prevent future moral lapses. However, learning is difficult under these circumstances. Cooperation in all blame games breaks down. Individuals retain selective memories of who said what to whom. The inquisition-like quality of these periodic quests for accountability attract rumour and innuendo.

To make sure that there is accountability and that responsibility is not so easily diffused in organizations, there is a tendency to try to reduce specialization. This results in the flattening of organizational structures. The call to multi-functional teams with generalists or those trained across functions is part and parcel of the effort to create greater accountability in the contemporary organization. This solution is rooted in the belief that when people are trained to do and understand more than one specialty, they do not "assume" that others will take care of what they leave undone. When Volvo created the holistic work team, now common in manufacturing, which would put together and be responsible for all the parts of each car they manufactured, it was felt that a solution to the diffusion of responsibility problem was at hand.

It seems, however, that celebration was premature. The move to holistic teams, generalist rather than specialist workers, and flattened rather than tall organizations, has increased worker involvement and certainly intensified the possibilities for both workaholism and escalation, but it has not, despite the claims, made firms more accountable. In the new teams, in the flattened organizations, there are still deep and meaningful debates over who is and who is not responsible for problems, including moral transgressions. These debates occur because there are three very distinct and specialized rationalities that accompany activities in even the most flat and democratic of contemporary organizations.

In Figure 6.8 we see an explanation of why it is that despite efforts to decrease specialization to flatten and democratize organizations, diffusion of responsibility endures. The logic in Figure 6.8 is based on the belief that for organizations to remain viable, they must locate and establish three distinct but interrelated rationalities as the basis for competent action and decision making. Each rationality—technical, political, and social—is necessary, but not sufficient. The greater the number of specialists in an organization, the more likely these can become imbalanced. Thus, in an organization predominately made up of engineers, we might expect technical rationality to prevail even under circumstances where the problem may best be handled by either social or political rationality. Or, in an organization dominated by the expansionist leanings of those who favour mergers and acquisitions, we may find that political rationality is privileged.

Technical rationality sees the good world as the efficient one. Energy is expended on making organizational decision-making more efficient. The organization acknowledges its constraints and competition and seeks to reduce scarcity and succeed competitively by cutting down on resources, lessening the time to production, and reducing poor quality products and services. To be technically rational is to be able to justify your position by pointing towards its proven efficiency over other alternatives. In all organizations, technical rationality must exist, but it must be balanced by an outlook that looks to the social and political rationalities of the option taken. This balance is hard to achieve merely by flattening organizations or moving towards generalists. It is, I believe, best achieved by consciously seeking to place individuals and groups that represent these three forms of specialized rationality on teams, committees, and task forces that are making key decisions.

Political rationality sees the good corporate world as one in which the organization is positioned strategically to acquire future resources and to deal flexibly with all contingencies. Political rationality focuses on brokering deals and securing resources with favourable terms. Actions and decisions taken in the organization are not, as in technical rationality, merely means to increase efficiency in the same action patterns. Political rationality, and those who carry its interests, attempts to discern when to shift the direction of the organization and turn those with technical rationality to finding efficiencies within new action patterns. Charismatic leaders setting new visions for the organization, brokers setting new deals with suppliers and contractors, and innovators claiming new territory into which the organization can expand are examples of organizational players utilizing political rationality.

Social rationality, often equated by business ethics students with "moral rationality," focuses upon creating harmony in the workplace. The function of social rationality is to minimize conflict and create a sense of organizational integration. Social rationality privileges empathy as a means of producing solidarity in the working unit. Social rationality facilitates. It helps bring together discordant views and creates procedures for arriving at negotiable and acceptable outcomes. In organizations in which social rationality prevails, the quest for harmony may, in the eyes of some, become very time demanding, and much that is creative in conflict and competition may be forfeited. However, it is an error to think of social rationality as moral rationality. While harmony is a value worth cherishing, we cannot, as is clear in the dirty hands problems, rely on any one rationality to carry the day.

To lessen the diffusion of responsibility and create accountability, it is wise to have systems in which technical, political, and social rationality are brought together in the decision-making procedures and action patterns. Without this we create simplicity traps. Simplicity traps, essentially the reliance upon a single form of rationality, create accountability problems and enhance the diffusion of responsibility. Technical rationality speaks directly to the ability of organizations to improve and move towards greater efficiencies over time. This addresses the reality of both resource constraints and competition. Systems are responsible for both the costs and the benefits that are created in their pursuit of technical rationality. Political rationality requires that we are cognizant of and take responsibility for the deals we broker and the strategic changes we both embrace and promise to others. Systems are responsible for both the costs and benefits that are created in their ongoing pursuit of political rationality. Last, social rationality is inclusive and attempts to reduce conflict and discordance in organizations. It is the organization's commitment to harmony. Systems are responsible for the costs and benefits they generate in their efforts to create and sustain social rationality.

In the diffusion of responsibility, whether thought of under the auspices of the specialization engendered by teams, task forces, and committees, or under the rubric of the imbalance possible when organizations attempt to bring together the three forms of rationality, the probability is high that good persons intending to do good can get their hands dirty. In the specialization version of the diffusion of responsibility, good people working in committees, task forces, and teams often get into situations where no one is responsible for the group's decision. This leads, as we have seen, to a lack of clear direction and leadership as controversies blow up. The tendency is to scapegoat innocent players. In the diffusion of responsibility due to the imbalance of the three necessary rationalities, good people intending to do good can get their hands dirty when the rationality is neither informed by nor takes into account the other two forms. This leads to good people becoming caught in simplicity traps. Simplicity traps exist when doing good is made too simple. Using technical rationality, political rationality, or social rationality alone produces a simplicity trap. When we are in a simplicity trap we lose sight of the larger issues of accountability required in organizations.

Dirty hands problems in business as illustrated in our examples—workaholism, groupthink, escalation, and the diffusion of responsibility—will not go away just because we are studying business ethics. We will still, as Gellerman (1986) makes clear, rationalize our actions so as to remove any taint of dirty hands from them. We can recall the way Buzz McCoy, Stephen, the New Zealanders, and the Japanese, while challenging themselves on the trail to Muklinath, managed to pass along responsibility for the sadhu so that, in the end, a near-starving man was left at 15,000 feet to fend for himself. Some of us will become lost in workaholism, seeking to use our workplace as a means of working through our search for wholeness, self-esteem, and genuine membership. Others will find themselves in escalation processes, throwing caution to the wind and overriding all indications that their selection was a costly error. Our description of some of the processes underlying "dirty hands" in business is not an argument for the continuance of questionable moral behaviour; rather, it is a suggestion that morality is an ongoing problem that must be confronted. We cannot simply assume, since we are well-intended and believe ourselves to be "good" people, that we have not in our committee work or in our professional bodies created the very conditions that give rise to dirty hands.

In the next chapter we turn to the last of our descriptive treatments of everyday moral processes in organizations, and we look at whistle-blowing. It is clear that when we are involved in organizational life, there may be times we stumble onto troublesome knowledge about our organization and its members' behaviour. We may find ourselves powerless to rectify the situation. When we decide to go public and call others' attention to what we believe to have happened, we open up a very interesting and even dangerous can of worms.

CASES AND QUESTIONS

CASE 6-1   Apex: Deep in the Big Muddy

Apex Sports Wear has expanded its line of sports clothes to the point where its logo is now worn boldly on the chests of many of the richest people on the planet while they golf, ski, and sail. The company has grown prosperous by sticking to a simple but consistent line of action. Manuel Fernandez, the president and chief architect of Apex's massive growth, has presided over his sports clothes empire by investing heavily in advertising—using celebrities and high-profile public figures to tout his sportsware—keeping costs down by contracting out the bulk of labour to countries where labour costs and regulations are low, and vigilantly monitoring the quality of these garments by putting the finishing touches on them (packaging, logo, labels) in one of three small outlets (California for the North and South American market; Marseilles for the European, Mid-eastern and African markets; and Singapore for the Asian, Australian, and Indian markets).

The formula has been successful. Fernandez, born in Brazil, educated at the University of Toronto and the London School of Economics, and now a citizen of the Cayman Islands, has been proud of his ability to deliver solid value to his stockholders, satisfy the demands of an exacting clientele, and avoid the costly and troublesome management-union relations faced by the majority of his competitors. Mr. Fernandez not only believed in his system, but knew that the key rested in the vigilant monitoring of the quality of work done by his subcontractors in third world countries. To this end he had hired a solid company, Kravitz, Johnson, and Sing Importers and Exporters, whose connection to small needleworkers in these lands was unsurpassed. Fernandez saw Apex's use of Kravitz, Johnson, and Sing as both the broker and monitor of Apex's subcontracts as the key element in their strategic ascendancy in the industry.

In 1994, the early warning signs of trouble for Apex came innocuously in the form of a page-four story in a community newspaper in San Jose, California. A student in the local community college had written a piece for the paper that suggested that it was common knowledge in his village in Sierra Leone that the world-famous Apex brand used child labour, poor working conditions, and supported corrupt local politicians in the manufacture of their very expensive sportswear. The author, K.P. Sholo, drew out his description by quoting from letters from his cousins who had been engaged by Apex to do piece work. The article drew little attention from the media as it was seen as an opinion piece, written by a not overly-credible journalist for a paper that is given away free to householders.

Fernandez's attention was drawn to the article by the head of Apex's public relations department, Anthony Storer. Fernandez put together an advisory committee to help him determine whether he should distance himself from Kravitz, Johnson, and Sing and make sure that Apex Sports Wear turned its back on child labour. Fernandez himself was genuinely unaware and upset by the possibility that Apex was engaged in these practices and was eager to take the committee's advice. He placed Milo Schwartz, the head of the California Division, Pierre Bonneau from France, Maxwell Gee from Singapore, and Rubin Kravitz from Kravitz, Johnson, and Sing on the committee. The first three were at the helms of their respective geographical divisions. Rubin Kravitz was there to defend Kravitz, Johnson, and Sing's position. All four men were long-time friends and each had been involved in Apex for twenty years. The committee, after a day of deliberation, suggested that Manuel Fernandez stay the course and remain with the strategic plan that had brought the company success for years. The use of child labour was standard practice in the countries where Apex

was subcontracting; moreover, the children were far better off working than starving on the streets or being driven to child prostitution. Fernandez decided to stay away from the controversy.

The seed was planted and within the next three years articles questioning the ethics of Apex appeared in the *New York Times, The Wall Street Journal, Washington Post, Manchester Guardian*, on television in programs like *60 Minutes*, and on public community programs and news magazines throughout the world. During the early outbreak of mounting faxes, Fernandez not only denied the issues but escalated his commitment to retain the broker and monitoring function in Kravitz, Johnson, and Sing Importers and Exporters. By the fourth year, a group called Consumers For a Healthy Planet set up a rather effective boycott that drove the affluent consumer away from Apex Sports Wear.

Apex Sports Wear closed its doors four and a half years after the page-four story in a community newspaper in San Jose, California.

QUESTIONS

1. Describe the dirty hands problem that Manuel Fernandez of Apex Sports Wear has got himself into. What are the flaws in Apex Sports Wear's strategic plan? Why has it been so successful in the past?

2. What role, if any, does groupthink play in helping to get Manuel Fernandez into his dirty hands problem? What could have been done by Mr. Fernandez to cut down on the groupthink dynamics?

3. What could Manuel Fernandez and Anthony Storer, the head of Apex's public relations department, have done to verify the existence or non-existence of child labour used by the subcontractors of Apex? If it were found that Apex was using child labour in its subcontracting, what should it do? If it were not using child labour, what then should it do?

4. What would you advise that Manuel Fernandez do with the argument made by Milo Schwartz, Pierre Bonneau, Maxwell Gee, and Rubin Kravitz that, even if Apex were inadvertently using child labour, in these third world countries the children so employed were far better off?

5. What role does the diffusion of responsibility have in the dirty hands at Apex Sports Wear? What recommendations would you make now to curb this diffusion of responsibilities?

6. What role do escalation processes play in Manuel Fernandez's stubborn refusal to heed public opinion? What recommendations with regard to escalation processes do you think would, if implemented, help to get Apex through its dirty hands problem? At the stage of the boycott by Consumers For a Healthy Planet, what could Apex and Manuel Fernandez have done?

CASE 6-2 Dr. Raymond Vagelos at RPV Diagnostic: Too Much, Too Fast

Dr. Raymond Vagelos was the CEO at Riverton, Pikers and Vagelos (RPV) Diagnostic, a company that specialized in developing new technologies for the early diagnosis and treatment of cancer. The company, under the direction of Dr. Raymond Vagelos, had risen from obscurity to become a leading contender in the race to develop and patent a diagnostic procedure using tests on saliva samples to detect breast cancer in women. Dr. Vagelos and his silent partners, Martin Pikers and Matthew Riverton, were poised to move into a lucrative lead in the race to bring this technology to market.

Dr. Vagelos was a true believer in the RPV saliva test. He became so central in the race at RPV Diagnostic that he pretty much moved into the research facility in the vicinity of Hamilton, Ontario. Dr. Vagelos worked sixteen-hour days, seven days a week. His marriage, no doubt due to his workload, disintegrated. His two children, Keith, aged six, and Margaret, aged nine, are under the care of their mother, who has recently remarried. Dr. Vagelos had visitation rights, but in the past two years saw his children just once and this was to take them

on a trip to Ithaca, New York, where a conference on breast cancer was being held. After the weekend, both Keith and Margaret complained to their mother and stepfather that their father had given them money to go to a movie and take a taxi back to the hotel while he went out to Cornell University to hear an important paper on the problems of saliva testing for breast cancer.

Dr. Vagelos was recognized by his colleagues in the field as a genius. He was driven. In the race to be the first to bring a prototype of the diagnostic test for medical approval, he had been ruthless. He plundered the competition in search of the best minds working on saliva tests for cancer detection. He offered 30–40 per cent higher salaries than the competition. He offered stock options that surpassed his rivals. To get Bruce Dillinger, a young scientist important to the team, Dr. Vagelos had RPV Diagnostic provide the adventurous scientist with a customized sportscar fitted to Dr. Dillinger's specifications. However, Dr. Vagelos hired only those scientists whose views corresponded to his own. There are important arguments and debates in the field of breast cancer detection using alternate tests. Dr. Vagelos supported his "one view" approach by arguing that it is the only way to get anywhere quickly. He is famous for his statement, "You can't win the race if you take the time to talk about the different tracks that one might race upon."

To keep his special team lean and mean, Dr. Vagelos put together a cohesive group of very bright, very motivated true believers. One of them, Dr. Roger Wideen, completed a series of experiments that purported to show a very high success rate on the RPV saliva test. Dr. Vagelos and the team at RPV Diagnostic were excited about the findings. It would raise the profile of RPV and the value of their stock. Nevertheless, a review of Dr. Wideen's work by one of the individuals refereeing the study for publication in the journal *Diagnostic Testing: The Cancer Review,* took extreme exception with the experimental protocol used in Dr. Wideen's study. This individual argued that the statistical technique used in Dr. Wideen's multi-trial experiment inflated the data in a manner that required a re-testing of the data.

Dr. Vagelos called his hand-picked team together to decide whether to go public with Dr. Wideen's results and bypass the criticism raised by one of the three reviewers. The other two raised doubts and recommended that the paper be modified, but neither questioned the findings themselves. Dr. Dillinger and the other seven members of the team gave Dr. Vagelos a green light.

RPV increased its commitment to the saliva test along the lines of Dr. Wideen's study, raising over $8,000,000 and sinking it all into the project. One year later, in an attempt to replicate Dr. Wideen's study in a laboratory in France, a storm erupted. The scientific community began to argue that RPV Diagnostic had been fabricating its data. The tests done by Dr. Wideen were based on poor statistical procedures. The

findings, it was argued, were an artifact of the experimental design and the statistics used. Within a year, RPV Diagnostic's stocks went from a high of $82.00 per share to $14.00. A large number of scientists, even those on the project team, left for better pay. The silent partners, Martin Pikers and Matthew Riverton, took up a lawsuit against Dr. Raymond Vagelos to recover their losses.

Dr. Raymond Vagelos, the mastermind behind the three-year wonder known as RPV Diagnostic, took his own life. He left his two children, ex-wife, and partners with very confusing memories. When questioned, they all still think he was a brilliant man, a good man, but a man who pushed too much, too fast.

QUESTIONS

1. What sort of dirty hands problem surrounded RPV Diagnostic? How, in your view, did Dr. Raymond Vagelos contribute to dirty hands at RPV Diagnostic? What role does workaholism play in the dirty hands at RPV Diagnostic?

2. Why, in your view, was Dr. Raymond Vagelos so driven? What good can come out of this sort of dedication? What harm can arise from it? In this case, do the harms outweigh the benefits?

3. What role does groupthink play in generating dirty hands at RPV Diagnostic? What, in your view, could have been done to curtail the effects of groupthink in this instance? What role could Dr. Raymond Vagelos have played in helping to curtail the propensity for groupthink at RPV Diagnostic?

4. What role do escalation processes play in the dirty hands at RPV Diagnostic? What could RPV Diagnostic have done to control the escalation process? What role did the escalation processes, groupthink, and workaholism play in contributing to Dr. Raymond Vagelos' suicide?

5. If you were Martin Pikers or Matthew Riverton, what could you have done, and at what stage, to curtail the dirty hands problem at RPV Diagnostic? Were the salaries paid by RPV and the perquisites, like the customized sportscar for Dr. Dillinger, in line with industry norms? What does this tell us about the organizational culture at RPV Diagnostic?

6. What role does Dr. Roger Wideen play in the dirty hands at RPV Diagnostic? Was Dr. Roger Wideen a bad man seeking to further his scientific reputation and make a fortune? Was Dr. Roger Wideen a victim of the dirty hands processes at RPV Diagnostic? What do you think is likely to happen to the future career of Dr. Roger Wideen within his area of research? Why?

| CASE 6-3 | **Keith Morgan, Consulting Engineer: Reminiscences of Dirty Hands** |

Following the completion of a consulting project, Keith Morgan, an engineer for a large manufacturer of electronic equipment in North America, told me that business ethics was going to be an ongoing factor in his employment. Keith tells the following story about when he was fresh out of the University of Alberta and in his first job:

"The first, but certainly not the last time a boss ever told me to lie was about twenty years ago, when I had just been promoted to the head of the engineering department in a firm that manufactured process-control computers. The company had just sold a computer system to a Japanese firm, which paid a premium for a fixed delivery date since it required the computer for a new contract.

"About a week before the deadline I realized that we were not going to deliver the computer on time, so I spoke with the vice president of marketing. My recommendation was that we alert the customer about the late completion date and return their premium. The vice president of marketing sent it to the vice president of operations, who sat on it for three weeks before sending it to the vice president of our Asian division, where it sat for a further week. Mr. Seto, the key individual at the Asian division, finally routed it to the legal department. The legal department, headed by Karen Wellesley, closely studied the contracts. They discov-

ered that if the Japanese company took the computer from our facility for at least 24 hours, then the premium of about $100,000 (US) would be ours. Once a day had gone by, we would alert the client that we had just found a glitch in the computer, recall it, and promise to repair it at no cost to them. This way, Karen Wellesley (or was it Mr. Seto? or maybe the people in operations?) pointed out, we would save face, pocket the premium, and have a good chance of being seen by our Japanese client as a good friend.

"Personally, I was uncomfortable with this set-up since it offended my sense of craft, workmanship, and integrity. However, I had only been with the company for six months, I had a young family to support, and I guess I justified the whole incident by blaming myself and my people in the engineering department for not getting the job done on time. Anyway, I never was asked my opinion on the set-up; I was merely copied on the faxes and memos that buzzed between and among the vice presidents of marketing, operations, and legal. They all just assumed that they were helping out us "boobs" in engineering who had dropped the ball.

"The set-up went as planned. We in engineering had the computers in good enough shape that the flaws would not be detected within 24 to 72 hours. The Japanese took possession of the entire order of made-to-measure computers. They were delighted. We took them out for scotch and steaks. Before the computers could leave the country, we phoned to say we had discovered a minor glitch and would be glad to repair them—free of charge—and get them back as soon as possible. We said that this was part of our service, a sort of follow-up. They were delighted. In fact, they came back in two years with an order triple the size of the first.

"I felt extremely 'dirty' when at Christmas an extra bonus of $8,000 was added to my paycheque with a note from the vice president of marketing, saying, "Thanks, Keith. You deserve at least 8% of the bounty." I quit three months later, believing I had found a company that did not require that I distort my basic principles in order to take care of my family and do the kind of work that I love. I was wrong. Out of the five companies I have worked for in the past twenty years, all but one was almost identical to that first one."

QUESTIONS

1. What sort of dirty hands exist in the large manufacturer of electronic equipment that once employed Keith Morgan? What is shady in their operation? When, in your view, do they cross the line from sharp practices to shady practices? What argument can you make that has as its major premise that there is no shady practice here?

2. What role does diffusion of responsibility play in this case? Who is responsible for the decision on how to handle the late delivery of computers to the Japanese clients?

3. What factors surrounding Keith Morgan and his job make him a pawn in the dirty hands problem? What could Keith have done to maintain his principles? Would this have cost him? Why?

4. What role do processes of escalation play in the decision? Once the decision has been framed in a particular way, why does it become harder and harder to question? To whom do you think Keith Morgan should have directed his questions? Would they have been heard? What could Keith Morgan do to help make these questions audible?

5. Since they were not found out, it could be argued that the company for which Keith Morgan worked did the right thing. Make this argument. Now show what costs were borne despite the company's retention of the premium and its satisfaction of the important Japanese client.

6. What would you have done with the $8,000 bonus received by Keith? Once you feel that your hands are dirty, what do you think you can do to get them clean?

THE BLOWING OF WHISTLES, TILTING OF WINDMILLS, AND ROCKING OF BOATS

Whistle-blowers, as we know, are employees who believe their organization is engaged in illegal, dangerous, or unethical conduct. Usually, they try to have such conduct corrected through inside complaint, but if not, the employee turns to government authorities or the media and makes the charge public. Usually whistle-blowers get fired. Sometimes they may be reinstated. Almost always their experiences are traumatic and their careers and lives are profoundly affected.

Alan F. Westin
Whistle-Blowing! Loyalty and Dissent in the Corporation (1981)

In journalism, the term "muckraker" is applied to investigative reporters and newshounds who specialize in prying open the dirty hands of powerful individuals, organizations, and institutions. This is their job; they help make the powerful accountable. They are often well-paid and—when they excel at their task—celebrated. Whistle-blowers are, however, a very different breed, as Alan F. Westin makes clear in *Whistle-blowing! Loyalty and Dissent in the Corporation* (1981). Whistle-blowers attack while still employed by, or soon after leaving the organization that they impugn. They are not paid for their revelations. Often they face retaliation from a society that seems to erect clear norms against "finking" or acting the "squealer," and whose advice is, "don't make a big deal of it."

The etymological roots of the term "whistle-blower" (Safire, 1978:796)—the image of an employee "blowing a whistle"—is rather counterintuitive. Usually one who blows the whistle is the dominant authority in a social or gaming situation. The referee or umpire who blows the whistle in a sporting competition is the impartial official entrusted with enforcing the rules of play. The same can be said of the traffic constable who blows the whistle to capture our attention while orchestrating the rush-hour crush of pedestrians, automobiles, and cyclists. Likewise, the lifeguard at the public beach or pool blows the whistle to alert us of the danger of drowning. Employees who complain about organizational wrongdoing carry the whistle rather precariously. Rather than blowing it as a trusted authority figure, the employee blows the whistle in desperation. The whistle-blower is drawing attention in the hopes that help will arrive to make right what he or she believes to be morally problematic.

In this chapter we shall focus on whistle-blowing as a process in which moral accounts of organizational behaviour are at odds. Someone believes that dirty hands exist in his or her workplace and must decide whether or not to surface this perception and make it public. There are five major participants in the whistle-blowing process (see Figure 7.1). The first is the whistle-blower, who—triggered by his or her interpretation of an illegal, immoral, or illegitimate event within the organization—feels compelled to act so as to make right the wrongdoer's actions by an act of public disclosure. The group or individual selected as the outlet for the whistle-blower's tale of wrongdoing is the second participant. This participant/group can vary from internal players such as a shift supervisor, to external stakeholders including media or a professional association whose code of ethics prohibits the behaviour (or omission of such) enacted by the wrongdoers and to which they are members. It is important to remember that the whistle-blower's allegations of wrongdoing are not substantiated at the beginning of the whistle-blowing process. The relationship between participant one (the whistle-blower) and participant two (the whistle-blowing outlet) is primarily a communication process (Seeger, 1997) wherein the whistle-blower alleges through the outlet the ethical, illegal, or otherwise harmful wrongdoing of the organization.

The third participant in the process is the whistle-blower's target—the alleged wrongdoer and possessor of "dirty hands." The allegation may be tied to specific persons, parts of the organization, or those power-brokers who are believed to be accountable for breaches. The wrongdoer may have engaged actively in the wrongdoing or simply failed to act in a situation in which one would expect accountability. The fourth participant in the whistle-blowing process is the organizational and societal members whose interest and sympathies may be caught by the whistle-blower or by his or her target. Like bystanders to an event, these individuals may take up the moral account of the whistle-blower, turn on him or her, or remain largely indifferent. When bystanders remain indifferent, the whistle-blowing incident usually has a short life in the public's attention. When bystanders rise in moral indignation, there is a good chance that the whistle-blowing process will generate an in-depth look at the organization and its activities. When bystanders pronounce the whistle-blower as a weirdo, nonconformist, idealist, or attention-seeker, the most probable outcome for the whistle-blower is corporate and social retaliation.

The fifth and final participant in the whistle-blowing process is society at large, wherein we ascertain the long-term costs and benefits of our attitudes towards the process. It is in this context that we determine the question posed by Marcia Miceli and Janet Neer in *Blowing*

FIGURE 7-1 **Five Participants in the Whistle-Blowing Process**

Participant	Moral Account	Strategies for Action
Whistle-Blowers	Whistle-blowers take a position of principled dissent wherein the whistle-blowers claim that it is their duty to call attention to and attempt to rectify behaviours by members of their organization that are seen as illegal, immoral, or costly.	The whistle-blowers must seek to have their interpretation of the triggering event taken as legitimate by those to whom they have selected to blow the whistle. The whistle-blowers must select the appropriate channel and level of whistle-blowing.
Whistle-Blowers' Outlets	Whistle-blowers' outlets are the people, committees, or even institutions such as the law that whistle-blowers select to disclose their allegations.	The whistle-blowers' outlet can attach themselves as judicial body to the allegations or distance themselves from it.
Whistle-Blowers' Targets	Whistle-blowers' targets take a position of attempting to neutralize and de-legitimize the moral account of the whistle-blowers.	The whistle-blowers' targets attempt to make the whistle-blowers (their motives, personalities, need for attention, etc.), not their message, the issue.
Organizational and Societal Bystanders	Organizational and societal bystanders take a position of: (a) ignoring both the whistle-blowers and the whistle-blowers' targets; (b) allying themselves with the powerful whistle-blowers' targets; or (c) allying themselves with the principled dissent of the whistle-blowers.	The organizational bystanders can elect to get information about the controversy experienced in the debate between the whistle-blowers and the whistle-blowers' targets, or remain aloof.
Society at Large	Society at large takes an ambivalent position on whistle-blowing, encouraging it under the call for "accountability," but in many specific instances, portraying whistle-blowers as tattlers, squealers, and finks.	Society at large can provide incentives or disincentives for whistle-blowers. Protection from retaliation, fair procedures hotlines, and an open and free press can create conditions for greater dialogue.

the Whistle, when they ask whether whistle-blowers are heroes and corruption fighters "who represent society's last line of defense against organizational misconduct," or "are they—as others believe—company traitors who reveal (company) secrets for their own glorification?" (1992:1). If whistle-blowers are seen by society as heroes—as Davids battling against corporate Goliaths—we would expect incentives for people to come forth with truthful tales of corporate wrongdoing. Where whistle-blowers are seen as serving the long-term good of society, we would expect those who repress, rebuff, and retaliate against whistle-blowers and their families to be viewed as villains. However, in contexts in which whistle-blowers are seen as "rat finks," "squealers," "snitches," or "tattle tales," where norms of team loyalty preside, then whistle-blowers and the whistle-blowing process will be seen as a nuisance, often a costly one. In these contexts it is believed that society is best served when employees keep silent and avoid publicly shaming those who provide their employment.

With the five participants in mind, we will examine the five key stages in the typical whistle-blowing process. In business ethics, whistle-blowing offers us insight on how difficult it is to tell the truth in the face of power and have one's voice taken seriously. It is easy to see whistle-blowing as a David-and-Goliath struggle in which the forces of good seek to imbue the large, unthinking, and amoral organization with a moral compass. However, as we shall see, this black and white view hides as much as it reveals.

THE WHISTLE-BLOWING PROCESS

There is a general agreement on definitions of whistle-blowing. Sissela Bok views whistle-blowing as a new label generated by our increased awareness of the ethical conflicts encountered at work. "Whistle-blowers sound an alarm from within the very organization in which they work, aiming to spotlight neglect or abuses that threaten the public interest (1983:261). Gene G. James notes that "whistle-blowing is an attempt by a member or a former member of an organization to bring illegal or socially harmful activities of the organization to the attention of the public (1980:100). Janet Near and Marcia Miceli define whistle-blowing as "the disclosure by organization members (former or current) of illegal, immoral, or illegitimate practices under the control of their employees, to persons or organizations that may be able to effect actions" (1985:4). These definitions delineate the basic parameters of the whistle-blowing process and distinguish it from other instances of "voice" (Hirschman, 1970) used by members to "speak out" (Elliston, 1984) about what they see as misconduct.

The basic parameters of the whistle-blowing process concern four key issues: (1) an individual or group (the whistle-blower) within an organization or recently involved with it "interprets" an event or series of events undertaken by the organization and licensed or enacted by some of its members as a form of non-trivial wrongdoing; (2) the whistle-blower is not sufficiently powerful to rectify directly the perceived wrongdoing; (3) in an attempt to rectify the wrongdoing, for motives that can be framed as altruistic or self-serving, the whistle-blower attempts to make his or her interpretation of the wrongdoing a matter of public record; and (4) the content of the whistle-blower's information has the potential to rock the status quo, but the determination of whether the wrongdoing is actual and necessitates sanctions is not made easily until the process has ended.

Given these four parameters, it is important to distinguish whistle-blowing from other forms of "voice" used in power-asymmetric conditions in organizations. A complaint by a subordinate regarding a superordinate's favouritism does not, in itself, become an instance of whistle-blowing. Even if the subordinate should exit as a consequence of the alleged favouritism, we still would not have a bona fide case of whistle-blowing. Whistle-blowing entails raising one's voice—in a metaphorical manner—to a third party in order that pressure be placed upon the perceived wrongdoers to right their wrong. If an employee believes that a superior is acting with favouritism and selecting cronies for advancement despite the apparent existence of more senior and competent players, and that employee, in an act of dissent, goes outside normal channels, persists, and raises a stink, then we have the start of the whistle-blowing process.

The "voice" or "speaking out" by subordinates in an instance of whistle-blowing does not follow the usual channels of reporting. Internally, whistle-blowing arises when the structural mechanisms intended to deal with reports of wrongdoing either fail to hear the whistle-blower altogether, or hear the whistle-blower but are perceived to avoid dealing with the wrongdoing. Whistle-blowing, when it moves externally, does not follow the usual public relations routes, but is intended to place the organization—and, more specifically, the wrongdoers within it—in a negative light. Some whistle-blowing episodes start internally and escalate until, as voices rise in discordance, they are heard outside. In others, the whistle-blower sees that the organizational culture is not supportive of dissent and thus whistle-blowing may move to, say, the media or a professional association before it is fully appreciated by the powers that be within the organization. In both internal and external instances, the distinction between a complaint and whistle-blowing rests on the fact that in the former there is no effort made to use "public shaming" or the involvement of third parties to pull the perceived wrongdoer into line.

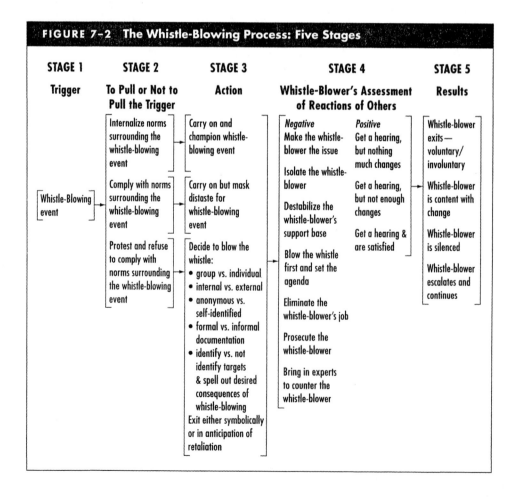

FIGURE 7-2 The Whistle-Blowing Process: Five Stages

STAGE 1	STAGE 2	STAGE 3	STAGE 4		STAGE 5
Trigger	To Pull or Not to Pull the Trigger	Action	Whistle-Blower's Assessment of Reactions of Others		Results
Whistle-Blowing event	Internalize norms surrounding the whistle-blowing event	Carry on and champion whistle-blowing event	*Negative* Make the whistle-blower the issue	*Positive* Get a hearing, but nothing much changes	Whistle-blower exits— voluntary/ involuntary
	Comply with norms surrounding the whistle-blowing event	Carry on but mask distaste for whistle-blowing event	Isolate the whistle-blower Destabilize the whistle-blower's support base	Get a hearing, but not enough changes	Whistle-blower is content with change
	Protest and refuse to comply with norms surrounding the whistle-blowing event	Decide to blow the whistle: • group vs. individual • internal vs. external • anonymous vs. self-identified • formal vs. informal documentation • identify vs. not identify targets & spell out desired consequences of whistle-blowing Exit either symbolically or in anticipation of retaliation	Blow the whistle first and set the agenda Eliminate the whistle-blower's job Prosecute the whistle-blower Bring in experts to counter the whistle-blower	Get a hearing & are satisfied	Whistle-blower is silenced Whistle-blower escalates and continues

Figure 7.2 outlines the five phases or stages in a typical, albeit stylized, whistle-blowing event. Figure 7.3 provides a detailed case of whistle-blowing to illustrate the five stages. We will begin by first describing each stage as a sequence in the whistle-blowing process, and then discussing the options available at that stage. To close each stage, we will describe it as it seemed to occur in the case of "Roger Whitelaw at Quasar Research Laboratories (QRL)."

FIGURE 7-3   Roger Whitelaw at Quasar Research Laboratories (QRL)

Roger Whitelaw, a chemist, family man, and elder in his church, specializes in developing chemical processes for removing carcinogenic contaminants from soil prior to its use for residential housing and the development of public facilities such as schools and playgrounds. Whitelaw was hired by Quasar Research Laboratories (QRL) to head a project intended to revolutionize soil clean-up by using a new, cheaper, more reliable, and environmentally friendly chemical filter system. QRL believed that this system, tied to the company's core competence and brought to the market quickly enough, would provide QLR with a substantial lead over its competitors.

Whitelaw, his wife Charlotte, their six children, and Charlotte's invalid mother all adapted well to their move to Toronto. The Whitelaws saw Canada as a good country in which to bring up children, and looked with favour upon Toronto's public school system and medical care facilities. QRL purchased for the Whitelaws a respectable 7-bedroom, 3,200-square-foot home in Toronto's Don Mills area. The house was to be theirs, rent-free, for five years, and if Whitelaw stayed with QRL longer than that, the house would be given to them outright. Whitelaw was to receive $240,000 per year, a company car, and 20 per cent of any profits QRL made with the new chemical screen process as long as he remained in the employ of QRL.

Roger Whitelaw began to assemble a practical "ground team" of scientists to complement the more theoretically-minded scientists QRL had assembled for the project. He hired three colleagues from previous job sites: Carlos Fuentes, an excellent soil diagnostician and a master in the use of lasers to activate complex chemical processes; Marla Mitchell, a specialist in filter cleaning and the use of water-borne techniques; and Matthew Kelley, a chemist with an aptitude for the use of plants, trees, and vegetative protein matter as cleansing techniques. All three were moved to Toronto at great expense and with great expectations by QRL. All three were active members in the church in which Roger Whitelaw acted as an elder, and all three were exceptional in their fields.

The project team Whitelaw put together included himself, his three new hires (Fuentes, Mitchell, and Kelley), and four theoretically-minded scientists who had been in the employ of QRL for a minimum of ten years each—Abraham Cohen, Ralph Peters, Daniel Marcus, and Allen Manus. The eight unanimously decided that the best way they could gel as a team would be to review—from a chemist's perspective—QRL's last ten projects, and determine where the company's technical competence rested.

The "Whitelaw team" sought the permission of the chief operating executive, Mr. Robert Sculley, to obtain data covering the last ten projects and to access the users of these sites to take soil samples and audit the sites' retention of their chemical forms. After consulting QRL's board, Sculley gave the team a double green light.

Marla Mitchell was put in charge of reviewing data, a process never before done at QRL. Allen Manus was given the task of soliciting permission from site users before

FIGURE 7-3 Continued

visiting the sites to inspect their soils. Annual soil inspections previously had been sub-contracted to Technology Laboratories, who filed their findings with both the operating arm of QRL and the municipal government. Manus was to probe deeper and look at health data for site users as well as users' satisfaction with QRL efforts. The research wing at QRL was looked on as a bunch of prima donnas by the operating branch. The operating component, by far the larger of the two, brought in the bulk of revenues and employed 90 per cent of QRL's 420 employees. It was Robert Sculley's recognition that the "real money" rested in patents for the techniques and not for the actual work, that had led to QRL's expansion and heavy investment in the Whitelaw group. The operating branch suspected that the research group, if it succeeded, would cost them jobs and change the company's locus of power, making it a place for PhDs rather than hard-working employees.

Marla Mitchell finished her analysis of QRL's data within one month. She was aghast. It seemed that under the field operating head of Mike Peterson, the company had not actually conducted all the work for which it had been contracted. In the last eight of the ten sites (the first two were worked under Jacques Lussiers, Mike Peterson's predecessor), the soil removal had not gone to the depth specified by the clients and required by the law. Mitchell was certain that under Peterson, QRL had short-changed its clients, pocketed enormous profits, and was now exposing site users to health dangers. Mitchell sat on her data, waiting for Allen Manus to make his preliminary findings known to the group; she wanted to make sure she had not made an error.

Allen Manus was astounded. His data showed that, unbeknownst to the public, the rate of cancers being reported by site users in eight of the ten projects was significantly greater than those of control sites. Moreover, the soil tests taken by Manus did not jive with Technology Laboratories' scores, which consistently underreported the contaminant levels by a factor of nearly 500 per cent. It was Manus's conclusion that these sites were still unfit for human habitation.

On 17 April 1998—exactly seven months to the day that Roger Whitelaw had signed his contract at QRL—the Whitelaw group held its weekly Friday meeting to hear the preliminary reports of Marla Mitchell and Allen Manus. It was to have been a perfunctory meeting intended to close off the week in an amiable fashion. When the group heard the reports' findings they were devastated.

Probing and close examination of the data by other members confirmed the reports' views. An interesting schism occurred. When Whitelaw asked the seven team members what they should do with the data, the group split. The new members—Fuentes, Mitchell, and Kelley—were unequivocal in their assertion that this was a scandal that had to be made right. Allen Manus joined them in asking for action. They insisted Whitelaw speak to Robert Sculley, point the finger at Mike Peterson and Technology Laboratories, and warn those who were living, sleeping, and eating on ground that was capable of making them ill. Three of the four team members who had been at QRL for a much longer time—Cohen, Peters, and Marcus—all insisted that the group undertake more research before it went off in all directions and brought the company into disrepute. They made it clear that QRL could not now rehabilitate these sites without tearing down the relatively new and expensive structures that had been built. This statement—and with it the realization that the Whitelaw group held the company's fate in its hands—caused Roger Whitelaw to call for two more weeks of analysis before they decided upon a course of action.

FIGURE 7-3 **Continued**

Daniel Marcus, a good friend of Robert Sculley, was terribly upset. He felt that the new "Bible belt" scientists had no sense of loyalty to the firm and were hell-bent on causing trouble. Marcus believed that the data used by Allen Manus, "an old-timer," was good, but that it was too difficult to determine cancer rates in such a short period of time. Moreover, the data used by Marla Mitchell did not take into account the particular soil type at the river junctures pouring into Lake Ontario. Since the keep soil shifted there, the newly-contaminated soil at that depth did not indicate that it was due to the failure of QRL to complete its specified contract. Marcus conjectured that perhaps a great deal of the land in that area included superficially "clean" sites contaminated at deeper levels.

Daniel Marcus went to see Robert Sculley with his thoughts and conjectures on what the Whitelaw group had unearthed. Sculley put together a team of chemists headed by Simon Raymond to look into the original data given to the Whitelaw group. On the advice of his brother-in-law, an oncologist at Sunnybrook Hospital, Sculley hired Dr. Louise Sarchesse to investigate the health claims of Allen Manus. Marcus gave Sculley the handouts that Mitchell and Manus had made available to the Whitelaw group at the April 17th meeting.

At the May 1st Friday meeting of the Whitelaw group, after much soul-searching, data crunching, internal debate, and discussion, it was decided that the group should empower Roger Whitelaw with the task of bringing Sculley up to date with their findings, and ask him to strike a taskforce to ascertain how to best rectify the situation for the residents and users of the sites in question and, simultaneously, to minimize the long-term economic fallout to QRL. It was clear that if QRL were forced into receivership as a consequence of their suspicions, not only would the sites remain contaminated, but one of the firms with the highest probability of solving the problem would be sidelined.

Daniel Marcus, unable to dissemble any longer, revealed that he already had made available Mitchell's and Manus's results to Sculley, and that the company already was setting up a taskforce headed by Simon Raymond and an outsider, Dr. Louise Sarchesse. The Whitelaw group saw this as an attempt by Marcus to help Sculley prepare a defense against their team. In fact, Matthew Kelley speculated that Sculley may have been apprised of Peterson's shallow-cleaning technique and use of false data from Technology Laboratories. Abraham Cohen told Kelley that he was way off base, and that Sculley was a man of integrity. Cohen conjectured that Mike Peterson was a man accustomed to living above his income, and that he likely had pulled a nasty trick on Sculley and QRL.

Roger Whitelaw calmed the ruffled feathers of his team, had a few harsh words for Marcus's inability to wait the two weeks agreed upon by the group, and suggested that it was too early to rush to conclusions or place blame. The task at hand was to present Sculley with the data, await his actions, and lend a hand in dealing with the problem. Only then, if it seemed that Sculley was trying to conceal good science and protect QRL by endangering the lives of site inhabitants and users, would Whitelaw, on behalf of the group, go to the press.

On 4 May 1998, Whitelaw went to Sculley armed with twenty-six pages of factual documentation on the severe problems in eight of the ten sites analyzed by the Whitelaw group. Whitelaw told Sculley that he was aware that Daniel Marcus had leaked some of this data earlier, but that the group was unanimous, including Marcus, in requesting that QRL seek to rectify the situation. In the eventuality of QRL's attempt to stonewall or conceal the data, Whitelaw made it very clear that he and members of his group would go to the press, the municipal government, and community activist groups.

FIGURE 7–3 Continued

Robert Sculley insisted that Whitelaw's data was being closely examined by unbiased third parties; that lawyers from the company would be in touch with each member of the team to point out the "confidential" clause in the contracts they had signed regarding "data" belonging to QRL; and that starting the following week, Daniel Marcus, Abraham Cohen, and Ralph Peters were to be taken off his team and a new research team headed by Marcus was to be put in place. Sculley made it clear that within three months Whitelaw was to fire two of his team and Marcus was to hire two. Sculley informed Whitelaw that this had been passed by the Board of Directors. It was felt that competing research teams was the best way to assume that QRL's long-term research goals could be met.

Roger Whitelaw left the meeting in disgust. He now felt that Sculley was going to sit on the data and issue a series of contradictory data-sets that would bury the issue in a sea of techno-talk. On 9 May 1998, QRL issued a press release indicating that in an effort to ascertain ways to more safely and effectively deal with the important issue of soil contamination, they were investigating reports on the condition of soil on more than 300 sites cleaned during the last 40 years. QRL assured the public that they were a company seeking excellence and, to this end, had established two rival research teams—the Whitelaw group and the Marcus group—that were taking two different approaches to soil contamination. The press release went on to detail how QRL fosters debate and controversy in its pursuit of excellence.

Roger Whitelaw was not a stupid man. He realized that Robert Sculley and forces he had yet to fully fathom were playing hardball. In his own press release, issued with Fuentes, Manus, Mitchell, and Kelley, Whitelaw attempted to point out that eight of ten contaminated soil sites worked on by QRL still had toxic readings above the legal limit for residential use. The story emphasized the failure of Technology Laboratories to monitor the soil conditions in a manner that met the specifications done by Allen Manus of QRL. The reaction to the release was swift and alarming. Residents of the specified sites demanded a government inquiry into the allegations and insisted that compensation be made available to residents, if Whitelaw's facts were correct, to bring QRL, Technology Laboratories, and even the government itself, if justified, to court.

Sculley reacted to Whitelaw's press release by both issuing one of his own and firing Allen Manus for breaching his confidentiality agreement. As well, Whitelaw was told that due to his own breach of the confidentiality clause, QRL was no longer going to underwrite his housing costs. Beginning the following month, $3,480 was to be deducted from his monthly salary. Mrs. Whitelaw suddenly found that previously friendly interactions with the spouses of QRL employees were now on hold. The Whitelaw children found that the children of employees at QRL, many of whom went to their school, began to make cruel jokes and isolate them at the lunchroom tables. The eldest Whitelaw child received a black eye in a skirmish over accusations that his father was a "traitor."

What was left of the Whitelaw group met to work out their strategy. Manus, who was given three months notice and a year's severance pay, told the group he was taking a job with a Swiss consortium and cutting his losses before QRL further bloodied his reputation. Fuentes noted that he was taking a job with an Argentinean firm. Both, however, stated that if Whitelaw, Mitchell, and Kelley were willing to press the issue, they would show up for an inquiry, law case, or public forum to give expert testimony. Whitelaw thanked his team members but realized how their positions at QRL were precarious. The Whitelaw team, by the end of the year, had all gone elsewhere.

The story that Roger Whitelaw had started drew some interest in the Toronto media. The QRL study issued by Dr. Louise Sarchesse and Simon Raymond in August 1998 essentially showed that soil contamination was a problem in large parts of what had

> **FIGURE 7-3 Continued**
>
> formerly been industrial sites in Toronto and vicinity, but that the health problems associated with this were minor. Moreover, in a worldwide list of cities with soil contamination problems, Toronto ranked relatively favourably 68 out of 100. The government, seeing a way out of the mess, cut the inquiry down as a means of showing the public that its electoral promise of smaller and more frugal government was more than idle chatter.
>
> The fright caused by Roger Whitelaw's press release did generate a three-week downward spiral in the value of QRL's shares. Since the company bought up the shares at this reduced price, it profited very nicely when the shares shot up following the successful deflection of public scrutiny. On 28 June 1998, Roger Whitelaw announced that he was leaving QRL to take up a post with a large American company—a competitor of QRL.

Stage 1: The Event as a Trigger

Stage 1 can be called the whistle-blowing event. It functions as the trigger to initiate the whistle-blowing process. Without it the process cannot start. The whistle-blowing event is an action or the omission of an action that the whistle-blower perceives to be immoral, illegal, or illegitimate in a non-trivial sense. The event, in the eyes of the whistle-blower, is an act of wrongdoing committed by those in the organization who benefit at the expense of others. It is the "potential" whistle-blower's belief that he or she has seen or heard something that suggests that dirty hands exist in the corporation. In the view of the whistle-blower, this wrongdoing must be recognized to be rectified.

The whistle-blower may "happen" upon the trigger event by accident or be asked to join the alleged wrongdoers. Regardless, the whistle-blower is appalled. However, in most trigger events, the whistle-blower lacks sufficient power to rectify the situation through his or her own actions. The whistle-blower must get others to see the trigger event as he or she does; get others to rectify the situation. This is no easy task. The whistle-blower must avoid retaliation from those who feel that the whistle-blower's call for help is problematic. The whistle-blower must get good, credible proof of the costly, injurious, and/or immoral nature of the trigger event. The whistle-blower must be able to remain credible despite the efforts of others to cast aspersions regarding his or her purported version of the trigger event.

Typically, a non-trivial breach in moral behaviour involves the wrongdoers in causing intentional or unintentional harm to innocent others. Passing off products, food, or soil—as in the case of Roger Whitelaw (see Figure 7.3)—as safe, is an instance of a non-trivial breach in moral behaviour. An example of a trivial breach in moral behaviour could be "calling in sick" on a sunny day. In Stage 1, the line between what is and is not trivial rests solely in the hands of the whistle-blower. However, it is clear that the more trivial the event, the harder it is to push it through all five stages of the whistle-blowing process (see Figure 7.2).

It is important to realize that in many whistle-blowing incidents the whistle-blower knows something is wrong, but lacks a full understanding of what forces rest beneath the surface of what was observed. The ambiguity of the "real" meaning of events in organizations frequently is modified as we move on from Stage 1. However, in this first stage it is clear that the whistle-blower—whether by being in the wrong place at the wrong time or by checking out earlier suspicions—arrives at the conclusion that wrongdoing has occurred and that something must be done. This "something" can be to blow the whistle, but it may be to investigate further, to confer with family members, to speak to the perceived wrongdoer, or to remain silent and bide time.

In our fictitious case of Roger Whitelaw at QRL, Stage 1 of the whistle-blowing process was dependent on the inadvertent discovery that eight of the ten soil samples revealed that soil contamination and illness rates of site users was higher both than is permissible by law and reported by Technology Laboratories. The initial motive of the Whitelaw team was neither to check up on nor to monitor QRL's work on previous jobs. Rather, the research team sought to get a baseline reading of QRL's core competence in treating soil contamination before developing a new chemical filter system. After unearthing unfavourable results, Whitelaw and his group decided to wait two weeks, think about their options, and meet again.

The event was non-trivial. It was the belief of most (but not all) team members that many residents were being exposed to dangerous toxin levels from still contaminated soil. The government believed the soil was healthy since Technology Laboratories, a firm subcontracted by QRL, which allegedly carried out annual soil analyses, had each year given the sites a clean bill of health. Lastly, the team believed that all eight of the ten sites that remained at high levels of contamination were overseen by one QRL executive, Mike Peterson. All eight members of the Whitelaw team, with the exception of Daniel Marcus, seemed to be eager to set things right.

Stage 2: The Decision to Pull the Trigger

Once an individual or group has experienced Stage 1, the trigger event, the decision must be made whether or not to pull the trigger and give public voice to their suspicions. Alternatives exist. Potential whistle-blowers can remain silent. They can give voice to their suspicions, but keep it tied to the standard reporting channels. When and if nothing is forthcoming that alters the behaviour of the alleged wrongdoers, they may, in good faith, feel that they have done all they can. Or, they can decide that they cannot live with themselves if they stifle. These last few blow the whistle. This minority, for a welter of reasons, decides to protest. They become, in many cases, organizational dissidents (Balk, 1996; Graham, 1986; Miceli and Near, 1996). Whether brave and principled, foolhardy and short-sighted, or principled and deeply committed, whistle-blowers persist where—as studies by social scientists (Callahan and Dworkin, 1994; Dozier and Miceli, 1985) reveal—most of us simply remain silent or engage in token gestures.

A great number of potential whistle-blowing cases get cut off at Stage 2. When faced with the prospect of calling attention to the wrongdoing or wrongdoers, many freeze and decide to remain mute. We can distinguish two forms of muteness that stifle the whistle-blowing process. In the first, the potential whistle-blower convinces him or herself that what he or she had initially interpreted as a wrongdoing is—on closer and more thorough examination—not one at all. In this case, the internal alarm that went off after Stage 1 is voluntarily turned off at Stage 2. By talking to others and seeing different points of view, the individual re-frames or reinterprets his or her initial labelling of the wrongdoing. At times, like all dirty hands processes in business life (see Chapter 6), this is just a rationalization for the desire to conform, remain obedient to significant others, and reap the rewards of being a loyal and true member of the organization. At other times, this re-framing is a genuine insight into the complexities of business. I recall being outraged when a consultant with whom I worked on a job assisting in a whistle-blowing incident in the pharmaceutical industry began to deliberately provoke our client by questioning the client's moral integrity. It was only later on that I learned how she used this provocation to help the client realize both the urgency of the problem and the personal integrity it would require to make it right.

A different form of muteness, actually a form of compliance, arises when the potential whistle-blower believes that a wrongdoing has been perpetrated, but would rather sit on the fact than go to either internal or external publics with the allegation. Rather than re-framing the interpretation, as in the first form of muteness, the potential whistle-blower at-tempts to bury or suppress it. Some anticipate that they will not be believed—they are too new in the firm; their data or evidence is too sketchy; or the power and credibility of the (per-ceived) wrongdoers is too high and secure. Others comply because they believe that going public will jeopardize their career; they will be unable to focus on actual work due to the de-manding fuss that will most probably ensue and no doubt escalate. Still others remain mute for fear of retaliation from those who see the protester as a "snitch," or worse—a traitor.

Whether their silence is due to the internalization of new standards through the acts of socialization, re-framing, and reinterpretation, or to compliance with the dominant orga-nizational culture, those who remain silent do not blow the whistle. However, from a be-havioural point of view, the two form of muteness differ. The individual who "sees the light" and adjusts his or her perception of morally suspect behaviour to see it as a form of good citizenship, is likely to engage in this behaviour him or herself and to socialize other members of the organizational culture in such a way that they too learn to respect this behaviour. On the other hand, the individual who suppresses or buries his or her inter-pretation of the triggering event still sees it as immoral, illegal, and/or illegitimate. This potential whistle-blower stifles voice in the anticipation that the cost of protest and action is too high to bear. However, this individual is unlikely to actively socialize other orga-nizational members to this behaviour. More importantly, if and when a whistle-blower emerges to carry the costs of the protest, this individual and those like him or her will ally themselves with the reformer.

Those who do pull the trigger at Stage 2 remain entrenched in their initial interpretation of the triggering event as a wrongdoing, and they are willing to protest this perceived wrong. Protest in this context is understood as giving "voice" to the initial interpretation, or using "exit" to make it explicit that one is quitting out of protest over the organization's com-plicity in the wrongdoing (Hirschman, 1970, 1974). Jill W. Graham, in "Principled Organizational Dissent: A Theoretical Essay," gets at our notion of protest in Stage 2 in her definition of principled organizational dissent as "the effort by individuals in the work-place to protest and/or to change the organizational status quo because of their conscientious objections to current policy and practices" (1986:2). As one intensifies and escalates a protest, both the perception by others of one's disloyalty to the firm and the probability of the firm retaliating for this perceived disloyalty mount.

In the case of Roger Whitelaw's team, the decision to pull or refuse to pull the trigger cre-ated a split decision. Whitelaw, the potential whistle-blower, was sensitive to the different reactions of the team's newcomers and old-timers to the disturbing data unearthed. He de-cided to wait two weeks and then, if the data remained firm, follow the orthodox or ex-pected chain of command and provide the findings to Robert Sculley, QRL's CEO. His decision illustrates the scientist's need for verification of data as a means of ascertaining and clearly documenting the evidence. However, at Stage 2, Whitelaw's intention was to begin a loyal, internal "call for help" in making right what had been wrong.

Daniel Marcus short-circuited Whitelaw's plan by deciding to pre-empt the provision of the data and its interpretation to Sculley. Perhaps in the belief that he spoke for other long-term members of the organization, Marcus suggested to Sculley that possible alternative explana-tions existed for what—if Whitelaw had his way—would be the ruin of the company. Sculley was warned by Marcus. Marcus acted as an internal whistle-blower, going outside the recognized chain of command and seeming to protest Whitelaw's interpretation of the data. There is some controversy in seeing Daniel Marcus as a whistle-blower if one views whistle-blowing as an altruistic act intended to reform the status quo. On the surface, Marcus seemed to be rationalizing and defending the status quo. However, it is clear that within the Whitelaw group he represented a minority view and seemed to be pre-emptively protesting their next move.

STAGE 3: THE ACTION STAGE

Stage 3 in the whistle-blowing process involves the act of whistle-blowing itself. Blowing the whistle involves choices, all of which impact the next two stages in the process. For our purposes, there are five choices that must be made when blowing the whistle. Figure 7.4 outlines these choices, providing both reasons why a rational whistle-blower would select one over another and how each choice would be framed from an ethical point of view. It is important to realize that these five critical choices are not all available to all whistle-blowers in all whistle-blowing contexts, and that the ordering of them is not intended to indicate a decision sequence.

The first critical choice a whistle-blower must make before taking action in Stage 3 is whether to blow the whistle as an individual or to seek allies and protest the Stage 1 wrongdoing

---

FIGURE 7-4   Five Critical Choices When Blowing the Whistle

Choices	Reasons for Selecting One Over the Other	Ethical Framing
Group vs. Individual Whistle-Blowing	People choose to ally themselves with others in group whistle-blowing because it increases credibility, diminishes the strength of retaliation by the firm, and provides one with many voices. The group seeks to identify the firm's moral transgression as a group.	Group whistle-blowing lowers the possibility of others framing the protest as a psychological idiosyncrasy. However, the perceived political status of the group within corporate life enhances the likelihood that others will frame the protest as nothing but vested interests.
Internal vs. External Whistle-Blowing	Choosing to start the whistle-blowing process by going inside vs. outside is related to the whistle-blower's perception of the likelihood of being heard by the organization. When the trust is high that one will be heard, whistle-blowers usually select the internal route. When the perception that one will not be heard and, in fact, one may be retaliated against, the whistle-blower usually takes the external route.	Internal whistle-blowing is framed as showing more loyalty than is external whistle-blowing. This is a corporate perspective. External whistle-blowing is framed, in the public's eye, as a peek into the back rooms of corporate life. Both internal and external whistle-blowing raise concerns regarding organizational practices.

FIGURE 7-4 Continued

Choices	Reasons for Selecting One Over the Other	Ethical Framing
Anonymous vs. Self-Identified Whistle-Blowing	It is now possible to blow the whistle anonymously or to identify oneself as the source of the information. Anonymous whistle-blowing is selected when the group or individual doing the whistle-blowing fears reprisals, would like to initiate the process but remain aloof as it intensifies. Individuals and groups self-identify when they feel strongly and cannot avoid involvement.	The anonymous whistle-blower is framed as lacking the power of their convictions. People are suspicious, when the situation requires anonymity, that there are likely to be several different forms of hidden agendas. Self-identified whistle-blowers show the courage of their convictions, but they are more likely to suffer retaliation.
Formal vs. Informal Documentation	This is often related to the medium one elects to use when blowing the whistle. Talking to others or using the telephone are relatively informal. Presenting data at an internal organizational inquiry or a public press forum are relatively formal.	Formal documentation of the wrongdoing is framed as more publicly available and verifiable. It is, however, more open to refutation by competing experts. Informal documentation relies almost entirely on the credibility of the whistle-blower.
Identify the Targets and Consequences to Be Dealt Out to the Whistle-Blowers vs. Allow Others to Do So	In blowing the whistle, one has to decide whether, in telling one's case, one identifies the wrongdoers or presents the facts and allows others to both identify them and attribute the moral label of "wrongdoers" to those identified.	Should the whistle-blower stick "just" to the facts or to their interpretation and diagnosis? Or should this be left to a less involved and more objective participant?

as a group. Although the bulk of informed literature on the topic of whistle-blowing (Brabeck, 1984; Ewing, 1983; Glazer and Glazer, 1987, 1989; Miceli and Near, 1992, 1994, 1996; Nader *et al.*, 1972; Vinten, 1994) seems to assume that it is individuals and individuals alone who engage in whistle-blowing, this assumption is not borne out by my experience as an ethics consultant in North America, Europe, and Asia. In practice, I have not found it at all rare for whistle-blowers to decide to disclose information as a team or group. The logic is that a team has a greater chance of being taken seriously; it is more difficult to dismiss whistle-blowing as nothing but the psychological idiosyncrasy of a weirdo or troublemaker when a group of employees is involved. As well, the use of symbolic exit or indeed the threat of exit by a group—as all union members know—is more certain to be heard by management.

Why, then, does the literature assume that it is individuals who blow the whistle? I would conjecture three reasons for this assumption. First, even when a group does blow the whistle, as issues tend to be identified with a leader/spokesperson they often—as in the case involving Roger Whitelaw—become associated in the public eye with a single individual. Second, group whistle-blowing is framed less altruistically; the motives of groups are debased more easily and seen as a form of vested interests and organizational politics. Third and last, as the pressure rises in the whistle-blowing process and retaliation or the threat of it raises its head, the group often dissolves, at times leaving the most committed individual to take the heat.

The reasons for electing to whistle-blow at Stage 3 as an individual rather than in a group rest on: (1) the degree of suspicion one has regarding others' complicity in the wrongdoing; (2) the need for speed of action and adaptation to the moves and countermoves likely to be made by one's detractors in Stage 4; (3) the need for consistency in the reportage of the triggering event in order to prevent the discrediting of one's "voice" in the documentation; and (4) the ability to exit from the whistle-blowing process without explicitly letting down others within a group. On the other hand, the reasons for selecting to whistle-blow in a group rather than as an individual rest on: (1) a belief that there is safety in numbers; (2) the possibility of using multiple or a group threat of exit to draw attention to the protest; (3) the diminished ability of skeptical others to reduce whistle-blowing to the idiosyncratic "weirdo" or "troublemaker" labels that often befall outspoken individuals; (4) the ability in a group to divide the labour required to blow the whistle effectively (attend inquiries, provide data, give press conferences) so that whistle-blowing does not detract from individual job performance; and (5) the diffusion of responsibility to the group should, in the course of time, the whistle-blowing process turn out to be misconstrued and seen as frivolous or downright erroneous.

The second critical choice the whistle-blower can make in Stage 3 is to decide between blowing the whistle internally or publicly shaming the organization by turning to external outlets such as the media, government regulators, the tax department, trade associations, activist groups, and the like. When the whistle is blown internally, remember that the whistle-blower does not follow the "normal" or expected chain of command. At Stage 3 we are interested only in where one "starts" in blowing the whistle and not, in fact, where one eventually ends up. It is possible to elect to start blowing the whistle internally at Stage 3 and—if one's voice goes unheard or is not acted upon—to escalate one's efforts and turn to external outlets. Conversely, one can elect to initiate the action of whistle-blowing by going to external outlets and then—once taken seriously by internal players—moving the action into the firm.

The "internal vs. external" distinction in the literature on whistle-blowing (Barnet, 1992a; Farrell and Peterson, 1982; Keenan, 1990; Near and Miceli, 1987) is a simplification of a larger problem that faces whistle-blowers at Stage 3: to whom will one blow the whistle? The "internal vs. external" framing of this problem only helps the whistle-blower to narrow the frame, and draws attention to the fact that corporate retaliation against whistle-blowers is intensified when the whistle is blown externally and in a public and incriminating way with little or no warning to the focal organization (Elliston, 1982b; Miceli and Near, 1989; Near and Jensen, 1983; Parmalee *et al.*, 1982). Farrell and Peterson (1982) use this notion to argue that "real" whistle-blowing occurs only when the whistle is blown outside the organization. This presumption assumes that in hardball whistle-blowing events, the most effective source of aid in righting the corporate wrong is not found within the corporation.

Farrell and Peterson (1982) are not wrong. At times, external whistle-blowing is more effective and more likely to stir up scandal than internal whistle-blowing. But one can argue equally that external whistle-blowing may take the issue out of the hands of the corporation and the whistle-blower and result in a solution that disappoints both. Alternatively, external whistle-blowing may bolster the organization's resolve to stand firm; to some, compromising under

FIGURE 7-5 Examples of Internal and External Outlets for Whistle-Blowers

Internal Outlets

Example:	*Reason for Selection:*
Union	Easy to access for unionized employees. Acts as an effective countervailing power to management. Can mobilize the troops.
Supervisor	Often the normal route for disclosure issues. Should be elected when the incumbent is seen as unbiased and open to the issue.
Internal Committee	Companies often have already developed internal committees anticipating problems in this area: e.g., sexual harassment. If they exist and are seen as more than token efforts at saving face, they should be employed.
CEO	Possesses the power to make things happen, and relatively quickly. If one has access, a good case, and an open CEO, this is a good bet.
Mentor	When one is trying to decide which outlet to select, if one has a wise and well-connected mentor, one may be advised to check out one's options first.
Ombudsperson	If one seeks a fair and impartial hearing for one's voice that can aid one to develop or to drop the protest, this is a good option.
Board of Directors	This is an outlet difficult for the typical employee to access, but one interested in the long-term reputation of the firm.
Internal Auditor	This outlet is, in effect, an outsider collecting data on the firm; if the information can be made credible, this is a powerful outlet.

External Outlets

Example:	*Reason for Selection:*
Media	Captures a wide public with often sensational coverage. Avoid when the issues requires restraint and careful analysis.
Government in Power	Is an effective outlet when the government in power champions the "cause" at the root of a whistle-blowing incident.
Professional Body	If the organization is tied closely to a credential-granting or professional body with a code of ethics that is being violated, and one has time and very good documentation, this may be a good option.
Police	When push comes to shove and when one is dealing with an issue of criminal behaviour, this is a good outlet. Have facts ready and be prepared for lawyers.
Activists/Corporate Critics	Providing one's documents to activists and corporate critics may intensify one's perception as a traitor, but it will likely get the data in the hands of those eager to put it into play.
Government in Opposition	At times, the opposition in government is more receptive to critiques of the status quo than the government. It may be possible to take this outlet and have the issue brought to a head.

FIGURE 7-5   Continued

External Outlets

Courts	A costly outlet that is time-consuming and often requires deep pockets and patience. Recommended when (wealthy) others are backing the issue.
Stockholders	Difficult to reach except at annual meetings. If they see the issue as germane to their investment strategy, they can be very helpful.

public pressure is much more difficult than modifying one's views with internal negotiations. Moreover, it can be argued that involuntary compromises, those that require persistent monitoring by external bodies, tend to be resisted in practice by organizational cultures.

It is wise to see the whistle-blower at Stage 3 as having the option of selecting to start whistle-blowing internally or externally and moving between them as the process reveals more information to the participants. Moreover, even if the whistle-blower elects to start, let us say, internally, he or she must still select who will serve as the most effective internal outlet for the disclosure. Figure 7.5 provides an array of options available to whistle-blowers, and the logic of selecting one over another. In making this selection, the whistle-blower must make sure that his or her documentation of the triggering event is in a form that can be understood by the outlet; that the whistle-blower's time and finances fit the requirements of the outlet; that the whistle-blower is willing to be questioned, poked, and prodded by those in the outlet; and that the whistle-blower feels comfortable with the fact that once he or she tells others, they will re-frame the data to suit their purposes.

To whom one elects to give voice in blowing the whistle is not restricted to one and only one of the outlets listed in Figure 7.5. Going to the media can be seen as trying to talk to both the firm's stockholders and/or to its CEO. Looking internally, going to the union is also a way to blow the whistle to one's supervisor. Yet the business ethicist counselling a whistle-blower must make it clear that going to the union in order to get to the supervisor has very different results and meaning than going to the supervisor first. The sequence taken in selecting the outlet(s) is very important for the eventual outcome of the whistle-blowing process. Electing to go to one's mentor and then, without heeding one's mentor, giving the data to activists and corporate critics, and then soliciting the support of the firm's stockholders, will certainly complicate matters. A less tension-filled sequence might be to go to one's supervisor with a specified timeline for action; if this is not forthcoming, go to the CEO; if this provides no results, go to the media.

The third critical choice the whistle-blower must make at Stage 3 is whether or not to blow the whistle anonymously or to self-identify (Elliston, 1982a; Elliston *et al.*, 1985a, 1985b). For authors who portray whistle-blowing as an act of courageous altruism (Barrie, 1996; Glazer and Glazer, 1989; Weinstein, 1979; Westin, 1981), it is conflicting to provide whistle-blowers with the option of keeping their identity anonymous. If one seeks to study only stellar examples of principled dissent backed by personal conviction and unflinching bravery, then the exploits of "Deep Throat" in instigating the resignation of Richard Nixon will not be seen as an instance of whistle-blowing, nor would anonymous e-mail messages, confidential sources in journalism, or leaks by unknown members of one corporation to another.

One selects anonymity because one anticipates that the corporation is likely to retaliate. Stage 4 in the whistle-blowing process—the reactions of others—documents more completely the sorts of retaliation possible. While the motive for anonymity is apparent, the ability to achieve it while still effectively blowing the whistle is less clear. Five factors make anonymous whistle-blowing difficult: (1) the pursuit of anonymity causes bystanders to suspect the motives of anonymous whistle-blowers; (2) there is a norm in many cultures that the accused must be able to "face" his or her accuser; (3) the anonymous whistle-blower will be unable to appear at inquiries, depositions, press conferences, and other representative forums; (4) the anonymous whistle-blower cannot threaten to exit as a symbolic form of using voice; and (5) the anonymous whistle-blower does not have the same freedom of selecting a sequence of possible outlets as does the self-identified or known whistle-blower.

Making one's identity known in the act of whistle-blowing lends a sense of principled dissent and clarity of motive to one's endeavour. There are three specific reasons for taking off the mask or coming out from behind "a reliable source said" quotations: 1) it is clear that representing oneself lessens the likelihood of being either misrepresented or having one's views colonized by others with different agendas; 2) there is a probability that in the course of whistle-blowing one's identity will become known, at which point an initial attempt to remain anonymous will provoke questions regarding one's motive and character; and 3) to avoid the moral quandary that arises if and when innocent others are suspected of—and even retaliated against—initiating the call for reform.

The fourth critical choice that must be made at Stage 3 is how to document the alleged wrongdoing. Whistle-blowers seek to call wider attention to what they see as a situation in which a wrongdoing, if left unchecked, will not only flourish, but as a consequence bring harm to innocent others. However, to get others to pay attention is not always easy. It is necessary to communicate allegations to selected outlets in such a manner that they are seen as credible. To simplify matters, we can reduce this choice to selecting either a formal or an informal means of documentation.

Formal documentation of allegations is most appropriate when the whistle-blower is addressing either those above him or her in the corporate hierarchy or an external outlet. With formal documentation, the whistle-blower should pinpoint the trigger event with facts that can be substantiated using objective data—e.g., time, place, data entries, video footage, account data, and corroborative statements of witnesses including names, phone numbers, and addresses. The plausibility of the data should be emphasized by pointing to the whistle-blower's experience and character, by establishing his or her job history with supporting reference letters from credible gatekeepers within the system. The beauty of formal documentation is that when it is done well, it can be used to get attention from more than one outlet. It requires that those who seek to deny the allegation speak to the documented facts.

Paradoxically, formal documentation is often hard to obtain by those who need it most. If one is a minor player in a large corporation it can be difficult to requisition account data, or gain access to video surveillance material or even the appointment books of key personnel. Nevertheless, the often "invisible" nature of secretaries, clerks, and the like provides them with access to data. A question I am frequently asked is whether it is right to take data necessary to document one's case without corporate permission. My response is always to caution the potential whistle-blower that such an act of trespassing and data thievery may, in time, be used against them, but that the only way to call effective attention to the wrongdoer is to capture the wrongdoing in clear data.

Informal documentation works best when the whistle-blower is a relatively high-status player within the organization. This whistle-blower will usually find that others are willing to set up an inquiry and begin a probe into allegations. There is a rather unfortunate tendency in the literature to frame whistle-blowing in a "David vs. Goliath" paradigm, where the whistle-blower (David) is out-muscled by his adversary. In many of the whistle-blowing episodes I have worked, the whistle-blower has been blowing the whistle on his or her peers. This peer whistle-blowing can rely on either informal or formal documentation. As well, there are times when an individual or group well-placed in an organization seeks to blow the whistle on a wrongdoer of lesser status. Whistle-blowing downward in corporate settings has its own difficulties; the more formal the documentation in instances of this sort, the more the whistle-blowing process can be framed as a witch hunt.

A final point drawing attention to the "formal vs. informal" documentation option is the use of legal counsel or an advisor to help clarify what is and is not convincing documentation. It is hard for the typical whistle-blower to understand whether or not he or she possess plausible documentation. The whistle-blower may be: 1) too close to his or her perception and interpretation; 2) often unaware of who it is that should hear his or her views; 3) lacking a view of the bigger picture, including the retaliatory potential and legal issues that may ensue. Figure 7.6 is a compilation of the sort of sound advice a typical lawyer or mentor would give to a potential whistle-blower. It is highly advised that one seek advice on the specifics of one's allegations before charging off to tilt windmills and rock the boat.

The fifth and last of the critical choices to be made by the whistle-blower at Stage 3 in the process is whether or not to identify the targets or wrongdoers, and what should be done to rectify the situation. Whistle-blowing that focuses on wrongdoers is accusatory, and whistle-blowing that suggests what should be done to right the wrong is corrective. If one elects to connect these two, one is setting oneself up to try and take charge of the whistle-blowing process. This is demanding. It requires not only a solid repertoire of strategic moves, but also the resources to take charge. The greater the whistle-blower's resources, the more difficult it is for those in the organization to imagine continuing without him or her.

However, many whistle-blowers not only are viewed as dispensable, but their very act of whistle-blowing increases this likelihood. In these instances, which are by far more frequent, the whistle-blower would be wise to raise suspicions and allow others to take charge of precisely who are the wrongdoers and what should be done to rectify their wrongdoing. This "call for help" perhaps is authenticated most easily when the members called see that the actions of the wrongdoers, if left unchecked, will cause irreparable damage. People are willing to probe and investigate when this makes them look good and when it can be argued that the investigation will be in the best interests of all. To accomplish this the whistle-blower cannot just hope for the best—they must be prepared for a fight.

In the case of Roger Whitelaw, the option of internal whistle-blowing was made impracticable by Daniel Marcus's pre-emptive move to inform the CEO of the Whitelaw team's data and concerns. In response, Robert Sculley selected a new team to investigate the claims. By the time Roger Whitelaw approached Sculley to blow the whistle, the event had been framed by Sculley in such a way that Whitelaw felt that internal whistle-blowing was no longer a viable option. Acting on behalf of what he no doubt believed to be the best interests of QRL, Sculley began playing hardball with those whom he perceived were acting with disloyalty towards QRL. With the internal option closed, Whitelaw's only choice was to blow the whistle externally. In terms of the five critical choices at Stage 3 in the whistle-blowing process, Whitelaw leaned towards a group whistle-blowing function which, as the

FIGURE 7–6 Ten Survival Tips for Whistle-Blowers

Survival Tip	Reasoning
1. Ask yourself if the wrongdoing is non-trivial, immoral, or whether it is simply a questionable business policy with which you disagree but others have good reasons to support.	A potential whistle-blower has a strong obligation to make sure the allegations are well-founded.
2. Whistle-blowing is an irreversible process. Before beginning it, talk to your family, close friends, and intimates about your decision to blow the whistle.	If you elect to challenge the system, you must get the permission and support of your social support system.
3. Be clear about what, in business terms, you expect to be altered if your whistle-blowing is successful. Have a plan for what you will do when the process is over.	Clear objectives are necessary if you are to know how and when to lessen your involvement in the process.
4. Be alert and discreetly attempt to learn of other people in the organization who have data on the wrongdoing. However, protect yourself.	It will be difficult to tell allies from foes. Allies may try to warn you off. Foes may act friendly and try to get information from you.
5. In the midst of your whistle-blowing, keep up your work and continue to do your job thoroughly. Stay on your best behaviour with both superiors and peers.	Bear in mind that your past performance will be reviewed and efforts will be made to discredit you—perhaps even fire you.
6. Invest some funds to get a legal opinion from a good lawyer or whistle-blowing specialist. Know how to best defend yourself and what to expect.	Experts not only give advice; their presence on your team is a signal to others that you are serious.
7. Keep copies of all relevant documents and records that you issue throughout the process. Keep a diary or factual log of events.	You will be questioned and re-questioned. Consistency is your ally. If facts change, show how and where they fit into your new story.
8. In presenting your version of the facts, do not embellish. Do not use caricatures or simplify the events to make them easier to understand.	In efforts to discredit your version of events, others will attempt to show that you do not understand the true depth of events in the situation.
9. Develop relationships with people in the corporation who are trustworthy and can keep you informed.	Things will change quickly. Information is power. You must remain informed.
10. Understand that, if the going gets rough, you must be prepared to exit. Have plans for this possibility worked out.	Whether you win or fail in your own eyes, you must get on with your life. At some point you must leave these events behind you.

process advanced, weighed more and more squarely on his shoulders alone. Whitelaw and his compatriots did nothing to mask their identities. When they blew the whistle externally to the press, they used formal documentation rather than spelling out who had done what and what ought to be done to right the wrong.

Stage 4: Assessing the Reactions of Others

Stage 4 of the whistle-blowing process focuses on how others, both inside and/or external to the organization, are believed to react to the whistle-blower's disclosure. Figure 7.7 provides a comprehensive overview of the strategies taken by those who, for diverse reasons, seek to avoid the costs that whistle-blowers impose upon individuals, departments, organizations, and even systems. Their motives vary from the self-interested desire to avoid punishment, to the genuine belief that the whistle-blower is making a mountain out of a mole hill, making vague accusations accompanied by weak documentation.

Whether one blows the whistle internally or externally, others' reactions to disclosures are not at all easy to predict. I have worked on aiding whistle-blowers who, by the nature of their disclosures, I thought would be deeply discredited by their employer, only to find them most appreciative of the assistance provided by the whistle-blower. On the other hand, I have been involved with whistle-blowing episodes that I thought would be supported by the employee's organization and society at large in which the whistle-blower was torn apart and discredited; they lost their job, had their marriage destroyed, and at the end found themselves without confidence, depressed, and dependent upon medication to buoy their spirits.

Whistle-blowing is not for the faint-hearted. Most whistle-blowers blow the whistle only once in their lifetime. As a rule, they are not particularly savvy to the five critical choices in Stage 3 of the whistle-blowing process, nor are they aware of the seven counter-strategies in Stage 4. Generally speaking, it is their lack of awareness of the following stage and their prevailing belief that they are right that makes whistle-blowers both easy victims to those who seek to discredit them and relentless in their pursuit of what they see as the "truth." Most whistle-blowers are well-intentioned people who stumble into knowledge of an event they not only find reprehensible, but which they feel they must correct. They are not powerful enough to right this wrong through direct action, but whistle-blow in order to draw the attention of bystanders.

Bystanders who hear the whistle-blower's call for help but remain aloof have been neutralized. This may be due both to the effective strategies of those who seek to neutralize and discredit the whistle-blower—combined with the often ineffective counter-strategies of the ill-prepared whistle-blower—and also to the relatively low status that our society accords whistle-blowing. Whistle-blowers frequently are seen as disloyal to the hand that feeds them. Their act of dissent and protest is unsettling to those of us taught not to call attention to ourselves, to work within the system, and to defer to legitimate power. The whistle-blower is an archetype of the crusader on a moral or holy mission—but ours is a very secular society.

The whistle-blower implicitly asks us to join in the risky venture of righting a wrong. Most of us decide to sit on the sidelines and let those involved thrash it out. Why do we prefer to remain neutral? First and most prevalent, because we believe we do not have enough clear information to judge the event. Second, because we tend to wonder about the psychological makeup of those who blow the whistle while most others remain mute. Third, because most citizens believe that the principled dissent of the whistle-blower must make its principled position clear. This is commonly obscured when altruistic cases of whistle-blowing get

FIGURE 7-7 Seven Strategies for Neutralizing and Discrediting Whistle-Blowers/Whistle-Blowers' Counter-Strategies

Strategy	Counter-Strategy
1. Make the whistle-blower the issue. This is an effort to take the focus off the content of the message (disclosure) and turn it on the messenger. Typically, aspersions are cast on the whistle-blower's motive, character, previous work history, and private life.	1. The whistle-blower must turn the focus to the disclosure by making these documents the focus. To do so, there should be a clear wrongdoing with others enriching themselves and/or harming innocent others.
2. Isolate the whistle-blower. This strategy emphasizes taking the whistle-blower out of contact with potential allies.	2. To overcome the isolation, the whistle-blower must keep ongoing contact with his or her support base.
3. Destabilize the whistle-blower's support base. This strategy attempts to utilize a "divide and conquer" approach to the whistle-blower's support base.	3. To overcome efforts to destabilize the whistle-blower's support base, the whistle-blower must build confidence in a positive outcome.
4. Blow the whistle on oneself first and set the agenda. This strategy seeks to diffuse the impact of the whistle-blower's message by taking a pre-emptive whistle-blowing foray.	4. The whistle-blower can counter with two strategies: one proactive and the other reactive. Proactively, the whistle-blower can avoid signalling his or her whistle-blowing message; reactively, the whistle-blower must try to build the case out of the data used in the pre-emptive strike.
5. One of the hardball strategies is to eliminate the whistle-blower's job. This is often done so as to appear tied to larger economic, policy, or strategic issues being put into place by the firm.	5. Document all dates. If a whistle-blower is laid off after a whistle-blowing event and believes that this is motivated by a desire to silence the message, the whistle-blower should seek a good employment lawyer.
6. One of the most frequent ways to silence whistle-blowers is to prosecute them or threaten to take them to court for such issues as breach of confidentiality, employment-contract violation, or giving away trade secrets.	6. If one is going to back down upon the threat of prosecution, do not blow the whistle. If one anticipates that others will attempt to prosecute for frivolous reasons, take first mover's advantage by trying to prosecute them.
7. Others may bring in experts and hired guns to discredit the disclosure.	7. The whistle-blower can try to raise public consciousness by producing eye-witness testimonials of everyday people.

reported in the same way as those acts that are intended to save a job, help a career, or to increase the flow of resources to a department.

When we look at Figure 7.7, we can see why and how the power to retaliate and make life difficult for whistle-blowers thrives in the power structure of the typical organization. Those who seek to discredit and neutralize the whistle-blower's power base usually have deeper pockets, greater access to experts, greater knowledge of the wider context in which the whistle-blowing event is embedded, and the power to demote, promote, isolate, and fire the whistle-blower. For their part, whistle-blowers can only escalate the shrillness of their whistle-blowing by escalating their efforts to publicize the disclosure and bring shame, reputation damage, and in time, change to the status quo within the organization. In the first strategy available to the neutralizer, efforts are made to discredit the whistle-blower by making him or her, and not the content of the disclosure, the focus of attention. In whistle-blowing cases I have been a party to, this usually occurs when spokespersons on behalf of the "firm as a whole" allude to the whistle-blower's past history of mental health problems, alcohol or substance addiction, stress-related illnesses, family problems, credit or financial debt issues, checkered work history, and the like. Essentially, the strategy is to plant in the public record a red flag regarding the character and thereby credibility of the whistle-blower. The tacit or unspoken question is whether or not this self-nominated whistle-blower is a trustworthy interpreter of complex events.

The whistle-blower, in his or her counter-strategy, must stay with the facts. Going toe-to-toe on character innuendo is not possible; it detracts from the facts and tends to loosen the focus. This strategy moves the whistle-blower's case into the realm of interpretation. Once there, the whistle-blower is in trouble. His or her credibility has already been impugned; to correct this perception is not furthered by seeming to bad-mouth those with whom one works. In fact, this plants the idea that one is not a team player and may harbour personal animosity towards one's targets. If, however, the whistle-blower seeks to get at the character of his or her targets, he or she must get others in the organization to come forward with this sort of "supportive" testimonial.

The neutralizers recognize this potential countermeasure and often seek to isolate the whistle-blower. This second strategy emphasizes taking the whistle-blower out of contact with potential allies. This is a particularly useful strategy when the whistle-blower has only threatened to blow the whistle, or begins by first blowing the whistle internally to a small group who seeks to keep, for whatever motive, the content of the disclosure quiet. The isolation can involve a transfer of the whistle-blower to a new location, a demotion, a promotion, or placing him or her on special assignment. The idea in this strategy is simple—with new and/or indifferent co-workers, the whistle-blower is less likely to mobilize sympathy or appreciation. A second variation is to transfer the whistle-blower to a new dead-end task and/or location. Then, if and when the whistle-blower goes public, it is always possible to imply that as a reaction to his or her transfer the employee seems to have taken on a disgruntled and mean-spirited view of the firm.

To overcome the neutralizers' efforts to isolate, the whistle-blower must persist in keeping together and developing a network of allies, both in the organization and among the organization's stakeholders. It is highly recommended that the whistle-blower establish ongoing lines of communication with those willing to support and provide information to build the case and improvise within the case as the neutralizers begin their strategic moves. Would-be supporters need to see that the whistle-blower already has some very powerful players on-board. The whistle-blower should develop—outside of company time—a good e-mail, newsletter, or telephone system that builds the support base; there should be key lieutenants entrusted and empowered to help coordinate efforts.

Once the whistle-blower has built a support base, the neutralizers will attempt to destabilize it using a "divide and conquer" approach. Like the whistle-blower, members of the support team may find themselves transferred. They may find that excellent performance evaluations become scarce and that resources of all sorts await those who are willing to shift their support away from the whistle-blower. Strong and overt allies of the whistle-blower may find themselves demoted or even released from the firm. The neutralizers seek to make the support base ineffectual by flooding it with members who are willing to act as "double agents."

To counter this effort to destabilize the whistle-blower's support base, the whistle-blower must build confidence in a positive outcome. The support base must believe in the possibility of achieving this outcome. The whistle-blower can buoy the confidence of the support group by demonstrating small victories—the joining of a new, high-status member from the organization, a report supportive of the whistle-blower's position, evidence of growing public concern and interest in the issue. As well, the whistle-blower would do well to document all efforts of the neutralizers to unjustly pick upon members of the whistle-blower's support base. If an inquiry is held, these acts taken as a whole may be used to reveal a pattern of vindictive actions. To stabilize the whistle-blower's support base it is necessary continually and clearly to apprise the support group of the latest developments.

To blow apart any effort of the whistle-blower to develop a support base within the organization and among its stakeholders, the neutralizers may attempt to control the agenda by taking a pre-emptive whistle-blowing foray. This strategy is used when the neutralizers feel that the whistle-blower has a good case. By blowing the whistle first and in a way that can be controlled, the neutralizers increase public perception of them as being part of the solution rather than the problem. This controlled whistle-blowing effort usually implicates large parts of the organization. It tends to avoid specific targets. Moreover, the firm that is seen to monitor itself, and do so in a way that the public perceives as voluntary, is not likely to be seen as stifling whistle-blowers. This strategy inoculates the firm. In episodes where a genuinely uncontrolled whistle-blower emerges and threatens action, the neutralizers can point to the past history of the firm and its tight monitoring to substantiate its view of the whistle-blower as nothing but a disgruntled employee or a wild-eyed radical.

The whistle-blower can counter the neutralizers' pre-emptive whistle-blowing strategy using one of two counter-strategies. In a proactive manner, the whistle-blower can avoid signalling his or her whistle-blowing message. This, of course, makes it less likely that the neutralizers can pre-empt and control the whistle-blowing process by setting its agenda. However, there is a tendency in the court of public opinion to give high points to whistle-blowers who first try to work out their issues of dissent and disclosure within the firm. A second and more reactive counter-strategy is for the whistle-blower to use the harmless pre-emptive strike initiated by the neutralizers to start a genuine inquiry. The key is to take the control out of the pre-emptive whistle-blowing strategy by building momentum. The momentum is best built by getting people to ask pointed questions within what was initially planned as a tame process.

The fifth strategy employed by the neutralizers is to eliminate the whistle-blower's position. This is usually tied to a downsizing exercise in which, due to economic conditions or a disappointing quarter, certain redundant or unnecessary positions will be cut. The layoff typically occurs before the whistle-blower's message is disseminated widely. This hardball tactic works. When the whistle-blower, one of a larger group of laid-off employees, begins to vent, it is framed by the neutralizers as nothing but a desire for vengeance and a display of hard feelings. Moreover, the whistle-blower's allies and support group can be cast likewise in this light. The neutralizers frame themselves as economically responsible. The whistle-blower or whistle-blowers are framed as victims of large, impersonal, economic forces.

The key to the whistle-blower's counter-strategy is to document all dates and begin, where possible, to video or tape-record key events. If a whistle-blower is laid off after or during a whistle-blowing event and believes that this was motivated by a desire to silence, he or she should seek a good employment lawyer. With the dates and documentation of events, a suit for unjust dismissal should be part of the whistle-blower's efforts to be heard. To further establish such a case, the whistle-blower should research the downsizing history of the firm and draw out any anomalies that attach themselves to the whistle-blower's lay-off. This counter-strategy diminishes in impact if it cannot be shown that the dismissal followed the whistle-blower's first pronouncement of his or her intentions.

The sixth and, in my experience, very common strategy used by neutralizers is to threaten whistle-blowers with prosecution or take them before some quasi-judicial board for such alleged issues as breach of confidentiality, giving away trade secrets, or violation of professional conduct. This threat to tie up the whistle-blower in costly courts or in the procedures of professional and/or in-house committees impedes the whistle-blower's freedom. While in court, for example, defending him or herself, the whistle-blower must refrain from talking publicly about certain issues; while under professional or in-house investigation, procedures limit the whistle-blower's ability to speak freely and openly. As well, such procedures take up a great deal of the whistle-blower's time, concentration, and capital. During his or her appearance in these contexts, credibility as a moral crusader is not greatly enhanced.

The counter-strategy here is for the whistle-blower to strike first and strike hard. If the whistle-blower anticipates that others will attempt to prosecute for strategic reasons, he or she may be wise to take the first mover's advantage. If one is worried that prosecution may be used to silence the whistle-blower, it may prove wise to work in a group. If, however, one is unable to anticipate that the neutralizers will act in a litigious manner, it is important for the whistle-blower to try to use the courts, in-house tribunal, or professional association to hear facts relevant to the disclosure. This can be done by tying the defense to the whistle-blowing status.

The last or seventh strategy utilized by those seeking to neutralize a whistle-blower is to bring in experts and hired guns to discredit the disclosure. This strategy attempts to move the problem towards "official" data discussions—law, science, medicine, psychiatry—where long, technical discussions may move the story off the front pages of the press. The paid experts and spin doctors remain to do remedial work on the corporation's post-whistle-blowing reputation. These experts are very expensive and often very good. They work as spokespersons for the firm, crisis managers, and special project problem solvers. They are well-connected and thoroughly knowledgeable in their fields of expertise. The neutralizers often hire a team of experts to help neutralize the whistle-blower and thereby save the firm from headaches. The hiring of the expert team is often supported by those who seek to retain their jobs, maintain their dividends, and keep their subcontracts with the firm.

The typical whistle-blower cannot go head-to-head with the experts, hired guns, and spin doctors hired by the neutralizers. Rather, the counter-strategy in this case is to keep the whistle-blowing disclosure on the front burners of public consciousness. The whistle-blower and his or her support base must put forward eyewitness testimonials of everyday people. This pushes the technical data out of the media and focuses on the costs to everyday people. The testimonials must be eye-catching and throw light on the whistle-blowing disclosure. If this is not possible, then it is wise to build a war chest and either hire experts, or get them to donate their time and talent to the cause. Raising both money and free expert advice is only possible when the whistle-blower makes the case more than a parochial business concern, and rather an issue that must be dealt with by society.

In the case of Roger Whitelaw, Stage 4 came as a very rude shock. Sculley and QRL played hardball with that faction of the group that seemed determined to back the substance of the press release issued by Whitelaw. Several typical strategies (see Figure 7.7) were followed by Sculley, including Strategy 4 (blow the whistle first and set the agenda). Prior to Whitelaw's press release, Sculley issued one of his own in which he re-framed the issue so it seemed that QRL was acting as a good corporate citizen investigating, at its own expense, soil contamination. When Whitelaw released his "bombshell," to many it seemed that this was simply part of a larger study undertaken by QRL, a company seeking to learn more about how to do its work better. This attempt to foreshadow and colonize the content of the whistle-blower's disclosure was possible because Daniel Marcus signalled Whitelaw's intention early on.

A second strategy used by Sculley and QRL combined Strategy 3 (destabilize the whistle-blower's support base) and Strategy 5 (eliminate the whistle-blower's job). To destabilize and eliminate jobs, Sculley divided the Whitelaw group into two factions—the Marcus faction and the Whitelaw faction—and used this recognized split between old-timers and newcomers to fire Allen Manus, the only old-timer who was taking an active and committed stance in blowing the whistle. Three things damaging to Whitelaw and the active whistle-blowers were accomplished with this one-two punch. First, Sculley made it clear to both internal and external constituents of QRL that these two factions were exploring contradictory views on soil contamination, and that this healthy rivalry was planned to maximize QRL's research insights. This meant that when the groups disagreed, QRL would have one long-serving group of experts pitted against another new group. The disagreement would be seen as part of the corporate design. Second, by removing Manus, Sculley gave a warning—particularly to the old-timers—that despite their long tenure at QRL, they were far from indispensable. Third and last, Sculley served notice to the newcomers that their centrality to the future of the company and its objectives was under review.

The final strategy employed by Sculley and QRL to silence the whistle-blowers was Strategy 6 (prosecute them or threaten to take them to court). Sculley fired Manus for failing to adhere to "confidentiality" guidelines set in Manus's initial contract with QRL. The others could read the writing on the wall. They had all signed similar agreements. This fear of prosecution, of losing their jobs, took its toll. Manus left to take a job with a Swiss consortium; Fuentes announced his departure for an Argentinean firm. The Whitelaw group had, as far as whistle-blowing potential was concerned, been neutralized.

Stage 5: Results of the Whistle-Blowing Process

Whistle-blowing processes do not always end easily or, for that matter, happily. Stage 5 emphasizes the results or possible aftermath alternatives from the vantage of the whistle-blower. These results can best be portrayed within the context of two generalized outcomes (see Figure 7.8). In the first, labelled outcome A, the whistle-blower believes that he or she has been heard. Conversely, in outcome B, the whistle-blower feels that despite great effort, he or she has not been heard. Outcome A can lead to options A1 or A2. In A1—the best of all possible worlds from the view of the whistle-blower—not only is the whistle-blower heard, but as a direct consequence of his or her actions, others do what the whistle-blower considers to be the right thing. In A1 the call for help either brought bystanders into the

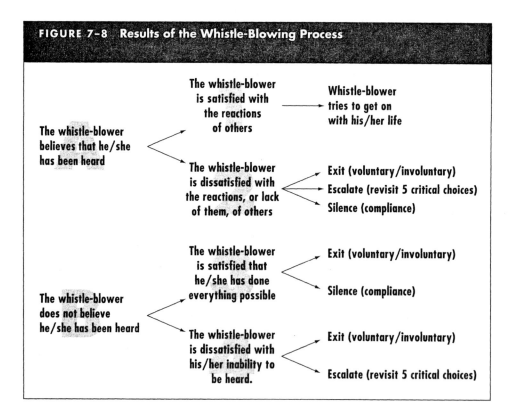

FIGURE 7–8 Results of the Whistle-Blowing Process

fray or the threat of this was sufficient to turn the tide. Even in successful whistle-blowing processes marked by an A1 result, one should realize that the whistle-blower may still suffer recriminations in his or her attempt to return to "life as usual" in the firm.

Other complications arise, even in A1 outcomes, when the changes to the status quo ushered in by the whistle-blower satisfy some but not others in the process. I have seen and experienced several variations of this theme. In one instance, the whistle-blowing episode at Stage 3 was rooted in a group rather than pushed forward by an individual. The group persisted and at Stage 5 the majority were satisfied with the outcome—but a minority felt that the concessions made by the organization were too few and too late. This minority decided to persist. They re-triggered the whistle-blowing by going to a government inquiry and seeking to have the issue examined further. Another instance of an A1 outcome leading to complications occurred in a company that responded to a long, drawn-out whistle-blowing event surrounding corporate benefits for same-sex couples. Those protesting this issue were satisfied with the outcome. Society at large, however, skewered the well-intentioned firm in the press. Other members of the firm complained that the position taken was out of line with family values. Several members voluntarily exited, claiming the reasons for their departure were directly related to the benefits offered to same-sex couples.

A second outcome often overlooked by the literature on whistle-blowing (Casal and Zalkind, 1995; Chambers, 1988; King, 1997) is when the whistle-blower believes he or she is heard, but remains dissatisfied with the reactions or lack of them. Outcome A2 positions are underemphasized for two reasons. First, it remains a belief that satisfaction with being heard equals a successful whistle-blowing process. This position assumes too much. Being heard is necessary, but not sufficient. It is possible that the whistle-blower selects an outlet in the action stage (Stage 3) of the process who hears the whistle-blower and attempts to rectify the wrong, but lacks the power and connections to do so. The second reason is that managers in organizations generally argue that they have treated a whistle-blower fairly when they provide them with a hearing. This position can be simply tokenism. The hearing is provided and reports are written, but when the dust settles, the reports sit in their big, black binders on the desks of individuals who write whistle-blower policies for corporations (Barnet, 1992b), but who may not act too readily upon the contents of these messages. The whistle-blower, however, seeing the seriousness with which the process is taken, believes that in time the wrong will be righted. This hope can fade, and along with it the whistle-blower's initial satisfaction.

Then there are those whistle-blowing processes that result in generalized B outcomes, where the whistle-blowers do not believe that they have been heard. In Stage 4—the whistle-blower's assessment of the reactions of others—the whistle-blower may feel that he or she has been retaliated against, discredited, or neutralized. In short, that the protests fell either on deaf ears or were re-framed so as to lose meaning and intensity. In outcome B3, the whistle-blower, believing that he or she has done as much as is possible, packs it in, either exiting or choosing to be silent. The exit, of course, can be voluntary or involuntary. The whistle-blower can quit in disgust with the stonewalling and concealment tactics of the firm. After all, most of us do not react well to character assassination, isolation, or efforts by our co-workers to discredit us. Moreover, most of us cannot afford to lose our job or have our professional reputation damaged by being linked to a highly public and costly whistle-blowing event. Studies reveal that even when whistle-blowers win the day, their reputations as rising stars or competent players in the industry take a severe knock (Anonymous, 1997; Casal and Zalkind, 1995; Feliu, 1990; Miethe and Rothschild, 1994).

Silence of the compliant sort results in B3 outcomes, when the whistle-blower is beaten but unwilling to exit voluntarily and the firm sees no reason to make a martyr out of the discredited or neutralized player. Organizations fear making martyrs out of defeated whistle-blowers for three reasons: 1) they do not want the whistle-blower to become a rallying cry for future generations of employees who seek to protest; 2) they fear the possibility of a backlash from the public at large; and 3) they would like the ordeal to be forgotten and remain buried. The existence of a martyr or perceived victim of a large corporation can be dredged up years later and made into a movie, become the subject of a best-selling book, or otherwise cause complex and unexpected damage to an organization's reputation.

The last outcome, B4, is one in which the whistle-blower believes that he or she has not been heard, remains dissatisfied, and still seeks to carry the issue forward. In these outcomes, as in A2 outcomes, the whistle-blower may, despite having come to the end of the process, decide to re-trigger it. This is usually seen as a form of escalation in which the whistle-blower revisits the five critical choices in the action stage of the whistle-blowing process. For example, the whistle-blower may decide to move from internal to external sources, to formalize the documentation and involve legal counsel, or to drop his or her anonymity and self-identify. The escalation is, within a game theoretical framework, an attempt to realign moves and see how opponents counter. Long, drawn-out whistle-blowing processes can do this for several iterations of the five-stage process. In the B4 outcome, the whistle-blower does not become compliant and pack it in, going back to his or her job. If the whistle-blower cannot take the escalating costs and personal involvement entailed in B4 escalation, he or she exits.

In the B4 outcome, the whistle-blower can be dismissed by an organization unwilling to sustain the employment contract of what they see as a costly troublemaker. In this instance, the firm looks for means to fire the whistle-blower for activities that are cause for legal dismissal and are peripheral to the whistle-blowing event. Strategies vary in different organizations. Some increase the whistle-blower's workload with a transfer, new responsibilities and even a raise, or special project germane to his or her job precisely when the whistle-blower's time is taken up with the whistle-blowing process. Then, as work performance falls, the corporation moves to dismiss. Other firms prefer to avoid the "gotcha" strategy and fire the employee with ample severance pay, willing to deal with the further possibility of an unjust dismissal case. It is, they feel, worth it to finally get rid of the troublemaker.

Voluntary exit in the B4 outcome is tied to a strategic effort of the whistle-blower to be heard or even to use the exit as a means of calling attention to the perceived wrongdoing. Three variations of the voluntary exit exist in B4 outcomes. The first, as in B3 outcomes, has the whistle-blower symbolically attaching the exit with his or her dissatisfaction over the ineptitude or even complicity of the organization in obfuscating or stonewalling over the whistle-blowing process. The second variation has the whistle-blower leaving the firm and working full-time—either with donated money or as part of a not-for-profit social movement—in fighting the old fight as an ex-employee. Ex-employees with unfulfilled grievances form an important, often passionately involved, component of activist groups that take as their mandate to monitor and hound the socially irresponsible organization. The third variation sees the whistle-blower using voluntary exit in order to provide external bodies—government inquiries or muckraking, investigative journalists—with data that they could not divulge while an employee.

In the case of Roger Whitelaw, the Stage 5 results were rather disappointing if you believe that two corporations (QRL and Technology Laboratories) and various individuals may have knowingly lined their pockets at their expense of others' health and well-being. If, however, you believe that QRL is a rather good company working in a field that is still unable to reduce toxins as well as it would like, and that the data was interpreted by Whitelaw and his colleagues in a fashion overly critical of QRL, then you may not be disappointed with the results.

From the perspective of Whitelaw and his colleagues, outcome B3 best encapsulates their view. They felt retaliated against: Manus was fired for breach of confidentiality; Sculley appointed others to negate the team's analysis of the data; and Whitelaw and his family found themselves increasingly isolated. Whitelaw did not believe that they had been heard, by either QRL or the general public, and while dissatisfied with the outcome, he believed they had done all they could. With the exception of Allen Marcus, the whistle-blowers all left to take up employment with other firms in the same industry.

Their exits were not symbolic; no attempts were made to draw the attention of others to their leaving as a form of protest. They left quietly—each, perhaps, attempting to keep his or her reputation as an employee with excellent prospects intact. They were eager to leave the event behind as a fight they had entered but not won. QRL remained not only economically viable, but received a large infusion of cash from making judicious decisions in the market. David Marcus was, in short time, given Roger Whitelaw's job. Sculley increased his own attractiveness as a potential CEO with a larger firm. The trigger is lost. There is little likelihood that the issue will be raised again.

Each whistle-blowing process works its way through the five stages schematized in Figure 7.2 in a rather unique way, but each process calls our attention to the role of the individual or group as one who can hold the organization accountable, albeit often at great personal cost. This descriptive treatment of the whistle-blowing process functions as a reminder that the values we act on in organizational settings are being scrutinized and can be made public. In society, we cannot rely solely upon whistle-blowers to activate controversies over what is and is not acceptable behaviour by organizations. In the next three chapters we turn our attention to the controversial processes we are currently debating in our efforts to bring the values operative in organizations in line with changing values and issues in society at large.

CASES AND QUESTIONS

CASE 7-1 **The Weasel and the Prince at Environmental Logistix Incorporated**

Keith Slater, Barbara Rawlins, and Inerjit Singh graduated from the "Environmental Studies" Program at York University in Toronto and returned to their hometown of Calgary, infused with idealism and determined to set up a principled company to do environmental consulting and impact studies for developers. "Slater, Rawlins and Singh Ltd." was founded when each of the partners borrowed or begged $20,000 from their families, lovers, and friends. For the first two years, the small company made a reasonable reputation for itself as a straight-shooter and competent provider of environmental services to large firms and government agencies; despite this, the three partners barely made a living. Each had a $20,000 debt growing with interest payments, and after paying overhead and "necessary" bills, each earned less than $18,000 per year. They were working sixty-hour weeks, but were barely living above the poverty line.

The three partners were aware that in order to catch a break they would have to invest some of their hard-earned cash in networking and going to industry shows and meetings. At the Seattle Conference on Environmental Assessment Techniques, Keith Slater met and impressed Vincent Murray, Vice President of operations at Environmental Logistix Incorporated. Environmental Logistix Incorporated is a large environmental services company op-

erating internationally out of its head office in San Francisco and carrying on operations in more than forty countries. Vincent Murray was in charge of looking for talent to outsource some of Environmental Logistix's contracts. He invited Slater and his partners down to San Francisco to see what they could do for Environmental Logistix.

At first, the relationship between Slater, Rawlins and Singh Ltd. and Environmental Logistix went like clockwork. Within three years, ninety per cent of the Calgary company's business was with Environmental Logistix. The company was flourishing. Keith, Barbara, and Inerjit were not only out of debt, but were now beginning to earn what all of them considered to be a substantial income. They had moved their premises within Calgary to reflect their newfound success, and hired four employees to keep up with the work. The honeymoon period, as Barbara Rawlins liked to refer to those early years, came to a screeching halt when the three discovered that Martha Clegg, another environmental specialist working on a contract with Environmental Logistix, was taking bribes to get questionable material through the environmental review process in Brazil. The mishap that tore the clockwork precision out of the relationship between Slater, Rawlins and Singh Ltd. and Environmental Logistix went as follows.

Vincent Murray and Environmental Logistix had won a bid to do the environmental impact and assessment studies on a series of airports to be built by a consortium of private corporations, government agencies, and union bodies in Brazil. The two-year contract involved working closely with the Brazilian consortium. Murray decided to throw Martha Clegg together with Slater, Rawlins and Singh Ltd. to handle the Brazilian deal. Clegg was very familiar with the key players in the Brazilian consortium because her husband, Manuel Halperin, was a high-ranking player in the consortium. The three Calgarians were to take control of the technical elements and leave the schmoozing to Clegg.

Three months into the project, it became apparent to Keith, Barbara, and Inerjit that all was not above board in the Brazilian airport project. Martha Clegg was taking and giving payments to officials to assure that all parties to the consortium were happy. This became evident when she came to Keith, Barbara, and Inerjit and offered them part of the $300,000 (US) she had made in transacting her deals. At times, Martha used bribes to remove impediments. For example, she used $25,000 (US) to quiet a small bird-loving group from raising a fuss about the nesting grounds likely to be destroyed by the runway lights in one location. At other times, Martha took money from the members of the consortium to make sure things went in a particular manner. One member stood to make a fortune on land he owned if the planned airport would have its retail space facing his property. For a sum of $100,000, Martha not only assured him of this, but made it so.

Keith, Barbara, and Inerjit were stunned. They immediately contacted Vincent Murray in San Francisco, who seemed nonplussed. He asked them if they were being asked to compromise any of their assessments. They said they were not, but had found irregularities in the way in which the Brazilian consortium seemed to be interpreting their assessments. Vincent asked if anyone on site or involved in the project was complaining about Martha Clegg or the environmental assessment as a whole. To the best of their knowledge, everyone seemed very happy. In fact, insisted the Calgarians, this is precisely how Martha Clegg was employing the "slush fund"—to make people happy.

Murray told Keith, Barbara, and Inerjit that "when in Rome, do as the Romans," and that no one knew this or did it any better than Martha Clegg. The Calgarians were stunned into silence. The next day they called a lawyer. In a week they had blown the whistle to the press in Brazil, the United States, and Canada. The news made a big splash in the Brazilian press, putting the airport project on hold for a year and resulting in a new start-up for the project. (Martha Clegg was again placed at the helm by Environmental Logistix.)

After the news hit the paper, Murray acted swiftly. Keith, Barbara, and Inerjit had their contract pulled. Each was given two weeks pay and a one-way air ticket to Calgary. Within days of arriving home, they received a registered letter from Environmental Logistix's lawyer drawing their attention to the confidentiality clause in the initial contracts they had signed, and pointing out that they would be sued if and when they made public any details of the work they had done while in the employ of Environmental Logistix. A week later, Murray phoned and told the three Calgarians that they were nothing but weasels. He told them that he would do all he could to keep the three environmentalists from ever working on a big project in the field again. Within a year of its rise to economic success, Slater, Rawlins and Singh Ltd. of Calgary closed its doors. Keith Slater is now a developer of ski chalets in Whistler; Barbara Rawlins owns a florist shop in Edmonton; and Inerjit Singh is a graphic designer for a high-technology company making Web sites.

QUESTIONS

1. In your view, did the whistle-blowers in this case plan their whistle-blowing process in a rational manner? Did the outlets selected make sense? Was the whistle-blowing target(s) clear? Why, in your view, did organizational and societal bystanders remain largely indifferent to the whistle-blowers' call for help?

2. While hindsight provides us with 20/20 vision, what would you have recommended that Keith Slater, Barbara Rawlins, and Inerjit Singh have done to improve their chances of being heard? Looking at the results (Stage 5) of the whistle-blowing process in this case, would this be an A2 or a B4 outcome? Discuss.

3. What concessions, if any, should Keith Slater, Barbara Rawlins, and Inerjit Singh have made for doing a job in a country with different attitudes towards the use of a broker to cement deals? Was Martha Clegg actually using bribery? From Vincent Murray's position, make a moral argument defending his hiring and protection of Martha Clegg, even in the face of the information made public by Slater, Rawlins and Singh Ltd.

4. What retaliatory measures did Vincent Murray engage in to make sure that Keith Slater, Barbara Rawlins, and Inerjit Singh did not persist in their efforts to blow the whistle? What counter-strategies might the whistle-blowers have employed to block this effort to muzzle them?

5. Would you have blown the whistle in this case? If so, why? If not, why not? Which of the ten survival tips for whistle-blowers do you think helped you decide? Who, in your view, is injured because of the activities of Martha Clegg of Clegg Consulting and Vincent Murray of Environmental Logistix Incorporated?

6. Were Slater, Rawlins and Singh Ltd. acting as princes or weasels? Why, in your view, is our society so ambivalent in its attitude toward whistle-blowers? What can be done in society to make whistle-blowing more acceptable?

CASE 7-2	From Whistle-Blowing to Social Movement Foundation at Chemical World Incorporated

Dominique Wong graduated with honours in chemistry from Simon Fraser University and was soon hired by Chemical World Inc.'s Asian plant just outside Bangkok. Wong was a gold-medal student whose award-winning paper explored new techniques for measuring health problems in chemical workers. This paper, co-authored with his advisor, was considered by people within the industry as a seminal contribution. Wong was pleased and somewhat unnerved when Chemical World offered him more than twice the salary and far greater perquisites than any of the other six firms bidding for his services. Not wanting to look a gift horse in the mouth and

eager to put some distance between himself and his parents, Dominique Wong set off for the suburbs of Bangkok.

Chemical World had a growing reputation in Asia for being rather cavalier in its exposure of workers to toxic materials. In a cutthroat, competitive business, Chemical World was a low-cost, bulk supplier of chemicals. It specialized in industrial solvents and fertilizers for agri-business. We can speculate now that Chemical World laid out a fortune to acquire the promising young specialist because it was felt that he would be willing to give Chemical World's handling of chemicals a high grade. Milton

Choo, the CEO of Chemical World's plant, was worried that his trained employees were taking up employment with the competition, and he was concerned about a legal case in which a group of long-time employees of Chemical World were seeking recompense for their failing health—particularly the high incidence of blindness. The workers, in a case that was gathering momentum in the Asian press, were attributing their maladies to the unnecessary changes associated with their work at Chemical World.

Within a month of Dominque Wong's arrival, he was given the task, under the direction of Ben Okuda, the director of occupational safety and health, to author a report assessing both the overall health and safety measures operating at Chemical World's Asian plant and evaluating the state of the techniques used to protect its employees from illness and medical problems. Wong initially protested that he did not yet know enough about the plant and its operations to complete an assessment of the size and scope requested by Ben Okuda. Wong relented when he was told that the report would be used to put earlier studies in line. He reasoned that all he would have to do was stick to the earlier authors' methodology and attach new data.

Wong was shocked when given the earlier set of studies. They were, in his eyes, a whitewash of some very deep and real problems. He devised a methodology of his own and began to rank the dangers of working with chemicals at Chemical World. Okuda queried Wong about his report and was assured that he was making excellent progress. Wong was. He had received unexpected help and cooperation from the workers at the plant, who realized he was an honest man interested in trying to realistically assess health dangers.

When Wong gave a copy of his report to Okuda he was told to rewrite it in line with the findings of the earlier studies. Wong refused to alter his findings or to suppress them by hiding them in ineffectual measurement techniques. Within the day, he received a phone call from Milton Choo requesting that he dine with him that evening. During the meal, Choo first offered Wong a promotion to vice president of research and development within one year if the young man rewrote his report. When Wong politely refused, Choo suggested that he would have to see that Wong's position was made redundant. Okuda had been given directives to downsize his unit from thirty-two employees to twenty, and since Wong was the most recent employee, no doubt he would have to be cut. Wong, quite aware of the hardball being played, told Choo to go to hell. Choo reminded Wong that employees who could not keep their tempers in check at Chemical World would never be given satisfactory letters of recommendation. The two parted with hardly another word.

Wong documented each and every word spoken by Choo. He took the name of the waiter, asking him to confirm that a rather emotional exchange had taken place. Wong went to his office immediately and took all the memos and previous studies that had been given to him by Okuda, and spent the next three days collecting testimonials from those workers and middle management at Chemical World who were sympathetic to a rigorous and truthful assessment of the safety concerns. On the fourth day, he was fired.

Three days after his dismissal, Wong brought his data and documentation to the newly-emergent workers' group called Chemical Workers for Safe Workplaces. Wong's participation in the group's efforts was instrumental in the creation of an ongoing regulatory agency monitoring occupational safety and health in the workplace. Wong is now head of the agency and an active campaigner in the field of workplace justice. Dominique Wong is a firm believer that whistle-blowers can make a difference.

QUESTIONS

1. What did Dominque Wong do to increase his probability of being a successful whistle-blower? Should he have done some research on Chemical World before joining it? Do you think red flags should have gone up when Chemical World agreed to pay him more than twice the salary other firms were offering and with better perquisites?

2. From the perspectives of Mr. Choo and Mr. Okuda, what plans did Chemical World have for the gold medal winning student in chemistry? Why did they expect Mr. Wong to go along with their plan? Who would be injured if Mr. Wong complied?

3. What is the trigger event in this whistle-blowing process? What retaliatory strategies did Chemical World attempt to utilize to neutralize Mr. Wong? How did Mr. Wong cope with these strategies? What counter-strategies did Mr. Wong utilize so effectively?

4. Using the "Five Critical Choices When Blowing the Whistle," assess Mr. Wong's choices. Which do you feel were key in helping him prevail despite a decided lack of power compared to Chemical World?

5. Analyze the results in this whistle-blowing process. Why does the existence of a social movement or group like Chemical Workers for Safe Workplaces make it less likely that things will slip back into their old pattern?

6. Why is society at large the winner in this whistle-blowing case? Is this always the outcome in successful whistle-blowing cases?

CASE 7-3 Mr. Seeger's Warped World

Jonathan Seeger had been with New Paper Publishing (NPP) for over fifteen years and been passed over for promotion at least eight times. Seeger was a perfectionist and was poor at prioritizing in his work as a children's book editor. Rather than find a life outside of his job, or even become immersed in his work routines, Seeger was a very bitter man. He held Karla Jamieson, the head of children's publishing at NPP, responsible for his lowly status. He plotted and schemed, biding his time until he could get back at her.

Seeger planned his revenge nightly, living for the opportunity to degrade Jamieson, who was unaware of the loose cannon she was harbouring in her department. Usually on Thursdays, Jamieson had Charles Schacter stay late and work with her on the pile of unsolicited manuscripts that kept growing. Schacter was a married man with two children, and in August he took his family to Old Orchard Beach for a month of rest and relaxation. During August, Seeger took his place in trying to make a dent in the pile of unsolicited manuscripts.

One evening, while watching television, Seeger came across a program in which an employee ruined his supervisor's career by falsely accusing him of having sexual relations with a colleague. The light went on in Seeger's scheming mind. The next day, he put an anonymous e-mail on the NPP system accusing Karla Jamieson and Charles Schacter of having an ongoing Thursday night tryst. Seeger signed the e-mail, "The Whistle-Blower." NPP was all abuzz with the rumour. Jamieson and Schacter were called into the offices of Lawrence Cambridge, the president of NPP, and asked to provide some insight on the e-mail. Obviously, neither could.

Within a month of the episode, Schacter left NPP to take a job elsewhere. Jamieson still wondered what she had done to deserve the nasty accusation. Although nothing was said, her movement up the ladder at NPP was put on hold.

However, Seeger was far from finished. About a year later, Seeger, who had taken Schacter's place on the Thursday evening efforts to reduce the manuscript pile, went to Lawrence Cambridge's office and told him that Jamieson had made unwanted sexual advances. Cambridge asked if he would put his accusations in writing. Seeger complied.

Within a month, Karla Jamieson was knee-deep in efforts to clear her name in an in-house investigation of Seeger's allegations. Seeger quickly perceived that within the "he said, she said" context of the investigation, he had little chance of pushing home his version of events. Jamieson, despite the buzz over Charles Schacter, had many close friends at NPP. Seeger was a loner and disliked by most employees. To short-circuit the investigation, he complained to the Provincial Ombudsperson that his serious charges were being treated frivolously at NPP. Seeger insisted that in this in-house "kangaroo court" he felt he could receive no justice.

Lawrence Cambridge was stunned by Seeger's accusation. NPP had hired a professional mediator and negotiator and made sure that they followed the provincial guidelines for in-house investigations into sexual harassment. Jamieson was equally stunned. Due to Seeger's complaint to the Provincial Ombudsperson, a special committee under the auspices of the Ombudsperson's office was to conduct the inquiry. The inquiry lasted two years. It cost the taxpayers an estimated $1.2 million. During this period, Jamieson was suspended from work and after two months received no pay whatsoever from NPP. Seeger was kept on the payroll throughout the provincial inquiry. In the end, after enormous legal costs and the break-up of her marriage, there was found to be insufficient evidence to determine whether or not Karla Jamieson had sexually harassed Jonathan Seeger.

Karla Holmes, having gone back to her maiden name, was not rehired at NPP, nor was she able to secure a position in the publishing industry. Karla Holmes eventually remarried and, with her husband, operates a trailer park in the Great Lakes area. Jonathan Seeger still works at the same job at NPP. His disposition, on the whole, has not improved at all.

QUESTIONS

1. Is Mr. Jonathan Seeger a genuine whistle-blower? If yes, why? If not, why not? What motivates him? What motivates most whistle-blowers?

2. How was the anonymous initial disclosure romantically linking Karla Jamieson and Charles Schacter useful in Jonathan Seeger's effort to set up Karla Jamieson? Was Charles Schacter acting rationally when he left New Paper Publishing one month after the accusation? Did this make things better or worse for Karla Jamieson? If better, why? If worse, why?

3. At what point, in your view, does this become a whistle-blowing case? How is society at large impacted by dysfunctional or fraudulent whistle-blowing processes? How was the reputation of New Paper Publishing impacted by Jonathan Seeger's complaint to the Provincial Ombudsperson?

4. What can we do in organizations, and in society, when whistle-blowers target innocent others as their victims and then portray themselves as the genuine victims? How do we encourage functional whistle-blowing, but discourage dysfunctional whistle-blowing?

5. What would you suggest is a fair and just thing to do with Jonathan Seeger? Is he a well man? What, in your view, causes a person to project their bitterness onto another person as Jonathan Seeger did?

6. What could Karla Jamieson have done to protect her reputation from the likes of Jonathan Seeger? What can we do in organizational cultures to curtail the misuse and abuse of dysfunctional or disingenuous whistle-blowing?

C h a p t e r

ENVIRONMENTAL
ETHICS AND
BUSINESS

*Why should corporations bother about the natural environment? ...
Unrestrained economic and industrial growth have bestowed a grand
standard of living on people in developed countries. Yet survival of
corporations and industries depends on the survival of the earth's
ecosystems. Only with corporate greening can corporations—the main
engines of economic development—be make ecologically sustainable*

Paul Shrivastava
*Greening Business: Profiting the
Corporation and the Environment* (1996)

The use of the colour green to designate an emerging attitude towards nature and the natural
environment by business, as Paul Shrivastava (1996) makes clear, is a response to the belief that the earth's ecosystem—the very basis for healthy life on the planet—is being threatened. Calls for the "greening" of organizations (Allenby and Richards, 1994; Bhat, 1996;
Davis, 1991; Schmidheiny, 1992) are, as we shall see in this chapter, an effort—at times simply token—to heed the public cry for a new ethos of the environment. The public concern
and awareness of environmentalism as an issue concerning business and the economy is
relatively recent.

In 1962 Rachel Carson, in *Silent Spring*, focused international attention on the deadly
effects of DDT and chemical pesticides. Carson's groundbreaking work, written in accessible
prose by a veteran scientist and nature-lover, evoked a passionate response. The damage

we were doing to ourselves, other species, and the ecosystem, Carson proposed, was not a result of malicious intent, nor did it reveal itself in an obvious fashion. Rather, in our desire to feed greater and greater numbers of humans and livestock at lower prices and with less back-breaking labour, we have succumbed to pesticides, weed killers, and chemicals. While their use has boosted our ability to support more and more humans, we have and continue to put into jeopardy the soil and water that support the long-term viability of the ecosystem. Rachel Carson envisioned a future in which accumulating groundwater and airborne chemicals would create an uncontrolled chemical soup capable of devastating consequences.

Within a year of Carson's work, Stewart L. Udall's *The Quiet Crisis* (1963), in which the term "environmental crisis" was born, had achieved sufficient public legitimacy to warrant a glowing introduction by John F. Kennedy. Paul and Anne Ehrlich's *The Population Bomb* (1971) and Barry Commoner's *The Closing Circle: Nature, Man and Technology* (1971) rounded out the first volley of books warning us that running the planet with a "business as usual" framework entailed fairly predictable and devastating risks—increased shortages and/or lack of purity in air, water, and food; soil erosion and leaching; desertification of agricultural land, increasing famine and epidemics; growing rates of allergies and immune disorders; and decimation of the forests.

This evocation of what in Biblical times would be explained as the wrath of God, a modern-day series of plagues, with great debate between and among scientists on any one area of imminent threat, has been recognized as the environmental crisis. Figure 8.1 outlines the general contours of what is being called the environmental crisis (Cantril and Oravee, 1996; Rogers, 1994; White, 1993). The list of dangers, perceived or real, include: resource depletion, the greenhouse effect, water shortages, stratospheric ozone depletion, species extinction, population growth, forest decimation, hazardous toxic waste, and acid rain. The role of business, that which Shrivastava (1996) calls "the main engine of economic development," is deeply implicated. Business is seen as both a force contributing to the environmental crisis and, on the other hand, one which can play an important role in turning the threat aside.

To capture this dual perception of business in the call for a new and meaningful relationship to the environment, first we will look at public reactions to the environmental crisis; then we will investigate how business managers conceive of the environment very differently than do committed environmentalists; and finally we will turn to the different shades of green that accompany the call for a marriage of environmental and business ethics.

REACTIONS TO ENVIRONMENTAL CRISIS

Figure 8.1 provides us with a moderately alarmist reaction to the environmental crisis. I use the designation "moderately alarmist" because there are four very distinct but not unrelated frames of reference in which we can make sense of the literature and public discussion surrounding the environmental crisis. People react to crises very differently. The Chinese see "crisis" as Janus-faced, simultaneously presenting intensified risk and great opportunities. Each of the four reactions outlined in this section depicts the environmental crisis—and the opportunities it offers—quite differently. We will look at each of these four reactions in turn, outlining its internal logic, and then spelling out the implications for business ethicists. A basic outline of this is provided in Figure 8.2.

FIGURE 8-1   Ten Major Threats to Planet Earth: The Environmental Crisis

1   **Resource Depletion:** Renewable resources such as fish and timber are being depleted at unsustainable rates; non-renewable resources such as fossil fuels and some metals and minerals are in urgent need of conserving. In Canada, our experience with both the east and west coast fisheries speaks to the reality of this issue. There are fears that efforts to correct for this, for example, fish farming or aquaculture, are prone to failure as the high use of antibiotics in fish food raises health problems for consumers.

2   **The Greenhouse Effect:** The greenhouse effect represents the warming of the atmosphere by carbon emissions, industrial pollutants, and the burning of forests. The atmosphere is unable to cope with the plethora of gases emitted into it. These gases, such as carbon dioxide, methane, nitrous oxide, and CFCs, block infrared radiation build-up and are increasing the temperature of the earth's surface and its atmosphere. It is conjectured that sea levels will rise due to thermal expansion and the melting of ice. Rising temperatures will destroy crops, flood low-lying coastal areas and, in time, require the shifting of human settlements.

3   **Water Quality/Shortages:** While 70 per cent of the planet's surface is covered by seawater that is too costly to transform to potable water, the safety and availability of water is no longer assured. Water pollution, climate change, soil leaching, and a build-up of salt in 10 per cent of the world's irrigation areas spell trouble. Mismatches of water supply with demand and high transportation costs make water scarce in several highly-populated parts of the world. Countries dependent on water supplies whose rivers originate in other countries have gone to war for water. India and Pakistan, Chile and Bolivia, Jordan and Syria, Syria, Iraq, and Turkey have all been involved in water-related conflicts.

4   **Stratospheric Ozone Depletion:** The ozone layer, which protects the earth from harmful solar ultraviolet radiation, is being destroyed by chemicals. Chlorofluorocarbons (CFCs) found in refrigeration, aerosols, and foams are used for many industrial processes. Despite a ban on CFCs, they flourish in the underground market. Despite their numerous industrial uses, the harmful effects of CFCs outweigh their benefits. Increased ultraviolet radiation due to ozone depletion causes skin cancer, eye damage, and immune response system suppression. Wheat, rice, corn, and soybeans can be adversely impacted by increased ultraviolet radiation.

5   **Species Extinction:** Due to the expansion of human settlements, the burning of forests, pollution of plant and animal habitats, use of pesticides, and the like, more than 50 plant and animal species cease to exist forever, or become extinct, each and every day. This reduces biological diversity, leading to a simplified and more vulnerable ecosystem. This is made most clear in the recognition that some of the plants and herbs now extinct may have held important medicinal properties. From an aesthetic point of view, the loss of a species is the loss of an important aspect of what makes our planet whole, beautiful, and healthy.

6   **Population Growth:** The world's population is increasing exponentially and concentrating in urban spaces. At present rates, the population doubles every 40 years. This brings an immense rise in human use of resources. From 1950 to 1990, while the planet's human population doubled, the number of registered automobiles increased more than 7.25 times, energy consumption increased 400 per cent, and metal consumption rose 600 per cent. While the population growth is putting pressure on the environment, so is the concentration of population in supercities.

FIGURE 1–1   Continued

Supercities, or clusters of cities in a bio-region occupying prime agricultural lands, require foodstuffs and resources to be transported from a great distance and increase the transportation nightmare that seems to trap all urban centres.

7 **Forest Decimation:** One billion hectares of forests have disappeared since the end of World War II. Within the 4 billion hectares of forested land that exist world-wide, only 1.5 billion hectares are undisturbed primary forest. Most specifically, the decimation of forests is advanced in the rain forest regions where the rain forests play a central role in the well-being of the planet by converting carbon dioxide into oxygen. The rain forests, which cover one-fourteenth of the earth's land surface, are being destroyed at the rate of 40 hectares (100 acres) every minute of every day.

8 **Widening Income Disparities:** The rich are getting richer and the poor are not only getting poorer but more numerous. According to the World Commission on Environment and Development, more commonly known as The Bruntland Commission (1987:8), the best predictor of sustained environmental degradation is acute poverty. Acute poverty reduces choices; coal is burned, forests are decimated, rivers are polluted and, ironically, population growth soars. In economic terms, the richest 20 per cent of humans on the planet enjoy about 83 per cent of the measurable wealth on the planet, while the poorest 1.4 per cent can lay claim to only 1.4 per cent. This widening gap is likely to continue pressure towards political strife, social disruption, and mass migration of economic refugees.

9 **Hazardous and Toxic Waste:** Disposing of waste, particularly the non-biodegradable, and especially the hazardous and toxic, remains a challenge that we have not been able to meet. Increased garbage disposal destroys both renewable and non-renewable materials. Industries currently use about 100,000 chemicals worldwide, and thousands of new chemicals are being introduced each and every year. Toxicity information on many of these chemicals is scanty. Each and every day, one million tons of hazardous waste must be disposed of on the planet. Many efforts to dispose of this waste are poorly designed, close to drinking water, children's schools, and animal habitats.

10 **Acid Rain:** Coal-burning power stations, ore smelters, and heavy manufacturing plants emit enormous amounts of sulphur dioxide. Automobiles and power plants produce nitrous oxide. These gases are converted into sulphuric acid, nitric acid, ammonium sulphate, and ozone. This is expected to intensify as mass consumption comes to China and India. This is expected in the next decade. Deposition of sulphur dioxide and nitrogen oxide causes acidification of freshwater lakes and streams. Acidic deposition, called acid rain, infects lakes and streams, killing fish and aquatic plants, as well as damaging the life support systems of trees and forests.

The Anti-Environmentalists

The first reaction has been to deny the existence of an environmental crisis and to proclaim "business as usual." These modern-day Pollyannas (e.g., Julian Simon and Herman Kahn, 1984) not only deny what they see as the "doomsday logic" of the radical environmentalists, but present a comforting and soothing vision of the planet's future. Anti-environmentalists are fully familiar with the general contours of the environmental crisis, but they see this as

---

FIGURE 8-2 The Four Reactions to the Environmental Crisis

Reaction	Logic	Implications for Business Ethics
Anti-Environmental Backlash	Sees little immediate alarm in the environmental crisis. Views the environmental crisis as exaggerated and rooted in the psychological make-up of environmentalists.	Argues for a business-as-usual point of view. Places a great deal of faith in the radical separation between humans and the natural environment. It is the task of humans to improve upon nature.
Opportunistic Environmentalism	Views the environmental crisis as a real opportunity to create new products, services, and ideas that reach an environmental market for goods and services.	Argues that the environmental crisis has helped to reshape consumer preferences, giving rise to new green or "new age" markets. Satisfying these markets—reduce, repair, reuse, and recycle—is an important adaptation to the crisis.
Reform Environmentalism	Acknowledges the threat of the environmental crisis as one that can be turned around by extending and evolving an ethic that reduces the human separation from nature.	Argues that the environmental crisis is the outcome of humans' anthropocentric instrumentalism. What is needed is a truly eco-centric ethic for business. This is made most explicit in the call for sustainability.
Radical Environmentalism	Rings the alarm, insisting that radical action is needed quickly. The environment that includes the built environment will fall apart within two generations.	Argues that we need to take direct action to protect trees, lakes, endangered species, and living habitats. Our first responsibility is to the biosphere or to the living planet called Gaia (Lovelock, 1979). The stance is counter-authoritarian and deeply reverential of simplicity and early cultures.

---

alarmist claptrap. Ronald Bailey, in *Ecoscam: The False Prophets of the Ecological Apocalypse* (1993), argues that the rhetoric of those espousing ecological disaster is misguided and deceptive. Ben Waltenberg, in *The Good News is the Bad News is Wrong* (1984), insists that the proclamations of alarmist environmentalists are nothing but a cacophony of exaggeration, poor science, and inept forecasting drawn together in an idealization of a golden age of pastoral bliss that never was.

Committed environmentalists see the anti-environmentalists as in denial—they refuse to admit the necessity of changing their behaviour in the face of growing factual evidence. The radical environmentalists see the anti-environmentalists as a significant element in the perpetuation of the crisis. The anti-environmentalists do not see themselves as denying the existence of the environmental crisis; they see themselves as firm believers in the ability of the human species to master its problems through the disciplined application of science, the creation of incentives for innovation in problem areas, and the continued investment in and improvement of technology.

Dixie Lee Ray and Lou Guzzo in *Trashing the Planet* (1993), and Dixie Lee Ray in *Environmental Overkill: What Ever Happened to Common Sense?* (1993), exemplify the very popular view that, due to science, technology and human inventiveness, we are on the whole far better off today than we have ever been. Ray believes that the hoopla surrounding the environmental crisis is a projection of the confused and somewhat neurotic thinking of a small, affluent, educated group—amplified by the popular press—which has been unable to put its ideals into practice and rather childishly sees its values as speaking as the voice of prudent planetary wisdom. Ray believes that in its extreme form environmentalism serves as a secular religion. It uses science to create a cosmology in which "hard times," even "doom," awaits those sinners who do not take up the correct environmental values. Ray sees environmentalism as a social movement aimed at changing the behaviour of *Homo sapiens* in line with what is, in the long run, in their best interest.

The skepticism towards the environmental crisis raised by Bailey (1993), Ray (1993), Ray and Guzzo (1993), and Waltenberg (1984) is far more interesting to business ethicists than the term anti-environmentalism implies. There are ten basic positions in the lexicon of environmentalism with which they feel uncomfortable. They, except for Michael Lewis in his work, *Green Delusions* (1992), tend to see reform and radical environmentalism as sharing premises that in themselves are problematic. These premises include:

1. Civil disobedience, even eco-sabotage, may be required to protect the biosphere.

2. Technology is a force that is accelerating the deterioration of the natural environment.

3. Animals, trees, perhaps even rivers, should be given rights that begin to approximate those given to humans.

4. Markets and competition intensify the profligate use and abuse of scarce resources.

5. Globalization eradicates local cultures and sets the stage for mass consumption.

6. Economics is usable to evaluate key elements of the natural environment.

7. Science and scientists, in the degree to which they are beholden to big business and funding agencies, fail to take the interests of the natural environment to heart.

8. It would benefit the planet if urban citizens adapted a more primal lifestyle and returned, to some degree, to the land.

9. Consumerism, mass consumption, and dependence upon big business for the satisfaction of one's needs is problematic.

10. Inequalities in wealth must be reduced, even radically so, if the political and ecological problems of the planet are to be reduced.

While any one of these ten points may seem sensible, when taken together they worry many people. The worries are expressed in different forms. Some fear the licensing of "eco-anarchism," whereby anything that is believed to benefit the natural environment is supportable. Others fear what has been labelled "eco-fascism." The committed environmentalists' position is not only firm, but is argued with a sense of superiority, bolstered by the belief that all those who disagree are supporting a status quo which, given the environmental crisis, is doomed. To make their arguments even stronger or more "fascistic," the "moderate" and "radical" environmentalists take a holistic position in their approach, which generally contends that to heal the planet, we must think and act not on discrete parts of the problem—as do the opportunistic environmentalists—but rather we must embrace environmentalism as a full commitment.

The anti-environmentalists view all environmentalists as pretty much the same. Their fears express deep reservations regarding the amount and types of change to the status quo that are being demanded. They see them as an active lobby group, tending at times to simplify complex issues in black and white terms. In fact, the anti-environmentalists worry about the explicitly moral form of argumentation used by environmentalists. They feel uncomfortable with talk that refers, often passionately, to good and evil, and trust the objective and more dispassionate discourse of science and scientists. Not surprisingly, anti-environmentalists see environmentalists—particularly committed ones—as woolly-headed romantics, with their fascination for tribal cultures, natural healing, pantheistic forms of spirituality, and cooperative forms of ownership.

Looking ahead to Figure 8.5, we see how the anti-, the opportunistic, the reform, and the radical environmentalists take very distinct and often opposing positions with regard to the forces believed to be the underlying causes of the crisis. The anti-environmentalists are true believers in the status quo. What is required is more and better technology driven by competitive markets and the continued desire to create human goods and services that produce wealth and add value to hard-working, disciplined human beings. There is no doubt, in the lexicon of the anti-environmentalists, that *Homo sapiens*, as rational, tool-making beings, are the masters of the planet. Resources are in the service of human needs.

While the anti-environmentalists differ least from the opportunistic environmentalists, differences do exist. The anti-environmentalists applaud the opportunistic environmentalists' exploration of green capitalism, but they deplore green capitalists' demands for favoured treatment by governments and their pestering marketing campaigns that claim the moral high road. The anti-environmentalists often strategically employ the case of the "third world" or developing societies to hammer home their disagreements with the opportunistic environmentalists, who, they argue, seek to introduce products and services that in their eyes protect the environment and thereby help to reduce the urgency and probability of some elements of the crisis. However, as the anti-environmentalists are quick to point out, usually this is accomplished by raising the price of goods and services and thereby putting these even further beyond the reach of citizens and organizations in the third world.

The anti-environmentalists take umbrage too with the reform environmentalists, who they see as questioning the basic environmental premises of economies of scale, global and competitive markets, and the anthropocentric nature of all human relations with the environment. The anti-environmentalists firmly believe that large systems rooted in economies of scale are the powerhouses behind the increasing application of better and more innovative technology, the continued success of adaptation of our species, and the ability to grapple with bigger and more pressing problems.

The reform environmentalists see "small as beautiful" and seek to work with a notion of "fit" or "appropriate" technology. While the anti-environmentalists applaud what they see as the globalization of markets and the intensification of competition in global markets, the reform environmentalists seek to develop regional economies rooted in bio-regions. The reform environmentalists worry when commerce and organizational transactions are divorced from the "reality" of the climate, species patterns, habitat, and other biological anchors. Lastly, and perhaps most divisive between anti- and reform environmentalists, is the latter's belief that *Homo sapiens* are placing themselves falsely at the head of the biological hierarchy—and particularly the adult male of the species. The anti-environmentalists see this call for expanding rights to others, including other species, as a peculiar pipe dream. Those, like women and members of developing nations, who can and will enter the fray, will win their rights. Other species, such as the spotted owl or baby seal, should be preserved only if there is a market to support and nurture them.

The "social Darwinian" principles of the anti-environmentalists, wherein the world is a jungle in which some thrive and survive while others slowly starve and perish, is not the image of nature maintained by radical environmentalists. They see nature not "red in tooth and claw," but as the "fertile mother." These images are as different as night and day. The most fevered rivalry played out in the media regarding the environmental crisis is between the anti- and radical environmentalists. The heat, rather than light, produced on these occasions is often confusing. To simplify the debate for sound bites, anti-environmentalism is often associated with business and the business community, while radical environmentalism is assumed to be connected to those who seek to save the planet from imminent environmental disaster.

The economy of this simplification and its "dramatic" effect make it as ideal a form of entertainment as WWF wrestling. The realty is more complex. Business is not simply anti-environmental, just as radical environmentalism cannot be simplified as anti-business. The radical environmentalists, in an effort to awaken a somewhat inertial public, stridently call attention to those people, nations, institutions, and technologies that they believe exacerbate the crisis. It is in this manner, as we saw in Chapter 4, that radical environmentalists often create "issues management" crises for organizations.

However, radical environmentalists form organizations to get their ideas across. To "awaken" the public, the radical environmentalists use marketing techniques, raise finances, enter into strategic ventures, form joint alliances, and have become important players in the global market. This is not a criticism of Greenpeace, The Sierra Club, or other global organizations of their kind. These organizations or not-for-profit businesses do possess an ideology that espouses the use of minimal hierarchy, volunteerism, and environmentally friendly office supplies. Nevertheless, they use state-of-the-art computers and technology. Mailing lists of donors are kept in careful repair. Solicitation of members and donations necessitates an increasingly trained staff to put order and sophisticated business acumen into brochures, door-to-door solicitation, and management of public events.

Getting the radical environmental message across is big business, albeit not the same category of big business as strip mining, clear-cut logging, or the genetic engineering of new agri-business companies. We might say that as radical environmentalism increases its effectiveness, the more businesslike it becomes in getting its message to more and more people as efficiently as possible. The message is anti-business only in the sense that it identifies specific businesses as exploitative, rapacious, and polluting. However, it should be clear that as radical environmentalism gets its message across by becoming more businesslike, it both facilitates the evolution of new business forms and states of consciousness, and may be compromising its message. All organizations will find that their structure and processes have an impact upon their output.

The anti-environmentalists' view of saving the world is not heard very clearly in the rivalry with radical environmentalists. The public apprehension of arguments for the status quo is always heard most easily and defended as correct most righteously by those who find themselves privileged by and in the status quo, and by those who believe they soon will be, if the rules remain intact. Ironically, both the wealthy and many of the poorest citizens on the face of the planet remain staunch anti-environmentalists. The former, it is clear, stand to gain materially and socially from the continuation of "business as usual." The latter fear the loss of their jobs and the likelihood that changes in the rules pertaining to the extraction of fossil fuels and minerals, requirements for pollution abatement, and the cutting and/or burning of forests will, in fact, severely impair their ability to move from the status of developing to developed nation states.

From the perspective of the "world as system," the poor feel that efforts by the wealthy to introduce population control, shut down mines, and reduce the harvest and/or clearing of the forests for agricultural purposes are part of a larger conspiracy. At the aggregate level of nations, the developing nations insist that the developed nations who achieved their wealth by strip mining, forest decimation, pollution, and large population growth now seek to prohibit others from enjoying the fruits of immediate gratification and ready, if not always prudent, use of resources. At the individual level, with little hope of alternative employment, the poor tremble at the prospect of firms—or indeed whole industries—being forced to close down or cut back on their operations due to the desire to save a stream from pollution or a plant or animal species from extinction.

To the anti-environmentalists, saving the planet requires faith in and reliance upon the market to reallocate incentives to the best and brightest minds to solve problems as and when they are apprehended. This belief in human intelligence, problem solving, and the application of technology is the only way to live in an uncertain world, which cannot be run while indulging a belief that there is one and only one crisis we will face in the next sixty years—the environmental crisis. To restructure society using this framework leaves us vulnerable and over-invested in dealing with what may not turn out to be a crisis at all.

The Opportunistic Environmentalists

The ethics of the opportunistic environmentalists will probably strike contemporary Canadian business ethics students as far more in tune with their perceptions of business than the anti-environmentalist reaction.

Business, if it is anything, is capable of seeing opportunities in new markets, social ideologies, and economic trends. To the opportunistic environmentalist, the public perception of both the plausibility of the environmental crisis and the manner in which it is creating a demand for new environmentally friendly products and services is a fact to be cheered. The environmentalists hear the slogans of the call for a conserver society (Henion and Kinnear, 1979; Trainer, 1995; Valaskakis, 1979), not as a denial of consumerism, but as the stimulus for demand for products made of recycled paper, cars that use electric batteries, and houses that are more energy efficient. The call to "reduce, repair, reuse, and recycle" is heard by the anti-environmentalists as a retreat from the pursuit of innovation and the application of new technology to problems; the opportunistic environmentalists hear the trumpets sounding for innovation, new forms of socially responsible consumerism, and the development of new environmentally friendly technologies.

While the anti-environmentalists struggle to reveal to the public the false, exaggerated, or hidden agendas beneath the admonition of those proclaiming the environmental crisis, the opportunistic environmentalists see the possibilities of new green businesses using green management techniques and green technology as forces that can, in time, help to soften the harsh edges of the crisis (David, 1991; Harrison, 1993; Hopfenbeck, 1993). If we think of the colour green as designating an attitude towards rethinking environmental ethics, then we would paint the opportunistic environmentalists as "light green," the reformers as "green," and the radicals as "dark green." The anti-environmentalists are not green at all.

The opportunistic environmentalists rest uneasily between the anti- and the reform environmentalists in their commitment to reform. Like the anti-environmentalists, they share the belief that markets, technology, and good management are positive forces. However, they do recognize the scope and intensity of the environmental crisis (although it does not alarm them particularly). The opportunistic environmentalists agree, at least tacitly, with the anti-environmentalists that business—even light green business—is intended to serve and make life happier for humans. Their position is rooted in an instrumental view of the relationship between humanity and the natural world, in which humans, acting responsibly, must conserve and innovate in order to return the relationship between mankind and nature to a balance.

Where the opportunistic or light green environmentalists differ from the reformers is in their desire to minimize the cost to human progress and material growth of returning to that balance. The opportunistic environmentalists accomplish this by fixing their analysis on the firm and not the economy as a whole. They emphasize low-cost, voluntary options in which planned change is not only possible, but may prove profitable. The reform environmentalists worry that the real problem is not solved simply by the good intentions of bright people in search of fair profits. They worry about unintended effects at the systems level. At this level, even small amounts of chemicals discharged into a river system by firms eager to act in a light green manner can, in time, create a toxic chemical stew. The reform environmentalists are aware that in the "commons," that is, the domain managed by no particular entrepreneur or owner, environmental problems intensify.

Essentially, the light greens see the environmental crisis as an opportunity for the management of established firms to engage in planned change, such as policies of "eco-efficiency" to reduce, repair, reuse, and recycle, or otherwise remain efficient while turning to green modes of production (Elkington and Burke, 1987; Hutchinson and Hutchinson, 1996; Smith, 1993). For new firms, or for those established firms interested in securing a new and—in the eyes of the environmental opportunists—growing market niche (the green consumer), management can engage in forms of green marketing (Ottman, 1993, 1998; Peattie, 1995; Waskik, 1996). In both instances, the opportunistic environmentalists view the managers of organizations as possessing the freedom to introduce environmentally friendly and profitable changes into the firm. Planned change is voluntary. The managers select the time, organize the process, and have some control over the cost and duration of the change.

The opportunists, unlike the reform and radical environmentalists, do not envision the need by stakeholders to force unwanted changes upon particular firms. The opportunistic environmentalists do not want to slow down growth, but would like to re-channel it. Eco-tourism can replace tourism. The service organization, with its high-tech, low-pollution operations, can replace the smoke-belching factory. Smaller, more fuel-efficient cars and buses can replace the larger, gas-guzzling vehicles. Eco-efficiency essentially seeks to address the transformation subsystem of all firms and get them to engage in seven basic planned alterations. These include attempts to:

1. minimize the material intensity of goods and services
2. minimize the energy intensity of goods and services
3. move towards the gradual elimination of toxic dispersion
4. increase opportunities of material recyclability
5. maximize the sustainable use of renewable resources
6. extend product durability
7. enhance incentives for firms that reduce, repair, reuse, and recycle

If one is a committed environmentalist in either the reform or radical environmentalist category, opportunistic environmentalism can seem like a hoax (Plant and Plant, 1991) or a selling-out of ideals (Welford, 1997). Both "eco-efficiency" and "green marketing" do not challenge the set of business ethics with a set of environmental ethics. As Figure 8.3 makes clear, both the anti-environmentalists and the opportunistic environmentalists firmly root their convictions in business ethics. While opportunistic environmentalists are willing to tinker with the business process, in no way, shape, or form do they entertain a turnaround in the basic values of business.

The light greens do not cross too far over into a rethinking of orthodox business ethics. It is not mother nature who knows best; it is humans, who in the acts of organizing and harnessing technology, can and must bring value to nature. The value to be brought to nature and the natural world is "use" value. Nature is a resource. Opportunistic environmentalists would like to slow down our use of natural resources by encouraging firms to conserve, substitute renewable for non-renewable resources, and engineer technical processes in such a way as to make them more environmentally friendly. Essentially, the opportunistic environmentalists have little problem with putting the machine in the garden. Their view is that the machine, with the aid of enlightened managers, designers, planners, and programmers, can be used to tend satisfactorily to the garden.

When it comes to the question of scale (see Figure 8.3), the opportunistic environmentalists believe that efficiency and effectiveness can be related to economies of scale. Size is viewed as the result and one of the rewards of successful growth. Just as the anti-environmentalists are unequivocal in their proclamation that "bigger is better," the opportunists are not averse to large global corporations. The light greens argue that it is the corporation's attitude and actions towards the natural environment that are central, not its size. The "small is beautiful" position of the more committed environmentalists in both the reform and radical reactions to the environmental crisis, sees large-scale organizations and technology as inherently problematic. They are too likely to forfeit their tie to the local community and the bio-region. They increase dependency. Even if operated by well-intended specialists, they make great demands on the natural environment. Like a large city, the scale of large organizations leaves a large footprint upon the planet. Large-scale enterprise requires more resources for its survival, generates more waste, and demands a greater share of diminishing resources than do smaller enterprises. Moreover, argue the committed environmentalists, due to their size, we become dependent upon them. They are the key engines of economic growth, jobs, and a prime source of tax revenue for governments. When they become too environmentally costly, often we are too dependent to act rationally. Like addicts to harmful substances, we turn a blind eye to the environmental costs and emphasize the immediate benefits.

FIGURE 8-3   Ideological Tensions Between Environmentalists and Business Persons

Environmental Ethics	Business Ethics	Nature of Tension
Nature knows best. Humans are inextricably part of nature and will become wise only when they return to their rightful role in nature.	**Humans know, or will know, best.** Humans are separate from nature and seek to improve upon it. Nature is seen as a resource to be used.	The environmentalist sees the business person as an anthropocentric instrumentalist; that is, as a person who uses others and nature to advance him or herself. The business person looks at the environmentalist as an idealistic romantic.
Small is beautiful. Environmentalists argue for the systematic dismantling of large organizations, systems, and administrative apparatus in favour of smaller, user-friendly systems.	**Economies of scale are vital.** Business persons believe that large size can increase efficiency. Size is viewed as the outcome, and one of the rewards, of successful growth.	The business person views the environmentalist as failing to appreciate the relationship between size and efficiency in the market context. The environmentalist sees the business person as failing to see the unintended consequences of large-sized, centralized, and hierarchical systems.
Economic markets must be modified to reflect biocentric values. Economic markets reflect a human concern with use value, immediate gratification, and neurotic forms of status-seeking.	**Economic markets effectively reflect consumer demand and supply.** Things, ideas, people, and wildlife are worth precisely what others are willing to pay for them.	The business person sees the environmentalist as an alarmist whose alarm has gone off too early. The market is the timing device. The environmentalist sees the market as a flawed warning device as it only measures things in short, consumer-use time, not in species-related or biological time.
Ecologically sustainable systems should be tied to their region or local market. The slogan "think globally, act locally" reflects the view that action and learning make sense only in context.	**Successful businesses increase their probability of sustained success by operating globally.** Globalization is the mark of a business that is successfully adapting to change.	The business person insists globalization enhances learning. The environmentalist sees the business person as colonizing all parts of the globe with promises of consumer goods. This homogenizes local cultures and fosters dependence upon large corporations.
Progress is non-linear. The good life, the environmentalists argue, ends by leaving little trace or footprint upon nature.	**Progress is linear.** The good life is lived when one accumulates resources and transfers these to wealth in order to leave one's mark.	The business person sees the environmentalist as engaged in a flight of fantasy, confusing progress with a regression to a primal, even primitive, state of being. The environmentalist sees the linear conception of progress as a self-serving delusion.

This discordant reaction to the scale of enterprise and technology between those espousing orthodox business ethics and those claiming to speak on behalf of the environment, is reflected in the similarly contradictory views of another systems-level notion—the market. The opportunistic environmentalists, like the anti-environmentalists, extol the virtue, clarity, and necessity of competitive markets. Markets quickly and accurately reflect changes, via price, in the way humans value goods and services. In the new corporate environmentalism lauded by the light greens, the market provides a true reflection of the growing demand for environmentally friendly goods, services, and production processes. Their position is that being green not only increases the probability of boosting sales, but also of enhancing one's corporate reputation (see Chapter 9). In fact, the light greens argue that enhancing one's corporate reputation provides one with an edge over the competition. The light greens envision a future in which, due to the competitive nature of markets, the growing demand for green products and services will spur firms to "out-green" one another. The winners, the light greens insist, are not only the green firms and their stakeholders, but the planet earth as well.

This "good news" story of the beneficence of competitive markets is not shared by those who claim to speak for the natural environment. Both reform and radical environmentalists believe that *Homo sapiens* rely too heavily on markets to evaluate priorities, and thereby determine values at a systems level. Markets that rely on demand and supply fail to take account of the value of nature in its actual state. Trees, for example, take on cash-in-hand value when cut. Nature must, in human terms, be used if it is to have market value. Even wilderness, the idea of nature in its primal state, is valued in market terms only if used to satisfy human needs for escape, recreation, and spiritual and aesthetic fulfillment. Committed environmentalists worry about the market's inability to deal with the value of nature outside of its use value, and also the way in which markets help humans justify their selection of short-term, human-centred forms of gratification over long-term, biocentric values.

The opportunistic environmentalists praise globalization and the internationalization of markets as factors that will both stimulate the "greening" of business and help to diffuse innovative green business processes throughout the world. The committed environmentalists, on the other hand, view sustainable economic systems as best developed within regional or even bioregional terms. The tension between the ideologies of "globalization" versus "regionalization" can be traced to assumptions made about how wealth and knowledge are diffused. The opportunistic environmentalists assume that as the world's wealth and knowledge are amassed, everyone gains—although not necessarily equally. The committed environmentalists worry that the wealthy get even more wealthy and have access to greater power through knowledge than do the poor. And in a great many instances, the circumstances of the poor may be further reduced when more power and wealth is amassed by the wealthy.

The opportunistic environmentalists believe that globalization enhances markets worldwide. It provides firms with incentives to learn the needs of new regions. In time, globalization raises the economic and material well-being of those who reside in the world's less developed nations. Globalization not only brings jobs and business to these regions, but also raises the standards of living. As poverty in the developing world is reduced, more affluent consumers who have the time, interest, and knowledge of the seriousness of the environmental crisis are introduced into the equation. Moreover, thanks to globalization, these new green consumers will be able to purchase products that help to reduce, repair, reuse, and recycle. This combination of the creation of the "green consumer" and the availability of relatively inexpensive, reliable, and environmentally friendly goods and services, even in the most remote corners of the planet, is part and parcel of the opportunistic worldview.

The committed environmentalists, whether of the green or dark green variety, do not buy into this uplifting tale of global redemption and salvation through globalization and the internationalization of markets. Rather, while reminding us to "think globally," reform and radicals alike insist that we must "act locally." Globalization enriches the wealthy nations. What "trickles down" to the third world are poorly paid jobs that cannot be done cheaply enough in the first world. In the thinking of committed environmentalists, the plants that first world nations build in third world contexts are built for a welter of motives. At times, they are so located in order to sidestep more stringent environmental and occupational safety and health regulations operative in more developed economies. At others times, they are opened up to saturate indigenous cultures with values and products previously available only in advanced nations. On this point, the opportunistic environmentalists and the committed environmentalists are in agreement. However, the committed environmentalists see this "new market" as a dysfunctional form of learning. They see functional learning as tied to useful knowledge of the region, local market, and culture; globalization, on the other hand, is depicted as robbing the local region of its unique adaptations. Rather than becoming more powerful, the knowledge they learn fosters a dependence upon the values and culture of the first world. Globalization, insist the committed environmentalists, provides third world citizens with the "trickle down" economies of poorly paid, often dangerously toxic work; on the cultural side, globalization decontextualizes third world culture, creates dependence upon symbols and images from distant cultures, and fosters a homogenous global response to unique third world problems. Ironically, the committed environmentalists argue, this is all done in the name of innovation and progress.

The ideological tension between views in line with traditional business ethics and those that claim to speak for the environment is probably greatest over the idea of progress—what this is, how to measure it, and who, in fact, should benefit from it. Within the world views of the anti- and opportunistic environmentalists, progress is linear. Although the former holds this view more aggressively than the latter, the good life lived in a progressive system occurs when resources are accumulated, then transferred to wealth within the context of markets, and then used to better the human condition. The view of history uniting anti- and opportunistic environmentalists is of time and time's passage as a ladder. Over time, our species, due to its intelligence, hard work, and ability to defer gratification and learn from mistakes, is ascending this ladder. This view of time also recognizes movement down the ladder, but in applying our rationality we can reduce our lapses.

The anti-environmentalists, of course, see no problem with continuing to climb the ladder step by step. The opportunistic environmentalists see the environmental crisis as a challenge to this continued ascent. However, it is a challenge that can be managed by applying the principles of conservation, reduction, recycling, reusing, and other innovations to the heart of the enterprise. In the opportunistic environmentalists' conception of progress, sustainable development is seen as a minor slow-down, and prudent consumption of resources is not a radical revision or reformulation of the values of business. It is envisioned as a logical necessity to divert ecological disaster and continue to climb the ladder of progress. The anti-environmentalists and the opportunistic environmentalists see the good life in the new, shining options available to consumers. Neither imagines that in the past of ancient Babylon or Greece, or in the lives of the indigenous peoples of Canada or Australia, values far more compatible with the environment can be found.

The committed environmentalists, particularly the radicals or dark greens, argue that material progress is neither necessary nor sufficient to establish spiritual and environmental notions of progress. The reform or green environmentalists also feel that the blatant materialism of consumer-based societies requires radical revision. Rather than depicting progress as a ladder, the committed environmentalists see progress as a complex series of spirals.

The possibilities of ascent and descent in this view are tied to more than material indicators of progress such as the number of cars, telephones, or computers per 100,000 people. Rather, they are tied to spiritual development, our ties to the earth, sea and sky, and our ability to join with others (including other species) in extending rights and privileges. It is the sole pre-occupation with the ladder of material progress and, simultaneously, the neglect of our spiritual development and relationship with biocentric values that has left us so vulnerable and imbalanced. Moreover, to right this imbalance, the reform and radical environmentalists insist that the traditional values of the business community require more modification and revision than that established by the opportunistic environmentalists.

Before we leave the light greens and turn to look more carefully at the critiques of the reformers and radicals, we must see the function played by the opportunists in communicating environmental ethics to the mainstream business community. The light greens are vital to contemporary efforts to merge business and environmental ethics. They speak easily and well about how to take existing firms and make them more environmentally friendly. Theirs is a point of view that speaks to concrete actions and benefits. They are sympathetic to the constraints faced by business and understand that the prime directive of 99 per cent of the organizations on the planet has little to do with "saving planet earth" from environmental crisis. The light greens are seeing that it is possible to make organizations more responsive to the costs they impose upon the planet. In pointing towards the development of this responsiveness, they are not blowing the whistle, rocking the boat, or tilting at windmills—rather, they would like to leave the organizational power structure in place. To make business responsive, we must: (1) educate consumers to demand environmentally responsive products and services; (2) create incentives for firms who act in an environmentally friendly manner; and (3) introduce techniques on cost-efficient and effective means of acting in an environmentally friendly way into the curriculum of managers, architects, urban planners, and the like.

The Reform Environmentalists

When Donald Van DeVeer and Christine Pierce called their book *People, Penguins, and Plastic Trees: Basic Issues in Environmental Ethics* (1986), they were pointing at one of the three basic issues that separate reform environmentalism from opportunistic environmentalism. The "greens" differ from the light greens in: (1) making a strong and meaningful distinction in the use of the term "environment" when applied to humans, penguins, and plastic trees; (2) viewing nature and the natural world as requiring rights and entitlements; and (3) believing that the instrumental use or abuse of nature by humans requires vigilance by organizations whose goal is to speak for and act as agents for the integrity of natural systems. On the whole, the reform environmentalists are an eclectic group (Brown, 1981; Callicott, 1994, 1996; Everenden, 1992; Nash, 1989; Stone, 1974, 1987; Suzuki and Knudston, 1992) who see the light green or opportunistic environmentalists as well-intended but misguided in their belief that eco-efficiency in itself is sufficient to cope with the environmental crisis.

The reform environmentalists are much clearer than either the anti- or the opportunistic environmentalists in seeing that the term "environment" as used in a typical management textbook is at odds with its use in a book written to train ecologists. The reform environmentalists make explicit that in systems theory there are three basic and quite different systems (see Figure 8.4). There are systems that are managed for human purposes and goals, which are designed, operated, and controlled by humans. There are natural systems such as the society of penguins, which, even in our wildest fantasies, seem to have no specifically human purpose. These "natural systems" include humans at a biological level, but exclude us when it comes to managed systems such as the city, the legal system, or the modern corporation. The third type of system is the mixed or hybrid system. An example of the hybrid system is a river system with several electric dams and cities built along its banks. The hybrid system combines elements of the natural system and the managed system in some combination.

The four reactions to the environmental crisis—anti-, opportunistic, reform, and radical environmentalists—conceive of the three systems types very differently. The anti-environmentalists would like to shift the balance of power on the planet so as to decrease the scope of the natural environment and shift it towards the managed environment. This position is unabashedly pro-business and technology. It sees nature as a reservoir of resources and a rather troublesome source of many of the storms, plagues, and famines that strike *Homo sapiens*. The light greens, or opportunistic environmentalists, point to the need to promote hybrid systems in which the environment clearly is under the control of the managerial system, but is so with eco-efficiency. The light greens would like human dominion over the planet to grow, but they caution a prudent form of enlightened self-interest for those who operate managerial systems.

The reform environmentalists change the equation. They believe that the natural environment is presently deeply scarred and imbalanced. Unlike the opportunistic environmentalists, they do not see hybrid systems, when increasingly brought under the auspices of managed environments, as righting this imbalance. Rather, the reformers seek to articulate a series of voices that claim to speak for and as agents of the underrepresented natural environment. To them we must recover, preserve, and increase the domain of natural systems. They call for the responsible organization of environmental groups. As in our discussion of tertiary stakeholders in Chapter 3, we can portray the reform environmentalists as levelling an explicit critique of orthodox business ethics. This critique bolsters the values of natural systems, calling for a recognition of the holistic principle whereby humans, other species, and the biosphere are intricately connected and, as a consequence, rights should be extended to other species, including the land and the sea as living systems.

The radical environmentalists push the envelope of the priority of natural systems over managed systems to its logical extreme. The liberal, moral pluralism of the reform environmentalists is found wanting by the radicals, who see the natural system as sacred. It is the life force. They see the momentum of postmodern corporatism, globalization, and the information revolution as denuding natural systems at warp speed. The radical environmentalists call for direct action to change the direction and locus of power in management systems. They champion the introduction of deep ecological educational principles into the earliest years of public education. They support bold moves of what they see as civil disobedience whereby individuals must take action against what are currently "legal" crimes against nature. They also argue in eco-feminism that women, when given power within the corporate structure, will employ it to support a resurgence in natural systems.

Of the four perspectives, the reform position is the most subtle and perhaps challenging to understand. Relative to the radicals, reform environmentalists are constructive critics. They see the status quo in business as flawed. In Figure 8.4 we see how the reformers break with both the anti- and the opportunistic environmentalists in lauding the supremacy of anthropocentric instrumental values as the centre of the prevailing business ethic. The reformers argue that in order for our species in its present condition to be responsible for our actions, we must take a long-term view of sustainability. We must begin to care for poster-

FIGURE 8-4 Six Positions on the Prevailing Business Ethic

Position	Anti-Environmentalists...	Opportunistic Environmentalists...	Reform Environmentalists...	Radical Environmentalists...
Failure to care for posterity or future generations	Claim that greater access to information, better scientific knowledge, and a more informed public indicate that we are at an all-time high in planning for the future.	Insist that with the proper incentives and market demand, the system will pay more attention to posterity or future generations.	Argue that time is short. We must reformulate our centralized and inefficient planning system and move to a more participatory mode.	Claim that future generations are being deprived of their heritage. We must extend rights to future generations, other species, and the biosphere itself.
Affluence breeds over-consumption and waste	Argue that consumption is the pump that primes the economy; consumption produces greater benefits than costs.	Insist that neither affluence nor waste is a problem if channelled into environmentally friendly practices.	Accept the view that affluence breeds over-consumption and waste; however, this can be dealt with by educating the public	Insist that everything and everybody is a commodity. Activism and direct action are needed to constrain over-consumption.
Spiritual malaise prevails as humans see themselves as separated from nature and the environment	Argue that this is a period of spiritual renewal and a reawakening of the quest to explore space, create virtual realities, and establish a Garden of Eden, albeit one engineered to satisfy human needs.	Insist that the demand for spirituality and proximity to nature are being met through wilderness parks, heli-skiing, eco-tourism, courses on meditation, alternative healing, and the like.	Accept the view that humans must repair the schism whereby they see themselves as separate from and in control of nature and the physical environment.	Insist on idealizing the spiritual life of societies that hold a pantheistic view of the environment. They see the need to return to a cosmology that places nature at the centre.
There is an over-reliance on technology	Argue that technology is the most promising means of improving the planet earth, reducing disease, conserving species, and providing an ample food supply.	Insist that new and environmentally friendly technologies will emerge if there is a demand for these products and services.	Argue that technology must be "appropriate." Appropriate technology is user-friendly, easy to repair, non-polluting, and environmentally friendly.	Insist that technology is an extension of a human-centred ethic and adopt a view of technology as fostering dependence and addictive behaviour.
The question of scale is skewed towards the assumption that bigger is better	Argue that bigger is indeed better and use the ideas of globalization, economies of scale, and stability to make their case.	Insist that scale is determined by the market. Large scale is best at mass-batch production of goods; small systems are best at tailoring to local needs.	Accept the view that small is beautiful. Small systems adapt swiftly, are easier to repair, and create fewer problems.	Insist that direct action, radical politics, and activism be employed to make large government, business, unions, and organizations realize their central role in the present environmental crisis.
Poverty breeds political strife and over-population	Argue that poverty is a problem that can be reduced by developing the resources and technology of the third world and thereby helping them.	Insist that poverty is a problem that can best be reduced by bringing new, cheap, environmentally friendly products into the developing nations.	Accept the view that poverty breeds political strife and over-population, and see the solution in educating the poor to population control, self-sustaining agricultural patterns, and job re-training.	Insist that poverty and its companions — political strife and over-population — can be dealt with only with a radical redistribution of wealth and its entitlements.

ity and future generations. If we rely on the invisible hand of the market to motivate us to become green, we will start too late and end too early.

The reformers re-frame the idea of sustainable development in a way that challenges the opportunistic environmentalists' assumption that sustainable development is possible through the adoption of environmentally innovative processes, leaving economic growth and profits intact. The reform environmentalists see sustainable development as requiring a very real reduction in the material well-being of both developed and developing nations to achieve the long-term ecological integrity of the planet. While they recognize the "small victories" approach of the opportunistic environmentalists, they see it as ultimately doomed to failure since its attendant goals are to stimulate consumption and bolster the growth of profits.

Consumption—more realistically, over-consumption—plays a part in the reform environmentalists' critique. The goal of managed systems is growth, even in the poorest societies. Growth requires an escalating commitment to consumption in order to prime the pump of the economy. The reform environmentalists are not arguing that all firms as managed systems grow equally quickly, but that the value beneath the managed system is growth for growth's sake. This goal stimulates and triggers a vast expanse of obsolescence, over-consumption, and waste, all detrimental to maintaining the ecological integrity of planet earth. As such, growth must be modified; consumption must be brought in line with the carrying capacity of the planet. Appealing to the logic of household management, the reform environmentalists argue that we cannot take more from the planet than we put back and expect to continue this imbalance indefinitely.

To explain the persistence of this imbalance and our refusal to address it on a daily basis, the reform environmentalists speculate on the existence of a spiritual malaise. The assumption that humans can thrive best by separating themselves from nature is a product of wishful thinking. Humans, insist the reformers, wish to live without death, disease, and discomfort. Our species, with the help of the marketing arm of managed systems, creates the fantasy that in the built environment of products and services it is possible to satisfy all our needs, remove our problems, and become significant. The postmodern equation is simple—when you confront a problem, look for the solution in the managed systems of information, services, technologies, and goods. The reform environmentalists think this alienation from nature creates an infantile, pampered, and dependent society unable to face the important spiritual crisis necessary to be truly in this world.

To rectify this spiritual malaise, the reform environmentalists recommend that we turn away from the reveries of quick-fix consumption and utopian technologies to satisfy our needs for companionship and stimulation. They worry that our dependence on technology and its promise of a virtual reality—a version of a managed system that is like a natural system—will not only deepen our spiritual malaise, but will give technology the status of an elixir. The reformers press us to modify unrealistic expectations of technology as a form of deliverance from our troubles. They call for "appropriate" technology—technology that is task-specific, environmentally friendly, easily repaired, and perceived as a tool rather than a solution.

As we noted earlier, part of their perception of the need to modify our expectations and reliance upon technology is related to the reform environmentalists' critique of scale. The reformers do not believe that bigger is better with reference to technology, nor with any other aspect of the managed and hybrid systems. The reform view is grounded in the ideology that small is beautiful, and that only when the units are small can we hope to achieve balance in large systems. This reasoning would have seemed acceptable to Adam Smith, who conceived of an economy in which all firms were small price takers and none could dominate by establishing a price independent of the market. The present fascination with the entrepreneur and the small business enterprise, when coupled with a growing distaste for large government, business, and labour organizations, speaks to a growing public recognition that small can be beautiful. But the public still looks to the large, dominating corporation and public monopoly when it seeks essential services, reliable and vital goods, and important economic services. The reform environmentalists would like to see us reduce the size, scale, and scope of our basic control units within the managed system on the planet.

Their argument, when pushed to its conclusion, is that small is beautiful because small systems both adapt swiftly and tie their adaptations to the specific needs of a given region. Large systems do not adapt swiftly or well; they create great inequities between those at the top and those at the bottom. In fact, the reform environmentalists see the origins of poverty not in the natural system—famines, floods, diseases—but in the poorly-managed distribution strategies of large managed systems—the multinational corporations. Whether publicly or privately owned, these large managed systems fail to adapt to the bioregions in which they operate. They colonize and bring rapid infusions of apparent wealth, but like sugar in the bloodstream it provides only short-term stimulation. Poverty must be dealt with by developing regional self-sustaining economies. The reform environmentalists argue that political strife, poverty, and overpopulation are intensified by imbalances wrought by the large managed system in bioregions still tied to subsistence agriculture and rudimentary technologies.

The imbalances in question can be understood by examining two of the reformers' key suggestions. The conception of "sustainable development" and the notion of the need for a "biocentric" world view both seem to be working their way from the reform environmentalists' critique of orthodox business ethics into the public consciousness. Outside of the opportunistic environmentalists' translation of these ideas, they have not made it into mainstream business practices. They remain—as I remind my students—challenges for the next generation of businessmen and women.

The easiest way to understand reforms' challenge that business must adapt a more biocentric world view is to turn to the "naturalistic" assumption that most members of the business community use in living in a world of natural, hybrid, and managed systems. The naturalist assumption is that we in this world are guided by two very different spheres of morality; there are ethics that attach themselves to managed systems and there are ethics that attach themselves to natural systems. We will admit that taking apples or pears from a farmer's field is theft (although of the type practised by many a hungry child). However, picking fruit from wild fruit trees is neither theft nor an act that requires one to look over one's shoulder or worry about the consequences. To take another example: getting someone to paint your house necessitates that you pay for his or her services. You may quibble over the quality of the service, but payment is required nonetheless. Getting an ox to help you work the farm, on the other hand, requires no direct payment to your assistant. Lastly, dumping waste into international waters that are treated as natural systems would involve symbolic penalties, sanctions, and public condemnation. These consequences pale in comparison to what would occur if the same incident took place in a managed system such as a lake used as the source of drinking water and recreation for a group of estate owners.

The reform environmentalists insist that the schism between what is right and good in managed systems is severely out of whack with what is deemed right and good in natural systems. Moreover, this schism is detrimental to the long-term integrity of the planet as a whole. It is not biocentric, but anthropocentric (as in the case of the anti-environmentalists) or "corpocentric" (as in the case of the opportunistic environmentalists). Anthropocentrism places humans at the centre and as the prime beneficiary not only of managed systems, but also of hybrid and natural systems. Some justify this view by pointing to the Biblical suggestion that mankind was created in the image of God; others point out that human dominion over the planet is due to the intelligence and problem-solving abilities of our species.

In Figure 8.5 we see that the anti-environmentalist position is the least biocentric of the four reactions to the environmental crisis. In terms of anthropocentrism, anti-environmentalists

FIGURE 8-5 Biocentric Views of Business Ethics

View	Anthropocentrism	Land Ethic	Biodiversity
Anti-Environmentalists	Take a human-centred perspective. What is deemed "good" is that which creates material wealth.	Do not see that natural systems—land, air, water—require any special status in the managed system. They are resources.	See no great value in preserving natural systems. Problems will be solved as they emerge.
Opportunistic Environmentalists	Take a "corporate-centred" perspective that is designed to reward those who create environmentally friendly innovations.	Would like to try to reduce the impact of managed systems on natural systems, but the relationship between the managed system and the natural system is still that of a user and a resource.	Speak to biodiversity, but use it primarily as a rhetorical device within green marketing. Natural systems are a resource.
Reform Environmentalists	Argue that species and biological systems like the rain forests must be given rights. The "eco-centric" view sees humans as just one of the groups seeking to interact with the natural system.	Insist that a land ethic or the treatment of natural systems be viewed as an integral part of business ethics. Firms that preserve and enhance the biosphere should be championed as ethical and rewarded; firms that degrade the biosphere should be vilified and penalized.	See the need to avoid putting all our eggs in one basket. To protect and enhance biodiversity, and argue for active legislation regarding endangered species and penalties for firms that destroy habitats of some rare species.
Radical Environmentalists	Not only argue an "eco-centric" view, but license civil disobedience. Those who fail to treat the natural system with all the respect they treat the managed system are criminals.	Extend the land ethic to a point where humans and non-human species should not be differentiated. Natural systems should not only have rights, the rights given to them should supercede and take priority over managed systems.	See biodiversity as an essential element in returning natural systems to their health. They call for re-education, activism, and the establishment of militant organizations and political parties to protect biodiversity.

extol the human use and exploitation of natural systems as a primary directive of doing good. The opportunistic environmentalists modify this view by taking a corpo-centric perspective, which suggests that we ought to do good by supporting those corporations that talk and act eco-efficiently. This view is still human-centred; it is motivated by a desire to simultaneously ward off the negative consequences of the environmental crisis and reward those corporations that take a leading role in reducing, repairing, reusing, and recycling. Profits go to the managed systems that use resources most effectively.

The reform and radical environmentalists extend a biocentric view, which places ecology rather than human beings or corporations at its centre. The reformers argue that non-human species and/or natural systems such as rain forests must be given rights. This eco-centric view sees humans as just one of the groups dependent upon and seeking to interact with natural systems. The failure of our species to preserve the integrity of natural systems is not dangerous simply in that it ushers in environmental crisis, but because it cuts us off from its vital connections to healing and rejuvenating sources. Humans, insist the reform environmentalists, require a change in their instrumental, human-centred, and (material) growth-oriented values. We must see ourselves as part of nature, view other species and natural systems as ends in themselves, and develop simple or less demanding expectations with regard to material growth.

The radical environmentalists go further in their call to eco-centrism. They see the need to curtail human arrogance as calling for those fully committed to the integrity of natural systems to engage in acts of civil disobedience. Those who fail to treat natural systems with all the respect granted to managed systems, should be dealt with as we do other criminals. The radicals see the need for committed environmentalists to take an active role in righting the wrongs inflicted—in the name of progress—on natural systems. We must live, they argue, in a world that uses the term "natural justice" to provide full justice to what is genuinely natural.

The second issue related to extending a biocentric view is what the reform environmentalists call the "land ethic." This term and the related body of literature that has grown up around it, seeks to extend Aldo Leopold's celebrated and controversial statement: "A thing is right when it tends to preserve the integrity, stability, and beauty of the biotic community. It is wrong when it tends otherwise" (1989:246). In this view, humans are just one species among many, and it is not clear that within the "biotic pyramid" human status should be more central or even more elevated than that of natural systems such as land, water, and air. No systems can thrive without these three; many systems, argue the reformers, can and have thrived without humans.

The anti-environmentalists remain confused by Aldo's notion of the land ethic. In their understanding, land attains its value only when it becomes the property of owners who use or lease its resources. To the anti-environmentalists, a thing is right when it tends to advance the wealth of people, particularly those who have access to resources. It is wrong to squander wealth. In this view, the idea of humans as part of a biotic community is lost. Humans own the biotic community and their task is to operate it for their personal benefit. The opportunistic environmentalists modify this view by extending value to the preservation of the integrity, stability, and even beauty of the biotic community. After all, in the end this is good business; it only makes sense to preserve and protect one's resource base. The radical environmentalists insist that we go beyond "preserving the integrity, stability, and beauty" of the biotic community and seek to make the land ethic a sacred principle. The land, rivers, streams, and air are alive; the whole planet is a living, breathing, and experiencing system.

The final way that reform environmentalists make their case for biocentrism is through "biodiversity." biodiversity refers to the number, variation, and health of the species—plant and animal—in a natural system. The reactions to the issue of biodiversity range from the anti-environmentalists' perception of it as a romantic, even pantheistic flirtation, to the radicals' version of it as a sacred tenet.

Not surprisingly, the anti-environmentalists do not rank highly the value of biodiversity. The idea that pests, wolves, and other species that interfere in instrumental human activities should be protected strikes the anti-environmentalists as ludicrous. Equally, land that would be used for subdivision and bring money into the economy ought not to be set aside to preserve a rare species of plant. The anti-environmentalist argument is simple—it makes sense to preserve natural systems and/or non-human species only when it is highly probable that their future "use value" will greatly surpass their present use value. The anti-environmentalists are ardent believers that the nature of progress necessitates that humans turn natural systems into managed systems, and that those species that cannot make the transition can be managed in zoos, theme parks, and other educational facilities.

The opportunistic environmentalists take up the idea of biodiversity precisely where the anti-environmentalists abandon it. They see the idea of biodiversity as an opportunity for firms to expand public consciousness through "green marketing," in which certain products or services are portrayed as contributing to planetary biodiversity, or wherein a portion of the profits will go to encourage and promote biodiversity. Businesses in the "new age" areas of natural health, alternative medicines, and herbal remedies often utilize the idea of biodiversity as supporting the view that little-known plants and fungi can be of immense aid in protecting the human immune system, lowering stress, and providing a sense of well-being. The actual business of directly protecting species and creating organizations—mostly not-for-profit—to protect species and natural systems has fallen to the reform and radical environmentalists.

The reform environmentalists view biodiversity as an essential value in articulating a biocentric world view. In the reform lexicon, biodiversity speaks to the health of natural systems and concomitantly to those, like humans, who are dependent upon these natural systems. The reform environmentalists view the present trajectory of species extinction and the exploitation of natural systems as problematic, because—unlike the anti-environmentalists—they believe that the emphasis upon present "use value" depletes resources. It creates a situation in which humans put all their eggs in one basket, increasing our vulnerability to unexpected events. To cushion this risk and to show respect for other species, reform environmentalists suggest that we eliminate the wanton and careless destruction of plant and animal species, and treat animals (particularly higher animals) with respect, avoiding cruelty and unnecessary experimentation. The reform environmentalists view the cramped lives and production-line treatment of many animals, particularly in the slaughtering process, as problematic.

To put their views into practice, reform environmentalists have been and are creating organizations and not-for-profit societies whose purpose is to promote the biocentric worldview—eco-centrism, the land ethic, and biodiversity. These organizations, such as Greenpeace, Earthscan, and the Sierra Club, raise money in order to put environmental ethics into practice. They often include different factions, moving along the spectrum from light green to dark green. Their members come from many walks of life, including many of the largest corporations on the planet. If one were to characterize their main positions, they would fall into the biocentric views of the reform environmentalists.

The wilder or deeper commitment—depending upon your point of view—to the bio-centric perspective is held by the radical environmentalists. To the radicals, biodiversity is not a choice—it is a sacred element. In this view, the planet as a whole is an organism whose fragility is tied to the ongoing interdependence of the specific and natural systems that go into it. Human systems that seek to manage the planet by removing the rain forests—the lungs of the organism—are endangering not only themselves but all the other species and natural systems. The radicals insist that this must stop. biodiversity is the only certain way to ensure that the great force of nature remains viable. Those who seek to take risks with their own capital ought to be applauded; those who take risks with the planet in order to increase their own capital ought to be vilified.

The Radical Environmentalists

The radical environmentalists position themselves as fierce critics of instrumentalism, anthropocentrism, short-termism, patriarchy, and growth. Moreover, and directly to the point, they see these values reflected, championed, and amply rewarded in the business community (Bookchin, 1991; Cramer, 1998; Taylor, 1995; Zimmerman, 1994). The radicals come in several distinct intellectual stripes, but they all, in some way, see the business community as a primary engine of the intensifying environmental catastrophe closing in upon the planet. The deep ecologists (Devall and Sessions, 1980; Drengson and Inoue, 1995; McLaughlin, 1993) ground their views in the "eco-philosophy" of the Norwegian philosopher, Arne Naess (Naess, 1983; Naess and Sessions, 1984; Reed and Rothenberg, 1993). They call for the radical restructuring of postmodern corporate values. The environmental activists (Grefe, 1995; Marietta and Embree, 1995; Mitchell, 1970; Muir and Veenendall, 1996) speak to the need to take direct and effective action to curb the abuse and exploitation of natural resources. Finally, the eco-feminists (Diamond, 1994; Gaard, 1993; Merchant, 1992; Turpin and Lorentzen, 1996) attribute a great deal of the responsibility for the environmental crisis to the persistence of patriarchy and, with it, the exclusion of women with their ethics of caring from the centre of corporate power.

We get a sense of the urgency and alarm with which the radicals treat the environmental crisis by comparing and contrasting their views on sustainable development with those of the anti-, opportunistic, and reform environmentalists. Figure 8.6 outlines the differing perspectives. Sustainable development is a concept used by those attempting to draw some conclusions regarding the good life and what it means. More particularly, the issue at stake is what the balance should be between our need for economic growth and our need for a deeper and more significant relationship with natural systems in which water is potable, air is clean, non-human species are healthy and abundant, and soil is fertile.

The anti-environmentalists see the need for balance between natural and managed systems as a false and misleading issue. It is a false issue, they insist, because it presupposes that there is a clear and obvious distinction between natural and managed systems. In the lexicon of the anti-environmentalists there is no such thing—the entire planet, whether we like it or not, is a managed system. Humans now must utilize their abilities to problem solve in order to produce innovative solutions to planetary problems, both those they cause and those that nature itself generates. It is misleading to question the balance because the question assumes that the answer requires humans to pull back in their attempts to manage the problems on planet earth. The anti-environmentalists do not believe that "nature knows best." Not only does this belief mislead, but it can lead to dangers.

FIGURE 8-6   Four Views of Sustainable Development

View	Sustainable Development	Implications for Business Ethics
Anti-Environmentalism	Anti-environmentalists rail against the notion of deliberately restructuring economic growth to deal with the environmental crisis. To the anti-environmentalists, sustainability smacks of interventionism, planning, and the regulation of free markets (Bailey 1993; Hoyt, 1994; Krieger, 1973; Rowell, 1996).	Anti-environmentalists' position on sustainable development emphasizes explosive economic growth where and whenever possible. Solutions to the environmental crisis are easier to solve when growth is transferred to wealth.
Opportunistic Environmentalism	Opportunistic environmentalists see sustainable development as an occasion to provide new goods and services to help restore a balance between managed and natural systems. This growth-oriented view heralds new eco-efficient techniques as the best way to accomplish sustainable development (deSimone, 1997; Fussler and James, 1996; Mansell and Wehn, 1998; Pedler, 1997).	Opportunistic environmentalists view sustainable development as an issue in corporate innovation, adaptation, and learning. They see the corporation as a force for sustainable change. They do not query issues of how much growth is the right amount, or the human-centred nature of even innovative organizations.
Reform Environmentalism	Reform environmentalists view sustainable development as an essential means of putting environmental ethics into practice. Sustainable development entails a substantial reduction and redistribution of the economic growth patterns on the planet (Henderson, 1996; Hutchinson, 1997; Frankel, 1998; Strong, 1995).	Reform environmentalists have set the growth reduction in economic terms at a level that threatens corporations. This is particularly so in developing economies. The business community seeks to avoid regulation from government concerning environmental issues.
Radical Environmentalism	Radical environmentalists look at sustainable development as a revolutionary doctrine. Putting it into practice requires a restructuring of the economic, social, and political order (Dobkowski *et al.*, 1998; Foreman and Haywood, 1987; Goldsmith and Hildyard, 1988; Sachs and Peterson, 1995).	Radical environmentalists' conception of sustainable development challenges the business community at its core. It vilifies the business community as one of the primary engines of an impending ecological nightmare.

Anti-environmentalists see the danger in the call to sustainable development as a hidden or latent call to intervene in the everyday working of efficient markets. To create a balance, insist the anti-environmentalists, requires a modification to the status quo. They are concerned that this modification—whether it takes the form of environmental regulations, higher taxes to repair environmental degradation, newfangled ideas such as auctioning off polluting rights, or new curricula on environmental values early in childhood education—will be more of a problem than a solution. The irony in the anti-environmentalists' position is that, although they see humans as the epitome of practical intelligence on the planet, they would rather rely upon the invisible hand of the market than depend directly on their intelligence. You cannot solve a problem that does not exist, and the environmental crisis must not be used as a Trojan horse. Once we accept it, claim the anti-environmentalists, we begin to dismantle our most effective means of assuring continued prosperity on the planet—open, competitive, and non-regulated or planned markets.

The opportunistic environmentalists see sustainable development in a different light. They utilize the distinction between natural and managed systems as an issue in the search for the good life. In practice, this means that light greens view the environmental crisis as real and requiring a redirection of the problem-solving abilities and material acumen of our present corporate system. During the processes of industrialization and the push away from the land into urban and increasingly urbane development, we became less and less sensitive and efficient in our treatment of natural systems. The opportunistic environmentalists believe that we can regain our balance, find a sustainable relationship between resource use and environmental enhancement, by shifting our attention to environmentally friendly and eco-efficient means of managing. It is possible to grow (stimulate consumption) and thereby heighten corporate productivity if: (1) consumption is rooted increasingly in green goods and services; (2) production stays with firms who reduce, repair, reuse, and recycle; and (3) markets emerge that reinforce practitioners of both (1) and (2).

The opportunistic environmentalists paint an optimistic scenario quite distinct from that of the anti-environmentalists. The opportunistic environmentalists believe that, within the pursuit of sustainable development, it is both possible to grow economically and to enhance, preserve, and safeguard the natural environment. The anti-environmentalists' position is that it is impossible, unnecessary, and both bad business and bad social policy to preserve, enhance, and safeguard the natural environment; rather, all our emphasis should be placed upon accelerating our ability to use resources and build an environment that improves upon natural systems. Interestingly, the two often exaggerate the differences in their positions. The anti-environmentalists accuse the opportunistic environmentalists of catering to the views of those who want material well-being but are unwilling to take the risks that accompany innovation and exploration. On the other hand, the opportunistic environmentalists see the anti-environmentalists as unable to adapt to the clear signals of both the marketplace and the scientific data on the environmental crisis. To their eyes, the anti-environmentalists are carrying on as if we were in the midst of the industrial revolution, acting as if there were no need to recognize limits to natural resources.

The rejoinder of the anti-environmentalists is that rather than being mired in the industrial revolution, they are citizens of the new information age. They see themselves as post-modern ambassadors. They extol technology and trumpet Internet commerce. They champion biotechnology and genetic engineering. They see themselves as heralding "virtual environments" that are totally synthetic constructions. It is they who are eager to colonize space and utilize the materials therein to add to the commercial wealth of our species and the planet earth. It is the anti-environmentalists who are most eager to explore mechanical life units, where half-robot/half-human species may be able to adapt to our coming world.

The reform environmentalists view sustainable development as an urgent issue. Unlike the opportunistic environmentalists, who view sustainable development as totally compatible with economic growth and continued material well-being, the reformers argue that to heal the damage already existing in the natural environment, humans must be willing to accept a rather discernible reduction in our growth rate and material affluence. The reform environmentalists do not single out business or business ethics as the prime culprit in the call for a reorientation of social values. They would like to educate and inform citizens in both the developed and developing nations that balance between managed and natural systems is possible only if the short-term gratification of material consumption or the view of nature as a "problem" can be altered to admit other conceptions.

In Figure 8.7 we see how the reform environmentalists' conception of nature attempts to both produce and widen a sense of "intrinsic" value with regard to relationships with nature. Where the anti-environmentalists see nature as a problem and a commodity, and join the opportunistic environmentalists as viewing it as a resource, the reformers conceive of nature as a source of pleasure and even as a miracle. It is the radical environmentalists who push the conception of nature from the mytho-poetic and spiritual realm of miracles to the idea of nature as a revolutionary force and exemplar. These views of nature are suggestive rather than definitive. They highlight the manner in which nature is not a static conception, but is—to use the jargon of postmodern social scientists—socially constructed.

The radical environmentalists' conception of sustainable development is tied closely to their conception of nature as a revolutionary force and an exemplar of the good life. To the radicals, sustainable development is a revolutionary doctrine. This certainly is not the "business as usual" view that girds the position of the anti-environmentalists. The view that eco-efficient business, emphasizing green products and services, is in itself sufficient to usher in sustainable development is viewed by the radical environmentalists as a hoax and a cover-up. It is a hoax, they insist, because it purports to heal massive hemorrhaging in the natural environment by placing a bandage on the surface of the life-threatening problem. It is a cover-up because it permits consumers who buy goods and services from green businesses to believe that they are significantly contributing to the abatement of the problem; furthermore, it permits citizens in general to believe that they can rely upon a segment of the business community to heal the breach with nature.

While the radical environmentalists applaud the well-meaning intentions of the reform environmentalists, they see the reformers' call for a reorientation of values as lacking urgency. It is perfectly satisfactory to espouse "eco-centrism" and argue for rights for animals and natural systems, but this is talk without action. Talk without action is good for introducing incremental change. Incremental change is excellent for issues on which we can deliberate for several generations before we act. However, the environmental crisis, insist the radicals, is not such an issue. It is a crisis. It has a close horizon. It requires action—now.

While the reform environmentalists are given to a rather philosophical approach to environmental ethics, the radical environmentalists are not. They see business and the business community as forces that impair efforts to achieve sustainable development. In their call for direct action, the radical environmentalists call for active intervention by "eco-warriors." Those who exacerbate the environmental crisis are clearly "enemies of the planet." Those whose rate of pollution is in the bottom quartile, who clear-cut, who strip-mine, who hasten the demise of endangered species, who make or release chemicals that threaten eco-systems, are all enemies. In building a logic where enemies exist, the radical environmentalists implicitly license a fight that can be seen as a holy war or a struggle for natural justice.

FIGURE 8-7 Six Conceptions of Nature

Conception of Nature	Nature's Role	Relevance to Business Ethics
1. **Nature as a Problem** (Emphasized by anti-environmentalists)	Nature requires managing. It is the source of death, disease, floods, storms, crop damage, and the like. We seek to prepare ourselves for earthquakes, tornadoes, and other "natural" disasters.	Licenses and encourages the belief that we must, where we can, intervene in nature in order to reduce the harm it can cause.
2. **Nature as a Commodity** (Emphasized by anti-environmentalists and opportunistic environmentalists)	Nature is bought and sold, not merely as a resource (see Nature as a Resource), but now as a commodity.	Nature becomes a commodity when it is seen as desirable, hard to access, and requiring specialized knowledge, skill, or gear.
3. **Nature as a Resource** (Emphasized by anti-environmentalists and opportunistic environmentalists)	Nature is the basic building block in the creation of wealth. As a resource, nature is transformed from its original state and made useful—therefore valuable—to humans.	Things, and even people, take on value in their use. The good world is consumed. It, when consumed, produces happiness and utility in the consumers. Environmental ethics asks us whether nature has an intrinsic value.
4. **Nature as a Source of Pleasure** (Emphasized by reform environmentalists)	Those of us who speak of ourselves or another as a nature lover understand the mytho-poetic aspects of the sounds of a stream bursting with salmon or the smell of an alpine meadow.	The pleasurable potential of nature is built into business ethics in three ways: (1) nature is associated with leisure; (2) nature is considered to be a source of rejuvenation and renewal; and (3) nature is seen as a set of symbols used to market one's goods and services.
5. **Nature as a Miracle** (Emphasized by reform and radical environmentalists)	Nature is the source of solutions to many problems. This takes two forms: (1) the pantheistic form in which God reveals him/herself in nature and the natural; and (2) the secular form in which nature is taken as a basic model for human affairs.	Nature must be kept pure. It is the source of awe and a model for integrated problem solving. In the pantheistic form, nature embodies the good and should be taken as an article of faith. In the secular form, nature is a template of the reasonable and the rational.
6. **Nature as a Revolutionary Force and Exemplar** (Emphasized by radical environmentalists)	Nature is conceived of as a force of renewal and regeneration. It is a template of the good and, from it, humans should learn how to live in harmony with their own species, fellow creatures, and natural systems.	Rather than being formulated as a means of making a living, business becomes a means of living. This living stresses harmony, biodiversity, "eco-holism," spirituality, and the ethics of caring.

At this point, let us suspend our reaction to the rather heroic self-placement of the radical environmentalists in their view of the struggle. In their conception of a holy war, the radicals join the reform environmentalists in conceiving of nature as a miracle. Nature, in this view, is the source of solutions to many of our problems. Note that this is in direct opposition to the views of those—the anti-environmentalists—who see nature as the source of many of our problems (disease, natural disasters, famine). As nature is a miracle, we must get in touch with its healing powers. Those who can and do so become empowered to bring this message to those who are not yet mindful. The message in the holy war takes a form that has a "new age" quality. The view is pantheistic. Nature is imbued with a sense of the holy. It is the centre of planetary symmetry, balance, and grace. In this view, we cannot become spiritually full or whole if we cut ourselves off from or seek to dominate nature. We must get in touch with nature, regain our balance, and therein discover or rediscover the sense of awe and wonderment that is only possible, insist some radicals, for those in touch with nature.

The war imagery embedded in the struggle for natural justice takes a far more secular form, although the rhetoric and intent still speak to a desire to radically reformulate the status quo. In this view, nature is a revolutionary force and an exemplar of the good life. Nature, in its untrammelled state, is far more than a commodity or a resource bin—it is the basic model for a more egalitarian, interdependent, participative, and self-managing system. Rather than seeking to dominate, we must learn from nature how we can attain a sense of justice that is rooted in respect for others—including other species—and a recognition of the interdependence of natural systems—including human systems. The radicals argue that this need to align human justice with planetary justice cannot proceed in the abstract; it must be tied to specific, achievable actions.

In regards to action, the radicals join the reformers in supporting environmental organizations whose mandate is to monitor environmental issues. Where the reformers rely on moral persuasion or government lobbying to issue tighter environmental regulations, the radicals push further. Radical environmentalists are not averse to forms of corporate or community activism. Environmental activists are true-believers in their role as committed agents for the cause of altering the relationship between nature and humans. Their techniques run the gamut from activities of questionable legality—tree spiking, monkey wrenching, damage to property, inflammatory journalistic/media attacks, and other forms of "eco-terrorism"—to the clearly legal—boycotts, media campaigns, public rallies, and financing of particular political parties. Insofar as there is an escalation of adversarial activity between some corporations and some radical environmentalists, there is also, ironically, a tendency for each to learn from the other. Environmental radicals have been quick to learn the marketing, strategic management, and financial techniques of corporations; businesses soon learned to emulate the radical environmentalists' rhetoric, ability to mobilize community spokespersons, and rapid response patterns.

Our concern, however, is not with how business sees radical environmentalists as a problem in issues management, but to feather out what values the radicals seem to espouse in their efforts to gain respect for and an appreciation of natural systems. It is unfair to attempt to capture their ideas as existing solely in opposition to others. The spokespersons emerging to give voice to the radical position are articulate (see Figure 8.8). They have fire in their bellies. Their views, although expressed with varying emphases, hang on five basic positions: voluntary simplicity, green politics, eco-feminism, eco-activism, and eco-holism. Each of these views takes a serious look at how to change the status quo; each holds nature, natural systems, and primal peoples and their relationship to nature in high esteem.

The radical environmentalists see wisdom in the ways of primal people. This wisdom is centred on their ability to relate to nature as the source and continuance of life. Voluntary simplicity, insist the radical environmentalists, is far more than a call to return to the ways of our elders or to emulate the views of the tribal shaman. Rather than extolling traditionalism or

FIGURE 8-8 The New Ecological Order: Radical Environmentalists' Views

View	Basic Premise	Impact on the Business Community
Voluntary Simplicity	The radical environmentalists believe that early and primal people carry great wisdom in their teachings and lifestyles. To return to the traditional ways is impossible, but to adopt a life of voluntary simplicity is a virtue (Devall, 1988; Elgin, 1981; Epstein, 1995; Neihardt, 1932).	The radical environmentalists' call for the pursuit of voluntary simplicity is seen as an attack upon the primary pump of the economy— consumption.
Green Politics	The radical environmentalists advocate that committed environmentalists must take politics seriously. To this end, they have begun to run legitimate political campaigns on a one-issue platform—the green issue (Capra and Spretnak, 1984; Coleman, 1994; Kassman, 1997; Luke, 1997; Rainbow, 1993).	The business community worries about the single-issue nature of green politics and challenges its anti-development and anti-corporate positions.
Eco-Feminism	A segment of the radical environmentalists holds the view that women, when in positions of power within the corporate and economic system, will revolutionize the relationship between our species, the economic order, and nature (Gaard, 1998; Cheny, 1987; Merchant, 1992, 1996; Plumwood, 1993; Warren, 1987, 1990, 1997).	The growing recognition that many organizations are run as patriarchal fiefdoms with an elite (old boys' network) challenges the view of business as a privileged, male domain.
Eco-Activism	The radical environmentalists believe that it is necessary to engage in boycotts, eco-sabotage, and civil disobedience as a means of calling attention to organizations that exploit and abuse nature (Bahro, 1986; Pearce, 1991; Pepper, 1993; Szasz, 1995; Taylor, 1995).	The radical environmentalists' eco-activism has alienated many citizens. The business community now addresses eco-activism as an "issue to be managed."
Eco-Holism	The radical environmentalists see nature as one integrated organism (which includes humans). The managed, or built, environment can be returned to natural systems status only if humans are willing to relinquish the assumption that they are "king of the hill" (Lee, 1995; Marietta, 1995; McLaughlin, 1993; Zimmerman, 1994).	To implement eco-holism, radical environmentalists advocate introducing deep ecology into the school system at an early age. Orthodox business persons see this as brainwashing and shudder at their perception of the anti-business implications of this curriculum.

romanticizing tribal life, the radical environmentalists see voluntary simplicity as a choice by postmodern citizens to become self-reliant. The maxim "less is more," often used with reference to design, captures some of the spirit of the radicals' position on voluntary simplicity. In a sense, voluntary simplicity asks us to reformulate our notion of wealth. In the eyes of the radical environmentalists, the wealthy person is the one who takes care of their needs most directly and is thus most self-reliant. Three paths towards voluntary simplicity are to: (1) attempt to keep your needs few by refusing to buy into the consumer myth of happiness; (2) learn to satisfy your needs where and whenever possible by your own actions, knowledge, and ability; and (3) learn to find pleasure in the routines you elect to satisfy your needs. Voluntary simplicity is a call to self-reliance and an extolling of the simple pleasures—make your own garden, grow your own food, build your own house, create your own job, bake your own bread and, most importantly, dream your own dreams.

The radical environmentalists insist that this call to voluntary simplicity is not rooted in a disdain for community or the idea of governance. On the contrary, the radicals take both community and politics as important, albeit reformulated, elements in the new ecological order. Green politics roots the idea of power in the community. The emphasis here is upon inclusivity, equalitarianism, and integrity. Integrity, in the context of green politics, is tied to the ethics of care. The responsibility of the community and its governing agents is to provide for and include those unable to speak for themselves. The inability to speak is related to the fact that existing political arenas recognize only those with the power to impose their will upon events. This reinforces and nurtures this form of power. It excludes the power of the wind, the sun, and the mighty rivers. While it is clear that even in green politics, rivers, wind, and the sun do not vote, the vested interests of natural systems must be made evident in political terms.

The radical environmentalists argue that one of the current impediments in realizing the ethics of care in politics is the persistence of patriarchy. A large and vocal segment of the radical environmentalists claim that "eco-feminism" is a necessary antidote to patriarchy. Eco-feminism sees women as a potentially liberating force in the ecological new order. Women, suggest the radicals, are much more sensitive of the role of nature and the natural in the creation of value. As they rise to prominence within the community, we can expect a greater sensitivity to the forces of nature, a far greater emphasis upon inclusivity, and a movement away from dominance, control, and mastery as signs of competence.

This willingness to explore new options is at the centre of "eco-activism" in the new ecological order. The new ecological order is rooted in a continued quest to speak actively for nature and against those whose treatment of natural systems is costly. It is this call, often to act "above" the law, that creates the largest amount of negative publicity for the radical environmentalists. Nevertheless, it remains the only way, other than the reformers' emphasis upon education, to grapple with the immediacy of the issues and call attention to the fact that there are no isolated infractions. The eco-activism of the radical environmentalists is a call to vigilance. Materials deposited in stream beds in distant and remote settings do become part and parcel of the food chain. There is, insist the environmentalists, no place that is out of sight in the eyes of eco-activists. The contamination of the soil, air, and water due to nuclear testing is no simple issue. The jurisdictions that permit this, for whatever reason, cannot control the adverse effects upon others.

The eco-activism of the radical environmentalists is best and most sympathetically understood if one appreciates their notion of "eco-holism." Essentially, eco-holism expresses the view that the planet and all within its gravitational pull are best understood as one living, integrated system. At present, this is a system with a malfunctioning immune system. To the radical environmentalists, the environmental crisis is not a series of separate indicators of systems trouble. It is more than a series of red flags. It is the confirmation that the system as a whole is ill—very ill. Moreover, the cure cannot be effective by managing each system in isolation. The eco-holism of the radical environmentalists is a reminder that we require more than small victories to put the planet's immune system back together again.

What we learn in this chapter is that aligning business and environmental ethics is no simple affair. To a large degree, we must locate ourselves along a continuum of realignments. At present, it is my belief that the business community in postmodern contexts such as Canada rests somewhere between the anti-environmentalist and the opportunistic or light green views. From my visits to Germany, I believe that in the postmodern context, the business community—with the prodding of the Green Party—increasingly recognizes the reform environmentalist position. Worldwide, however, it seems that despite the ideological inroads made by sophisticated and educated opinion leaders, business remains somewhere between the anti- and opportunistic environmentalist positions. This augers well for continuing debate in the field of business ethics, but no immediate consensus on aligning business and the environmental ethic is at hand.

In the next chapter, we illustrate two interrelated arguments in aligning business and changing social values: the legitimacy thesis, which we shall develop by exploring how organizations build, use, and, at times, misuse "reputational capital"; and the reflection thesis, whereby we shall plumb the costs and benefits of the controversial view that "workplace diversity" is necessary to align organizations to and with changing social values.

CASES AND QUESTIONS

CASE 8-1	The Three Partners Who Couldn't Create a Business Plan

Samantha Fine, Ricardo (Ricky) Martinez, and Gavin Wagner are in their early thirties. They became friends through a shared fascination with and dedication to outdoor pursuits. They met for the first time three years ago when they were assigned as workmates by a subcontractor hired by Macmillan Bloedel to plant trees outside of Squamish, British Columbia. The experience cemented their relationship and confirmed their desire to start a meaningful whale watching and eco-tourist company off Robson Bight in the Straight of Georgia. Samantha, Ricky, and Gavin agreed that

once each had raised $25,000, they would meet for a long weekend at Dunsmuir Lodge outside Victoria and create a business plan, which they hoped would permit them to borrow another $150,000 from a banker (who happened to be a golfing buddy of Samantha's father).

Samantha, an only child and quite accustomed to getting her own way, had graduated with a Master's degree in sociology from the University of Western Ontario. She had concentrated her attention on the changing attitudes of Canadians toward the idea of wilderness. Her professors thought she was a very gifted analyst, but worried about her tendency to wax poetic (at times mystically so) about the spiritual peace and harmony possible when urbanites get "in touch" with nature and the natural. Ricky was the fourteenth of sixteen children. Born in Puerto Rico, Ricky had hitchhiked across North America when in his teens. His most enduring and heartfelt employment came at the age of twenty-five. As a skipper hired by a large company, he was given total control over a whale watching and coral diving boat that serviced the eco-tourist trade off the island of Maui. Ricky had immigrated to Canada in anticipation of eco-tourism activities near Vancouver. The last of the trio, Gavin, was the most driven to succeed materially. The son of a steelworker from Hamilton, Ontario, Gavin had become estranged from his family. Gavin worked as a musician in clubs across Canada and supplemented his quest to retire by age forty with whatever jobs he could get his hands on. Gavin had worked as a house painter, zoo attendant, and bowling alley manager, and briefly operated a submarine sandwich franchise in Regina.

On a hot Friday in August, the "three amigos," as Ricky was fond of calling them, met at Dunsmuir Lodge to determine the business plan they were to present to Mr. Hiscox at the Granville Branch of the Bank of Montreal. Each, as agreed, had secured $25,000 to start their business in eco-tourism. Despite their friendship, the three amigos left the lodge on Monday evening, frustrated with their inability to arrive at a working plan. In fact, the disagreements were so riveting and, in their eyes, so irreconcilable, that they agreed perhaps they would be served best by letting their friendship lapse.

Samantha, the most assured of the three, began the discussion by pointing out that this was their great opportunity to show people how Native or indigenous peoples in North America lived in harmony with nature.

Samantha envisioned setting up a wilderness experience company working out of rental premises in downtown Victoria. The company would offer guided hiking and adventure trips in northern British Columbia, Yukon, and Alaska. Rather than look for an elite clientele who could pay top dollar, Samantha felt that the company should focus on inner-city youth and sign contracts with sponsors, private corporations, government agencies, and not-for-profit organizations such as the YMCA or Greenpeace. Samantha portrayed the wilderness experience as one in which the youths be introduced to the underlying world view of environmentalism in subtle but meaningful ways; they would be made aware of the deadly problems of a predominantly consumer-run, patriarchal society, and be taught how to adopt an outlook of voluntary simplicity. Ricky and Gavin, who had been sitting quietly, staring out the window at the lush rainforest at the edge of the lodge, began to roll their eyes.

Samantha concluded in a flourish, pointing out that once inner-city youth embraced the Gaia principle, they would no longer be shackled by the values that kept them prisoners of a culture that admired the quick fix of drugs and the opportunistic reliance upon lotteries, gambling, and the movement of the stock market to measure its good fortune. Gavin thanked Samantha for her presentation and asked politely how much she estimated the three partners would earn in the first year. Unhesitating, Samantha responded that the company would be set up as a not-for-profit organization, enabling the sponsors to realize some tax benefits on their investment. Twice a year, the company would take out advertisements in relevant community newspapers, celebrating the sponsors and recognizing them as good corporate citizens. Ricky asked Samantha again what salary the three could expect from the not-for-profit company. Once again, Samantha was forthright; this could only be a supplement to their "real" jobs. She expected that they would have to defer drawing a salary for at least the first three years.

Ricky, flustered by Samantha's ideas, suggested that before they began questioning her plan, perhaps it would be wise if he and Gavin presented their own plans. Then the three could see the range of options. Ricky then rolled in an overhead projector to show the transparencies he had prepared that bore the title Alpha Eco-Tourism Incorporated, Founders: Samantha Fine, Ricardo Martinez and Gavin Wagner. Ricky used a laser pointer to call attention to a picture of a two-pronged business venture that would enhance and take advantage of the whale watching boom in and around the Strait of Georgia, particularly near Robson Bight.

The first prong of Ricky's idea was to leverage Alpha Eco-Tourism into the whale watching business by opening a floating tuck shop that sold organic foods, sunscreen, binoculars, and other items to eco-tourists. The floating operation would follow the fleet and service its needs. The second prong showed that after five years, with each partner drawing a salary of $45,000 per year, the company would own a first-class boat that could be refitted to become the first whale watching restaurant on the heavily-touristed waters. Ricky whipped out diagrams showing how the initial tuck shop and catering business could be altered to its new function. The boat would be fitted with state-of-the-art sound baffles to stifle the engine noise that otherwise might negatively impact the whale pods. It would have eco-efficient septic tanks and sophisticated pollution control devices. With its sumptuous meals, their company would be able to attract those leery of stepping into a Zodiac or smaller boat.

Ricky suggested that within eight years Alpha Eco-Tourism would be able to purchase a second boat that should be operated off the Baja peninsula, drawing tourists from southern California and Mexico. Projecting

beyond that, he believed that Alpha Eco-Tourism should franchise the concept and sell the eco-tourist business to responsibly-minded entrepreneurs in areas that could support the concept. Ricky concluded by saying that he was eager to make it possible for people to experience the awe of the whale and the beauty of a pod moving unfettered through the territory it has travelled for thousands and thousands of years.

Gavin smiled and thanked Ricky, and nodded appreciatively at Samantha who seemed rather taken aback by Ricky's scheme. Gavin cut to the bottom line immediately. Gavin felt the new company, which he referred to as ZED Educational Cruises Incorporated, should utilize the capital to purchase a small cruise ship from a Vancouver-to-Alaska cruise company currently seeking to upgrade. Gavin felt, as he put it, that they could score a very pretty price since the company seemed eager to sell to someone outside of its competitive market.

Gavin said that ZED Cruises would be in the environmental education business, but with a big difference: it would have a small but sophisticated casino for after-hours diversion. ZED Cruises would hire lecturers from local universities, select destinations suitable to a corporate clientele, and provide cruises to perhaps Hawaii or Bali. The courses would be bona fide explorations of sophisticated techniques useful to corporate types interested in environmental impact assessments or in training competent spokespersons to represent their position on environmental issues. The casino would compensate for the relatively low price of the cruises, and the ship could dock as a floating casino house.

Gavin pointed out how the Cayman Islands were ideal headquarters for ZED Cruises. He had been assured that the casino could be licensed and the company registered with a minimum of hassle. He was certain that in following his plan they would make money, live interesting lives, and contribute to the economy. Gavin felt that the environmental education offered would prove beneficial to corporate types, but that this could be left in the hands of the professors and consultants they would hire. Likewise, the running of the casino would be placed in the hands of experienced professionals. The three amigos would be brokering the relationships, organizing orders from travel agents, and exploring new destinations. Gavin felt confident that they could retire at about age forty-five.

After two days of bitter wrangling, no plan met a middle ground. Samantha was horrified by Gavin's crass, business-as-usual attitude, and the opportunistic bent of Ricky's notion of dining while whale watching. In Samantha's mind, they both had "sold out." She was not throwing away her $25,000 and going into debt for another $25,000 to become a restaurateur or casino hostess. Ricky was stunned by Samantha's failure to realize that he was not supported by a wealthy family, nor was he going to inherit a fortune when his parents died. He had to work and get paid for a good and honest effort to bring people back to nature. Ricky saw Gavin as coming close to advocating quasi-illegal activities. The haste-to-wealth routine in Gavin's plan seemed to be using environmentalism as a front. The combination of casino and tax-exempt status were the keys; environmentalism was just a means to a tax-exempt status. Gavin, for his part, could not understand why his two friends were so frightened to seize the day and think like business people. Once they were wealthy, they could do whatever they wanted to bring inner-city kids to nature or get families out to experience the joys of whales at sea.

At 4:00 p.m. on Monday, much to their despair but with the agreement of all, Samantha Fine left a message on Mr. Hiscox's voice mail stating that Samantha, Ricky, and Gavin thanked him for his kind offer to back their plan, but they had decided to forego the partnership. At 5:00 p.m., the three boarded the ferry and knew that, at least in the short-run, their lives had taken a bit of a change. The great dreams each had were now on hold.

QUESTIONS

1. Which of the three amigos seems, in your view, to have come closest to the views of a radical environmentalist? Why? Do you think his/her business plan would pass the scrutiny of the banker, Mr. Hiscox? If so, why? If not, why not?

2. Which of the three amigos seems, in your view, to come closest to the views of a reform environmentalist? Why? Do you think his/her business plan would pass the scrutiny of the banker, Mr. Hiscox? If so, why? If not, why not?

3. Which of the three amigos seems, in your view, to fall somewhere between an anti-environmentalist and an opportunistic environmentalist? Why? Do you think his/her business plan would pass the scrutiny of the banker, Mr. Hiscox? If so, why? If not, why not?

4. From their business plans, how do you think Samantha Fine, Ricardo (Ricky) Martinez, and Gavin Wagner would react to each of these statements?

   (a) "small is beautiful"

   (b) "the environmental crisis is imminent"

   (c) "globalization is good and healthy"

5. Of the three plans presented, which do you feel expresses your values most closely? Are your views of the environment compatible with your concerns over your career, security, and financial well-being? If they are compatible, what do you think can be done to sustain this? If they are not compatible, what do you feel you can do to make this more possible?

6. If two of the three friends were to cut a deal and join business plans, which two do you think it would be? Why? What compromises do you feel each would have to make?

CASE 8-2 Green Lake Park: The Wolves and the Fires

Green Lake Park encompasses an area of nearly five million hectares of federal parkland in Canada. The park includes two national wildlife refuges, six national forests, the last refuge and habitat of a breed of wolves, a major tourist resort, and five large timber contracts. Each year, dozens of fires burn within the Green Lake area, many as a result of lightning. In most years, the fires extinguish themselves naturally, burning little more than an acre or two, but once or twice in a decade the fires become extensive enough to threaten both the tourist and the timber trades. The wolves have no trouble whatsoever adapting to the fires by altering their terrain. The fighting of the fires, however, requires a chemical which, even years later, seems to produce birth defects in the already endangered wolf population.

In the public policy debate over how to best deal with the trade-offs between the wolves, lumber, and tourism in Green Lake Park, four positions have come forward. They are summarized below. The first is by Tony Abbott, a spokesperson for the group of firms that own the timber rights to selective patches of the park. Second is Patricia Rogers, a spokesperson for the Parks Board. Claude Desjardins, a spokesperson for Canadian Wilderness Advocates, and Robert Anderman, the Mayor of Glacier Town, complete the agenda.

Tony Abbott's position:

"To keep Green Lake viable, there must be economic returns. Currently it costs $180 million in taxpayers' money to run just this one park. Professor Lewin, an expert on cost-benefit analysis at Canada's Northern University notes that if we were to remove logging and logging-related commerce from the park, the cost to taxpayers would more than double to approximately $405 million. This doubling does not take into account that once the forest contracts are relinquished, no one will be maintaining the logging roads. Except for the major highway into Glacier Town, the logging roads provide the major arteries into the park. Currently the Park Board's own figures reveal that of the 520,000 visitors to the park who go beyond Glacier Town, 18 per cent do so by water and 82 per cent do so by logging roads and hiking. The forest companies presently spend $120 million on the maintenance of existing logging roads and the construction of new ones.

"Efforts to remove our licenses (most of which hold good until the year 2022) will, of course, dearly cost the taxpayers and the Park Board. The foregone earnings for abandoning our contracts will come to approximately $1 billion. We are assured by our lawyers that such a case is likely to be in the courts and remain unresolved for five to twelve years. During this time, the failure to protect our timber—whether to save the wolves or for some other reason—will leave us open to adding our lost revenue to our total demands.

"Our view is simple—we have contracts entered into in good faith; we contribute greatly to the operations of the park; and we cannot let our forests go up in smoke and our investors' capital diminish because there is a chemical fire retardant that adversely affects the reproductive potential of the wolves. To show our good faith, we are prepared to make a $100,000 contribution to Dr. Galico at the University of Northern Canada, who is eager to begin research on altering the negative impact of the present fire retardant."

Patricia Rogers' position:

"We at the Parks Board try to represent all of Green Lake, and especially those who cannot speak for themselves. Our mandate is to provide park users with a relationship to nature and natural systems that they cannot experience by driving down any highway in Canada. We seek to preserve and provide access to nature for many users, as long as these uses remain compatible. When conflicts occur in the use pattern, we must first provide the participants with a way to make their views known and, second, attempt to help the participants find a compromise. If that is not possible, our last task is to establish a policy in which none of the participants feel themselves to be the loser.

"It is imperative we underline that our primary goal is to preserve and provide access to nature for non-commercial purposes. This is what distinguishes us from a private hunting sanctuary, a nature theme park, or a government agency that exists to license resource rights. I am not unaware that running a park can cost a great deal of money and that a good deal of this can be made from permitting motels, cabins, and privately-owned hot springs to run on park land. It is clear that both Glacier Town and the forest industry are important elements in our economic reality.

"However, our mission is not primarily economic. Our mission is to make sure that wilderness has rights and that Canadians of all social classes and economic status can, when they follow the rules, find a place in this park. The wolves are under our protection, as are the people we admit into the park. We at the Parks Board would like to protect the wolves from their demise due to the fire retardant. However, it is clear that without this fire retardant we are endangering the forest industry directly and Glacier Town indirectly. We understand that if we are forced to "pull" the contracts of the forest companies, business in Glacier Town will be adversely affected. Currently, one dollar in every four spent in Glacier Town comes directly or indirectly from the forests. Of the 2,400 permanent residents in Glacier Town, 500 have permanent or part-time jobs in the forests of Green Lake.

"Yet, if we must bite the bullet, we will. We believe that we cannot act as if our livelihood was not first and foremost that of living in a wilderness park. Without this, in the long run, we have nothing but another forest town trying to start a tourist industry. Once there is no wilderness, I believe the tourists will go elsewhere. Our task is to protect wilderness. In this discussion tonight, it means extending rights to the wolves. They are our neighbours. Moreover, without them, and the elk and the eagles, I'm not sure any of us would be here tonight."

Claude Desjardins' position:

"I am here tonight on behalf of Canadian Wilderness Advocates. Both previous speakers confuse me. Abbott seems to be threatening us like a child who believes that once he is dead all will mourn him. Yes, the forest industry is worth a lot of money in our economy, but it is also ruining the park. The wolf issue brings this to the fore, but it has always been there. When the forest industry goes, we will, in time, not only adjust, but thrive. I prefer Ms. Rogers' point of view, but it does not go far enough. In the best of all worlds, Ms. Rogers would like the status quo—a world in which participants who have conflicting uses of wilderness work these out. The forest companies, however, do not use nature—they abuse it. The forest companies in the vicinity not only denude the forest, but bring great rumbling trucks down narrow roads in the middle of nowhere.

"What we need is a recognition of the sacred nature of our task. We are keepers of wilderness. We have a holy task. In the future, or maybe even today, when the city asphalt is hot and people can't sleep, what do they do? They dream. They dream about being fully alive in a canoe with a full moon opening up a vista of a great glacier and, in the background, the eerie howl of the wolves. We cannot live this dream by breaking the park up into users' ghettos—this section for the wolves, this section for the lumber barons, this section for the television-watching tourists, this section for the townies. The whole park—all 5 million hectares—is a living, breathing organism. To see it as this and live with it means that we cannot cut out its lungs and pray that they grow back. The trees, after all, are the lungs of the great being that is Green Lake."

Robert Anderman's position:

"Geez, I don't know about you, but I'm happy in Green Lake. There are opportunities in this town for great expansion. As president of Glacier Town's Chamber of Commerce, I recognize that we are caught between two cultures that seem in this, our Garden of Eden, to be at odds. On the one hand, we have the passionate environmentalists like my good friend and neighbour, Claude Desjardins; on the other hand, we have the pragmatic business types like old Tony Abbott (who I've known since grade ten). The difference between us and other communities is that we, as a community, live under the auspices of the Federal government or, more clearly, Patricia Rogers' Parks Board. This means that we must, as she made clear, attempt to reconcile the two and bring business into the wilderness such that both gain.

"With the wolves' endangerment from the fire retardant, this is a challenge. To meet the challenge, I recommend that we try to develop means of detecting the outbreaks of fire early on in the cycle. This would mean that we could control the fires without resorting to the heavy-duty fire retardant that is killing off the wolves. To detect fires earlier, I recommend that we use the sys-

tem presently employed in Oregon where they have tightened up the grid system of fire watching. At present in Green Lake, we have six manned fire-watch stations to cover 5 million hectares. In Oregon, they have moved to an automated fire grid run by three individuals for areas as large as Green Lake. The system works by planting heat sensors in the soil. The cost per sensor is about $11,000, and to wire Green Lake with this tighter grid would cost, I have been told, something in the order of $34 million. I believe we could get the Parks Board, the Federal government, the Provincial government, the forest companies, and the citizens of Glacier Town to make good on this.

"Remember—don't fight, innovate. Good environmentalism is always good business and vice versa."

QUESTIONS

1. What, in your view, is the environmental position adopted by Tony Abbott? Is he a dark green, green, light green, or not a green at all? Why? Do you think Claude Desjardins' characterization of Tony Abbott's position is fair? If yes, why? If not, why not?

2. What, in your view, is the environmental position adopted by Robert Anderman? Is he a radical environmentalist, reform environmentalist, opportunistic environmentalist, or an anti-environmentalist? How do you think those who work in the existing fire towers will feel about Robert Anderman's solution? What implementation problems do you foresee in Robert Anderman's heat sensor solution at Green Lake?

3. What is the implicit message in Patricia Rogers' position? Is she a dark green, green, light green, or anti-environmentalist? Why? How, in your view, can Patricia Rogers of the Parks Board extend rights to the wolves?

4. What seems to be Claude Desjardins' solution to the trade-off between the endangered wolves and the timber industry in Green Lake? Is he a radical environmentalist, reform

environmentalist, opportunistic environmentalist, or anti-environmentalist? Why? What do you think Claude Desjardins means when he calls the task of being "keepers of the wilderness" a holy task?

5. Of the four positions laid out by Tony Abbott, Patricia Rogers, Claude Desjardins, and Robert Anderman, which strikes you as best and why, in regard to the following:

(a) the procedures to be followed

(b) a solution

(c) a philosophy of life

(d) the costs of change

6. Of the four positions taken by Tony Abbott, Patricia Rogers, Claude Desjardins, and Robert Anderman, which view (or combination of views) exemplifies nature as a:

(a) source of pleasure

(b) miracle

(c) commodity

CASE 8-3   Risa Benedix Does Time

Risa Benedix's father, a corporate lawyer in Montreal, Quebec, was called early one August morning by a colleague in Chicago, Illinois, to inform him that his daughter had been apprehended breaking into the research facilities of Everenden Pharmaceuticals. Ralph's colleague asked him if he would fly out to attend the preliminary hearing the next morning to lend support to the view that Risa was from a good family. Ralph blurted his sleepy assent. He turned to his wife, Rachel, tapped her lightly on the forehead and said, "Gotta go, Risa's in trouble again." Rachel responded in a half sleep, "Oh no—this time she may go to jail."

On the plane, Ralph Benedix went over his daughter's career with the law. Risa was now twenty-four years old. She was a graduate of the University of Montreal where she had studied comparative religion. Her honours project was on the spiritual significance of animals in early-Christian doctrine. The work was considered brilliant and was published by a not-for-profit organization seeking to mobilize interest in the animal rights movement. Risa soon became heavily involved in the movement, taking on the role of secretary for the north east division of North American Animal Rights Advocates. Risa started living, breathing, and sweating ani-

mal rights issues. Two years previously she had been reprimanded for being caught writing slogans—"People cannot be at peace when they slaughter animals cruelly" and "Imagine being fattened up so you can bring more money to your murderers"—on the walls of a meat rendering factory and slaughterhouse in Montreal. Last year she had been warned and barred from the campus of the University of New England for breaking into their animal research facilities and letting loose 68 cats, 290 experimental mice, and 11 dogs. In the New England University caper, Ralph had given $8,000 (US) to the school to cover their costs. Since they were not eager for publicity, only a warning was issued.

In February of this year, Risa and three of her friends from the North American Animal Rights Advocates had raided a mink farm in the Laurentian Mountains north of Montreal and set free over 700 mink. The four were apprehended when they fully admitted to the crime in a public press conference. Risa protested that "it is never a crime to free a life from wrongful imprisonment and sure death." The four, helped by a rather sympathetic judge and the fact that none had previous criminal records, were warned that if they were apprehended in similar illegal acts they would be imprisoned. The four, aided by their families, paid the fine of $5,000 to cover the court expenses and the cost of the 200 mink that still seemed to be at large.

Ralph Benedix was awakened from his thoughts by the pilot's announcement that the plane was approaching O'Hare airport. At Jim Bird's office, Ralph learned that Risa was apprehended breaking into the animal research facilities at Everenden Pharmaceuticals when she had set off an alarm. On her person, Risa had wire cutters and a sack of posters with animal rights slogans. Jim Bird told Ralph that the best he could do was to get Risa deported. This offense would bar her from legal entry into the United States or its protectorates for a minimum of five years. The deportation would also be recorded in the Canadian court system and could activate any previous warnings. However, Jim Bird expected that since Risa seemed hell-bent upon bringing up her commitment to the North American Animal Rights Advocates and was proud of her record of wall writing, sloganeering, and animal liberation activities, she would probably do small time (one to six months).

Jim Bird asked Ralph to talk to his daughter and convince her not to parade her commitment to the animal rights movement. The courts, insisted Jim, were taking a dim view of radical causes using the media attention generated by a trial to advance their positions. "Ralph," Jim said, "I know she is a fully-grown woman and an extraordinarily brilliant one at that, but if you could get her to stay off the stand and only answer 'yes' or 'no' to the questions, I believe I could get her deported." Ralph understood what he was being asked to do. "When can I see Risa?"

Risa seemed glad to see her father. They had always been close. She asked how Rachel was and told Ralph that he need not have travelled so far; that she was ready to do her time, but that she was always glad to see him. Ralph told Risa that he too was glad to see her, but that the occasion lacked

spontaneity. Risa smiled. Ralph asked Risa what she intended to tell the judge the following day. Risa unhesitatingly responded that she would tell the truth. Ralph now took his turn to smile. "You can, of course, tell the truth to the judge just by answering the questions posed with a simple yes or no."

"Odd you should say that," Risa said. "That's pretty much what Mr. Bird has been telling me—but I can't." Risa went on to tell her father that this would not be representing her true beliefs about the exploitation, abuse, and crimes being legally perpetuated by Everenden Pharmaceuticals. The tears in Risa's eyes caught the light coming in from the window and Ralph knew that his daughter was speaking from conviction. "Dad, I know it sounds nuts, but I want to go to sleep in a world where I know that being human means not only treating humans with respect—and we have a long way to go on that one—but also treating animals with the same respect."

"But, Risa," Ralph interjected, "you are throwing away a brilliant career and a wonderful loving disposition." Ralph went on to portray jail as hardly a finishing school for those eager to see humans acting with dignity. "Serving time is a stigma," insisted Ralph. "It follows you around like an albatross. Years from now, people will not know that the record represents the innocent, loving idealism of a heroic woman. What they will see is simple, nasty, and sadly true— you are a criminal."

Risa walked over to her father, kissed him lightly on the cheek, and said, "I know, Dad, but I must do what is real. If we all fake our feelings in order to make out okay, look what happens."

Risa was given a six-month jail sentence and a stern warning that more awaited her if she persisted in her adolescent and misplaced idealism. Ralph wept on the plane back to Montreal and wondered if he really understood why he admired his daughter.

QUESTIONS

1. What justification do you think Risa Benedix has for her eco-activism? Employing the "six conceptions of nature" discussed in this chapter, that, in your view, comes closest to Risa Benedix's view? Why?

2. Critically examine the following from the position of an anti-environmentalist:

    (a) the break-in at Everenden Pharmaceuticals

    (b) the animal release at New England University

    (c) the graffiti and sloganeering on the walls of the slaughterhouse in Montreal

    In your view, should acts of personal conscience take precedence over the law? If so, when and why? If not, why not?

3. Is Risa Benedix acting, in your view, as the judge who sentenced her seemed to think—with adolescent or misplaced idealism—or as Ralph Benedix would like to believe—as brave questioner in a world whose values probably should be questioned? Support your position.

4. How would an opportunistic or light green environmentalist act if they found themselves in Risa Benedix's shoes? Speculate on what path you think the North American Animal Rights Advocates organization would take if its members were primarily opportunistic environmentalists. What profitable business could this group spin off?

5. What sort of defense do you think the owners and stockholders at Everenden Pharmaceuticals, the researchers in the animal facilities at New England University, and the owners and employees at the Montreal slaughterhouse could bring to bear on Risa Benedix's position? Which of these defenses do you think is the most convincing? Why?

6. What is the difference, in your opinion, between Risa Benedix's position and those of a terrorist fighting passionately for what he or she believes is a higher principle? When do freedom fighters differ from terrorists?

REPUTATIONAL CAPITAL AND DIVERSITY IN THE WORKPLACE

The age of the ethical consumer has arrived. Ethical consumers do not leave their conscience at the door of the store when looking for the best deal. They want to know who is behind the familiar name on the product. They want to know whether the parent organization is making unsavoury investments in another country. Or what political platform it supports. Or what stand it takes on their issues.

John Smythe, Colette Dorwood, and Jerome Rebeck
Corporate Reputation: Managing the New Strategic Asset (1992)

John Smythe and his colleagues (1992) argue that society is changing and businesses must adapt. In their view, contemporary consumers increasingly are interested in the ethical portfolios of the firms with which they do business. Consumers not only seek a good price, but, as well, seek to enter into a relationship with a firm they see as trustworthy, reliable, and reputable. Smythe and his colleagues are working in an area that has become known as "business and society" (Castro, 1996; Marcus, 1998; Post *et al.*, 1996; Sawyer, 1979), which broadens the questions posed by the environmental ethicists in their concern for business. Within the hands of the sociologically-minded business and society analysts, the question "How does the machine fit into the garden?" is altered to read "How does business fit into the changing society?" Those taking this approach to business ethics view the newly-emergent social concerns and organizational regard for reputation as an adaptation to the changing demands society places upon business.

Essentially, social scientists who employ the business and society lens to make sense of the interest in business ethics seek to use either or both the "legitimacy thesis" and the "reflection argument" to overcome the "radical separation view." The radical separation view, which is the implicit target of business and society analysts, suggests that where and whenever possible, business should be treated as an analytical category separate from society. This is more than a bookkeeping function. We have already seen this point of view in "the job of business is business" argument and in the rather captivating idea that business is a game—a special game with rules that are unwarranted in the more cooperative sphere of our personal existence. The plausibility of the radical separation view is maintained in social systems where work is separated from leisure, family from business, and one's home or private identity is radically separated from one's work or public identity.

The business and society theorists are interested in the forces that are helping to break down or slowly erode the once rigid boundary that separated the conception of a private self in a moral world from the self at work in an amoral world. The business and society theorists view the radical separation argument as untenable in the emerging postmodern context. Social trends and business trends are converging. In Figure 9.1 we see how five social and five business trends converge to help break down the radical separation between business and society. The theorists insist that these forces are helping to reformulate the relationship between business and society. The new technology of the information superhighway, the cellular phone, and the possibility of Internet commerce, just as examples, mean that the line between work and non-work, between the social self and the business self, is changing. Increasingly we work at home. We are on call. Due to the two-career family and the growing number of single-parent families, we must learn to balance work and family.

In the convergence of forces outlined in Figure 9.1, we see that as a society we no longer can separate work from other aspects of our social existence. Globalization, social marketing, downsizing, and the flattening of the corporation all have significant implications for how we think about and structure our social existence. Moreover, and equally germane, the business community is impacted by changes in the social structure of society—the changing nature of what was once the traditional family, the explosion in part-time, seasonal, and contingent workers, the growth of consumerism, and alterations in the views of retirement and the aged.

In attempting to indicate the newly-emerging view of business and society, analysts point in two interrelated directions. The first, the legitimacy thesis, argues that organizations of all sorts—public sector, not-for-profit, and profit-oriented—must not only vie for capital to remain viable, but must as well create a positive reputation. Without legitimacy (Blumenberg, 1983; Brown, 1997, 1998; Brummer, 1991; Pava and Krausz, 1997; Pfeffer and Salancik, 1978), organizations become vulnerable. Society changes their access to resources. It imposes a higher cost upon their operations than would be the case for an organization that is seen as reputable and held generally in high regard in society. Currently, the plight of the tobacco industry (Glantz, 1996; McCowan, 1995) or those companies that engage in clear-cut logging (Devall, 1994; Marchak, 1983) can be used as examples of what can occur to firms as their legitimacy is questioned. Within the legitimacy thesis, organizations that genuinely engage in behaviours and decisions that enhance their reputation are not only building reputational capital, but are playing a key role in defining the ethical firm in postmodern society.

The second approach used within the business and society view of business ethics focuses on the need and ability of organizations that seek to act ethically to reflect the social, demographic, and technical changes occurring in society (Boyett and Boyett, 1995;

FIGURE 9–1   Social and Business Trends Converge in the Business and Society Perspective

Business Trends		Social Trends	
Trend	**Implications**	**Trend**	**Implications**
Home Offices: The trend is facilitated by firms outsourcing labour and providing incentives for flexible work arrangements (Gottlieb *et al.*, 1998; Kugelmass, 1995; Minoli, 1995).	This trend helps to break down the fixed notion that home and office are separable. This requires integration of one's values at home and those at work.	**Altering Family Structures:** Dual-career couples, single parents, and "latch key kids" place greater pressures on families to integrate work and family (Bohen and Viveros-Long, 1981; Neal, 1993; Parasurman and Greenhause, 1997).	This trend requires one to use one's capital from work to pay for help to attend to one's children and ailing parents. The trade-off requires constant monitoring.
Information Superhighway: New information technologies like the Internet tie the neighbourhood to the workplace (Cameli, 1996; Egan, 1994; Menzies, 1996).	This trend towards the wiring of our homes and lives (cellular phones, Internet) means that, no matter where we are, we are on call. Work is never far away.	**Consumer Movement:** The consumer seeks active engagement and knowledge about the products and services on the market (Crocker and Linden, 1998; Gardiner and Gardiner, 1976).	This trend indicates that the days of the passive consumer are long gone. Consumers seek to break down the corporate wall of secrecy and access information pertinent to their lives.
The Flattening of Corporations: New organizational structures require greater "role" and personal involvement in corporate teams (Belbin, 1996; DiBella and Nevis 1998; Galbraith, 1994; Senge, 1990).	This trend towards flattening the corporation requires that workers increasingly supervise themselves and become committed to the values of the corporation.	**Greater Education:** As populations increase their years of education, they also increase the questions they ask. As people question more, simple obedience diminishes (Cassidy and Faris, 1987; Dixon, 1992; Hamilton, 1990; Lawton *et al.*, 1995).	The more educated the individual, the greater his/her desire to make sense of the big picture and to integrate views with an understanding of key patterns and forces.
Greater Reliance on Social Marketing: Businesses increasingly seek to promote and advocate social issues like literacy (Fine, 1990; Martinez and Aries, 1997; Steckel and Simons, 1992).	The implication of this trend is that the public increasingly associates business with social causes and issues. Political lobbying, corporate advocacy, and sponsorship of cultural events are all part of the mix.	**Moonlighting, Part-Time and Contingent Work:** The person with many part-time or seasonal jobs tries to integrate work and leisure in new ways (Belows, 1989; Danesh, 1991; Rivage, 1992).	This trend signals that the new worker must piece together a work lifestyle over time. This attempt to job pattern involves an awareness of how to combine work and play.
Organizations Are Moving Into the Third Sector: Volunteers are emerging to do what has previously been considered paid work (Anhier and Siebel, 1990; Hudson, 1995; Rifken, 1995).	The implications of this commercialization of the third sector make it more difficult to separate business from social affairs.	**Retirement is Taking on New Meaning:** On the whole, people are now living longer and more healthy lives. New careers now often follow retirement (Bytheway, 1989; Walker, 1996; Williamson *et al.*, 1992).	This trend indicates that retirement is taking on new meaning. It is no longer a simple formula to separate work and one's golden years.

Dertouzos, 1997; Drucker, 1995; Kempner *et al.*, 1974; Pol and Thomas, 1997). The role of ethical business in the "reflection argument" is to adapt to a social world that is increasingly diversified and driven by escalating and unpredictable change. In this turbulent social world, the ethical organization provides stability, yet remains open to change. It reflects and responds to emergent social needs, a diversifying world in which women, ethnic and racial minorities, the handicapped, youth, and others previously excluded or relegated to the periphery by the predominantly white "old boys' network," are integrated into and made part of the corporate elite.

To illustrate the logic of both the legitimacy thesis and the reflection argument in the business and society approach to business ethics, we will turn first to an examination of the dynamics of reputational capital, and then to the processes underlying the postmodern call for diversity in the workplace. These issues must not be thought of as radically opposed. Each argues for convergence in business and society. Moreover, one may utilize diversity programs to enhance one's corporate reputation or, vice versa, use one's positive corporate reputation to attract and maintain a talented and diversified workforce.

Figure 9.2 illustrates how in the quest for reputational capital, firms seek to enhance goodwill, establish a public corporate persona, and reduce the costs of securing resources in business operations. In illustrating the reflection argument, we will focus on how organizations that seek to diversify their workforce threaten the corporate elite, raise the expectations of the previously marginalized, and lead to active and ongoing debates over how to measure and deal with merit in organizational life.

REPUTATIONAL CAPITAL

There is a delightfully apocryphal story that gets at the root of what is intended by the term reputational capital. At the height of his wealth and success, the financier Baron de Rothschild tells the story of an acquaintance who, due to his relentless business acumen, had won the Baron's approval and was subtly petitioning him for a rather large loan at rather good rates. It is said that the Baron replied, "I won't give you a loan myself, but I will walk arm-in-arm with you across the floor of the stock exchange and soon enough you shall have willing lenders to spare" (Kilduff and Krackhardt, 1994). True to his prediction, Rothschild's acquaintance benefited greatly by the reputation-enhancing stroll he took across the stock exchange floor. That walk helped to build reputational capital.

Charles Fombrun, in *Reputation: Realizing Value From the Corporate Image* (1996:81), writes that "corporate reputations have bottom line effects." Enhancing the corporate reputation increases the organization's goodwill. It functions like a healthy immune system in the biology of an individual. When a firm establishes a positive reputation, it has—in the reputational capital associated with it—a strategic asset, which if put to good use can help to ward off problems and retain its health in the midst of the stresses and problems that accompany business. As in the case of Rothschild's acquaintance, firms with solid reputations can find many lenders willing, at good rates, to venture a risk. Communities will often compete with one another to locate a firm with an excellent reputation. It is these highly reputed firms that "star employees," those who can pick and choose their employers, select as their workplaces.

This should come as no surprise. If ever you have renovated your home, sought a restaurant for a special occasion in a city you do not know, or looked for a new dentist, you most likely relied on what others told you about the renovator, the restaurant, or the dentist. You

---

FIGURE 9-2 Illustrating the Legitimacy Thesis and the Reflection Argument

Legitimacy Thesis

Dynamics of the Argument

Organizations exist in a social context. This social context can confer or retract legitimacy based on the perception of the organization, its actions, and the personnel associated with it. In conferring legitimacy, society believes that the organization is likely to confer greater benefits than costs, will not harm innocent others, and will act fairly and in line with prevailing notions of justice. Firms that have their legitimacy questioned for any one of these reasons will find that it costs more to operate. Regulatory bodies, lending institutions, and consumers increase their demands. Management must seek to regain its legitimacy in order to carry on.

Application: Reputational Capital

In practice, firms seek to manage their "legitimacy" by managing the corporate reputation. Corporate reputations are fickle. They can be enhanced or lost. Managing the organization's reputation involves four components: (a) marketing; (b) public relations; (c) corporate social affairs; and (d) crisis management. Organizations that fail to achieve reputational capital are frequently perceived as engaging in unethical and shoddy practices. Once a company has been labelled as unethical, reputation management goes into high gear.

Reflection Argument

Dynamics of the Argument

Organizations exist in a social context. To thrive in this context, organizations must strive to reflect the social, demographic, and technological changes occurring in society at large. The ethical organization acts in line with these changes. It produces stability, yet remains open to change. Firms that fail to reflect societal, technological, and demographic changes fail to adapt to current issues and problems. They bear the economic cost of the firm using dated equipment or operating with outmoded social values. Their failure to adapt to social change creates organizational cultures out of touch with prevailing social norms.

Application: Diversity in the Workforce

In practice, we can look to the idea of diversity in the organizational workforce as a means of operationalizing the reflection argument. Firms that seek a diversified workforce would like their organizations to reflect the demographic composition of the societies in which they operate. This challenges the idea that corporations are bastions of power for a fixed elite. In many countries, like Canada, this is a male, white, "old boys" network that tacitly colludes to use its merit criteria to exclude or limit the power of women, minority ethnic and racial groups, and others.

---

sought information to make a decision in which you could not directly test the product or services in question. The more important your decision—or the more time and capital that ride on its outcome—the more likely you will gather information on reputation. This insight is, of course, the basis for firms and corporations investing heavily in creating a brand name, establishing a unique look, and projecting consistently positive images of themselves, their products, and their corporate identity (Gregory and Wiechmann, 1991).

Reputations are built and, with this, firms enhance their legitimacy. In terms familiar to students of business ethics, legitimacy increases when the evaluations people make of organizations and individuals are perceived to be in line with their own values (Bromley, 1993). When people, often at the level of affect or emotion, approve of what they believe to be the values of others, they not only reduce their skepticism, as we have learned in our discussion of trust, but they are willing to enter into exchanges with these reputable others. Then, too, reputations can be lost. With this loss, society, through its various publics, begins to question and probe. Issues of illegitimacy, at least in the eyes of some publics, emerge. This loss diminishes reputational capital. It adds to the stress of doing business. It curtails a firm's degree of freedom, for as reputational capital diminishes, monitoring by authorities such as government bodies increases.

In other words, winning or—put less competitively—securing a positive reputation, is valuable. It has bottom line effects. Reputation, as Stephen Nock points out in *The Costs of Privacy: Surveillance in America* (1993), is a form of capital rooted in information and in the information society. It is Nock's belief that a positive reputation, as uncertainty in society rises, is an ideal form of capital. It is portable. It adapts to change easily. It can be made meaningful in an international context. It is, argues Nock, suspect players and suspect populations who bear the high costs of surveillance in the information society. These populations, unlike those with positive reputations, can make no claim to other know-how or "know-who." Know-how, for example, as expressed in credentials or proof of one's success under ordeals, is taken as a sign for low surveillance. This person, organization, or public agency is a competent player. Know-who, as embodied in reference letters or friendships with "reputable others," also suggests that such a one will be able to get a bank loan, for example, more easily. (Rothschild's friend in our story had "know-who.") Nock draws our attention to how, in a decontextualized social world, reputation contextualizes. Positive reputation lowers social, political, and economic barriers; negative reputation, on the other hand, raises these barriers.

It is this decontextualization of the social world, a phenomenon often given the code name "change" by students of organizations, that gives rise to the search for information about "reputation" as a means of reducing one's uncertainty. Individuals, organizations, industries, and even nation states seeking reputations in international political affairs understand this. As a consequence, actors at all levels in the postmodern world seek to control and manage their reputations. We have witnessed this rush to seek a positive reputation as occupations increasingly seek professional status. This involves the ability to prove know-how and know-who. Professionals claim know-how in their credentials. Know-who is generated in the professional use of peer review and reliance upon peer evaluation. This world of reputational identity is one of creating a good impression. In an important sense, to be postmodern is to be an impression manager—one who seeks to manage how others evaluate his or her reputation. He/she may be either genuinely sensitive to others or, as it were, deceptive and manipulative in seeking to raise reputational capital.

In business within the information society, reputation is an asset that has strategic importance. One seeks to enhance one's reputation and to both utilize this asset by wisely investing it in certain lines of actions and by banking or storing it for use at the appropriate time. Within the strategic use of reputation, it is important to realize that one's actions not only have consequences for one's own reputation, but can affect others. The whistle-blower, as we have seen in Chapter 7, not only puts his or her own reputation on the line, but seeks to alter the reputations of those targeted. The Nobel Prize laureate, in this sense, not only raises his or her reputational profile, but confers this upon all who can claim an association with him or her. Universities that seek to enhance their reputations may use a strategy, among others, of publicizing the number of Nobel Prize winners who have been or are in their employ. The strategic development and use of reputation, like Midas's touch, can backfire. King Midas, who was granted his wish that all he touched would turn to gold, was horrified when his food turned to gold, and devastated when, upon touching his much-beloved daughter, she turned into a golden statue.

We must use reputation wisely or it can turn nasty on us. A university that publicly proclaims itself the proud home of several Nobel Prize winners must be wary that they don't all decide to leave and in a very public fashion. Industries that publicly proclaim their excellent industrial relations policies must be aware that they are creating a public image, chock full of expectations, which can be severely trampled with a very public and nasty strike. Companies that proclaim themselves as "green" and utilize this to attract consumers must be consistent. They cannot be shown, in an independent study, to be merely average compared to others in their environmental actions. To create a reputation—positive or negative—is to create expectations. It is clear that the strategy of how and when to best develop and use reputational capital is far more complex than to simply state that a positive reputation is good and should be one of the goals of ethically sensitive managers.

In actual organizational contexts, reputations are not merely a one-to-one correspondence between how an organization would like to be seen and how it actually is perceived and effectively evaluated by others. In Figure 9.3 we see both an overview of the dynamics in play in building, defending, and using reputational capital at the level of the organization, and instances of ethical quandaries that can occur at each of these stages. There are, of course, various ways to make sense of the dynamics at play in this model. Jarrell and Petzman (1985) and Borenstein and Zimmerman (1988) analyze the importance of a firm's reputational capital by quantifying the impact on a shareholder wealth of product recalls and airline crashes, respectively. Landon and Smith (1997) attempt to capture the dynamics of reputational capital in their analyses of consumers' views of Bordeaux wines. Moving from an economic to a more sociological perspective, Lahno (1995), Herbig and Milewicz (1994), and Shenkar and Yuchtman-Yaar (1997) explore the dynamics of reputation building and reputation loss as a function of trust, credibility, and standing, respectively. Others with a more psychological lens to the reputational capital dynamics, explore how fear of losing one's reputation can cause difficulties in balancing work and home relationships (Kydd and Ogilvie, 1990), and play havoc with the everyday process of self-evaluation and the confidence one normally vests in a healthy notion of self.

In Figure 9.3, the five stages of the model of reputational capital at the organizational or corporate level are: (1) the corporate identity stage; (2) the corporate image field stage; (3) corporate reputation crystallization; (4) reputational capital assessment; and (5) reputational capital in use. This model, culled from the existing literature, underscores the business and society theorists' concern for legitimacy. First we will review each of the five stages in the reputational capital model, indicating at each stage how the dynamics at play create ethical problems. Before we turn to diversity in the workforce as an instance of the reflection argument in a business and society perspective on business ethics, we will look at what the growing literature in the field of reputational capital and reputation management suggests are the organizational traits that increase the probability of generating a stable positive reputation in the postmodern world.

Corporate Identity

In Chapter 2 of Thomas Garbett's book, *How to Build a Corporation's Identity and Project Its Image* (1988), the author asks the question "Will the real corporation please stand up?" and then proceeds to show his readers that this is in fact more difficult to respond to than it seems. Just as individuals are in pursuit of their identity, so too, organizations and those

FIGURE 9–3   Instances of Ethical Quandries in the Five-Stage Reputational Capital Model

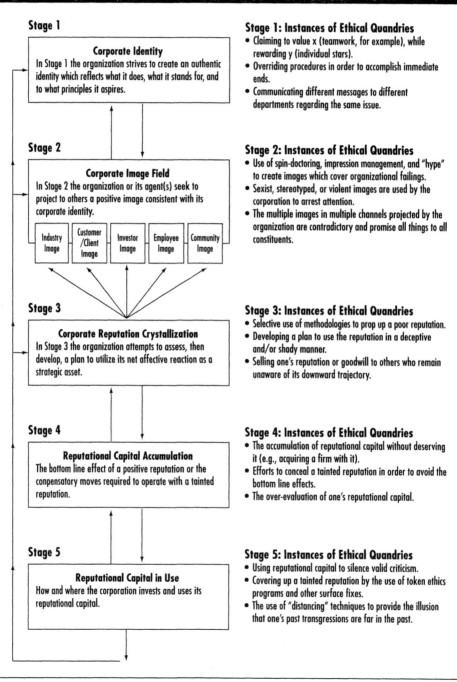

Stage 1

Corporate Identity
In Stage 1 the organization strives to create an authentic identity which reflects what it does, what it stands for, and to what principles it aspires.

Stage 1: Instances of Ethical Quandries
- Claiming to value x (teamwork, for example), while rewarding y (individual stars).
- Overriding procedures in order to accomplish immediate ends.
- Communicating different messages to different departments regarding the same issue.

Stage 2

Corporate Image Field
In Stage 2 the organization or its agent(s) seek to project to others a positive image consistent with its corporate identity.

| Industry Image | Customer /Client Image | Investor Image | Employee Image | Community Image |

Stage 2: Instances of Ethical Quandries
- Use of spin-doctoring, impression management, and "hype" to create images which cover organizational failings.
- Sexist, stereotyped, or violent images are used by the corporation to arrest attention.
- The multiple images in multiple channels projected by the organization are contradictory and promise all things to all constituents.

Stage 3

Corporate Reputation Crystallization
In Stage 3 the organization attempts to assess, then develop, a plan to utilize its net affective reaction as a strategic asset.

Stage 3: Instances of Ethical Quandries
- Selective use of methodologies to prop up a poor reputation.
- Developing a plan to use the reputation in a deceptive and/or shady manner.
- Selling one's reputation or goodwill to others who remain unaware of its downward trajectory.

Stage 4

Reputational Capital Accumulation
The bottom line effect of a positive reputation or the conpensatory moves required to operate with a tainted reputation.

Stage 4: Instances of Ethical Quandries
- The accumulation of reputational capital without deserving it (e.g., acquiring a firm with it).
- Efforts to conceal a tainted reputation in order to avoid the bottom line effects.
- The over-evaluation of one's reputational capital.

Stage 5

Reputational Capital in Use
How and where the corporation invests and uses its reputational capital.

Stage 5: Instances of Ethical Quandries
- Using reputational capital to silence valid criticism.
- Covering up a tainted reputation by the use of token ethics programs and other surface fixes.
- The use of "distancing" techniques to provide the illusion that one's past transgressions are far in the past.

who have a stake in them attempt to pursue and come to terms with the corporate identity. Corporate identity is an attempt to both capture and shape the commonly understood features used by those concerned to characterize how an organization approaches the work it does, the product it makes, the industry it competes within, and the customers or clients and investors it serves. Charles Fombrun writes that "corporate identity derives from a company's experience since its founding, its cumulative record of successes and failures" (1996:37). Others (Blake, 1971; Olins, 1978, 1990; Simpson, 1987) concur in viewing corporate identity as the baseline agreement, albeit tacit and unstated, that emerges among corporate participants as to what the organization is, does, and stands for.

Corporate identity is, as Garbett (1988) points out, the perceived "personality" of the organization. It is related to the organization's culture, but rests at the surface of the culture where the manifestly observable and easily recorded events in the organization's collective experience are registered. There are two very different sets of forces that shape the corporate identity. First are the participants' direct impressions. These are formed directly, not shaped by identity campaigns created by management to help mediate aspects of its corporate identity. Identity campaigns, the second force, are active interventions by management or its agents to shape the identity of the firm in such a way that problems may be solved.

In an organization largely satisfied or secure with its corporate identity, the direct impression of participants is the predominate force contributing to the baseline agreement regarding it; in organizations dissatisfied or insecure with their corporate identity, the use of identity campaigns will prevail. Identity campaigns are directed both to internal and external constituents. As Wally Olins, a prominent British consultant, notes, "there is no consensus among organizations that purport to practise corporate identity on what it is precisely that they do" (1990:157). Some firms direct their attention to changing the "mission statement" or corporate philosophy, others revise the architecture of their offices, while still others emphasize logo redesign and visual graphics, or even new store layout, as ways to achieve the "improved" corporate identity.

In Stage 1 of the five-stage reputational model, corporate identity is a shifting and open search for the collective's "self concept" (Fombrun, 1996:227). It summarizes, albeit with considerable differences in points of view, how the company thinks of itself and how it would like to be seen on the outside. It is clear that before the organization seeks to project and control its images in the multiple-image field, it must have some stable conception of itself from which to project and grow these images. In organizations with poorly formulated corporate identities, the image often prevails over the identity. This style-over-substance position alarms critics of companies who invest heavily in image promotion campaigns and advertising that seems to be cut off from their corporate identity.

From a business ethics perspective, the corporate identity stage in the five-stage model of reputational capital is worthy of reflection. Figure 9.3 provides examples of quandaries to help stimulate reflection. The quandaries emerge because corporate identity is not fixed at base but is an emergent consensus. Even the participants in this "identity conferring" are not fixed. The baseline reading for who should define the identity of the organization— employees, managers, government regulators, clients, investors, and the like—is not easily resolved. In my work as president of a consulting company, which specializes in providing services to organizations with ethics quandaries, I am struck by how frequently those who contact our group would like to solve an ethical dilemma by putting it into perspective within the corporate identity. "Dr. Wexler," they say, "we have been in operation for twenty-six years and not once have we had a case of sexual harassment. Now we stand to lose all our hard-won reputation because of the bloated libido of an employee who seems to be going through his mid-life crisis."

The desire to see ethical lapses as a departure from the authentic personality of the organization and its true identity is all too common. Corporate identities that are healthy and secure absorb news of the company's faults and seek to redress them. Sickly corporate identities, rooted in insecurities, seek to treat the news of a failure or an ethical lapse as an act that ought not to be counted since it is a deviation from the organization's ideal identity. There is danger and difficulty in increasing the distance between the ideal identity, or the problem-free identity, and the actual behaviour of the organization and its participants.

This leads to the sort of splitting that should worry organizational participants. For example, organizations that unintentionally split their ideal corporate identity from their actual identity are similar to those heavy drinkers who excuse bad behaviour while intoxicated, since it is not rooted in the "real" person. This splitting, as indicated in Figure 9.3, can lead to organizations claiming to value x (e.g., teamwork) in their ideal corporate identity, while in their actual corporate identity rewarding y (e.g., generating an individual star system of recognition and reward). Companies that engage in this splitting and justify it in the name of pursuing the ideal corporate identity are like chameleons on a Persian rug. They can justify overriding their standard operating procedures in order to accomplish immediate and desirable ends, and then excuse the override as nothing but a lapse from the ideal adherence to procedures.

What we learn at Stage 1, corporate identity, is that organizations with a high probability of earning a reputation that is consistent, positive, and sustainable, try to create an authentic identity that genuinely reflects what they do, what they stand for, and to what principles they aspire. This, of course, is easier said than done. Organizations that succeed at this do not substitute their aspirations for an account of their actions. They see themselves, to use a well-worn metaphor, "warts and all." The managers of these firms do not hide the warts, nor make them "unmentionables," for in practice I have learned that in organizational life, the more that is made "unmentionable," the less authentic is the corporate identity. We make events, ideas, and people "unmentionable" by refusing to hear from or of them, by ignoring them as part of our identity, and seeing them as instances of aberrant behaviours, accidents, and other "one off" categories.

The Corporate Image Field

The relationship between identity (Stage 1) and image (Stage 2) in the five-stage model of reputational capital is similar, in psychological terms, to the relationship between who we think we are (identity) and what others make of us (image) (Gray, 1986; Ind, 1992; LaBorde, 1993; Selame and Selame, 1988; Wynbrandt and Wynbrandt, 1992). Those whose corporate reputations are multiple (i.e. where an organization may be viewed as having excellent products but be a bad place to work) are attending to Stage 2 of the reputational capital model. In this stage, organizations attempt to use information and communication channels to influence how key others—competitors, clients (consumers), investors, employees, and communities—see them. When we seek to evaluate the postmodern organization, we can rely on our direct experience with the collectivity in question or with a series of images amplified by the electronic media, print, and the grapevine or rumour mills that operate in communities (Borden and Harvey, 1998; Koenig, 1985).

In Figure 9.4, we see that in some image-creation ventures, such as those strategically placed in the company's annual report or in advertising campaigns, the focal organization and its management or management's agent (public relations firm, advertising agency) have a great deal of control over the image. Under these conditions, there is a deliberate effort to project a positive image by attempting to satisfy the particular public to which the image is primarily directed. On the other hand, management often has little or no control over other images in the corporate image field. These occur, for example, when a company reacts to its public portrayal following or even during an unexpected organizational crisis or

FIGURE 9.4 Degrees of Managerial Control in the Corporate Image Field

Control Levels	Image Management Action	Examples of Image Targets
High Control	• Producing annual reports containing images of corporate performance over the past year and appraisals of the following year.	Investors
	• Developing an advertisement campaign that emphasizes the firm's product performance as superior to that of its competitor.	Competitor/Clients
	• Placing, with the help of the firm's communication department, a story in the press extolling the behaviour of a particular employee.	Employees/Clients/ Community
Medium Control	• Hiring a public spokesperson with high community recognition, visibility, and credibility as a figure with whom the firm and its products or services want to be associated.	Community/Clients
	• Entering into contests or standing ratings in which companies will be publicly ranked on specific criteria like social responsibility, product excellence, workplace enjoyment, etc.	Industry/Employees/ Community (depending on the criteria in the ranking)
Low Control	• Reacting to an unexpected and very public disaster, accident, or crisis in which the organization is central.	Investors/Clients
	• Publicly apologizing for failing to live up to societal norms and expectations.	Investors/Clients
	• Recalling products or being compelled to submit briefs to a regulatory commission.	Employee/Clients/ Community

public disaster in which the firm is portrayed as the villain, or when a company and its elite are compelled by a court or regulatory commission to provide public information that is less than flattering. In these instances, where management's image control is weak and negative images of the firm prevail, the strategy is to try to minimize the fallout from the negative imagery (Pinsdorf, 1987).

In the corporate image field, reputations are both made and destroyed. Three points should be kept in mind regarding reputation building and reputation destruction in Stage 2. First, there are both very active corporate image field players and also relatively passive players. The active image field players seek to crystallize their image into a reputation by consciously targeting audiences and studying them to understand whether or not their "investment" in image making is worth the cost. These active players may select to "go after" investors, clients or consumers, employees, or competitors in their own industry or the community at large. They may elect to use philanthropy and the publicity that surrounds it to influence their image in the community as a whole, or they may use and promote their company's application of "flex time" as a way to positively influence both existing and prospective employees. Most of us are familiar with company's active efforts to establish unique brand recognition and company identification through logos, product design, and spokespersons with high visibility as a means of influencing clients.

On the other hand, firms with a relatively passive image field presence hope to indirectly influence clients or consumers, investors, industry competitors, employees, and communities at large. Rather than attempt to project a controlled positive image to the right audience at the right time, or to minimize existing negative images in the corporate image field, passive image players rely on a direct relationship with their client, investor, industry competitor, employee, or community at large. In the passive image strategy, firms tend to be embedded in local markets where direct contact and word-of-mouth works best. In this view, it is believed that competence—understood as the ability to satisfy clients with reliable products and services, to return ample and growing dividends to investors, to build an organizational culture that provides for employees, to develop recognition and healthy relations with one's competitors, and to attend responsively to the needs of the community at large—will provide a positive reputation.

While it is possible to vilify the active corporate image field player and lionize the passive player, this only makes sense if one believes that players are using their image building as a form of spin doctoring—that is, to cover up some deficiency or lack of competence. However, if one sees most firms as competent—and markets as efficient in weeding out those less competent—then image building is one more strategic asset with which to compete. In other words, a competent firm in an industry, one adhering to the passive corporate image field strategy, should grow slowly and do well using direct influence means and relying upon word of mouth to capture the attention of potential clients, investors, employees, and the like. On the other hand, another firm in the same industry with equal competency in these areas but willing to siphon off some of its capital for active corporate image building will increase its probability of reaching new markets more quickly and be able to spot within existing markets new audiences for its image.

The second of the three points germane at Stage 2 of the reputational capital model is the fact that active image making may negatively impact other audiences' perceptions of an organization's image. In our discussion of corporate social responsibility we learned how one must be cognizant of the possible trade-offs between, for example, employees who seek to use corporate wealth to improve their fate within the company and investors who seek to take corporate wealth in their return on investment. Corporate image building—in practice, not in theory—has this dynamic built into it. A concerted and self-conscious effort of a firm to bolster its image to the community at large may entail giving a larger proportion of money to philanthropic causes than has been the case in previous years. Moreover, and in line with the logic of active image building, the firm would seek to maximize public recognition of its generosity, particularly within the community. However, if the firm has at the same time cut investors' dividends and frozen employee salaries, one can expect reactions to include wonder at why and how in the midst of relative hardship the firm has turned beneficent.

It is in the context of these trade-offs among or between audiences in the corporate image field that we can speak of image making as entailing certain dangers. Not only is it possible to alienate one audience by playing up a certain image with another, but this fragmenting of audiences and views may lead to difficulties in developing a unified or crystallized image, as we shall see in Stage 3. The fragmenting of image fields and, concomitantly, the emergence of a generalized confusion regarding the overall or crystallized reputation occurs when active image field players overwork the image field and, as with Humpty Dumpty, can no longer bring the different audiences back together again (Baker, 1993).

The third and last point to consider is that the more active a firm becomes in the corporate image field, the higher it raises its audiences' expectations. In an increasingly hyper-competitive business world, there is a tendency to match competitors' image building efforts and seek to go one better. This is not problematic until the image is raised, in competition with others, but the firm cannot back it up. The skepticism in many areas of applied ethics between "talking the talk" and "walking the walk" is clear. What is less clear is that this can lead to the firm winning the image war, but losing its reputation.

As an example, imagine a worldwide retail chain of cosmetic stores promoting itself as green. It touts itself as taking a leading role in promoting the Amazon rain forest by buying products from its indigenous peoples to offset their financial dependence and thereby reduce their need to sell timber. As well, the organization promotes itself as a friend to environmental causes, and creates in its image building campaign the suggestion that when one purchases hair conditioner from it one is helping to further the work of environmentalists. Moreover, its owners, managers, and employees believe themselves to be on the cutting edge of "green"—harbingers of a "dark green" world. Then a series of articles appears ranking the company pretty much in the middle of the pack, relative to others in its industry, vis-à-vis green issues.

Raising expectations, particularly by firms doing so with active image campaigns, may require that they be held responsible for their creations. In the corporate image field, there is a competitive push towards the use of "hype" spin doctoring and impression management techniques for firms wanting to prop up their images. This hazy land of hyperbole that we call image building is an important source of public information about organizations. Moreover, we in the postmodern society rely upon these fleeting and changing images to make important decisions about where to invest our time, money, and attention. The ethics of image making—the use of sexist, stereotypical, or violent images to capture attention—is part of the visual and acoustic world that is becoming our virtual reality. While we hope that each new generation deciphers the codes in these images and remains conscious of what is real and valuable and what is false, there is a large price to pay if we are wrong.

Corporate Reputation Crystallization

Corporate reputations are elusive and difficult to pinpoint. "As evaluators rate a company," writes Charles Fombrun in *Reputation: Realizing Value From the Corporate Image*, "against a peer group, an overarching reputation crystallizes from the plethora of images produced" (1996:37). In Stage 3 of the reputational capital model, the diverse images of the firm held by various publics at the corporate image stage of the model (Stage 2) are put together by the general public and evaluated by the firm. In this sense, corporate reputation can best be understood as the overall estimation in which a company is held by its constituents. "A corporate reputation," writes Fombrun, "represents the 'net' affective or emotional reaction—good or bad, weak or strong—of customers, investors, employees, and the general public to the company's name."

Just as celebrities and those with high visibility put together a reputation despite the diverse images created by themselves and established by magazines, critics, and association with different projects and product endorsements, so too, firms in their quest for a favourable reputation must both put together a reputation and assess it over time (Braudy, 1986; Marshall, 1997; Rein *et al.*, 1987). It is important to realize that organizations both invest in and plan to create a reputation (Markham, 1972). Some industries, including fashion and entertainment industries, place this strategic asset high up on their wish list. Others, such as construction companies and those who contract to large firms, seek to establish their reputation more for industry insiders than for the general public. Keeping with the legitimacy thesis, we would expect those organizations acting outside of the public acceptance—illicit drug dealers, motorcycle gangs, and money launderers—to shun the spotlight and seek to remain reputationally invisible (Kydd *et al.*, 1990; Szwajkowski and Figlewicz, 1997).

The crystallization of corporate reputation is no simple affair. It is rooted in three interrelated data fields, each used to get a reading on the overarching reputation attained at any point in time by the firm. The first data field, and the one used most frequently, is how much money the firm is investing in creating a positive image or in minimizing reputational costs incurred. The firm that spends like a drunken sailor on public relations neither expects nor easily accepts a mounting tide of newspaper accounts in which its reputation is maligned. In the same manner, an organization that increases its spending on an advertising campaign to foster brand identification expects results. Its managers do not anticipate recognition of their distinct services or products to falter.

This "troubleshooting" view of reputational assessment treats corporate reputation crystallization as a problem when either the investment (time, money and/or talented personnel) fails to achieve its objectives or when, given consistent investment over time, reputational problems increase. In the troubleshooting view of reputational assessment, quietness is measured as success. When the firm's overall reputation is mired by the credibility of consumers threatening boycotts, employees warning of imminent and disruptive strikes, or competitors running discrediting advertisement campaigns, then managers' troubleshooting antennae go up. When these antennae go up, there is a recognition that the firm is experiencing undesirable reputational capitalization.

On the other hand, when all is quiet on the reputational front, managers using the troubleshooting view of reputational assessment assume that all is well. This passive form of monitoring identifies problems in crystallization relatively late. On the whole, using this approach undervalues reputational crystallization when it is successful and overvalues it when it has failed to match expectations. Undervaluing is not the result of a conscious decision by management. Management does little when reputational issues are quiescent. Rather than increasing investment in order to sustain this desirable state of affairs, firms that use the troubleshooting approach increase their investment only when the reputational crystallization falls sufficiently below expectation.

The second data field used to assess a firm's overarching reputation is the myriad of corporate and organizational rankings published by a diverse series of institutions and media outlets. *Fortune* and *Business Week* in the United States, *The Globe and Mail*, *The National Post*, and *The Investor's Digest* in Canada, to name just a few, print authoritative lists of organizations in different categories. These are ranked—using some objective indices and other more subjective assessments of industry insiders and, at times, representative views of their constituents—and disseminated to the general public. These "third party" rankings or standings (Shenkar and Yucktman-Yaar, 1997) may be seen as credible by the general public since they are not controlled directly by the corporations themselves, typically are widely disseminated, and are often publicized. For example, the edition of *McLean's* containing their annual ranking of the best Canadian universities is by far the best-selling edition of this weekly Canadian magazine.

These rankings vary from the presence of stars or asterisks grading films or restaurants in local newspapers, to rankings by national organizations and publications, to corporate contests where awards typically are made in five basic categories: (1) products; (2) work processes; (3) ethics or social performance; (4) environmentalism; and (5) leadership. These do not exhaust the award categories; they merely point to areas in which reputational crystallization is possible. Product awards tend to be industry-specific competitions that compel judges to make comparisons between companies. Process awards recognize outstanding organizational processes, human and information systems processes, or overall quality management. Social performance awards, such as VanCity's Ethics in Action Award, judge nominated companies on their commitment to social responsibility and community contribution. Environmental awards honour organizations that are judged to have made an outstanding effort to promote energy efficiency, minimize pollution, or provide an example for others to follow. General leadership awards honour CEOs for their contributions to management or entire organizations for their ability to innovate consistently over time.

These public ratings, rankings, awards, and contests help to crystallize both public and inside assessments of a firm's reputation. They help to solidify or unify the fragmented corporate images that prevail in Stage 2 of the five-stage reputational capital market. Moreover, they have a strong secondary effect; they create criteria that managers who hope to rise in the rankings or to win the coveted award must take into account in future efforts. Managers are attentive to those activities and improvements they must engage in because they know that a company's reputation in such a public forum matters.

The third and last data field used by firms to get a reading on their overarching reputation is their efforts to develop their own techniques for measuring reputation or else delegating this task to an agency or research firm (Garbett, 1982; Olins, 1978, 1990). In Figure 9.5 we get an overview of some of the basic methods used by firms or agencies to assess whether an organization's reputation has crystallized or remains mired in the field of corporate images. The costs and benefits for the methodologies in question indicate that firms that use this third data field are investing in a customized and clear reading of their reputation and its perception.

Firms that employ the customized approach to the third stage of the five-stage reputational capital model are regularly on the alert for "faulty" reputation crystallization. Faulty repu-

FIGURE 9-5   Six Techniques for Assessing Reputational Crystallization

Technique	Basic Approach	Costs and Benefits
1. Recognition Studies (also called awareness, attitude, or familiarity studies)	Quantitative surveys establish the degree of recognition and the attitudes held by those in the organization's image field. These can be used as a one-time study to establish information about the image of the organization, or these studies may be repeated during or after an attempt to change the organization's image.	Good recognition studies are very expensive. They often require hiring a marketer or marketing research company. The sample must be pertinent and the aim of the study clear. The benefits rest in a baseline reading of the image field from key constituents.
2. Opinion Studies	Quantitative surveys on various public issues of importance to the organization usually deal with social subjects. The findings of opinion studies can be used to provide the organization with areas it might like to project its image. As well, the data can be used to bolster existing image strengths.	Opinion studies are very popular, but care is required. Opinion polls on controversial subjects will require care in order not to associate the company with the controversy. The benefits of opinion studies are that they provide the organization with a map of the changing image field.
3. Qualitative Depth Interviews	Qualitative depth interviews can be used to uncover deep feelings, underlying motivations, and ideas of selected respondents. These can be community leaders, early users of innovations, or any sample whose views of the organization image may help to fasten upon specific areas in order to strengthen them.	Qualitative depth interviews give data that requires careful interpretation before it is used to work upon aspects of the image. The intent is to analyze and understand a key group or real feelings and motivations. The process must be done professionally. The benefits rest in trying to understand what lies beneath the surface of the image.
4. Community Studies	Qualitative and quantitative surveys and interviews are done in select communities served by the organization. Efforts to plumb the depth, or lack of it, in community affect towards the company, its operations, and its products requires a careful series of questions combining a fixed response option with open-ended options.	Community studies are difficult to do well. The sampling requires attention to detail. The cost is high. The results cannot be generalized when the approach is effective. Done well, the study emphasizes the unique characteristics of the neighbourhood or community.
5. Focus Groups	Small groups, with between 6 and 12 people recruited from the desired target audience, concentrate on a subject under the direction of a moderator. The aim is to explore the opinions, beliefs, and attitudes concerning the subject. The data is qualitative.	The key benefit of this technique lies in the ability of the moderator to create conditions whereby the group is indeed willing to explore and reveal its beliefs, attitudes, and opinions.
6. One-on-One Research	Interviewing with specific material such as advertisement concepts or copy can be done one-on-one as well as in focus groups. One-on-one eliminates any chance of group bias.	The benefits of the one-on-one rest in the ability to focus on specific text or concepts. The costs are high since a moderator is used in each one-on-one. The data also requires careful analysis.

tation crystallization is equivalent to an early warning sign that in some aspect of its activities a firm is receiving "significant" reputational hits, which have the capacity to impact its overall affective public ranking. Vigilant firms are the most sensitive regarding reputation and the potential loss of goodwill. However, it is not always clear whether those who are most sensitive remain so because they seek to change their behaviours, products, or work processes in line with the demands of constituents, or whether they gain this information in order to persist in their behaviours, products, etc., and utilize it in order to silence, appease, or convince others that their worries are groundless.

At Stage 3—corporate reputation crystallization—ethical quandaries flourish. First, firms can and do use the methodologies selectively to prop up poor reputations. Managers have careers to consider; when firms take reputational hits sufficient to impact the overall corporate reputation, managers often seek to cover their backsides. So, second, they produce studies which, due to selective sampling or the manipulation of the wording, purport to show that all is well. These "inside" studies are neither supervised by others, nor is their data scrutinized by third parties trained in social-scientific research. Poorly designed or deliberately misleading studies provide a false impression of the overall reputation. As a baseline reading, this impression will be taken as a serious data point from which to plan future reputational strategies.

Third, this false baseline can be used, for example, to sell a firm's reputation or goodwill to others who remain unaware of its downward trajectory, or the data can be entered as solid, clear, and indisputable in contests and awards that employ company-supplied data. These shady practices are dishonourable. They use the cloak of scientific objectivity associated with good, balanced research for their own purposes. When questioned about their use of selective data-gathering devices or the selective reporting of results, firms frequently distance themselves. They point with alarm, feigned or otherwise, to the company they contracted for the study or to the individual who may have made a series of mistakes.

On the positive side, when they act in good faith, those firms that are sensitive to their overall reputation hear complaints early and act most propitiously to put them right. Most firms do not use the appearance of objective scientific data to cover up their blunders. Most do not mobilize and pay for experts to tell them what they would like to hear. Most experts who do applied social-scientific research are professionals; they act with integrity. They do not use methodologies selectively. They do not report data selectively. They deliver bad news and interpret it as such to their clients when the data collected leans in that direction.

Reputational Capital Accumulation

Goodwill, or positive reputational capital, that results from sustaining an overall positive reputation is the goal of most firms that seek to make reputational capital work for them. At Stage 4, firms seek to accumulate and manage the goodwill that results from a positive reputation, or they seek to distance themselves from accumulating reputational hits (Brucato and Smith, 1997; Ching and Holsapple, 1992; Goldsmith, 1997). Organizations at Stage 4 must not only attain reputational capital from their overarching reputation, they must be able to store it for future use.

Most forms of capital—such as profits accruing to a firm, human resources, and even technology—can be both easily deferred and stockpiled. Reputational capital, on the other hand, is difficult to accumulate for future use in dealing with possible reputational downturns. In fact, one of the important elements in Stage 4 is that as firms increase their positive overall reputation, they raise public expectations that more of the same is likely to follow. We are shocked when a firm that has achieved a stellar reputation for dealing honestly, fairly, and sensitively with its constituents is caught, as it were, in a reputational hit. This creates cognitive dissonance or tension in the way in which we make sense of the world. On the other hand, a firm that frequently takes reputational hits—whether due to its abysmal record on environmental issues, long history of labour strife, or an ongoing rash of investor calls for management resignation—prepares us for its next hit. We are neither shocked nor surprised when it occurs. We do not experience cognitive dissonance when we learn that a firm with a history of reputational lapses has just been found in another.

How firms accumulate reputational capital varies. In essence, there are three overall strategies: the vigilant reputational accumulator strategy (VRAS); the self-promotional accumulator strategy (SPAS); and the reactive minimizer accumulator strategy (RMAS). Each strategy, as outlined in Figure 9.6, has different underlying reasons for its rational selection and is associated with different ethical quandaries. Many firms see their reputational capital strategy as solely a function of their marketing department. They do not see how it links to human resource strategies, financial acquisition strategies, or technology replacement strategies.

VRAS is practised by the firm that seeks not only to compete with others for reputational capital, but to do so by tying its accumulation to the planning cycle. Such a firm invests heavily in crystallizing its reputations, and then accumulates the reputational capital for use in anticipated important issues. This firm increases its attentiveness to reputation enhancing as it approaches issues (new product launch, labour negotiations, plant relocation, search for new CEO) and seeks to use its reputational capital to lubricate these situations. The VRAS firm monitors the corporate image field (Stage 2) and attends to reputational crystallization (Stage 3) in such a manner that it accumulates reputation just before it seeks to use it.

Logically, the VRAS firm is rooted in the belief that to let reputational capital accumulate without using it is a waste. The VRAS firm uses its corporate capital judiciously. It uses some reputational capital to increase the likelihood of making more, and it dips into its accumulation in periods of anticipated high need. There is a built-in temptation in this strategy for the firm to use its accumulated reputational capital to help cover up or otherwise gloss over ethical lapses in corporate practices.

The second strategy for reputational capital accumulation, SPAS, is used by the firm that sees the costly monitoring and slowness inherent in VRAS as problematic. This firm seeks to promote its reputation far beyond its actual crystallized reputation. It tends to substitute promotions for reputation-building activities. In terms of reputational capital, the strategy is to avoid the gradual reputation-building activities of VRAS in lieu of treating reputational capital as a form of self-fulfilling prophecy. This view purports that the more the firm says or pays others to say about its good reputation, the more others will believe it.

The conflation of promotional investments with reputational capital accumulation in the very philosophy of the SPAS firm creates a problem for the trusting consumer, employer, investor, or society at large. Hype—the use of hyperbole and exaggeration in a convincing and skilful fashion—can permit a firm with low crystallization of reputation to appear as if it has actually accumulated substantial reputational capital. Firms that excel at SPAS do not appear to be blowing their own horns; rather, they seem to be receiving genuine praise and testimonials. The "infomercial" or use of product promotions in movies and even in newscasts sets the tone for ethical discussion regarding SPAS firms.

FIGURE 9-6 Three Strategies for Reputational Capital Accumulation

Strategy	Approach to Reputational Accumulation	Ethical Quandaries
Vigilant Reputational Accumulator Strategy (VRAS)	The firm seeks to monitor reputational capital closely and to tie the accumulation cycle to its planning cycle. This strategy accumulates reputational capital and then directs it towards key issues (new product launches, labour negotiations) that it anticipates may be eased by using the reputational capital strategically.	The firm that uses the VRAS may be tempted to use the accruing reputational capital to cover up or conceal ethical lapses. The appeal to the firm's good name can be used as a way to deflect well-intended criticism.
Self-Promotional Accumulator Strategy (SPAS)	The firm seeks to promote its reputational capital as a reality far above its actual crystallized reputation. It covets publicity, fame, and recognition. It seeks the spotlight. Publicity is the royal road to reputation. It is more interested in how many times its name is mentioned than what context it is mentioned in.	The firm that uses the SPAS accumulates reputation by claiming it in image outlets in which it can control the image content. This conflates reputation with hype.
Reactive Minimizer Accumulator Strategy (RMAS)	The firm seeks to avoid competing in the costly arena for reputational capital. It prefers that nothing be said or written about it. This lowers others' expectations and provides the company with a low profile.	The firm that uses the RMAS tends to be difficult. It prefers anonymity, often electing to own and operate companies at a distance.

The last of the three strategies for reputational capital accumulation actually shuns the spotlight. The firm employing RMAS avoids competing for reputation, preferring to go unnoticed. Even when it acts in the international arena, it elects to do so without fanfare. The RMAS firm reacts minimally when it takes a reputational hit. This accumulation strategy, or perhaps more appropriately an anti-accumulation strategy, rests on the belief that a response—even a good response—to a reputational hit merely prolongs its impact and leads to controversy. The firm that uses RMAS avoids controversy.

The strategy of avoiding attention, either positive or negative, leads to the use of secrecy, confidentiality, and a low profile as a means of establishing credibility and accumulating power in the business context. A low profile often entails a firm having complex ownership patterns with key players being hard to trace. Operating at a distance, keeping a low profile, and preferring minimal external monitoring, while obviously a strategy that minimizes complaints from constituents, does not lend itself to the information openness and accessibility required to create a dialogue over ethical issues in the business community.

Taken together, the three strategies for reputational capital accumulation indicate that one ought not simplify reputational analysis by assuming that all firms seeking to enhance their reputation will act more ethically. This view, by and large, satisfies the general conditions in the VRAS, but fails to do so with firms using SPAS or RMAS. The SPAS firm conflates hype with reputation and seeks to use its promotional activities as a substitute for a close examination and monitoring of reputational issues. The RMAS firm values and extols the benefits accrued from purposefully seeking and investing in a low profile. All three strategies indicate that reputation, even if one shuns it and seeks a low profile, must be put to use.

Reputational Capital in Use

Figure 9.7 provides an overview of those traits that reputational analysts (Dickson, 1984; Fombrun, 1996; Garbett, 1988; Gray, 1986; Olins, 1978, 1990; Riahi-Belkaoui and Pavlik, 1993) view as likely to bring a positive reputation. In all three strategies discussed above— VRAS, SPAS, RMAS—firms seek to avoid negative reputational hits. Using VRAS and SPAS, firms actively seek reputational capital, albeit of different sorts. The RMAS firm invests its energies in avoiding the high profile that accompanies reputational capital. It is more likely to invest in traits such as community service or openness with information than would a SPAS firm. The SPAS firm, with its flair for promotion, would most likely emphasize traits such as client-friendly services and achievement awards.

This fifth and final stage—reputational capital in use—indicates that firms not only accumulate reputational capital, but must put it to use. In the legitimacy thesis, a good reputation lowers transaction costs. Some firms will use this benefit to serve as a deterrence to others (those with no reputation) attempting to enter their domain. Some will use it to create a lucrative franchise system wherein along with the franchise outlet is sold the organization's good name. Others, when selling their organization, may charge a premium for their goodwill or reputation. Some will use their reputation to influence government commissions or regulatory bodies germane to their operations. Others will use their reputational capital to get more of the same, through good works such as promoting literacy or helping to set up a hospice. Some will do so even without insisting upon having their name placed prominently before the public.

Within the business and society perspective, analysts interested in the legitimacy thesis try to make sense of which options in reputational capital use will be selected by a particular firm and which will broadly characterize business in a particular society. There is a tendency to speculate on the need for a full-bodied stakeholder view of business ethics as a means of tempering the self-interested model of organizational and economic behaviour. In practice, most organizations and those who manage them realize that a good reputation yields marketplace advantages. Within the business and society perspective, two scenarios prevail. In the first, stakeholders seeking to move the organization towards their view, perceive of the possibility of using the threat of embarrassing the firm to their advantage. This is an optimistic view. It sees business as responsive to the values of society. In the second scenario, organizations use reputational techniques—image campaigns, infomercials, branding strategies— to keep stakeholders bamboozled. In this view, things in reputational circles are not only not what they seem, but this state of affairs is a creation of organizations that would like both to reduce their transaction costs and carry on their activities without too much alteration.

Both of the above scenarios speak to Stage 5, reputational capital use. Reputational capital used ethically ties the corporate image of the organization to its use of capital. These firms

FIGURE 9-7 Reputational Capital in Use: Seven Traits of Organizations with Positive Reputations

Trait	Reason for Reputational Impact	Link to Reputational Capital
1. Organizations that are perceived to serve the community.	These companies appear to be honouring the unwritten contract that good firms are a blessing and a benefit to the communities in which they operate.	Communities that believe in a corporation can help to carry it through hard times; they expect the organization to do likewise for the community if the need arises.
2. Organizations that are perceived as capable of dealing with crises and emergencies.	These companies appear to be ready for all eventualities. This enhances a sense of trust and a perception of competence.	The perceived preparedness of the organization raises the confidence of those who might otherwise question its legitimacy.
3. Organizations that have won competitive awards for products, services, community relations.	These companies are seen by the public as winners. By the same token, losing or ranking lower than expected can be reputationally devastating.	Winning awards or ranking high relative to others brings the organization to the attention of many heretofore unaware of its potential.
4. Organizations that are perceived to have excellent human resource policies.	These companies are seen by the public as dealing fairly with their workers. This perception increases the likelihood that employees will speak positively of the firm.	When the organization is seen as unfair in its dealings with employees, others realize that conflict and bad press are not far behind.
5. Organizations that are seen to deal with their profits fairly.	These companies satisfy investors, employees, the community, and government by using their profits to secure a satisfied group of stakeholders.	As stakeholders are satisfied, they are more likely to remain committed to the organization and see it as possessing potential.
6. Organizations that are perceived to be open with information and accessible.	These companies are seen as willing to let others have access. They are not seen as secretive, manipulative, or scheming.	Openness indicates that the organization has nothing to hide. This lowers concern. It raises trust. It indicates confidence in the organization's abilities.
7. Organizations that are perceived as customer- or client-friendly.	These companies are seen as offering high quality goods or services at a fair price with good follow-up. Clients and consumers are likely to return.	Return business due to satisfied customers or clients enhances the powerful effect of "word-of-mouth" reputation building.

walk their talk. They use their reputations to become more responsive to their stakeholders and to society at large. What is germane in the ethical use of reputational capital is that these organizations realize that how they use their reputational capital has an impact on the first two stages of the five-stage reputational capital model. In examining the model (see Figure 9.3), note the feedback loop from Stage 5 to Stages 2 and 1, which highlights the endless nature of the reputational cycle. As the firm uses its reputation, others have their early perceptions of the firm and what it stands for either confirmed or violated. Firms using reputational capital use it to act out a principled set of values.

Reputational capital used unethically disrupts or violates the early Stage 1 and Stage 2 promises of the organization. These firms do not walk their talk. They use their reputational capital to stifle valid criticism. They use their good name to distance themselves from lapses in ethical behaviour and from poor and/or insensitive decisions. They call upon impeccable testimonies and support from the powerful and the well-placed to compensate for their weaknesses. They do not use their reputations to become more responsive to their stakeholders and to society at large. In their operations, the use of reputational capital increasingly distances itself from the corporate identity stage or the corporate image field. In a dysfunctional manner, they increase the distance between how they are seen by those close to them or those at a greater psychological distance. Rather than seeing the reputational cycle as endless, those who use their reputational capital unethically see it as a solution to an organizational problem. Upcoming problems rather than a principled set of values determine the use of this reputational capital.

In both ethical and unethical uses of reputational capital, the organization must not only manage its reputational capital, but in putting it to use the organization will be evaluated. Moreover, and pertinent to the "reflection argument," in acting out its values in society, the firm must make sure that as social values change, its own actions are seen to reflect these values. To make sense of the reflection argument, let us look at the reasoning for "diversity in the workplace."

DIVERSITY IN THE WORKPLACE

One of the best and most controversial illustrations of the "reflection argument" within the business and society perspective can be accessed by examining the contemporary call for ethical organizations to respond to the changing nature and composition of society by increasing workplace diversity (Baytos, 1995; Cox, 1991, 1993; Fernandez, 1981, 1991, 1993; Hopkins, 1997; Taylor, 1995). Society, as we have seen in our discussion of postmodern business ethics, is no longer homogenous. Differences prevail. Those who speak for the reflection argument in its diversity form contend that the characterization of the corporate work setting as the domain of the white, male, Christian, heterosexual who is the sole breadwinner of his family is no longer an accurate portrayal (Asante and Davis, 1989; Hemphill and Haines, 1997; Ferguson, 1984; Kaplan and Lucas, 1996). The reflection theorists argue that as societies become more complex, heterogeneous, and polyglot with the mixing of races, religious views, age categories, lifestyle and sexual preference patterns, regional identities, cultures and, of course, the mass entry of women into the workforce, organizations must adapt and respond. Those which respond ethically and sensitively bring new blood with new ideas and ways of thinking about work into the organization; others clamour to maintain the status quo.

Figure 9.8 illustrates how diversity concerns go beyond the "usual suspects" of race and gender. The call for age diversity in the workplace makes the demographically sensitive point that if organizations seek to reflect the societies in which they operate, they must

FIGURE 9-8 Nine Key Diversity Categories

Diversity Category	Logic of the Diversity Category
Age	Age diversity refers to a workplace with a representation of age groups. Workplaces that lack age diversity tend to have a large percentage of employees in a particular age group. Within demographic parlance, age groups are referred to by such terms as "baby boomers," "echo generation," "generation X," and "golden agers."
Culture	Cultural diversity refers to an individual's affinity to, identification with, or association with a particular cultural dimension, which may include but is not limited to the following: race, ethnicity, nationality, or colour. Workplaces that lack cultural diversity hire, retain, and promote along a homogeneous cultural dimension.
Disability	Disability diversity refers to an individual's identification with some type of visible and/or invisible impairment, which may include but is not restricted to the following: physical, mental, visual, and hearing. Workplaces that lack disability diversity hire, retain, and promote the able-bodied.
Gender	Gender diversity refers to the workplace which wholly or predominately hires, retains, and promotes either males or females. In society today, the issue of gender diversification refers to the tendency of workplaces to hire, promote, and retain men at a rate far surpassing that of women.
Geography	Geographic diversity refers to an individual's identification with or sense of belonging in a particular geographic location, which may include but is not limited to the following: country, region, city, and province. Firms that lack geographical diversity hire the predominant number of workers from a preferred geographical area.
Language	Language diversity refers to an individual's linguistic identity, which includes but is not limited to the following: monolingual, bilingual, multilingual. Workplaces that lack language diversity hire, retain, and promote employees from one language group.
Race	Racial diversity refers to an individual's racial background, which in a workplace with racial diversity includes a mixing of people with different racial characteristics in varying positions of power and privilege in the organization. Race discrimination is prohibited by law, but many racial groups find it hard to access positions of power in the corporate world.
Sexuality	Sexual diversity refers to an individual's sexual orientation, which may include but is not limited to the following: heterosexual, homosexual, lesbian, bisexual, celibate, transsexual, transvestite. Workplaces that lack workplace diversity hire solely from one category.
Spirituality	Spiritual diversity refers to an individual's religious or spiritual affiliation, which may include but is not limited to the following: Christian, Moslem, Jewish, Mormon, agnostic, atheist, pantheist. Workplaces that lack spiritual diversity hire, retain, and promote individuals predominately from one spiritual alternative.

avoid the tendency to let their memberships slip into a narrow age band. Cultural diversity, an issue made prominent by the desire of many firms to operate in the lucrative international context, makes the point that organizations that operate in and/or sell to customers and clients from different cultures and/or lifestyles should reflect these in their workforce. Champions of disability diversity argue that the ethically responsive firm hires, retains, and promotes the disabled worker and helps to create a workplace climate in which all individuals can compete and excel. Gender diversity, as distinct from sexual diversity, refers to the role of women in the workforce; sexual diversity pertains to an individual's sexual orientation and questions whether or not gays, lesbians, and bisexuals are being discriminated against in the processes of hiring, evaluation, retention, and promotion.

From obscure categories like geographical diversity, to much more prominent ones such as racial diversity, we get a sense that those who utilize the reflection argument are insisting that in order to act as ethical agents, organizations cannot seriously think of themselves as separate entities existing apart from society. In keeping with this point of view, advocates of diversity programs root their arguments in one or more of these three positions: (1) due to societal and business changes, workplace diversity is both inevitable and ought to be anticipated by well-managed organizations; (2) effective diversity programs neither can be initiated nor run under duress or by government and/or legal decree, but must be motivated by the rewards to be accrued to both organizational members and top management; and (3) those who oppose well-run diversity programs fail to appreciate points one and two and are acting to protect and buffer the powers of an entrenched organizational elite.

The Inevitability of Workplace Diversity Programs

Workplace diversity programs are initiatives by organizations to communicate, train, recruit, mentor, promote, and involve employees in opening the organization to competent representatives from the diversity categories discussed in Figure 9.8. Although the specific argument for the inevitability of workplace diversity varies among its advocates (Chemers *et al.*, 1995; Fine, 1995; Golembiewski, 1995; Nancoo and Ramcharon, 1995; Wilson, 1996), the central logic remains the same. The same forces that create the volatile and fragmented nature of postmodern society not only fuel international business and raise the material expectations of citizens, but also create the conditions for a politicization of issues relevant to workplace participation. Groups that have been kept peripheral to real organizational power want in. The fanciful ideology espoused by the hippie generation—"turn on, tune in, and drop out"—is now looked upon as a curiosity by social groups tired of their outsider status. They want "in" and they want "up," for the organization stands for material well-being, challenging work, and an entry into where "the action" is believed to be—the international arena.

The advocates of workplace diversity not only argue that heretofore excluded or marginalized groups want in, but also that demographic, socio-political, economic, and moral forces are conspiring to make it increasingly difficult for organizations to ignore the opportunities this brings. In Figure 9.9 we get an overview of how women's groups, the disabled, ethnic minorities, racial minorities, and older workers are not only seeking a new role in the corporation, but being aided by changes in both business and society. For instance, in Figure 9.9 we look at how economic forces cited by advocates of workplace diversity—internationalization or globalization of business, the burgeoning wealth of China and large parts of the developing world, rising consumer involvement, and the commercialization of the household—all create demands on organizations to broaden the base from which they hire, retain, and promote.

FIGURE 9-9 The Four Forces Facilitating Workplace Diversity

Economic Forces

Examples

- Globalization or internationalization of business
- Increasing wealth in the third world
- the commercialization of the household
- rising consumer involvement

Socio-Political Forces

Examples

- The emergence of the women's movement
- Recognition of the voting power of immigrants, ethnic groups, and minorities
- Gay and lesbian power
- Activism and political lobbying of the disabled and aged

Workplace Diversity

Initiatives

Examples

- Diversity statements
- Diversity training programs
- Diversity recruiting programs
- Diversity mentoring programs
- Diversity promotion programs
- Diversity-related employee involvement

Groups

Examples

- Women
- The disabled
- Ethnic minorities
- Racial minorities
- Other cultures
- Younger and older workers

Moral Forces

Examples

- Greater protection for minorities in society
- Extension of rights to those with different lifestyles and backgrounds
- recognition of the need to apply social norms of fairness in the workplace
- desire to use voluntary forms of workplace diversity as a hedge against systematic discrimination

Demographic Forces

Examples

- Rising number of single-parent families
- Altering immigration patterns
- Fewer children, born later in a woman's life
- aging population

As organizations internationalize, they turn away from the nation state as the basis for their hiring. The internationalization or globalization of business (Amin, 1997; Dunning, 1993; Johnston, 1990; Swanson, 1993) requires that the organization act with sensitivity to racial, religious, and ethnic groups, whether clients or employees. The attractiveness of these "new" groups is amplified by the fact that in many instances, such as China and parts of eastern Europe, the opening of markets and growing consumer affluence are magnets to profit-seeking organizations intent on moving into the international market. Even on the domestic front, the new-found affluence of gays and lesbians (Miller, 1992), the elderly (Thorson, 1995), and women (Edwalds and Stocker, 1995) makes these markets difficult to miss.

It is no longer possible to market to consumers and clients when they are not represented in the workforce of the organization offering the goods and services. Rising consumer involvement (Laarksonen, 1994; Nava, 1992) entails two interrelated forces: first, from stakeholder approaches to business, it is clear that consumers seek to get their views heard by the organization; and second, organizations that seek to innovate must find out what their customers and clients think and how they will use the product or service. Many clear-headed firms know that if their employees think like their customers, they will have an easier time anticipating both opportunities and problems. As these clients increasingly come from other cultures, other racial groups, and other lifestyles, many responsive firms see the benefit of hiring competent representatives of these groups.

Within the examples of the economic forces illustrated in Figure 9.9, it is clear that the rising commercialization of the household has drawn business into the small details of people's homes. As households "contract out" and increasingly commercialize daycare, dog walking, and even grocery shopping, businesses that move into this arena do so with an eye to knowing the values of their clients. Servicing the household and doing it well requires an understanding of the lifestyle, religious views, ethnic foods, and preferences that mark one household from another. According to the advocates of workplace diversity, this is possible only if organizations are sufficiently heterogeneous to capitalize on differences with a high degree of commercial relevance.

The sociopolitical forces outlined by the champions of workplace diversity point towards the rise of the women's movement (Belenky *et al.*, 1986; Morgan, 1996), the politicization of the disabled (Ingstad and Whyte, 1995; Weaver, 1991), gays and lesbians (Kahn, 1997; Winfield and Spielman, 1995) and the emergence of ethnic groups and racial minorities as important constituents in the political arena (Bannerji, 1993; Palumbo-Liu, 1995). The women's movement, in both its liberal and radical forms, has given voice, political clout, and credibility to women seeking to gain entry and rise in the corporation. In its radical form, the women's movement is focused upon the problem of the "sticky floor," which refers to the reality that once women are hired, they do not rise as quickly to positions of power as do men with equal education and performance records. The liberal-leaning women interested in workplace diversity point towards the problem of the "glass ceiling." This invisible barrier stops upwardly-mobile corporate women in their tracks, while men of comparable education and performance records steam right on by and up the hierarchy. Both radical and liberal proponents of gender diversity meet in agreeing that "comparable worth," wherein both men and women who engage in comparable tasks and do so with equal competence, should receive equal compensation.

Within the North American context, women's organizations have become an active political and social force with implications for workplace diversity. Women have been the vanguard in calling for diversity training (Brislin, 1989; Ford and Fisher, 1996; Loden, 1996; Wheeler, 1994). They have made it perfectly clear that sexual harassment (Baridon and Eyler, 1994; Collier, 1995; Wall, 1992) in the workplace will be monitored vigilantly. They have led the fight for subsidized daycare (Fernandez, 1986; Shaw, 1982), mentoring programs (Kram, 1985; Megginson and Clutterbuck, 1995), flex-time (Frederick and Atkinson, 1997; Simmons, 1996), and corporate recognition of the home-office via telecommuting (Christensen, 1988; Jackson and Van Der Wielen, 1998). Women's groups have not been adverse either to using the courts or to lobbying governments in order to achieve their ends. Few would doubt that organizations now respond to women quite differently than they did at the end of World War II. Nevertheless, the gap between men's and women's earnings for similar work remains large. Openly lesbian, Black, Native, and disabled women have found it harder than white, able-bodied women to ride the crest of the women's movement. There is a backlash (Faludi, 1991; Friedan, 1997) in the women's movement organized by women who seek to return to their sex its rightful feminine status as homemakers, mothers, and enchantresses.

Quieter in its public exposure is the growing power and politicization of a group that until the 1980s remained quite peripheral to workplace concerns (Burkhauser and Haveman, 1982). The disabled have created a new image for themselves through the disabled Olympics. They have lobbied hard and long—using moral persuasion, medical research, and adept social marketing—to convince the public that when they can do the job they should be hired. Governments, on the whole, have been supportive, frequently offering incentives to those organizations that hire disabled workers.

All groups interested in promoting the socio-political forces that make for workplace diversity seek to lever their power. Coalitions between and among groups within the diversity categories are a phenomenon often alluded to as "the rainbow coalition." Aided by a bevy of consultants in what Heather McDonald (1993) calls the "diversity industry" and Frederick Lynch (1997) labels "the diversity machine," the rainbow coalition lobbies government and places pressure on organizations to implement diversity programs. Raising, or even threatening to raise the spectre of organizational discrimination against such groups can be an effective strategy for raising the stakes for organizations that refuse to take diversity programs seriously. In this regard, government organizations and the public service are particularly susceptible.

In commenting on the socio-political forces (see Figure 9.9) surrounding workplace diversity, some worry about the political correctness or PC elements (Friedman and Narveson, 1995; Kurzweil and Phillips, 1994; Schmidt, 1997). In their eyes, these are inherent in workplace diversity initiatives and in the very ideology that pervades workplace diversity. Advocates of diversity programs dismiss this view as nothing but a conservative backlash in which members of the old corporate elite confuse their "personal freedoms" with their privileged positions. On the other hand, those who accuse workplace diversity initiatives of political correctness point out that policing and monitoring of both the participation and promotion rates of special interest groups is itself a form of discrimination and special treatment. Those who worry about political correctness believe that the "ethics police" will replace sound managerial decision making. They claim that these do-gooders are largely naive dupes or fronts for those who claim a new status beneath the rubric of the diversity categories. They worry that the ideology of "inclusiveness," made acceptable beneath the banner of workplace diversity programs, institutionalizes the power of nothing but special interest groups.

Despite this foray into the cultural wars (Lakoff, 1996; Howard, 1997) that permeate discussions of political correctness, workplace diversity is being facilitated by moral forces (see Figure 9.10), which are demanding that we as a society, using the courts and other institutionalized forms, provide greater protection for minorities. The concern for the rights of women, Blacks, Natives, the elderly, and others is an important force in paving the way for the acceptability of workplace diversity issues.

Workplace discrimination (Armstrong and Armstrong, 1994; Handa, 1994; Rasi and Rodriquez-Noques, 1995) is viewed as reprehensible. It excludes individuals based on prejudice. This prejudice sees a group as different (often inferior) and, as such, denies access to individuals within it. We act rationally when we seek to fight against discrimination on the basis of the traditional categories—colour, gender, age, religion, culture—for if we fail to take a stance there, we may find other categories—obesity, baldness, smoking, shortness—becoming as firmly entrenched. We are all in a category that can be potentially discriminated against. Any one of us may find ourselves in a car accident and, as a result, wake up in the hospital with severe spinal or head injuries. Workplace diversity programs serve as a hedge against systemic discrimination.

In keeping with the instrumental tone of morality in the postmodern society, diversity programs, it has been argued, increase workplace empowerment (Dew, 1997; Johnson and Redmond, 1998), foster teamwork (Jackson, 1992; Syer and Connolly, 1996), and accelerate organizational learning (Lassey, 1998; Senge, 1990). These "selling points" are emphasized in the literature, not as "get rich quick" approaches to business, but as ways to foster fairness in the workplace. The quest for fairness in the workplace is particularly poignant in a period in which organizations have been rather merciless in their use of downsizing (Downs, 1995; Gottlieb and Conkling, 1995)—a tool to purge organizations of deadwood, introduce new technology, and signal a new direction to investors. In this context, many in society, particularly those who have lost their jobs and not found their way back into the system, feel betrayed. It can be argued that workplace diversity programs are one of the strategies used by organizations to ease this sense of betrayal, introduce new and highly-motivated workers, and signal to others an altered attitude towards those who show loyalty to the organization.

Organizations that simultaneously implement workplace diversity programs while downsizing create a confusing series of signals in the moral force field. Rather than seeing workplace diversity as a hedge against discrimination and a force for fairness in the workforce, it is viewed as a technique used to both cover up and, in some senses, to justify downsizing. In its cover-up capacity, workplace diversity is seen as a distraction. As a justification, workplace diversity is seen as a step in re-engineering the organization. Downsizing capitalizes on the "new blood," using it to replace larger numbers of employees with more seniority.

However, most workplace diversity programs are not Machiavellian efforts to cut costs, downsize, or re-engineer. Within the dominant moral force field, they are an attempt to apply the social norms of fairness in the workplace and protect minorities against workplace discrimination. If, as argued here, workplace diversity programs are inevitable, then business would prefer to implement, manage, and monitor these programs before they are imposed by governments, the courts, or special regulatory bodies. The motives of business are mixed. They are interested in putting their imprimatur on the norms of fairness to be used in managing, and they are interested in retaining control over the cost, implementation, and timing of the diversity programs. Diversity programs can be understood as part and parcel of the managerial strategy of the organization, or as a severe limitation and constraint upon managerial actions.

The final force for workplace diversity is the changing nature, composition, and age structure of the population. Demographic changes are aggregate changes in divorce rates, fertility, age or retirement, and lifespan, to name a few. Societies such as Canada are undergoing immense changes in this realm—changes that increase the inevitability of workplace diversity programs. For instance, new waves of immigration, now from Asia, the Caribbean, and Eastern Europe, are replacing traditional influxes of Northern Europeans. Women are having fewer children, increasingly heading single-parent families, marrying later, and receiving higher levels of education than ever before. In some Canadian professional schools, like medicine and law, women now exceed men in admissions. Add to this an aging population and we have all the ingredients for a strong demand for workplace diversity.

What the demographers (Dreman, 1997; Ferraro, 1997; Ginsburg and Rapp, 1995; Halli *et al.*, 1990; Huntington, 1996; Joy, 1992) are telling us is that postmodernity brings with it a fragmented, heterogeneous, and polyglot society. This is not accidental. It comes about as national boundaries are lowered and migration patterns depart from older, stable routes. It means that families are getting smaller and smaller and becoming more mobile. The population is becoming concentrated in urban areas where organizations providing employment are plentiful. It also means that very educated and talented people, often with different languages, lifestyles, and cultural views, must be integrated into the organization. As well, increasingly societies are immersed in two very different spheres of social and demographic concerns—the local and the cosmopolitan (Brennan, 1997; Cvetkovich and Kellner, 1997).

Demographers and sociologists tell us that in postmodern contexts the local sphere is diminishing in size and importance while the cosmopolitan sphere is increasing. The local realm refers to the relatively clear patterns and social practices that have persisted in a geographical region over time. In the local realm, tradition prevails. This emphasis upon tradition limits accessibility to outsiders and creates a sphere of social activities and practices with a high degree of homogeneity. The cosmopolitan realm, on the other hand, refers to the way societies integrate, assimilate, and explore social practices, including ideas, products, foods, and trends that have been developed elsewhere. The cosmopolitan realm both accelerates and is accelerated by the internationalization of business, new migration patterns, and the like. As the cosmopolitan realm within a social system rises in scope and importance, new techniques such as workplace diversity are adopted.

While advocates of workplace diversity insist that it is inevitable, the more careful and restrained among them readily acknowledge that all workplace diversity efforts are not equally effective. The three areas where a breakdown in effectiveness is typical are: 1) the failure of top management to champion initiatives in workplace diversity; 2) the motives for implementing the initiatives; and 3) the creation of unrealistic expectations surrounding the initiatives.

Effectiveness and Workplace Diversity

The results of established workplace diversity programs have been mixed (Bantel and Jackson, 1989; Golembiewski, 1995; Hemphill and Haines, 1997). Some companies, like Dupont (Scales and Emery, 1996), Digital Equipment Corporation (Walker and Hanson, 1992), and IBM (Childs, 1996) swear by their diversity programs, while others have found them to be costly and highly disappointing in both integrating the organization's workforce and providing it with a competitive advantage (Cross and White, 1996; Norton and Fox, 1997). In their highly readable book, *Diversity Directive: Why Some Initiatives Fail and What To Do About It* (1997), V. Robert Hayles and Armida M. Russell outline the areas where we can separate effective from ineffective diversity initiatives. Marlene Fine, in *Building Successful Multicultural Organizations* (1995), hones in on the criteria that lend success to organizations attempting to cross cultures, and Marilyn Loden's *Implementing Diversity* (1996) takes a hands-on approach to delineating the successful implementation process for workplace diversity programs.

The reflection argument seeks to make sense both of the need for workplace diversity in a changing society and of how to most effectively implement the ideas of diversity. On the whole, three areas of concern are shared in this literature: 1) the need for top management to both symbolically and actually champion workplace diversity initiatives; 2) that the motives for those implementing the program remain in line with the needs of top management, employees, and the organization's stakeholders; and 3) the workplace diversity initiatives must be portrayed realistically to their users. Let us examine the logic of each in turn. We will pay somewhat more attention to the "variation in motives" concern because it goes beyond the usual reasoning employed by those attempting to discuss how and why some workplace diversity issues are successful while others fail.

The first explanation for the management of successful workplace diversity programs is that the organization's top management not only license the idea but actively champion it and are seen to sustain this commitment over time. This meaningful and committed involvement by top management bypasses tokenism (Cohen and Swim, 1995; Jackson *et al.*, 1995), signalling that key structural aspects, incentives, and even issues of promotion will be impacted by the diversity program. In this regard, we can think of two very different images of diversity program implementation. The first, which we shall call the "weak diversity position," is best understood when employees of an organization seek to win diversity concessions from top management. In practice, typically this results in a diversity implementation scenario that is truncated. The battle, using a military metaphor, is waged over recruitment. Reluctantly, and as pressure mounts, top management agrees to increase its "shortlisting" of candidates for new jobs. Often implementation is delegated to the human resource department.

In the weak diversity position, the signalling is all wrong. Top management's reluctance to embrace the program is registered subtlety in the organizational culture. Those "others" who make their way into the organization, buoyed by the support of lower participants, will soon have their way barred. The process is subtle. Organizations using teams in the workplace often set up the newcomers in their own and separate work teams. This "apartheid" between the old and established non-diversity teams and the new diversity teams creates tensions. Mentors who otherwise would willingly give their time and know-how to the "new blood" may hold back. Their reticence originates in a recognition that this may not be the best use of their time and energy. The absence of top management support for the workplace diversity program leaves this change initiative without direct levers to power. As a result, it is often stillborn.

In the "strong diversity position," due to the willingness of top management to champion the innovation, the signalling of the initiative is tied to the levers of power. In these instances, the probability of implementing a program that goes beyond the shortlisting of job applicants from the organization's selected diversity categories is highly likely. In the strong diversity position, the champions of the program not only can *plan* to develop, retain, promote, and reward competent diversity category applicants, but they also have the wherewithal to implement these plans. This signals that new members from the diversity categories will not be shunted into their own teams, but integrated into the existing assemblage of teams that function within the organization. This encourages those with a facility for mentoring to invest their time and effort in working with talented newcomers who seek to make their mark.

The second area of concern regarding the effectiveness of diversity programs is motive. In Figure 9.10 we see an overview of five different but interrelated motives for those championing diversity initiatives. Within this framework, the "effectiveness" of the diversity program must be understood relative to the purposes and goals of those strategically investing their time, capital, and reputation.

The first motive—and least acceptable to advocates of workplace diversity—is to implement the initiative under duress. The organization employs a "quick and dirty" diversity

FIGURE 9-10 Five Motives for Workplace Diversity

1. Diversity under duress

Basic Premise	Structure	Limitations	Effectiveness
This is a situational adaptation by a firm to a pressing problem. Diversity programs are offered as a gesture to help take the heat off a firm.	Structures are ad hoc and temporary. Leadership is delegated downward. These programs are structured so that they can be closed down after the heat is off.	These diversity programs are tokenistic. They do not have the support of management. New entrants under program auspices are stigmatized and kept separate.	These diversity programs are effective when they buy the focal organization time to settle down the source of the duress.

2. Diversity by government or legal decree

Emphasis is upon equal opportunity, or eliminating discriminatory practices that have been tolerated far too long, or upon preferred treatment for groups that have been discriminated against in the past.	These are bureaucratically structured in compliance with the law and governmental monitoring. They are seen by firms as a costly imposition.	These diversity programs are seen as imposed from outside. Attempts to remedy past wrongs is not seen as the responsibility of the organization.	These diversity programs are effective when the bureaucracy established to oversee the initiatives receives few complaints and satisfies the political motives at play.

3. Diversity as a means of internationalizing or globalizing business

As firms globalize, they must learn to operate in several cultures, languages, religions, etc. Diversity in the workforce is one way to prepare for the tolerance required to manage differences.	These are structured in an international context where geographical divisions must learn to deal with consumers and co-workers from other cultures, regions, religions, and language groups.	These diversity programs are often trumped up as providing mobility routes for previously excluded groups. In practice, the socialization of talent is often kept within a set region.	These diversity programs are effective when they facilitate the organization's effort to globalize or cross cultures with minimal problems.

4. Diversity as a competitive strategy

As firms seek to compete for talented workers and clients in other groups, they increasingly see diversity as a strategy to help them innovate, adapt, and grow.	These are structured so that the results of the diversity programs can be assessed against the bottom line. The programs grow where they produce results.	These diversity programs are pragmatic efforts to gain an advantage. As long as they provide this advantage, they are maintained.	These diversity programs are effective when they enhance the ability of the organization to compete with others in its industry.

5. Diversity by members (managers and employees) of the organization

Firms that internalize the value of diversity are committed to the programs. This is reflected in an organizational culture that values the differences and mobility of those who do the tasks.	These are structured so that decision processes and incentives will induce those who have been marginalized, but are competent, to advance. These extend opportunities to employees with different work histories and approaches to problems.	These diversity programs require long-term, intensive effort with high costs and a continual need to learn as problems emerge. True-believer commitment can impede aspects of the programs that are not working.	These diversity programs are effective when they are successful at integrating "new blood" into the organization in such a way that it is accepted by the organizational culture and internalized into everyday practice.

program as a situationally adaptive strategy to a pressing problem. The problem can emerge from active and public complaints by those within diversity categories, or it can occur when, in its efforts to internationalize a geographically-dispersed firm, head office compels reluctant divisions to initiate diversity programs. Firms doing the majority of their work for government or other publicly sensitive organizations may find that their contractual obligations require them to achieve certain workplace diversity objectives. Within this "under duress" motive, the structures used to create the programs are ad hoc and temporary. As in the "weak diversity position," management treats these programs as gestures. They are considered effective when they satisfactorily take the heat off the firm without deeply impacting either the organizational culture or the power structure within the firm. When the problem lifts, the diversity initiative often falls into neglect.

As in the first motive, in the second, effectiveness is foisted upon the organization. These diversity initiatives occur when government or the legal forces of the land impose measures that emphasize equal opportunities or attempt to eliminate discriminatory practices. The structure is rule-laden and bureaucratic, and attempts are made to monitor the organization's compliance. These diversity programs are effective from the point of view of government and the legal system when they accomplish the goal of bringing organizations more in line with society's needs (as defined by legal and political institutions). From the organization's vantage, these programs are often an encumbrance. They raise levels of paperwork, increase transaction costs, and generally impose a bureaucratic monitoring device in an area that the organization believes ought rightfully remain a prerogative of management.

The third motive for implementing a diversity program is that it helps the organization adapt to the international or global market. As firms globalize, they must learn to operate in several cultures and languages and, of course, appeal to customers and clients from diverse backgrounds, traditions, and lifestyles. In this context, diversity programs are seen as a means to an end. Top management is often keen on the initiative since it is tied to the firm's strategic direction. While a great deal of fanfare often attends workplace diversity programs initiated in this context, the probability of sustained interest is dependent on the payout. Such workplace diversity programs are effective when it is truly believed that they are instrumental in the firm's success in globalizing and, as such, should be retained and built upon. They are far less effective when they are not seen as providing a competitive advantage. In these cases, diversity programs are relegated to the sidelines while other tools are sought to provide the quick fix the firm is seeking to gain the advantage in its efforts to internationalize.

The fourth motive is also instrumental in conception. Workplace diversity programs are seen as a "generalized competitive strategy" to accomplish five desirable ends: (1) to attract the best and the brightest by bringing in, promoting, and identifying competence in new and under-explored populations; (2) to foster innovation by ushering in new ideas with the new blood; (3) to facilitate better relations with consumers since the diverse workforce reflects the different points of view and lifestyles found in the population at large; (4) to reduce conflict by creating conditions in which cooperative teams and teamwork flourish; and (5) to enhance organizational learning as new blood with new ideas makes its way into the organization. The idea that diversity programs are a silver bullet helps sell them, but may damn them as well by raising expectations too high too quickly. The effective diversity program, in this context, creates a problem-solving ability that enhances the firm's competitive advantage.

The fifth and final motive—and the one most favoured by advocates of workplace diversity initiatives—occurs when the members of the organization, both top managers and employees, seek to add to the organizational culture by internalizing the strength of values that come with new blood. This is reflected in organizations that seek to grow and challenge themselves by dealing with the hard problems of "difference." This approach requires long-term, intensive effort, with the recognition of high costs and few, if any, immediate or obvious economic rewards. There is a recognition that effective workplace diversity programs stretch and challenge the status quo within the organization by introducing "new blood" with great potential.

An effective workplace diversity program, to some degree, depends upon the motive for its implementation. In the literature on this topic, which implies that the ethical organization is responsive to workplace diversity, there is a tendency to assume the fifth and most intrinsically-based motive as the starting point. While this helps make the case, it neglects the fact that when diversity programs are introduced to companies, the easiest selling strategy is to emphasize the benefits and downplay the costs. These conditions set the stage for the third and last explanation for the failure of diversity programs: in a nutshell, they are hyped and oversold. Overselling the diversity program dramatically lowers its probability of success.

There are four main causes behind the failure to realistically portray workplace diversity programs. First, advocates often have to override a very vocal and strong corporate opposition simply to get the resources to create a diversity program. In doing this, advocates often oversell. Second, there is no single strong template or prototype. Where workplace diversity advocates succeed in getting the resources and authority to implement a program, they frequently find that in putting it into practice they must improvise, at times radically modifying their initial conception. In a related fashion, a third explanation builds on the improvisational quality of many workplace diversity programs, but attributes the ongoing need for modification to new groups—both within and outside the corporation—who demand increasing input. Fourth—and least ethically supportable—is the desire of the organizational elite to use these programs to gloss over and provide the appearance of a corporation that is responsive and sensitive to the needs of groups previously excluded or underutilized in the organizational world.

We are left with the question: are workplace diversity programs capable of delivering their advocates' promises? If we look at motives one though four in Figure 9.10, we can come to a rapid conclusion that diversity programs are a sure winner. First, they can help as a situational adaptation to the organization's immediate problems and pressures. Second, token efforts to assemble a diversity program can help dissuade government and the long arm of the law from imposing its own solutions to diversity problems. Third, firms can use diversity programs to help them enter lucrative global markets and achieve strategic goals such as innovation, teamwork, organizational learning, improved consumer and community relations, and bolstering the quality of personnel. However, the propensity to oversell the idea of diversity sets expectations high and opens the door for those who argue that these programs are not all that their advocates claim. The critics' attack on workplace diversity mobilize ideas on two very different fronts, which will be explored in the next section.

The Critics of Workplace Diversity

The critics of workplace diversity are not portrayed in a flattering light by its advocates. They are portrayed as powerful ostriches—powerful because they are acting to protect the dominant (white, male, Christian) corporate elite, and ostriches because they refuse to take their heads out of the sand and see how society has changed. Meanwhile, the critics (Bernstein, 1994; Kuran, 1995; Lasch, 1994; Lynch, 1991, 1997; McDonald, 1993; Taylor, 1992) see workplace diversity as a costly, ineffective, and largely ill-conceived intervention that creates a terrible precedent by establishing that all future minority groups can argue for entry into the workplace solely on the basis of their minority status. The most reasonable critics concede that some minorities have an extremely good case, but in their rush to right the wrongs of society, diversity advocates view this as a form of compromise, and are unwilling to rank the rights of diversity categories.

In Figure 9.11 we see an overview how the critics of workplace diversity see disadvantages where the advocates see only benefits. To the critics, the advocates' reasoning is circular. They assume that when they talk about and insist upon the virtues of workplace diversity initiatives that the programs will be effective. This, insist the critics, achieves the desired objectives—lower costs, diminished conflict, enhanced customer service, quality management, systems flexibility—by fiat.

The critics assert that diversity programs in operation frequently increase costs. This rise in costs occurs as monitoring increases to deal with increased grievances and to handle the bureaucratic structure concomitant with the procedural justice issues that accompany workplace diversity programs. The critics point out that these programs do not diminish conflict, but either intensify it in the short term or, more provocatively, suppress it; in the long term many firms with seemingly effective diversity programs are likely to ignite a spark that explodes long-suppressed gender, racial, or religious hostilities.

In each of the seven problem areas in Figure 9.11, the advocates see workplace diversity as a key to the solution; the critics see it as the solution only in very rare circumstances. For example, if we look at the two problem areas called customer service and system flexibility, we can note how each sutures its logic in a diametrically opposing fashion. To the advocates of diversity programs, customer service will be enhanced when and if workplace diversity is implemented, because in the opening of the workforce to "difference," it will be more agile in dealing with the increasingly heterogeneous postmodern clientele. The critics of workplace diversity agree that this seems imminently logical. What they disagree with is that the desired scenario portrayed by workplace diversity advocates is not usually forthcoming in practice. In fact, workplace diversity has a large probability of adversely impacting customer service. In organizations where customer service is already satisfactory, tinkering with new personnel who must learn their task on the job complicates the customer-organization transaction. Customers seek smooth, known, and uncomplicated exchange transactions. Speed, insist the critics, is the essence of the postmodern transaction. Why complicate it by going back to the small-town version where shared values and knowledge of kind was essential? The future emphasizes self-service, machine-client interactions, and polite but equally impersonal exchanges to all clients.

In the eyes of the advocates of workplace diversity, systems flexibility is enhanced. The logic is simple but persuasive. Employees with diverse views drawn from different categories will remain sensitive to emergent issues. They will be better able to anticipate and deal with changes and tolerate the ambiguity that is a hallmark of postmodern existence. The critics agree with the idea that workplace diversity will increase divergent views within the organization, but rather than tie this to systems flexibility, they warn that for many, divergent views make it more difficult to take action. This is particularly so, given that in most workplace diversity initiatives a preference for teamwork is held out as central to the initiative. The critics' concern is with how a divergence in views, under a rubric of consensus, may impede rather than facilitate systems flexibility.

FIGURE 9-11 The Case For and Against Workplace Diversity: Seven Selected Problem Areas

Problem Area	Advantages of Diversity	Disadvantages of Diversity
1. Costs	Cost savings will occur because with an effective diversity program the best people are put to the right task. Thwarting diversity suppresses and underutilizes talent.	Costs will rise. Implementing diversity programs will add both costly levels of bureaucracy and monitoring to the personnel function of the organization.
2. Customer Service	Customer service will be improved, since the greater the diversity in employees, the greater the probability that the desires of customers with different needs and problems will be met.	Customer service will be impaired. Diversity programs complicate the workplace. Exchange patterns slow down and become uncertain when employees fail to see things the same way.
3. System Flexibility	Employees with diverse views and values are sensitive to emerging issues. This increases system flexibility.	Too many divergent views make it difficult to take action. Workplace diversity jeopardizes system flexibility.
4. External Regulators	When organizations successfully and voluntarily implement diversity programs, the probability of external bodies such as courts and governments imposing their views diminishes.	If organizations start, persist, and make a big thing about their diversity efforts, external bodies such as governments will demand more.
5. Conflict	Conflict between employees and between the organization and its stakeholders will diminish as the organization becomes sensitive to the needs and values of others.	Conflict will increase over time as diversity compels people and groups who often do not get along to search for mutual interests. They often do not find these.
6. Quality Management	Diversity programs empower and utilize teams to enhance the continuous evaluation and adjustment of work processes to ensure high quality at low prices.	Diversity programs lower the probability of effective quality management by fostering the continual need for consensus. This wastes time and lowers productivity.
7. Internationalization	Workplace diversity helps organizations move to global markets since it enhances openness to many languages, cultures, lifestyles, and races.	Workplace diversity programs give the illusion of moving the firm towards global markets; in fact, they simplify the problems of internationalizing.

In Figure 9.11, the critics' point is that in each of these seven problem areas, advocates of workplace diversity gloss over the possibility that their well-intentioned programs can go awry. The critics hold doubts even with the concerns of internationalization and external regulators. They argue that workplace diversity simplifies the massive preparations a firm ought to engage in before planning to enter the international market. While hiring people from other countries is a logical and necessary step, including this within the ideological framework of a diversity program politicizes a function that need not become politicized. Throwing domestic Blacks, Natives, the disabled, women, and other diversity categories into efforts at internationalization is to assume that the views of domestic minorities and those of recruits in other cultures—often the elite in these cultures—are similar. This can complicate, confuse, and impair serious efforts at internationalization.

As far as the idea that organizations ought to anticipate workplace diversity in order to short-circuit government and/or legal intervention, the critics remain skeptical. They argue that if organizations start, persist, and utilize workplace diversity as a public relations tool to enhance their reputations, then external bodies such as government and the courts, pleased at these gains, will raise the stakes and increase their demands. In fact, the critics insist, the actual process is more circuitous. The adoption of diversity programs raises the expectations of special interest groups. When their expectations are not met by the organization, they may petition the government, utilizing documentation from the firm itself in making their case credible, winning public sympathy, and creating an image of the organization as callous, in violation of its own principles, and hypocritical.

The second criticism levelled by those who oppose workplace diversity initiatives focuses on whether or not making the organization more responsive to minority groups is equivalent to making it more responsive to society. Unlike the first criticism, the second is primarily rhetorical. However, it has implications for those who use the business and society perspective to argue, within the reflection argument, that ethical organizations reflect the society in which they operate. The advocates of workplace diversity claim that society is changing and, by adopting workplace diversity initiatives, ethical organizations can assimilate these changes and become responsive in the new social context. The critics claim that to reflect society, organizations must avoid "catering" to special interest groups. They do not reflect society. In fact, they represent vocal minorities who are capable of using voice in order to get their views heard.

This argument rests on who it is that organizations should be responsive to when they seek, whether for intrinsic or extrinsic motives, to be responsive to society. The critics of workplace diversity argue that organizations cannot turn to special interest groups as their basic barometer of responsiveness, as this creates three interrelated problems: 1) it tends to reinforce those special interest groups that can mobilize public attention; 2) it establishes a precedent that makes it difficult to refuse entry to future minority groups or diversity category candidates; and 3) it often unintentionally discriminates against the silent majority.

Both of our business and society theses—the legitimacy thesis and the reflection argument—indicate that our understanding of how and why businesses align themselves with changing social values is still in its generative stage. As the quest for reputational capital intensifies in the postmodern context, business images and values spill over into our social values. Conversely, we discover that there is a demand that organizations take a leading role in articulating inclusive, participatory, and just social values. In the final chapter we turn our attention to what happens to business ethics in a technologically changing society where our views of what is and is not possible help to determine our views of the good world.

CASES AND QUESTIONS

CASE 9-1	Knolls Real Estate Ltd. Seeks to Repair its Reputation

Shannon Vogel was stunned. She almost spilled her morning coffee on her cat when she read the business section in *The Bay City Monitor*, the local newspaper. The article was about Shannon's ex-employer, Emory Knolls, and his efforts to turn around the flagging reputation of his company. The article by Douglas Katz, a reputable journalist who Shannon knew personally, claimed that Knolls Real Estate (KRE) was embarking on a two-pronged strategy. First, KRE was in the process of acquiring rival Sunny Cove Realtors Inc., a well-known local real estate firm. Second, Emory Knolls and KRE were going to set the record straight by initiating a diversity program and an ethics training program for all employees and commissioned sales agents. Katz went on to refresh the reader's mind regarding the recent history of KRE.

It was only too well that Shannon knew the recent history of KRE. Shannon had worked for KRE as Emory Knolls' executive assistant for the last year. In fact, she had only begun her job at Sunny Cove Realtors two months before. The last two months had been fun and stimulating. Work at Sunny Cove Realtors was a challenge. Mr. Kinney, who ran Sunny Cove, was a clear-headed, honest dealer. He treated people fairly, with respect, and sought to make money by providing excellent information and service to his clientele. On the other hand, Shannon refers to her stint with KRE as "the most miserable period of my life."

This period came to a rather abrupt end seven months ago when six employees, including Shannon Vogel, blew the whistle on Emory Knolls and KRE. The group of four agents and two office staff had first gone to Emory Knolls himself to voice their concerns, but he only scoffed at their efforts and dismissed them as nuisances who would be fired if they persisted with their malicious misinformation. With a great deal of secrecy which, in hindsight, looked silly to Shannon, "the KRE six" as they were soon dubbed in the Canadian newspapers, went to Douglas Katz. Receiving good coverage from *The Bay City Monitor*, they were advised by their lawyer to register their complaints with the Bay Valley Real Estate Board. When Emory Knolls, true to his word, fired the six employees, they took KRE to court for wrongful dismissal and were each awarded $60,000 in an out-of-court settlement.

"The KRE six" had done their homework on effective whistle-blowing. With the help of Shannon Vogel's access to KRE's files, they documented each step of their accusation. They each kept a journal of the dates, times, and places of key conversations. To most conversations they could and did provide witnesses or supporting evidence. The complaints that "the KRE six" made public can be summarized as follows:

1. KRE, with the full knowledge of Emory Knolls, was paying standard commissions to all its real estate agents, but charging more for the services it offered to its agents (signs, office space, secretary, answering system, referrals, etc.) if they were young, Asian, Black, and/or women. Karla Ward, the third highest-selling real estate agent of the thirty-two at KRE, was earning (after service charges) less than Ron Woodward, the

fourteenth highest producer. There were no exceptions, nor any clear justification for this discriminatory practice.

2. KRE, with the full knowledge of Emory Knolls, was acting in a conflict of interest when it had Cisco Appraisers—a firm owned by Mr. Knoll—appraise houses for prospective clients and then use third parties to purchase the undervalued houses. This ruse, documents revealed, was particularly successful with older, retired clients. In all cases, KRE, under the guise of the third parties, resold the properties within a year and at a substantial profit. The profit went 20% to the third party buyer, and 40% each to Cisco Appraisers and KRE, both owned by Emory Knolls.

3. KRE, with the full knowledge of Emory Knolls, instructed its real estate agents to attempt to knowingly hide structural damages and significant repairs due to fire, flood, or pest infestations from its prospective buyers.

4. KRE, with the full knowledge of Emory Knolls, sought to use insider knowledge of the opening of a new municipally-funded marina to purchase housing tract land proximate to the site. The information in question was provided by Emory Knolls' son, Peter Knolls, who is a councilman in the Bay Valley area. With the information, Emory Knolls purchased land at $2.8 million which, after the announcement of the marina, was estimated to be worth $6.4 million.

5. KRE, with the full knowledge of Emory Knolls, persisted in keeping Harry Clark, the highest performing real estate agent at KRE, in the company despite the existence of seven written complaints of sexual harassment by fellow employees. Mr. Clark, it seems, could not keep either his hands or his sexually-loaded sense of humour to himself. All seven complaints were submitted in writing to Mr. Knolls. Three of the seven had also gone with their complaints to the Bay Valley Real Estate Board. The record shows that both Mr. Clark and Mr. Knolls agree that Mr. Knolls never spoke to Mr. Clark about this matter.

The consequences of this very public airing of dirty laundry was devastating to KRE. The Bay Valley Real Estate Board fined KRE $10,000 and insisted that it immediately hire a consulting firm to help implement an ethics program and workplace diversity initiative. The out-of-court settlement, including lawyers and settlements to the sexual harassment complainants cost KRE roughly $500,000. But what was most problematic was the drop-off in the number of clients, both commercial and residential, willing to trust their real estate needs to KRE. In the first three months after the public debacle, Emory Knolls calculated that the value of his business fell by at least fifty per cent. Harry Clark and the majority of the other top producers at KRE were leaving the firm. They could make more money elsewhere. It was clear, given the revelations regarding KRE's operations, that they owed little loyalty to this company. Even on a personal level, the impact was devastating. Krolls' son, Peter, lost his job on the city council and refuses to speak with his father. Tina, his wife, was threatening to move to Toronto. Everywhere she went in Bay Valley people pointed and stared. She no longer received invitations from her neighbours.

Emory Knolls, although still quite certain that he had done nothing too wrong except get his neighbours and industry envious at his success, called in Delta Image Consultants from Toronto to assist him in remaking his corporate reputation. Emory Knolls and Keith Slater, the consultant sent from Delta, hit it off from the start. Their plan, reported quite accurately by Douglas Katz of *The Bay Valley Monitor*, was to: (a) set in motion a series of public events in which Emory Knolls would apologize for his transgressions and suggest he was opening a new chapter in his life; (b) purchase the highly reputable and respected Sunny Cove Realtors, now owned by the aging Mr. Kinney; (c) change the name of the company from Knolls Real Estate to New Sunny Cove Realtors; and (d) make a big public announcement regarding the state-of-the-art ethics program and new workplace diversity issues initiatives that New Sunny Cove Realtors (working with Keith Slater of Delta) would establish.

Emory was pleased with this plan. In the first weeks of implementing it, he and Keith Slater ran into two problems that they handled in the following way. The first problem was with Mr. Kinney of Sunny Cove Realtors. He was quite willing to sell his company to Mr. Knolls, but wanted to stay on for a year at a salary of $30,000 just to see that the transition went smoothly. Actually, Mr. Kinney was worried that, despite the epiphany claimed by Mr. Knolls, some rough edges seemed to exist. Emory Knolls and Keith Slater huddled on this proposition. They decided to increase the price paid for Sunny Cove Realtors by $300,000, bringing the total to $2,300,000, and permit Mr. Kinney to act as the chairperson of an "advisory" committee. This position was an honorary one. Its duration was to be two years. The two other committee members were to be selected by Mr. Knolls.

6. The second problem was what to do with the three Sunny Cove Realtor employees like Shannon who were part of what became known as "the KRE six." These employees, after receiving their settlement from KRE and with their expertise intact, had sought and received employment with Sunny Cove and Mr. Kinney. Mr. Knolls was outraged at the six. In fact, without them he would still be on the fast track to real wealth. Keith Slater and Emory Knolls worked out that, since there was going to be a great deal of redundancy when the two firms merged, it would be wise to fire the three whistleblowers. But they would do this judiciously. Two, including Shannon, would be dismissed (along with thirty others) in the big downsizing that accompanied the merger. During this time, much would be made of retaining one of the initial "KRE six." After a year, they would make things so difficult for the last member that he would leave on his own.

QUESTIONS:

1. How does Knolls Real Estate Ltd. (KRE) illustrate the legitimacy thesis used by business and society analysts? What costs were incurred by Emory Knolls and KRE when it had its legitimacy questioned? Do you believe that the questioning of legitimacy in the case of KRE was justified? If yes, why? If not, why not?

2. Using the five-stage model of reputational capital as the basis for your response, is the reputation repair planned by Emory Knolls and Keith Slater of Delta Image Consultants likely to succeed? Have they worked out how at stage one (corporate identity) they will integrate the identities of the staff and employees at KRE with the staff and employees at Sunny Cove Realtors in order to create New Sunny Cover Realtors? How, for example, is the imminent firing of Shannon Vogel going to provide for an assessment of stage five (reputational capital in use)?

3. From your point of view, is Mr. Kinney selling out if he accepts Emory Knolls' offer to add $300,000 to his offer to purchase Sunny Cover Realtors if Mr. Kinney accepts the advisory chair rather than stay on the company payroll for a year? Do you think Mr.

Kinney was right to suspect Mr. Knolls' rapid conversion to the position of a socially responsible businessman? If yes, why? If not, why not?

4. What did Peter Knolls do that was so reprehensible from a principled, ethical point of view? In this example of insider trading, what costs are borne by the community? What was wrong with Emory Knolls' ownership and use of Cisco Appraisers? Why, in your view, did Emory Knolls do nothing about the complaints he received regarding Harry Clark?

5. Using the three strategies for reputational accumulation discussed in this chapter, which, in your view, best describes the one

that Emory Knolls and Keith Slater plan for New Sunny Cove Realtors? The Bay Valley Real Estate Board is trying to encourage Emory Knolls to adopt which strategy? Why?

6. Do you think that the ethics program and the workplace diversity initiatives planned by Emory Knolls and Keith Slater are an attempt to change the basic philosophy in the new company? If so, why? If not, why not? What do you recommend Shannon Vogel do after she is dismissed from New Sunny Cove Realtors? Do you think that this is retaliation for her whistle-blowing activity? If yes, why? If not, why not? What justification do you think Emory Knoll will utilize when he dismisses Shannon Vogel?

CASE 9-2 Dragonfly Clear Water Incorporated

Jacques Gendron took over the helm of Dragonfly Clear Water Incorporated (DCWI), the manufacturer and bottler of Dragonfly—a non-carbonated bottled water—after Gordon Fleming had let the firm's reputation sag. Dragonfly had slipped from being the third best-selling bottled water in Canada and eighth overall in North America, to ninth in Canada and twenty-third in North America. Ken Chew, editor of *Beverage Industry News*, attributed DCWI's downward trajectory directly to the bad press the company received from having been boycotted by the Natives of Mighty Mountain Territory. "Dragonfly is noted for its smooth taste, excellent visual appeal, and first-rate brand recognition, but is presently saddled with a sullied reputation. Until it can check its negative association with suicides in the Native community of the Mighty Mountain tribe, we recommend that investors look elsewhere."

Gordon Fleming had failed to anticipate that a dispute with Canada's Department of Native Affairs and the Mighty Mountain tribe might hold the image of Dragonfly hostage in the public's mind. Fleming had

worked hard to build DCWI's solid corporate identity as an environmentally friendly conglomerate with a heart. He had marketed successfully the glacier waters of the Mighty Mountain Territory as "The Water of Purity." Brand recognition had soared. The bottle label and DCWI's corporate logo portrayed a stylized Native lad bending over to drink from a quickly rushing stream, with a dragonfly hovering inquisitively over his left shoulder. Employees loved working for DCWI. It was ranked at number 68 in the best 100 places to work in North America. Investors were impressed by its potential and, during Fleming's tenure, shares on the stock exchange rose from $12.32 per share to $18.91. In the community at large, DCWI had a first-rate reputation as a good corporate citizen. It was known throughout North America as the primary sponsor of the disabled Olympics and a strong advocate of shelters for the homeless. In fact, DCWI held the real estate rights on twenty-three properties in inner-city neighbourhoods, which it leased for a very moderate fee to not-for-profit organizations.

The wheels came off when, 2,000 miles from DCWI's head office, Bobby Seal, a fifteen-year-old from the Mighty Mountain tribe, committed suicide and was followed within a month by two of his friends. The tribe reacted with a fierce cry of outrage. They called for more jobs for their youth, more social workers, and greater employment of Natives on the tribal lands. Chief Henry Windfield pointed out how the DCWI plant at the base of Mighty Mountain glacier employed only one Native out of sixty-four workers, and he was the night watchman. Within a short period of time, Windfield and the tribe blockaded the road into the small DCWI plant at the base of the glacier.

Gordon Fleming reacted calmly and well to this news. The firm had a two-year supply of Dragonfly in its system. If there were really a need to bring workers in and out of the small plant they could use a helicopter. Fleming ordered all but five of his sixty-four employees in the vicinity to return to headquarters to be reassigned work in DCWI's plants and distribution centres throughout North America. Lastly, with the assistance of Joseph Pape in the public relations department, Fleming issued a press release expressing DCWI's deep concern regarding the social plight of the Natives in the Mighty Mountain Territory, and offered to pay for an educational counsellor to work with and in the tribal community for one year. The press release also pointed out that of its 1,300 employees throughout North America, 7 per cent were Natives, putting DCWI in the top quartile of businesses employing Native North Americans.

Fleming's easy-going and rational response did not evoke the expected results. The government decided to strike an investigation to look into the grievances of the Mighty Mountain tribe. Dr. Roger Pilon, an anthropologist from the University of Northern Canada, was given the mandate to write a report. Meanwhile, the blockade con-

tinued. The Natives refused DCWI's offer of an educational counsellor, and Chief Windfield looked straight into the television cameras and said, "Dragonfly is a drink for those who don't mind seeing young Natives commit suicide." With an international audience poised to receive his image, Chief Windfield picked up a bottle of Dragonfly, pointed to the label and said, "Do you see that Native lad? That was Bobby Seal. He died at the base of a glacier that makes millions of dollars for DCWI—the makers of Dragonfly."

The clip was played over and over again on CNN. It seemed to be the story of the week. It had all the makings of a modern tragedy. This was exacerbated when Dr. Roger Pilon made public his preliminary findings. The Mighty Mountain tribe was portrayed as a community in trauma, spiritually and psychically numbed. They had an unemployment rate of 62 per cent and few future prospects. Due to the arrival of companies like DCWI and Hardy Ames Timber Company, they had abandoned their cultural roots in hunting, fishing, and trapping, but with nothing actually forthcoming from these companies. Bobby Seal and the other youth of Mighty Mountain were victims. They were caught in the tension between the tribal images of the noble warrior, hunter, and trapper and the postmodern image of the Native as the educated knowledge worker.

The Association of Groups for the Advancement of Native Rights seized upon the Bobby Seal case. They replicated the Dragonfly bottle label with the words "Remember Bobby Seal" in place of "Dragonfly." Labels were distributed to their members in thirty-two major North American cites. Within two weeks, the bottled-water drinking population—primarily an urban group—was associating Dragonfly with the suicidal behaviour of young Natives.

The damage was done. DCWI was no longer thought of as the large conglomerate with a heart—it was perceived as the company responsible for the death of Native kids. Sales plummeted. Stock prices joined in this downward rush. Employees were confused and the industry at large began to dismiss DCWI as a contender. Several competitors were already beginning to hover. Fleming and Pape attempted to use DCWI's accumulated reputational capital to help ward off this negative image. Roosevelt Sykes, the president of Gimme Shelter, appeared in an advertisement for Dragonfly in which he pointed out how DCWI had helped provide shelter for more than 1,000 homeless people each night for the past 4 years. Carolyn Matthews, the disabled swimmer with the winning smile, appeared in an advertisement campaign in which she thanked Dragonfly and DCWI for making her dreams come true. However, the harder Pape and Fleming tried, the further the company plummeted.

Jacques Gendron's approach to the problem was very different. Within a week of arriving at DCWI Gendron visited Chief Windfield and the parents of the three boys who had committed suicide. Gendron asked Windfield if he could address the tribe. Chief Windfield responded that it would be an honour, saying, "No Chief or Elder from DCWI had ever come as a guest to Mighty Mountain tribe." That night, in an assembly in the recreation centre on Mighty Mountain, Jacques Gendron told the tribe about his vision.

First, he apologized for the manner in which DCWI had neglected the tribe. He pointed out that the Mighty Mountain glacier was the source of DCWI's good fortune, and that the tribe were the keepers of "The Water of Purity." They had to work together to assure that the death of Bobby Seal and his friends would not be for nothing, but would bring them together. Gendron asked the parents of Bobby Seal and his friends to rise. He asked, on behalf of DCWI, that they forgive them for their shortcoming.

The tribe clapped as each parent got up, and in a solemn voice, said "I do." Gendron thanked them all and asked to meet with the Band Council to discuss some of the ways in which DCWI and the tribe could heal their wounds. Chief Windfield invited Jacques Gendron to his house to get to know one another. Gendron spoke about his grandchildren, his cottage in the woods, and his love of hiking. Chief Windfield spoke of his grandchildren, the new smokehouse the tribe was building, and his fascination with opera. They parted, each satisfied that the other was trustworthy.

A month later, Jacques Gendron returned to meet with the Band Council. He invited the Council to come to DCWI's headquarters to meet its Board of Directors. In response to the Band Council's apprehensions, Chief Windfield said, "I am getting to know Mr. Gendron and I think he has wisdom. I recommend that we take him up on this opportunity."

When the Mighty Mountain Band Council arrived at DCWI, they were encouraged to wander about and speak with employees. The Council saw a workplace alive with purpose and commitment. Many employees expressed their sincere sympathies for Bobby Seal and his two friends. The Council was impressed; they felt they were involved with people who could be trusted. Later that day, Jacques Gendron introduced each member of the Board of Directors. Chief Windfield provided introductions to his Band Council. After seven hours of heart-to-heart discussion a rough plan of action was worked out. Twenty-five to thirty per cent of the jobs at DCWI's Mighty Mountain plant were to be filled by Native residents. A college fund would be set up for five young tribal members, funded by DCWI but operated by the Band Council. The Board of Directors unanimously agreed to place Chief Henry Windfield on the Board. The Band Council agreed to help Dragonfly present its deal with the Mighty Mountain tribe to the public. To commemorate the three young suicide victims, DCWI agreed to change its label to include the words, "Remember Bobby Seal." The Band Council agreed to help disseminate the company's new image, wherein the memory of Bobby Seal was to be presented as a testament to a future where big business and the Native community can help one another.

The new label hit the streets after three weeks of an advertisement campaign that highlighted the Mighty Mountain/DCWI agreement. Chief Windfield talked about the Bobby Seal College Fund as television cameras focused on Native workers walking into DCWI's Mighty Mountain plant. The Association of Groups for the Advancement of Native Rights liked the deal so much they offered to disseminate the new logo throughout their urban network. Within six months, the downward trajectory at DCWI was heading north. When the stock price hit $15.29 per share, Mr. Chew's advice was unequivocal: "DCWI has rid itself of its reputational hit; we expect a steady and perhaps not all that slow rise to about $21.00. DCWI is a buy."

QUESTIONS:

1. Using the "legitimacy thesis," discuss what Gordon Fleming did to jeopardize DCWI's reputation. Using the "reflection argument," discuss what Gordon Fleming did to jeopardize DCWI's reputation. Why did Gordon Fleming's rejoinder to Chief Henry Windfield miss the mark?

2. In your view, is Chief Henry Windfield's outrage at DCWI justified? If yes, why? If not, why not? Why, in your opinion, did the Mighty Mountain tribe blockade the road to the small DCWI plant at Mighty Mountain glacier?

3. What role did Roger Pilon's government report have in fanning the flames of the controversy? What role did the Association of Groups for the Advancement of Native Rights have in fanning the flames of the controversy? Why was Gordon Fleming's use of DCWI's accumulated reputational capital ineffective in dampening the growing controversy?

4. How did Jacques Gendron use the five-stage model of reputational capital differently than Gordon Fleming? Which, in your view, crystallized the corporate reputation as a large conglomerate with a heart? How did this crystallization open DCWI for attack by Chief Henry Windfield and the Mighty Mountain tribe?

5. Why, in your opinion, did Gordon Fleming not visit Chief Henry Windfield in the Mighty Mountain Territory? What did Jacques Gendron do during his visits to the Mighty Mountain tribe that earned their respect?

6. How did Jacques Gendron refocus the feedback tie between reputational capital in use (Stage 5) and DCWI's corporate identity (Stage 1) and DCWI's corporate image field (Stage 2)? Why is the fit better in Jacques Gendron's re-framing than was the case in Gordon Fleming's?

CASE 9-3 **The Diversity Debate at Blue Sky Personnel**

Kai Lundberg, an apparently healthy man, was found dead of a heart attack in the executive suite at Blue Sky Personnel. Lundberg was the founder and chief architect of the firm's growth over the past eighteen years. Under his direction, the temporary office assistance agency had become a world leader in providing office assistance and technical personnel to high-tech offices, military projects, and the medical community. With its headquarters in Canada, the firm had branches in forty-one countries and provided highly

trained personnel on short- or long-term contracts to a list of prominent businesses. Blue
Sky's reputation was legendary, with its
motto, "We provide you with ability and we
guarantee this." Dissatisfied clients were always reimbursed.

In the midst of mourning Kai Lundberg's
unexpected death, the Board of Directors
sought to replace their charismatic leader.
Within two months, and after receiving 842
serious applications, a shortlist of 18 was
created. The executive search company,
Brock and Viger, was hired to visit those
shortlisted, talk to their colleagues, verify
their resumes, and present an overview to
the Board. At the end of the process, two
excellent candidates remained—Heather
Barkley and Ken Habibi. Both were in their
late forties, energetic, and had executive experience and excellent industry connections.
Heather Barkley had founded and operated
Technical Assistance Personnel, which Blue
Sky had always found to be a top-notch
competitor. Barkley's company had been
acquired by Micro-Digital Computers and
been made the centre of their new personnel
development program. Ken Habibi was currently vice president of Blue Sky's main
rival regarding military projects. Expert
Systems Manpower was not fully developed
in either private sector high-tech industries
or the medical community. Within the industry, Habibi was known as an excellent
administrator and a knowledgeable player
in backroom deals.

In the extensive interviews that followed,
it became clear that there was one big difference between the candidates. They took
very different directions in their proposals
vis-à-vis what they would do to prepare Blue
Sky Personnel for the future. Barkley believed that Blue Sky Personnel was out of
touch with the changes occurring in the different societies in which the firm operated.
She handed out a detailed set of charts and
diagrams to illustrate how in France, for ex-

ample, the firm employed a ratio of fourteen men to every woman—and these
women functioned in relatively low-paying
clerical jobs. Of the men hired by Blue Sky's
French operation, only five per cent were
of North African descent. Bringing the discussion closer to home, Barkley pointed out
that in Canada Blue Sky Personnel hired
only one woman for every nine men and, as
in France, these women were at the lower
end of the pay scale. Of the male employees,
only one in eighteen was French Canadian.

Several board members started fidget-
ing with their papers until Barkley said, "I
am not a radical feminist or a bleeding heart
liberal. I am a hard-nosed business person."
She demonstrated that in those countries
where Blue Sky Personnel's profile fit the
profile of society at large, profits were
roughly twelve per cent higher than in countries where the profiles were out of whack.
In her opinion, this was no spurious correlation. Establishing workplace diversity targets in which Blue Sky Personnel moved
towards society's changing profiles made
good sense, because only then were workers
in touch with the changing needs of clients.
This strategy, insisted Barkley, was not a
compromise of talent. Blue Sky Personnel
would still look for the very best and brightest, as revealed in objective tests. They
would hire and promote on the basis of
merit. But only by establishing and meeting workplace diversity targets would Blue
Sky Personnel retain its competitive edge
in the international market. With her conclusion, the Board broke into applause.
Many felt they had their future CEO.

Three days later, Ken Habibi faced the
board. Habibi argued that what Blue Sky
Personnel was doing now, it must simply do
better. Habibi pointed out Blue Sky
Personnel's successful history of identifying
elite workers in those societies in which they
did business and bringing them into the fold.
Elite workers were not necessarily those who

scored highest on exams or who came first in their class. They were men with connections, breeding, and class. They were leaders. Habibi argued that Blue Sky Personnel had become a leader in its field by hiring leaders and treating them fairly. Blue Sky Personnel had not joined in the manpower rental of secretaries and domestics and retail salesgirls, but had stayed with the rental of technical analysts, special project engineers, scientists, and systems analysts. Habibi suggested that Blue Sky Personnel rise to the future by beginning to gather personnel with the skills to work on cyberspace projects, establish secure economic transactions for Web commerce, and deal with the opportunities of virtual reality. Blue Sky's clientele, insisted Habibi, want their elite manpower to help guide them through the thicket of new technologies. The Board broke into applause. Many felt they had their future CEO.

QUESTIONS:

1. From your point of view, which of the two candidates do you think the Board will hire? Why? How do Heather Barkley and Ken Habibi use the "reflection argument" to come to different conclusions? Whose use of the reflection argument is more elitist? Why?

2. Take the pro-diversity position of Heather Barkley and attempt to show how increasing workplace diversity at Blue Sky Personnel would increase:

   (a) organizational learning

   (b) systems flexibility

   (c) satisfaction with customer service

3. Take the anti-diversity position of Heather Barkley and attempt to show how increasing workplace diversity at Blue Sky Personnel would:

   (a) increase the incidence of conflict among and between workers

   (b) increase the incidence of external regulation by government

   (c) result in greater overall costs

4. If Ken Habibi succeeds Kai Lundberg as the CEO of Blue Sky Personnel, what ethical quandaries do you see arising from each of the following?

   (a) Ken Habibi's past association with military projects

   (b) minority groups

   (c) third world nationalists

5. If Heather Barkley succeeds Kai Lundberg as CEO of Blue Sky Personnel, what problems do you think she is likely to experience in implementing a diversity program? What, in your view, will make for an effective diversity program at Blue Sky Personnel?

6. Is Ken Habibi's fascination with getting Blue Sky Personnel to focus on new technologies incompatible with Heather Barkley's focus on workplace diversity? If yes, why? If not, why not? If Heather Barkley were to implement workplace diversity initiatives at Blue Sky Personnel, should she, in your opinion, use the same program for each of the three client groups (high-tech industries, military projects, medical communities), or try to tailor the diversity programs to suit the clientele?

ENCOUNTERS WITH TECHNOLOGY: ETHICS AND CHANGE

Chapter 10

Technology = change. The faster the pace of technological advancement, the faster the pace of business. Indeed, technology is changing from mainframes in the seventies, to stand alone PCs in the 1980's, to networks of servers in the 1990's. Today we are poised to enter a new age, an age where business, like the PCs they connect together, form cooperative, open networks of skill sets. Essentially we are steadily moving from an era of hierarchical organizations where information must find its way down a labyrinth of special interest and power cliques to a more networked structure where information is the only master.

Jessica Keyes
Technology Trendlines (1995)

What are the ethics to be in a business world where—if Jessica Keyes is correct—change is ubiquitous, information is central, and skill sets must be updated constantly to master the code or program at the heart of this technologically-wired world? To begin to answer this question, let me relate a story told by a colleague over dinner some weeks ago. The tale may be true, or perhaps it is simply an apocryphal dinner-party anecdote for the millennium.

During my colleague's brief trip to Barcelona to discuss her recent work on the "virtual organization" and its applications to the international financial service industry, she became aware of the sort of ethical issue she suspected would become more apparent as we begin to employ smart machines in human or robotic form. With an eye to promoting his upscale eatery, a local restaurateur had replaced all his busboys—those who stack dishes, bring water, and set the tables—with state-of-the-art robots. Initially the entrepreneur's plan had gone as expected; patrons lined up not simply to eat his food, but to catch a glimpse of the future. All this was brought to a rather sharp halt, sighed my colleague, when a robot, replacing a stainless steel steak knife, inadvertently plunged the utensil deep into the ribcage of a diner.

Veracity aside, the story was sufficiently plausible to evoke a lively debate. One group, seeing technology as a liberating tool and a promising means of disburdening our species of future discomfort, lamented the plight of the injured patron, but painted both him and the entrepreneur as heroes in an ongoing experiment. However, the philosopher at our table, recognizing the potential threat made by technology, framed the event as an issue of product safety. In her view, people who own and seek to profit from technology (the restaurateur), those who license potentially harmful technology (the government or professional association), and those who create it (the manufacturer) ought—with varying degrees of immediacy—to be held responsible for the diner's injury.

After a few bottles of wine, two other ways of framing the ethics of technology emerged. A consultant made the point that technology is neither a "promise" nor a "threat," but an "instrument of power." Technology, especially new technology, calls forward the need for new experts and, in time, positions of power for individuals, groups, and organizations who possess or control it. This led to the recognition that our debate over technology as a promise or a threat went beyond the injured diner in Barcelona to include the shape of the world we are creating. Technology is a "portal to a new age." As such, it provides both clues to our discontent with the world as we find it, and intimations of the good world that we believe can be created.

For most of us, the technology encounter is happening at each and every moment of our lives. We live in what Marshall McLuhan called the "technological environment" (1964), wherein technology is ubiquitous. It is the application of organized knowledge to practical tasks by ordered systems of people and machines. Technology is not only the machines or devices we use to make our lives easier, but also the ideas and systematic practices or techniques developed to get things done. It is difficult for most of us to get a sense of technology because our very sense of existence is shaped by our continuous reaction with it. Think of it—the pencil, Librium, polyester, rollerblades, calculus, computers, information retrieval systems, voice mail, the alphabet, sampling procedures—all are instances of technology.

The purpose of this chapter is twofold. The first is to examine more closely the four prevailing ways of framing technology in postmodernity. Figure 10.1 outlines the organizational and ethical implications of framing technology as (1) a promise, (2) a threat, (3) an instrument of power, and (4) a portal to a new age. The second purpose is to enlarge upon the idea of technology as a portal to the new age, in order to speculate about the following: (1) the ideological battles over appropriate technology and organizational structure; (2) the ethics of the virtual organization and virtual reality; and (3) the future of business ethics in the technological environment.

FIGURE 10-1 Four Technological Frameworks: Organizational and Ethical Implications

Framework	Basic Premises	Organizational Implications	Ethical Implications
Technology as a Promise	In this framework, technology is associated with the idea of progress. Technology lightens the load. It disburdens. It democratizes social and political life.	Technology is central to all applications of rationality, including organizations. It solves problems. High-tech organizations seek to use technology as a competitive advantage.	Ethics is a means of stabilizing and examining how to best use, apply, and distribute the harms and benefits that result from societal experimentation with technology.
Technology as a Threat	In this framework, technology is associated with anxiety and a loss of control. Technology speeds things up. It de-skills. It makes people dependent.	Technology is a problem in organizations. It must be updated constantly. It requires that people dumb down in the workplace. It breaks down.	Ethics unmasks and reveals the limits of technology. It is one means of limiting the abuses that can result from technology.
Technology as an Instrument of Power	In this framework, technology is associated with power and the creation of privilege. He or she who controls technology wins power. Technology itself is neutral.	Technology is a source of power in organizations. Those in the organization who control it are central. They are not easily substituted by others.	Ethics is a means of keeping the uses of technology fair so that the powerful who control the technology do not exploit those who are subservient to it.
Technology as a Portal to a New Age	In this framework, technology is associated with massive societal, political, and economic change. Some see the new age optimistically; others see it pessimistically. Both optimists and pessimists agree that the new age presents challenges.	New organizational structures like the "virtual organization" are speculated to require a totally new managerial skill set. Technology is the future of organizations.	Ethics is a means of linking the values of the past with the newly-emerging and imminent virtual realities. Ethics emphasizes enlightened choices. It provides a vocabulary to humanize the technological options that await us.

TECHNOLOGY AS A PROMISE

In his work, "The Impact of Technology on Ethical Decision Making," Robert Nisbet makes the point that "technology is the application of rational principles to the control or re-ordering of space, matter, and human beings" (1971:41). It is a powerful tool that—if used wisely and well—represents our species' best chance to progress and flourish. Other species can fly, run more swiftly, and have greater physical strength than us. However, in harnessing our intellect to applied systems of control—indeed, in re-ordering nature, including human nature—we have developed devices with which we can fly, move at speeds that surpass the leopard, and act with the grip and strength of the elephant. Without these devices we are a species with a rather limited adaptive capacity.

Those who frame technology as a promise (Ciborra, 1993; Kranzeberg, 1977; McCorduck, 1985; Michie, 1985; Rouse, 1993; Stokes, 1991) build upon this logic and retain a general optimism regarding the benefits to be accrued by continually improving upon technology. On the whole, within this perspective, technology is an enabler. It disburdens. In *Technology and the Character of Contemporary Life* (1984), Albert Borgmann links the disburdening qualities in the promise of technology to a gradual elimination of scarcity (in the economist's sense) and thereby to a life of increasing fulfillment, physical well-being, and eventual liberation from the irksome aspects of daily life. Bernard Gendron, in *Technology and the Human Condition*, writes that utopian technology advocates "believe that it [the application of technology] will eliminate scarcity and disease, that it will significantly improve communication and education, and it will undermine the environmental conditions that reinforce aggression, prejudice, sectarianism, nationalism, oppression, and exploitation" (1977:3).

Figure 10.2 provides an overview of the promises of technology for society as a whole and for the organization within society. The former illustrates the rather optimistic values girding this view of technology; at the organizational level we see its implications as applied in the workplace. The logic of seeing technology as a promise is easy to assimilate since it fits our daily, often unthinking, reliance on technology. Those of us who wear corrective lenses to improve our vision, or use a computer to aid our work, understand how technology makes life easier. This understanding is intuitive and often unconscious. Even those who see technology as a threat and a source of many social ills will adjust the thermostat when cold and turn on the lights when entering a darkened room.

The manifest nature of certain enabling aspects of technology ought not to detract from the fact that this belief in the promise of technology is probably the strongest and most ubiquitous "faith" expressed by postmodern citizens. Technology demands faith because its payoff rests in the future, a future that can be fully achieved only by increasing our reliance on and raising our investment in the promise of technology. At the societal level, technology and those who act as its agents promise the following: (1) progress; (2) dignity; (3) discovery; (4) egalitarianism; and (5) convergence. The promise is subtle and sophisticated. On the one hand, it is embodied in the existent devices, ideas, and orderly systems of practice that already we are using to make our lives easier; on the other hand, it tantalizes the imagination with new possibilities, still easier ways of fulfilling our desires, and worlds which will soon be here (Dyson, 1997). The historian, Daniel J. Boorstin, in *The Republic of Technology: Reflections on Our Future Community* (1978), explores how technology creates "enthusiasm irreversibility"—a sense of being buoyed up and carried onward by a series of waves of accumulating technology.

FIGURE 10-2 Technology as a Promise: Five Societal and Organizational Premises

Societal Premises

Progress: Technology "disburdens." It leads to a reduction of hardship and misery through the production of material wealth and well-being. It accelerates material production.

Dignity: Technology elevates the human soul. It helps to release humans from the most trying forms of toil. It liberates humans from many dreaded diseases. It provides time for worship, contemplation, and self-realization.

Discovery: Technology stimulates the search for new technology. It provides time and incentives for the pursuit of novelty. It enhances and supports the break with tradition. It places incentives on the search for the new and better.

Egalitarianism: Technology permits, in time, greater access of the masses to what was once the domain of the elites. Technology applied to mass markets democratizes. It provides common access to goods, services, and ideas.

Convergence: Technology standardizes. Over time, this standardization creates the removal of irksome differences. It increases efficiency and results in the sharing of a common material culture among different nation states and societies.

Organizational Premises

Problem Solver: Technology focuses, grounds, and improves human problem solving. Technology fixes. Technological fixes are quick, codifiable, easily transmitted to others.

Task Enrichment: Technology, particularly high technology, empowers. It facilitates the movement of decision power down the hierarchy. It facilitates the use of individuals' discretion on the job. It provides greater autonomy to individuals.

Innovation: Technology accelerates the ability of the organization to develop novel products, organizational responses, and techniques. Technology bolsters research and development.

Adaptation: Technology permits the organization to respond to challenges with novel structures. It creates new responses to clients and other stakeholders by permitting greater decentralization and quicker response.

Control: Technology heightens the ability of the organization to reduce uncertainty. Technology helps to create order, hold people and departments accountable, and measure deviations from a desired state of affairs.

The idea of progress (Burgen *et al.*, 1997; Gastil, 1993) embodies this idealization of the rewards to be reaped from a continued investment in technology and the research and development that accompany it. Science is believed to be the theory that girds and gives rise to the practices embodied in technology. Those who see technology as a prime mover in the historical conception of progress see it also as the building block for the betterment of the human species (Estes, 1988; Owen, 1974). Technology amplifies human productive efforts, creating efficiencies and economies of scale that, when managed ably, generate material wealth and well-being. In fact, technology raises standards of living, helps reduce debilitating illnesses, enhances leisure time, and generally improves the quality of life of those who have access to it. What ties technology to progress is not merely its apparent benefits, but its potential power to ameliorate. Technology, like science, claims to be self-reflexive. Both improve with age. Science improves itself by eliminating error and developing more rigorous tests; technology improves itself by applying science and by continually having to meet the test of increasingly competitive and demanding markets.

At the organizational level, the general promise of technology is focused on its ability to enhance the organization's capacity to solve problems (Couger, 1995; Gaither, 1990; Leonard-Barton, 1995). Computer-aided decision-making programs (Schutzer, 1991; Zahedi, 1993), technology-based information systems (Alter, 1996; Checkland and Holwell, 1998), and socio-technical systems linking workers to machines used in the production process (Passmore, 1988; Taylor, 1993) now flourish. Technology enhances. It fixes. The technological fix is particularly attractive in organizational contexts as it is codifiable, easily transmitted to others, and generates results. When and if the results are not as anticipated, the technology can be altered. When the results are in line with expectations, technology enables reliable, repetitive success.

Both the promise of progress at the societal level and the promise of problem solving at the organizational level hold implications for those interested in confronting moral worlds. Business ethics reminds us that progress at any cost is unacceptable. The discipline of business ethics poses the question of values and, in this instance, asks us to formulate a direction for progress. It insists, for example, that progress achieved by enslaving and exploiting others is very different from the idea of progress that is sought by providing others with autonomy. At the organizational level, business ethics adds the question of values to the seemingly objective notion of a "technological fix." Two sorts of value-laden questions are asked. The first looks at the "problem-free" aftermath of technology use. Do problem-solving technologies solve the problems in question, or do they merely transfer the problems to others, or delay our need to deal with them? The second asks about the possible interaction between the technology and its users in the problem-solving process. Is the "fix" embedded in the technology injurious to its users? Does it create a dependency? Does it, over time, "dumb down" its users?

Business ethics imposes a context and insists on a value system in making sense of the promises of technology. When we turn to the second promise of technology—dignity at the societal level and task enrichment at the organizational level—we are prepared to probe the issues and ask under what conditions these premises hold true. The promise that technology elevates the soul by releasing humans from trying forms of toil is true within an enlightened liberal conception of dignity (Stetson, 1998). This posits that humans, when provided with leisure and more comfortable surroundings, will use this for contemplation, worship, self-realization, and discovery, all of which build dignity (Harris, 1997). This celebration of technology is rooted in a rather uplifting model of human beings, who are presumed to employ technology in ways that are beneficial to both the self and the wider community. It is a model that ignores the possibility that humans will accelerate their use of technology to menace and devastate others within the context of war, or to create efficient means of mass murder, genocide, and destruction (Burleigh, 1997; Fasching, 1993).

At the organizational level, the promise of dignity is rooted in a literature that sees technology as enriching the workplace and, more specifically, the task (Fink, 1992; Taylor, 1980; Yorks and Whitset, 1989). It is clear that empowerment (Gould *et al.*, 1997; McLagen and Nel, 1995)—the shifting of significant decision-making power downwards within the hierarchy—can be assisted by the new information technologies (Turban *et al.*, 1996). This is particularly so when the technology increases the discretion, autonomy, and responsibilities of the user. This promise of task enrichment must be contextualized by consulting those whose jobs and workplaces ostensibly are being enriched. Moreover, efforts to assess the job satisfaction of employees before and after the introduction of new "task enriching" and empowering technology must be examined. We cannot move from the good intentions of champions of technology to the assumption that the consequences are always equally good.

The third promise of technology at the societal level is that it will stimulate the discovery and/or invention of new technology (Bresnahan and Gordon, 1997; Fox, 1996; Norman, 1993); at the organizational level, it is the promise of innovation and creativity (Blackwell, 1991, Plsek, 1997; Rhodes and Wield, 1994; Voyer and Ryon, 1994). Both promises speak to technology's ability to guide us into the future with greater certainty and speed than without it. As investment in technology increases, so too does the curiosity of those seeking ample rewards for their efforts. As reliance upon technology increases, people use it to mediate between and among existing technologies to repair, modify, and upgrade technology. The spread of technology is facilitated as prices lower, users come into contact with non-users, and large pools of older technology become accessible.

Implicit in both notions—discovery and innovation—is the insistence that traditional (or what in postmodern society we call "low-tech") is distinguished from high-tech (Diwan and Chakraborty, 1991; Peterson, 1993; Umseem, 1986). Low-tech refers to routines and devices that have been assimilated within the use pattern of the society or organization. High-tech refers to novel, still exploratory technologies that are believed to have an open-ended future. The ballpoint pen is low-tech; the computer is high-tech. The promises of discovery and innovation speak to a state of mindfulness that is necessary when working and living with high technology. High-tech or cutting-edge technologies symbolize and embody a break with tradition. They promise a future of faster, better, and more, and they excite and accelerate what technology utopians call the "pursuit of excellence."

Business ethics contextualizes discovery and innovation by forcing a recognition that novelty for the sake of novelty, or faster for the sake of faster, are ethically problematic justifications. In the midst of the fascinating emotions that accompany the experience of rigorous competition, we must be reminded that novelty and speed can lead down some very dismal roads. Technology must not be thought of as the accelerator pedal and ethics as the brake pedal, but that ethics serves as our conscience and technology as our continuing search for gratification.

The advocates of utopian technology respond to the notion that technology is a force that has a conscience by pointing out how, over time and at the societal level, the proliferation of technological improvements creates greater equality and the democratization of information (Brown, 1988; Diamond, 1997; McLean, 1989). At the organizational level, the proponents of technology (Meindl *et al.*, 1996; Merry, 1995; Zammuto, 1982) argue that it permits greater access by the masses to what once was solely the domain of the elite. This occurs in the world of material goods and, increasingly, the world of information and ideas.

Egalitarianism is enhanced in the world of goods by applying techniques of mass production (Biggs, 1996; Pine and Davis, 1993) and automation (Burns, 1993; Mody and Wheeler, 1990) to the production process itself. In the world of information and ideas, the revolution in information technology—Internet, satellites, cable—has meant that information about the world, conjectures by the finest minds, and data of all sorts increasingly are available in even the most remote locations and to those who for centuries remained unaware of events outside their local communities.

At the organizational level, notions of both the increasing capacity and greater availability of information (including the possible lowering of prices to consumers) are tied to the promise of reducing the vulnerability of organizations. As with all promises of technology discussed here, this explicitly asserts that greater investment in new and appropriate organizational technology ultimately will prove beneficial. Due to their increased and more flexible production processes, their ability to lower prices when required and to modify their technologies when appropriate, organizations will be in a far better position to compete (Tyson, 1997) and survive the dynamics of uncertain markets. Managers in organizational environments marked by rapid and unpredictable change can improve their success rates when they use state-of-the-art information technology and train their personnel to apply it properly. The idea that uncertainty in business can be reduced by access to and use of continually improving technologies has become a major feature in the turn-of-the-century marketing campaigns of computer companies.

Business ethics poses the question of how technology alters power in human systems. The assumption that—given time—power goes to the people, is treated less as a truism than a particular theory of history—a theory that tacitly equates progress with democracy. But in contextualizing the promise of greater equality in the works of technological utopians, ethicists ask whether technology can be employed to deny access, to buttress the powers of the existent elite, and to disenfranchise those who seek status and voice. The use of technology to foster inequalities addresses the contemporary ethics of the wealthy employing private police armed with state-of-the-art technology to assure that wealth—no matter how it was attained—remains with its "rightful" owners. At the organizational level, business ethicists remind us that it is not merely the use of technology to help the organization adapt that is in question, but the *fair* use of this technology. Business ethicists ask us to probe the use of polygraphs, drug testing, and hidden surveillance cameras on employees to reduce organizational problems. If the technology in question is useful, and if using it helps the organization diminish its uncertainty but at the same time infringes upon the freedoms of its members, should it be entertained?

The last of the five promises of technology is the belief that it reduces irksome differences that divide society; indeed, that technology facilitates convergence (Baumol *et al.*, 1994; Inkeles, 1998; Kerr, 1983; Leer, 1996; Mowlana, 1996). At the organizational level, technology is promised to enhance control (Harrington, 1991; Lorin, 1995; Stacey, 1991; Wickens, 1995). Convergence is the implicit assumption used by most forecasters to predict that we are moving towards a global village. Technology standardizes. The use of shared weights and measures, computer software, and modes of transport mean that, given time, the differences that mark societies disappear. A strong form of technological determinism would insist that this is inevitable; a weak form, which prevails in most versions of contemporary technological utopias, insists that material culture converges. Political, social, and economic reactions of local communities to this convergence are far less predictable. The promise in the idea of convergence rests, as in the idea of "globalization," in the increased sharing of material culture. A new age of efficiency, prosperity and cooperation is at hand.

The optimism surrounding convergence at the level of inter-societal exchanges is bolstered by a belief that, at the organizational level, technology enhances control. Or, put otherwise, technology reduces the likelihood of things getting out of control. Due to modern technology we are assured that stock markets today will prevent us from the likes of the stock sell-off that led to the Depression. Technology enhances our ability to move towards convergence, engage in mass exercises of organization, and yet still stay under control. Technology stimulates accountability. It provides reliable feedback on dangerous deviations from the desired state of affairs, it helps eliminate uncertainty, and creates the order, reliability, and standardization upon which good managers flourish.

From an ethics perspective, both convergence at the societal level and control at the organizational level are placed into context by querying their desirable threshholds. It seems that both convergence and control can turn nasty if pursued beyond a certain point. When one reads dystopian novels such as George Orwell's *1984: A Novel* (1961) or Aldous Huxley's *Brave New World* (1946), one realizes that both convergence and control can be overdone. Convergence, when pushed beyond the threshold, can lead to a woeful homogeneity and a crushing loss of local identity; control, when pushed beyond the threshold, can annihilate spontaneity and diminish personal freedom.

As foreshadowed in the works of Orwell and Huxley, technology can be seen as having a dark side. Let us now turn to a view of technology as a menace and a threat, a view that questions technology as a problem solver and the road to progress. It is lodged in a perspective that is ushering in what Leften Stavrianos (1976) calls the "coming dark age," Stephen Hill (1989) sees as "the tragedy of technology," and Ernest Brown laments in *Futile Progress: Technology's Empty Promise* (1995).

TECHNOLOGY AS A THREAT AND MENACE

My family was stunned. We had moved to Vancouver from Toronto and taken temporary rental accommodation on the twenty-second floor of a high-rise building with state-of-the-art conveniences and a grand view of Burrard Inlet. Within the first week of our tenancy, the electricity in our area of the city "went down" for two days, thanks to the unhappy coincidence of a freak storm and the subsequent damage to a key generator that required a part that had to be shipped from Montreal. Had you told me—as I wheezed my way up twenty-two flights of stairs while carrying groceries—that technology was a promise, I would have muttered something like, "Yeah, a very menacing and precarious promise." A similar utterance is still, no doubt, on the lips of an acquaintance whose birth defects were caused by his mother's innocent desire to subdue morning sickness by taking an anti-nausea pill called thalidomide.

While the promise of technology is rooted in the belief that applied rationality and technology are the preferred evolutionary strategies of our species, as we saw in Chapter 8 in our discussion of radical environmentalism, the promise wears thin when the machine is believed to be destroying the garden. From a rational perspective, when calculations conclude that the costs of technology far outstrip the benefits, technology may be one very large error (Ellul, 1964, 1980, 1990; Gimpel, 1995; Ramo, 1983; Scorer, 1977; Woodward, 1980). The technological naysayers see the optimists as blinded by their faith, much as an earlier age of faith entailed unquestioning religious conviction. They argue that the new "smart" or high-tech devices, ideas, and techniques must not be accepted on the basis of their promises, but should be held up for serious probing and questioning (Brown and Hutchings, 1972; Glendinning, 1990; Sassower, 1997).

Within these two rational orientations, two quite different intellectual temperaments characterize technological naysayers. The postmodern Luddites (Ezrahi *et al.*, 1994; Papworth, 1995; Roszak, 1994; Steffen, 1993; Vacca, 1973) see technology as a force that must be smashed. There are no ifs, buts, or maybes in this view. Technology is an albatross. It dehumanizes and demoralizes. It burdens. It creates waste, obsolescence, and pollution, and leaves in its wake very little—if any—real privacy or dignity. Typically the postmodern Luddite hails from or has experienced an urban environment plagued by massive problems—congested highways, high cancer rates, polluted air, sick buildings, waste—despite state-of-the-art technological devices. The postmodern Luddite identifies technology as the force responsible for his or her feeling that things are out of control and, worse, that this state of affairs is accelerating at a rapid rate. On the other hand, the technological skeptics (Barbour, 1993; Burke and Ornstein, 1995; Giarini and Louberge, 1978; Salomon and Lebeau, 1993; Thomas, 1994), who also see technology as a threat and menace, rather than smash it, insist that we resist technology except when it proves itself. The technological skeptics claim that we must sift slowly through the heap of offerings, being more selective and sparing in our technological adoptions. Technology should only be brought into our lives when it proves to be user-friendly, lowers dependence upon experts and centralized authority, enhances curiosity and playfulness, can be easily repaired, and is beneficial to the natural environment.

The postmodern Luddites' negative attitude towards the promise of technology can be framed in three separate but interrelated manners. In the first, we can think of postmodern Luddites as nostalgic for an earlier, less technology-dependent age. In the second, we can think of them as arguing a strong form of humanism in which technology is seen as detracting from, rather than adding to, the attainment of our potential. In the third, we can consider them as cautionary seers who see in our rush into the future a foreboding doom. The technological skeptics, on the other hand, seem to make a distinction between technology and the promise of technology. Just as we remain skeptical when we hear the word "new" used to hype a product, so too the technological skeptics remain aloof upon hearing the promise of technology. To the technological skeptics, technology should be assimilated only when it has proven itself.

Technological utopians are outraged by postmodern Luddites, arguing that they simply are unable to grow and inculcate the new ideas and techniques necessary in this age of pervasive technology. They are perceived as nostalgic and somewhat romantic in their desire to return to an earlier age—not one without technology, but an age with technologies that are fully familiar and do not challenge their conceptions. On the other hand, the technological skeptics—in the eyes of the utopians—seem to want all the benefits of technology, but are unwilling to take the risks. Their "slow down" mentality is seen as implicitly stifling the robust experimental stage of technology development by calling for greater regulations and longer testing times, including more time between the invention of technologies and their diffusion to the public. From the vantage of the technological utopians, the skeptics would treat all technologies as if they were to undergo the scrutiny we now expect of innovations in the pharmaceutical industry.

Figure 10.3 provides an overview of the technological naysayers' premises. In this figure, the views of the technological skeptics and the postmodern Luddites are combined, and the emphasis locates how these views of technology as a threat make sense at both the level of society as a whole and at the level of the organization. Compare Figures 10.2 and 10.3 for an overview of the difference between those who view technology as a promise and those who see it as a threat.

The technological naysayers should not be dismissed by business ethicists. Their values are rooted in a very different model of the person than that employed by the technological utopians. The naysayers want us to face the future as self-reliantly as we are able. We cannot, they argue, continue to misuse and abuse the planet's resources in the name of a di-

FIGURE 10-3 Technology as a Threat: Five Societal and Organizational Premises

Societal Premises

Illusion of Progress: Technology creates degeneration and regression. Rather than increasing the quality of life on the planet, it threatens the ecosystem, creates dependency, fosters inequality, and reduces flexibility.

Disenchantment: Technology standardizes and rationalizes. It produces conformity and reduces the very differences that lead to curiosity. Technology de-spiritualizes. It secularizes and reduces the importance of the sacred in society.

Dependence: Technology not only reduces curiosity, but systems in society become dependent on it. When technology "goes down," the system grinds to a halt. This dependence creates vulnerability and reduces flexible options.

Elitism: Technology in society, far from fostering egalitarianism, actually creates elitism. The new technologies serve as barriers to entry to the new world of power for the poor and voiceless.

Homogeneity: Technology creates much more divergence than convergence in society. The rich get richer; the powerful get more powerful. Multinational firms benefit, but few of the benefits are passed on to third world citizens.

Organizational Premises

Problem Maker: Technology is intended as a solution, but inevitably causes problems. Technology breaks down. It creates obsolescence. Technology creates externalities like pollution and increases the need of the organization to expand.

De-Skilling: Technology reduces work to a series of repetitive activities. The new smart technology actually dumbs down its users. Rather than enrich tasks, technology dilutes them. People at work are increasingly programmed.

Quick Fixes: Technology is relied on to pull people out of problems and extricate them from danger. Because of this belief, organizations often rely on a technical quick fix rather than dealing with problems as they appear.

Increased Vulnerability: Technology often provides organizations with confidence in their abilities to adapt, but actually, by placing all their eggs in one technological basket, they increase their vulnerability.

Illusion of Control: Technology can, and often does, get out of control, resulting in nuclear meltdowns, industrial accidents, train collisions, genetic aberrations, and birth defects. Technology, when it goes out of control, is more than just human error.

rection we insist is the correct one. Progress is neither inevitable, nor is it captured by making humans more comfortable (Ferrarotti, 1985). We are enveloped in what Ian Reinecke (1984) calls "the electronic illusion," a belief that if we become masters of our technology, we shall, in fact, master our destiny. This, insist the naysayers, is far from true. Technology is not a simple solution; it is also the source of complex, deep, and pervasive problems. Michael Shallis (1984) calls the total immersion in the god-like status of the smart machine a form of "silicon idolatry." This reliance breeds a false sense of confidence. Herbert Schiller (1996) sees the information highway as nothing but a feeding frenzy that lends strength to the emergence of an even stronger and all-watchful "big brother," and greater inequality between the information-rich and those without access to the highway. David Shenk (1997) sees the new information technologies as generating a "data smog," which, far from helping us, drowns us in an information glut.

There is a conspiratorial edge to the technological naysayers' orientation. Things are not what they seem; surface promises must be examined thoroughly. Indeed, when placed at the centre of society, technology disenchants (Germain, 1993; Phelan, 1980). Rather than spiritually uplifting our species, technology standardizes and rationalizes. In the pursuit of the comfortable, we lose sight of the sacred (Mander, 1991; Taitte, 1987). We become dependent not only on the technology itself, but on a cabal of technologically-experienced users and owners (including those who provide access and license technology). As is made clear in Figure 10.3, technology fosters neither egalitarianism nor personal freedom. Technology ushers in waves of new technical elites (Clarke, 1981; Gould, 1966; James, 1996), whose aim is to gain personal wealth, accrue status and power, and establish a legitimate basis for their privilege in society as a whole. This global technical elite is no new manifestation of a more enlightened elitism. Far from being a force for worldwide unity and convergence, the global technical elite seeks to divide and conquer. This is a highly homogeneous group when it comes to social, political, and moral values, and those within it use their access to and control of technology to exclude those who they perceive as a threat.

This picture of a self-serving technical elite flies in the face of the image served up by the technological utopians, of a society with the democratizing force of technology at its centre. The naysayers turn this picture upside down, portraying a world that is being stripped slowly and irreversibly of its ethical core, with its notions of dignity, justice, and respect for the other. The commercialization and commodification of organ transplant banks, the more effective use of biological agents and new viruses in warfare, the cloning of animal life, the surreptitious employment of information technology to construct data banks and profiles of citizen consumers, or the use of the Internet and information highway to disseminate pornography hardly refer to a world made more just or ethically sensitive. The naysayers claim that technology accelerates our ethical quandaries. New technologies introduce new ways to violate trust, exploit, derogate, and closely while unobtrusively monitor others.

This dark side of our species, insist the technological naysayers, does not quietly disappear when we move from plunging a sword into the belly of our enemy to detonating a nuclear device or unleashing lethal air- or water-borne bacteria. The hard work of ethics rests not in technical engineering, but in enhancing opportunities for humans to better understand the direct impact of their actions upon the world. Within organizations, technology is a force for removing direct contact. It distances and speeds things up. It is a problem maker. Technology breaks down. It accelerates obsolescence. It increases the probability of large-scale industrial accidents. It reduces humans to numbers in the name of enhanced efficiency. It often creates unintended consequences for the health of users, latent problems that are difficult to assess at the time of usage. Technology is costly to acquire, and once it becomes the industry standard, barriers to new entrants become apparent. Technology must be changed with some frequency, but once one commits to technology, it is difficult to reverse one's commitment. It is only possible to alter the technology in which one elects to invest one's time, capital, and energy.

Technology in organizations "de-skills" (Crompton and Jones, 1984; Myles, 1987; Osterman, 1996; Wood, 1982). The technological naysayers insist that technology reduces work to a series of somewhat repetitive actions or programmed ideas. The new smart technology is vested in devices, techniques, and programmed ideas that recalibrate themselves as more information becomes available. But as technology gets smarter, so to speak, people who use it or rely on it become more dependent and less likely to think for or by themselves. De-skilling occurs when work becomes simplified, or reduced to what John W. Collis (1998) labels one of the seven fatal management sins—the belief in a simplistic fix. In organizations, technology lends itself to the belief that it is possible to engage in a quick fix (Kilmann, 1989). As organizations rely more and more on allegedly improved technologies, they become more complex. Paradoxically, tasks become simplified, but organizational structures become more complex. Quick fixes using technology can be applied to the task easily and well. This often gives managers the illusion that they are in control of the organizational structure as a whole. However, the technological naysayers not only insist that they are not in control, but that managers are often unaware of the degree to which their organizations are out of control.

The ethical point made by technological naysayers echoes throughout the business and society orientation to business ethics. Organizations that accomplish their goals—making profits, healing the diseased, providing security for citizens—cannot simply assume that achieving their goals—made all that more possible by technology—can be done at the expense of ethical principles. Using productive technology that causes repetitive strain injury (Pecina and Bojanic, 1993), or that jeopardizes salmon streams through the release of industrial toxins, may enhance the organization's probability of achieving its narrowly-defined goals, but it does little to enhance its claim of being ethical. Being ethical requires being responsible not only for the benefits that accrue as a consequence of using technology, but for the costs as well.

Unlike either the utopians—who see only the promise of technology—or the naysayers—whose view is limited to its threats—the "power analysts" see technology as an instrument of power (see Figure 10.4). To the power analysts, technology alters influence and structures, and results both in power accruing to specific groups, and being taken from or denied to others.

TECHNOLOGY AS AN INSTRUMENT OF POWER

It was the summer of 1966, a year before Expo was to triumph in my hometown of Montreal. Employment opportunities were so good that already I had saved enough money for my university tuition, with time left over to see some of the world. Eighteen years old and sporting fashionably long hair, I decided it would be "radical" to head out to San Francisco and pick up on what then seemed to be the centre of all the action. I responded to a "U-Drive" advertisement looking for licensed drivers to take cars from Montreal to points west. I was offered a Cadillac (what now would be called a land yacht) to drive to Portland, Oregon.

The deal seemed sweet. I had to pay for gas and would receive $200 in US funds when I delivered the car, in good shape, to an address in Portland. The first few days went swimmingly. I had a large Caddy, university credentials, a credit card in good standing, and my whole future lay in front of me like the open road. The Cadillac hugged the road like a tank. It conferred status. Everywhere I went people were open and friendly. The officials at the roadside hostels where I bunked were pleasant. When asked for identification, I would show them my passport, driver's licence, and university enrolment card, and they invariably made the decision that I should be given a small, private or quiet room rather than the barracks that seemed set aside for hardcore nomads and the homeless.

About a hundred miles south west of Chicago, I was rudely awakened from my comfortable nap in the back seat of the car. The knife-wielding desperado took the car keys, the Cadillac, all my identification, including my credit card and passport, and my knapsack, and then insisted that I strip off and place my clothes in the trunk of the car. Clad in just my underwear and with not a dime to my name, I walked barefoot through the hot night to a farmhouse, where I was given permission to phone the authorities. State Trooper Alvin Burn filled in the necessary forms, reassuring me that the state police would report my stolen passport for me. As my parents were vacationing in Europe, the only call I made was to cancel my credit card. With ten dollars borrowed from Alvin Burns, a rag-tag set of clothing provided by the town church, and a letter from Alvin outlining my plight, I was off to continue my pilgrimage.

What happened in the next twelve days of "living rough" taught me a lesson I never forgot—that without access to technology and the power it confers, it is a very different journey out there. Without the Cadillac, passport, credit card, or university ID, and wearing shabby clothes, I was treated shabbily. Just as the first three days had been a dream, the last twelve were a nightmare. I was now relegated to the crowded, often flea-ridden bunks at roadside hostels. Local constabularies ushered me off freeways and threatened on four different occasions to deport me to the nearest border town. My letter from State Trooper Alvin Burns carried little weight outside his jurisdiction. In fact, I was placed in jail to sleep on two separate nights. Frequently I was asked by those willing to give me a lift to climb aboard and sit and/or keep an eye on the animals in the flatbed.

Technology, as power analysts (Bacharach and Lawler, 1980; Kipnis, 1990; Mintzberg, 1983; Perrucci and Potter, 1989; Pfeffer, 1981, 1992; Zuboff, 1988) make clear, and as I discovered in my youthful pilgrimage to San Francisco, is an instrument of power. Once I lost access to the Cadillac, credit card, and proof of my education, the world, at least in power terms, altered. Power analysts are interested in technology as conferring power on some people or groups in society and depriving others (Auletta, 1997; Evan, 1981; Finlay, 1987; Scarbrough and Corbett, 1992; Sussman, 1997). Power is related to authority. Power can be thought of as the ability of A to get B to do A's bidding. Authority, on the other hand, is the ability of A to get B to do A's bidding by convincing B that this is what B would do even if A were not around. A and B can be understood as persons, groups, organizations, or even larger systems like societies or nation states. Thus, once a nation state possesses nuclear arms, this technology confers power upon it. Moreover, this power often changes the dynamics between the now nuclear nation state and those with whom it has ongoing grievances. The recent nuclear testing by India and Pakistan attests to the emergence of new dynamics.

The relationship between altered technology and the emergence of power dynamics is at the basis of the logic used by power analysts. Technology changes relationships (Rusher, 1988; Vallas, 1993). The automobile gives rise to suburban development. Suburban development, in turn, shifts the power away from the city centre to the malls that serve as satellite consumer-catchment basins. The use of e-mail within postmodern organizations has altered the power base of many middle managers from an experiential and hands-on expertise in communication to the technical developments of the news group and e-mail culture. Within the recent proclivity towards downsizing in organizations, one of the justifications for cutting deeply into the population of middle managers is the emergence of e-mail as an excellent means of facilitating communication between and among employees. As computers move from expensive mainframes to accessible household items, shopping via the Internet emerges, threatening the power base of old-guard retailers of certain standardized commodities such as books or cars.

Figure 10.4 presents an overview of who or what receives power from technological change, how this occurs, and what implications it has for organizations. From a business ethics perspective, each power scenario leads us into very different territory. Looking briefly at each of the five scenarios in the power analysts' framing of technology, try and work out how each lends itself to the perspectives of technology as a promise and technology as a threat or menace.

The first power scenario is one where changes in technology confer power on the existing societal (Kingston and Lewis, 1990; Newman, 1979; Zweigenhaft and Domhoff, 1998) or corporate elite (Carroll, 1986; Clement, 1975, 1977; Korten, 1995; Schwartz, 1988). Elites, within the vocabulary of the power analysts, are those whose power within a system is sufficiently great to permit them to make key decisions. In a nutshell, the elite are the powerful. When technology bolsters the already powerful, it serves to fortify the established order. An example of this power scenario at the level of society would be military technology that is deployed to subdue domestic terrorists or revolutionaries intent on upsetting the established elite. An example at the organizational level would be a new information technology used by the dominant corporate elite to enhance their decision-making autonomy. Business ethicists become concerned when technology—and the power it confers upon the elite—is employed to reduce the elite's readiness to deal with the grievances and perceived injustices given voice to by the non-elite.

The second power scenario explores how and when changes in technology confer power on technical analysts or emerging experts (Albert and Bradley, 1997; Bereiter and Scardamalio, 1993; Clegg and Palmer, 1996) who, as a consequence of their new-found power, challenge the existing elite. It is in this sense that introducing new technology into a system politicizes (Dizard, 1985; Mansell and Silverstone, 1996; Sclove, 1995). Technological change enhances opportunities for the emergence of new experts (Chafetz, 1996) who can, under the right circumstances, parlay their expert power into capital that challenges the established elite. In societal terms, the emergence of the "new" wealth in the hands of computer whiz-kids like Bill Gates of Microsoft illustrates how quickly within the postmodern context the emerging expert can break into the established elite. At the level of the organization, we can note how CEOs with backgrounds in engineering sciences tempered with years of industry experience are being replaced by a new generation of CEOs whose education is in information sciences or marketing. Business ethicists should be concerned that the emerging new elite remains true to its social responsibilities.

In the third power scenario, new technologies confer power upon the privileged, and thereby—albeit at times unintentionally—deny it to the masses. The privileged (Daenzer, 1993; McIntosh, 1988; Scott, 1994; Tullock, 1989) have either sufficient discretionary capital or a position in society to claim power over others. Servants, not surprisingly, see privilege in the faces of those who hire them; feminists, for that matter, see it in the way that from birth onwards males are granted special favours. In society, technologies that confer power upon the privileged are either too costly for most folks (the executive jet), or, like much of the new information technology, are tacitly designed to penalize women users (Rothschild, 1983; Stabile, 1994; Wajcman, 1991). At the organizational level, new technologies that, for

FIGURE 10-4 Technology as an Instrument of Power: Five Power Scenarios

Basic Premise	Implications for Organizations	Implications for Business Ethics
1. *Power to the Traditional (Managerial) Elite:*		
The power of technology accrues to the existing power elite. Technology ostensibly is used to generate change, but this change is primarily under the control of the traditional elite.	Technological change is a top-down process. It is intended to keep the top in power and reinforce its authority.	When technology reinforces the power of the status quo, business ethicists become concerned with the ability of the powerful to hear and deal with justice issues.
2. *Power to the Technical Analysts or Emerging Experts:*		
The power of technology goes to the new technical analysts or emerging experts. These individuals design, format, alter, and interpret technology.	In organizational life, technological change often reduces the power of the old dominant coalition in management and provides leverage for the emergence of a new technical elite.	When technology ushers in a new technical elite, business ethicists become concerned with the ability of the new elite to establish fair procedures for dealing with grievances and ethical quandaries.
3. *Power to the Privileged:*		
The power of technology goes to the privileged. It is costly. It requires credentials or training.	In organizational life, technological change empowers those with privilege—access, capital, position, credentials, training. It is denied to others.	When technology ushers in more power to the privileged and the gap between the haves and the have-nots grows, then business ethicists seek to make sure that the have-nots are not exploited.
4. *Power to the Masses:*		
Technology democratizes. It is readily accessible, user-friendly, and empowers its users.	In organizational life, technological change is implemented in a bottom-up process. It empowers the everyday employee.	When technology ushers in more power to the masses, business ethicists are concerned with whether or not the technology creates dialogue and a search for the good life.
5. *Power to the Technology Itself:*		
The power of technology is embedded in the technology itself. Technology that has this quality becomes indispensable.	In organizational life, technological change can result in greater power to the technology. All others feel a net loss in power.	When technology creates power for itself, business ethicists' concerns are for establishing the rights of participants and the limits of the use of technology.

example, bolster the budgets of departments that already receive the lion's share of resources, easily fall within the parameters of this third power scenario. Business ethicists must attend to what is a reasonable gap between the haves and the have-nots and, more pressingly, how technology is impacting this relationship.

The fourth power scenario, "power to the masses," at first glance seems to be diametrically opposed to the idea of "power to the privileged." It is, if we think of society as altering only one technology at a specific time. It is not, if we think of society as capable of introducing both the executive jet and the mass-produced and entirely reliable Timex watch. Technology that confers power to the masses democratizes. Currently in society there is a vivid and certainly interesting debate over whether the Internet actually confers power to the masses or whether it is a platform for the privileged. In organizations, technology that confers power to the everyday worker empowers; like the technologies used to support the idea of "teamwork" (Hackman, 1990; Romig, 1996; Wellins *et al.*, 1994), it is an example of the type four power scenario. When technology does confer power to the masses, business ethicists need to examine longitudinally whether or not the power is transferred, and whether it is used in a way that leads to the good life. Commentators looking back at a half-century of television—a technology that was to have empowered the masses, stimulated a new age of democratic politics, and enlightened the populace in their leisure pursuits—now have grave concerns regarding its once apparent relationship to the good life (Marc, 1995; McKibben, 1992; Powers, 1990; Winn, 1987).

The fifth and final power scenario made explicit in Figure 10.4 confers power to the technology itself. This is clearly a departure from the idea of technology as a device, program, or system designed and operated by and intended to serve the wishes of its users. We have already discovered how technology can become more costly than planned, how it can lead to unintended consequences, and how it can be used to harm others intentionally. In the fifth scenario, "power to the technology itself," the technology takes on a life of its own. This can be said to happen in three interrelated ways: (1) the technology is tied inextricably to its users either biologically, as in the case of pacemakers, contact lenses, or plastic hip replacements, or mechanically, like an airplane in flight to the fate of its passengers and crew; (2) the technology is tied systematically to the lives (both human and non-human) of those who are often unaware of their dependence on technological systems—water systems, transportation systems, electrical systems, telecommunications systems, etc.; and (3) the technology is perceived to be "worth" so much in real economic terms that we question seriously whether or not we should retain the particular technology even if its use causes the loss of lives, negatively impacts natural systems, or can, under predictable circumstances, turn unreliable. When technology or technologically-based systems take on a life of their own, this is precisely when we require that they—and those who are part of their operations—act as moral entities.

This fifth scenario opens up the frequently discussed idea (Borgmann 1984, 1995; Franklin, 1990; Mitcham, 1994) that as technology confers power upon itself, it is a portal to a new age—a force of revolutionary change. In this view, "technological new agers" see that the shape of the future is taking on a new bent due to the role of technology. The revolution in question, implicit in this new age view, can be filtered through the perception of either "technology as a promise" or "technology as a threat or menace," but no matter which perception is selected, all technological new agers believe that there will be immense ethical implications wrought by the new technologies.

TECHNOLOGY AS A PORTAL TO A NEW AGE

The technological new agers (Boaz, 1997; Drexler and Peterson, 1991; Grossman, 1995; Peters, 1996; Pool, 1997; Want, 1995) view technology as a key determinant of the future, at both societal and organizational levels. As with most futurologists, the technological new agers are dealing with a complex welter of trends and patterns. Within this whirlwind of change, they attempt to discern and make credible a dominant pattern. I recall my puzzlement when years ago my sister repeated the phrase heard frequently in health food circles that "you are what you eat." It seemed to me twenty years ago (and still does now), that one's self, for all intents and purposes, is far more than a system for the ingestion and digestion of particular food sources. My sister reminded me then (and still does now) that the food you eat is one of the few basic building blocks of your self over which you have control, engage in daily choices, and can alter these choices to make a significant difference in how you feel, act, and heal when you become ill.

My point here is that technological new agers, whether they filter their view of the upcoming new age through the "promise" or "threat and menace" view of technology, make a similar point: "we are becoming the technologies we use." To use a technology is to enter into an interaction that has, over time, the power not only to change your life but the nature of life within your family, organization, or even society. A family without a television orders its time, leisure activities, and its world view very differently from one whose family room is, in fact, the TV room. An organization that provides employees access to e-mail and reinforces their use of it to communicate ideas throughout the plant is a different organization than one that uses memos. A society with nuclear power and the application of nuclear energy to military ends is a very different society from one that both has no nuclear capacity nor seeks to develop it.

Technology, in the thinking of technological new agers, shapes and lends identity to the future. We in the business school have been particularly partial to this form of technological determinism. We acknowledge the industrial revolution (Stearns, 1993; Thompson, 1973) as a clear departure from the agrarian revolution based primarily upon the introduction of new technologies which, as we say, changed the world. Now many technological new agers have called an end to the industrial revolution, seeing the postmodern context as one that is grounded in the service revolution (Bell, 1973; Howard, 1995; Pitsch, 1996), information technologies and computerization (Estabrooks, 1995; Lacy, 1996; Wells, 1997), the new knowledge workers (Kirn and O'Hare, 1997; Mohrman *et al.*, 1995; Winslow and Bramer, 1994), the digital age (Lynch and Lundquist, 1996; Tapscott, 1996; Tapscott *et al.*, 1998) and, as we shall explore in the next section, the ideas of virtual reality and the virtual corporation (Oravec, 1996; Thierauf, 1995; Whittle, 1997). Thus, as technology changes, particularly significant technology, it alters the basic fabric of the business community. It is in this sense, as we noted in our discussion of postmodern business ethics in Chapter 2, that business in a society rooted in credit card exchanges is very different from business in a society requiring exchange with cash on hand.

In Figure 10.5 we see an outline of five schools of thought currently used to make sense of the relationship between technology and the impending future. The five paradigms are: (1) the device paradigm; (2) the smart machine paradigm; (3) the Frankenstein paradigm; (4) the new spirituality paradigm; and (5) the immersion paradigm. Our interest rests in both the basic premises of the paradigms and, more importantly, the implication of each for future business ethicists. This topic is important because it leads us to speculate not only on the future and how changes—particularly in technology—will affect businesses and their operations, but on what role business ethics will play in this new age.

David Bolter, in *Turing's Man: Western Culture in the Computer Age* (1984), captures the reasoning of the technological new agers when he maintains that we tend to think of ourselves in the image of our technologies. In Bolter's view, after the industrial revolution we began to think of ourselves as if we were machines. Late into this period we believed that when someone faltered in their abilities to transact normal routines, they were said, like machines, to have "broken down" or, indeed, to have suffered a "breakdown." In the present, a period that Bolter and others (Alberts and Papp, 1997; Hope and Hope, 1997; Rowland, 1997) characterize as the early stages of the information age, we think of ourselves as information processors; we no longer break down, but suffer from "overload." When technology subtly impacts the language we use to make sense of ourselves and our propensities to falter, then we must assume that it has an impact on what we consider to be fair, rational, and just.

The Device Paradigm

The new age addressed in the device paradigm is one of gadgets and conveniences that are intended to make life in the world easier. In the device paradigm, technology is a means to an end. It is conceived of as a tool or utensil. This is the "faster, better, more" vision of technology applied to the future (Allen, 1977; Davis and Wessel, 1998; Jasinowski, 1998; Morrison, 1996; Verduin, 1995). The future is engineered. It is the result of applied and improved rationality. It is more efficient than the present. In this future, the managed and built environment is extended. New synthetic materials are applied to devices. Invention and experimentation, guided by good science and stimulated by market demand, accelerate the diffusion of innovation. This is a future of science, engineering, and planning.

On the whole, the device paradigm as a portal to a new age reassures us that the future will be an improvement upon the past. The device paradigm supports the notion of progress, albeit through good science, competitive markets, and a healthy economy. Technology, in this story of our future, is under our control. These are machines; they are not complicated systems or sufficiently smart to learn how to redesign themselves or recalibrate and set new goals for their activities. The good life in the device paradigm is fulfilled in a future in which our needs are met in ways that are "better," "faster," and "more." Those who are concerned about the device paradigm worry about three aspects of it: first, that in its quest to accelerate innovation, systems that espouse the device paradigm may be engaged blindly in change for change's sake; second, that the increased use of technology as a device to smooth over that which makes us anxious may actually result in the population becoming dependent upon or "drugged" by these devices; and third (and related to the second concern), that reliance upon devices in the future can make people mindless or uncritical and unthinking.

The Smart Machine Paradigm

The smart machine paradigm views the new age as one in which machines are no longer simple devices, but systems capable of information processing, memory, learning, and even self-design (Bailey, 1996; Briscoe and Caelli, 1996; Dennett, 1998; Kurzweil, 1990; Mazlish,

FIGURE 10–5 Technology as a Portal to a New Age: Five Paradigms of New Age Thinking

Facet	Basic Premises	Implications for Business Ethicists
The Device Paradigm	This is the faster/better/more view of technology applied to the future. It amplifies the known, but does not frighten. Those who raise fears point to the speed-up and loss of mindfulness.	Business ethicists try to remind those caught up in the hurly-burly of the business community that the "good life" is not achieved merely by acquiring a system or technology that is faster, better, and creates more, but one that is directed to an end that is ethically desirable. The device paradigm loses sight of the end and tends to idealize the means.
The Smart Machine Paradigm	This is the view that smart machines increasingly will take a larger and larger role in the cerebral and decision-making activities of our species. The smart machines speak of a future in which human intelligence is machine enhanced.	Business ethicists are noticing the already-relevant tendency to "blame the computer" when accounting for errors in business activity. It is entirely possible, in the age of the smart machine, that this attribution of responsibility will accelerate. Business ethicists worry about accountability when smart machines are seen, not merely as the tools of decision, but as the decision makers.
The Frankenstein Paradigm	This is the dystopian view that the new technology will take us to hell in a hand-basket. We are creating technological monsters that will haunt us. The nuclear bomb is just an appetizer.	Business ethicists are concerned about technologies that psychologically, physically, and socially injure others, including non-human species. In the rush to market new technologies, we often do our experimentation in the market. This nurtures commerce, but also may nurture the Frankenstein paradigm.
The New Spirituality Paradigm	This is a reflection of the new age metaphysics being ushered in by the new technology. The idea that God is a code or that fractals are a form of mandala show the tendency in society for technology to influence spirituality.	Business ethicists, on the whole, applaud the connection between the new technology and spirituality. Where concern is evident is in the increasing attempt to define the good life in technological terms. The closed nature of technological systems gives an illusion of completion and control to this form of spiritual musing.
The Immersion Paradigm	This is a belief that the new technology will be pervasive, that it will alter our cognition and experience of reality. We will be, as it were, wired to the technology.	Business ethicists' views on virtual reality are still, as is the topic itself, in their infancy. It can be speculated that there will be a concern with the immersion paradigm as an escape from reality and a shirking of one's responsibilities.

1993; Nilsson, 1998; Turban, 1992). In a classic distinction between mind and body, we might note that while technology in the device paradigm enables the human body, technology in the smart machine paradigm enables the human mind. In the smart machine paradigm, the organization uses technology to make sense of the rapidly changing world. The cybernetic functions of intelligent governance (Espejo, 1996; Hogan, 1998; Zuboff, 1988) mean that, in the future society and the future organization, key functions such as decision making, predicting and forecasting, and even learning (Baldi and Brunak, 1998; Wehenkel, 1998) will occur not merely with the help of smart machines and systems, but with these at the centre. Recent victories by the smart machine, "Deep Blue" over chess masters indicates the plausibility with which this future is envisioned.

In a future in which—if proponents of the smart machine paradigm are correct—the technologies of information processing, signal recognition, and symbol interpretation will become more central in the important "minded" activity that must be done in society, business ethicists become concerned. Questions abound. What or who is to be accountable when, as a consequence of a smart machine's actions or lack of them, serious loss and/or injury is inflicted upon unsuspecting others? What are the rights of intelligent machines? Are they to be non-existent or are they to be similar to those of higher animals or even to corporate entities? What is the role of the programmer to the smart machine when the smart machine overrides the program and acts, as it were, independently? Can or should smart machines be able to veto or negate the wishes of a majority of people casting a vote on an issue in which the machine clearly is agreed to be the most knowledgeable expert?

The smart machine paradigm opens up a Pandora's box of ethical questions which, if its proponents are correct, await the next generation. As I write this book in 1999, most of my colleagues who work within the smart machine paradigm are extremely confident that in another decade, say by the year 2010, we will be surrounded by machines that increasingly will combine aspects of the device and smart machine paradigms. Robots will, in an important sense of the word, learn, and will be able to alter their behaviours in ways unanticipated by those who program them. Computers as we currently know them will be more than fancy word processors, advanced calculators, and conduits to the World Wide Web; they will be ramps to a new virtual reality. Personally, I look forward to these prospects, but I am well aware that others cringe at the idea of a future in which machines will become empowered, think, use language, and possess intelligence, albeit artificial intelligence.

The Frankenstein Paradigm

Those who balk at the future as seen through the portal of the smart machine paradigm get their view of the future from what—leaning on the influential work of Mary Wollstonecraft Shelley (1823)—I call the Frankenstein paradigm. In this view (Athanasiou, 1996; Dobkowski *et al.*, 1998; Rivage-Seul and Rivage-Seul, 1995; Rollin, 1995; Tenner, 1996), technology leads to hell in a handbasket. As in the tale of Frankenstein, which over the years has taken on a prominent role in postmodern popular culture (Glut, 1973; Turney, 1998), efforts to make technology take on the attributes of intelligent persons can only end in disaster. In Shelley's novel, the disaster emerges out of the hubris of science and the scientists who feel that life can and must be made artificially. The artificial intelligence that emerges in Shelley's world of the early eighteenth century is lost, and, without its place in nature, it becomes monstrous and out of control in search of vengeance. Some read this modern telling of an old story as an admonition that humans ought not play God; others see it as the punishment that goes to those who are so very lonely that they seek to "make" their perfect companion.

More contemporary versions of the Frankenstein paradigm portray technology as rife with unintended consequences. Each technology seems perfectly rational within its context or usage sphere. However, when technology is taken all together, we are unaware of the concoction that we have inadvertently brewed and that we now, to extend the metaphor, drink on a daily basis. A second way into the contemporary Frankenstein paradigm is to imagine a future in which smart machines are implanted in, so to speak, human bodies. This new person-machine hybrid also worries those who fear the new world order being born beneath the rubric of the new reproductive technologies (Ginsburg and Rapp, 1995; Kaplan and Tong, 1994). Cloning humans, or even sheep, suggests that technology is no longer the enabler—it is the source of life. Within the Frankenstein paradigm, there is a longing for a world held in balance by forces other than human intelligence and cunning. There is longing—some would label it romantic—for humans to conquer their inner dark forces before they project them outwards and empower them in the new technological future.

The New Spirituality Paradigm

The new spirituality paradigm envisions a future where humans, influenced by the new technology, will be able to conquer their dark side and become more fully-realized, spiritual beings. This literature (Abraham, 1994; Cade and Coxhead, 1979; Herbert, 1993; Hutchinson, 1986; Varela *et al.*, 1991; Wolf, 1986) portrays a future in which technology both helps to recover the idea of the sacred and stimulates the search for spiritual growth. As Imants Baruss points out in *Authentic Knowing: The Convergence of Science and Spiritual Aspirations* (1996), the new spirituality paradigm seeks to use the idea of technology as a bridge to help bring science and spirituality together. Relative to the three other paradigms of technology as a portal to a new age that we have discussed, the new spirituality paradigm is the only one that directs technology into the human psyche and, as well, seeks to define explicitly the good life outside of instrumental reasoning.

Biofeedback (Danskin and Crow, 1981; Schwartz, 1987), whereby an individual gets wired to receive feedback on their reactions both physiological and psychological to various conditions, can be seen within the new spirituality paradigm not only as an aid to relaxation and the diminishment of stress, but also as a means of self-knowledge and enlightenment (Boyett and Boyett, 1995; Fox *et al.*, 1997; Schecter, 1995). At the organizational level, the new spirituality paradigm has its advocates (Brisken, 1998; Guilloy, 1997; McLagan and Christo, 1995; Secretan, 1996). These advocates argue that the new information technology moves organizations from a competitive emphasis on vertical structures where power prevails, to more horizontal structures where cooperation and even compassion can thrive (Klein and Izzo, 1998; Percy, 1997). In *Art Meets Science and Spirituality in a Changing Economy: From Competition to Compassion*, Louwrien Wijers (1996) compiles the arguments for the emerging centrality of spirituality in the information age. Three factors conjoin: first, the new technology stimulates the search for possible worlds, alternative views, and ideas of how to be truly awake or mindful in a world that calls for constant adaptation to change; second, the new technology creates what Sally Helgesen (1995) calls a "web of inclusion" that fosters deeper and more meaningful forms of collaboration among participants in the business community; and third, the new technology enhances and facilitates a sense of awe and a recognition of the sacred in its ability to help establish the ubiquity of pattern in even the most random occurrences. This last point leads to what Steven R. Holtzman (1994) calls the very holy nature of "digital mantras" and the new metaphysics of virtual reality (Heim, 1993).

In exploring the new age spirituality paradigm we learn that as we change our world with our technology, we alter how we conceive of the good life and our role within it. Spirituality in the new age spirituality paradigm fastens on the new technology as a symbolic expression of new possibilities (Zaleski, 1997)—some inspiring, others terrifying—but all, insist the new age spiritualists, part of the world-in-the-making. It is this idea of the world-in-the-making that leads us to the fifth and last of the paradigms treating technology as a portal to the new age.

The Immersion Paradigm

The immersion paradigm sees the new technology as so pervasive that not only is it altering our cognitive experience in a subtle way, but it is altering our very notion of reality (Dixon and Cassidy, 1998; Levy, 1997; Markley, 1996). In the immersion paradigm, we are not at the "portal" of a new age but, rather, we are in the very thick of it. Our conception of reality as a fixed Archimedean point has not only been dislodged; we are now increasingly wired to a world that not only enhances multiple perspectives, but that can create a simulated, virtual, or alternate reality convincing enough for us to elect to immerse ourselves within the experience of it (Grantham, 1993; Wang, 1997; Zhai, 1998).

Within the immersion paradigm (Jones, 1995; Pimentel and Teixeira, 1993; Rheingold, 1991, 1994; Schroeder, 1996; Stuart, 1996; Woolley, 1992), the present is malleable, replicable, and storable. Virtual reality as a technology (Chorafas and Steinmann, 1995; Dodsworth, 1998; Powers, 1997) refers to a three-dimensional, computer-generated simulation of reality with visual, aural, and tactile dimensions that produces an environment in which a user or users can be immersed and with which they can interact. Virtual reality has been referred to by many of its most keen adherents as a "three-dimensional form of consensual hallucination." This is because virtual reality is a technology that permits data or information to be visualized, heard and/or felt as software transforms information to stimulate either a real or imagined environment. This environment, actually an uninhabitable, computer-generated space, is called "cyberspace," and many in the know are claiming it as the new business frontier (Cordell, 1997; Kitchin, 1998; Martin, 1996).

To understand the logic of the immersion paradigm, let us begin with a brief introduction to how—using an example of virtual technology at the individual level—we can generate a virtual environment sufficiently real to "suspend disbelief" and become the very stuff of credible cyberspace. By mounting on one's head a pair of goggles equipped with a set of small video monitors with the appropriate optics, a stereoscopic image is produced before one's eyes. This image is continuously updated and adjusted by the computer so that the visual stimuli are altered in the appropriate way as one moves one's head. In this way, one finds oneself completely surrounded by a stable, three-dimensional world. In addition to the goggles, one may wear stereo headphones and special "data" gloves, or even an entire bodysuit wired with position and motion transducers to transmit to others (and to represent to oneself) one's image and activity in the virtual world. This virtual, visual, tactile, and aural world can be generated in either "real time," the time of action by the computer, or it can be pre-processed and stored in the computer's memory, or it can exist elsewhere and be encoded or "videographed" and transmitted to the user.

The uses of virtual reality are, its adherents suggest, limited only by our imagination and the willingness of users to enter and engage in economic transactions in cyberspace. Business has become extremely interested in creating the virtual corporation (Davidow and Malone, 1992; Grenier and Metes, 1995; Hale and Whitlan, 1997). At this point in time, the use of the actual goggles, glove, or bodysuit and stereo headset tied to the computer program is limited to architects and designers who run their clients through the experience of living in a not-yet-built house, or for training physicians or military personnel in the skills required in particular simulated situations. But where virtuality as a concept flourishes in business is in creating a viable and secure cyberspace on the Internet for commercial transactions (Cronin, 1997; Kalakota and Whinston, 1996; McCarthy, 1996); utilizing the Internet and virtual technology to create networked organizations that remain connected to other organizations via the development of networks to outsource work and build collaborative platforms or strategic alliances (Chisholm, 1998; Judson, 1996; Metes *et al.*, 1998); and, lastly, to explore cyberspace as a means of bringing new ideas to the market in a more direct, client- and employee-friendly manner (Creighton and Adams, 1998; Czerniawska and Potter, 1998; Goldman *et al.*, 1995).

Experiments on "virtuality," whether in the commercial arena or in society at large, must not be confused with a future that is virtuous. As we immerse ourselves—speaking literally—in computer-generated environments, and become familiar with the World Wide Web, traditional ethical quandaries—privacy, fairness, integrity—do not disappear at all. They take on new form (Bowyer, 1996; Dodsworth, 1998; Edgar, 1997; Kling, 1996; Weckert and Adeney, 1997). Business ethics remains a dynamic attempt, not only to synthesize the classical moral formulations of the moral philosophers, but to apply these insights to the world that is being made by the new technologies with which we are experimenting. In the next section, we turn to the role of business ethicists in the new technologically-grounded information society.

BUSINESS ETHICS IN AN AGE OF PERVASIVE TECHNOLOGY

Michael Dertouzos, in his eminently readable book, *What Will Be: How the New World of Information Will Change Our Lives* (1997), calls into question, among other things, how ethically unprepared we are for the technologies we are unleashing in the midst of the information revolution. As a species, we seem able to create technical innovation at a more rapid rate than we can develop a value consensus, or even a polite public dialogue on how, when, and who should employ these technologies—if, indeed, they are to be employed at all. Should food be irradiated? In countries such as Canada, the answer is no; in the United States, the response is resoundingly positive. With the present state of cryogenics, should authorities license the operation of commercial outlets intending to freeze the bodies of a near-dead, pay-for-service clientele until medical science has developed a cure for their ailments? Given the new surveillance techniques beamed off satellites, should consumers, employees, or the general public in commercial spaces have their activities unobtrusively monitored? Is it ethical to sell data collected on unsuspecting consumers to third parties? Are we, with the new wired capabilities of the Internet, going to implement a more direct form of democracy where the public as a whole votes on key issues of the day?

These questions are in the domain of the business and applied ethicists. These sorts of questions, like the field of business ethics itself, are growing. There is a very real hunger for models, perspectives, techniques, theories, methodologies, and certainly answers to these sorts of questions. This is not accidental, nor (in my admittedly biased outlook) simply a matter of a fad or a fashion. Technology tests our stable consensus. We experienced an uprooting in the industrial revolution and now, once again, another major dislocation in the information revolution. Our postmodern reaction has left us very stimulated and poised creatively for new options, but largely unable to fathom a sense of deeper meaning and shared direction with those around us. This is true in the very public, very powerful, managed environment we call our organizations.

We are, in these contexts, extremely anxious and uncertain. In an important sense of the word "right," we want to know what is right so that we can move towards that deeper meaning and shared direction that we believe eludes us. It is in this context that modern or, as I am prone to say, postmodern business ethics emerges. It is not a discipline that answers questions. In my view, business ethics is at its best when it helps individuals, groups, and organizations pose questions that aid them to locate their positions and values within an argument field. The absence of a value consensus has made it appealing to train aspiring business participants, whether they aspire to roles in management, labour, or social activism, to understand the cross-cutting currents of positions operating in their organizational worlds.

Confronting moral worlds, even in the midst of their very technical surfaces, is the task of business ethicists. Figure 10.6 provides an overview of five different but interrelated roles played by business ethicists or those, like yourself, receiving formal training in business ethics. Each role reflects a different way of thinking about the function and relevance of business ethics in a technologically-driven society. To practice business ethics in a self-conscious manner is not only to understand the basic premises of a body of knowledge, but also to comprehend how others in society—and, of course, in the business community—are likely to make sense of that role. The role of the business ethicist as both an occupational category and/or a specialty practised by personnel in an organization is not a static entity.

When I first started teaching and doing business ethics consulting for firms more than two decades ago, the business ethicist was seen primarily as someone to be brought into the firm to stabilize issues. The role of the business ethicist as a stabilizer was, and still is, to bring parties in a dispute over values together. In the contemporary context—and germane to the introduction of new technology—those who rail against the new technology as "de-skilling" their craft hold different views from those who see the new technology as enriching jobs in the organization. The collision of these contrary views can destabilize and lead to extraordinarily costly problems. The business ethicist as a stabilizer is someone who utilizes his or her skills to help create policies, training programs, and contexts in which breakdowns in the value consensus can be brought into line.

As a stabilizer, the enemies of the business ethicist are ignorance, intolerance, and the failure of participants in a dispute to be clear and forthright in airing their views. Conflict is not the enemy. Unnecessary conflict that breeds uncertainty, fosters instability, and results in inward-looking, clique-like behaviour from participants is dysfunctional. The role of the business ethicist is to anticipate the emergence of dysfunctional conflicts, whether between participants within an organization or among stakeholders in the organization's primary, secondary, or tertiary environments. In keeping with our reasoning throughout this text, the business ethicist who helps the firm cope with dysfunctional conflict moves that organization in the direction of becoming a good corporate citizen.

FIGURE 10-6 The Role of Business Ethics in an Age of Pervasive Technology

Role	Function	Relevance
Business Ethics as a Stabilizer	Within this view, business ethics helps to stabilize human behaviour in times of extreme change. It helps to create standards or guidelines where the law is believed to be either mute or unhelpful. It helps create shared expectations and a recognition that a shared ethos is indispensable in the life of the business community.	Business ethics fosters the view that, in the midst of extreme changes due to the technological revolution, there is an enlightened and rational means of re-instilling stability, shared expectations, and a communal ethos.
Business Ethics as a Guide to Action	Within this view, business ethics is seen as adding value to planning, decision making, and action taking in the business community. Business ethics enhances one's ability to anticipate the reactions of others to one's planned action. This ability permits one to create realistic priorities and to ask pertinent questions when impeded by others.	Business ethics fosters the view that business entails dealing with points of view that are both rationally defensible and opposed to others. Business ethics speaks to the ability to negotiate logically in a highly diversified and complex world of differing views.
Business Ethics as a Conspiracy	Within this view, business ethics is seen as a form of implementing political correctness and, under the guise of dialogue, silencing those whose views are not fashionable. In this view, business ethicists are acting as the paid toadies of the social do-gooders or others. Their services can be bought.	Business ethics fosters the view that business entails doing what is right. There is, and should continue to be, a serious debate over what is right. Those who feel that business ethicists can adversely affect their turf will not be happy; others will be highly committed.
Business Ethics as a Specialized Expertise	Within this view, business ethics is seen as a specialized academic or consulting specialty with its own experts. The job of the business ethics expert, whether hired as a consultant or as an ongoing employee, is to solve ethical quandaries, assure the reputation of the firm, and maintain an ethical organizational culture.	Business ethics fosters the view that there is a specialized body of knowledge which, when mastered, enables professional ethicists to diagnose, plan, and help solve corporate ethical quandaries.
Business Ethics as a Public Dialogue	Within this view, business ethics is seen as a means of giving voice to issues that otherwise might be buried in the operations of the postmodern organization. These issues, when made public, foster inquiry, debate, and media examination. The public dialogue heightens recognition of ethical issues.	Business ethics fosters the view that business is not separate from other spheres of human endeavour. This holistic focus means that business ethicists seek to make debate and argumentation in business public and relevant to society as a whole.

The role of business ethics and the business ethicist as a stabilizer is made all the more relevant because the business ethicist is viewed as taking a perspective that is not necessarily that of top management. To be effective, business ethicists cannot produce stability when they are seen as part and parcel of an advocacy position within the value-rooted dispute. Business ethicists achieve their credibility by viewing the destabilizing issue from the perspective of the right thing to do—not the most expedient. Most organizational players quickly realize that stability achieved through the quest for justice is quite distinct from stability achieved through brokering a deal. It is in times of great uncertainty and technological change that many diverse participants in the organizational context look for a form of stability that seems to meet the test of higher principles rather than the test of temporary compliance.

A second role played by business ethicists, and one quite prominent in the information age, is as a guide to action. In this regard, business ethicists provide or sell information to organizations that is viewed as adding value to planning, decision making, and action taking within the business community. The information runs the gamut, from how to write effective corporate codes of ethics, to much more idiosyncratic notions such as how to best deal with the owner/operator of a mid-sized firm who shows early signs of Alzheimer's disease. This information can be provided in different forums, formats, and contexts. Training sessions, special reports, advisory committees, and consulting projects all provide the context for the provision of information. In exchanging information in an organizational context, business ethicists, as professionals, must try to walk the talk. Within the cash-for-information nexus outlined here, business ethicists must avoid, for example, sugar-coating their views to keep the client satisfied, promoting old ideas as if they were new, or selling generic or boilerplate formulations as if they were handcrafted for the client.

In guiding corporate action, business ethicists seek to promote corporate social responsibility within the realistic constraints of the problems, issues, and opportunities faced by the corporation. The action fostered by business ethicists is informed by the diverse points of view heard in the organization. Action that is responsible is, in the lexicon of business ethicists, responsive. Those who act on behalf of the whole must be held accountable for both the procedures they utilize to set their actions and, of course, for the consequences that ensue as a result of the actions. It is in this way that business ethicists seek to make sure that action is valuable in two senses: first, that it is tied to a procedure that is fair; and second, that the consequences of the action neither injure nor exploit innocent others.

The third way in which business ethics and business ethicists are seen in an age of pervasive technology is as part of a conspiracy. As a practising business ethicist, this is not a view or role I find particularly flattering, but it would be irresponsible to portray the role of the business ethicist without the warts. In this view, business ethicists are seen as implementing forms of political correctness. Business ethicists are seen as ethics police, know-it-alls, telling others what is and is not acceptable or rational conduct. White males, for example, who believe they have lost their jobs or the prospects of them to women or Natives, can, with some anger, point to the diversity programs spearheaded by business ethicists as the source of their undeserved trouble.

In viewing business ethics as a conspiracy, there is a belief that business ethicists are acting as toadies and legitimizing agents for social do-gooders. The conspiracy rests less in the explicitness of the values at play in the perception of business ethicists as ethics police, than in the assertion that in the face of business ethics organizational participants do not give voice to their true and authentic views, but attempt to say what they believe is politically correct. Rather than fostering truth telling and engendering valuable advice as guides to action, business ethicists actually help to impose a polite and acceptable ethical surface upon corporate life—a stability that those adhering to the conspiracy point of view insist is far from reliable. In fact, in small groups, people make fun of the way they are "supposed" to act in public.

The view of business ethics as a conspiracy should not be swept under the rug. As business ethics explores what is right and proper conduct in business circles, it will make enemies and critics. In an example we all see working itself out in organizations around us, smokers are genuinely disturbed by their increasing ostracism and banishment to special facilities. To many who feel that their privileges or "rights" are being curtailed by those who "claim" to speak for the "good life," these spokespersons are nothing but charlatans. They are frequently portrayed as stripping individuals of their liberties and helping to create, often in the name of minority rights, a highly conformist future. From this—a perspective of curtailed freedoms—it is easy to see how business ethicists, among others, are tarred with a backlash reaction and seen as part of a bigger conspiracy.

Partially as a way to protect themselves from accusations of conspiracy, and certainly as a way of increasing their professional legitimacy, business ethicists are staking out a claim as a body of specialized experts. In books such as this, business ethicists are staking out a body of knowledge that is the domain and, in another sense, the working capital of the business ethicist. There is a movement within the profession from the academic setting, particularly of the moral philosopher working from a philosophy department, to the business ethicist as a professional and active member of the business community. As this shift occurs there is an increased worry about the relationship between theory or reflection, on the one hand, and practice or ethical problem solving on the other.

The role of the business ethicist is to contribute to a body of knowledge that enhances both reflection on ethical quandaries and practical means to solve these ethical quandaries. Contributions to the profession establish how business ethics practitioners can change both theory and practice. In writing this book, I hope to influence, albeit in a modest manner, a generation of aspiring business students to think seriously about turning their talents and energies to business ethics. It is both a means of establishing personal satisfaction in earning one's living, and of contributing to building a body of knowledge and practice. It is a profession and an occupation that calls upon one to become involved not only with new ideas and technologies in the workplace, but to integrate these with changing conceptions, socially bound, of the good life and what one must do to move towards it.

Lastly, business ethics and ethicists create the opportunity for a public dialogue over issues that remain controversial. It is a working edict of all the business ethicists I have worked with over the years that to make something undiscussable is to refuse to face what it is that causes fear, embarrassment, or shame. Part of the task of the business ethicist is to surface the undiscussable by providing others with the belief that controversy is not to be shunned. The enemy of business ethics is not the existence of evil, but the slide into moral muteness. Moral muteness arises in groups, departments, organizations, and social systems when people refuse to talk about irksome ethical issues because, in doing so, they fear they will cause trouble and be penalized.

The role of the business ethicist is to create a context in which giving voice to one's moral views is seen as part of one's responsibility in the community. To create this context, the business ethicist attempts to show in talk and action that we cannot separate ethics out from our economic, technical, and political worlds. To confront the existence of our world in business as a moral world is to understand business ethics. To practice business ethics, one must seek to join in and contribute to the public dialogue on how to pass our time on the planet in a way that meaningfully contributes to the "good life."

CASES AND QUESTIONS

CASE 10-1 | **Paul Desauteils Writes the Autopsy for the Kranzer Low Radiation Video Display Terminal (VDT)**

Paul Desauteils is a Master of Business Administration student at the local university, who, for his MBA project, is doing a study exploring why the Kranzer Low Radiation Video Display Terminal, manufactured by Kranzer Electronics Limited between 1995 and 1998, failed. Dr. Claire Wolfson, the Dean of the Faculty of Business Administration, has been contacted by Robert Kranzer, the President of Kranzer Electronics Limited, to help him make sense of the failure of an innovative new technology into which he had poured over $12 million. Dr. Wolfson turned to her best MBA candidate and apprised him of an opportunity to complete his project in his area of interest—excellent technologies that fail.

Paul Desauteils met Robert Kranzer at the suburban office of Kranzer Electronics Limited in the summer of 1998. Despite the age difference between the two men, they quickly became good friends. To satisfy both the requirement for his MBA project and the curiosity of Mr. Kranzer, Paul Desauteils decided to conduct a series of interviews with the key players in the creation, development, marketing, and failure of the Kranzer Low Radiation VDT. As well, Paul asked for and was granted permission to access all the files and documentation surrounding the Kranzer Low Radiation VDT. The five major interviews conducted in July of 1998 were with the following:

1. Mr. Robert Kranzer, President and CEO of Kranzer Electronics

2. Mr. Philip Fletcher, Director of Research and Development, Kranzer Electronics

3. Martha Liston, Special Project Manager of the Kranzer Low Radiation VDT Project, Kranzer Electronics

4. Mr. Norton Hoyt, Director of Marketing, Kranzer Electronics

5. Mr. Kenji Morishima, Director of Research and Development, CRK Computers of Canada

An abridged version of Paul Desauteils' field notes, taken at the interviews for each of the key participants, is as follows.

Robert Kranzer

Background: From *Who is Who in Canadian Business*, I found that Mr. Kranzer is a trained engineer who spent sixteen years working for CRK Computers of Canada where he implemented several successful technical innovations. In 1987 he started up Kranzer Electronics Limited, which has become a leader in optics applied to voice recognition systems and retina recognition devices used in surveillance and property protection. Kranzer Electronics employs 942 full- and part-time employees and enjoys sales of $651 million.

Major Projects: Robert Kranzer had begun to pay attention to VDTs when, in 1975, Swedish scientists reported an unusually high number of VDT operators complaining of eye difficulties, and a 1977 Swedish National Board of Occupational Safety Health Study found that 85% of all Scandinavian Airline System Employees who worked with VDTs experienced blurred vision, temporary near-sightedness, and a significantly high percentage of cataracts in later life. It was speculated by this early study that electromagnetic fields surrounding VDTs were responsible. It has been known since the 1960s that all electronic devices create an electromagnetic field. However, the strength of the magnetic fields from these appliances falls off with distance. VDTs, however, require ongoing proximity and many operators are required to work for eight to twelve hours at a time before their VDTs.

Other studies piqued Mr. Kranzer's curiosity on the possible relationship between VDT use and eye problems. In the late 1970s, the Newspaper Guild of New York charged that VDTs posed a threat to the eyes of copy editors. The Bell Telephone Laboratories in Murray Hill, New Jersey, conducted tests that demonstrated that prolonged exposure to the electromagnetic field created by VDTs could have detrimental health effects on workers. Mr. Kranzer's curiosity was raised when, in a series of controversial studies, it was speculated that VDT exposure could adversely affect the health of the fetus when pregnant women were exposed to the electromagnetic field surrounding VDTs. In 1983, the Canadian Centre for Occupational Health and Safety recommended that pregnant workers be relieved of VDT work and noted that lead aprons were ineffective for deflecting or absorbing the electromagnetic field around VDTs.

Idea: Mr. Kranzer's idea, while still working at CRK Computers, was to develop a low priced, low radiation VDT. Mr. Kranzer felt that, since the scientific data on the impact of VDTs was still controversial, it would be wise to price the new, safe VDT within $65–$100 of the cost of a regular computer monitor. In 1993, having gone out on his own, Mr. Kranzer, with the aid of Philip Fletcher, began to work on the design of what they would later call the Kranzer Low Radiation VDT.

Mr. Philip Fletcher

Background: From Personnel File 411 of Kranzer Electronics, I found that Mr. Fletcher, a PhD in electronic engineering from Cornell University, is a long-time friend and colleague of Mr. Robert Kranzer. They worked together at CRK Computers on several successful technological innovations. Mr. Fletcher's performance appraisals revealed a driven and dedicated man capable of great concentration and focus. The failure of the Kranzer Low Radiation VDT seems to have deeply impacted Mr. Fletcher's confidence.

Major Points: Mr. Fletcher joined Mr. Kranzer when he started Kranzer Electronics with the explicit understanding that he would be entrusted with the actual development of the Low Radiation VDT. Mr. Fletcher felt that the lowering of the radiation in the electromagnetic field of the VDT could be accomplished by experimenting with the placement of the major video board. Over time, Mr. Fletcher and Mr. Kranzer reduced the measurable radiation by 60 per cent while only raising the cost of production by 10 per cent. The patents for the Kranzer-Fletcher technique were successfully granted in 1994. Mr. Fletcher pointed out how he felt that he and Mr. Kranzer were sitting on a fortune. Mr. Fletcher provided the following newspaper clippings that were coming out at approximately the time the product was being fine tuned:

- Seven of thirteen pregnant women who worked at Air Canada's check-in counter at Montreal's Dorval Airport reported miscarriages. The press speculated on VDT connections.

- Six of ten pregnant VDT operators at Sears Roebuck's South Regional Office in Dallas, Texas reported miscarriages. A seventh operator gave birth to a premature infant who died.

- It was revealed that seven pregnancies among clerks in the accounts department of Surrey Memorial Hospital in Vancouver, British Columbia resulted in three miscarriages, one premature birth, one infant with a club foot, one infant in need of eye surgery, and one infant with digestive tract abnormalities.

Idea: Mr. Fletcher's technical innovation succeeded. His reliance on newspapers to collect the rising VDT scare does not square with the scientific and governmental account of the relationship between VDTs and health problems. My Internet search shows that, at this time, the Ontario Ministry of Labour, after investigating the relationship, noted "We left no stone unturned to find a case where a single machine emitted a dangerous level of radiation .... There is not a single scrap of evidence to indicate any danger from VDT radiation." In the United Stated, the House Committee on Science and Technology opened hearings on VDTs and concluded that, at this time, no action was required other than to recommend that standards be developed to measure radiation in the electromagnetic field of VDTs.

Ms. Martha Liston

Background: From *Canadian Women in Business* and Personnel File 642 of Kranzer Electronics, I found that Ms. Liston had been a representative on the Canadian Equestrian Team in world competitions, a vigorous exponent of management education for women (as evidenced by her current role as president of the not-for-profit organization Women in Business), and a first-rate project manager. Ms. Liston's previous work experience at Future Technological Enterprises and SQM Consulting Engineers indicates a very accomplished project manager accustomed to bringing technology projects in on time and within budget.

Major Points: Ms. Liston felt that the Low Radiation VDT project had gone excellently.

The team, made up of Ms. Liston and four specialists in electromagnetic emissions, worked well together. Mr. Fletcher and Mr. Kranzer both championed the project by giving it adequate funds and a fast-track development ramp. Ms. Liston felt that the team had not only risen to the technical challenge, but had done so within budget and on time. Ms. Liston did express worries at that time as to whether the health scare would stick or just pass on by. Ms. Liston openly speculated that she felt that the large computer firms and governments had vested interests in keeping the issue quiet—the computer companies because the possibility of adverse health effects impacted their clients, the government because it was a primary user of computers and stood to lose millions if litigation by unionized workers in the public sector led to pay-outs for eye problems, birth defects, and other health-related issues.

Idea: Ms. Liston's speculation on the strategic intent of the large computer firms and government is unlikely, in my view. But a point she brought up that deserves further work in my project concerns the question "Why didn't other firms or government agencies begin to think about lowering the emissions in VDTs?" Ms. Liston implicitly believes they did just that, but were unwilling to go public since this public admission might leave them legally responsible for those claiming adverse health effects from VDTs.

Mr. Norton Hoyt

Background: From Personnel File 592 of Kranzer Electronics, I found that Mr. Hoyt is an extremely gifted and creative man. He had founded Hoyt and Rivera Communications Ltd. in 1982 and joined Kranzer Electronics in 1994 when his partner, Mr. Jose Rivera, was struck by lightning while playing golf. Mr. Hoyt's specialty is marketing high-tech products and he is known in the industry for his ability to take complex issues and portray them simply.

Major Points: Mr. Hoyt did not like the advertisement potential in the Kranzer Low Radiation VDT. The association between VDTs and health is seen in the public's mind as a paranoid's perception. VDTs are seen positively. They are gateways to the future. They make our work easier. They permit us access to heretofore unmined information resources. They enhance our ability to escape from the humdrum of every day and play video games. My job was to remind them that VDTs could be bad for their health. To do this, I had to avoid a shrill tone that would scold them. It is this scolding tone that, Mr. Hoyt conjectured, leaves anti-smoking ads so ineffective. Mr. Hoyt says the lack of formal scientific and medical recognition of the role of VDTs is a problem. The typical VDT buyer was a large corporation interested in price, reliability, and service follow-up. The home consumer, as well, was interested in price, visual clarity, and service. In focus groups done on VDT buyers, very few mentioned health in their purchasing decisions.

Idea: Mr. Hoyt, unlike Mr. Kranzer and Mr. Fletcher, saw a large distinction between the stories of VDT health-related problems in the newspapers and the willingness of authorities in science, medicine, and government to publicly support these views. Mr. Hoyt feared that a company that solved a problem that others did not take seriously would be put in the awkward position of having to sell the problem before it could reap the rewards of selling the solution.

Mr. Kenji Morishima

Background: From *Who is Who in Canadian Business* I found that Mr. Morishima is a much-travelled veteran of technological innovation in computer monitors. Mr. Morishima worked for IBM, World Technology, and CRK Computers in both its Japanese Division and, more recently, in its Canadian region. Mr. Morishima has a reputation for his knowledge of the field and key players.

Major Points: Mr. Morishima was candid in his views and quite willing to speculate in explaining the failure of the Kranzer Low Radiation VDT. Mr. Morishima felt that the industry, as a whole, genuinely looked at the Kranzer innovation as an effective way to lower radiation emissions in the electromagnetic field of the VDT. Without breaking patent laws, most of the VDT manufacturers had learned from Kranzer. In fact, Mr. Morishima went on to say, recent emission readings by high-end radiation emitters are now at about the level of the early Kranzer low radiation prototypes. What the industry had done was remain silent on the issue while they sought diligently to lower radiation emissions. They were encouraged by governments to do so. In fact, when Kranzer Electronics first came out with its advertisement campaign to sell the Kranzer Low Radiation VDT, the industry held its breath. They were relieved when "health and the computer" did not become part of the public agenda. This would have greatly impaired its introduction into both home and workplace. Mr. Morishima felt that Mr. Kranzer had been sacrificed by an industry interested in getting its product accepted. Companies in the field of technical innovations must first agree on what is good for the industry before they begin to innovate. If you innovate in such a way that the industry sees the innovation as a potential problem—as in bringing up the association between health and VDTs—you will be frozen out of the game. Kranzer Electronics, despite its genius for problem solving, was frozen out of the game. Since Mr. Kranzer is such a valuable player, the big boys, Mr. Morishima conjectured, held back and real damage happened only on the special project and not to Kranzer Electronics as a whole.

Idea: Mr. Morishima points to a future where firms collude to ease out troublemakers. Kranzer Electronics inadvertently became a troublemaker when it sought to draw attention to the growing public association between VDTs and adverse health The future is one in which technology must be made faster, better, and more—even if all the glitches are not yet removed.

QUESTIONS

1. Despite the fact that the Kranzer Low Radiation VDT failed, how could Paul Desauteils frame the conclusion of his MBA project to show "the promise of technology"? In this view, did the industry solve the "possible" problem between the electromagnetic emission field surrounding VDTs and eye problems or birth defects and miscarriages? If yes, how? If not, why not?

2. How could Paul Desauteils frame the conclusion of his MBA project to bolster the credibility of those who see "technology as a threat"? Is the evidence collected by Robert Kranzer and Philip Fletcher regarding the harmful effects of VDTs persuasive? If so, why? If not, why not?

3. What, in the comments of Martha Liston and Norton Hoyt, could Paul Desauteils employ to frame the conclusion of his MBA project to bolster the credibility of those who argue that "technology is an instrument of power"? In this view, why did the computer industry refuse to actively pursue the possible adverse

effects of VDTs? Who gained and who lost power in the failure of the Kranzer Low Radiation VDT?

4. What, in the comments of Kenji Morishima, the industry veteran from CRK Computers, could Paul Desauteils employ to frame the conclusion of his MBA project to bolster the credibility of those who argue that "technology is a portal to a new age"? Which of the five new age paradigms (see Figure 10.5), or which combinations of these, best summarizes the views of Mr. Morishima? Why?

5. If you were using Paul Desauteils' interviews with Robert Kranzer, Philip Fletcher, Martha Liston, Norton Hoyt, and Kenji Morishima to write an MBA project in business ethics, how would you analyze the computer industry's desire for silence or an end to the controversy over VDTs and health? How could business ethics be useful in this case in establishing public dialogue?

6. While hindsight offers 20/20 vision, what advice do you think Paul Desauteils could give to Robert Kranzer regarding how to best learn to avoid a repeat of the failure of the Kranzer Low Radiation VDT? Look at the advice you are offering Robert Kranzer from the point of view of a business ethicist. From the point of view of a business ethicist, what would you question? Why?

CASE 10-2   The Pleastine Pill: High-Tech Doping in Sports

For the first thirty-three years of his life, Allen Jennings was an ideal citizen. He played by the rules. A genuine genius, he accelerated his education and graduated from Harvard at age twenty-three with a PhD in chemistry. Shortly afterwards, Allen married Brenda, went to work for a major pharmaceutical company in San Francisco, and fathered two children, Sally and Micah. Within a year of working with a team looking at ways to boost the immune system, Allen came up with what is now called the

"Ricoh-Jennings Cocktail," used as one of the early and effective AIDS treatments.

The Jennings lived frugally. Both Allen and Brenda were advocates and practitioners of voluntary simplicity. They opened their summer cottage to inner city children and their parents for three weeks each summer. They gave ten per cent of their earnings to their church. Brenda organized and ran the church choir. The family embodied generosity and warmth. It all came to a crushing halt when Brenda and the children, on a visit to Brenda's mother in Belfast, fell victim to a car bomb. Twenty-nine people, including eight-year-old Sally, were killed instantaneously. Brenda was left in a coma—she would be machine dependent for what remained of her life—and Micah suffered second-degree burns over ninety per cent of his body.

Within a year it became clear that, even given Allen's simple personal needs, his medical coverage, and his salary, he would need at least $200,000 a year for some time to see both his son and wife through their medical bills. Brenda Jennings required 24-hour, intensive medical care. Her coma could persist or come to an end within a month or two. It was not certain whether, should Brenda awaken, she would require further medical care. In the meantime, she was hooked up to a respirator, dialysis system, and vital-sign monitoring equipment in the Intensive Care Unit of The Worthington Memorial Hospital. Two floors down, in the Burn Unit, Micah Jennings was in critical condition. Micah's face, upper torso, and feet required reconstructive surgery. His physicians speculated that if Micah survived his burns he would probably require extensive psychiatric treatment.

Allen Jennings entered a period of depression. Those around him did what they could to buoy his spirits. His neighbours brought him meals and tended his garden. Allen spent hours each day at the hospital visiting his wife and son. Every Friday at 7:00 p.m. he went to the cemetery to place flowers at Sally's grave. His employer sought to make allowances for his growing absence from work. He was given stimulating problems to work on in the hopes that it would help him focus his mind and return to his earlier level of productivity. The problem he was working on was how to chemically stimulate or boost the immune system to rid it selectively of other chemicals. Despite his despondency and "loner" attitude to his research, Allen was progressing on what he called the Pleastine Pill.

A year after the car bombing Allen realized he had debts for medical services exceeding $400,000. Brenda was still totally machine dependent, but showed some signs of improvement. Micah required five or six more surgical interventions. His psychiatric treatment was very expensive and likely to go on for years. Allen's salary was $82,000. Life in the Bay Area was costly. Allen sold the summer cottage and put the family home on the market. He moved into a rooming house near the laboratory, anticipating that he would purchase or rent more spacious accommodation once his son and wife were released from the hospital. Allen was well aware that at the rate things were going he could be in debt several million dollars within five years.

Allen had a very good disposition when it came to living with debt. However, what made him desperate for money was the possibility of a new exploratory procedure on brain-damage coma cases being done by an Argentinean physician, Luis Brunel. Dr. Brunel was willing to use the facilities at The Worthington Memorial Hospital to try his procedure on Brenda Jennings. To expedite matters and secure the facilities, rent the machinery, and fly Dr. Brunel and his team to San Francisco required Allen to write a cheque for $300,000, to be followed in one year with another $150,000. Allen was stymied. He was already in the process of exhausting his creditors.

The following day, a light bulb went on in Allen's head. The Pleastine Pill he had been developing as a new weapon in the fight against AIDS might, he ruminated, have another function. Allen was aware of the controversy surrounding athletes' use of substances to enhance their physical performance. Insofar as the technique involved the ingestion of steroids for strength and speed, the Pleastine Pill would mask detection within the present testing procedures. Allen Jennings had inadvertently discovered that the pill would cover all traces of steroid use.

Within two months, Allen had contacted Mr. Rickards, a bright but shady chemist who headed the PRT Sports Medicine Group. Once Allen demonstrated the ease with which the Pleastine Pill masked the detection of steroid use, and how simply it could be manufactured, Mr. Rickards offered Allen $1 million in a one-time deal to abandon his research on the Pleastine Pill, label it a failure, and give the formula for its manufacture to Mr. Rickards. Mr. Rickards assured Allen that the pill would be called the "Q Pill," and would be filtered to athletes in such a way that neither he nor Allen would ever be implicated. He added that the Q Pill would cause little damage, since the athletes in question were already taking steroids and the pill was merely a guarantee that they would not be caught.

Allen was not concerned by Mr. Rickards' shabby rationalizations—his focus was fixed directly on Dr. Brunel and the experimental surgery for Brenda. Allen agreed to the deal. That year, twelve new world records were set—the highest ever in a non-Olympic year. With the experimental surgery, Brenda recovered her faculties and now is relearning basic speech patterns. Micah seems to be improving, and his doctors anticipate that in time he will be able to function at a high level. Allen Jennings now rents a small bungalow on Miller Avenue and is working hard to pay off $200,000 in remaining debts.

QUESTIONS:

1. What is Allen Jennings' ethical dilemma? What is the ethical dilemma involved with selling a drug like the Pleastine or Q Pill? Who gets hurt? Who benefits? Why does a drug like the one created by Allen Jennings put more pressure on athletes to use steroids?

2. Frame this case and its ethical dilemma as demonstrating "technology as a promise." Within this perspective, why is the technology not to blame for the problem? Who is? Why?

3. How can the story of Allen Jennings and the Pleastine or Q Pill be framed as one that supports the view of "technology as a threat or a menace"? What form of elitism is bolstered? How might one argue that this pill de-skills in the realm of athletics?

4. Employ the "technology as an instrument of power" framework to make sense of Allen Jennings' decision. Who, in your opinion, gets power from this technology? Will new counter-tests be required to detect the Pleastine or Q Pill? If so, how does this redistribute power? Why, in this contest for power, is there likely to be an ongoing escalation in technology to encourage the use of performance-enhancing substances, and also an escalation in technology to detect the presence of these substances? In power terms, why is this escalation occurring? What does this tell us about values in society?

5. From your perspective, what sort of portal to the future is represented by the Pleastine or Q Pill? Why? From your perspective, what sort of portal to the future is represented by the experimental brain surgery conducted by Dr. Brunel? Why? Which, in your view, dominates today? Why?

6. How do you feel about what Allen Jennings did? Do you think he should tell his wife and son about his decision? What do you think about his burying the possible positive uses of the Pleastine Pill under the "failed" research category? Did Allen Jennings act professionally? Why are some of us very sympathetic to Allen Jennings?

CASE 10-3 Pioneer Information Limited Explores Data Mining

"**S**nail" Carruthers and Kathy Jenkins founded Pioneer Information Limited (PIL) in 1992. With a small amount of capital from Redding Venture Capital Associates and an interest-free loan from Kathy's father, PIL has grown from a small company that flooded homes and offices with unwanted faxes to become one of the key players in Canada's data mining industry. Kathy and Snail (who received his nickname when he was a high school track star) started PIL when they first moved in together. Snail had graduated from the Business School at the University of Windsor; Kathy completed her Master's degree in philosophy at Guelph University. The two purchased six high-quality fax machines and set up their home business.

Snail had conceived of the idea of PIL in 1992, when he realized that Canada had no regulations regarding unsolicited or junk faxes, whereas in the United States authorities were and still are tough on the junk-fax industry. PIL would fax unsolicited advertisements across Canada and into the United States for a pay-for-service clientele. PIL, in its first year of operation, could pump out up to 150,000 pages an hour, charging advertisers up to 10 cents per page. With a large market, PIL did $3 million in its first year.

By 1994, both Snail and Kathy were taking $100,000 a year out of the company as salary. By this time, many other junk-fax companies had moved into the market. To keep one step ahead, PIL moved in two directions. First, it began selling customers' numbers and addresses to other companies, taking on the new role of list broker; second, PIL moved into the upscale fax advertising market serving clients who distribute information to professionals, including economic research firms, financial advisors, and stock management clubs. By 1996, the year the Canadian Radio and Television Commission began regulating junk faxes, PIL was in the data mining game. The company was now sufficiently large that Snail and Kathy decided to float the company on the stock market. Initial shares were offered at $5 and by mid-year they had more than doubled.

Data mining involves collecting, storing, and analyzing data about the minutiae of people's daily lives—what people eat, wear, watch, ride in, read, etc.—and sell it to other companies eager to market to particular client types. The data itself is mined every time you use your credit card, air miles card, Interac bank card, or private store cards such as the Safeway Members card and Zellers' Club Z card. Particular purchases that require information such as warranties or club memberships provide the very raw data of data miners like PIL. The data from these sources is immense. In Canada, for example, Interac expects to handle nearly 1.5 billion transactions at the rate of 42 per second. It has been estimated that approximately 40 per cent of all known consumer transactions in Canada leave an electronic trail.

To make huge profits, Snail and Kathy now have a staff of 46 full-time and 16 part-time technical specialists. To extract high rents in this rough-and-tumble business, companies explore two options. The first is to create and/or keep abreast of increasingly smarter software programs that can sift through wads of information and uncover patterns of consumer behaviour that most marketing professionals would never think to probe. A classic example of this correlation is the "beer and diaper connection." One data mining company, a rival of PIL, discovered that men who pop out to buy diapers in the evening are disproportionately likely to pick up a twelve-pack of beer on their way home.

The second option is labelled "mass customization." In mass customization, the data miners use a variety of sources of information to create client profiles. Data miners' clients use these services—and pay dearly for them—in order to determine what particular kind of person or organization is likely to became a customer. Extremely high prices are paid to data miners who can, after building the profiles, instruct their clients on what can be done to encourage that person's or company's patronage.

PIL is benchmarking two American leaders in the field and hopes to emulate their techniques. San Francisco-based Wells Fargo and Co., and MBNA Corp. of Wilmington, Delaware are at the forefront of the data mining revolution. They have developed advanced software programs that scan electronically the financial profile of hundreds of thousands of individuals and small businesses in order to pinpoint potential customers. Snail and Kathy are trying to emulate this software. Another source of data PIL is integrating into its data mining file is the Internet. Almost every major retailer in the world is now using—or planning to use—the Net to generate new business and in the process acquire more knowledge about its customers. Every time someone orders a book, for example, from the Seattle-based on-line bookstore, Amazon.com, that information goes immediately into the customer's personal file, adding to the store of data regarding his or her reading preferences, interests, and the like. Web site operators are employing this sort of information to direct specific kinds of advertising at people who seem, given their profile, to be receptive to these messages.

Thus, with the help of PIL, the Internet is now a gold mine for data miners. But PIL and the data miners have even bigger dreams. In a few years, it should be possible to data mine the television viewer just as the Internet user is now being mined. Snail and Kathy speculate that within months it should be possible for cable companies to monitor exactly the programs each of their customers views. In the hands of the data miners that information could be correlated with household demographics such as age and income so that advertisers could direct specific commercials at receptive audiences.

Snail and Kathy realize that data gathering and data mining businesses have exploded so swiftly that governments and activist groups interested in privacy have had little opportunity to take stock of the situation, let alone regulate it. Snail and Kathy buy and sell information about individuals' daily transactions; they are both well on the way to becoming multi-millionaires.

QUESTIONS:

1. Ann Cavoukian, Ontario's Information and Privacy Commissioner, addressed data mining by saying, "Data mining represents a major challenge to privacy because the companies who practice data mining cannot predict what uses the resulting information will have"; indeed, that data mining "may be the most fundamental issue that privacy advocates face in the next decade." Do you think she is exaggerating? If so, why? If not, why not?

2. From the point of view of businesses seeking new clients and customers, how would you frame PIL and data miners as fulfilling the "promise of technology"? From the point of view of society as a whole, how would you frame PIL and data miners as fulfilling the "promise of technology"?

3. How do data mining companies like PIL exemplify "technology as an instrument of power"? Who, in your view, gains most in this view of technology as an instrument of power (see Figure 10.4)? Why?

4. Make the case for the regulation of the data mining industry. Is this made more simple by the fact that data mining is done in an international context? What aspect of data mining would you regulate?

5. Make the case against the regulation of the data mining industry. Over time, who, in your view, will dominate this industry?

Why? Do you think Snail and Kathy of PIL would be for or against regulation of the data mining industry? Why?

6. If we take PIL and the data mining industry as an example of the way we will use smart machines and smart programs in the future, what sort of future awaits us? In this context, what is a good role for the business ethicist?

VIDEO CASE 1   Canadian Pacific Railway: Relocation, Rationalization, and Good Corporate Citizenship

Postmodern society is, as we are learning, continually changing. It challenges both management and public administrators to avoid complacency. Postmodernism often requires us to throw away old plans and begin to rethink our businesses, our business ethics, and our corporate images. This is happening at the once staid and venerable Canadian Pacific Railway. Under the guidance of its chief executive officer, R.J. (Bob) Ritchie, and his vice presidents, particularly Fred Green and Hugh MacDiamird, this company is attempting to revitalize itself and keep abreast of the changes that have taken place in the rail industry since Canadian Pacific Railway's inception in 1881.

The top management have found that revenues from the railroad operations have not kept up with expectations. Ironically, Canadian Pacific Railway's strength for future growth rests in the Canadian West, but it is in the East that the company has the bulk of its railroad investment. It is headquartered in Montreal, but trucking has made huge inroads in the East on the once lucrative railroad business. In 1997, Canadian Pacific Railway set five goals. These are:

1. to quickly review assets needed to grow the business

2. to accelerate the rationalization of new strategic resources

3. to continue reducing operating expenses

4. to improve customer service to generate satisfaction levels that translate into profitable growth

5. to turn around performance of the Eastern rail network

As the "operations" man at Canadian Pacific Railway, Fred Green has been put in charge of what can be called the most colossal make-over in Canadian corporate history. Canadian Pacific Railway's recent (1996) annual report states: "Canadian Pacific Railway is on the threshold of a new, exciting period in its history. We have adapted, changed, and transformed ourselves during the past ten years into a much more narrowly-based company." As part of its larger vision, the company has moved from employing 39,300 employees in 1993 to 20,150 employees in 1997. This near halving of personnel is reflected in the decision to move corporate headquarters to Calgary from Montreal and cut the 1,500 employees to 750 in the new Western head office. This move out of Quebec did not sit well with either the provincial government or the municipality of Montreal. Both felt that after years of providing jobs in the local economy, Canadian Pacific Railway was failing to act as a good corporate citizen. The governments in question felt despite the economic rationalization, the move was motivated by political considerations. They feared other large employers in Quebec would follow the lead of Canadian Pacific Railway.

Employees were shaken. Many of those who survived the downsizing had to leave long established neighbourhoods and routines to move to a new city. The relocation of Canadian Pacific Railway's headquarters has actually been a microcosm of their new organizational philosophy. In the move to Calgary, Canadian Pacific Railway cut the levels of administrative hierarchy from eleven to five. This new flat structure is intended to empower decision makers at a lower level in the company. Cooperation and teamwork are to be the operating principles of the new, leaner, more responsive Canadian Pacific Railway.

Despite this espoused change in values, some fear that companies like Canadian Pacific Railway are really failing to take the role of the good corporate citizen to heart. They fear that beneath the apparent velvet glove of the new forms of empowerment, there actually rests a concerted effort to break the spirit of unions, reduce benefits by reducing the number of workers and the number of full-time equivalents, and to make sure that, where and whenever possible, work can be contracted out. Others see Canadian Pacific Railway as an exemplar of the good corporate citizen—a firm that has seen the constraints and opportunities in its operations and moved to secure them for as many people as it requires to do the task and compete successfully. Canadian Pacific Railway has helped people relocate. It has been generous in its retirement, retraining, and severance packages to those it has let go. It has been forthright and honest in its attempt to make itself a viable national railway when railroads have fallen off the national agenda.

QUESTIONS:

1. In your view, is Canadian Pacific Railway showing the signs of a good corporate leader? If so, how do its actions confirm this? If not, what is it doing that worries you?

2. Do you think it is ethical for a firm like Canadian Pacific Railway to shift its headquarters from Montreal to Calgary? Would you feel the same if a large company in Canada decided to move its headquarters to Mexico?

3. Roy Dale, transfer #49, is a loyal employee. From his viewpoint, do you think his loyalty is being recognized at Canadian Pacific Railway? If yes, why? If not, why not?

4. How would a postmodern pessimist see the changes at Canadian Pacific Railway? How would a postmodern optimist see these changes? Which—the optimist or the pessimist—best captures your attitude? Why?

5. In your view, what complications ensue when a large corporation attempts to simultaneously reduce its employee base by half and save $125 million, while fostering greater cooperation, teamwork, and the empowerment necessary for faster decisions? Why do employees look at the conjunction of these factors differently than stockholders? In your view, what are the conditions under which downsizing is most adequately justified?

VIDEO CASE 2   *Privatizing Canadian Prisons: A Look at Social Responsibility*

Crime control, in postmodern contexts, is big business. We are all familiar with the explosive growth in Canadian businesses developing gated communities, renting out security and bodyguards, installing and monitoring alarm systems in both homes and offices, securing information systems from prying hackers, and setting up video surveillance systems in retail outlets. However, fewer people are aware that prisons are a booming growth sector increasingly under the eye of entrepreneurs. The United States, which incarcerates 600 individuals per 100,000 population (a world leader in this category), is much advanced in the privatization and franchising of prisons. Questions arise. Should business profit from those imprisoned for criminal activities? Are the governments and courts that operate and fill the prisons acting responsibly when they contract out these duties? Is the public as a whole being served well and protected by privatized prisons? Are those imprisoned treated in a fashion considered acceptable by the courts and governments who act as agents for the public? The reasoning on the issue of social responsibility in the privatization and franchising of prisons in the United States has been simple and pragmatic. Privatizing prisons saves taxpayers money.

Currently, as is made explicit in our video, many Canadian jurisdictions are eyeing the American experience with extreme interest. The provinces of New Brunswick, Ontario, Alberta, and Nova Scotia are putting out feelers on this issue. Canada is caught in the crossfire of several forces. Like the United States, Canada uses its prisons to control its citizens to a greater extent than most world nations of comparable stature (see Figure 1).

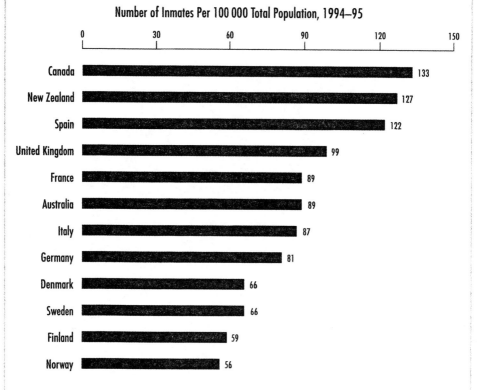

Number of Inmates Per 100 000 Total Population, 1994–95

Canada	133
New Zealand	127
Spain	122
United Kingdom	99
France	89
Australia	89
Italy	87
Germany	81
Denmark	66
Sweden	66
Finland	59
Norway	56

Moreover, both the size of the incarcerated population and the cost per prisoner within the Canadian correctional system are rising. The prisons, at both federal and provincial levels, are overcrowded, old, and soon will require massive and costly reconstruction. Added to this mix are two emergent social factors: first, the Canadian population seems far more concerned with deficit cutting than with the state of the correctional system and, if money is found for social services, Canadians place education, health, and child care far ahead of modernizing and expanding penitentiaries; and second, there is a new wave of Canadian entrepreneurs like Chris King of Brecknell

Corporation, Keith McGillvary, an architect from Nova Scotia, and SMC Lavelin Limited, who are eager to join experienced American prison operators such as Management Training Corporation (MTC) in using private capital and expertise to manage Canadian prisons.

The government of Nova Scotia is leading the way in exploring the prison privatization option. It is considering turning over 512 beds in Truro and 8 other outdated and crowded prisons to bids from the private sector. MTC, a company that already turns a $45 million (US) profit in the operation of its American prisons, is interested in partnering with Canadian firms in gaining entry into the $1.5 billion (Cdn) prison market. MTC's formula for success is simple and effective—they keep costs down by shaving from 10 to 20 per cent off what it costs at present to operate prisons in the public sector. In prisons like Marana, a minimum security prison in the heart of Arizona, MTC uses an open-floor design requiring fewer guards per prisoner than the typical prison. It avoids unionization. It cross-trains guards to do more than one task. Bill Rhoedde, the warden of Marana and former warden in the government-run prison system, extols the private prison's ability to innovate. Savings can be found in purchasing prison clothes, food, and furniture in the open market. Garbage disposal can be done in-house. Drug and vocational counselling can be subcontracted. Ron Russell, the head of MTC's prison division, points out that companies like MTC build, own, and operate the prison following rules set and monitored by governments and the courts. The private company charges the state a fixed sum per day per prisoner. When the contract expires the sum is renegotiated.

Karen Inman, a former waitress in a California steakhouse, exemplifies the new breed of private prison workers. In an eight-year period, Inman has worked her way up the MTC system to become the deputy warden at Marana. She is tough. She is decisive. Drawing on her earlier work experience, Inman feels that working in a prison and making it work is not all that different from running a steakhouse. Community security is a paid commodity. Those who provide this service, when disciplined, trained, and seasoned in competitive markets, deliver the best service. They use problem solving and the best techniques of efficient management to provide better service at better prices. Bill Houshley, the government inspector who makes sure that MTC and other private prison companies are doing what they say they will, gives them a clean bill of health. Houshley heads a small government-run group of inspectors who monitor and do spot checks in privately run prisons. He realizes that while the private prison firms have built and own the prisons, it is the courts that fill them and it is the government who is ultimately responsible for their operation.

Within Nova Scotia, the call for bids to privatize prisons has been an occasion for renewed interest in just who is and should be responsible for corrections. The prison guards in Nova Scotia and elsewhere in Canada are unionized. They see privatization of prisons as, among other things, a means for government to rid itself of unions. They worry that the "rent a guard" mentality will mean that guards will receive little, if any, training or professional status. They are concerned that when it comes down to a trade-off between prison property and guard safety, the privately run prison, given its interests, will opt for protecting property. Ed Foulkes, a spokesperson for the Nova Scotia Correctional Officers Union, wonders about the values of a society that permits people to profit off the backs of criminals. Foulkes and the union see the new "factory" prisons as holding out an initial promise of great savings, but in time delivering less effective services for higher costs. On the other hand, Fred Honesberger, the executive director of Nova Scotia Correctional Services, sees the new prison entrepreneurs as a breath of fresh air, who, if monitored properly, will deliver more effective prison services at lower costs.

It is not clear how the citizens of Nova Scotia feel. There are those who see the new prison entrepreneurs as the most socially responsible option. They will be bound by contracts. They will be cutting costs. They will be bidding competitively against other prison operators. On the other hand, there are those who feel that contracting out prison services is a failure to act responsibly. These individuals worry that businesses will seek to cut corners. They will unintentionally jeopardize community security and/or mistreat those incarcerated. The naysayers worry that private prisons will abandon this important social role when profits diminish or when much higher profits can be made elsewhere at less risk. These citizens envision a possible future in which large prison companies may find it in their best interests to lobby government to keep up a steady and growing flow of prisoners. While the future is not an open book, it is clear that within the next decade Canada will be making up its mind on whether or not prisons are a business just like any other.

QUESTIONS

1. Compare and contrast the "self-interested CSR model" with the "social contract perspective in CSR" as they pertain to the privatization of prisons in Canada. Which view best captures Karen Inman's views? Why? Which view best encapsulates the views of Bill Houshley and Fred Honesberger? Why?

2. Within the "stakeholder (management) model of CSR," who should represent the inmates in prisons? Who, in your view, would represent the inmates in the privatized prisons? What are the costs and benefits of the privatized prison in this regard?

3. Within the idea of "business as a community," discuss why Ron Russell and Chris King would be interested in arguing for the prison system as really an entrepreneurial community. Why would Ed Foulkes see it as a community of rational rules? Why do some critics of prison privatization worry about it becoming a community of fleeting exchanges? Over time, do you think government inspectors like Bill Houshley will be successful in making certain that it does not become a community of fleeting exchanges? If yes, why? If not, why not?

4. Why do Ed Foulkes and the unions in the existing correctional system distrust the prison entrepreneurs? At the systems level, can one create trust between the unions and the new prison entrepreneurs? If yes, how? If not, why not?

5. From an issues management perspective, what issues can the Nova Scotia government expect to arise if it accepts a bid to privatize Truro and eight other prisons? What advice would you give the government of Nova Scotia on how best to prepare for these issues?

6. If Canada, in time, decides to privatize some or all of its prisons, what sort of skill set—calculator, legislator, or interpreter—do you expect to rise to ascendancy? Why? Would this skill set fit your existing image of the warden, prison guard, or prison employee? If yes, why? If not, why not?

VIDEO CASE 3 **Oberto Oberti's Dream and the Environmental Review Process**

Many "green" businesses attempt to keep land in use without it being abused. These businesses create golf courses and ski hills and establish sites for recreational and eco-tourist usage. They argue that these uses of the land are much better for the environment than putting up high-rises, building factories, and paving the natural setting. Golfers, skiers, birdwatchers, and hikers all form an alliance of new green consumers who use their leisure time in such a way that it encourages the development of more green spaces. Oberto Oberti, a successful Vancouver architect and entrepreneur, has a dream that suits this version of green business but, despite all his energy and enthusiasm, he is finding it both difficult and extremely costly to find his way through British Columbia's Environmental Review Process.

Oberto Oberti grew up skiing in the Italian Alps. He is a man of dramatic passions and enthusiasms. Oberti's dream is to design, build, and, along with his investors, operate the highest, longest, wildest, year-round ski resort. The Purcell Mountains, lodged in the Columbia Valley in eastern British Columbia near the town of Inverness, is the home of Jumbo Glacier. This valley and Jumbo Glacier are a favourite haunt of wilderness hikers seeking to view the grizzly bear and other species in their natural habitat. Oberti recognizes this and seeks to ensure that Jumbo Glacier and the surrounding area is protected from concentrated forms of development. To open up the area and bring prosperity to Inverness and the smaller towns in the vicinity, Oberti, with money from American, Japanese, Italian, and Swiss investors, wants to create an alpine village with accommodations for 6,000 of the world's economic elite. The ski resort would be tied to helicopter skiing on the glacier. Other facilities would include all the luxuries demanded of this exacting clientele. The site planned by Oberti, with his architect's eye and entrepreneurial dreams, would outclass both Whistler and Banff.

Driven by a desire to bring both world-class skiing to North America and preserve the beauty of Jumbo Glacier, Oberti raised more than $5 million (US) to begin the project. In 1990, when Oberti first began his dream, he found that it was far easier to get foreign capital lined up for the $250 million (US) project than it was to get permission to proceed with the development. For five years Oberti has been butting heads with officials from the British Columbia Environmental Review Process. Most provinces, territories, and the federal government have a version of this process. In effect, the environmental review process is an effort to weigh the costs and benefits of developing sites viewed as environmentally sensitive. The cost-benefit analysis used in this context includes not only economic values, but also attempts to look at the impact of the proposed development upon the natural environment. This stakeholder approach awkwardly mixes a management stakeholder view with a stewardship stakeholder view, which frequently pits those with an economic perspective against those who resist it in the name of protecting the natural habitat.

Bob Camsil, a retired teacher and proprietor of the Blue Dog Cafe in Inverness, typifies the type of concerned citizen who joined the "Jumbo Coalition." With its 2,000 citizens, Inverness managed to mobilize a concerted and organized resistance to Oberti's plan for the development of Jumbo Glacier. The coalition was a mixture of environmentalists, activists, politicians, and concerned citizens. Like Bob Camsil, they saw Oberti's dream as a potential nightmare for the Columbia Valley and its ecological sustainability. Others pointed out that within a three-hour radius of Inverness, there are already twelve well-developed ski hills, none of which are operating at near capacity. Still others expressed concern with Oberti's attitude; in their eyes, he seemed patronizing in his self-serving desire to bring the Columbia Valley to a level of unheard prosperity. Many came to the valley expressly to escape the "keeping up with the Joneses" lifestyle that Oberti's seemed to promise.

The Jumbo Coalition was not a backwater group of small-town citizens willing to be "taken" by the slick, big-city businessman. They perceived themselves as already prosperous. They were committed to meeting Oberti and his experts on every level and at every opportunity. They operated a sophisticated Web page on the Internet through which they promoted their cause. They posted sample protest letters, petitions, and forms. All that was required was a signature from those citizens whose schedules inhibited a more active commitment to the coalition. From bumper stickers to actively lobbying members of parliament, Bob Camsil and the Jumbo Coalition sought to bury Oberti's alpine village and all that came with it.

In Cranbrook, BC, in the early days of winter 1995, five years and $5 million (US) into Oberti's efforts, twenty bureaucrats from three levels of government met with Oberti and his team and the Jumbo Coalition to determine the fate of Jumbo Glacier. The views of this committee were to go directly to the cabinet of the BC government. Oberti and his experts came well prepared. They provided five volumes of data collected by world experts in ski development projects, ecologists, and economists. The Oberti team provided testimonials. They worked hard in the time allocated to establish the benefits of the project. They sought to clear the air of doubts. Aside from a minor foray into the dropping of bombs to offset avalanche worries, the team did splendidly. Oberti believed that with his diligent work and the obvious merits of his project, all was in hand. Bob Camsil dropped a bomb of his own. The Jumbo Coalition produced a petition of 1,600 signatures from valley residents opposing the development. This had not been on the agenda's schedule. Taken aback by the inclusion of unexpected data, the Environmental Review Committee decided to postpone a decision.

Oberto Oberti vows he will persist in his fight. It is clear that as time drags on, Oberti's investors may begin to question the wisdom of spending more time and money on the possibility of another costly meeting at another future date. The Jumbo Coalition is happy; their valley is still a place for the grizzly, the elk, and other mountain species.

QUESTIONS:

1. Does Oberto Oberti's project represent a green point of view? Is his dream that of a radical environmentalist, reform environmentalist, opportunistic environmentalist, or none of the above? Explain your selection.

2. Even if Oberto Oberti feels that the Jumbo Coalition has acted unfairly and unethically, why can't he blow the whistle on them? Why, in your view, is whistle-blowing not an effective strategy in this case?

3. Does the point of view expressed by the Jumbo Coalition represent a green point of view? Is the view of the coalition that of a radical environmentalist, reform environmentalist, opportunistic environmentalist, or none of the above? Explain your selection.

4. In your opinion, does the environmental review process as depicted in this case effectively mediate the ideological tension between environmentalists and business persons? In the fight over the possible use of Jumbo Glacier, how are these ideological tensions brought to the fore? For which position do you feel the greatest sympathy? Why?

5. What, in your opinion, could Oberto Oberti have done to increase his chances of success in dealing with both the Jumbo Coalition and the environmental review process? Would these options, in your opinion, be ethical? Was Bob Camsil's unscheduled introduction of the petition before the Environmental Review Committee ethical? If yes, why? If not, why not?

6. What is Oberto Oberti's moral obligation to his investors? At what point and under what circumstances should Oberti request more funds to shepherd the project through the environmental review process? As an investor in Oberti's dream, given what you now know, would you continue to invest? If yes, why? If no, why not?

VIDEO CASE 4   ING Bank of Canada: Virtual Banking With Deep Pockets

As of August 1998, the number of North American adults surfing the Internet surged to 79 million compared to 18 million users in 1995. Nielsen Media Research reports that Canada is the country with the fastest growing proportion of its population on the information highway. Currently, 8.5 million Canadians over the age of 16 are regular Internet users. From 1997 to 1998, North American figures rose by 22 per cent, while Canadian figures rose by 36 per cent. In fact, Canadians are quickly gaining a reputation as early adopters of new technology. Canada also can claim to have the fastest Internet technology in the world—a fibre optic network that the Canadian development team says will be able to deliver the entire contents of the Library of Congress in one second. This new network for institutional users will be known as CAnet 3 and is scheduled to be active in October 1998. A similar Internet network in the works in the United States is expected to accomplish this same task in approximately one minute.

With a growing reputation as a "technology friendly" nation, Canadians increasingly are being selected as a sample population for businesses competing with high-tech delivery of services to try out their wares. The Canadian financial services industry, particularly the banks in Canada, are in the midst of shakedown and transition. Two forces are combining. The first force, as is made clear in Figure 1, is an explosion of new technologies used in banking. Once more, Canadians have taken to automated teller machines, debit cards, and home banking at a rate that outstrips all other nations. The second force is the opening of the heretofore stable and sheltered Canadian banking system to global competition. These two forces combine the ING Group's entry into Canada with ING Direct.

ING Group is the third largest financial services company in the world. It employs over 80,000 people in over 60 countries. It has full-fledged charter operations in over 50 countries. Headquartered in The Netherlands, the ING Group looks to Canada as an experiment. ING Bank of Canada, a member of the Canada Deposit Insurance

```
┌─────────────────────────────────────────────────────────────────────────┐
│                                                                           │
│     New Technologies Adopted by the Chartered Banks and Trust Companies   │
│                                                                           │
│  Customer sales and service applications:    Office or office automation technologies:  │
│  • Automated teller machines                 • Mainframe/minicomputers    │
│  • Automated cheque verification             • Word processing            │
│  • Pay by phone                              • Electronic filing          │
│  • Automatic debit/credit systems            • Microcomputers/personal computers │
│  • "Smart" cards (with installed microprocessors)  • Internal database management systems │
│  • Home banking                              • Local area networks        │
│  • Connect to retail point-of-sale network   • Computerized decision support networks │
│  • Computerized trust management             • Voice activated computers  │
│  • Computerized pension management           • Artificial intelligence/expert systems │
│  • Securities transfer/stockholder services  • Integrated work stations   │
│                                                                           │
│  Design technologies:                        Telecommunications technologies:  │
│  • "4th generation" computer language        • Private automatic branch exchange │
│                                              • Electronic mail            │
│  Electronic funds transfer (EFT):            • Voice mail                 │
│  • EFT interbranch                           • Facsimile with built-in microprocessor │
│  • EFT interbank                             • Satellite/microwave system │
│  • EFT corporate                             • Videotex                   │
│  • EFT commercial and retail accounts        • Video conferencing         │
│                                              • Fibre optics               │
└─────────────────────────────────────────────────────────────────────────┘
```

Corporation, seeks to operate ING Direct as an electronic bank. Yves Brouillette, President and CEO of ING Canada, seeks to compete with the Canadian banks without opening a branch. Rather, Brouillette seeks to offer better rates and better hours. For example (see Figure 2), in its advertisements in August 1998, ING Direct touted its investment savings account by claiming it "pays higher interest," "no service charges or monthly fees," "funds are never locked in," and "transfer by phone from wherever you are." ING Direct brazenly gives its interest rates to the competition and challenges consumers to do better. Yves Brouillette is confident that with the new technology, the deep pockets of the ING Group, and the absence of both a costly branch system and the personnel that accompany it, ING Direct will not only prove itself in Canada, but be used by the ING Group as a prototype of how to proceed in other nations.

Matthew Czepliewicz, the ING expert at Solomon Brothers in the United Kingdom, where ING has a firm hold in what was once a staunchly British system, suggests that ING is a force with which one must reckon. The ING Group has more than twice the assets of Canada's biggest bank (Royal Bank of Canada), an aggressive penetration strategy, and a willingness to bide its time before realizing the full array of profits possible in Canada. ING, as Czepliewicz insists, is setting the agenda for virtual banking. Others in Canada are moving into the arena, but concentrating only a small part of their attention and capital in this experiment. ING Direct is going at it with all its capital, all its attention, and all its time.

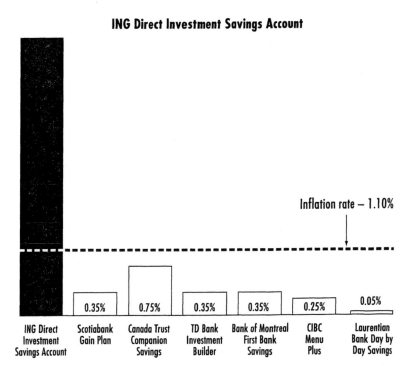

ING Direct Investment Savings Account

Inflation rate – 1.10%

ING Direct Investment Savings Account	Scotiabank Gain Plan	Canada Trust Companion Savings	TD Bank Investment Builder	Bank of Montreal First Bank Savings	CIBC Menu Plus	Laurentian Bank Day by Day Savings
	0.35%	0.75%	0.35%	0.35%	0.25%	0.05%

Chuck Wilson of Royal Bank's Direct Banking, Operations and Planning Division, is leading Royal Bank's efforts at on-line banking. It is clear that at present they are playing catch-up with ING Direct. The upcoming merger between Royal Bank and the Bank of Montreal, no doubt stimulated by ING and large global firms like it, is a mixed blessing. On the one hand, the merger will provide the new Canada mega-bank with sufficiently deep pockets to deal with the INGs of the world. On the other hand, the long-time loyalty of steady Bank of Montreal and/or Royal Bank customers may be disturbed by the merger. When customers are disturbed and shop for the best prices, ING may be able to walk away the big winner. Industry strategist Elizabeth Wright suggests that on the new banking frontier, old loyalties become suspect. These loyalties may be severely tested severely when, in order to meet ING rates, Royal Bank and the Bank of Montreal close down branches, cut employees due to redundancies created by the merger, and attempt to create a new corporate culture and reputation that satisfies both employees and customers.

Alan Wilkinson of the Financial Systems Group, NCR Canada, reminds us that Canadian banks have the home-field advantage, they have an excellent reputation, and the ability to match ING stride for stride in the technological aspects of this new frontier. However, we must remember it is not only who wins and who loses that concerns us, but how the technology itself is restructuring the human financial service industry and doing that threatens some and reveals great promises to others.

QUESTIONS:

1. What advantages do the big six Canadian banks have over ING Direct in establishing reputational capital? What strategies do you recommend Canadian banks, like Royal Bank, engage in to sustain their present advantage over ING Direct in reputational capital? How do you think the planned merger between the Royal Bank and the Bank of Montreal will influence each bank's reputational capital?

2. Using the "technology as a promise" framework, discuss how you would argue for the entry of ING Direct as an element in helping the financial services industry in Canada progress. How may ING Direct help in creating "convergence" and "discovery" in the Canadian financial services industry?

3. Employing the "technology as a threat" framework, discuss how you would argue for the entry of ING Direct as an element in creating "disenchantment" and "de-skilling" in the financial services industry in Canada. How can ING Direct create a "quick fix" reliance and actually cause more problems than it solves?

4. Within the "technology as an instrument of power" framework, does the use of electronic banking bring power to the masses or to the privileged? Support your views. Do you think that the new emphasis on electronic banking will bring added powers to the traditional managerial elite or will it foster the emergence of a new series of experts and technical analysts? Support your selection.

5. Reflect on the new technology in banking (see Figure 1) from (a) the new spirituality paradigm and (b) the smart machine paradigm in thinking about technology as a portal to a new age. What ethical quandaries regarding this case do you imagine are forthcoming, using the new spirituality paradigm as your reference point? What ethical quandaries about new technology in banking do you envision, using the smart machine paradigm as your reference point?

6. What role should nationalism play in the contest between ING Direct and the Canadian banks? Is the ideology of nationalism or internationalism more compatible with the new technology? Why?

Bibliography

Abraham, R. *Chaos, Gaia, Eros: A Chaos Pioneer Uncovers Three Great Streams of History*. San Francisco: Harper San Francisco, 1994.

Aguilar, F. *Scanning the Business Environment*. New York: Macmillan, 1967.

Akerstrom, M. *Betrayal and Betrayers: The Sociology of Treachery*. New Brunswick, NJ: Transaction Publishers, 1991.

Albert, S. and K. Bradley. *Managing Knowledge: Experts, Agencies and Organizations*. Cambridge: Cambridge University Press, 1997.

Alberts, D.S. and D.S. Papp. *Information Age: An Anthology on Its Impacts and Consequences*. Vol. 1 (Part 2), *Business, Commerce and Services*. Washington: National Defense University Press, 1997.

Albrow, M. *Bureaucracy*. London: Pall Mall, 1970.

Aldag, R.J. and S.R. Fuller. "Beyond Fiasco: A Reappraisal of the Groupthink Phenomenon and a New Model of Group Decision Processes." *Psychological Bulletin* 113 (1993): 533–52.

Allaire, Y. and M. Firsirote. "Theories of Organizational Culture." *Organization Studies* 15 (1984): 193–226.

Allen, T.J. *Managing the Flow of Technology: Technology Transfer and the Dissemination of Technological Information Within R&D Organizations*. Cambridge, MA: MIT Press, 1977.

Allenby, B.R. and D.J. Richards. *The Greening of Industrial Ecosystems*. Washington: National Academy Press, 1994.

Alvesson, M. and P.O. Berg. *Corporate Culture and Organizational Symbolism: An Overview*. Berlin: Walter de Gruyter, 1992.

Amin, S. *Capitalism in the Age of Globalization: The Management of Contemporary Society*. London: Zed Books, 1997.

Anhier, H.K. and W. Siebel. *The Third Sector: Comparative Studies of Nonprofit Organizations*. Berlin: Walter de Gruyter, 1990.

Anshen, M. "Changing the Social Contract: A Role for Business." In *Ethical Theory and Business*, edited by T.L. Beauchamp and N.E. Bowie. 2nd ed. Englewood Cliffs, NJ: Prentice Hall, 1983.

Ansoff, H.I. "Strategic Issues Management." *Strategic Management Journal* 1 (1980): 131–48.

Arent, R.P. *Trust Building With Children Who Hurt*. West Nyack, NY: Center For Applied Research in Education, 1991.

Argyris, C. *Overcoming Organizational Defenses*. Boston: Allyn and Bacon, 1990.

Aristotle. *Nicomachean Ethics*. Translated by T. Irwin. Indianapolis: Hackett Publishing Company, 1985.

Arkes, H. and C. Blumer. "The Psychology of Sunk Costs." *Organizational Behavior and Human Decision Processes* 35 (1985): 124–40.

Armstrong, P. and H. Armstrong. *The Double Ghetto: Canadian Women and Their Segregated Work*. Toronto: McClelland and Stewart, 1994.

Arrington, R.A. and R.N. Sawaya. "Managing Public Affairs: Issues Management in an Uncertain Environment." *California Management Review* 26 (1984): 148–60.

Arrow, K. *The Limits of Organization*. New York: W.W. Norton, 1974.

Asante, M.K. and A. Davis. "Encounters in the Inter-Racial Workplace." In *Handbook of International and Intercultural Communication*, edited by M.K. Asante and W.B. Gudy Kunst. Newbury Park, CA: Sage, 1989.

Athanasiou, T. *Divided Planet: The Ecology of Rich and Poor*. Boston: Little, Brown and Company, 1996.

Auletta, K. *The Highwaymen: Warriors of the Information Superhighway*. New York: Random House, 1997.

Bacharach, S.B. and E.J. Lawler. *Power and Politics in Organizations*. San Francisco: Jossey-Bass, 1980.

Bahro, R. *Building the Green Movement*. Philadelphia: New Society Publishers, 1986.

Bailey, J. *After Thought: The Computer Challenge to Human Intelligence*. New York: Basic Books, 1996.

Bailey, R. *Ecoscam: The False Prophets of the Ecological Apocalypse*. New York: St. Martin's Press, 1993.

Baker, L.W. *The Credibility Factor: Putting Ethics to Work in Public Relations*. Homewood, IL: Business One Irwin, 1993.

Baldi, P. and S. Brunak. *Bioinformatics: The Machine Learning Approach*. Cambridge, MA: MIT Press, 1998.

Balk, W.L. *Managerial Reform and Professional Empowerment in the Public Service*. Westport, CT: Quorum Books, 1996.

Bannerji, H. *Returning the Gaze: Essays on Racism, Feminism and Politics*. Toronto: Sister Vision Press, 1993.

Bantel, K.A. and S.E. Jackson. "Top Management and Innovation in Banking: Does the Composition of the Top Team Make a Difference?" *Strategic Management Journal* 10 (1989): 107–24.

Barber, B. *The Logic and Limits of Trust*. New Brunswick: Rutgers University Press, 1983.

Barbour, I.G. *Ethics in an Age of Technology*. San Francisco: Harper Collins, 1993.

Baridon, A.P. and E. Eyler. *Working Together: New Rules and Realities for Managing Men and Women at Work*. New York: McGraw Hill, 1994.

Barley, S. "Semiotics and the Study of Occupational and Organizational Culture." *Administrative Science Quarterly* 28 (1983): 393–413.

Barnet, T. "A Preliminary Investigation of the Relationship Between Selected Organizational Characteristics and External Whistle Blowing by Employees." *Journal of Business Ethics* 11 (1992): 949–59.

———. "Why Your Company Should Have a Whistle Blowing Policy." *SAM Advanced Management Journal* 57 (1992): 37–42.

Baron, D.P. *Business and Its Environment*. 2nd ed. Upper Saddle River, NJ: Prentice Hall, 1996.

Barrie, G. "Blowing the Whistle: Business Ethics and Accountability." *Political Quarterly* 67 (1996): 141–50.

Bartha, P. "Managing Corporate External Issues: An Analytical Framework." *Business Quarterly* 47 (1982): 78–90.

Baruss, I. *Authentic Knowing: The Convergence of Science and Spiritual Aspirations*. West Lafayette: Purdue University Press, 1996.

Baudrillard, J. *The Consumer Society: Myths and Structures*. Thousand Oaks, CA: Sage, 1998.

———. *The Mirror of Production*. St. Louis: Telos, 1975.

Baum, H.S. *The Invisible Bureaucracy: The Unconscious in Organizational Problem Solving*. New York: Oxford University Press, 1987.

Bauman, Z. *Intimations of Postmodernity*. London: Routledge and Kegan Paul, 1992.

———. *Legislators and Interpreters: On Modernity, Post-Modernity and Intellectuals*. Cambridge: Polity Press, 1987.

————. *Life in Fragments: Essays in Postmodern Morality*. Oxford: Basil Blackwell, 1995.

————. *Postmodern Ethics*. Oxford: Basil Blackwell, 1993.

Baumol, W.J., R. Nelson, and E.N. Wolff. *Convergence of Productivity: Cross-National Studies and Historical Evidence*. New York: Oxford University Press, 1994.

Baytos, L.M. *Designing and Implementing Successful Diversity Programs*. Englewood Cliffs, NJ: Prentice Hall, 1995.

Bazerman, M.H. *Judgment in Management Decision Making*. New York: John Wiley & Sons, 1998.

Beauchamp, T.L. and N.E. Bowie. *Ethical Theory and Business*. 2nd ed. Englewood Cliffs, NJ: Prentice Hall, 1983.

Beck, U., A. Giddens, and S. Lasch. *Reflexive Modernization: Politics Tradition and Aesthetics in the Modern Social Order*. Cambridge: Polity Press, 1994.

Belbin, R.M. *The Coming Shape of Organizations*. Oxford: Butterworth Heineman, 1996.

Belenky, M., B.M. Clinchy, N.R. Goldberger, and J.M. Tarule. *Women's Ways of Knowing: The Development of Self, Voice and Mind*. New York: Basic Books, 1986.

Bell, D. *The Coming of Post-Industrial Society: A Venture in Social Forecasting*. New York: Basic Books, 1973.

Belows, R.S. *The Contingent Economy: The Growth of Temporary, Part-Time and Subcontracted Workforces*. Washington: National Planning Association, 1989.

Bennis, W. and B. Nanus. *Leaders: Strategies for Taking Charge*. New York: Harper and Row, 1985.

Bentham, J. *A Bentham Reader*. Edited by Mary Peter Mack. New York: Pegasus, 1969.

Bereiter, C. and M. Scardamalio. *Surpassing Ourselves: An Inquiry Into the Nature and Implications of Expertise*. Chicago: Open Court, 1993.

Berle, A.A., Jr. and G.C. Means. *The Modern Corporation and Private Property*. New York: Macmillan, 1933.

Bernstein, R. *The Dictatorship of Virtue*. New York: Alfred A. Knopf, 1994.

Berquist, W. *The Postmodern Organization: Mastering the Art of Irreversible Change*. San Francisco: Jossey-Bass, 1993.

Bhat, V.N. *The Green Corporation: The Next Competitive Advantage*. Westport, CT: Quorum Books, 1996.

Bhide, A. and H.H. Stevenson. "Why Be Honest if Honesty Doesn't Pay?" *Harvard Business Review* (1990): 119–25.

Bigelow, B., L. Fahey, and J.F. Mahon. "Political Strategy an Issues Evolution: A Framework for Analysis and Action." In *Contemporary Issues in Business and Politics*, edited K. Paul. Lewiston, NY: Edwin Meelen Press, 1991.

Biggs, L. *The Rational Factory: Architecture, Technology and Work in America's Age of Mass Production*. Baltimore: John Hopkins University Press, 1996.

Bion, W.R. *Experiences in Groups*. New York: Basic Books, 1959.

Blackwell, B. *The Global Challenge of Innovation*. London: Butterworth-Heineman, 1991.

Blair, K. "Internet Use/Abuse Gets Employers' Attention." *Canadian HR Reporter*, 27 January 1997.

Blake, J.E. *A Management Guide to Corporate Identity*. London: Council of Industrial Design, 1971.

Blau, P.M. *Bureaucracy in Modern Society*. New York: Random House, 1956.

————. *Exchange and Power in Social Life*. New Brunswick, NJ: Transaction Publishers, 1989.

Block, P. *Stewardship: Choosing Service Over Self-Interest*. San Francisco: Berrett-Koehler Publishers, 1993.

Blumenberg, H. *The Legitimacy of the Modern Age.* Translated by R.H. Wallace. Cambridge, MA: MIT Press, 1983.

Boatright, J. *Ethics and the Conduct of Business.* Englewood Cliffs, NJ: Prentice Hall, 1997.

Boaz, N.T. *Eco Homo: How the Human Being Emerged From the Cataclysmic History of the Earth.* New York: Basic Books, 1997.

Bohen, H.H. and A. Viveros-Long, *Balancing Jobs and Family Life: Do Flexible Work Schedules Help?* Philadelphia: Temple University Press, 1981.

Boje, D.M. "Lessons From Premodern and Modern for Postmodern Management." In *Constituting Management: Markets, Meanings and Identities*, edited by G. Palmer and S. Clegg. Berlin: Walter de Gruyter, 1996.

———. "The Storytelling Organization: A Study of Story Performance in an Office Supply Firm." *Administrative Science Quarterly* 36 (1991): 106–26.

Boje, D.M., R.P. Gephart, Jr., and T.J. Thatchenkey, eds. *Postmodern Management and Organization Theory.* Thousand Oaks, CA: Sage, 1996.

Bok, Sissela, "Whistle Blowing and Professional Responsibility." In *Ethical Theory and Business*, edited by T.L. Beauchamp and N.E. Bowie. Englewood Cliffs, NJ: Prentice Hall, 1983.

Bolter, D. *Turing's Man: Western Culture in the Computer Age.* Chapel Hill: University of North Carolina Press, 1984.

Bonazzi, G. "Scapegoating in Complex Organizations: The Results of a Comparative Study of Symbolic Blame-Giving in Italian and French Public Administrations." *Organization Studies* 4 (1983): 1–18.

Bookchin, M. *Defending the Earth: The Debate Between Murray Bookchin and Dave Foreman.* Montreal: Black Rose Books, 1991.

Boon, S.D. and J.G. Holmes. "The Dynamics of Interpersonal Trust: Resolving Uncertainty in the Face of Risk." In *Cooperation and Presocial Behavior*, edited by R.A. Hinde and J. Groebel. Cambridge: Cambridge University Press, 1991.

Boorstin, D.J. *The Republic of Technology: Reflections on Our Future Community.* New York: Harper and Row, 1978,.

Borden, D.L. and K. Harvey. *The Electronic Grapevine: Rumor, Reputation and Reporting in the New On-line Environment.* Mahwah, NJ: Lawrence Erlbaum, 1998.

Borenstein, S. and M.B. Zimmerman. "Market Incentives for Safe Commercial Airline Operation." *American Economic Review* 78 (1988): 913–35.

Borgmann, A. "The Moral Significance of the Material Culture." In *The Politics of Knowledge*, edited by A. Feenberg and A. Hannay. Bloomington: Indiana University Press, 1995.

———. *Technology and the Character of Contemporary Life.* Chicago: University of Chicago Press, 1984.

Bowlby, J. *Attachment and Loss.* Vol. 2, *Separation: Anxiety and Anger.* London: Hogarth Press, 1973.

Bowles, M.L. "The Organization Shadow." *Organization Studies* 12 (1991): 387–404.

Bowyer, K.W. *Ethics and Computing: Living Responsibly in a Computerized World.* Los Alamitos, CA: IEE Computer Society Press, 1996.

Boyett, J.H. and Boyett, J.T. *Beyond Workplace 2000: Essential Strategies For the New American Corporation.* New York: Dutton, 1995.

Brabeck, M.M. "Ethical Characteristics of Whistle Blowers." *Journal of Research in Personality* 18 (1984): 41–53.

Braudy, L. *The Frenzy of Renown: Fame and Its History.* New York: Oxford University Press, 1986.

Brennan, T. *At Home in the World: Cosmopolitanism Now.* Cambridge, MA: Harvard University Press, 1997.

Bresnahan, T.F. and R.J. Gordon. *The Economics of New Goods*. Chicago: University of Chicago Press, 1997.

Brightman, H.J. *Group Problem-Solving: An Improved Management Approach*. Atlanta: Georgia State University Press, 1988.

Briscoe, G. and T. Caelli. *A Compendium of Machine Learning*. Norwood, NJ: Ablex Publishing, 1996.

Brisken, A. *The Stirrings of Soul in the Workplace*. San Francisco: Berrett-Kohler Publishers, 1998.

Brislin, R.W. "Intercultural Communication Training." In *Handbook of Intercultural Communication*, edited by M.K. Asante and W.B. Gudy Kunst. Newbury Park, CA: Sage, 1989.

Brockner, J., J.Z. Rubin, and E. Lang. "Face Saving and Entrapment." *Journal of Experimental Social Psychology* 17 (1981): 68–79.

Bromley, D.B. *Reputation, Image and Impression Management*. New York: John Wiley & Sons, 1993.

Brown, A.D. "Narrative, Politics and Legitimacy in an IT Implementation." *Journal of Management Studies* 35 (1998): 35–48.

———. "Narcissism, Identity and Legitimacy." *Academy of Management Review* 22 (1997): 643–54.

Brown, E. *Futile Progress: Technology's Empty Promise*. London: Earthscan, 1995.

Brown, H. and E. Hutchings, Jr. *Are Our Descendants Doomed? Technological Change and Population Growth*. New York: Viking, 1972

Brown, H.P. *Egalitarianism and the Generation of Inequality*. Oxford: Clarendon Press, 1988.

Brown, J.K. *This Business of Issues: Coping With the Company's Environment*. New York: Conference Board, 1979.

Brown, L.R. *Building a Sustainable Society*. New York: W.W. Norton, 1981.

Brown, W.S., R.E. Lubove, and R. Kwalwasser. "Karoshi: Alternative Perspectives of Japanese Management Styles." *Business Horizon* 37 (1994): 58–60.

Brucato, P.F., Jr. and D.H. Smith. "An Analysis of Firm Reputation in the Market's Reaction to Corporate Dividends." *Quarterly Review of Economics and Finance* 37 (1997): 647–65.

Brummer, J.J. *Corporate Responsibility and Legitimacy: An Interdisciplinary Analysis*. New York: Greenwood, 1991.

Bruono, A.F. and L.T. Nichols. "Stockholder and Stakeholder Interpretations of Businesses' Social Role." In *Business Ethics: Readings and Cases in Corporate Morality*, edited by W.M. Hoffman and J. Mills Moore. New York: McGraw Hill, 1990.

Buckler, S. *Dirty Hands: The Problem of Political Morality*. Brookfield, UT: Ashgate Publishers, 1993.

Burgen, A., P. McLaughlin, and J. Mittel-Strass. *Idea of Progress*. Berlin: Walter de Gruyter, 1997.

Burke, J. and R. Ornstein. *The Axemaker's Gift: A Double Edged History of Human Culture*. New York: Putnam, 1995.

Burkhauser, R.V. and R.H. Haveman. *Disability and Work*. Baltimore: Johns Hopkins University Press, 1982.

Burleigh, M. *Ethics and Extermination: Reflections on Nazi Genocide*. Cambridge: Cambridge University Press, 1997.

Burns, M. *Automated Fabrication: Improving Productivity in Manufacturing*. Englewood Cliffs, NJ: Prentice Hall, 1993.

Burrell, G. "Modernism, Postmodernism and Organizational Analysis 2: The Contribution of Michel Foucault." *Organizational Studies* 9 (1988): 221–35.

———. "Modernism, Postmodernism and Organizational Analysis 4: The Contribution of Jurgen Habermas." *Organizational Studies* 15 (1994): 1–19.

Bytheway, B. *Becoming and Being Old: Sociological Approaches to Later Life.* London: Sage, 1989.

Cade, C.M. and N. Coxhead. *The Awakened Mind: Biofeedback and the Development of Higher States of Awareness.* London: Wildwood House, 1979.

Callahan, E.S. and T.M. Dworkin. "Who Blows the Whistle to the Media, and Why: Organizational Characteristics of Media Whistleblowers." *Business Law Journal* 32 (1994): 158–84.

Callicott, J.B. *Earth's Insights.* Berkeley: University of California Press, 1994.

———. *Earth Summit Ethics.* Albany: State University of New York Press, 1996.

Cameli, A.P. *The Information Superhighway: Issues and Challenges.* Commack, NY: Nova Science Publishers, 1996.

Cammillus, J.C. and D.K. Datta. "Managing Strategic Issues in a Turbulent Environment." *Long Range Planning* 24 (1991): 67–74.

Canadian Conference of Catholic Bishops. *Breach of Trust, Breach of Faith: Child Sexual Abuse in the Church and Society.* Ottawa: Canadian Conference of Catholic Bishops, 1992.

Cantor, N. *Twentieth Century Culture: Modernism to Deconstruction.* New York: Peter Lang, 1989.

Cantril, J.C. and C.L. Oravee. *The Symbolic Earth: Discourse and Our Creation of the Environment.* Lexington: University Press of Kentucky, 1996.

Capra, F. and C. Spretnak. *Green Politics.* New York: Dutton, 1984.

Carr, A.Z. "Is Business Bluffing Ethical?" *Harvard Business Review* 46 (1968): 127–34.

Carroll, A.B. "The Pyramid of Corporate Social Responsibility: Toward the Moral Management of Organizational Stakeholders." *Business Horizons* 34, no. 4 (1991): 39–48.

Carroll, W.K. *Corporate Power and Canadian Capitalism.* Vancouver: University of British Columbia Press, 1986.

Carson, R. *Silent Spring.* Boston: Houghton Mifflin Company, 1962.

Casal, J.C. and S.S. Zalkind. "Consequences of Whistle Blowing: A Study of the Experiences of Management Accountants." *Psychological Reports* 77 (1995): 795–802.

Cassidy, F. and R. Faris. *Choosing Our Future: Adult Education and Public Policy in Canada.* Toronto: OISE Press, 1987.

Castro, B. *Business and Society: A Reader in the History of Sociology and the Ethics of Business.* New York: Oxford University Press, 1996.

Chafetz, M.E. *The Tyranny of Experts: Blowing the Whistle on the Cult of Expertise.* Lanham, MD: Madison Books, 1996.

Chambers, A. "Whistle Blowing and the Internal Auditor." *Journal of Business Ethics* 4 (1988): 192–98.

Chase, W.H. "Organizing for Our New Responsibility." *Public Relations Journal* 32 (1976): 14–15.

Chase, W.H. *Issue Management: Origins of the Future.* Stamford: Issue Action Publications, 1984.

Chemers, M.M., S. Oskemp, and M. Constanzo. *Diversity in Organizations: New Perspectives for a Changing Workplace.* Thousand Oaks, CA: Sage, 1995.

Cheney, J. "Eco-Feminism and Deep Ecology." *Environmental Ethics* 9 (1987): 115–45.

Chia, R. *Organziational Analysis as Deconstructive Practice.* Berlin: Walter de Gruyter, 1966.

Childs, T. "Managing Diversity: The IBM Experience." In *The Diversity Factor: Capturing the Competitive Advantage of a Changing Workforce*, edited by E.Y. Cross and M. Blackburn White. Chicago: Irwin Professional Publishing, 1996.

Ching, C. and C.W. Holsapple. "Reputation, Learning and Coordination in Distributed Decision Making Contexts." *Organization Science* 31 (1992): 275–97.

Chisholm, R. *Developing Network Organizations: Learning From Practice and Theory*. Reading, MA: Addison Wesley, 1998.

Chorafas, D. and H. Steinmann. *Virtual Reality: Practical Applications in Business and Industry*. Upper Saddle River, NJ: Prentice Hall, 1995.

Christensen, K.E. *The New Era of Home-Based Work: Direction and Policies*. Boulder: Westview Press, 1988.

Ciborra, C. *Teams, Markets and Systems: Business Innovation and Information Technology*. Cambridge: Cambridge University Press, 1993.

Clarke, M. *Fallen Idols: Elites and the Search for the Acceptable Face of Capitalism*. London: Junction Books, 1981.

Clawson, J. "You Can't Manage Them If They Don't Trust You." *Executive Excellence* 6 (1989): 10–11.

Clegg, S. *Modern Organizations: Organizational Studies in the Postmodern World*. London: Sage, 1990.

———. "Postmodern Management." In *Constituting Management: Markets, Meanings and Identities*, edited by G. Palmer and S. Clegg. Berlin: Walter de Gruyter, 1996.

Clegg, S. and G. Palmer. *Politics of Management Knowledge*. London: Sage, 1996.

Clement, W. *The Canadian Corporate Elite: An Analysis of Economic Power*. Toronto: McClelland and Stewart, 1975.

———. *Continental Corporate Power: Economic Elite Linkages Between Canada and the United States*. Toronto: McClelland and Stewart, 1977.

Clutterback, D. *How To Be a Good Corporate Citizen: A Manager's Guide to Making Social Responsibility Work—and Pay*. New York: McGraw Hill, 1981.

Cohen, L. and J.K. Swim. "The Differential Impact of Gender Ratios on Women and Men: Tokenism, Self-Confidence and Expectations." *Personality and Social Psychology Bulletin* 21 (1995): 876–82.

Coleman, D.A. *Ecopolitics: Building a Green Society*. New Brunswick: Rutgers University Press, 1994.

Collier, R. *Combating Sexual Harassment in the Workplace*. Philadelphia: Open University Press, 1995.

Collis, J.W. *The Seven Fatal Management Sins: Understanding and Avoiding Managerial Malpractice*. Boca Raton: St. Lucie Press, 1998.

"Commerce Courts P.R. Disaster." *The Globe and Mail* (Toronto), 6 June 1997.

Commoner, B. *The Closing Circle: Nature, Man and Technology*. New York: Knopf, 1971.

Connor, S. *Postmodernist Culture: An Introduction to Theories of the Contemporary*. Oxford: Oxford University Press, 1995.

Cook, K.S. *Social Exchange Theory*. Newbury Park, CA: Sage, 1987.

Cooper, R. "Modernism, Postmodernism and Organizational Analysis 3: The Contribution of Jacque Derrida." *Organizational Studies* 10 (1988): 479–502.

Cooper, R. and G. Burrell. "Modernism, Postmodernism and Organizational Analysis: An Introduction." *Organizational Studies* 9 (1988): 91–112.

Cordell, A.J. *The New Wealth of Nations: Taxing Cyberspace*. Toronto: Between the Lines, 1997.

"Corporate Culture: The Hard-to-Change Values That Spell Success or Failure." *Business Week,* 27 October 1980.

Couger, J.D. *Creative Problem Solving and Opportunity Finding*. Hindsdale, IL: Boyd and Fraser, 1995.

Courtright, J.A. "A Laboratory Investigation of Groupthink." *Communication Monograph* 45 (1978): 229–46.

Cox, T., Jr. *Cultural Diversity in Organizations: Theory, Research and Practice.* San Francisco: Berrett-Koehler Publishers, 1993.

―――. "The Multicultural Organization." *Academy of Management Executives* 5 (1991): 34–47.

Cramer, P. *Deep Environmental Politics: The Role of Radical Environmentalism in Crafting American Policy.* Westport, CT: Praeger, 1998.

Creighton, J.L. and J.W.R. Adams. *Cybermeeting: How to Link People and Technology in Your Organization.* New York: AMACOM, 1998.

Crocker, D.A. and T. Linden. *Ethics of Consumption: The Good Life, Justice, and Global Stewardship.* Lanham, MD: Roman and Littlefield, 1998.

Crompton, R. and G. Jones. *White Collar Proletariat: Deskilling in Clerical Work.* London: Macmillan, 1984.

Cronin, M.J. *Banking and Finance on the Internet.* New York: Van Nostrand Reinhold, 1997.

Cross, E. and B.M. White. *The Diversity Factor: Capturing the Competitive Advantage of a Changing Workforce.* Chicago: Irwin, 1996.

Crozier, M. *The Bureaucratic Phenomenon.* London: Tavistock Publications, 1964.

Cvetkovich, A. and D. Kellner. *Articulating the Global and the Local: Globalization and Cultural Studies.* Boulder: Westview Press, 1997.

Czerniawska, F. and G. Potter. *Business in a Virtual World.* London: Macmillan, 1998.

Daenzer, P.M. *Regulating Class Privilege: Immigrant Servants in Canada, 1940s–1990s.* Toronto: Canadian Scholars' Press, 1993.

Danesh, A.H. *The Informal Economy: Underground Economy, Moonlighting, Subcontracting, Unorganized Sector, Barter, Ghetto Economy, Second Economy.* New York: Garland, 1991.

Danskin, D.G. and M.A. Crow. *Biofeedback: An Introduction and Guide.* Palo Alto, CA: Mayfield Publishing, 1981.

David, A.R. *The Greening of Business.* Brockfield, VT: Graver, 1991.

Davidow, W.H. and M. Malone. *The Virtual Corporation.* New York: Harper Business, 1992.

Davis, B. and D. Wessel. *Prosperity: The Coming Twenty-Year Boom and What it Means to You.* New York: Times Business, 1998.

Davis, J. *Greening Business.* Oxford: Basil Blackwell, 1991.

Davis, J.H., F.D. Schoorman, and L. Donaldson. "Toward a Stewardship Theory of Management." *Academy of Management Review* 22 (1997): 20–47.

Deal, T.A. and A.A. Kennedy. *Corporate Culture.* Reading, MA: Addison-Wesley, 1982.

Deetz, S. *Transforming Communication, Transforming Business: Building Responsive and Responsible Workplace.* Creskill, NJ: Hampton Press, 1995.

DeGeorge, R. *Business Ethics.* 3rd ed. New York: Macmillan, 1990.

Denhardt, R. *In the Shadow of Organizations.* Lawrence: Regents of Kansas Press, 1981.

Dennett, D.C. *Brainchildren: Essays on Designing Minds.* Cambridge, MA: MIT Press, 1998.

Derrida, J. *Deconstruction in a Nutshell.* New York: Fordham University Press, 1997.

―――. *Dissemination.* Translated by B. Johnson. London: Athlone Publishing, 1981.

Dertouzos, M.L. *What Will Be: How the New World of Information Will Change Our Lives.* San Francisco: Harper Edge, 1997.

DeSimone, L.D. *Eco-Efficiency: The Business Link to Sustainable Development.* Cambridge, MA: MIT Press, 1997.

Deutsch, M. "Trust and Suspicion." *Journal of Conflict Resolution* 2 (1958): 265–79.

———. "Trust, Trustworthiness, and the F-Scale." *Journal of Abnormal and Social Psychology* 61 (1960): 138–40.

Devall, W. *Clearcut: The Tragedy of Industrial Forestry*. San Francisco: Sierra Club Book, 1994.

———. *Simple in Means, Rich in Ends: Practicing Deep Ecology*. Salt Lake City: Peregrine Books, 1988.

Devall, W. and G. Sessions. *Deep Ecology: Living as if Nature Mattered*. Salt Lake City: Gibbs M. Smith, 1980.

Dew, J.R. *Empowerment and Democracy in the Workplace*. Westport, CT: Quorum Books, 1997.

Diamond, I. *Fertile Ground: Women, Earth and the Limits of Control*. Boston: Beacon Press, 1994.

Diamond, J.M. *Guns, Germs and Steel: The Fates of Human Societies*. New York: W.W. Norton, 1997.

Diamond, M.A. *The Unconscious Life of Organizations: Interpreting Organizational Identity*. Westport, CT: Greenwood Press, 1993.

Diamond, M.A. and S. Allcorn. "Psychological Barriers to Personal Responsibility." *Organizational Dynamics* 12 (1984): 66–77.

DiBella, A.J. and E.C. Nevis. *How Organizations Learn: An Integrated Strategy for Building Learning Capability*. San Francisco: Jossey Bass, 1998.

Dickson, D.V. *Business Audits Public*. New York: John Wiley & Sons, 1984.

Diwan, R.K. and C. Chakraborty. *High Technology and International Competitiveness*. New York: Praeger, 1991.

Dixon, B.J. and E.J. Cassidy. *Virtual Futures: Cyberotics, Technology and Post-Human Pragmatism*. New York: Routledge, 1998.

Dixon, R.G. *Future Schools*. Toronto: ECW Press, 1992.

Dizard, W.P. *The Coming Information Age: An Overview of Technology, Economics and Politics*. New York: Longman, 1985.

Dobbins, M. *The Myth of the Good Corporate Citizen: Democracy Under the Rule of Big Business*. Toronto: Stoddart, 1998.

Dobkowski, M.N. and I. Wallimann. *The Coming Age of Scarcity: Preventing Mass Death and Genocide in the 21st Century*. Syracuse: Syracuse University Press, 1998.

Dodsworth, C. *Digital Illusion: Entertaining the Future With High Technology*. Reading, MA: Addison-Wesley, 1998.

Donaldson, J. *Business Ethics: A European Casebook*. London: Academic Press, 1992.

Donaldson, T. "The Third Wave." *Ethics Digest*, March 1989, 1–4.

Donaldson, T. and T.W. Dunfee. "Integrative Social Contracts Theory: A Communitarian Conception of Economic Ethics." *Economics and Philosophy* 11 (1995): 85–112.

———. "Towards a Unified Conception of Business Ethics: Integrative Social Contracts Theory." *Academy of Management Review* 19, no 2 (1994): 252–84.

Donaldson, T. and L. Preston. "The Stakeholder Conception of the Corporation: Concepts, Evidence and Implications." *Academy of Management Review* 20 (1995): 1–27.

Dostoevsky, F. *Crime and Punishment*. The Coulson translation. New York: W.W. Norton, 1975.

Downs, A. *Corporate Executions: The Ugly Truth About Layoffs—How Corporate Green is Shattering Lives, Companies and Communities*. New York: AMACOM, 1995.

Dozier, J.B. and M.A. Miceli. "Potential Predictors of Whistleblowing: A Pro-social Behavior Perspective." *Academy of Management Review* 10 (1985): 825–36.

Dreman, A. *The Family on the Threshold of the 21st Century: Trends and Implications*. Mahwah, NJ: Laurence Erlbaum, 1997.

Drengson, A. and Y. Inoue. *The Deep Ecology Movement*. Berkeley: North Atlantic Books, 1995.

Drexler, K.E. and C. Peterson. *Unbounding the Future: The Nanotechnology Revolution*. New York: William Morrow, 1991.

Drucker, P.F. "Introduction: This Post-Modern World." In *Landmarks of Tomorrow*. New York: Harper, 1957.

———. *Managing in a Time of Great Change*. New York: Dutton, 1995.

———. *The New Realities in Government and Politics; In Economics and Business; In Society and World View*. New York: Harper and Row, 1989.

———. "The New Society of Organizations." *Harvard Business Review* 70 (1992): 95–104.

———. *Post-Capitalist Society*. New York: Harper Business, 1993.

Drummond, H. "De-Escalation in Decision Making: A Case of a Disastrous Partnership." *Journal of Management Studies* 32 (1995): 265–81.

———. *Escalation in Decision Making: The Tragedy of Taurus*. Oxford: Oxford University Press, 1996.

Dunning, J.H. *The Globalization of Business*. New York, NY: Routledge, 1993.

Dutton, J.E., L. Fahey, and V.K. Narayanan. "Towards Understanding Strategic Issues Diagnosis." *Strategic Management Journal* 4 (1983): 307–23.

Dutton, J.E. and S.B. Jackson. "Categorizing Strategic Issues: Links to Organizational Action." *Academy of Management Review* 12 (1987): 76–90.

Dyson, F. *Imagined Worlds*. Cambridge, MA: Harvard University Press, 1997.

Edgar, S.L. *Morality and Machines: Perspectives on Computer Ethics*. Sudbury, MA: Jones and Bartlett, 1997.

Edwalds, L. and M. Stocker. *The Woman-Centered Economy: Ideals, Reality and the Space in Between*. Chicago: Third Side Press, 1995.

Egan, B.L. *Information Superhighways*. Boston: Artech House, 1991.

Ehrlich, P.R. and A. Ehrlich. *The Population Bomb*. New York: Ballantine Books, 1971.

Eisenstadt, S.N. *Power, Trust and Meaning*. Chicago: University of Chicago Press, 1995.

El Sawy, O.A. and T. Pauchant. "Triggers, Templates and Twitches in the Tracking of Emerging Strategic Issues." *Strategic Management Journal* 9 (1988): 455–73.

Elgin, D. *Voluntary Simplicity: Toward a Way of Life That is Outwardly Simple, Inwardly Rich*. New York: William Morrow, 1981.

Elkington, J. and T. Burke. *The Green Capitalists: Industry's Search For Environmental Excellence*. London: Gollance, 1987.

Elliston, F.A. "Anonymity and Whistle Blowing." *Journal of Business Ethics* 1 (1982): 167–77.

———. "Civil Disobedience and Whistle Blowing: A Comparative Appraisal of Two Forms of Dissent." *Journal of Business Ethics* 1 (1982): 23–28.

———. *Whistleblowing: Managing Dissent in the Workplace*. New York: Praeger, 1984.

Elliston, F.A., J. Keenan, P. Lockhart, and J. Van Schaik. *Whistle Blowing Research: Methodological and Moral Issues*. New York: Praeger Special Studies, 1985.

Ellul, J. *The Technological Bluff*. Translated by G. Bromiley. Grand Rapids: Eerdmans, 1990.

———. *The Technological Society*. Translated by J. Wilkinson. New York: Knopf, 1964.

———. *The Technological System*. Translated by J. Neugroshel. New York: Continuum, 1980.

Epstein, R.A. *Simple Rules for a Complex World*. Cambridge, MA: Harvard University Press, 1995.

Erikson, E.H. *Childhood and Society*. New York: W.W. Norton, 1963.

———. *Identity: Youth and Crises*. New York: W.W. Norton, 1968.

Espejo, R. *Organizational Transformation and Learning: A Cybernetic Approach to Management*. New York: John Wiley & Sons, 1996.

Esser, J.K. and J.S. Lindoerfer. "Groupthink and the Space Shuttle 'Challenger' Accident: Toward a Quantitative Case Analysis." *Journal of Behavioral Decision Making* 2 (1989): 167–77.

Estabrooks, M. *Electronic Technology, Corporate Strategy, and World Transformation*. Westport, CT: Quorum Books, 1995.

Estes, R. *Corporate Social Accounting*. New York: John Wiley & Sons, 1976.

———. *Trends in World Social Development: The Social Progress of Nations, 1970–1987*. New York: Praeger, 1988.

———. *Tyranny of the Bottom Line: Why Corporations Make Good People Do Bad Things*. San Francisco: Berrett-Koehler Publishers, 1996.

Etzioni, A. *The Moral Dimension: Toward a New Economics*. New York: The Free Press, 1988.

Evan, W.M. *Knowledge and Power in a Global Society*. Beverly Hills: Sage, 1981.

Everenden, N. *The Social Creation of Nature*. Baltimore: Johns Hopkins University Press, 1992.

Ewing, D.W. *Do It My Way or You're Fired. Employee Rights and the Changing Role of Management Prerogatives*. New York: John Wiley & Sons, 1983.

Ewing, R.P. *Managing the New Bottom Line: Issues Management For Senior Executives*. Homewood, IL: Dow Jones-Irwin, 1987.

Ezrahi, Y., E. Mendelsohn, and H. Segal. *Technology Pessimism and Postmodernism*. Dordrecht: Kluwar Academic Publishers, 1994.

Fahey, L. and W.R. King. "Environmental Scanning For Corporate Planning." *Business Horizons* 20 (1977): 61–70.

Fairholm, G. *Leadership and the Culture of Trust*. Westport, CT: Praeger, 1994.

———. *Organizational Power Politics: Tactics in Organizational Leadership*. Westport, CT: Praeger, 1993.

Fallows, J. "Tokyo: The Hard Life." *The Atlantic Magazine* 121 (1991): 24–26.

Faludi, S. *Backlash: The Undeclared War Against American Women*. New York: Crown, 1991.

Farrell, D. and J.C. Peterson. "Patterns of Political Behavior in Organizations." *Academy of Management Review* 17 (1982): 561–75.

Fasching, D.J. *The Ethical Challenge of Auschwitz and Hiroshima: Apocalypse or Utopia?* Albany: State University of New York, 1993.

Fassel, D. *Working Ourselves to Death: The High Cost of Workaholism, The Rewards of Recovery*. San Francisco: Harper, 1990.

Fawcett, G. *Living With Disability in Canada: An Economic Portrait*. Ottawa: Canadian Council on Social Development, 1996.

Feliu, A.G. "Whistle Blowing While You Work." *Business and Society Review* Winter (1990): 65–67.

Ferguson, K.E. *The Feminist Case Against Bureaucracy*. Philadelphia: Temple University Press, 1984.

Fernandez, J.P. *Child Care and Corporate Productivity: Resolving Family/Work Conflicts*. Lexington, MA: Lexington Books, 1986.

————. *The Diversity Advantage*. Lexington, MA: Lexington Books, 1993.

————. *Managing a Diverse Workforce*. Lexington, MA: Lexington Books, 1991.

————. *Racism and Sexism in Corporate Life*. Lexington, MA: D.C. Health, 1981.

Ferraro, K. *Gerontology: Perspectives and Issues*. New York: Springer-Verlag, 1997.

Ferrarotti, F. *The Myth of Inevitable Progress*. Westport, CT: Greenwood Press, 1985.

Fine, H. *Social Marketing: Promoting the Causes of Public and Nonprofit Agencies*. Boston: Allyn Bacon, 1990.

Fine, M.G. *Building Successful Multicultural Organizations: Challenges and Opportunities*. Westport, CT: Quorum Books, 1995.

Fink, S.L. *High Commitment Workplaces*. New York: Quorum Books, 1992.

Finlay, M. *Powermatics: A Discursive Critique of New Communications Technology*. London: Routledge and Kegan Paul, 1987.

Fisher, R. and W. Ury. *Getting to Yes: Negotiating Agreement Without Giving In*. Boston: Houghton, Mifflin, 1981.

Fombrun, C. *Reputation: Realizing Value From the Corporate Image*. Boston: Harvard Business School Press, 1996.

Forcese, C. *Commerce with Conscience?* Montreal: International Centre for Human Rights and Democratic Development, 1997.

Ford, K.J. and S. Fisher. "The Role of Training in a Changing Workplace and Workforce: New Perspectives and Approaches." In *Managing Diversity: Human Resource Strategies for Transforming the Workplace*, edited by E.E. Kossek and S.A. Lobel. Cambridge: Basil Blackwell, 1996.

Foreman, D. and B. Haywood. *Ecodefense: A Field Guide to Monkeywrenching*. 2nd ed. Tucson: Nedd Ludd Books, 1987.

Foucault, M. *The Order of Things*. New York: Vintage, 1970.

————. "The Subject and Power." In *Michel Foucault: Beyond Structuralism and Hermeneutics*, edited by H. Dreyfus and P. Rabinow. Chicago: University of Chicago Press, 1982.

Fox, A. *Beyond Contract: Work, Power and Trust Relations*. London: Faber, 1974.

Fox, F.V. and B.M. Staw. "The Trapped Administrator: Effects of Job Insecurity and Policy Resistance Upon Commitment to a Course of Action." *Administrative Science Quarterly* 24 (1979): 449–71.

Fox, M. *Returning to Eden: Animal Rights and Human Responsibility*. Malabar, FL: R.E. Krieger, 1990.

Fox, M., M. Toms, and J. Toms. "Work, Passion and the Life of the Spirit." In *The Soul of Business*, edited by Michael Toms. Carlsbad, CA: Hay House, 1997.

Fox, M.A. and R.T. Hamilton. "Ownership and Diversification: Agency Theory or Stewardship Theory." *Journal of Management Studies* 31 (1994): 69–81.

Fox, R. *Technological Change: Methods and Themes in the History of Technology*. Amsterdam: Horwood Academic Press, 1996.

Frankel, C. *In Earth's Company: Business, Environment and the Challenge of Sustainability*. Gabriola Island, BC: New Society Publishers, 1998.

Frankel, M.S. "Professional Codes: Why, How and with What Impact?" *Journal of Business Ethics* 8 (1987): 109–15.

Franklin, U. *The Real World of Technology*. Toronto: Anansi Press, 1990.

Frederick, C. and C. Atkinson. *Women, Ethics and the Workplace*. Westport, CT: Praeger, 1997.

Frederick, W.C. *Values, Nature and Culture in the American Corporation*. New York: Oxford University Press, 1995.

Freeman, R.E. *Strategic Management: A Stakeholder Approach*. Boston: Pitman, 1984.

Freeman, R.E. and W.M. Evan. "Corporate Governance: A Stakeholder Interpretation." *Journal of Behavioral Economics* 19 (1990): 337–59.

Freeman, R.E. and D.R. Gilbert. *Corporate Strategy and the Search For Ethics*. Englewood Cliffs, NJ: Prentice Hall, 1988.

Freeman, R.E. and R.A. Phillips. "Efficiency, Effectiveness and Ethics: A Stakeholder View." In *Human Action in Business: Praxiological and Ethical Dimensions*, edited by W.W. Gasparski and L.V. Ryan. New Brunswick, NJ: Transaction Publishers, 1996.

Freud, A. *The Ego and the Mechanisms of Defense*. Rev. ed. New York: International University Press, 1966.

Freud, S. *Inhibitions, Symptoms and Anxiety*. Vol. 20. London: Hogarth Press, 1926.

Friedan, B. *Beyond Gender: The New Politics of Work and Family*. Washington: Woodrow Wilson Center Press, 1997.

Friedland, N. "Attribution of Control as a Determinant of Cooperation in Exchange Interactions." *Journal of Applied Social Psychology* 20 (1990): 303–20.

Friedman, J. and M.M. Baumil. *Betrayal of Trust: Sex and Power in Professional Relationships*. Westport, CT: Praeger, 1995.

Friedman, M. *Capitalism and Freedom*. Chicago: University of Chicago Press, 1962.

———. "The Social Responsibility of Business is to Increase Its Profits." *New York Times Magazine*, 13 September 1970.

———. "The Social Responsibility of Business is to Increase Its Profits." 2nd ed. In *Ethical Theory and Business*, edited by T.L. Beauchamp and N.E. Bowie. Englewood Cliffs, NJ: Prentice Hall, 1983.

Friedman, M. and J. Narveson. *Political Correctness: For and Against*. Lanham, MD: Rowman and Littlefield, 1995.

Fussler, C. and P. James. *Driving Eco-Innovation: A Breakthrough Discipline or Innovation and Sustainability*. Washington: Pitman, 1996.

Gaard, G. *Ecofeminism: Women, Animals and Nature*. Philadelphia: Temple University Press, 1993.

———. *Ecological Politics: Ecofeminism and the Greens*. Philadelphia: Temple University Press, 1998.

Gagliardi, P. *Symbols and Artifacts: Views of the Corporate Landscape*. New York: Aldine de Gruyter, 1992.

Gaither, N. *Production and Operations Management: A Problem-Solving and Decision-Making Approach*. Chicago: Dryden, 1990.

Galbraith, J.R. *Competing With Flexible Lateral Organizations*. Reading, MA: Addison-Wesley, 1994.

Gallagher, H.P. *By Trust Betrayed: Patients, Physicians, and the License to Kill in the Third Reich*. New York: Henry Holt, 1990.

Gambetta, D. "Can We Trust Trust?" In *Trust: Making and Breaking Cooperative Relations*, edited by D. Gambetta. New York: Basil Blackwell, 1988.

Garbett, T. *How to Build a Corporation's Identity and Project Its Image*. Lexington, MA: Lexington Books, 1988.

Garcia, G. "Death of a Manager." *Time Magazine*, 8 August 1988, 23.

Gardner, H. *The Quest For Mind: Piaget, Levi-Strauss and the Structuralist Movement*. Chicago: University of Chicago Press, 1981.

Gastil, R.D. *Progress: Critical Thinking About Historical Change*. Westport, CT: Praeger, 1993.

Geertz, C. *The Interpretation of Cultures*. New York: Basic Books, 1973.

Gellerman, S. "Why 'Good' Managers Make Bad Ethical Choices." *Harvard Business Review* 64, no. 4 (1986): 85–90.

Gendron, B. *Technology and the Human Condition*. New York: St. Martin's Press, 1977.

Germain, G.G. *A Discourse on Disenchantment: Reflections on Politics and Technology*. Albany: State University of New York, 1993.

Giarini, O. and H. Loubergé. *The Diminishing Returns of Technology*. Translated by M. Chapman. Oxford: Pergamon Press, 1978.

Giddens, A. *Modernity and Self Identity: Self and Society in the Late Modern Age*. Cambridge: Polity Press, 1991.

Gilligan, C. *In a Different Voice: Psychological Theory and Woman's Development*. Cambridge, MA: Harvard University Press, 1982.

———. "In a Different Voice: Women's Conception of Self and of Morality." *Harvard Educational Review* 47 (1977): 481–517.

———. *Mapping the Moral Domain: A Contribution of Women's Thinking to Psychological Theory and Education*. Cambridge, MA: Harvard University Press, 1988.

Gimpel, J. *The End of the Future: The Waning of the High-Tech World*. Translated by H. McPhail. Westport, CT: Praeger, 1995.

Ginsburg, F.D. and R. Rapp. *Conceiving of the New World Order: The Global Politics of Reproduction*. Berkeley: University of California Press, 1995.

Glantz, S.A. *The Cigarette Papers*. Berkeley: University of California Press, 1996.

Glazer, M. and R. Glazer. "Pathways to Resistance: An Ethical Odyssey in Government and Industry." *Research in Social Problems and Public Policy* 4 (1987): 193–219.

———. *The Whistle Blowers: Exposing Corruption in Government and Industry*. New York: Basic Books, 1989.

Glendinning, C. *When Technology Wounds: The Human Consequences of Progress*. New York: William Morrow, 1990.

Glut, D. *The Frankenstein Legend*. Metachen, NJ: Scarecrow Press, 1973.

Goffman, E. *The Presentation of Self in Everyday Life*. Garden City: NJ: Doubleday, 1959.

Goldman, R.M. and W.M. Hardman. *Building Trust: An Introduction to Peacekeeping and Arms Control*. Aldershot, UK: Ashgate, 1997.

Goldman, S., R.M. Nabel, and K. Preiss. *Agile Competitors and Virtual Organizations: Strategies for Enriching the Customer*. New York: Van Nostrand, 1995.

Goldsmith, E. and N. Hildyard. *The Earth Report: Monitoring the Battle For Our Environment*. London: Mitchell Beazeley, 1988.

Goldsmith, R.E. "Reputation: Realizing Value From Corporate Image." *Service Industries Journal* 17 (1997): 354–58.

Golembiewski, R.T. *Managing Diversity in Organizations*. Tuscaloosa: University of Alabama Press, 1995.

Goodpaster, K.E. "The Concept of Corporate Responsibility." *Journal of Business Ethics* 2 (1983): 1–22.

Goodpaster, K.E. and J.B. Matthews, Jr. "Can a Corporation Have a Conscience?" In *Ethical Theory and Business,* edited by T.L. Beauchamp and N.E. Bowie. Englewood Cliffs, NJ: Prentice Hall, 1983.

Gottlieb, B., E.K. Kelloway, and E.J. Barham. *Flexible Work Arrangements: Managing the Work-Family Boundary*. New York: John Wiley & Sons, 1988.

Gottlieb, M. and L. Conkling. *Managing the Workplace Survivors: Organizational Downsizing and the Commitment Gap.* Westport, CT: Quorum Books, 1995.

Gould, J.M. *The Technical Elite.* New York: A.M. Kelley, 1966.

Gould, S., K.J. Weiner, and B.R. Levin. *Free Agents: People and Organizations Creating a New Working Community.* San Francisco: Jossey-Bass, 1997.

Grace, D. and S. Cohen. *Business Ethics: Australian Problems and Cases.* Oxford: Oxford University Press, 1995.

Graham, Jill W. "Principled Organizational Dissent: A Theoretical Essay." *Research in Organizational Behavior* 8 (1986): 1–56.

Granovetter, M.S. "Economic Action, Social Structure and Embeddedness." *American Journal of Sociology* 91 (1985): 481–510.

Grantham, C.E. *The Digital Workplace.* New York: Van Nostrand Reinhold, 1993.

Gray, J.G. *Managing the Corporate Image: The Key to Public Trust.* Westport, CT: Quorum Books, 1986.

Greenleaf, R.K. *Servant Leadership: A Journey in the Nature of Legitimate Power and Greatness.* New York: Paulist Press, 1977.

Grefe, E.A. *The New Corporate Activism: Harnessing the Power for Grassroots Tactics for Your Organization.* New York: McGraw Hill, 1995.

Gregory, J.R. and J.G. Wiechmann. *Marketing Corporate Image: The Company as Your Number One Product.* Homewood, IL: NTC Business Books, 1991.

Grenier, R. and G. Metes. *Going Virtual: Moving Your Organization Into the 21st Century.* Englewood Cliffs, NJ: Prentice Hall, 1995.

Grossman, L.K. *The Electronic Republic: Reshaping Democracy in the Information Age.* New York: Viking, 1995.

Guilloy, W.A. *The Living Organization: Spirituality in the Workplace.* Salt Lake City: Innovation, 1997.

Guy, M.E. *Ethical Decision Making in Everyday Work Situations.* New York: Quorum Books, 1990.

Habermas, J. *Legitimation Crisis.* Boston: Beacon, 1973.

———. *Moral Consciousness and Communicative Action.* Translated by C. Lenhardt and S.W. Nicholson. Cambridge, MA: MIT Press, 1990.

Hackman, R.J. *Groups that Work (And Those That Don't): Creating Conditions for Effective Teamwork.* San Francisco: Jossey-Bass, 1990.

Hale, R. and P. Whitlan. *Towards the Virtual Organization.* London: McGraw Hill, 1997.

Halli, S., F Trovato, and L Dreidger. *Ethnic Demography: Canadian Immigrant, Racial and Cultural Variations.* Ottawa: Carleton University Press, 1990.

Hambrick, D.C. "Fragmentation and Other Problems CEOs Have in Their Top Management Teams." *California Management Review* 37 (1995): 110–27.

Hamilton, S. *Apprenticeship for Adulthood: Preparing Youth For the Future.* New York: Free Press, 1990.

Hampden-Turner, C. *Corporate Culture: From Vicious to Virtuous Circles.* London: Hutchinson Business Books, 1989.

———. *Maps of the Mind: Charts and Concepts of the Mind and Its Labyrinths.* New York: Collier Books, 1981.

Handa, J. *Discrimination, Retirement and Pensions.* Aldershot, UK: Avebury, 1994.

Handy, C. *Understanding Organizations.* 3rd ed. London: Penguin Books, 1985.

Hardin, G. "The Tragedy of the Commons." *Science* 162 (1968): 1243–48.

Hardin, R. "Trustworthiness." *Ethics* 107 (1996): 26–42.

Harmon, W. "Why the World Business Academy?" *World Business Academy Perspectives* 3 (1992).

Harrington, H.J. *Business Process Improvement: The Breakthrough Strategy for Total Quality, Productivity and Competitiveness.* New York: McGraw Hill, 1991.

Harris, G.W. *Dignity and Vulnerability: Strength and Quality of Character.* Berkeley: University of California Press, 1997.

Harrison, E.B. *Going Green: How to Communicate Your Company's Environmental Commitment.* Homewood, IL: Business One Irwin, 1993.

Hatch, M.J. *Organization Theory: Modern, Symbolic and Postmodern Perspectives.* New York: Oxford University Press, 1997.

Hawken , P. *The Ecology of Commerce: A Declaration of Sustainability.* New York: Harper Collins, 1993.

Hayles, V.R. and M.R. Armida. *Diversity Directive: Why Some Initiatives Fail and What To Do About It.* Chicago: Irwin Professional Publishing, 1997.

Heath, R.L. and R.A. Nelson. *Issues Management: Corporate Public Policy Making in an Information Society* Beverley Hills: Sage, 1986.

Heim, M. *The Metaphysics of Virtual Reality.* New York: Oxford University Press, 1993.

Helgesen, S. *The Web of Inclusion: A New Architecture for Building Great Organizations.* New York: Doubleday, 1995.

Hemphill, H. and R. Haines. *Discrimination, Harassment and the Failure of Diversity Training: What To Do Now?* Westport, CT: Quorum Books, 1997.

Henderson, H. *Building a Win-Win World: Life Beyond Global Economic Warfare.* San Francisco: Berrett-Koehler Publishers, 1996.

———. *Creating Alternative Futures: The End of Economics.* New York: Berkely Publishing Corporation, 1978.

Henion, K.E., II and T.C. Kinnear. *The Conserver Society.* Chicago: American Marketing Association, 1979.

Herbert, N. *Elemental Mind: Human Consciousness and the New Physics.* New York: Dutton, 1993.

Herbig, P. and J. Milewicz. "A Model of Reputation Building and Destruction." *Journal of Business Research* 31 (1994): 28–31.

Hill, S. *The Tragedy of Technology.* London: Pluto Press, 1989.

Hirschhorn, L. *The Workplace Within: Psychodynamics of Organizational Life.* Cambridge, MA: MIT Press, 1988.

Hirschman, A.O. "Exit, Voice and Loyalty: Further Reflection and a Survey of Recent Contributions." *Social Science Information* 13 (1974): 7–26.

———. *Exit, Voice and Loyalty: Responses to Decline in Firms, Organizations and States.* Cambridge, MA: Harvard University Press, 1970.

Hodgetts, R.M. *Modern Human Relations at Work.* Chicago: Dryden Press, 1984.

Hogan, J.P. *Mind Matters: Exploring the World of Artificial Intelligence.* New York: Ballantine Books, 1998.

Holtzman, S.R. *Digital Mantras: The Languages of Abstract and Virtual Worlds.* Cambridge, MA: MIT Press, 1984.

Hope, J. and T. Hope. *Competing in the Third Wave: The Ten Key Management Issues of the Information Age.* Boston: Harvard Business School Press, 1997.

Hopfenbeck, W. *The Green Management Revolution: Lessons in Environmental Excellence.* Englewood Cliffs, NJ: Prentice Hall, 1993.

Hopkins, W.E. *Ethical Dimensions of Diversity.* Thousand Oaks, CA: Sage, 1997.

Horton, T.R. and P.C. Reid. *Beyond the Trust Gap: Forging a New Partnership Between Managers and Their Employees.* Homewood, IL: Business One Irwin, 1991.

Howard, A. *The Changing Nature of Work.* San Francisco: Jossey-Bass, 1995.

Howard, R.E. "Human Rights and the Culture Wars." *International Journal* 53 (1997): 94–102.

Howell, D.J. *Environmental Stewardship.* Westport, CT: Begin and Garvey, 1997.

Hoyt, J.A. *Animals in Peril: How "Sustainable Use" is Wiping Out the World's Wildlife.* Garden City Park: NY: Avery Publishing, 1994.

Hudson, M. *Managing Without Profit: The Art of Managing Third Sector Organizations.* London: Penguin Books, 1995.

Huntington, S.P. *Clash of Civilization and the Remaking of World Order.* New York: Simon and Schuster, 1996.

Husted, B.W. "Trust in Business Relations: Directions For Empirical Research." *Business and Professional Ethics Journal* 8 (1989): 23–40.

Hutcheon, L. and J Natoli, eds. *A Postmodern Reader.* New York: State University of New York Press, 1992.

Hutchinson, A. and F. Hutchinson. *Environmental Business Management: Sustainable Development in the New Millennium.* London: McGraw Hill, 1996.

Hutchinson, C. *Building to Last: The Challenge for Business Leaders.* London: Earthscan, 1997.

Hutchinson, M. *Megabrain: New Tools and Techniques for Brain Growth and Mind Expansion.* New York: William Morrow, 1986.

Huxley, A. *Brave New World.* New York: Harper and Row, 1946.

Ind, N. *The Corporate Image: Strategies for Effective Identity Programmes.* London: Kogan Page, 1992.

Ingstad, B. and S.R. Whyte. *Disability and Culture.* Berkeley: University of California Press, 1995.

Inkeles, A. *One World Emerging? Convergence and Divergence in Industrial Societies.* Boulder: Westview Press, 1998.

Jackall, R. *Moral Mazes: The World of Corporate Managers.* New York: Oxford University Press, 1988.

Jackson, P. and J.M. Van Der Wielen. *Teleworking: International Perspectives, From Telecommuting to the Virtual Organization.* London: Routledge, 1998.

Jackson, P.B., P.A. Thoits, and H. Taylor. "Composition of the Workforce and Psychological Well Being: The Effects of Tokenism on America's Black Elite." *Social Forces* 74 (1995): 543–62.

Jackson, S.E. "Team Composition in Organizational Settings: Issues in Managing an Increasingly Diverse Workforce." In *Group Processes and Productivity,* edited by S. Worchel, W. Wood, and J.A. Simpson. Newbury Park, CA: Sage, 1992.

Jacques, E. *The Changing Culture of a Factory.* London: Tavistock Publications, 1951.

———. "Social Systems as a Defense Against Persecutory and Depressive Anxiety." In *New Directions in Psychoanalysis,* edited by M. Klein, P. Heimann, and R.E. Money-Kryle. New York: Basic Books, 1955.

James, G. *Business Wisdom of the Electronic Elite: 34 Winning Management Strategies From CEO's at Microsoft, COMPAQ, Sun, Hewlett-Packard, and Other Top Companies.* New York: Times Business/Random House, 1996.

James, G.G. "Whistle Blowing: Its Nature and Justification." *Philosophy in Context* 10 (1980): 99–117.

Jameson, F. *On Postmodernism*. London: Verso, 1997.

———. *Postmodernism, Or the Culture of Late Capitalism*. Durham: Duke University Press, 1991.

Janis, I.L. *Groupthink: Psychological Studies of Policy Decisions and Fiascoes*. Boston: Houghton Mifflin Company, 1982.

———. *Victims of Groupthink*. Boston: Houghton Mifflin Company, 1972.

Jarrell, G. and S. Petzman. "The Impact of Product Recalls on the Wealth of Sellers." *Journal of Political Economy* 93 (1985): 512–36.

Jasinowski, J. *The Rising Tide: The Leading Minds of Business and Economics Chart a Course Towards Higher Growth and Prosperity*. New York: John Wiley & Sons, 1998.

Jenson, J. and R. Mahon. *The Challenge of Restructuring: North American Labor Movements Respond*. Philadelphia: Temple University Press, 1993.

Johnson, R. and D. Redmond. *The Art of Empowerment: The Profit and Pain of Employee Involvement*. London: Pitman, 1998.

Johnston, C.G. *Globalization: Canadian Companies Compete*. Ottawa: Conference Board of Canada, 1990.

Jones, S.G. *Cybersociety: Computer-Mediated Communication and Community*. Thousand Oaks, CA: Sage, 1995.

Joy, R.J. *Canada's Official Languages*. Toronto: University of Toronto Press, 1992.

Judson, B. *Net Marketing: How Your Business Can Profit From the Online Revolution*. New York: Wolff New Media, 1996.

Kahn, A.D. *The Many Faces of Gay: Activists Who Are Changing the Nation*. Westport, CT: Praeger, 1997.

Kahneman, D., J. Knetsch, and R. Thaler. "Fairness as a Constant in Profit Seeking: Entitlements in the Market." *The American Economic Review* 76 (1986): 728–41.

Kalakota, R. and A.B. Whinston. *Frontiers of Electronic Commerce*. Reading, MA: Addison-Wesley, 1996.

Kant, I. *The Moral Law*. 1785. Reprint, edited and translated by H.J. Paton. London: Hutchinson, 1948.

Kaplan, L.J. and R. Tong. *Controlling Our Reproductive Destiny: A Technological and Philosophical Perspective*. Cambridge, MA: MIT Press, 1994.

Kaplan, M. and J. Lucas. "Heterosexism as a Workplace Diversity Issue." In *The Diversity Factor: Capturing the Competitive Advantage of a Changing Workforce*, edited by E.Y. Cross and M. Blackburn White. Chicago: Irwin Professional Publishing, 1996.

Kassman, K. *Envisioning Ectopia: The U.S. Green Movement and the Politics of Radical Social Change*. Westport, CT: Praeger, 1997.

Keenan, J.P. "Upper-Level Managers and Whistle Blowing: Determinants of Perceptions of Company Encouragement and Information About Where to Blow the Whistle." *Journal of Business and Psychology* 5 (1990): 223–35.

Kempner, T., K. Macmillan, and K. Hawkins. *Business and Society: Traditional and Change*. London: Allen Lane, 1974.

Kerr, C. *The Future of Industrial Societies: Convergence or Continuing Diversity*. Cambridge, MA: Harvard University Press, 1983.

Kets de Vries, M.F.R. *The Irrational Executive: Psychoanalytic Studies in Management*. New York: International University Press, 1984.

———. *Life and Death in the Executive Fast Lane: Essays on Irrational Organizations and Their Leaders*. San Francisco: Jossey-Bass, 1995.

———. *Organizations on the Couch: Clinical Perspectives on Organizational Behavior and Change*. San Francisco: Jossey-Bass, 1991.

Kets de Vries, M.F.R. and D. Miller. "Leadership Styles and Organizational Cultures: The Shaping of Neurotic Cultures." In *Organizations on the Couch: Clinical Perspectives on Organizational Behavior and Change*, edited by M.F.R. Kets de Vries. San Francisco: Jossey-Bass, 1991.

————. *The Neurotic Organization: Diagnosing and Changing Counterproductive Styles of Management*. San Francisco: Jossey-Bass, 1984.

Keyes, J. *Technology Trendlines*. New York: Van Nostrand Reinhold, 1995.

Kidder, R.M. *How Good People Make Tough Choices*. New York: William Morrow, 1995.

Kiesler, C.A. *The Psychology of Commitment*. New York: Academic Press, 1971.

Kilduff, M. "Deconstructing Organizations." *Academy of Management Review* 18 (1993): 13–31.

Kilduff, M. and D. Krackhardt. "Bringing the Individual Back In: A Structural Analysis of the Internal Market for Reputation in Organizations." *Academy of Management Journal* 37 (1994): 87–108.

Kilduff, M. and A. Mehra. "Postmodernism and Organizational Research." *Academy of Management Review* 22 (1997): 453–81.

Killinger, B. *Workaholics: The Respectable Addicts*. Toronto: Key Porter Books, 1991.

Kilmann, R.H. *Managing Beyond the Quick Fix: A Completely Integrated Program for Creating and Maintaining Organizational Success*. San Francisco: Jossey-Bass, 1989.

Kilmann, R.H., M. Saxton, and R. Serpa. *Gaining Control of the Corporate Culture*. San Francisco: Jossey-Bass, 1985.

King, G. "The Effects of Interpersonal Closeness and Issue Seriousness on Blowing the Whistle." *Journal of Business Communication* 34 (1997): 419–36.

King, W.R. "Strategic Issue Management." In *Strategic Planning and Management Handbook*, edited by W. King and D. Cleland. New York: Van Nostrand Reinhold, 1982.

————. "Using Strategic Issue Analysis." *Long Range Planning* 15, no. 4 (1987): 45–49.

Kingston, W. and L.S. Lewis. *The High Status Track: Studies of Elite Schools and Stratification*. Albany: State University of New York Press, 1990.

Kipnis, D. *Technology and Power*. Berlin: Springer-Verlag, 1990.

Kirn, S. and G. O'Hare. *Cooperative Knowledge Processing: The Key Technology for Intelligent Organizations*. Berlin: Springer-Verlag, 1997.

Kitchin, R. *Cyberspace: The World in the Wires*. New York: John Wiley & Sons, 1998.

Klein, E. and J. Izzo. *Awakening the Corporate Soul*. New York: Midpoint Trade Books, 1998.

Kling, R. *Computerization and Controversy: Value Conflicts and Social Choices*. San Diego: Academic Press, 1996.

Klockars, C.B. "The Dirty Harry Problem." In *Moral Issues in Police Work*, edited by F.A. Ellison and M. Feldberg. Totowa, NJ: Rowman and Allanheld, 1985.

Klonoski, R.J. "Foundational Considerations in the Corporate Social Responsibility Debate." *Business Horizons* 34, no. 4 (1991) 9–17.

Koenig, F. *Rumor in the Marketplace: The Social Psychology of Commercial Hearsay*. Dover, MA: Auburn House Publishing, 1985.

Koestenbaum, P. *Leadership: The Inner Side of Greatness*. San Francisco: Jossey-Bass, 1991.

Kohlberg, L. *Essays on Moral Development*. San Francisco: Harper and Row, 1981.

————. *Moral Judgment Interview and Procedures for Scoring*. Cambridge, MA: Center for Moral Education, Harvard University, 1976.

Kohlberg, L. and R. Kramer. "Continuities and Discontinuities in Children and Adult Moral Development." *Human Development* 12 (1969): 93–120.

Kohlberg, L., C. Levine, and A. Hewer. *Moral Stages: A Current Formulation and a Response to Critics*. New York: Karger, 1983.

Kohut, H. *The Restoration of the Self*. New York: International University Press, 1977.

Korten, D.C. *When Corporations Rule the World*. San Francisco: Berrett-Koehler Publishers, 1995.

Kram, K.E. *Mentoring at Work: Developmental Relationships in Organizational Life*. Glenview, IL: Scott Foresman, 1985.

Kramer, R.M. and D.M. Messick. *Negotiation as a Social Process*. Thousand Oaks, CA: Sage, 1995.

Kranzeberg, M. "Technology as Liberator." In *Technology at the Turning Point*, edited by W. Pickett. San Francisco: San Francisco Press, 1977.

Kreiger, M.H. "What's Wrong With Plastic Trees?" *Science* 179 (1973): 446–55.

Kugelmass, J. *Telecommuting: A Manager's Guide to Flexible Work Arrangements*. New York: Lexington, 1995.

Kuhn, T. *The Structure of Scientific Revolutions*. Chicago: University of Chicago Press, 1970.

Kuran, T. *Private Truths, Public Lies: The Social Consequence of Preference Falsification*. Cambridge, MA: Harvard University Press, 1995.

Kurzweil, E. and W. Phillips. *Our Country, Our Culture: The Politics of Political Correctness*. Boston: Partisan Review Press, 1994.

Kurzweil, R. *The Age of Intelligent Machines*. Cambridge, MA: MIT Press, 1990.

Kydd, C.T. and J. Ogilvie. "I Don't Care What They Say, as Long as They Spell My Name Right: Publicity, Reputation and Turnover." *Group and Organization Studies* 15 (1990): 53–74.

Laarksonen, P. *Consumer Involvement: Concepts and Research*. London: Routledge, 1994.

LaBorde, A. *Corporate Image: Communicating Vision and Values*. New York: Conference Board, 1993.

Lacy, D.M. *From Grunts to Gigabytes: Communications and Society*. Urbana: University of Illinois Press, 1996.

Ladd, J. "Morality and the Ideal of Rationality in Formal Organizations." *Monist* 54 (1970): 488–516.

Lahno, B. "Trust, Reputation and Exit in Exchange Relationships." *Journal of Conflict Resolution* 39 (1995): 495–510.

Lakoff, G. *Moral Politics: What Conservatives Know That Liberals Don't*. Chicago: University of Chicago Press, 1996.

Landa, J. *Trust, Ethnicity and Identity: Beyond the New Institutional Economics of Ethnic Trading Networks, Contract Law and Gift Exchange*. Ann Arbor: University of Michigan Press, 1994.

Landon, S. and C.E. Smith. "The Use of Quality and Reputation Indicators By Consumers: The Case of Bordeaux Wines." *Journal of Consumer Policy* 20 (1997): 289–323.

Lasch, C. "Revolt of the Elites." *Harper,* November 1994, 39–49.

Lassey, P. *Developing a Learning Organization*. London: Kogan Page, 1998.

Latane, B. and J.M. Darley. *The Unresponsive Bystander: Why Doesn't He Help?* New York: Appleton-Century Crofts, 1970.

Lawton, S.B., J. Freedman, and H.J. Robertson. *Busting Bureaucracy to Reclaim Our Schools*. Montreal: Institute for Research on Public Policy, 1995.

Layard, R. and S. Glaister. *Cost-Benefit Analysis*. Cambridge: Cambridge University Press, 1994.

Lee, M. *Earth First: Environmental Apocalypse*. Syracuse: Syracuse University Press, 1995.

Leer, A. *It's a Wired World: The New Networked Economy*. Oslo: Scandinavian University Press, 1996.

Leona, C.A. "A Partial Test of Janis' Groupthink Model: Effects of Group Cohesiveness and Leader Behavior on Defective Decision-Making." *Journal of Management* 11 (1985): 5–17.

Leonard-Barton, D. *Wellsprings of Knowledge: Building and Sustaining the Sources of Innovation.* Boston: Harvard Business School Press, 1995.

Leopold, A. *A Sand County Almanac and Sketches Here and There.* 1949. Reprint. Oxford: Oxford University Press, 1989.

Lerbinger, O. *The Crisis Manager: Facing Risk and Responsibility.* Mahway, NJ: Lawrence Erlbaum, 1997.

Levitt, T. "The Dangers of Social Responsibility." *Harvard Business Review* 36 (1958).

Levy, P. *Collective Intelligence: Mankind's Emerging World in Cyberspace.* Translated by R. Bononno. New York: Plenum Trade, 1997.

Lewington, J. "Grappling With an Ethical Question: How Much is Too Much?" *The Globe and Mail* (Toronto) 27 March 1997, C1.

Lewis, J.D. and A. Weigert. "Trust as Social Reality." *Social Forces* 63 (1985): 967–85.

Lewis, M.W. *Green Delusions: An Environmentalist Critique of Radical Environmentalism.* Durham: Duke University Press, 1992.

Loden, M. *Implementing Diversity.* Chicago: Irwin Professional Publishing, 1996.

Logsdon, J.M. and D.R. Palmer. "Issues Management and Ethics." *Journal of Business Ethics* 7 (1988): 191–98.

"Looking Back at Ten Years in the Business Ethics Field." *Business Ethics*, July/August 1991.

Lorin, H. *Doing It Right: Technology, Business and Risk of Computing.* Greenwich, CT: Manning, 1995.

Lovelock, J.E. *Gaia, A New Look at Life on Earth.* Oxford: Oxford University Press, 1979.

Luhman, N. *Trust and Power.* New York: John Wiley & Sons, 1979.

Luke, T.W. *Ecocritique: Contesting the Politics of Nature, Economy and Culture.* Minneapolis: University of Minnesota Press, 1997.

Lynch, D.C. and L. Lundquist. *Digital Money: The New Era of Internet Commerce.* New York: John Wiley & Sons, 1996.

Lynch, F. *The Diversity Machine: The Drive to Change the "White Male Workplace."* New York: Free Press, 1997.

———. *Invisible Victims: White Males and the Crisis of Affirmative Action.* New York: Praeger, 1991.

MacGowan, J. "Lives Lived: Gunther Voss." *The Globe and Mail* (Toronto), 29 August 1997, A26.

Machiavelli, N. *The Prince.* Translated by W.K. Merriott. London: Dent, 1968.

MacIntyre , A. *After Virtue: A Study in Moral Theory.* Notre Dame: University of Notre Dame Press, 1981.

Mander, J. *In the Absence of the Sacred: The Failure of Technology and the Survival of the Indian Nations.* San Francisco: Sierra Club Books, 1991.

Manley, W.W., III. *Handbook of Good Business Practice.* London: Routledge, 1992.

Mansell, R. and R. Silverstone. *Communication by Design: The Politics of Information and Communication Technologies.* Oxford: Oxford University Press, 1996.

Mansell, R. and U. Wehn. *Knowledge Societies: Information Technology for Sustainable Development.* New York: Oxford University Press, 1998.

Marc, D. *Bonfire of the Humanities: Television Subliteracy and Long-Term Memory Loss.* Syracuse: Syracuse University Press, 1995.

Marchak, P.M. *Green Gold: The Forestry Industry in British Columbia*. Vancouver: University of British Columbia Press, 1983.

Marcus, G.E. *Corporate Futures: The Diffusion of the Culturally Sensitive Corporate Form*. Chicago: University of Chicago Press, 1998.

Marietta, D., Jr. and L. Embree. *Environmental Philosophy and Environmental Activism*. Lanham, MD: Rowman and Littlefield, 1995.

Marietta, D., Jr. *For People and the Planet: Holism and Humanism in Environmental Ethics*. Philadelphia: Temple University Press, 1995.

Markham, V.W.R. *Planning the Corporate Reputation*. London, UK: Allen and Unwin, 1972.

Markley, R. *Virtual Realities and Their Discontents*. Baltimore: Johns Hopkins University Press, 1996.

Marshall, P.D. *Celebrity and Power: Fame in Contemporary Culture*. Minneapolis: University of Minnesota Press, 1997.

Martin, J. *Cultures in Organizations: Three Perspectives*. New York: Oxford University Press, 1992.

Martin, J. *Cybercorp: The New Business Revolution*. New York: AMACOM, 1996.

Martinez, K. and K.L. Ames. *The Material Culture of Gender, the Gender of Material Culture*. Winterther, DE: University of New England Press, 1997.

Mathews, M.C. *Strategic Intervention in Organizations: Resolving Ethical Dilemmas*. Newbury Park, CA: Sage, 1988.

Mazlish, B. *The Fourth Discontinuity: The Co-evolution of Humans and Machines*. New Haven: Yale University Press, 1993.

McCarthy, J.L. *Commerce in Cyberspace*. New York: Conference Board, 1996.

McCorduck, P. *The Universal Machine: Confessions of a Technological Optimist*. New York: McGraw Hill, 1985.

McCowan, R. *Business, Politics and Cigarettes: Multiple Levels, Multiple Agendas*. Westport, CT: Quorum Books, 1995.

McCoy, B.H. "The Parable of the Sadhu." *Harvard Business Review* May-June (1997): 54–64.

McDonald, H. "The Diversity Industry." *New Republic*, 5 July 1993, 22–25.

McFarland, J. and G. Keenan. "Harassment Suit Put Heat on Big 3." *The Globe and Mail* (Toronto), 10 September 1997, A1, A7.

McIntosh, P. *White Privilege and Male Privilege: A Personal Account of Coming to See Correspondences Through Work in Women's Studies*. Wellesley: Wellesley College, Center for Research on Women, 1988.

McKibben, B. *The Age of Missing Information*. New York: Random House, 1992.

McLagan, P.A. and N. Christo. *The Age of Participation: New Governance for the Workplace and the World*. San Francisco: Berrett-Koehler Publishers, 1995.

McLaughlin, A. *Regarding Nature: Industrialism and Deep Ecology*. Albany: State University of New York, 1993.

McLean, I. *Democracy and New Technology*. Cambridge: Polity Press, 1989.

McLuhan, M. *Understanding Media*. New York: Signet Books, 1964.

McMillan, C.J. and V.V. Murray. "Strategically Managing Public Affairs: Lessons From the Analysis of Business-Government Relations." *Business Quarterly*, Summer 1983, 94–100.

Megginson, D. and D. Clutterbuck. *Mentoring in Action: A Practical Guide for Managers*. London: Kogan Page, 1995.

Meindl, J.R., C. Stubbart, and J. Porac. *Cognition Within and Between Organizations*. Thousand Oaks, CA: Sage, 1996.

Meir, Golda, *My Life*. New York: Putnam, 1975.

Menzies, H. *Whose Brave New World? The Information Highway and the New Economy*. Toronto: Between the Lines, 1996.

Menzies, I.E.P. "A Case in the Functioning of Social Systems as a Defense Against Anxiety: A Report on a Study of the Nursing Service of a General Hospital." *Human Relations* 13 (1960): 95–121.

Merchant, C. *Earthcore: Women and Their Environment*. New York: Routledge, 1996.

———. *Radical Ecology: The Search for a Livable World*. New York: Routledge, 1992.

Merry, U. *Coping With Uncertainty: Insights for the New Sciences of Chaos, Self-Organization and Complexity*. Westport, CT: Praeger, 1995.

Metes, G., J. Gundry, and P. Bradish. *Agile Networking: Competing Through the Internet and Intranets*. Upper Saddle River, NJ: Prentice Hall, 1998.

Miceli, M.P. and J.P. Near. *Blowing the Whistle: The Organizational and Legal Implications for Companies and Employees*. New York: Lexington, 1992.

———. "The Incidence of Wrongdoing, Whistle-Blowing and Retaliation: Results of a Naturally Occurring Field Experiment." *Employee Responsibilities and Rights Journal* 2 (1989): 91–108.

———. "Listening to Your Whistle Blowers Can Be Profitable." *Academy of Management Executives* 8 (1994): 65–72.

———. "Whistle Blowing as Antisocial Behavior." In *Antisocial Behavior in the Workplace*, edited by G. Greenberg and R. Giacalone. Thousand Oaks, CA: Sage, 1996.

Miceli, M.P., B.L. Roach, and J.P. Near. "The Motivations of 'Deep Throat': The Case of Anonymous Whistle Blowers." *Public Personnel Management* 17 (1988): 281–96.

Michalos, A. "The Impact of Trust on Business International Security and the Quality of Life." *Journal of Business Ethics* 9 (1990): 619–38.

Michie, D. *The Knowledge Machine: Artificial Intelligence and the Future of Man*. New York: William Morrow, 1985.

Miethe, T.D. and J. Rothschild. "Whistle Blowing and the Control of Organizational Misconduct." *Sociological Inquiry* 64 (1994): 322–47.

Mill, J.S. *Collected Works*. Toronto: University of Toronto Press, 1963.

Miller, N.I. *Out in the World: Gay and Lesbian Life From Buenos Aires to Bangkok*. New York: Random House, 1992.

Minirth, F. *The Workaholic and His Family*. Grand Rapids: Baker Books, 1981.

Minoli, D. *Analyzing Outsourcing*. New York: McGraw Hill, 1995.

Mintzberg, H. *Mintzberg on Management: Inside our Strange World of Organizations*. New York: Free Press, 1989.

———. *Power in and Around Organizations*. Englewood Cliffs, NJ: Prentice Hall, 1983.

———. *Structure in Fives: Designing Effective Organizations*. Englewood Cliffs, NJ: Prentice Hall, 1983.

Mishra, A.K. "Organizational Responses to Crises: The Centrality of Trust." In *Trust in Organizations: Frontiers of Theory and Research*, edited by R.M. Kramer and T.R. Tyler. Thousand Oaks, CA: Sage, 1996.

Mitcham, C. *Thinking Through Technology: The Path Between Engineering and Philosophy*. Chicago: University of Chicago Press, 1994.

Mitchell, J.C. *Ecotactics: The Sierra Club Handbook for Environmental Activists*. New York: Pocket Books, 1970.

Mody, A. and D. Wheeler. *Automation and World Competition: New Technologies, Industrial Location and Trade*. London: Macmillan, 1990.

Mohamed, A.A. and F.A. Wiebe. "Toward a Process Theory of Groupthink." *Small Group Research* 27, no. 3 (1996): 416–30.

Mohrman, S.A., S. Cohen, and A. Mohrman. *Designing Team-Based Organizations: New Forms For Knowledge Work*. San Francisco: Jossey-Bass, 1995.

Molm, L.D. *Coercive Power in Social Exchange*. Cambridge: Cambridge University Press, 1997.

Moorhead, G., R. Ference, and C.P. Nuk. "Group Decision Fiascoes Continue: Space Shuttle Challenger and a Revised Groupthink Framework." *Human Relations* 44, no. 6 (1991): 539–50.

Morgan, R. *Sisterhood is Global: The International Women's Movement Anthology*. New York: Feminist Press of the City University of New York, 1996.

Morrison, J.I. *The Second Curve: Managing the Velocity of Change*. New York: Ballantine Books, 1996.

Mount, E., Jr. *Professional Ethics in Context: Institution, Images and Empathy*. Louisville, KY: Westminster Press, 1990.

Mowlana, H. *Global Communication: The End of Diversity?* Thousand Oaks, CA: Sage, 1996.

Muir, S.A. and T.L. Veenendall. *Earthtalk: Communication for Environmental Action*. Westport, CT: Praeger, 1996.

Myerson, D., K. Weick, and R. Kramer. "Swift Trust and Temporary Groups." In *Trust in Organizations: Frontiers of Theory and Research*, edited by R.M. Kramer and T.R. Tyler. Thousand Oaks, CA: Sage, 1996.

Myles, J. *The Expanding Middle: Some Canadian Evidence on the Deskilling Debate*. Ottawa: Statistics Canada, 1987.

Nader, R., P.J. Petkas, and K. Blackwell. *Whistle-Blowing: The Report on the Conference on Professional Responsibility*. New York: Grossman, 1972.

Naess, A. "The Deep Ecology Movement: Some Philosophical Aspects." *Philosophical Inquiry* 8 (1983): 10–31.

Naess, A. and G. Sessions. "Basic Principles of Deep Ecology." *Ecophilosophy* 6 (1984): 3–7.

Nancoo, S.E. and S. Ramcharon. *Canadian Diversity: 2000 and Beyond*. Mississauga: Canadian Educators Press, 1995.

Nas, T. *Cost-Benefit Analysis: Theory and Application*. Thousand Oaks, CA: Sage, 1996.

Nash, L. *Good Intentions Aside: A Manager's Guide to Resolving Ethical Problems*. Boston: Harvard University Business School Press, 1990.

Nash, R. *The Rights of Nature: A History of Environmental Ethics*. Madison: University of Wisconsin Press, 1989.

Natoli, J. *A Primer to Postmodernity*. Oxford: Basil Blackwell, 1997.

Nava, M. *Changing Cultures: Feminism, Youth and Consumerism*. Newbury Park, CA: Sage, 1992.

Neal, M.B. *Balancing Work and Caregiving for Children, Adults and Elders*. Newbury Park: Sage Publications, 1993.

Near, J.P. and T.C. Jensen. "The Whistle-Blowing Process: Retaliation and Effectiveness." *Work and Occupations* 10 (1983): 3–28.

Near, J.P. and M.P. Miceli. "Organizational Dissidence: The Case of Whistleblowing." *Journal of Business Ethics* 4 (1985): 1–16.

————. "Whistle Blowers in Organizations: Dissidents or Reformers?" *Research in Organizational Behavior* 9 (1987): 321–68.

Neck, C.P. and C.C. Manz. "From Groupthink to Teamthink: Toward the Creation of Constructive Thought Patterns in Self-Managed Work Teams." *Human Relations* 47 (1994): 929–39.

Neihardt, J.G. *Black Elk Speaks*. Lincoln: University of Nebraska Press, 1932.

Neu, D. "Trust, Contracting, and the Prospectus Process." *Accounting Organization and Society* 16 (1991): 243–56.

Nevis, E.C., J. Lancourt, and H.G. Vassall. *Intentional Revolutions: Seven-Point Strategy for Transforming Organizations*. San Francisco: Jossey-Bass, 1996.

Newman, P.C. *The Canadian Establishment*. Toronto: McClelland and Stewart, 1979.

Nilsson, N.J. *Artificial Intelligence: A New Synthesis*. San Francisco: Morgan Kaufmann Publishers, 1998.

Nisbet, R. "The Impact of Technology on Ethical Decision Making." In *The Technological Threat*, edited by J. Douglas. Englewood Cliffs, NJ: Prentice Hall, 1971.

Nock, S. *The Costs of Privacy: Surveillance in America*. New York: Aldine de Gruyter, 1993.

Nohria, N. and J.D. Berkley. "The Virtual Organization: Bureaucracy, Technology and the Implosion of Control." In *The Post-Bureaucratic Organization*, edited by C. Hecksher and A. Donellon. Thousand Oaks, CA: Sage, 1994.

Norman, A.L. *Informational Society: An Economic Theory of Discovery, Invention and Innovation*. Boston: Klewer Academic Publishers, 1993.

Norton, D.L. "Character Ethics and Organizational Life." In *Papers on the Ethics of Administration*, edited by N.D. Wright. Provo, UT: Brigham Young University Press, 1988.

Norton, J.R. and R.E. Fox. *Changing Equation: Capitalizing on Diversity for Effective Organizational Change*. Washington: American Psychological Association, 1997.

O'Toole, J. "Do Good, Do Well: The Business Enterprise Trust Awards." *California Management Review* 33, no. 3 (1991): 9–24.

Oates, W. *Confessions of a Workaholic*. Nashville: Abingdon Press, 1971.

Olins, W. *Corporate Identity: Making Business Strategy Visible Through Design*. London: Thames and Hudson, 1990.

————. *The Corporate Personality: An Inquiry Into the Nature of Corporate Identity*. New York: Mayflower Books, 1978.

Oravec, J.A. *Virtual Individuals, Virtual Groups: Human Dimensions of Groupware and Computer Networking*. Cambridge: Cambridge University Press, 1996.

Orwell, G. *1984: A Novel*. New York: New American Library, 1961.

Osterman, P. *Broken Ladders: Managerial Careers in the New Economy*. New York: Oxford University Press, 1996.

Ottman, J.A. *Green Marketing*. Lincolnwood, IL: NTC Business Books, 1993.

————. *Green Marketing: Opportunity for Innovation*. Lincolnwood, IL: NTC Business Books, 1998.

Ouchi, W. *Theory Z*. Reading, MA: Addison Wesley, 1981.

Owen, G.L. *The Betterment of Man: A Rational History of Western Civilization*. New York: Putnam, 1974.

Palumbo-Liu, D. *The Ethnic Canon: Histories, Institutions and Interventions*. Minneapolis: University of Minnesota Press, 1995.

Papworth, J. *Small is Powerful: The Future as if People Really Mattered*. Westport, CT: Praeger, 1995.

Parasurman, S. and J.H. Greenhause. *Integrating Work and Family: Challenges and Choices for a Changing World*. Westport, CT: Quorum Books, 1997.

Parmalee, M.A., J.P. Near, and T.C. Jensen. "Correlates of Whistleblowers' Perceptions of Organizational Retaliation." *Administrative Science Quarterly* 27 (1982): 17–34.

Passmore, W.A. *Designing Effective Organizations: The Sociotechnical Systems Perspective*. New York: John Wiley & Sons, 1988.

Pauchant, T.C. and J.J. Mitroff. *Transforming the Crisis-Prone Organization: Preventing Individual, Organizational, and Environmental Tragedies*. San Francisco: Jossey-Bass, 1992.

Pava, M.L. and J. Krausz. "Criteria For Evaluating the Legitimacy of Corporate Social Responsibility." *Journal of Business Ethics* 16 (1997): 337–46.

Pearce, F. *Green Warriors: The People and the Politics Behind the Environmental Revolution*. London: Bodley Head, 1991.

Peattie, K. *Environmental Marketing Management: Meeting the Green Challenge*, London: Pitman, 1995.

Pecina, M. and I. Bojanic. *Overuse Injuries of the Musculoskeletal System*. Boca Raton, FL: CRC Press, 1993.

Pedler, M. *The Learning Company: A Strategy for Sustainable Development*. New York: McGraw Hill, 1997.

Pellegrino, E.D., R.M. Veatch, and J.P. Langon, eds. *Ethics, Trust and the Professions: Philosophical and Cultural Aspects*. Washington: Georgetown University Press, 1991.

Pepper, D. *Eco-socialism: From Deep Ecology to Social Justice*. London: Routledge, 1993.

Percy, I. *Exploring Spirituality: Going Deeper Into Life and Leadership*. Toronto: Macmillan, 1997.

Perrow, C. *Normal Accidents: Living With High-Risk Technologies*. New York: Basic Books, 1984.

Perrucci, R. and H.R. Potter. *Networks of Power: Organizational Actors at the National, Corporate and Community Levels*. New York: Aldine de Gruyter, 1989.

Peters, B. and J.L. Peters, eds. *Corporate Stewardship of the Environment*. New York: Conference Board, 1991.

Peters, G. *Beyond the Next Wave: Imaging the Next Generation of Customers*. London: Pitman, 1996.

Peters, T. and R.H. Waterman. *In Search of Excellence: Lessons From America's Best-Run Companies*. New York: Warner Books, 1982.

Peters, T.J. and N. Austin. *A Passion for Excellence*. London: Collins, 1985.

Peterson, J. *High Technology and the Competition State: An Analysis of the Eureka Initiative*. New York: Routledge, 1993.

Pfeffer, J. *Managing With Power: Politics and Influence in Organizations*. Boston: Harvard Business School Press, 1992.

———. *Power in Organizations*. Marshfield, MA: Pitman, 1981.

Pfeffer, J. and G. Salancik. *The External Control of Organizations: A Resource Dependence Perspective*. New York: Harper and Row, 1978.

Phelan, J.M. *Disenchantment: Meaning and Morality in the Media*. New York: Hastings House, 1980.

Pheysey, D.C. *Organizational Cultures: Types and Transformations*. London: Routledge, 1993.

Piaget, J. *The Moral Judgement of the Child*. Translated by M. Gabain. New York: Free Press, 1965.

———. *Structuralism*. New York: Basic Books, 1970.

Pimentel, K. and K. Teixeira. *Virtual Reality: Through the New Looking Glass*. New York: Intel/Windcrest, 1993.

Pine, B.J. and S. Davis. *Mass Customization: The New Frontier in Business Competition*. Boston: Harvard Business School Press, 1993.

Pinsdorf, M.K. *Communicating When Your Company is Under Siege: Surviving Public Crisis*. Lexington, MA: Lexington Books, 1987.

Pitsch, P.K. *The Innovation Age: A New Perspective on the Telecom Revolution*. Indianapolis: Hudson Institute, 1996.

Plant, C. and J. Plant. *Green Business: Hope or Hoax?* Philadelphia: New Society Publishers, 1991.

Plsek, P.E. *Creativity, Innovation and Quality*. Milwaukee: ASQC Quality Press, 1997.

Plumwood, V. *Feminism and the Mastery of Nature*. London: Routledge, 1993.

Pol, L.G. and R.K. Thomas. *Demography for Business Decision Making*. Westport, CT: Quorum Books, 1997.

Pool, R. *Beyond Engineering: How Society Shapes Technology*. New York: Oxford University Press, 1997.

Post, J.E. "The New Social Contract." In *Is the Good Corporation Dead?* edited by J.W. Houck and O.F. Williams. London: Rowman and Littlefield, 1996.

Post, J.E., W.C. Frederick, and K. Davis. *Business and Society: Corporate Strategy, Public Policy and Ethics*. New York: McGraw Hill, 1996.

Power, M. "Modernism, Postmodernism and Organization." In *The Theory and Philosophy of Organizations: Critical Issues and New Perspectives*, edited by J. Hassard and D. Pym. London: Routledge and Kegan Paul, 1992.

Powers, M.J. *How to Program a Virtual Community*. Emeryville, CA: Ziff-Davis Press, 1997.

Powers, R. *The Beast, The Eunuch, and the Glass Eyed Child: Television in the 80's*. San Diego: Harcourt, Brace & Jovanovich, 1990.

Rainbow, S. *Green Politics*. New York: Oxford University Press, 1993.

Ramo, S. *What's Wrong With Our Technological Society—And How to Fix It*. New York: McGraw Hill, 1983.

Rasi, R.A. and L. Rodriquez-Noques. *Out in the Workplace: The Pleasures and Perils of Coming Out on the Job*. Los Angeles: Alyson Publications, 1995.

Raspa, D. "The CEO as Corporate Myth-Maker: Negotiating the Boundaries of Work and Play at Domino's Pizza Company." In *Symbols and Artifacts: Views of the Corporate Landscape*, edited by P. Gagliardi. New York: Aldine de Gruyter, 1992.

Rawls , J. *A Theory of Justice*. Cambridge, MA: Harvard University Press, 1971.

Ray, D.L. *Environmental Overkill: Whatever happened to Common Sense?* Washington: Regnery Gateway, 1993.

Ray, D.L. and L. Guzzo. *Trashing the Planet: How Science Can Help us Deal With Acid Rain, Depletion of the Ozone, and Nuclear Waste (Among Other Things)*. Washington: Regnery Gateway, 1993.

Reed, P. and D. Rothenberg. *Wisdom in the Open Air*. Minneapolis: University of Minnesota Press, 1993.

Regan, T. *All That Dwells Therein: Animal Rights and Environmental Ethics*. Berkeley: University of California Press, 1982.

Reich, C. *Opposing the System*. New York: Crown Publishers, 1995.

Rein, I.J., P. Kotler, and M.R. Stoler. *High Visibility*. New York: Dodd, Mead, 1987.

Reineke, I. *Electronic Illusions: A Skeptic's View of Our High-Tech Future*. New York: Penguin Books, 1984.

Renfro, W.L. *Issues Management in Strategic Planning*. Westport, CT: Quorum Books, 1993.

Rheingold, H. *The Virtual Community: Homesteading on the Electronic Frontier.* Reading, MA: Addison Wesley, 1994.

———. *Virtual Reality.* New York: Summit Books, 1991.

Rhodes, E. and D. Wield. *Implementing New Technologies: Innovation and the Management of Technology.* 2nd ed. Oxford: NCC Blackwell, 1994.

Riahi-Belkaoui, A. and E.L. Pavlik. *Accounting for Corporate Reputation.* Westport, CT: Quorum Books, 1993.

Rifken, J. The End of Work: *The Decline in the Global Labor Force and the Dawn of the Post-Market Era.* New York: Putnam, 1995.

Rivage, V. *New Policies for the Part-Time and Contingent Workforce.* Armonk, NY: M.E. Sharpe, 1992.

Rivage-Seul, D.M. and M. Rivage-Seul. *A Kinder, Gentler Tyranny: Illusions of a New World Order.* Westport, CT: Praeger, 1995.

Robinson, B.E. *Work Addiction.* Deerfield Beach, FL: Health Communications, 1989.

Rogers, R.A. *Nature and the Crisis of Modernity: A Critique of Contemporary Discourse on Managing the Earth.* Montreal: Black Rose Books, 1994.

Rollin, B.E. *The Frankenstein Syndrome: Ethical and Social Issues in the Genetic Engineering of Animals.* Cambridge: Cambridge University Press, 1995.

Romig, D.A. *Breakthrough Teamwork: Outstanding Results Using Structural Teamwork.* Chicago: Irwin Professional Publishing, 1996.

Rosenau, P.M. *Post-Modernism and the Social Sciences: Insights, Inroads and Intrusions.* Princeton: Princeton University Press, 1992.

Ross, J. and B.M. Staw. "Organizational Escalation and Exit: The Case of the Shoreham Nuclear Power Plant." *Academy of Management Journal* 36 (1993): 701–32.

———. "Expo 86: An Escalation Prototype." *Administrative Science Quarterly* 32 (1986): 274–97.

Roszak, T. *The Cult of Information: A Neo-Luddite Treatise on High Tech, Artificial Intelligence and the True Art of Thinking.* Berkeley: University of California Press, 1994.

Rothschild, J. *Machine Ex Dea: Feminist Perspectives on Technology.* New York: Pergamon, 1983.

Rotter, J.B. "Generalized Expectations for Interpersonal Trust." *American Psychologist* 26 (1971): 443–52.

———. "A New Scale for the Measurement of Interpersonal Trust." *Journal of Personality* 35 (1967): 651–65.

Rouse, W.B. *Catalysts for Change: Concepts and Principles for Enabling Innovations.* New York: John Wiley & Sons, 1993.

Rowell, A. *Green Backlash: Global Subversity of the Environmental Movement.* New York: Routledge, 1996.

Rowland, W. *Spirit of the Web: The Age of Information From Telegraph to Internet.* Toronto: Somerville House, 1997.

Ruchala, L.V., J.W. Hill, and D. Dalton. "Escalation and the Diffusion of Responsibility: A Commercial Lending Experiment." *Journal of Business Research* 13 (1996): 15–31.

Rusher, W.A. *The Coming Battle For the Media: Curbing the Power of the Media Elite.* New York: William Morrow, 1988.

Ryan, K.D. and D.K. Oestrich. *Driving Fear Out of the Workplace: Creating the High-Trust, High-Performance Organization.* 2nd ed. San Francisco: Jossey-Bass, 1998.

Sachs, A. and J.A. Peterson. *Eco-Justice: Linking Human Rights and the Environment.* Washington: Wordwatch Institute, 1995.

Safire, W. *Safire's Political Dictionary.* 3rd ed. New York: Random House, 1978.

Salancik, G. "Commitment is Too Easy." *Organizational Dynamics* 6, no. 1 (1977): 62–80.

Salomon, J.J. and A. Lebeau. *Mirages of Development: Science and Technology for the Third Worlds.* Boulder: L. Rienner, 1993.

Sartre, J.P. *Les Mains Sales.* In *No Exit and Three Other Plays,* translated by L. Abel. New York: Vintage Books, 1960.

Sassower, R. *Technoscientific Angst: Ethics and Responsibility.* Minneapolis: University of Minnesota Press, 1997.

Sawyer, G.C. *Business and Society: Managing Corporate Social Impact.* Boston: Houghton Mifflin Company, 1979.

Scales, B. and M. Emery. "Diversity at Dupont: The Strategic Diversity Plan." In *The Diversity Factor: Capturing the Competitive Advantage of a Changing Workforce,* edited by E.Y. Cross and M. Blackburn White. Chicago: Irwin Professional Publishing, 1996.

Scarbrough, H. and J.M. Corbett. *Technology and Organization: Power, Meaning and Design.* London: Routledge, 1992.

Schaef, A. and D. Fassel. *The Addictive Organization.* San Francisco: Harper and Row, 1988.

Schecter, H. *Rekindling the Spirit in Work.* Barrytown, NY: Station Hill Openings, 1995.

Schein, E. *Organizational Culture and Leadership.* 2nd ed. San Francisco: Jossey-Bass, 1992.

Schiller, H. *Information Inequality.* New York: Routledge, 1996.

Schmidheiny, S. *Changing Course: A Global Business Perspective on Development and the Environment.* Cambridge, MA: MIT Press, 1992.

Schmidt, A.J. *The Menace of Multiculturalism: Trojan Horse in America.* Westport, CT: Praeger, 1997.

Schriener, J. "Tree Hugging Tactics." *The Financial Post,* 21 June 1997, 8.

Schroeder, R. *Possible Worlds: The Social Dynamics of Virtual Reality Technology.* Boulder: Westview Press, 1996.

Schultz, M. *On Studying Organizational Cultures: Diagnosis and Understanding.* Berlin: Walter de Gruyter, 1994.

Schutzer, D. *Business Decisions With Computers: New Trends in Technology.* New York: Van Nostrand, Reinhold, 1991.

Schwartz, H.S. "Acknowledging the Dark Side of Organizational Life." In *In Search of Meaning: Managing for the Health of Our Organizations, Our Communities and the Natural World,* edited by T.C. Pauchant. San Francisco: Jossey-Bass, 1995.

———. *Narcissistic Process and Corporate Decay: The Theory of the Organization Ideal.* New York: New York University Press, 1990.

Schwartz, M. *The Structure of Power in America: The Corporate Elite as a Ruling Class.* New York: Holmes and Meier, 1988.

Schwartz, M.S. *Biofeedback: A Practitioner's Guide.* New York: Guilford Press, 1987.

Sclove, R. *Democracy and Technology.* New York: Guilford Press, 1995

Scorer, R.S. *The Clever Moron.* Boston: Routledge and Kegan Paul, 1977.

Scott, J. *Poverty and Wealth: Citizenship, Deprivation and Privilege.* London: Longman, 1994.

Scott, W.R. *Organizations: Rational, Natural and Open Systems.* 3rd ed. Englewood Cliffs, NJ: Prentice Hall, 1992.

Secretan, L. *Reclaiming Higher Grounds: Creating Organizations That Inspire Soul.* Toronto: Macmillan, 1996.

Seeger, M.W. *Ethics and Organizational Communication.* Cresskill, NJ: Hampton Press, 1997.

Selame, E. and J. Selame. *The Company Image: Building Your Identity and Influence in the Marketplace.* New York: John Wiley & Sons, 1988.

Senge, P.M. *The Fifth Discipline: The Art and Practice of the Learning Organization.* New York: Doubleday, 1990.

Sethi, S.P. *Advocacy Advertising and Large Corporations: Social Conflict, Big Business Image, the News Media, and Public Policy.* Lexington, MA: D.C. Heath, 1977.

———. "Institutional/Image Advertising and Idea/Issue Advertising as Marketing Tools: Some Public Policy Issues." *Journal of Marketing* 43 (1979): 68–78.

Shallis, M. *The Silicon Idol.* Oxford: Oxford University Press, 1984.

Shaw, S. *Better Daycare for Canadians: Options for Parents and Children.* Ottawa: Canadian Advisory Council on the Status of Women, 1982.

Shaw, W.H. and V. Barry. *Moral Issues in Business.* 5th ed. Belmont, CA: Wadsworth Publishing, 1992.

Shelley, M.W. *Frankenstein or the Modern Prometheus.* New York: Woodstock Books, 1993.

Shenk, D. *Data Smog: Surviving the Information Glut.* San Francisco: Harper Edge, 1997.

Shenkar, O. and E. Yuchtman-Yaar. "Reputation, Image, Prestige and Goodwill: An Interdisciplinary Approach to Organizational Standing." *Human Relations* 50 (1997): 1361–81.

Shrivastava, P. *Greening Business: Profiting the Corporation and the Environment.* Cincinnati: Thompson Executive Press, 1996.

Sievers, B. *Work, Death, and Life Itself: Essays on Management and Organization.* Berlin: Walter de Gruyter, 1993.

Simmel, G. *The Philosophy of Money.* Boston: Routledge and Kegan Paul, 1978.

Simmons, S. *Flexible Working: A Strategic Guide to Successful Implementation and Operation.* London: Kogan Page, 1996.

Simon, J. and H. Kahn. *The Resourceful Earth: A Response to Global 2000.* New York: Basil Blackwell, 1984.

Simpson, M. *Corporate Identity: Name, Image and Perception.* New York: Conference Board, 1987.

Sinator, M. "Building Trust Into Corporate Relationships." *Organizational Dynamics* 16 (1988): 73–79.

Smiricich, L. "Organizations as Shared Meanings." In *Organizational Symbolism,* edited by L.R. Pondy, P.J. Frost, G. Morgan, and T.C. Dandridge. Greenwich, CT: JAI Press, 1983.

Smith, A. *An Inquiry Into the Nature and Causes of the Wealth of Nations,* ed. R.H. Campbell and A.S. Skinner. Oxford: Clarenden Press, 1976.

Smith, D. *Business and the Environment: Implications of the New Environmentalism.* London: Chapman, 1993.

Smythe, J., C. Dorwood, and J. Rebeck. *Corporate Reputation: Managing the New Strategic Asset.* London: Century Business, 1992.

Soloman, R.C. *Ethics and Excellence: Co-operation and Integrity in Business.* Oxford: Oxford University Press, 1992.

Soloman, R.C. and K.R. Hansen. *Above the Bottom Line: An Introduction to Business Ethics.* New York: Harcourt, Brace & Jovanovich, 1983.

Stabile, C.A. *Feminism and the Technological Fix.* New York: St. Martin's Press, 1994.

Stacey, R.D. *The Chaos Frontier: Creative Strategic Control for Business.* Oxford: Butterworth Heinemann, 1991.

Stavrianos, L.S. *The Promise of the Coming Dark Age*. San Francisco: W.H. Freeman, 1976.

Staw, B.M. "Knee-Deep in the Big Muddy: A Study of Escalating Commitment to a Chosen Course of Action." *Organizational Behavior and Human Performance* 16 (1976): 27–44.

Staw, B.M. and J. Ross. "Behavior in Escalation Situations: Antecedants, Prototypes and Solutions." In *Research in Organization Behavior*, Vol. 9, edited by L.L. Cummings and B.M. Staw. Greenwich, CT: JAI Press, 1987.

Stearns, P.N. *The Industrial Revolution in World History*. Boulder: Westview Press, 1993.

Steckel, R. and R. Simons. *Doing Best By Doing Good: How to Use Public-Purpose Partnerships to Boost Corporate Profits and Benefit Your Community*. New York: Dutton, 1992.

Steffen, J.O. *The Tragedy of Abundance*. Niwot, CO: University Press of Colorado, 1993.

Stetson, B. *Human Dignity and Contemporary Liberalism*. Westport, CT: Praeger, 1998.

Stoeffels, J.D. *Strategic Issues Management: A Comprehensive Guide to Environmental Scanning*. Oxford: Elsevier, 1994.

Stokes, S.L. *Controlling the Future: Managing Technology-Driven Change*. Wellesley: QED Information Sciences, 1991.

Stone, C.D. *Earth and Other Ethics: The Case for Moral Pluralism*. New York: Harper and Row, 1987.

———. *Should Trees Have Standing? Legal Rights for Natural Objects*. Los Altos, CA: Kaufmann, 1974.

———. *Where the Law Ends: The Social Control of Corporate Behavior*. New York: Harper and Row, 1975.

Strong, M. *After Rio: The Questions of International Institutional Reform*. Ottawa: National Round Table on the Environment and the Economy, 1995.

Stuart, R. *Design of Virtual Environments*. New York: McGraw Hill, 1996.

Sussman, G. *Communication, Technology and Politics in the Information Age*. Thousand Oaks, CA: Sage, 1997.

Suzuki, D. and P. Knudston. *Wisdom of the Elders: Honoring Sacred Native Visions of Nature*. New York: Bantam Books, 1992.

Swanson, C.L. *The Dilemma of Globalization: Emerging Strategic Concerns in International Business*. Greenwich, CT: JAI Press, 1993.

Syer, J. and C. Connolly. *How Teamwork Works: The Dynamics of Effective Team Development*. New York: McGraw Hill, 1996.

Szasz, A. *Ecopopulism: Toxic Waste and the Movement for Environmental Justice*. Minneapolis: University of Minnesota Press, 1995.

Szwajkowski, E. and R.E. Figlewicz. "Of Babies and Bathwater." *Business and Society* 36 (1997): 362–86.

Taitte, W.L. *Traditional Moral Values in an Age of Technology*. Dallas: University of Texas Press, 1987.

Tapscott, D. *The Digital Economy: Promise and Peril in the Age of Networked Intelligence*. New York: McGraw Hill, 1996.

Tapscott, D., A. Lowy, and D. Ticoll. *Blueprint to the Digital Economy: Creating Wealth in the Era of E-Business*. New York: McGraw Hill, 1998.

Tarnas, R. *The Passion of the Western Mind: Understanding the Ideas That Have Shaped Our World*. New York: Harmony Books, 1991.

Taylor, B.R. *Ecological Resistance Movements: The Global Emergence of Radical and Popular Environmentalism*. Albany: State University of New York Press, 1995.

Taylor, C. *Dimensions of Diversity in Canadian Business: Building a Business Case for Valuing Ethnocultural Diversity.* Ottawa: Conference Board of Canada, 1995.

Taylor, J. *Paved With Good Intentions.* New York: Carroll and Graf, 1992.

Taylor, J.C. and D. Felten. *Performance by Design: Sociotechnical Systems in North America.* Englewood Cliffs, NJ: Prentice Hall, 1993.

Taylor, L.K. *Not For Bread Alone: An Appreciation of Job Enrichment.* London: Basic Books, 1980.

Teger, A. *Too Much Invested to Quit.* New York: Pergamon, 1980.

Tenner, E. *Why Things Bite Back: Technology and the Revenge of Unintended Consequences.* New York: Knopf, 1996.

Thierauf, R.J. *Virtual Reality Systems for Business.* Westport, CT: Quorum Books, 1995.

Thomas, R.J. *What Machines Can't Do: Politics and Technology in the Industrial Enterprise.* Berkeley: University of California Press, 1994.

Thompson, A. *The Dynamics of the Industrial Revolution.* New York: St. Martin's Press, 1973.

Thompson, C. "State of the Union." *The Globe and Mail Report on Business*, April 1998, 72–82.

Thompson, J. *Organizations in Action.* New York: McGraw Hill, 1967.

Thompson, K.F., ed. *Classics of Western Thought: Middle Ages, Renaissance and Reformation.* 3rd ed. New York: Harcourt, Brace & Jovanovich, 1980.

Thorson, J.A. *Aging in a Changing Society.* Belmont, CA: Wadsworth Publishing, 1995.

Tober, E. "The Scapegoat as an Essential Group Phenomenon." *International Journal of Group Psychotherapy* 22 (1972): 320–32.

Toffler, B.L. *Tough Choices: Managers Talk Ethics.* New York: John Wiley & Sons, 1986.

Trainer, F.E. *The Conserver Society: Alternatives for Sustainability.* London: ZED Books, 1995.

Tullock, G. *The Economics of Special Privilege and Rent Seeking.* Boston: Klewer Academic Publishers, 1989.

Turban, E. *Expert Systems and Applied Artificial Intelligence.* Toronto: Macmillan, 1992.

Turban, E., E. Mclean, and J. Whethebe. *Information Technology for Management: Improving Quality and Productivity.* New York: John Wiley & Sons, 1996.

Turney, J. *Frankenstein's Footsteps: Science, Genetics and Popular Culture.* New Haven: Yale University Press, 1998.

Turpin, J. and L.A. Lorentzen. *Gendered New World Order: Militarism, Development and the Environment.* New York: Routledge, 1996.

Tyson, K.W.M. *Competition in the 21st Century.* Delray Beach, FL: St. Lucie Press, 1997.

Udall, Stewart L. *The Quiet Crisis.* New York: Holt Rinehart and Winston, 1963.

Umseem, E.L. *Low Tech Education in a High Tech World: Corporations and Classrooms in the New Information Society.* New York: Collier Macmillan, 1986.

Vacca, R. *The Coming Dark Age.* Translated by J.S. Whale. Garden City, NJ: Doubleday, 1973.

Valaskakis, K. *The Conserver Society: A Workable Alternative for the Future.* New York: Harper and Row, 1979.

Vallas, S.P. *Power in the Workplace: The Politics of Production at AT&T.* Albany: State University of New York Press, 1993.

Van De Veer, D. and C. Pierce. *People, Penguins, and Plastic Trees: Basic Issues in Environmental Ethics.* Belmont, CA: Wadsworth Publishing, 1986.

Varela, F.J., E. Thompson, and E. Rosch. *The Embodied Mind: Cognitive Science and Human Experience*. Cambridge, MA: MIT Press, 1991.

Velasquez, M.G. *Business Ethics: Concepts and Cases*. 2nd ed. Englewood Cliffs, NJ: Prentice Hall, 1988.

Verduin, W.H. *Better Products Faster: A Practical Guide to Knowledge-Based Systems for Manufacturers*. Burr Ridge, IL: Irwin Professional Publishing, 1995.

Vinten, G. *Whistle Blowing: Subversion or Corporate Citizenship?* New York: St. Martin's Press, 1994.

Voyer, R. and P. Ryon. *The New Innovators: How Canadians Are Shaping the Knowledge-Based Economy*. Toronto: J. Lorimer, 1994.

Waite-Stupiansky, S. *Building Understanding Together: A Constructivist Approach to Early Childhood Education*. Albany: Delmar Publishers, 1997.

Wajcman, J. *Feminism Confronts Technology*. Cambridge: Basil Blackwell, 1991.

Walker, B.A. and W.C. Hanson. "Valuing Differences at Digital Equipment Corporation." In *Diversity in the Workforce: Human Resource Initiatives*, edited by S.E. Jackson. New York: Guildford, 1992.

Walker, J. *Changing Concepts of Retirement*. Aldershot, UK: Arena, 1996.

Wall, E. *Sexual Harassment: Confrontation and Decisions*. Buffalo: Prometheus Books, 1992.

Waltenberg, B. *The Good News is the Bad News is Wrong*. New York: Simon and Schuster, 1984.

Wang, C.B. *Techno Vision II: Every Executive's Guide to Understanding and Mastering Technology and the Internet*. New York: McGraw Hill, 1997.

Want, J.H. *Managing Radical Change: Beyond Survival in the New Business Age*. New York: John Wiley & Sons, 1995.

Warren, K.J. *Ecofeminism: Women, Culture and Nature*. Bloomington: Indiana University Press, 1997.

———. "Feminism and Ecology: Making Connections." *Environmental Ethics* 9 (1987): 3–20.

———. "The Power and Promise of Ecological Feminism." *Environmental Ethics* 12 (1990): 125–47.

Wartick, S.L. and R. Rude. "Issues Management: Fad or Fashion?" *California Management Review* 29 (1986): 124–40.

Waskik, J. *Green Marketing and Management*. Oxford: Blackwell Business, 1996.

Weber, M. *The Theory of Social and Economic Organization*. 1924. Edited by A.H. Henderson and T. Parsons. Glencoe, IL: Free Press, 1947.

Weckert, J. and D. Adeney. *Computer and Information Ethics*. Westport, CT: Greenwood Press, 1997.

Wehenkel, L.A. *Automatic Learning Techniques in Power Systems*. Boston: Klewer Academic Publishers, 1998.

Weinstein, D. *Bureaucratic Opposition*. New York: Pergamon, 1979.

Welford, R. "Rediscovering the Spiritual Dimensions of Environmentalism." In *Hijacking Environmentalism: Corporate Responses to Sustainable Development*, edited by R. Welford. London: Earthscan, 1997.

Wellins, R.S., W.C. Byham, and G.R. Dixon. *Inside Teams: How 20 World-Class Organizations Are Winning Through Teamwork*. San Francisco: Jossey-Bass, 1994.

Wells, B.B. *The Computer Revolution*. Commack, NY: Nova Science Publishers, 1997.

Westin, A.F. *Whistle Blowing! Loyalty and Dissent in the Corporation*. New York: McGraw-Hill, 1981.

Wexler, M.N. "Expanding the Groupthink Explanation to the Study of Contemporary Cults." *Cultic Studies Journal* 2 (1995): 1–23.

———. "The Negative Rite of Scapegoating: From the Ancient Tribe to the Modern Organization." *International Journal of Group Tension* 3 (1993): 293–307.

Wheeler, D. and M. Sillanpää. *The Stakeholder Corporation: A Blueprint for Maximizing Stakeholder Value.* London: Pitman, 1997.

Wheeler, M. *Diversity Training.* New York: Conference Board, 1994.

"Whitchurst: Chemist, Lawyer, War Hero, Whistle-Blower." *Chemical and Engineering News* 75 (1997): 26–27.

White, R.R. *North, South and the Environmental Crisis.* Toronto: University of Toronto Press, 1993.

Whitehead, A.N. *Dialogues of Alfred North Whitehead.* Boston: Little Brown, 1954.

Whittle, D.B. *Cyberspace: The Human Dimension.* New York: W.H. Freeman, 1997.

Whyte, G. "Diffusion of Responsibility: Effects of Escalation Tendency." *Journal of Applied Psychology* 76, no. 3 (1991): 408–15.

Wickens, P. *The Ascendant Organization: Combining Commitment and Control For Long-Term Sustainable Business Success.* New York: Macmillan, 1995.

Wijers, L. *Art Meets Science and Spirituality in a Changing Economy: From Competition to Compassion.* London: Academy Editions, 1996.

Williams, B. "Politics and Moral Character." In *Public and Private Morality,* edited by S. Hampshire. Cambridge: Cambridge University Press, 1978.

Williamson, O.E. "The Economics of Organization: The Transaction Cost Approach." *American Journal of Sociology* 87 (1981): 548–77.

———. *Markets and Hierarchies: Analysis and Antitrust Implications.* New York: Free Press, 1975.

Williamson, R.C., D. Rinehart, and T. Blank. *Early Retirement: Promises and Pitfalls.* New York: Insight Books, 1992.

Willis, A. "The Ethical Pitfalls of Fun in the Sun." *The Globe and Mail* (Toronto), 15 August 1997, B10.

Wilson, T. *Diversity at Work: The Business Case for Equity.* Toronto: John Wiley & Sons, 1996.

Winfield, L. and S. Spielman. *Straight Talk About Gays in the Workplace: Creating an Inclusive, Productive Environment For Everyone in Your Organization.* New York: AMACOM, 1995.

Winn, M. *Unplugging the Plug-in Drug.* New York: Viking, 1987.

Winslow, C.D. and W.L. Bramer. *Future Work: Putting Knowledge to Work in the Knowledge Economy.* New York: Macmillan, 1994.

Wolf, F.A. *The Body Quantum: The New Physics of Body, Mind and Health.* New York: Macmillan, 1986.

Wood, S. *The Degradation of Work: Skill, Deskilling and the Labour Process.* London: Hutchinson, 1982.

Woodward, K. *The Myths of Information: Technology and Postindustrial Culture.* Madison, WI: Coda Press, 1980.

Woolley, B. *Virtual Worlds: A Journey in Hype and Hyperreality.* Oxford: Basil Blackwell, 1992.

World Commission on Environment and Development. *The Bruntland Report.* New York: United Nations, 1987.

Wrightsman, L.S. "Personality and Attitudinal Correlates of Trusting and Trustworthy Behaviors in a Two-Person Game." *Journal of Personality and Social Psychology* 4 (1966): 328–32.

Wrightsman, L.S. *Social Psychology in the Seventies.* Pacific Grove, CA: Brooks/Cole, 1972.

Wynbrandt, J.L. and T.C. Wynbrandt. *Creating a Winning Corporate Image.* New York: Conference Board, 1992.

Yamagishi, T. and K. Sato. "Motivational Bases of the Public Goods Problem." *Journal of Personality and Social Psychology* 50 (1986): 67–73.

Yergin, D. and J. Stanislaw. *The Commanding Heights: The Battle Between Government and the Marketplace That is Remaking the Modern World.* New York: Simon and Schuster, 1996.

Yorks, L. and D.A. Whitset. *Scenarios of Change: Advocacy and the Diffusion of Job Redesign in Organizations.* New York: Praeger, 1989.

Zahedi, F. *Intelligent Systems for Business: Expert Systems and Neural Networks.* Belmont, CA: Wadsworth Publishing, 1993.

Zaleski, J.P. *The Soul of Cyberspace: How New Technology is Changing Our Spiritual Lives.* San Francisco: Harper Edge, 1997.

Zammuto, R.F. *Assessing Organizational Effectiveness: Systems, Change, Adaptation and Strategy.* Albany: State University of New York Press, 1982.

Zand, D.E. "Trust and Managerial Problem-Solving." *Administrative Science Quarterly* 17 (1972): 229–39.

Zenter, R. "Issues and Strategic Management." In *Competitive Strategic Management*, edited by R.B. Lamb. Englewood Cliffs, NJ: Prentice Hall, 1984.

Zerbe, R.O. and W.D. Dively. *Benefit-Cost Analysis in Theory and Practice.* New York: Harper Collins College Publishers, 1994.

Zhai, P. *Get Real: A Philosophical Adventure in Virtual Reality.* Lanham, MD: Rowman and Littlefield, 1998.

Zimmerman, M. *Contesting Earth's Future: Radical Ecology and Postmodernity.* Berkeley: University of California Press, 1994.

Zuboff, S. *In the Age of the Smart Machine: The Future of Work and Power.* New York: Basic Books, 1988.

Zucker, L.G. "Production of Trust: Institutional Sources of Economic Structure, 1840–1920." In *Research in Organizational Behavior*, Vol. 8, edited by B.M. Staw and L.L. Cummings. Greenwich, CT: JAI Press, 1986.

Zweigenhaft, R.L. and W.G. Domhoff. *Diversity in the Power Elite: Have Women and Minorities Reached the Top?* New Haven: Yale University Press, 1998.

Index

Page numbers in bold indicate figures.